DATE DUE

DEMCO 38-296

OPERA PRODUCTION

and

ITS RESOURCES

THE HISTORY *of* ITALIAN OPERA

Edited by LORENZO BIANCONI *and* GIORGIO PESTELLI

Part II / Systems

VOLUME 4

OPERA PRODUCTION

and ITS RESOURCES

Edited by

Lorenzo Bianconi *and* Giorgio Pestelli

TRANSLATED BY LYDIA G. COCHRANE

The University of Chicago Press

CHICAGO & LONDON

LORENZO BIANCONI is professor of musical dramaturgy at the University of Bologna.
He is the author of *Music in the Seventeenth Century.*   GIORGIO PESTELLI is professor of music
history at the University of Turin and music critic for *La Stampa.* He is author of
The Age of Mozart and Beethoven.

The University of Chicago Press, Chicago 60637
The University of Chicago Press, Ltd., London
© 1998 by The University of Chicago
All rights reserved. Published 1998
Printed in the United States of America
07 06 05 04 03 02 01 00 99 98   5 4 3 2 1

ISBN (CLOTH): 0-226-04590-0

Originally published as *Storia dell'opera Italiana,* vol. 4:
Il sistema produttivo e le sue competenze, © 1987 E.D.T. Edizioni di Torino.

Chapter 2 is based in part on John Rosselli's book,
The Opera Industry in Italy from Cimarosa to Verdi, © 1984, Cambridge University Press.

Library of Congress Cataloging-in-Publication Data

Storia dell'opera italiana.   English
    The history of Italian opera / edited by Lorenzo Bianconi and
Giorgio Pestelli.
        p.   cm.
    Includes bibliographical references and index.
    Contents: — pt. 2. Systems. v. 4. Opera production and its
resources.
    ISBN 0-226-04590-0 (v. 4: alk. paper)
    1. Opera—Italy.   I. Bianconi, Lorenzo.   II. Pestelli, Giorgio.
ML1733.S7513   1998
782.1'0945—dc21   97-25421
                                                              CIP
                                                              MN

This book is printed on acid-free paper.

Contents

List of illustrations / ix

Preface / xi

List of Abbreviations / xix

1 Opera Production to 1780

FRANCO PIPERNO   1

1. *Court Operatic Spectacles* / 2

2. *Court Opera and Commercial Opera* / 7

3. *Traveling Companies: The Cooperative, Organized Diffusion
   of Commercial Opera* / 14

4. *Impresarial Opera: Ends and Means; the Single Impresario
   and Impresarial Associations* / 16

5. *The Impresario and the Theater Public* / 28

6. *Municipal Opera Houses and Collective Management
   in the Eighteenth Century* / 31

7. *Ballet and Its Mechanisms of Production* / 43

8. *The Production and Diffusion of Opera Seria* / 49

9. *The Production and Diffusion of Intermezzi and Comic Opera* / 60

   Bibliographic Note / 73

2 Opera Production, 1780–1880

JOHN ROSSELLI   81

1. *Opera as the Expression of a Hierarchical*
    and Conservative Society / 81
2. *The Economic Vicissitudes of the Opera Industry* / 89
3. *The Strong Arm of Authority* / 99
4. *The Profession of the Impresario* / 114
5. *The Labor Market* / 129
6. *The Impresario and the Public* / 146
    Bibliographic Note / 160

3 Opera Production from Italian
   Unification to the Present

FIAMMA NICOLODI   165

1. *Opera in the New Italy: Municipal Theaters*
    and Impresarial Management / 165
2. *The Role of Singers, Joint Stock Companies, and Publishers* / 177
3. *The Giolitti Era: From the* Politeama *to the First* Ente Autonomo / 188
4. *The Fascist Regime: Tradition and Transformation* / 192
5. *The New Republic: Reconstruction and the "Consumer Society"* / 208
6. *The Corona Act and the Current Situation* / 218
    Bibliographic Note / 224

4 The Librettist

FABRIZIO DELLA SETA   229

1. *A Problem of Conscience* / 229
2. *The Seventeenth Century* / 232
3. *The Eighteenth Century* / 240

4. The Nineteenth Century / 255

5. From the Nineteenth to the Twentieth Century / 273

    Bibliographic Note / 286

5 The Opera Composer

ELVIDIO SURIAN   291

1. Social Background / 301

2. Schooling, Professional Training, Apprenticeship / 302

3. Entry into the Production System, Career, Opera Production / 309

4. The Creative Process: Work Methods and Schedules / 327

6 The Opera Singer

SERGIO DURANTE   345

1. The Court Singer Mounts the Theatrical Machine / 346

2. Church, Theater, and School / 353

3. From Modena to Bologna: Criticism and Growth / 367

4. The Virtuosi: Background, Training, Itineraries, Specialties / 372

5. An Italian "School": Images and Economic Conditions / 388

6. Bel Canto: The Market and the Myth / 395

7. The Voice Mirrored / 406

    Bibliographic Note / 410

Index of Names / 419

Index of Operas and Ballets / 433

Index of Theatrical Venues / 438

Illustrations

Following page 108

1. Poster for *La calma fra le tempeste, overo Il prencipe Roberto fra le sciagure felice,* Reggio Emilia, 1684
2. Poster for *Il Maurizio,* Modena, 1689
3. Poster for *Arsace* and *I veri amici,* Modena, 1719
4. Poster for *Vologeso re de' Parti,* Reggio Emilia, 1741
5. Announcement for *Artaserse* and *Alessandro nell'Indie,* Sassuolo, 1750
6. Poster for *Le contadine bizzarre,* Modena, 1764
7. Price list for tickets and boxes, Genoa, 1772
8. Calendar of public entertainments, carnival, Modena, 1791
9. Poster for the spring opera season, Turin, 1782
10. Poster for *Enea e Lavinia,* Genoa, 1796
11. Announcement in Italian and French for the postponement of a performance at the Teatro alla Scala, Milan, 1799
12. Poster for *Il podestà di Chioggia, Il filosofo,* and *Che originali!,* Genoa, 1802
13. Poster for *La Cenerentola,* Naples, 1818
14. Announcement of an evening benefit for Salvatore Paradisi, choreographer and *primo ballerino,* Imola, August, 1836
15. Announcement of a performance of the second act of *Il nuovo Figaro* and the first act of *Il furioso,* Imola, 1839
16. Poster for *Ernani,* Teatro La Fenice, Venice, 1844
17. Announcement of the division into two evenings for the performance of *Mefistofele* at the Teatro alla Scala, Milan, 1868

Following page 268

18. Poster for the premiere of *La Gioconda,* Milan, 1876
19. Poster for *Aida,* Teatro La Fenice, Venice, 1881

20. Poster for the carnival season 1884–85, Teatro Comunale, Ferrara

21. Poster for the Columbian Festival performance of Donizetti's *La favorita,* Teatro Carlo Felice, Genòa, 1892

22. Poster for the carnival and lenten season 1893–94, Teatro Regio, Turin

23. Poster for *Tristano e Isotta (Tristan und Isolde),* Teatro Comunale, Trieste, 1906

24. Poster for the performance of *Otello,* Como 1899, in celebration of the centenary of Alessandro Volta's invention of the electrical battery

25. Poster for the Verdi centenary celebrations, Teatro Regio, Parma, 1913

26. Poster for the Verdi centenary celebrations, Busseto, 1913

27. Poster for the Verdi centenary, Amphitheater of Verona, 1913

28. Poster for *Parsifal* and *Andrea Chénier* at the Amphitheater of Verona, 1924

29. Poster for Arrigo Boito's *Nerone,* Bologna, 1924

30. Poster for *La figlia di Iorio,* Milan, 1906

31. Poster for *Héllera,* Turin, 1909

32. Poster for *Tosca,* Rome, 1900

33. Poster for *Turandot,* Milan, 1926

Following page 396

34. Anton Maria Zanetti, caricature of Farinelli in *Catone in Utica,* 1729

35. Pierleone Ghezzi, caricature of Farinelli

36. Engraving facing the title page of the ode, *In lode del signor Carlo Broschi detto Farinello, musico celebre* [In praise of signor Carlo Broschi called Farinello, celebrated singer], 1734

37. Bartolomeo Nazari, portrait of Carlo Broschi, 1734

38. Jacopo Amigoni, group portrait commissioned by Farinelli, ca. 1750

39. Jacopo Amigoni, portrait of Farinelli, ca. 1750–52

40. Corrado Giaquinto, portrait of Farinelli

41. *Il Parnaso canoro* [The Parnassus of Song], print by Antonio Fedi

42. The first photograph of Enrico Caruso in stage costume

43. Enrico Caruso, caricature of himself as Dick Johnson in *La fanciulla del West*

44. Stage photo of Enrico Caruso and others in *La fanciulla del West*

45. Publicity notice from *Theater Magazine,* December 1919

46. Enrico Caruso, still photograph from the film *My Cousin,* 1918

47. Enrico Caruso, photograph, embarkation for America, 20 October 1914

48. Enrico Caruso, photograph, on board an airplane

49. Enrico Caruso, paper doll

Preface

Odd as it might seem, when they first appeared in 1987–88, these volumes were the first history of Italian opera. Everyone is aware of the major role that opera has played (and continues to play) in our musical life; nonetheless, scholars working individually or in teams have never before attempted to recount its entire history. This lacuna is even more striking when we think of the large numbers of historical works available in the related fields of Italian political history, literature, and art.

Surely the universality of music—a tenacious and fallacious myth—is not a reliable guide for the enterprise at hand. Judging merely from the technical vocabulary adopted throughout the world, a history of Italian opera might seem to be the history of opera plain and simple, along with a few major secondary derivations and ramifications. Yet although we have histories of French opera, German opera, and English opera motivated by national pride and an interest in tracing the relationship of these lesser traditions to the trunk from which they branched off, there is no history of Italian opera. Even on the historiographical plane, the notion of "Italian opera" as a coherent object of historical study has been belittled and indeed denied aesthetic autonomy in the name of a more authoritative historical and musical tradition—the German one, born of romantic idealism, developed by nineteenth-century historicism, and, in the operatic field, influenced in large measure by the Wagnerian model. The German historical tradition (on which, incidentally, modern music history was founded) saw Wagnerian "music drama" as the supreme point of confluence of a number of currents—a notion that, by implication, reduced the great opera composers of the past to the rank of "precursors." It interpreted the history of opera as a succession of goal-oriented, connected events, and it resorted to a series of antitheses (melodrama/music drama; closed form/open form; bel canto/harmonic expression; convention/adherence to nature) as keys to the comprehension of opera's evolution. That scheme led, however, to eliminating Italian opera from the historical map or at least to marginalizing it as an incongruous mixture of heterogeneous elements, some of which were deemed noteworthy but only insofar as they contributed to the predetermined objective. To cite one example, romantic historiography and aesthetics, judging the eighteenth-century "reform" of *dramma per musica* a posteriori, saw it as a reaction against and a rejection of Italian opera, whereas in its time it was a development *within* the Italian operatic tradition.

As early as 1838 Gottfried Wilhelm Fink's study *Wesen und Geschichte der Oper* contained in a nutshell the outline of all future histories of the opera genre written in the German teleological mode. A century later, however, Hermann Abert, a historian with a much better grasp of the facts, still presented the same general viewpoint, essentially unchanged, in his *Grundprobleme der Operngeschichte*. This work, a virtual manifesto on historical research concerning opera, was read at the musicological convention in Basel in 1924, and it subsequently influenced several generations of German (and not only German) musicologists. Opera as a genre was presented in Abert's paper as the hero of a bildungsroman: after taking its first steps in humanistic, academic Florence, it suffered the unfortunate influences of Italian formalism (the da capo aria, coloratura), was then tempered by the brisk winds of French opera (the librettos of which had to withstand comparison to the dramatic works of Corneille and Racine), took cognizance of the good intentions of Agostino Steffani and Alessandro Scarlatti, reached its first height with Handel (rediscovered in the festivals of the 1920s in Göttingen), saw its horizons narrowed once more with Metastasio and Hasse, was regenerated through Gluck, Mozart, and romantic opera, and finally reached its goal in Wagner. It is hardly surprising that the names of Rossini, Meyerbeer, Verdi, and Puccini simply have no part in the descriptions of this "romance."

At the end of his study, Abert stated that the task of the historian of opera was "to discern some sense and some order in the multifarious vicissitudes of opera history." The present *History of Italian Opera* is based on quite different presuppositions. Rather than seeking cleanly traced lines or attempting to discover an order that creates unity out of diversity, it attempts to trace the accidental, disorderly, and tortuous course of a genre that has suffered a thousand mishaps and has developed under all sorts of material and spiritual constraints but that in Italy has nonetheless produced a thriving progeny and a robust and continuous tradition that has lasted for four centuries. That progeny and that tradition merit study in and of themselves.

During the last half century, research by scholars from many regions has produced a harvest of data and information on individual composers and librettists, particular sources, and specific episodes in the history of opera that has done more than offer a strong challenge to such categories as "musical drama." It has also proposed the national perspective as the most effective means for understanding the phenomenon of opera in the full range of its component parts, from the production of an operatic text—words and music—to the conventions governing its efficacy, from its realization under specific conditions as vocal music and as theatrical performance to the ways in which it circulated among different sorts of audiences. The history of Italian opera is also the history of a repertory that was created, maintained, and continually renewed in Italy; it is the history of Italian spectators, who attended performances of operas by Mozart, Meyerbeer, Gounod, Wagner, or Bizet as well as those by Italian composers; it is the history of the diffusion of Italian opera outside Italy and of how it was viewed from beyond the Alps, as seen in travelers' accounts of their "grand tours" during the eighteenth century or in nineteenth-century European novels.

A national characterization of this sort need not evoke the specters of *Volksgeist*. A great European intellectual, Carlo Dionisotti, offers proof of this in his *Geografia e storia della letteratura italiana*. Like Italian literature Italian opera has had a discontinuous and heterogeneous career precisely because Italy's cultural geography—not to mention its political geography—was (and still is) discontinuous and heterogeneous. Italy never had a hegemonic center or dominant capital city; it had a system of imperfect relations among a number of small and midsized centers, no one of which was truly self-sufficient and no one of which was completely "superfluous" to the smooth functioning of the system as a whole. This situation was evident in the diffusion and circulation of literary products (through manuscripts and books; through institutions and intellectual organizations) as well as in the diffusion and circulation of operatic spectacles. It was true from the first appearance of opera; it was true of the publicity and propaganda network that linked the courts of central-northern Italy (Florence, Mantua, Parma, Rome) in an unequal competition. It was even truer of the impresarial system: this extraordinary phenomenon spread, along with its repertory, at lightning speed from Venice to Bologna, Genoa, Milan, Florence, Lucca, Naples, and Palermo in the years roughly between 1640 and 1660. It was true of the market for opera seria in Italy during the eighteenth century and of the ramifications of that market north of the Alps; of the penetration of comic opera to all corners of Italy, even the most remote provinces, during the late eighteenth century; and of the nineteenth-century copyright laws, both before and after the unification of Italy in 1861, governing artistic and intellectual property. It is still true today concerning the application of laws currently regulating the operatic sector and the creation of new laws.

The history of Italian opera, like the history of any other form of culture in Italy that is not exclusively local, is of necessity a tale of sundry cities closely or loosely linked with one another. The laws that governed those connections were rarely dictated by any artistic "school"; far more often, they were determined by political or dynastic concerns or by intellectual or commercial ties among groups or individuals. A unified and homogeneous history of Italian opera in Italy can only exist as the history of a dynamic system of intertwined relations. For that reason local variants of the system, when they are seen in their national dimension, acquire a weight and a relevance that are necessarily obliterated in the abstract vision of a universal history of opera. Such local variants would be just as inevitably obliterated by the opposite perspective—that is, by a fragmented vision providing individual studies of each center of production (an old but persistent formula that has given us works on opera in Florence, Rome, Venice, Naples, and so forth).

Even the leading figures of opera in Italy did not necessarily perceive the full import and continuity of traditions and experiences. If we can readily imagine a determined reader able to keep abreast of the full range of Italian literary production (there really were such people in the eighteenth century, people such as Muratori, Maffei, Quadrio, Mazzuchelli, or Tiraboschi), it is unlikely that we can ever grasp all that is relevant to the history of opera. This is exactly because opera is a cultural product made not primarily of texts but of *events* — aesthetic events—whose literary and musical texts are merely their inert and imperfect instrument. Literary texts circulated easily and efficiently by means of books; spectacles were events that circulated slowly and irregularly from one theater to another and were subject to heavy constraints. One problem particular to the history of opera is often forgotten precisely because it is so basic: ascertaining how contemporaries—and later ages— conceived the overall image of Italian operatic tradition. Once again we can borrow a critical viewpoint, with necessary adjustments, from the history of literature.

In his *Literaturgeschichte als Provokation (Toward an Aesthetic of Reception)*, Hans Robert Jauss launched a new direction in the history of literature by shifting the aesthetic perspective from the older "aesthetic of production" to an "aesthetic of reception." It is in the processes of the reader's reception of a work and in the relationship of author, text, and readers that a historical sense of the literary work of art gradually coalesces. Every new work is directed toward a "horizon of expectation" constructed out of the shared literary experience of the collectivity of readers. Every new work enriches, confirms, modifies, changes, or on occasion overturns its reader's (or its readers') "horizon of expectation," and that work in turn becomes part of the shared horizon of expectation in a dynamic and shifting "dialogue" that is reflected in differing perceptions of the meaning of the work at various times and in various ages. If we replace the chain "author-text-readers" with "authors-theatrical event-spectators," we have a historically pertinent interpretive model that can be fruitfully applied to the history of opera in its national dimension—a dimension in which the idea of a collective subject called the "public," though somewhat stretched, still has a meaning. (The "public" was a noun introduced into the Italian vocabulary rather late, replacing the more usual term *spettatori*, and it was thanks to opera that the term became rooted in the civic and social experience of Italians.)

Practically speaking we can designate precisely the "horizon of expectation" of the people for whom operas were produced and document its range of action: it is equivalent to the seasonal program of any given theater in any given city, or better, to the sum of all operatic spectacles offered over the span of one or more generations to that portion of the city's population that frequented the opera house. By defining the operagoers' "horizon of expectation" as the makeup of the program and the current repertory, we can account for a phenomenon of primary importance: the changing "laws" that governed the duration, survival, and vitality of operatic works. These laws too were strongly national: the principles governing the natural selection and life expectancy of an Italian opera functioned in one manner in Italian theaters and quite differently in English, German, or French theaters, which meant that the opera's chances of continuing to exert an active influence on the cultural "horizon of expectation" of its audience and of being in turn influenced by its reception varied just as greatly.

The decline of the interpretive categories of the historicist school aside, there is another difficulty of a general nature that works against the prospects for a wide-ranging, general history of opera. Historians of opera, who long considered the subject simply a specialized branch of the history of music, have at last realized that the particular object of their investigation is highly heterogeneous. Neither a study of opera's musical forms and structures nor an investigation of the relationship between opera and the evolution of styles of musical composition in general provides an "explanation" of opera's history. The spectacular, visual, and gestural components of opera, its dramatic structure (in relation to the dramaturgy of the theater in general, literary and nonliterary), the institutional constraints on opera and on its production techniques—all these components determine "operatic theater" as a cultural phenomenon, and they all fall outside the special competence of the music historian. Nor should these multiple components be treated separately. Appending a history of the libretto, of vocal styles, or of set design to a history of the musical styles and forms of opera fails to do justice to the complex structure of the operatic phenomenon, in which each contributing factor counts not in and of itself but as the end result of an operation that subsumes it and transforms it. Rather than as a subject that remains exclusively within the sphere of the history of musical styles or dramatic forms, the history of operatic theater—a peculiar form of spectacle and the tangible manifestation of a continuity that contains a wealth of contradictions and a number of bottlenecks—will be studied in these volumes *juxta sua principia* as a phenomenon and a complex message reacting in synchrony with the social and cultural life it addressed. This means that vocal techniques, the writing of librettos, scene design, and other aspects of opera will be viewed *within* the phenomenon as a whole, not as subsidiary to its (presumed) quintessentially musical nucleus or as an accumulation of parallel notions complementing that nucleus.

This *History of Italian Opera* has been divided into two parts, *Events* and *Systems*. This separation of diachrony and synchrony is hardly novel but it is useful. It responds to practical demands, since it hopes to facilitate the reader's orientation within a complex topic involving multiple disciplines, both musicological and extramusicological. It also responds to demands of a more general and radical nature inherent in the aims of historical investigation. Historical studies have traditionally privileged the idea of history as movement, transformation, and progress, and at first sight this notion well suits the history of opera because—like political and civil history—it consists of *events* even more than it does of *texts*. But behind those events—which it is well to note were of an aesthetic nature and are memorable only as such— there lay an entire set of artistic conventions and social customs of rare solidity and persistence. At times these conventions and customs give the impression of inertia, whereas it might be more accurate to see them as the equivalent of an extremely complex, specialized form of artistic production that was, by its very nature, slow to evolve.

Today, and for several decades now, even those aspects of the history of opera that have remained inert and persisted intact seem worthy of the historian's attention. Description and comprehension of the historical picture now seems to include as essential elements not only a recounting of "how things really happened" but also the persistence and the tenacity of systems and structures. When we take a closer look at those systems and structures, we can see that they too were developing—just as events were—but much more slowly, so that our observation requires a special lens and a particular focus. If time in historical narration flows smoothly and uniformly, time in an account of structures proceeds with rhythms of its own that include long stagnant periods and sudden shifts, and it operates within a geography embracing a vast periphery as well as central areas. In short our division into the two levels of events and systems is based upon the obvious assumption that history is a picture to be interpreted from more than one perspective. History is a picture, but it is also a commentary on that picture, and thus it requires a mobile narrator—in the present case, an entire squadron of narrators—moving freely through time's museum, at times taking a broad, overall view of the general layout of that museum and at other times taking a closer look at one specific, circumscribed reality.

The portion of our *History* devoted to systems, which begins with this volume, is in turn divided into three sections. Volume 4, *Opera Production and Its Resources* (the present volume), contains a true "social history" of Italian opera theater, seen through its principal contributors, the librettist, the opera composer, the singer, and—even more basic to our story—the impresario, single or collective (from the prince to the speculator, from the eighteenth-century association of nobles to the subsidizing state of today). It is one thing to refuse to separate the study of vocal styles or librettos from an overall examination of operatic production (which risks dissolving into abstraction); it is quite another to describe—over the span of four centuries—the professional aspects and the social characteristics of the people who produced opera. Although the inertia of tradition weighed heavily on each one of the categories involved, the system of their reciprocal relations changed through time, imperceptibly but considerably, shifting their "pecking order" and relative importance. Today, for example, technological developments in the production and reproduction of operas—recordings first, then television and film—are subjecting the viscous body of ongoing tradition to notable stress, testing the elasticity of the system as a whole. *The History of Italian Opera* does not take the very most recent developments into specific consideration, but the reader should be able to sense their effects on the market and on taste.

The *spectacular* nature of Italian opera—and spectacle was also a system, in part inherent to opera and in part extraneous to it—occupies the entire fifth volume of this *History*. Devoting that amount of space to spectacle reflects a change that has come about in the historiography and the criticism of opera. Recent studies have turned away from a theory of opera that long and almost obsessively insisted on pairing text and music—that insisted on the "translation" into music of poetically expressed dramatic "states of mind"—and emphasize instead a tripartite view of opera as text, music, and spectacle, even asserting that opera must be seen in terms of musical and literary drama *as* spectacle. The old dichotomy between "drama," the realm of introspection (a positive, ideal value), and "theater," or "theatricality" (a negative value representing exteriority and aesthetic dissipation), no longer withstands scrutiny. This renewed sensitivity to spectacle and its demands is reflected in the chapters on aspects of opera either once considered irrelevant but now increasingly important—the role of the director—or, to the contrary, once prominent but now neglected—ballet. Until the end of the last century, the ballets were considered an essential component of any operatic "evening"; they were included in the price of the ticket and were just as important in the expectations of the ticket-holder as the opera itself.

The sixth and final volume in this *History of Italian Opera* considers the intensive and ongoing exchanges between Italian opera and the realms of literature and drama, aesthetics and ideology. Such exchanges involved a give-and-take of ideas, concepts, and myths; they also involved disagreements and clashes. On the one hand they have created a smoke screen that makes it difficult to draw the borderline between opera as seen by the literati and the reality of opera production; on the other they have contributed greatly to enlarging both the intellectual thrust of opera and the public's horizon of expectation. Operatic spectacle took on (and in Italy still enjoys) a prestige and a cultural importance that insiders—the *prime donne* and the *virtuosi*—were far from suspecting and perhaps do not even fully realize today. The first portion of the dual title of volume 6, *Theories and Techniques*, refers to three aspects and three systems vital to the artifact *opera in musica*: explicit theorization on opera (that is, opera as viewed by the literati); the dramaturgy implicit in opera and in the tacit assumptions of the opera composer (given concrete form in structural contrivances of tenacious persistence), and the metric and formal techniques consolidated and institutionalized by practice. The second portion of the title of volume 6, *Images and Illusions*, deals with the relations between Italian opera and culture in a broader sense—both the "low" culture of the popularization and vulgarization of opera and the "high" culture of exchanges with the literary elite. Until the late nineteenth century, when the genre became identified by its nation of origin, such relations were at times desired and yearned for and at other times negotiated and consummated.

Abbreviations

F = France; I = Italy. Collections within libraries follow the library siglum after a comma.

F-Pan	Paris, Archives Nationales
I-Bas	Bologna, Archivio di Stato
I-Bas, Comune	Bologna, Archivio di Stato, Archivio Storico del Comune di Bologna
I-Bca	Bologna, Biblioteca Comunale dell'Archiginnasio
I-Fas	Florence, Archivio di Stato
I-Fcomune	Florence, Archivio Storico del Comune di Firenze
I-Fn, CV	Florence, Biblioteca Nazionale Centrale, Carteggi vari
I-FOc, Piancastelli	Forlì, Biblioteca Comunale Collezione Piancastelli
I-Las	Lucca, Archivio di Stato
I-Ms	Milan, Museo Teatrale alla Scala
I-Mt	Milan, Biblioteca Trivulziana e Archivio Storico Civico
I-Nas	Naples, Archivio di Stato
I-PAi	Parma, Istituto Nazionale di Studi Verdiani (photocopies and transcriptions)
I-PAt	Parma, Archivio del Teatro Regio
I-PEA, Pacini	Pescia, Biblioteca Comunale, Fondo Pacini
I-Ras	Rome, Archivio di Stato
I-Rasc	Rome, Archivio Storico Capitolino
I-Rburcardo	Rome, Biblioteca Teatrale del Burcardo
I-Vas	Venice, Archivio di Stato
I-Vt	Venice, Archivio del Teatro La Fenice

ORGANIZATION NAMES

ACS	Archivio Centrale dello Stato (the Italian State Archives)
RAI	Radio-Audizione Italiana (the Italian Broadcasting System)
SIAE	Società Italiana degli Autori e Editori (the Italian Society of Authors and Publishers)

Opera Production to 1780

FRANCO PIPERNO

Between the early seventeenth century and the late-eighteenth century, anyone who attended an operatic spectacle saw the result of an extremely complex and carefully articulated cooperative effort involving a variety of different components and forces, each one of which could affect the final result in a unique and significant way. Opera was not a libretto or a score; it was not fine singing or stage design, choreography or drama. It was a combination of these and many other elements, all of which shaped the final product and were independent and interacting with one another. Opera always involved a considerable investment, both financial and organizational, and it required the combined efforts of a disparate workforce, each sector of which had its own particular technical field of expertise. Opera exploited motives and social distinctions that changed through time; it was promoted by individuals or groups for reasons that ranged from self-celebration to making a profit; it was put on by people who lent their talents for the occasion or who were specialized professionals. Here we shall be considering the overall picture of operatic spectacle as revealed by the means of production and consumption that slowly evolved between 1600 and the late eighteenth century. Rather than opera as an artistic phenomenon, we will be concerned with opera as a social and material phenomenon reduced to the concrete realities of its daily struggle with practical problems of a political, legal, and financial nature.

The discussion, which follows a chronological order, concentrates on the formation, evolution, and modification of three fundamental categories of persons who, for different reasons, were connected with operatic spectacle:

those who promoted it, those who performed and produced it, and those to whom it was addressed. In each of these categories we can discern three levels, defined according to social, entrepreneurial, and production criteria. These categories—and they were not totally self-contained—can be shown schematically.

Promoters
—The prince (spoken theater and opera in court and palace)
—Academies or civic associations (academic and institutional theater and opera)
—The impresario (commercial opera)

Performers
—Permanent, salaried personnel with nonspecialized skills
—Traveling troupes (organized, cooperative productions)
—Freelance specialized personnel

Audiences
—Courtiers (nonpaying, aristocratic audience)
—City elites (sponsorship by members of academies and civic groups)
—Paying audiences of composite and varied social status

1. Court Operatic Spectacles

Opera arose at the beginning of the seventeenth century in the Italian courts, places of residence where absolute sovereigns exercised power, and places of long-standing traditions and attitudes regarding spectacles. The overall aims of the organizational procedures, economic systems, and ideological scope were the same for opera as for all courtly spectacles in the sixteenth century: sumptuous productions using (on occasion, reusing) elaborate scenery made of materials of the highest quality;[1] employment of court personnel (from the carpenters to the court poet and the music director, the *maestro di cappella*); and the intention of celebrating the munificence of the sovereign, who was the promoter and ideological "director" of the spectacle, thus reaffirming his power.

The enormous monetary expenditures involved were calculated in terms of political and diplomatic affirmation rather than as profit and loss. Although there were clear differences in dramatic approach, musical style, and

---

1. For one exemplary case of the reuse of materials in a court theater, see Stuart Reiner, "Preparations in Parma—1618, 1627–28," *The Music Review* 25 (1964): 273–310. On the same spectacles, see also the full investigation and documentary reconstruction in Roberto Ciancarelli, *Il progetto di una festa barocca: Alle origini del Teatro Farnese di Parma (1618–1629)* (Rome: Bulzoni, 1987).

literary themes between, for example, the Florentine *intermedi* of 1589,[2] on the one hand, and *L'Arianna* of Ottavio Rinuccini and Claudio Monteverdi (Mantua, 1608), *Il trionfo di Partenope liberata* (Naples, 1649),[3] and *Eliogabalo* of Aurelio Aureli and Giovanni Antonio Boretti (Turin, 1678),[4] on the other, the differences in their systems of production, their modalities of exploitation, and their ideological ends were slight, even negligible. All these spectacles made notable use of astonishing scenic effects ranging from the aerial descent of the Fates and the Planets and the battle of the Pythians in the Florentine *intermedi* to the apotheosis of Ariadne in *L'Arianna* and the many set changes in *Eliogabalo*. All such entertainments employed the technical and musical personnel of the court and were put on in spaces adapted to theatricals in the palaces of the respective sovereigns. All were performed before a rigorously select public of persons in attendance by invitation and out of social obligation, who were seated in the hall in a manner that reflected social hierarchy. Finally, they all presented the spectators with an explicit political and ideological message, such as hopes for peace and prosperity (as expressed at the Medici-Lorraine wedding celebrations in Florence in 1589), praise of a political restoration (as enforced by Oñate, the Spanish viceroy in Naples, after Masaniello's revolt in 1647), or the eulogy of the monarchy as an institution (as in the new ending to *Eliogabalo* in Turin, in which the wedding of the dissolute Emperor Elagabalus was replaced by his assassination and the subsequent accession to the imperial throne of his just and enlightened successor, Severus Alexander).

At court, then, the mechanisms of operatic spectacle were set in motion with propagandistic and self-celebratory intent; they functioned as a means for political affirmation and as an *instrumentum regni* available to the absolutist centralized governments that began to take shape during the seventeenth century.[5] Court spectacles reproduced, on a smaller scale, the nature, structure, and ends of such governments: the new efficiency of the "state ma-

---

2. For a detailed description of the Florentine *intermedi* with critical documentation, see Nino Pirrotta, "La meraviglia, ohimè! degli intermedi," in *Li due Orfei: Da Poliziano a Monteverdi*, 2d ed. (Turin: Einaudi, 1975), 200–275, esp. 234–56, in English translation as "The Wondrous Show, alas, of the *intermedi*," chap. 5 in Pirrotta and Elena Povoledo, *Music and Theatre from Poliziano to Monteverdi*, trans. Karen Eales (Cambridge: Cambridge University Press, 1982), 173–236.

3. See Lorenzo Bianconi and Thomas Walker, "Dalla *Finta pazza* alla *Veremonda*: Storie di Febiarmonici," *Rivista italiana di musicologia* 10 (1975): 379–454, esp. 389–91.

4. Unlike the works previously mentioned, *Eliogabalo* was a revival and adaptation of a *dramma per musica* that had already been presented in Venice. See Mercedes Viale Ferrero, *La scenografia: Dalle origini al 1936*, vol. 3 of *Storia del Teatro Regio di Torino*, ed. Alberto Basso, 5 vols. (Turin: Cassa di Risparmio di Torino, 1976–83), 29–30.

5. On the absolute state see Perry Anderson, *Lineages of the Absolutist State* (London: New Left Books, 1974), and Alberto Caracciolo, ed., *La formazione dello stato moderno* (Bologna: Zanichelli, 1970).

chine" in the realms of warfare, diplomacy, bureaucracy, and taxation was reflected in the persuasiveness and seductiveness of a princely spectacle whose dramatic and musical essence centered on the solo presentation of the characters. Both operatic spectacles and the absolute state, with their complex and costly production mechanisms, were at the service of the same social elites and of the maintenance of their feudal privileges in an age marked everywhere by economic, social, and ideological revolt.

If the social circles for which court operatic spectacle was first created were extremely restricted, the diffusion of the works themselves was just as narrowly limited, particularly in comparison to the very intense written publicity they received. Court opera was the prerogative of the circles that had produced it; none of the examples mentioned above circulated outside the court at all. For one thing, the scenery could not possibly have been used in other theatrical spaces; for another, the theme of a work of this sort was explicitly connected with the place and occasion of its original performance. Moreover, these spectacles were by definition private and exclusive, and they were appreciated all the more for being unique and unrepeatable. It would have seemed a loss of status if a court could not do better than present a work that had already been performed elsewhere. The scores of the Florentine *intermedi* of 1589 and of *L'Orfeo* by Alessandro Striggio and Claudio Monteverdi (Mantua, 1607) were printed not in view of other possible productions but rather as "monuments" in perpetual memory of the spectacles' excellence. (If, on occasion, the existence of a printed score did give rise to the revival of a work on another stage, it was by chance and, in the eyes of the original promoters, improper.) After all, for the sovereigns who had financed the entertainment, the score, which only a few persons endowed with special skills could read, was of much less importance than descriptions of the performances in letters, diplomatic dispatches, and printed reports (at times with an accompanying engraving depicting the scenery) that told courts near and far of the magnificence and splendor of the spectacle and—by implication— of its sponsor.

Another element that discouraged the reuse or broader circulation of a work was the lack of a profit incentive in the courtly conception of operatic production, at least during the first two-thirds of the seventeenth century (if profit excludes the consolidation and enhancement of a court's "stock" in terms of prestige). When court operas were performed more than once, it was either for sheer enjoyment or to satisfy an erudite interest with a second hearing, or perhaps to provide an opportunity for a portion of the public that had been excluded from the first hearing (for lack of space or for reasons of protocol) to enjoy the princely spectacle. Lack of space was the reason for the repeat performance of *L'Orfeo* in Mantua, when "all the ladies of this city" who had been unable to crowd into the small hall to see the premiere on 24

February 1607 were invited to a second performance.[6] Erudite interests and pure pleasure motivated the operas promoted in Rome in the 1630s by the Barberini family and performed again in the same courtly and aristocratic circles in the years immediately following the first performances.[7]

The court put on operatic spectacles that offered an ad hoc image of itself. Since ostentatious display of wealth was one of the primary ends of the court spectacle, the production was magnificent and costly, but in allotting funds the sovereign destined the better part for the purchase of raw materials (textiles, wood, paint, cordage, wax, and the like) while making use of artisans and artists in his own service for technical tasks and artistic realization.[8] Such people ("singers, the engineer, craftsmen, musicians, the scene designer, the set painter, the costumer," and so forth)[9] were permanent, salaried court personnel for whom operatic spectacle differed from their routine duties only by its complexity and elaborateness. In and of itself, *opera in musica* demanded no professional specialization of them, and it offered them no special rewards. If anything, court personnel might feel some corporative resentment toward certain highly skilled performers (the singers, for instance, who were the most "visible" participants in the production) who were recruited from outside the court and handsomely paid. This is what happened in Turin at the court of "Madama Reale" (the duchess of Savoy) and at the viceregal Spanish court in Naples.[10] Although it caused a good deal of talk and required a major effort, operatic spectacle was only one of the official entertainments for which the prince's regularly salaried staff was responsible, perhaps not even the most important one, and certainly not the most frequent.

We need to consider not only why operatic court spectacles were put on but for whom—that is, who made up the targeted audience for such outlays

6. See the letter of Francesco Gonzaga to his brother Ferdinando (1 March 1607) quoted in Angelo Solerti, *Gli albori del melodramma*, 3 vols. (Milan: Sandron, 1904 reprint, 3 vols. in 1, Bologna: Arnaldo Forni, 1976), 1:69–70. A third performance of *Orfeo* was planned for spring 1607 on the occasion of a projected visit to Mantua by Carlo Emanuele of Savoy, but it failed to take place when the duke of Savoy canceled; see Iain Fenlon, "Monteverdi's Mantuan *Orfeo:* Some New Documentation," *Early Music* 12 (1984): 163–72, esp. 168–69.

7. See Margaret Murata, *Operas for the Papal Court 1631–1668* (Ann Arbor: UMI Research Press, 1981), appendix 1.

8. For an analytical and comparative study of administrative documents relating to a court opera (*Chi soffre speri*, sponsored by the Barberini family in 1639), see Lorenzo Bianconi and Thomas Walker, "Production, Consumption, and Political Function of Seventeenth-Century Opera," *Early Music History* 4 (1984): 209–96, esp. 215–21, 234–43.

9. Michele Timotei, *Il cortegiano, nel quale si tratta di tutti li offizii della corte* (Rome, 1614), quoted in Gino Benzoni, *Gli affanni della cultura: Intellettuali e potere nell'Italia della Controriforma e barocca* (Milan: Feltrinelli, 1978), 95–96.

10. See Viale Ferrero, *La scenografia*, 4, 28; Ulisse Prota-Giurleo, "Breve storia del teatro di corte e della musica a Napoli nei secoli XVII–XVIII," in *Il teatro di corte del Palazzo Reale di Napoli* (Naples: 1952), 19–158, esp. 30–31.

of money and organizational effort. The entire concept of a "public" for whom a work was produced was extraneous to courtly opera.[11] Court opera had spectators, to be sure—cultivated, well-to-do persons of high social rank who were capable of receiving, deciphering, and then ratifying the ideological and political signals (cryptic or explicit) that were woven into the spectacle— but the person for whose enjoyment the entertainment had been created and to whom it was principally directed was without question the patron himself. As with architectural projects or paintings, absolutistic royal patronage "meant that the king himself was the prime recipient of the works he had commissioned: he wanted them to reflect his greatness, to be a tangible representation of his power; and in fact everything displayed his crest, devices, ciphers, hereditary arms, images of his subjects' obedience."[12] Often, the prime function of the spectators of court opera was as an integral part of the ceremony, for which they provided a frame and an ornamental complement. In these cases, according to the situation, the public was "numerous," "most noble," "highly select," and as such contributed to the magnificence of the performance. The spectators' actual enjoyment was only secondary. Furthermore, this public had access to the spectacle at the prince's invitation, and attendance was part of a courtier's duties under court etiquette, much like attendance at a banquet, a tournament, a fireworks display, a coronation, or a marriage, all of which were official occasions of a grandiose, spectacular, and ritualistic nature whose purpose was to reaffirm the political establishment and demonstrate the power of the princely sponsor. The courtly public "suffered" a spectacle that was commanded from higher up, even in the sense that the courtiers had little say in the content or form of the entertainment. Consensus was unquestioned and taken for granted, and it mattered little whether it was sincere or inspired by a sense of duty. All performances were in any event officially a success.

One case in point is the highly acclaimed performance of Monteverdi's *L'Arianna* (Mantua, 1608). Yet unlike *L'Orfeo* of the previous year and *La Dafne* of the same year, the score for *L'Arianna* was not published—and publication customarily gave a work recognition, both musically and in the eyes of contemporary society and posterity. The audience became the principal target of the spectacle only when opera ceased being an emblem for and emanation of an absolute power and, above all, when the spectator who paid for his ticket became part of the economic picture. Only then did the public have

---

11. The modern meaning of *public* as a community or group of theatrical spectators was nearly unknown in the seventeenth century; see Bianconi and Walker, "Production, Consumption," 243.

12. Jean Starobinski, *L'invention de la liberté 1700–1798* (Geneva: Skira, 1964), quoted from *The Invention of Liberty, 1700–1798*, trans. Bernard C. Swift (Geneva: Skira, 1964; distributed in U.S. by World Publishing Co.), 14.

a way of demonstrating its enjoyment of the spectacle, deciding its fate, or shaping its form and contents. This power was not granted to the court public: the prince's choices were not open to debate.

2. Court Opera and Commercial Opera

During the first four decades of the seventeenth century, a number of courts adopted operatic spectacle as a form of conspicuous and official entertainment. After Florence came Mantua, and after Mantua came Piacenza, Parma, Turin, Ferrara, and Rome. In these cities operatic spectacles were not always the prerogative of the highest-ranking local court: in Rome, for example, the pope's personal court had obvious ethical and political reasons for avoiding such entertainments, but its role was taken over by the courts of the cardinals and nobles who gravitated around the papal court (first among them, the courts of Francesco and Antonio Barberini, nephews of Pope Urban VIII).[13] Similarly, there was no princely court in the university town of Padua. Spectacles were produced in that city by a noble, Pio Enea degli Obizzi, who also promoted and organized tournaments and theatrical festivities in Bologna and Ferrara.[14] In this period opera was not considered an autonomous form of theatrical spectacle but rather an integral part of mixed and composite entertainments, festivities "for the perfection of which a great variety of things was needed"[15]—music, drama, dance, singing, "magical" scenic effects, carousels, and more. One spectacular entertainment in this tradition turned out to be of prime importance: on 11 April 1636, Obizzi was the promoter of a tournament held in Padua that was preceded by a performance of *Ermiona,* for which he himself wrote the verse text and which was set to music by Felice Sances and performed by musicians for the most part from Rome.[16]

Although *Ermiona* was a prime example of the festive tradition and its concept of spectacle, some aspects of the work's production and the use made of it deserve comment, especially as regards its audience, which was more urban than courtly and more public than exclusive. First of all, *Ermiona* was

13. On this subject see Murata, *Operas for the Papal Court.*

14. See Bruno Brunelli, *I teatri di Padova dalle origini alla fine del secolo XIX* (Padua: Angelo Draghi, 1921), 72ff. On Obizzi's activities as a promoter of spectacles in Bologna, see Bianconi and Walker, "Dalla *Finta pazza*," 427–29; for his activities in Ferrara see Thomas Walker, "Gli sforzi del desiderio: Cronaca ferrarese (1625)," in *Studi in onore di Lanfranco Caretti,* ed. Walter Moretti (Modena: Mucchi, 1987), 45–75, esp. 47–49.

15. See the preface by Ascanio Pio di Savoia to the libretto for *Andromeda,* a theatrical festivity put on in Ferrara in 1638 (Ferrara, 1639), as quoted in Walker, "Gli sforzi del desiderio," 48.

16. On this performance see Pierluigi Petrobelli, "L'*Ermiona* di Pio Enea degli Obizzi ed i primi spettacoli d'opera veneziani," *Quaderni della rassegna musicale* 3 (1965): 125–41.

not written for a narrow courtly milieu but for an urban audience, larger numerically and of more varied social status. (In this it anticipated the appearance of public operatic theater in Venice, which followed soon after.) In Padua the audience (from the back rows to the front) included "the citizenry," "students" at the university and "aristocratic foreigners," "rectors and nobles of the Veneto," "gentlewomen" and "gentlemen." We know little about the precise social composition of the audience at court theaters, but what is striking about this testimony from a university city in a republican state—aside from the hierarchical seating arrangements, which much resembled the custom of the courts—is the presence of people of modest social rank ("citizenry" and "students") who presumably would not have been admitted to court spectacles in the capital city of a monarchical state. The civic nature of the performance was indeed explicitly stated on the middle of the proscenium arch, which was emblazoned with the insignia of the city authorities rather than the noble crests usually found at a court performance.[17] The new urban and public dimensions of the performance of *Ermiona* in Padua are the elements of greatest interest for marking out a transitional point between courtly operatic productions and the commercial productions under an impresarioso, inaugurated in Venetian theaters just one year later.

In hindsight, this shift is clearly discernible, but it was not the result of any brilliant initiative on the part of a farsighted patron. Rather, it was the consequence of the arrival of *opera in musica* in a state—the Venetian terraferma—that had no courts or absolute sovereigns but did have a widespread network of civic leaders and nobles. It is certain that the Paduan spectators of *Ermiona* (and, for all the more reason, audiences in Venice in the years that followed) viewed opera with new eyes and with a pragmatic attitude: because they gave less heed to the ideological and self-congratulatory elements in opera, they ultimately came to consider it as a form of civic entertainment. Hence opera became reproducible rather than unique, public rather than exclusive. This was precisely the case with the very first Venetian commercial opera, *Andromeda,* by Benedetto Ferrari and Francesco Manelli, performed in the Tron family's theater in the *contrada* of San Cassiano during carnival, 1637.[18]

A comparison between *Ermiona* and *Andromeda* is instructive in several ways. First, the cast of *Andromeda* was in part made up of the same people who had appeared in *Ermiona* at Padua in 1636. Perhaps because *Ermiona* had been a success, the company offered the same sort of spectacle in Venice

17. See Brunelli, *I teatri di Padova,* 75.

18. On the Teatro San Cassiano and *Andromeda,* see Nicola Mangini, *I teatri di Venezia* (Milan: Mursia, 1974), 33–42.

but with the substantial difference that in Padua Pio Enea degli Obizzi had acted as patron and coordinator for *Ermiona,*[19] whereas in Venice the artists themselves took on the risks and obligations of production. *Andromeda,* like *Ermiona,* was aimed at a large urban audience, but in Venice the potential audience was very large indeed because for the first time an operatic spectacle was put on in a space open to anyone who could pay the price of a ticket of admission. By that fact alone, opera became a commercial product. It should be noted, however, that the enterprise was an innovation only because for the first time an operatic spectacle was commercialized and open to a broader public than courtiers. Indeed, the modus operandi of the Ferrari-Manelli troupe in Venice had for some time been characteristic of commedia dell'arte companies that charged admission for spectacles they produced in a theater rented for that purpose.[20] When they transferred operations from Padua to Venice, the singers of *Ermiona* and *Andromeda* were the first to fit *opera in musica* into a preexistent production system of a commercial type—the system of the commedia dell'arte (which, incidentally, was the first professional theater of early modern times).

What the Ferrari-Manelli company offered for sale to the Venetian public was substantially the same entertainment given at court, but they put it on with limited technical means and, as they said, "completely at their own expense." They may perhaps have been slyly appealing to the Venetians' commercial instincts by stressing that the production was economical, whereas "similar operations by princes cost infinite amounts of money."[21] Princely munificence was money flung to the winds, but the meager sums spent by the Ferrari-Manelli company, and by others that were soon organized, became a commercial investment that aimed at producing a profit, or at least covering expenses.[22] Opera at court was like a book printed privately in a very limited edition; in a public theater, opera became like a paperback. The content was

19. Obizzi had made use of a network of contacts with noble and courtly circles for the recruitment of artistic personnel. His contacts with the duke of Modena can be documented; see Modena, Archivio di Stato, Archivio per materie: Letterati, busta 49 *bis.*

20. On the relations between the commedia dell'arte companies and musical troupes, see Nino Pirrotta, "Commedia dell'arte e melodramma," *Santa Cecilia* 3, no. 3, suppl. (1954): 23–37, also in Pirrotta, *Scelte poetiche di musicisti* (Venice: Marsilio, 1987), 147–71, and in English translation as "Commedia dell'arte and Opera," *Musical Quarterly* 16 (1955): 305–24. On the presence and activities of acting companies in Venice and the grafting of opera onto their production system, see Ludovico Zorzi, "Venezia: La Repubblica a teatro," in *Il teatro e la città: Saggi sulla scena italiana* (Turin: Einaudi, 1977), 237–91, esp. 252–58.

21. Preface to Ferrari-Manelli, *La maga fulminata,* also performed in the Teatro San Cassiano the following year (1638).

22. For a comparison of the costs and revenues of court opera and commercial, impresarial opera, see Bianconi and Walker, "Production, Consumption," 215–43.

the same, but the opera, appropriately labeled *mercenaria,* or commercial,[23] became a market commodity. Public operatic spectacle was deemed "by no means inferior to that practiced in various places by the magnificence of princes, with the sole difference that, while they offer its enjoyment out of their own generosity, opera in Venice has become business."[24] Opera's "becoming business" implied, above all, a difference in procedures that arrived at the same result: the nobility and patriciate of a republican state—Venice— procured by commercial means the same theatrical entertainment that the prince, in his munificence (and to bolster his magnificence), offered or imposed on his own subjects at court. The commercialization of opera had another and significantly different effect, however: when opera shifted to "mercenary" ends, it became an autonomous and individual form of spectacle and musical theater requiring particular, specialized systems of production and realization. At court, as we have seen, operatic spectacle was one means to an end, one component of a composite theatrical event, and one among many possible forms of spectacle. In the public theater it was instead an end in itself, a *res* considered and used for its own sake.

Court opera and commercial opera were two different, even opposed, modes of production and consumption applied to the same type of theatrical spectacle. They were not unaware of one another; indeed, they influenced one another. Commercial opera was marketed as a court product replicated on a business-oriented scale and offered for the enjoyment of a large and composite audience. Far from denying its prestigious, noble origins, it flaunted them for publicity purposes. A number of promoters of opera houses boasted of

23. See the three-part division of operatic spectacles—princely, academic, and "mercenary"—proposed and discussed in a treatise by Giovan Domenico Ottonelli in his *Della cristiana moderazione del teatro* (Florence, 1652), quoted in Ferdinando Taviani, *La commedia dell'arte e la società barocca: La fascinazione del teatro,* vol. 1 of *La commedia dell'arte: Storia testi documenti,* ed. Ferruccio Mariotti, 2 vols. (Rome: Bulzoni, 1969), 509–11. (The passage on *l'opera mercenaria* is also quoted in the present volume in chapter 6, 355–56.) When the term *commercial opera* is used in these pages it refers to the meaning that Ottonelli gave to the term *opera mercenaria* and the implications thereof.

24. Cristoforo Ivanovich, "Memorie teatrali di Venezia," in *Minerva al tavolino* (1681), 2d ed. (Venice, 1688), 361–453, esp. 381–82, portions of which are in Lorenzo Bianconi, *Il Seicento, Storia della musica,* vol. 4 (Turin: Edizioni di Torino/Musica, 1982), 298–306; quoted here from Bianconi, *Music in the Seventeenth Century,* trans. David Bryant (Cambridge: Cambridge University Press, 1987), 305. Ivanovich's *Memorie* presents the most authoritative description of the mechanisms of impresarial opera in its Venetian form (on which see the studies by Bianconi, Morelli, Walker, and others cited in notes 53 and 54). One very early example of the transfer of ideas between court opera and commercial opera (if not of their virtual identity) is *La Delia* of Guilio Strozzi: written in 1630–31 for a princely wedding but neither set to music nor produced on that occasion, the work was performed, with music by Manelli, as the inaugural production at the Teatro Santi Giovanni e Paolo in Venice in 1639 (see Bianconi and Walker, "Dalla *Finta pazza*," 410–11).

the princely rank, prestige, and dignity of their productions. In 1678, when the Grimani family of Venice spared no expense for the inauguration of the new Teatro San Giovanni Grisostomo with a performance of *Il Vespasiano* by Giulio Cesare Corradi and Carlo Pallavicino, the production was commercial in its production system and its context, and yet its intent and pretensions were princely by virtue of the new theater's grandeur and magnificence, its deliberately select public (determined by a higher ticket price than for other houses), and the self-celebration of its socially prominent promoters, presented metaphorically in the triumph of Emperor Vespasian.[25] Although court opera held firm to the demands of a high level of display and prestige and continued to eschew commercial ends, it did not disdain opening its doors to a paying public or adopting the production techniques of the impresarial theater—especially as regards the recruitment of personnel (singers, composers, set designers) and the circulation of repertory. Three examples will serve to illustrate this point.

From the outset, opera in Naples under the Spanish viceroys was conceived as an instrument of political propaganda as well as a courtly entertainment. To this end, viceroy Oñate made use of professional personnel from commercial opera, such as the traveling troupe of the Febiarmonici, who put on *La Didone* by Giovanni Francesco Busenello and Francesco Cavalli on 12 October 1650 in the Stanza del Pallonetto of the royal palace, a performance sponsored by Oñate with paid admission fees.[26] On 23 December 1652 Oñate inaugurated the new theatrical space in the royal palace with the highly political *Veremonda* of Giulio Strozzi and Cavalli, a work celebrating the victory of the king of Spain over the Catalonian rebels. In the following years relations intensified between the court theater and professional commercial troupes, and collaborative efforts multiplied. After 1653, genuine joint productions (or at least exchanges) took place between Naples and Venice, and the viceroys, instead of producing operas themselves, financed or acquired productions through the impresarial system, winning public approval simply for sponsoring them. With the opening of Naples' Teatro San Bartolomeo, arranged for by Oñate, the public and courtly dimensions of opera production were brought even closer together. In 1654 the Febiarmonici, who had been giving palace performances since 1650, moved to the public theater and shifted their operatic activities to a more impresarial style of management

25. See Mangini, *I teatri di Venezia*, 77–83.

26. "They charged 5 carlini per head at the door to those who wanted to come in to see [the opera], 2 carlini more for a seat, and 4 ducati for each box, one of which was occupied by the lord viceroy, who also paid for it." This was the report in the *Avvisi* of Naples of 18 October 1650, quoted in Bianconi and Walker, "Dalla *Finta pazza*," 379, and in Domenico Antonio d'Alessandro, "L'opera in musica a Napoli dal 1650 al 1670," in *Seicento napoletano: Arte, costume e ambiente,* ed. Roberto Pane (Milan: Edizioni di Comunità, 1984), 412.

with a performance of *Orontea regina d'Egitto* by Giacinto Andrea Cicognini and Francesco Cirillo.[27] *Alessandro vincitor di se stesso* by Francesco Sbarra and Antonio Cesti (1662) launched the practice of holding the first performance of an operatic spectacle in the theater of the royal palace (the Teatro di Palazzo), subsequently moving it to the Teatro San Bartolomeo. Eventually the viceroy financed public spectacles at the San Bartolomeo ("help with costs" is registered as early as 1662, under Peñaranda, and again in 1696, under Medinaceli)[28]—a financial aid that demonstrates that the viceroys fully grasped the political utility of opera. This early and explicit (but hardly unique) example of government participation in the administration of city theaters (in the form of both guidance and financial subsidy) was to become standard practice during the eighteenth century.[29]

In Turin opera productions remained typically courtly in their nature and their aims throughout the seventeenth century, but although they continued to serve as court entertainments, they soon came to be administered according to impresarial criteria. Count Giacomo d'Alibert, a man who had already been active in theatrical circles in Rome, sought a position in Turin as superintendent of theatrical spectacles, and he drew up a detailed proposal to the Savoy court for reinvigorating its theatricals. His suggestions included launching regular opera seasons for profit on the Venetian model; adapting opera to the local fashion for ballet in the French style; and offering a free first performance to encourage public interest. The idea behind these suggestions was that operatic spectacle increased the prestige of the sovereign and the prosperity of the state. It was not Alibert but the impresario Bernardino Bianchi who succeeded (after resolving a number of difficulties) in putting this program into effect in 1680. From that date on Turin had a court theater that was controlled and subsidized by the sovereign but charged admission and was administered by professionals working on contract. A number of the spectacles offered in Turin originated in Venice, in particular at the Teatro Santi Giovanni e Paolo and the Teatro San Giovanni Grisostomo, the latter

27. On problems concerning the attribution of this *Orontea* and other works with the same title, and on Francesco Cirillo, see Thomas Walker, "'Ubi Lucius': Thoughts on Reading *Medoro*," in Aurelio Aureli and Francesco Lucio, *Il Medoro,* ed. Giovanni Morelli and Thomas Walker, Drammaturgia musicale veneta, no. 4 (Milan: Ricordi, 1984), cxxxi–clx, esp. cxxxiv–cxl; see also Walker, "*Orontea* 'arrichitta': Un libretto veneziano a Napoli, 1654" (paper read at the conference on "La musica a Napoli durante il Seicento," Naples, 11–14 April 1985).

28. See Prota-Giurleo, "Breve storia," 26, 57.

29. On the theatrical scene in Naples summarized here, see Bianconi and Walker, "Dalla *Finta pazza*," 379–95; Prota-Giurleo, "Breve storia," 19–28; Lorenzo Bianconi, "Funktionen des Operntheaters in Neapel bis 1700 und die Rolle Alessandro Scarlattis," in *Colloquium Alessandro Scarlatti, Würzburg 1975,* ed. Wolfgang Osthoff and Jutta Ruile-Dronke (Tutzing: Schneider, 1979): 13–111, 220–27, esp. 17–18, 22–25.

owned by Vincenzo Grimani, who operated much like a theatrical agent in Venice for the Savoy court.[30]

From the mid-seventeenth century Reggio Emilia had a civic theater (the Teatro della Comunità) managed by a citizen group (known as the *soprastanti* [superintendents] of the theater) that took responsibility for its finances and organization. However, this theatrical society enjoyed subsidies (seemingly on a regular basis) from the dukes of Modena, Francesco II and Rinaldo d'Este, in whose territories Reggio lay. The dukes also furnished musical personnel (instrumental musicians and singers in the service of the court) and a set designer (the architect Tomaso Bezzi). In addition they took care of sizable budget deficits. For example, in 1696, on the occasion of the inauguration of the city's newly renovated theater, the ducal coffers were obliged to donate an additional 24,293 Modenese lire, "to be conceded out of the innate good will of His Royal Highness," which went to "fill in" the balance of the 13,680 lire "gift made by order of the Most Serene Patron," Duke Rinaldo. True, the theater of Reggio Emilia was a public, city theater, managed collectively and lucky enough to be able to count on a princely subsidy; nonetheless, it is equally appropriate to see it as an instrument of ducal policies—as a ducal theater removed from the court but over which the dukes exercised a large measure of administrative control, thanks to their financial aid and the personnel they furnished. The arrangement worked well both ways: the ducal subsidy permitted the theater in Reggio to achieve high-quality productions in substantial numbers, and the court at Modena, by publicizing the Reggio theater and its activities during the fairs held there in April and May, fostered the prosperity of both the city and the state, made the theater an attraction for those who attended the fairs, and, in the last analysis, gained luster and merit from having done so.[31]

Court theater and commercial theater were not separate, noncommunicating entities; they influenced one another and fed on one another, each in pursuit of its own ends.

---

30. See Viale Ferrero, *La scenografia,* 27–30, and Mercedes Viale Ferrero, "Repliche a Torino di melodrammi veneziani," in *Venezia e il melodramma nel Seicento,* ed. Maria Teresa Muraro (Florence: Olschki, 1976), 145–72. See also Stanislao Cordero di Pamparato, "Un duca di Savoia impresario teatrale e i casi della musica Diana," *Rivista musicale italiana* 45 (1941): 108–32, 237–63.

31. See Bianconi and Walker, "Production, Consumption," 283–84, 228–34. On the situation in Reggio in general, see Adriano Cavicchi, "Musica e melodramma nei secoli XVI–XVIII," in *Teatro a Reggio Emilia,* ed. Sergio Romagnoli and Elvira Garbero, 2 vols. (Florence: Sansoni, 1980), 1:97–133, esp. 107–19. See also Paolo Fabbri and Roberto Verti, *Due secoli di teatro per musica a Reggio Emilia: Repertorio cronologico delle opere e dei balli 1645–1857* (Reggio Emilia: Teatro Municipale, 1987).

3. Traveling Companies: The Cooperative, Organized Diffusion of Commercial Opera

When opera became commercial and took on the impresarial systems of production and administration, it spread rapidly; after the events of 1637 in Venice, performances that had once been occasional, private, and unique became ongoing, public, and replicable.[32] Opera first began to circulate thanks to a cooperative form of the impresarial system and traveling companies of singer-actors (such as Ferrari and Manelli's group, the Febiarmonici, and the Discordati) that took the organizational criteria and professionalism of the commedia dell'arte troupes as their models. The singers' companies even borrowed their itineraries from the traveling actors' troupes, and when two groups played the same town, they competed for the same audiences and often clashed violently.[33] Opera lacked the satirical bite of the commedia dell'arte, its hilarity, and its social criticism. Instead, opera's heroic, mythological, and romantic themes strongly reinforced the ideology of the ruling class that promoted and controlled spectacles (which were modeled, after all, on court opera). The public's appreciation of opera, however, was no less enthusiastic than for prose comedy. Audiences loved the histrionic fireworks, salacious witticisms, and intricate plots of the commedia dell'arte, but they were also fascinated by spectacular scenic effects, the seduction of song, and the courtly matrix of opera. For that reason the public's demands harmonized with the intent of the authorities, who favored operatic spectacle (or at least seldom opposed it) and who might even make deliberate political use of it.

In contrast to the stable (nontraveling), unspecialized personnel of court opera, these itinerant troupes were teams of technicians who specialized in putting on operas. The troupes arrived in a city with a show ready to be performed—with a text, a musical score, scenery, and singers. Either they

32. Obviously court opera did not die, even if, judging by relative numbers, it was much reduced by the spread of commercial opera and the establishment of urban opera houses operating in permanent structures. But in certain aspects court opera continued to receive the bulk of attention: stage design and techniques are much better documented for court opera than for commercial opera throughout the seventeenth century (see section 3 of Mercedes Viale Ferrero, "Theatrical Space and Scenic Space," chapter 1 of volume 5 of the present *History of Italian Opera*). Court opera's system of production and, even more, the complex of significations and motivations that it embodied, were perpetuated in certain aristocratic circles during the final two or three decades of the century under the special form of operas performed in country villas. The theatricals put on in the Contarini family's villa of Piazzola, in the villa at Pratolino by Ferdinando de' Medici, in the theater of Count Vitaliano Borromeo on Isola Bella, in the Chigi palace at Ariccia, and in the summer residences of other Roman nobles shared many of the characteristics of the court opera staged during the first forty years of the seventeenth century: an exclusive audience, erudite themes, a self-celebratory intent, and limited (or nonexistent) subsequent circulation of the work.

33. On the itinerant theatrical companies see Pirrotta, "Commedia dell'arte," and Bianconi and Walker, "Dalla *Finta pazza*."

rented a space in which to offer paid performances, handling administrative details themselves, or they might be engaged by the owner of a theater, who would take care of ticket sales. Such troupes represented an intermediate phase in the process of gradual specialization typical of the production system of opera. From the unique performance of court opera (a spectacle put on by court personnel who had other functions) it moved toward collectively organized itinerant companies, and it eventually arrived at a system of fully professional personnel—singers, set designers, composers, and orchestral musicians—operating in the free market, which became the rule after the mid-seventeenth century.

The history of opera during the 1640s and the 1650s is the history of traveling troupes of singers. A company of "Signori Academici Febiarmonici" performed *La finta pazza* by Strozzi and Francesco Sacrati in Piacenza in 1644. We find them giving the same opera and a few others (first, Giovanni Faustini and Cavalli's *Egisto* and, after 1649, Cicognini and Cavalli's *Il Giasone*) in other cities of north-central Italy—in 1644 in Genoa, in 1645 in Lucca and Florence, in 1646 and 1647 in Genoa and Milan, in 1648 in Turin and Milan, and in 1650 in Lucca, after which date the troupe remained permanently in Naples. In some of these cities the name "Febiarmonici" became synonymous with opera singers in general. Members of the company soon left to organize other troupes, some with the same name, some not (as with the Discordati), in Bologna, Ferrara, Rimini, Reggio, and other cities. Even more than opera's entry into the public theaters of Venice, it was the itinerant companies and their travels through the various states, provinces, and cities of Italy that directly determined the transformation of operatic spectacle away from the elitist and occasional genre that it had been in the courts and that spread it on a national scale. Many local operatic traditions and many permanent opera houses arose following the appearance and the residence of traveling companies. We have considered the case of Naples, where both the court theatrical tradition and that of the Teatro San Bartolomeo depended on the activities of the Febiarmonici. The Teatro Falcone of Genoa had an analogous history: after 1646–47, the Falcone made regular use of traveling companies. Opera was brought to Verona by Carlo Righenzi, a former member of the Discordati troupe, in 1665 (performing *Il Xerse* of Nicolò Minato and Cavalli).[34] In the long run, however, the boost that traveling companies had given to founding local opera traditions proved counterproductive for the troupes themselves: the proliferation and prosperity of permanent local institutions managed by an impresario and the establishment of fixed theatrical circuits

34. See Armando Fabio Ivaldi, "Gli Adorno e l'hostaria-teatro del Falcone di Genova (1600–1680)," *Rivista italiana di musicologia* 15 (1980): 87–152, esp. 142, and Bianconi and Walker, "Dalla *Finta pazza*," 401.

capable of recycling the repertory led to the decline of the itinerant companies. For example, Ferrari and Manelli, the first promoters of opera at Venice, no longer played that city after 1642–43; at best, their troupe appeared in theatrical centers, such as Piacenza, Parma, or Modena, that were slow to adopt the more stable impresarial system of organization found in the Venetian public theaters.[35]

4. Impresarial Opera: Ends and Means; The Single Impresario and Impresarial Associations

In mid-seventeenth-century Italy the impresarial form of operatic theater found fertile terrain in which to take root. From the public's viewpoint, opera was an efficacious response to a need, shared by a broad spectrum of society, for spectacle and theater—a need stronger than ever in an urban "mass" culture "guided" from above, as was the case in the seventeenth century.[36] Unlike the theater of the commedia dell'arte, opera met with few serious problems of censorship. Rather than being a destabilizing influence, it functioned as a vehicle for ideas expressing the dominant ideology (and, at times, as a vehicle for moralistic and didactic ideas, as in the librettos of Monsignor Giulio Rospigliosi, later Pope Clement IX). On occasion governments even used opera as a tool and a force for creating consensus.

From the viewpoint of the entrepreneurs, artists, and stage personnel, operatic theater opened a vast field for the display of talent and specialized skills. In the overall climate of economic recession characteristic of Italy in the mid-seventeenth century (which contributed greatly to nourishing the Italians' "yearnings for culture," their insecurity, their servility, and their scrambling for "protections" and posts),[37] the public market for operatic theater represented a creative activity that was gratifying in more ways than one. Some saw opera as an opportunity to create new jobs, precarious and unstable though they were; others saw it as a source of a second income that could supplement the salary paid them by an institution or earnings from their profession, art, or trade. Many of those who had a hand in the production of operas wore two hats: librettists were often lawyers (Faustini, Busenello, Giacomo Badoaro, Nicolò Beregan), secretaries or government functionaries (Strozzi, Maiolino Bisaccioni), teachers (Girolamo Gigli), physicians (Gio-

35. See Bianconi and Walker, "Dalla *Finta pazza*," 432.

36. For a discussion of these characteristics, with examples, see José Antonio Maravall, *La cultura del Barroco: Análisis de una estructura histórica* (Esplugues de Llobregat: Ariel, 1975), in English translation as *Culture of the Baroque: Analysis of a Historical Structure,* trans. Terry Cochran (Minneapolis: University of Minnesota Press, 1986).

37. See Benzoni, *Gli affanni della cultura.*

vanni Andrea Moniglia, Giovanni Cosimo Villifranchi, Antonio Salvi), or architects (Girolamo Frigimelica Roberti); for all of them, their literary activities were a marginal but welcome opportunity for earnings. Often the scene designers were also architects or civil or military engineers; singers and composers might be in the service of a private person, a potentate, or an ecclesiastical chapel (whose titles they flaunted in librettos). Impresarios frequently used earnings from another professional activity (musical or not) as the financial base for their impresarial initiatives. Until well into the eighteenth century, people involved in opera continued to have two professional careers. As operatic traditions and the markets for opera became more firmly established, however, the title and the post of *virtuoso* or *maestro di cappella* to a prince or a sovereign was more an embellishment, representing only a nominal protection (especially for singers) rather than a guarantee of a generous and regular stipend.[38]

From the viewpoint of its promoters and producers, on the one hand opera represented a form of investment that paid off in one way or another—either in monetary profits or enhanced luster—at a time when the Italian economy was stagnant. One might even say that the construction of theaters and the launching of operatic enterprises was one of the few forms of capital investment available in a society that still clung to land revenues. On the other hand, opera offered an ephemeral but prestigious civic entertainment, an opportunity for amusement eagerly sought by its target audience, and one to which its promoters could point with pride. The mercantilistic use that the republican capitals of Venice and Genoa were to make of opera are symptomatic of both aspects.

In Venice the city's loss of political and diplomatic prestige and its declining military and commercial power, together with the public debt, led noble families to seek new ways to invest their private wealth. Economic prospects and a desire for exhibitionistic display led them to see the opera house as a form of investment that would generate earnings as well as social prestige. In the case of the Grimani family, who opened the Teatro Santi Giovanni e Paolo and entered the competitive world of opera even before 1640, the two elements were clearly present. That theater, administered with prudence, cleverness, and a fine tactical sense both for business and for culture, turned out to be the most vital and the most durable of all the seventeenth-century Venetian opera houses. For the Grimani family it also worked to assert and consolidate their family's prestige in the eyes of Venice and all Italy. In 1660 the Grimanis brought into their service the impresario Marco Faustini, formerly of the rival

---

38. On this question see Sergio Durante, "Cantanti per Reggio (1696–1717): Note sul rapporto di dipendenza," in *Civiltà teatrale e Settecento emiliano,* ed. Susi Davoli (Bologna: Il Mulino, 1986), 301–7.

Teatro San Cassiano. In the meantime (1655–56) they had opened another theater, the San Samuele, which performed spoken drama only. Toward the end of the 1670s, when Francesco Santurini, impresario of the Teatro San Moisè and the Teatro Sant'Angelo, attempted to attract a broader public by offering half-price tickets, the Grimanis instituted the same policy at the Santi Giovanni e Paolo. At the same time, however, they also opened a luxury theater, the San Giovanni Grisostomo (1678), which had only full-price tickets and was (or claimed to be) the most prestigious and socially distinguished of the Venetian theaters. In 1687, in a move to forestall potentially dangerous competition from the renovated Teatro Vendramin at San Luca, the Grimanis forced Gasparo Torelli, who held the lease for the theater, to cede it to them as subtenants for the length of his contract with the Vendramin family, a tactic more typical of industrial and capitalistic political economy and a move that brought the San Luca within the Grimanis' theatrical sphere.[39] It is hardly surprising that the first historical treatise on *opera in musica*, Cristoforo Ivanovich's *Memorie teatrali di Venezia* (Venice, 1681), was dedicated to the Grimanis and, among its other aims, glorified and justified their theatrical operations.[40]

The situation in Genoa was similar. The Adorno family, who since 1602 had owned the Osteria del Falcone, an inn situated in a central commercial zone of the city, used portions of the structure to make a theater bearing their name, and in the mid-1640s they launched a regular program of theatrical activities. The Adornos saw operatic spectacle as a potentially profitable venture capable of replacing other sources of income that had dried up but also as an efficacious way of consolidating their family's prestige. They worked in collaboration with the managers of the Osteria del Falcone (whose signatures often appear on the dedications of librettos) and rented their hall to itinerant companies, prudently demanding payment one evening at a time, thus avoiding the risk of finding their lessees suddenly insolvent. Some members of the family—Giacinto Adorno in particular—took an active part in the artistic management of the theater, choosing works and casts on the basis of the success they had achieved in other opera houses.[41]

In Venice many patrician families—the Tron, Grimani, Vendramin, Marcello, and Giustiniani families, among others—became involved in theater ownership and management and in operatic production as a source, direct or indirect, of both revenue and prestige. If these many theaters guaranteed a lively competition (which was a strong incentive but also a chronic danger

39. See Mangini, *I teatri di Venezia*, 54, 56–61, 70–72, 77–83.

40. See note 24. On this brief treatise see Thomas Walker, "Gli errori di *Minerva al tavolino*," in *Venezia e il melodramma nel Seicento*, ed. Maria Teresa Muraro (Florence: Olschki, 1976), 7–20.

41. See Ivaldi, "Gli Adorno."

for the impresarial system), they also contributed greatly to the artistic and touristic attractions of a city past its prime that was grasping a last chance for international brilliance by developing a flourishing business precisely in art and tourism.[42] In Genoa, by contrast, only one family, the Adornos, initially showed interest in the theater. It was only in the early eighteenth century, with the opening of the Teatro Sant'Agostino (a real estate venture of Nicolò Maria Pallavicino's) and the reconstruction of the Teatro del Falcone (under Eugenio Durazzo, who took over its management from the Adorno family), that a limited degree of competition arose among these Genoese patrician families. Such competition was contained, however, and never as fierce and continuous in Genoa as it was in Venice and elsewhere. Carlo Goldoni's testimony of 1736 informs us, for instance, that during that period the Teatro del Falcone and the Teatro Sant'Agostino, both of which were managed by the impresario Francesco Bardella, alternated their operations every two years in order to avoid needless competition.[43]

Livorno's situation was significantly different from that of both Genoa and Venice. Livorno was the only city in Italy with a flourishing economy during the seventeenth century. Thanks to the institution of a free port, which gave it a strong position in the economic and mercantile expansion of northern European nations such as England and Holland, Livorno carried on an intensive foreign trade and had an expanding population.[44] In spite of the city's prosperity, Livornese society showed little interest in permanent operatic activities. When opera finally did take hold there, during the last fifteen years of the seventeenth century, it did so only thanks to the efforts of Ferdinando de' Medici, who had devoted a great deal of effort to controlling, promoting, and expanding the artistic and musical life of the entire grand duchy of Tuscany.[45]

Visions of profits and increased social prestige did not carry the same

42. In this connection the late eighteenth-century historian Carlo Antonio Marin said of Venice, "Its frequent spectacles, since they were for the most part splendid, attracted quantities of foreign people to admire them, thus the money that was spent for entertainment in part made up for the trade deficit." See his *Storia civile e politica del commercio de' Veneziani* (Venice, 1808), quoted in Zorzi, *Il teatro e la città*, 239.

43. See the "Prefazione" to volume 15 of Goldoni's *Opere* in the Pasquali edition, in Carlo Goldoni, *Tutte le opere*, ed. Giuseppe Ortolani, 4th ed. (Milan: Mondadori, 1959), 1:732.

44. See Ruggiero Romano, "La storia economica: Dal secolo XIV al Settecento," in *Dalla caduta dell'Impero Romano al secolo XVIII*, vol. 2, pt. 2 of *Storia d'Italia*, ed. Ruggiero Romano and Corrado Vivanti (Turin: Einaudi, 1972–76), 1813–1931, esp. 1917.

45. See Robert Lamar Weaver and Norma Wright Weaver, *A Chronology of Music in the Florentine Theater 1590–1750*, Detroit Studies in Musical Bibliography, nos. 30 and 70 (Detroit: Information Coordinators; Harmonie Park Press, 1978, 1993), 1:34–36. For a brief summary of operatic activities in Livorno during the seventeenth century, see Giovanni Orsini, *Il teatro di musica nella medicea Livorno (1644–1703)* (Livorno: Chiappini, 1913), which should be consulted with the information given in Elvidio Surian, "L'esordio teatrale del giovane Gasparini:

weight everywhere in the launching and consolidation of theatrical traditions. At Bologna, for example, the establishment of public theaters responded above all to the city's need for public institutions of entertainment in imitation of the Venetian model: the Teatro Formagliari, opened in 1641 and managed by the members of the Accademia de' Riaccesi, was frequented for the most part by the aristocracy; the Malvezzi, opened in 1653, was less exclusive socially, but when it was renovated in 1680 it became the most prestigious theater in the city; and the Teatro della Sala, the most popular of the city's theaters and the one with the lowest prices, gave operas only at irregular intervals and was owned by the municipality.[46] In Rome, musical theater had flourished under the Barberinis (a period that ended with the death of Pope Urban VIII in 1643), and it returned to favor with the arrival of Queen Christina of Sweden in 1656 and under the papacy of the Rospigliosi pope, Clement IX (1667–69). The opening of the Teatro Tordinona in 1671 was the result of pressure that the secular aristocracy, under the leadership of Christina and Count Giacomo d'Alibert, put on Pope Clement X to create a stable public institution to supplement the many small private theaters. At first that venture was successful, but later it was hindered by popes ill-disposed to tolerate theatrical spectacles (in fact, ready to condemn them as part of an illicit trade), to the point that in 1697 the morally strict Pope Innocent XII (Antonio Pignatelli) ordered the demolition of the theater building.[47] In Florence the aristocracy and the Medici court contributed funds for the reconstruction of the Teatro della Pergola, which put on few but prestigious spectacles composed especially for this theater and produced thanks to adequate financial backing from the grand-ducal court. The aristocratic Accademia degli Immobili was charged with management of the Pergola, whereas its contemporary, the Teatro di via del Cocomero owned by Nicolò degli Ughi, was first administered by the larger and socially more composite Accademia degli Infuocati and later by the Accademia dei Sorgenti. At the Cocomero the productions consisted

---

Alcune considerazioni sull'apprendimento e tirocinio musicale nel Seicento," in *Francesco Gasparini (1661–1727)*, ed. Fabrizio della Seta and Franco Piperno (Florence: Olschki, 1981), 37–54 n. 3.

46. On Bolognese theaters see Corrado Ricci, *I teatri di Bologna nei secoli XVII e XVIII* (1888; reprint, Bologna: Arnaldo Forni, 1965).

47. On Queen Christina of Sweden and Pope Clement IX as promoters and backers of operatic spectacles, see Per Bjurström, *Feast and Theatre in Queen Christina's Rome* (Stockholm: Nationalmuseum, 1966), and Margaret Murata, "Il Carnevale a Roma sotto Clemente IX Rospigliosi," *Rivista italiana di musicologia* 12 (1977): 83–99. On the Teatro Tordinona see Alberto Cametti, *Il Teatro di Tordinona poi di Apollo* (Tivoli: Chicca, 1938). The riotous and violent climate of the carnival season—particularly among the noble families of Rome, whose litigious outbursts for real or pretended motives of rank, precedence, and privileges caused a good deal of disorder in the city—helped to make theatrical life in Rome unacceptable to the popes. On this question see Margaret Murata, "The Church and the Stage in Seicento Rome" (paper read at the national meeting of the American Musicological Society, Philadelphia, October 1984).

for the most part of revivals of Venetian *drammi per musica*.[48] The academic cachet of these spectacles concealed a unique managerial system—theater administration by an association—that lay halfway between the court system and commercial opera.[49] This system aimed at combining the social and cultural prestige of court opera with the organizational and financial criteria of commercial management. Opera put on by a society or an academy involved the production of works chosen by a group of promoters (members of an academy or a citizen committee) who jointly financed the spectacle and usually directly managed the venture; often they were the theater's owners or at least those legally responsible for its activities. Such arrangements did not aim at earning a profit. Since the money taken in served to pay expenses and reduce the debt to the members of the association (an academy or the municipality), the promoters' aim was essentially to provide entertainment for themselves or, especially in the eighteenth century, to enhance the "decorum and advantage of the city." The productions, though not as splendid and rich as those at court, had ambitions in that direction: the prestige of a prince may not have been at stake, but there was still that of an honored committee of citizens or academicians. Although paid admissions did open up the theater to a larger audience, performances were also not as openly public as with "commercial" theate precisely because the spectacles were aimed at the enjoyment of the group that had promoted them, financed them, and on occasion absorbed losses.

Theater administration by a society of backers was a formula applied elsewhere than in Florence during the seventeenth century, in particular in cities without a court that had a citizen patriciate or a vital noble class. In Venice, for example, there was the case of the Teatro Novissimo, an anomaly in the city that created impresarial theater. During its brief (1641–45) but artistically illustrious life (it was the theater of the scene designer Giacomo Torelli and the singer Anna Renzi), the Novissimo offered opera exclusively. Furthermore, rather than occupying a preexistent theater building, it had been constructed anew—probably without boxes. The Novissimo was managed by a consortium of aristocrats and intellectuals who worked through an impresario to make it the most refined of the Venetian theaters, aiming perhaps more at fulfilling cultural and erudite expectations than at making money.[50] Similar

48. See Weaver and Weaver, *A Chronology*, 1:21–31, and in particular John Walter Hill, "Le relazioni di Antonio Cesti con la corte e i teatri di Firenze," *Rivista italiana di musicologia* 11 (1976): 27–47, esp. 28–36.

49. The management of the Pergola is treated in detail by William C. Holmes in *Opera Observed: Views of a Florentine Impresario in the Early Eighteenth Century* (Chicago: University of Chicago Press, 1993).

50. See Mangini, *I teatri di Venezia*, 62–66; Bianconi and Walker, "Dalla *Finta pazza*," 414–18.

circumstances arose in Pistoia, where in 1678 the Accademia dei Risvegliati promoted and financed the construction of a theater that they then managed on their own, and in Palermo, where the Teatro Santa Cecilia was the result of a joint venture involving the Unione di Santa Cecilia (a singers' organization), the city's aristocracy, and Viceroy Uzeda.[51] Such ventures were fewer, however, in the early, pioneering, and experimental phases of opera than in its later phase of expansion and consolidation. Theaters administered by a society or academy became more widespread during the eighteenth century, when this managerial system became the most typical of the opera house as a civic institution.[52]

Unlike the society-administered opera house (and, of course, unlike court theater), the theater under impresarial management was first and foremost the expression and the result of a professional activity aimed at making money.[53] The impresario was, professionally, an organizer of theatrical activities. He might work on his own or put his experience and skills at the service of others (a court, a civic group, a society, or an academy) as an independent contractor, functioning as administrator and director of the spectacles. On occasion the impresarial system involved collective or society management; when that was the case, risks and burdens were shared, just as in opera houses run by an academy. There are many known instances of this sort of joint management, ranging from the six singers who worked with Ferrari to produce *Andromeda* in 1637 to the "academy for reciting opera at San Cassan [Cassiano]," founded by Cavalli on 14 April 1638,[54] or from the "company" made up of Marco Faustini, Marc'Antonio Correr, Alvise Duodo, and Polifilo Zuancarli that operated in the Venetian theaters of Sant'Aponal (Sant'Apollinare), San Cassiano, and Santi Giovanni e Paolo in the 1650s and the 1660s[55] to the group of "Signori Interessati" involved in the management of the the-

51. On the Teatro dei Risvegliati see Alberto Chiappelli, *Storia del teatro in Pistoia dalle origini alla fine del secolo XVIII* (Pistoia: Officina Tipografica Cooperativa, 1913). On the Teatro di Santa Cecilia see Giuseppe Sorge, *I teatri di Palermo nei secoli XVI, XVII, XVIII* (Palermo: Industrie Riunite Editoriali Siciliane, 1926); on Palermo in general see Roberto Pagano, "La vita musicale a Palermo e nella Sicilia del Seicento," *Nuova rivista musicale italiana* 3 (1969): 439–66.

52. The most illustrious example of an opera house managed by a society or an academy is remote from Italy geographically, though not artistically: the Royal Academy of Music in London during the 1720s. See, in particular, Judith Milhous and Robert D. Hume, "New Light on Handel and the Royal Academy of Music in 1720," *Theatre Journal* 35 (1983): 149–67; Milhous and Hume, "The Charter for the Royal Academy of Music," *Music and Letters* 67 (1986): 50–58.

53. On the impresarial system see Bianconi, *Il Seicento,* 181–204, in English as *Music in the Seventeenth Century,* 180–89 and 190–204. See also Bianconi and Walker "Production, Consumption," 221–43.

54. See Giovanni Morelli and Thomas Walker, "Tre controversie intorno al San Cassiano," in *Venezia e il melodramma nel Seicento,* ed. Maria Teresa Muraro (Florence: Olschki, 1976), 97–120, esp. 98, 107–8.

55. See Bianconi and Walker, "Production, Consumption," 221–22.

ater of Reggio Emilia[56] or the four persons in Verona who, around 1690, had "made a company among themselves to have musical dramas performed in the prefectural theater of the city, called de' Temperati."[57]

Still, the most characteristic professional and commercial expression of impresarial management was the individual impresario. Chronicles, diaries, archival documents, and epistolary literature treat him as a curious, at times pathetic figure. They show him as a strategist of theatrical spectacle constantly assailed by financial problems, burdened with debts, besieged by creditors (singers, theater staff, and owners), avoided by debtors (box renters), and often crushed, even bankrupted, by the complexity of the financial machinery of operatic spectacles. This highly colored, dramatic image, although customary, is much in need of a closer look. First, it is an image contradicted by fact: financial ruin, legal persecution, singers' whims, composers' delaying tactics, the insolvency of the box renters, and a rowdy public failed to dissuade a legion of persons of varied social extraction and composite professional description from becoming impresarios.

Between the seventeenth and the early eighteenth centuries, a great variety of individuals became impresarios. Some came from the urban petty bourgeoisie; others, as we have seen, were men of law. There were also people who had already made a name in the theater world—a scene designer and librettist (Filippo Acciaiuoli); architects (the Mauro family), singers (Faustina Bordoni, Giovanni Battista Pinacci, Pasquale Cafaro—known as Caffariello—Antonio Lottini, and Domenico Guagni); composers (Cavalli, Giovanni Chinzer, Michelangelo Gasparini, and Antonio Vivaldi); painters (Sante Prunati from Verona and Sebastiano Ricci from Venice), and more. We also find aristocrats, such as Count Giacomo d'Alibert, who was involved, without great luck, in theatricals at Rome and Turin. There were even princes and sovereigns: Ferdinando de' Medici acted as an advocate for musical life in Tuscany, served as the "manager" of a prestigious theater in the Medici villa at Pratolino, and, together with the dukes of Mantua and Modena, worked to create performance circuits for singers; and Vittorio Amedeo II of Savoy served as an "importer" of Venetian operas to Turin, in collaboration with the Grimanis and others. It is clear even from this brief review of the impresarial role that it was often a "second job." Nobles and aristocrats took on impresarial tasks for pleasure, investing their own personal wealth in the ventures, at times at a total loss. The others made the impresarial role a strictly professional activity whose indispensable financial base came from another (profitable and hopefully stable) long-term activity.

56. Ibid., 228–29, and Cavicchi, "Musica e melodramma," 112.

57. See Vittorio Cavazzocca Mazzanti, "Un teatro veronese anteriore al Filarmonico," *Atti e memorie dell'Accademia di Agricoltura, Scienze e Lettere di Verona* 101 (1924): 77–91, esp. 82.

The chief inducement for the professional impresario must have been the prospect of financial gain to be derived from a capital investment in a promising commercial operation(or apparently promising, as judged by the liveliness of a market in continual expansion). Faustina Bordoni provides an interesting example of an impresario. She was a singer who knew the operatic market inside and out. During carnival 1729 Bordoni invested a portion of her savings (3,000 ducats) from two resoundingly successful years in London in the Teatro San Cassiano in Venice. Someone remarked, "If the opera does not succeed she will have lost her money and sung for nothing." Bordoni was undoubtedly aware of the risk, but, putting her faith in her own professional acumen, she bet on both artistic and financial success. Unfortunately, she was disappointed on both scores, because a rival theater—again the Grimanis' Teatro San Giovanni Grisostomo—responded to the challenge with the Venetian debut of a great castrato, Farinelli (Carlo Broschi).[58]

Paradoxically, the data available to us on the results of this type of investment are generally anything but encouraging. What we can glean from them is that the structure of the impresarial system was unstable and, for the most part, made operatic ventures uncertain and destined to fail; many chronicles and judicial acts relate clamorous personal bankruptcies. Nonetheless, we need to guard against being overly impressed by these data. They are vivid and dramatic, but they are also, at base, the only information that has come down to us on the financial results of theatrical ventures. There would have been little reason to publicize a balance sheet in the black, which may have been the normal expectation and the hoped-for and, for all we know, frequent result of such activities. Cases that "made the news" and elicited talk and scandal should perhaps be considered as striking exceptions to the rule and titillating topics for scandal-mongering chronicles and satires on mores (and, in the eighteenth century, even an inspiration for opera buffa libretto!) rather than as emblematic of an inherent tendency to failure in the profession of the impresario. Among such cases we may mention those of Giuseppe Polvini, dubbed "Faliconti," who died in Rome "loaded with debts and troubles" in 1741;[59] Francesco Santurini in Venice,[60] and Bernardino Bianchi in Turin.[61] Since the precariousness, the riskiness, and the uncertainty of the economic system underlying impresarial opera remained a constant, there must have

58. See Sylvie Mamy, preface to Domenico Lalli and Geminiano Giacomelli, *La Merope*, Drammaturgia musicale veneta, no. 18 (Milan: Ricordi, 1984), xxvii.

59. Pierleone Ghezzi gave this brief description of Polvini as the caption in his famous caricature of him; see Raimondo Guarino, "Il teatro dell'indifferenza: Questioni storiche e storiografiche sullo spettacolo inaugurale del Teatro Argentina," in *Il teatro a Roma nel Settecento* (Rome: Istituto della Enciclopedia Italiana, 1989), 1:421–44.

60. See Mangini, *I teatri di Venezia*, 45–46. and 73–75.

61. See Viale Ferrero, *La scenografia*, 31ff.

been a genuine prospect for earnings, for a balance sheet in the black, or else perhaps a prospect for some other type of incentive that needs to be defined in psychological and sociological rather than in economic terms. Similarly, the notion of the utility and necessity of the impresario's social function as an organizer of public entertainments and a mediator between theater people and the society for which operatic spectacle was destined must have been widely accepted. One indication is that many legal and financial differences were settled out of court. We cannot otherwise explain how a profession and a system of production that would seem, in light of the financial results known to us, to have been doomed to rapid extinction should have lasted so long—some two and a half centuries.

Just what were the risks that threatened the stability of the system of producing and financing commercial opera? Basically they lay in the contrast between the complexity of the organizational machinery of operatic spectacle and the uncertainty of its outcome, artistic and financial. The impresario's activity began with a sizable expenditure of money for a variety of things; it ended with the return of his investment through the sole and uncertain channel of sales—box rentals and admission ticket sales.[62] As he prepared the program for the opera season, the impresario's first step, typically, was to rent a theater.[63] That done, his next task was to procure the best singers available: singers, as we shall see, were the chief attraction of the spectacle and the most costly item in the impresario's budget. The impresario negotiated directly with the singers—who were often capricious, temperamental, and unpredictable—over their fees and their travel and lodging expenses.[64] There was al-

---

62. When a patron rented a theater box he or she had possession of it either for the duration of the season or for one or more years, including the right to furnish it and use it freely. Whether or not one had a box, an admission ticket was required for access to the evening's performance. With that ticket those who did not own a box could enter the pit (*la platea*), where they could watch the performance standing or could pay for an armchair (*uno scranno*). On this and other aspects of the organization and management of opera houses (Venetian theaters in particular), see Ivanovich, *Minerva al tavolino*, and the studies mentioned in notes 24, 53, and 54.

63. In larger Italian cities the carnival period, which ran from 26 December to Mardi Gras (but in Milan to "Fat Saturday," four days later), was the high point of the annual operatic season, when the greatest number of productions and the most prestigious ones were put on. In some towns, however, such as Reggio Emilia, Lugo, Senigallia, and others, the time when large commercial fairs were held had greater importance than carnival season for opera. Other times during the year when opera seasons occurred with some regularity were spring (after Easter), the summer months, and the autumn. This was particularly true of larger cities that had more than one theater and of smaller cities that took advantage of the slack time between the major fair seasons and carnival time to engage first-rank singers who normally sang only in the major centers.

64. See Bruno Brunelli, "L'impresario in angustie," *Rivista italiana del dramma* 5 (1941): 311–41. Brunelli's essay is based on the rich store of archival documents regarding the impresario Marco Faustini preserved in the Archivio di Stato of Venice, Scuola Grande di S. Marco, buste 188, 194. The same materials have been used, in a variety of ways, by Remo Giazotto, "La guerra

ways the danger that a better offer from a rival impresario would whisk away the star attraction from under his nose. Competition and personal rivalry put the fragile economic structure of individual managements to a hard test: on the one hand they determined the size of the singers' fees; on the other they made it necessary to contain ticket prices. Often they created an excess of supply over demand. Once the cast was set, the impresario needed to engage the house librettist to prepare the text of the drama. This step might not involve any out-of-pocket expenses, as the poet often made his money from the sale of the librettos, which he had printed at his own expense (although the impresario paid the printing costs if the libretto had already been used for a previous production).[65] Next the composer (who, incidentally, was paid a good deal less than the lead singers)[66] wrote the score, creating his music around the vocal characteristics of the cast that had been engaged. For the actual production itself, the largest budget items comprised lumber for the stage sets and flats, materials for lighting the theater, and yard goods for scenery and costumes.[67] Normally the impresario did not have enough ready cash to pay in advance for such raw materials or for the labor they required, so he would attempt to encourage advance payment of box rentals for the season.

The rental of boxes, then, as for subscriptions for opera and concert seasons today, involved signing a contract, ahead of time and sight unseen, for the shows on the program, and it was based on the notion that operagoers would attend performances assiduously and habitually (buying their admission tickets night by night). Advance sales meant that box rentals were one of the linchpins of the impresario's financial planning: it is conceivable that the Novissimo in Venice failed because it was a theater without boxes, hence its management could not depend on those relatively secure advance payments. In practice, however, the impresario often had to deal with dilatory

dei palchi: Documenti per servire alla storia del teatro musicale a Venezia come istituto sociale e iniziativa privata nei secoli XVII e XVIII," *Nuova rivista musicale italiana* 1 (1967): 245–86, 465–508; "Nel CCC anno della morte di Antonio Cesti: Ventidue [*recte* 21] lettere ritrovate nell'Archivio di Stato di Venezia," *Nuova rivista musicale italiana* 3 (1969): 496–512; and (to particularly good effect) by Carl B. Schmidt "An Episode in the History of Venetian Opera: The *Tito* Commission (1665–66)," *Journal of the American Musicological Society* 31 (1978): 442–66.

65. See Bianconi and Walker, "Production, Consumption," 238–39.

66. Exceptions to this rule include the fee paid to Francesco Cavalli in 1659 (2,480 Venetian lire), roughly as much as the average amounts paid to the singers in the cast: see Bianconi and Walker, "Production, Consumption," 224–25. Furthermore, in 1683 Alessandro Scarlatti received 500 scudi, as compared to the 700 scudi paid to Paolo Pompeo Besci, the star of the singing company; see Prota-Giurleo, "Breve storia," 37. Composers' fees could vary between a tenth and a half of the amounts paid to the leading singers; see the examples given in Bianconi and Walker, "Production, Consumption," 225 n. 50.

67. See Bianconi and Walker, "Production, Consumption," 215–34.

box renters. The impresario could count rents owed him as credits, but outstanding rents deprived him of the cash he needed to pay his own debts. As a consequence, impresarios often used boxes (and the rental fees attached to them) as a form of payment to their own creditors, a device that further contributed to the obvious precariousness of the economics of impresarial management and made it more vulnerable legally.[68] It was precisely delinquent box rentals that tipped the balance for the enterprising Santurini, the impresario of the Sant'Angelo in Venice from 1677 to 1683, and put him in the untenable financial position that led to his bankruptcy.[69]

Far from discouraging the impresarios, the precariousness of the system made them persevere in their activities, since the only concrete chance of remedying the results of an unsuccessful season lay in a happier outcome during the following one, hence in continued activity, come what may. What is more, the same precariousness required particular circumspection in organizational and managerial tactics. These included recycling scenery and music, creating circuits to enable a production to tour from one opera house to another, and carefully choosing theatrical offerings that would fit the taste of the public and best the competition. The reuse of materials was a vital, even indispensable, practice that amortized costs and brought down expenses. Everything from the lumber for the stage sets to the canvas for scenery and the materials for costumes was used again not only within the same season but from one season to another and even from one theater to another. This practice was simply an application of a basic law of survival in impresarial theater: the best result in terms of spectacle for the least output of money, or the "biggest bang for the buck."

The circulation—that is, the reuse—of the spectacle itself was closely connected to the reuse of materials. As theatrical life in Italy intensified, a number of provincial cities came to have opera houses, and they relied on productions from nearby capitals and larger centers of operatic production. In the late seventeenth century, for example, cities of the Venetian terraferma—Vicenza, Udine, Treviso, Bergamo, and Brescia—and more distant cities—Mantua, Pesaro, and Reggio Emilia—regularly offered reprises of Venetian productions. These borrowings were in fact so regular that we can suppose the custom to have been to some degree institutionalized. We know that a number of people involved in opera (among them the singer Antonio Scappi and the impresario Giovanni Orsatto) remounted productions of works from the Venetian repertory in provincial theaters, and that this happened so often that it cannot be attributed to chance. These provincial performances also throw light on organizational and cooperative criteria that helped the impresarial

68. See Morelli and Walker, "Tre controversie."
69. See Mangini, *I teatri di Venezia*, 73–75.

system to survive. A regular, smoothly functioning theatrical circuit brought obvious advantages to both the theater (and the impresarios) that produced the opera originally and owned the score and to the theater (and the impresario) that gave it a repeat performance. The first opera house increased its revenues and the second avoided having to pay for at least some budget items, if not most of them.[70]

The need for theatrical circuits and the ways those circuits operated eventually favored the creation of new opera houses, which in turn increased the geographic diffusion of operatic spectacle. Court opera had been limited initially to a few major cities, but with the production system of traveling companies, commercial opera reached a number of other towns, and thanks to its impresarial organizational structure, it spread throughout Italy. Beginning in the last twenty years of the seventeenth century, every city in Italy from Palermo to Trieste embarked on the construction of a theater for performances of opera and laid down plans for more or less regular operatic seasons. Usually the city's aristocracy or an enterprising impresario—combining the mirage of earnings with a notion of "decorum and utility" for the city— took the initiative and set up the operational and managerial mechanisms for an opera house. Capital cities were joined by smaller centers and satellite towns (Pistoia, Spoleto, Perugia, Vicenza, Pesaro) and by port and fair cities (Ancona, Reggio Emilia, Senigallia, Lugo). Operatic spectacle—that is, operatic theater as an organized business—took hold wherever there was money in abundance and a large potential audience. During the course of the eighteenth century, having a theater became a sort of ideal civic obligation that few municipalities in central and northern Italy chose to ignore.

5. The Impresario and the Theater Public

Impresarial theater management was thus based on making use of a production more than once, on the circulation of "texts" and personnel, on enlarging the audience for opera, and on a rising fashion for going to the opera house. Commercial opera of the impresarial sort was the kind most responsive to the tastes and the enjoyment of the public. Court opera, as we have seen, was produced for a restricted number of invited guests from whom consensus could be expected; opera sponsored by an academy or a society, although commercial, was for the most part consumed within the same social group that had financed it. Opera in an impresarial theater, to the contrary, was more open both in terms of number of spectators and social class. It

70. See Bianconi and Walker, "Production, Consumption," 285–93 (on Venetian circuits for repeat productions), 237–38 (on ownership of scores), 228–34 (on one case of a provincial theater's reliance on Venetian theater).

could be enjoyed by anyone who had the price of a ticket: in Venice: "the expense ... was no more than half a scudo, and nearly everyone in Venice could, without great inconvenience, spend that much, because money abounded there."[71]

In theory paid entrance offered unfettered access to the theater, but this was only in theory. In reality the social configuration of the audience in the impresarial opera house was not determined by the occasional operagoer who could, "without great inconvenience," purchase a ticket to the *platea* (pit) but rather by the habitual, customary spectator who came night after night, could afford to rent a box for the season, and might even "personalize" his box with his own furniture, decorations, and the family escutcheon. This typical spectator was thus an aristocrat or a wealthy burgher who, by assiduous attendance (some went every evening), appropriated the theater. On the one hand his presence lent the opera house social prestige, as he used it as his favorite place to meet friends, exchange conversation, or curry favor. On the other hand as a purchaser he could freely, openly, and often noisily manifest his pleasure or displeasure.[72] Theatrical institutions and performances open to the general public on payment of admission were indeed "public," but they were not "popular." For example, in Spoleto the Teatro Nobile (the theater's name reveals its social aspirations) was opened in 1667 for the "pleasure of gentlemen and ladies."[73] In Genoa, when the Teatro Falcone was under the direct management of the Adorno family (also the theater's owners), it was aristocratic by choice, and although it had paid admissions, its purpose was the entertainment of the leading families of the city. Only in 1677 did the Falcone open a third tier of boxes, "for the enjoyment of the ordinary people."[74] The expression, though snobbish, certainly did not refer to the stevedores in the port or even the artisan class but rather to the urban bourgeoisie—wealthy commoners who aspired to sharing the amusements of aristocratic circles.

This fashionable public of chatty, often quarrelsome people (who were

71. From a report by Francesco de' Pannocchieschi, coadjutor to the papal nuncio in Venice from 1647 to 1652, quoted in Pompeo Molmenti, *Curiosità di storia veneziana* (Bologna: Zanichelli, 1919), 317.

72. This was one reason for the rowdiness and capriciousness that reigned among Italian opera audiences. Foreign visitors—the French in particular—often remarked on this lack of discipline and contrasted the sociable, distracted habits of Italian audiences to their own compatriots' more critical and more composed enjoyment. On this question see Gerardo Guccini, "Esploratori e 'indigeni' nei teatri del '700: Un viaggio intorno al pubblico e alla sua cultura," *Biblioteca teatrale*, n.s., 4 (1987). See also James H. Johnson, *Listening in Paris: A Cultural History* (Berkeley and Los Angeles: University of California Press, 1995), on the behavior of French audiences.

73. See Oliviero Sansi, *Il Nobile Teatro di Spoleto (Caio Melisso)* (Spoleto: Panetto e Petrelli, 1922), 5.

74. Ivaldi, "Gli Adorno," 126.

more apt to clash over who should precede whom as they entered the theater than they were to complain of a singer who gave a mediocre performance or a poorly realized set) was the group that the impresario sought to please and with whom he curried favor. He had several ways to do so. The first was with scenic "marvels"—striking or ingenious sets and stage machines. Even when these became the rule, some theaters (the Novissimo in Venice, for one) still managed to make them seem extraordinary. Another was to make sure the libretto referred to local tradition: in Venice, for instance, it was tactful to mention Troy and the city's mythical Trojan origins.[75] Yet another was to pursue and publicize efforts to offer something new, albeit within the context of fixed formal, stylistic, thematic, and scenic conventions.[76] Or the impresario might promote his theater by lowering prices, a tactic used by Santurini at the Teatro San Moisè in Venice in 1674. Above all, however, the impresario's trump card in pleasing his audience (and his cross to bear when it came to balancing the budget) was his singers. It was clear from the outset that female "song birds" *(canterine)* and castratos *(evirati)* were opera's principal attractions. Leading singers were engaged by individual contract and were not usually part of the regular house company. They were always the impresario's greatest financial burden: principals were paid between two and ten times more than composers (and up to one hundred times what orchestral musicians received); the fees for the two lead singers might account for as much as half of the impresario's music budget. This situation continued, nearly unchanged, from the mid-seventeenth through the eighteenth centuries. Singers remained the largest budget item. Their hold on the public was immediate, and their contribution determined the success or failure of a production. Their exorbitant demands can be explained by a basic law of market economics: by the mid-eighteenth century it was considered legitimate to "pay a stipend of 6,000 zecchini to a singer whose reputation will bring in enough business in the city to turn a profit of 60,000 zecchini and bring in a gross of perhaps 600,000."[77]

So intense was the public's interest in singers that the entire machinery of operatic spectacle revolved around them. Impresarios attempted to sign up the best voices of the moment more than a year ahead, thus creating a free market for singers. Moreover, because the singers' contribution was artistically decisive, opera scores were conceived more and more as a showcase for

75. See Wolfgang Osthoff, "Maske und Musik: Die Gestaltwerdung der Oper in Venedig," *Castrum Peregrini* 65 (1964): 10–49, in Italian translation in *Nuova rivista musicale italiana* 1 (1967): 16–44; Bianconi and Walker, "Dalla *Finta pazza*," 412–13.

76. For a telling example of theatrical tactics in Venice, see Nino Pirrotta, "Il caval zoppo e il vetturino: Cronache di Parnaso 1642," in *Collectanea Historiae Musicae,* vol. 4 (Florence: Olschki, 1966), 215–26.

77. [Giovanni Cattaneo?], *La libertà del cantare* (Lucca, 1752), 50.

vocal exhibitionism. The distinction between recitative and aria developed in the late seventeenth century, and from all points of view—the composer's creative efforts, the care that singers put into execution, and the public's attention and enjoyment—the musical interest of the show focused increasingly on the aria. At the same time, rather than circulating the same score for an opera, as had been the rule in the days of traveling companies and had remained so when an entire production was "recycled," it became customary to reset the same libretto to new music tailored to the cast that had been engaged. When it proved feasible, a house composer might rework a previously used score or put together a pasticcio—a composite of music from several composers' settings of the libretto and sometimes even including music intended for other operas. A pasticcio had certain advantages, given that the music could be arranged by some obscure local musician.[78] Individual arias circulated much more frequently than entire scores. A copy of the aria might be printed up as a collector's souvenir of the performance or for use in domestic entertainments; a piece might become part of a singer's personal repertory among his or her "suitcase arias" *(arie di baule),* to be brought out, when the need arose, to replace a solo in another opera that was deemed unsatisfactory.

6. Municipal Opera Houses and Collective Management in the Eighteenth Century

By the end of the seventeenth century, when the impresarial system had spread to form an operational network covering nearly all the Italian peninsula, certain widely tested and successfully replicated production procedures had become firmly established. The theaters' efficiency increased, their geographic distribution stabilized, and their longevity grew. As time passed they became more and more consciously civic or governmental in character. The consolidation and replication of behavioral patterns and operational tactics found an excellent observer in Charles de Brosses, a Frenchman who made several visits to Italy. During a journey from 1739 to 1740, de Brosses wrote a brief summary of the production mechanisms of Italian opera as he saw them in theaters of the cities he visited (Bologna, Naples, and Rome).

78. On the pasticcio see *The New Grove Dictionary of Music and Musicians,* s. v. "Pasticcio," by Reinhard Strohm, and *The New Grove Dictionary of Opera* s. v. "Pasticcio," by Curtis Price. A good many case studies of the reworking and transformation of opera scores have appeared. For three of these, on different phases and periods during the latter seventeenth century, see Carl B. Schmidt, "Antonio Cesti's *La Dori:* A Study of Sources, Performance Traditions, and Musical Style," *Rivista italiana di musicologia* 10 (1975): 455–98; Surian, "L'esordio teatrale del giovane Gasparini" (here the name of the obscure local musician is known because he later became famous); and Lowell Lindgren, "I trionfi di Camilla," *Studi musicali* 6 (1977): 89–159.

> Here [in Italy] an impresario who wants to mount an opera for a winter obtains
> the permission of the governor, rents a theater, signs up singers and instrumentalists
> from various places, draws up an agreement with the workers and the scenogra-
> pher, and often ends up bankrupting them, like our own directors of provincial
> theater companies. For greater security the workers have boxes assigned to them
> as payment, which they then rent out at a profit. Every theater puts on two operas
> a winter, at times three. . . . Every year there are new operas and new singers.
> People do not want to see an opera, a ballet, scenery, or an actor whom they have
> already seen another year, unless it is some excellent work by Vinci or some very
> famous voice.[79]

De Brosses was speaking about the theatrical scene in Italy in the 1740s, but
what he had to say could easily have applied to any one of the impresarial
opera houses of the last twenty years of the seventeenth century.

In the early eighteenth century the impresarial system was not only settling
into a greater stability with individual ventures that enjoyed a longer life, it
was also experimenting with the operatic repertory. Certain aesthetic and social transformations produced specializations within opera that had important repercussions in the system of production. Out of a common source in
seventeenth-century spectacle—which was a mixture of tragic, comic, and
balletic elements—there emerged three distinct and autonomous genres, each
with its own form of production and its social uses. These in turn gave rise
to specializations in all sectors of production, from theaters to impresarios
and from writers to composers and performers. These three genres—the
tragic (which was *dramma per musica* stripped of its comic characters), the
comic (opera buffa and, with a notable difference in function, intermezzi),
and ballet—were henceforth considered to be separate, even though in practice they often coexisted (as discrete, independent elements, however) in one
composite theatrical spectacle. As *La gazzetta universale* of Florence reported
from Venice in 1777,

> Thursday is the reopening of our theaters [in Venice]: this year we have three of
> them for spoken drama, as many for opera buffa, and in just one the serious opera,
> *La Nitteti,* with music by the renowned Sig. Cavaliere Monza, is sung to great
> applause. There was a tremendous reception, however, for the ballets—to wit, *Il
> Coriolano* and *Il Telemaco,* the first choreographed by Sig. Canziani, the second
> by Mr. Le Picq, both famous in their profession.[80]

This newspaper notice summarizes several trends that emerged during the
eighteenth century: a gradual increase in the number of buffa over serious

79. Charles de Brosses, *Lettres familières,* ed. Giuseppina Cafasso and Letizia Norchi Cagiano de Azevedo, 3 vols. (Naples: Centre Jean Bérard, 1991; distributed by Boccard), 2:990–91.

80. *La gazzetta universale,* 11 January 1777, 20–21, from its Venice correspondent. The two
ballets were staged between the acts of Metastasio's *La Nitteti* at the Teatro San Benedetto.

operas; a greater interest in the entr'acte ballets with opera seria than in the opera itself; and mention of the composer (and not of the librettist), which indicates that the composer's role was becoming more central and more decisive, both in the production of opera and in the market as a whole. Before turning to the system of production specific to these three genres, however, we need to take a brief overall look at the gradual changes in opera in the late seventeenth century and at the innovations introduced in the eighteenth century.

In general, theatrical life in Italy during the eighteenth century became increasingly institutionalized and more and more conventional. Its financial structure was also less improvised, less random, and less approximate than in the seventeenth century. Opera management was never a flourishing financial success, nor was daily life in the opera houses without incident and tumult. Still, there were fewer clamorous cases of financial ruin, bankruptcy, and turbulence than there had been in theaters and among impresarios of the previous century. The opera house (unlike theaters for spoken drama, in spite of educational efforts on the part of many of the enlightened spirits of the age) now tended to be built of brick and mortar rather than of wood as before, and it still occupied a central position in the urban texture of the city. The opera house became an institution recognized by the governments; active on an ongoing basis, it was an expression of urban society and a meeting place and point of reference for a population that was increasingly aware of its role in the organizational and administrative life of the city. Theaters and theatrical institutions devoted to opera spread with the growth of urban populations and with the increasing political, economic, commercial, cultural, and bureaucratic importance of cities (whether or not the city was the actual seat of political power). By the end of the eighteenth century, not only the capitals and major tourist and commercial cities had an opera house but also such small towns and provincial centers as Senigallia, Lugo, Faenza, Camerino, Varese, Arezzo, Recanati, Siena, Prato, Alessandria, and Novara.

Italy's relative political stability after the War of the Spanish Succession (even more, after the treaties of Vienna in 1738 and of Aix-la-Chapelle in 1748) undoubtedly encouraged the building of opera houses. Still, the phenomenon is to be understood above all as both an indication and a result of the growth of bourgeois social strata that saw the opera house as a symbol of prestige, hegemony, and wealth (social promotion and cultural acquisition always go hand in hand). Such groups furthered the productivity of opera houses, financed their administration, and in general adopted opera as a way of confirming their new status and power, perogatives that once had belonged to the aristocracy. Not by chance, the administration of the majority of eighteenth-century Italian opera houses passed into the hands of associations of *cavalieri e cittadini;* the aristocrats who owned the theaters and in the previous century had often managed them directly (Adorno, Obizzi, Grimani, and others) were now reduced to renting out their buildings, fully equipped, to others (a more secure role in economic terms but socially less central).[81] Nor was it by chance that the increasingly conscious goal of providing civic entertainment affected the financial aims of opera. Launching or promoting an operatic venture came to mean, first and foremost, responding to urban social and cultural needs. Even the impresario, a figure who formerly often seemed an adventurous speculator, came to be more of an administrator—a professional whose job it was to mediate between the managers or proprietors of the opera house and the personnel who put on the performances.[82]

The longevity of eighteenth-century opera houses has already been mentioned, and in fact theaters that had an intense but brief and trouble-ridden life—like the Novissimo in Venice or the first Tordinona in Rome, to cite two quite different cases—were quite rare in the eighteenth century. The opera house had become an integral part of the customs of Italian urban society, and because citizens and governments took a part in its management and its administration (there was broad acceptance of the notion that a municipal theatrical institution had civic utility and filled a social need), the theater was able to continue regular operations even when its finances were precarious or it underwent a change in administration. As in the later seventeenth century, a theater's continued activity (even when contrary to reason) was intimately connected to its hope for survival and its prospects for revenue. In Naples in 1702, the Teatro San Bartolomeo was unexpectedly deprived of the "help with costs" (that is, the royal subsidy) indispensable for producing the program for the carnival season. In the interest of not wasting what they had already put into planning the program, some of the people most directly involved in the productions came to the aid of the theater (among them, Silvio Stampiglia and Alessandro Scarlatti, the librettist and composer of the second

81. In 1766 the Grimani family in Venice, once fiercely determined to dominate the theatrical life of the city, went so far as to sell the Teatro San Benedetto to an association of box renters that numbered eighty-five "gentlemen and merchants" (*cavalieri e mercanti*) when the theater was reconstructed in 1774 after a fire; see Mangini, *I teatri di Venezia*, 155–56.

82. Luigi Bernardo Salvoni, an impresario in Rome, declared in a document dated 1757, "Although I seem to be the impresario of the Teatro Argentina, the truth is that in that enterprise I am so in name only and have only supervisory powers, recognized and rewarded at the pleasure of the financial partners. Hence any act or payment made in my name must be done with monies from those same managers, and everything must be subservient to the profit or loss of the same"; quoted in Mario Rinaldi, *Due secoli di musica al Teatro Argentina*, 3 vols. (Florence: Olschki, 1978), 1:103. See also the document of the Reverenda Camera Apostolica quoted on page 35 (note 85). On the figure and the role of the impresario in the mid-eighteenth century, see Franco Piperno, "Impresariato collettivo e strategie teatrali: Sul sistema produttivo dello spettacolo operistico settecentesco," in *Civiltà teatrale e Settecento emiliano*, ed. Susi Davoli (Bologna: Il Mulino, 1986), 345–56.

work on the program, *Tito Sempronio Gracco*). Their gesture made the opera season possible, but it brought them no financial return.[83] It seemed imperative not to interrupt the activity of a theater; its very reason for being was to continue to arouse the interest of the public, to encourage the circulation of artistic personnel and the result of their efforts, and to provide an opportunity for employment, both immediate and eventual. This demand for continuity of operations at all costs (which had already appeared in the latter half of the seventeenth century) seems particular to the impresarial opera house, and when in the early eighteenth century impresarial management spread outside Italy to become an international phenomenon, we find the same need for continuity elsewhere. In London, for example, where the theaters directed by Handel and Heidegger had roughly the same organizational and operational structures as the Italian impresarial opera houses, catastrophic failures did not dissuade the managements from persisting in the same course, either in the hope of wiping out one season's debts with successes in the next or because even a failing venture was capable of providing social recognition, professional advantages, and income from other sources.[84]

Management by an association and the financial and legislative involvement of the government also contributed to keeping eighteenth-century Italian opera houses functioning continuously and reinforced their civic connection. Government backing brought a form of political control over the activities of the opera houses, but it also gave official sanction to their public and civic importance. In this regard, managing an opera house began to be endowed with a new force of representation and a legal solidity that greatly attenuated some of the worst threats to the theater's existence—directors too prone to risky adventures, boxholders quarreling over artistic choices or delinquent in their payments, riotous spectators, free admission, and more. For example, various laws concerning theaters clearly express concern over the financial and professional qualifications of the impresario. One document of the Reverenda Camera Apostolica of Rome (1755) on the management of the principal opera houses of the city—the Argentina and the Alibert—notes first that often impresarial contracts were not "sought by persons with capital to lose." The document goes on to state that in order to prevent theaters from falling "into the hands of unqualified persons," anyone taking on that responsibility should pay a security deposit of 3,000 scudi to demonstrate financial stability.[85] We can see in this explicit Roman document (but the situation was

83. See William C. Holmes, "Quindici letter inedite su Alessandro Scarlatti," in *La musica a Napoli durante il Seicento*, ed. Domenico Antonio d'Alessandro e Agostino Ziino (Rome: Torre d'Orfeo, 1987), 369–78.

84. See Judith Milhous, "Opera Finances in London, 1674–1738," *Journal of the American Musicological Society* 37 (1984): 567–92.

85. See Rinaldi, *Due secoli di musica*, 1:91.

similar in the rest of Italy)[86] the notion of the opera house as a common good, but we can also see a concern for its financial health and an interest in having its operations continue smoothly, even under the guidance of salaried personnel. Local theatrical life must be a source of pride, not a cause of unrest.

There are many examples of government intervention in the finances and administration of eighteenth-century opera houses and of the shift to impresarial group management.[87] As we have seen, a theater was built in Palermo as early as 1639 (the Santa Cecilia), and regular opera seasons were launched, thanks to the financial backing and joint support of the aristocracy, the Unione di Santa Cecilia, and Viceroy Uzeda. In 1710 in Milan, Eugenio of Savoy, the governor of the duchy, came to the aid of the impresario Antonio Peverelli with an edict stipulating that the servants of the nobles who owned boxes would be admitted to the theater only on payment of a ticket, thus putting an end to an abusive aristocratic practice that had frequently been the cause of scuffles in the Teatro Regio Ducale and of lost revenues for the unfortunate impresario. A fire destroyed the Milanese theater in 1717, and its rebuilding was financed by a society of gentlemen *(Società dei Cavalieri),* aided by a government subsidy. In return for their participation in this venture, the members of the society had proprietary rights to some of the boxes, and they also took over the management of the opera house. As a result the theater became a full-fledged civic institution, an integral part of the social structure of Milan, and an institution deeply embedded in the customs of the Milanese.[88]

A similar *Società dei Cavalieri* was formed in Turin in 1727, and King Vittorio Amedeo II entrusted it with the direction of the Teatro Regio. The king delegated to society the power to operate as a collective impresario and deal directly with the production personnel and artists. The society administered a capital fund that came, for the most part, from the coffers of the sovereign but also from the city and from the theater's income. The king's tastes dictated the choice of spectacle, and the city's aristocracy formed the primary audience. Paid admission was required, although a document from 1727 lists a total of 452 persons who had a right to free admission.[89] This particular formula for the production of operas and the management of opera

86. For Venice, see Mangini, *I teatri di Venezia,* 96.

87. On this particular type of theater management, see Piperno, "Impresariato collettivo e strategie teatrali," 345–48.

88. See Guglielmo Barblan, "Il teatro musicale a Milano nei secoli XVII e XVIII," in *Storia di Milano,* 17 vols. (Milan: Fondazione Treccani degli Alfieri, 1953–66), 12:947–96, esp. 968.

89. See Marie-Thérèse Bouquet, *Il teatro di corte: Dalle origini al 1788,* vol. 1 of *Storia del Teatro Regio di Torino,* ed. Alberto Basso, 5 vols. (Turin: Cassa di Risparmio di Torino, 1976), 109–26. The phenomenon of "exempt" *(esenti)* theater patrons (personalities of aristocratic rank, the military, the diplomatic corps) was fairly widespread in those Italian cities in which the opera house was an official institution serving to add prestige to the court or the local government. This was the case not only in Turin but also in Florence, Naples, Milan, Parma, and elsewhere.

houses was a compromise between the absolutist ethic of the court theater (as it had existed in the seventeenth century) and the public character and commercialism of the impresarial system. It can be found in a number of cities, such as Turin or Naples, that were seats of an absolute power. At Naples the custom of royal subsidy *(aiuto di costa)* to the Teatro San Bartolomeo was revived with the accession in 1734 of the Bourbon King Charles (and later extended to the Teatro San Carlo). The impresario of the San Bartolomeo, Antonio Carasale, was the right-hand man of the viceroy, from whom he took instructions regarding the repertory and which artists and musicians to engage.[90] The situation was similar at Parma under the Bourbon duke Filippo, where the opera house, an expression of the taste of the court and the product of its financial aid, was managed by the cultivated Guillaume du Tillot, a man of refined tasks and the general intendant to the royal house for theatrical spectacles. Royal financing was essential to the theater's survival: one French visitor observed that "the prince pays a part of the expenses and maintenance of the theater. Without that [aid], a city that is not very big and not wealthy would not have enough to continue to keep up a theater."[91] At Reggio Emilia, under the eighteenth-century dukes Rinaldo and Francesco III d'Este, the customary "gift" *(regalo)* of the court in Modena became either an ongoing subsidy or a guarantee that expenses would be covered in case of loss, and under Francesco III the government granted the theater a fixed sum in the form of a yearly "endowment" *(dote)* of 25,000 lire. The dukes provided a financial base for the theater at Reggio because they were persuaded of its importance for the fair held in that city in April and May, and hence for the state's economy. A prestigious theater offering first rate productions was an attraction for a vast public of merchants, tourists, and occasional visitors, and it contributed to the flourishing economy and the renown of the city. Moreover, the dukes exercised a good deal of control over the productions, which meant that the Reggio theater reflected their tastes, at times in opposition to the city patriciate's demands for autonomy. The theater of Reggio Emilia could stand as emblematic of the merging of court and public theater in the eighteenth century and of absolutist and impresarial management.[92]

90. See Prota-Giurleo, "Breve storia," 105–6.

91. Joseph-Jérôme Le Français de Lalande, *Voyage en Italie,* 2d ed., 9 vols. (Paris, 1786), 2:109–10. On Parma see Giuliana Ferrari, Paola Mecarelli, and Paola Melloni, "L'organizzazione teatrale parmense all'epoca del Du Tillot: I rapporti fra la corte e gli impresari," in *Civiltà teatrale e Settecento emiliano,* ed. Susi Davoli (Bologna: Il Mulino, 1986), 357–80.

92. See Odoardo Rombaldi, "Rapporti politico-amministrativi tra Modena e Reggio Emilia nella vita teatrale," in *Teatro a Reggio Emilia,* ed. Sergio Romagnoli and Elvira Garbero (Florence: Sansoni, 1980), 1:263–71, esp. 264–66. On the repertory of the theater in Reggio Emilia during this period see, in the same volume, Cavicchi, "Musica e melodramma," 120–32, and Antonio d'Orrico, "Il Teatro reggiano del Settecento: Dal modello ducale all'utopia giacobina,"

At Turin, Naples, Parma, and Reggio Emilia, the opera houses were more like state theaters than court theaters, as were the Pergola in Florence and the Regio Ducale in Milan. They were official theaters, fashionable places where the "right people" met.[93] Like the court theaters of the seventeenth century, they provided an opportunity for a show of luxury, splendor, and magnificence, but access was not denied to a paying audience. Such theaters made wide use of local artistic personnel, but they also relied on the circuits of impresarial theater for the engagement of singers, dancers, composers, and scene designers. These were clearly royal theaters and an emanation of a central power;[94] they were just as undeniably institutions for the pleasure of the citizenry, as demonstrated not only by their administrative organization and their public access but also by their location at the heart of urban life rather than in the privacy of the prince's palace. It is also true, though, that the civic dimension of an opera house could be expressed more fully and with greater conviction in cities in a republic or in those far from a seat of absolute power. The civic dimension of an opera house attained its most concrete form, as we have seen, in collective administration by an impresarial association and in the efforts, financial and legislative, of some local governments. Bologna had two theaters, the Malvezzi and the Formagliari, that were already administered in this fashion early in the century, and from around 1750 many other cities erected or renovated opera houses that were inaugurated under associative and collective management and with a government subsidy (Cremona, Teatro Nazari, 1747; Padua, Teatro Nuovo, 1751; Senigallia, Teatro Condominiale, or Pubblico, 1752; Verona, Teatro dell'Accademia Filarmonica, 1754; Bologna, Teatro Comunale, 1763; Milan, Teatro alla Scala, 1778; Novara, Teatro Nuovo, 1779, and more). In Genoa in 1772 a citizens' association was formed for the management of all the city's theaters: the senate of the republic granted the society an exclusive right to put on public spectacles, along with a right prohibiting other theaters from opening.[95]

223–45. See also Paolo Fabbri and Roberto Verti, "Struttura del repertorio operistico reggiano nel Settecento," in *Civiltà teatrale e Settecento emiliano,* ed. Susi Davoli (Bologna: Il Mulino, 1986), 257–75, 277–99.

93. Such theaters were the site not only of operatic spectacles but also of sumptuous festivities such as masked balls and cantatas staged on diplomatic occasions or to celebrate dynastic events.

94. Of course, such opera houses were closed when the reigning or governing house was in mourning. Thus the theater in Turin shut its doors from carnival to summer in 1773 to honor the death of Carlo Emanuele III of Savoy; the theater in Florence closed during carnival 1781 upon the death of Empress Maria Teresa, the mother of the grand duke of Tuscany, Pietro Leopoldo. This was the rule in all theaters in the capital cities of states governed by a sovereign but not in republics: in 1717 much of Milan was scandalized when the new Teatro Regio Ducale was inaugurated on the very day of the death of the Austrian governor who had ordered its construction.

95. See Armando Fabio Ivaldi, "L'impresa dei teatri di Genova (1772): Per una gestione sociale della cultura," *Studi musicali* 7 (1978): 215–36.

Rome, the capital of the Papal States, was a special case. At first glance it is hard to imagine that the local government, the expression of a theocratic state, would concern itself with Roman theatrical life, given that the papacy had a moral obligation to view the theater—particularly commercial theater—as an insult (or at least a threat) to morality and an inducement to vice and spiritual degradation. Indeed, the moral rigor of Innocent XI and Innocent XII injected a high degree of instability into Roman theatrical life during the latter seventeenth century. Nonetheless, during the course of the eighteenth century, beginning with the papacy of Clement XI (1700–1721), reasons of state gained the upper hand over reasons of morality. For political expediency and the best interests of the government, it became opportune to tolerate theatrical spectacles and other instances of license during carnival (except during Jubilee years and times when the papal throne was vacant), and although the "Edicts Concerning the Abuses of the Theaters" condemned excesses, they sanctioned the existence and the activities of the opera houses.[96] This tolerance demonstrates, paradoxically, the participation of the papal government in Rome's theatrical life. It was that tolerance that gave the theaters stability, that permitted continuity, and that helped Rome to become a major center for the production and consumption of opera. In 1733, with evident ideological inconsistency but equally evident political wisdom, Clement XII ordered the reconstruction of the Teatro Tordinona (with funds from the Reverenda Camera Apostolica!) as a solution to the perennial problem of the choice, distribution, and decoration of the boxes—a burning question that set off rivalries and kindled jealousy among the Roman nobility and the foreign embassies. Thus, aside from private theaters such as the Capranica, the Alibert, and the Argentina, the city could boast having an opera house with "government backing" in which "even all the boxes were the property of the state, and could be rented, one evening at a time, on a lottery basis, removing from them all characteristics of private ownership and permitting no distinction by crowns or noble escutcheons and no privileges of territoriality."[97]

It is clear that during the course of the eighteenth century, the combination of government interest, in the form of financial aid and legislation, and collective management by an association had a strong effect on Italian opera houses, securely connecting them to the fabric of urban life, to the habits of city dwellers, and to the economy of their respective places of activity. Collec-

96. See Bruno Cagli, "Produzione musicale e governo pontificio," in *Le muse galanti: La musica a Roma nel Settecento,* ed. Bruno Cagli (Rome: Istituto della Enciclopedia Italiana, 1985), 11–21. The "Editti sopra gli abusi dei teatri" mentioned here (Cagli, "Produzione," 35–36 and n. 85) show what an obvious, accepted thing it was for the papal government to take an official interest in the vitality and prosperity of Roman theaters.

97. Cametti, *Il Teatro di Tordinona,* 1:119–22.

tive management had two great advantages: from the social viewpoint, the persons deputized to run the opera house formed a citizen delegation that operated and administered the theater in conformity with its own tastes; from the economic viewpoint, when the impresarial role was collective, it permitted sharing the costs, risks, and possible losses.[98] Nonetheless, some of the administrative mechanisms characteristic of impresarial theaters in the preceding century persisted. For example, the most dependable and the largest revenues (second only to governmental subsidy) still came from fees for box rentals for the season. Boxes were often rented well before the season began, thus giving the management a way to predict both revenues and the program's drawing power. In the mid-eighteenth century contracts for the rental of boxes at the Teatro Argentina in Rome were drawn up during the preceding season, with half the subscription price due on signature.[99] If box rentals still provided the directors of an established opera house with their surest revenues, the societies that constructed new theaters also found the advance sale of boxes an efficacious way to collect the necessary funds. This procedure, which had been perfected in the seventeenth century (in Venice and elsewhere) and was used widely during the eighteenth century,[100] required the genuine participation of the citizenry, first for the construction, then for the management of the theater (often named "Comunale," "Comunitativo," or "di Comunità," whereas in the preceding century it had often been named simply "Pubblico"). The individual citizen, the government, and the impresario all had a particular role in the city's principal theatrical institution, and they all participated directly and actively in its activities.

The case of the Teatro Comunale of Bologna is typical. The Teatro Malvezzi, the most prestigious of the city's opera houses, had burned down in 1745, and in 1750 "various noble gentlemen and citizens of Bologna" (which

---

98. The convergence of these two elements, which aimed at maximizing the spectacular aspects of a form of entertainment financed by the same social class that benefited from it, is clearly discerned in the charter documenting the founding of a society of gentlemen to manage the Teatro Argentina in Rome in 1761: see Rinaldi, *Due secoli di musica,* 1:140. The document notes that performances of heroic opera "have never appeared with magnificence and pomp except when some noble gentlemen have taken the trouble to direct them." A group of aristocrats formed a society for that purpose, so that "such an enjoyable entertainment [would] not have to fall into nearly total deterioration, and [so that] the nobility will be able to enjoy all possible magnificence and pomp to ornament the aforesaid entertainments."

99. Rinaldi, *Due secoli di musica,* 1:80.

100. One seventeenth-century example outside Venice (among many others) is that of the reconstruction of the Teatro Malvezzi in Bologna in 1680: see Ricci, *I teatri di Bologna,* 120. For an eighteenth-century example see the description of the methods and phases of the construction of the Teatro Nazari of Cremona in Elio Santoro, *Il Teatro di Cremona,* 4 vols. (Cremona: Pizzorni, 1969), 1:29–91.

means both aristocrats and burghers) petitioned the senate for permission to erect a new theater, "necessary for the public convenience and dignity of the city." The citizens' committee lent the funds necessary to acquire the land for the opera house, the interest on which was to be due them until the loan had been repaid. The construction of the theater itself was financed by the papal government and the senate of Bologna, which meant that all the city's civic and administrative powers were involved.[101] In a number of other cases, such groups appear to have joined forces to help a theater in decline, to reconstruct one after a fire, or to offer a house financial aid in a difficult time. In Pavia in 1778, for example, the prohibition of games of chance deprived the impresarios of the Teatro Nuovo of the funds they needed in order to put on a carnival season, so they canceled the operas and ballets that had been scheduled (gambling was widespread in the theaters of the time and was an important source of their revenues).[102] From that time forward the boxholders contributed an annual fixed sum to insure that sufficient funds would be available to mount the productions.[103]

Thus the eighteenth-century Italian opera house was by definition a civic institution, not only by reason of its government subsidies and its associative management but also because its complex operational mechanisms offered opportunities for steady employment to local people, skilled professionals and unskilled labor alike, as orchestral musicians, stagehands, chorus members, carpenters, costumers, scene painters, lighting technicians, typesetters, legal consultants, and more. The opera house was a source of indirect revenue for the city's inns, taverns, and gaming places and for its merchants. The citizenry also profited from such attendant promotional and didactic activities as the schools of dance or singing that were started in the theaters of Turin, Pistoia, Pavia, and Parma.[104] Some theater revenues went into financing pub-

---

101. See Ricci, *I teatri di Bologna*, 167ff. Construction of the theater was completed in 1757, but due to financial difficulties the inauguration took place only in 1763. See also Wanda Bergamini, "Antonio Galli Bibiena e la costruzione del Teatro Comunale di Bologna," in *Due secoli di vita musicale: Storia del Teatro Comunale di Bologna*, ed. Lamberto Trezzini, 3 vols. (Bologna: Alfa, 1966), 1:79–99.

102. See John Rosselli, "Governi, appaltatori e giuochi d'azzardo nell'Italia napoleonica," *Rivista storica italiana* 93 (1981): 346–83.

103. See Elena Ferrari Barassi, "Osservazioni e commenti intorno agli spettacoli in musica nella Pavia settecentesca," *Bollettino della Società pavese di storia patria* 70/71 (1970–71): 99–130, esp. 122.

104. From the start the Teatro Regio in Turin had an active ballet school, run first by Claude Le Comte and later by Baldassare Armano; see Bouquet, *Il teatro di corte*, 180–89. In Pistoia after 1725 a room in the Teatro dei Risvegliati was rented to a ballet master who served the local aristocracy; see Chiappelli, *Storia del teatro in Pistoia*, 34. In Pavia the regulations drawn up for the Teatro Nuovo in 1771 mentioned various initiatives for young people's instruction in music

lic works in the city.[105] Finally, private individuals and religious institutions often drew sizable incomes from renting out rooms, rehearsal halls, storage spaces, and entire buildings to theater managers. How large a budget item such rentals might be can be deduced from the annual "pension" of 2,200 ducats that Naples' King Charles granted in 1737 to the Ospedale degli Incurabili to compensate the hospital for its loss of revenues from space it had previously rented to the Teatro San Bartolomeo, which had been replaced by the Teatro San Carlo.[106]

It should be noted, however, that in cities with more than one theater, only the principal house had this high civic function. This was the theater that had the most prestigious architecture, was placed at the center of the city, and possessed the best production facilities; a theater frequented by the highest social classes and that offered opera seria, by definition an "official repertory" of prestigious works. Such theaters included the Teatro Argentina in Rome, the Regio Ducale and, later, the Teatro alla Scala in Milan, the San Carlo in Naples, the Regio in Turin, the Santa Cecilia in Palermo, the Pergola in Florence, the Malvezzi (later the Comunale) in Bologna, and the Nuovo in Padua. Other, secondary theaters, smaller in size, of less glorious tradition, and with smaller audiences and less prestige, kept alive the impresarial system

---

and other related professions, in the interests of developing a pool of local talent; see Ferrari Barassi, "Osservazioni e commenti," 113. From 1757 on at Parma, Jean-Philippe Delisle directed a ballet school annexed to the Teatro Ducale, and after 1769 the theater also had a singing school directed by Francesco Poncini Zilioli; see *Dizionario enciclopedico universale della musica e dei musicisti: Il lessico,* s. v. "Parma," by Gian Paolo Minardi.

105. For example, a portion of the revenues of the Teatro Regio of Turin were earmarked for charitable work in prisons or for the Ospedale della Carità; see Bouquet, *Il teatro di corte,* 275, 297–98. In Bologna the revenues from some performances at the Teatro Formagliari went to finance public projects, for instance, the portico for the shrine of San Luca; see Ricci, *I teatri di Bologna,* 100.

106. See Benedetto Croce, *I teatri di Napoli dal rinascimento alla fine del secolo decimottavo,* 4th ed. (Bari: Laterza, 1947), 163. The custom of designating a portion of the income or the profit from public entertainments, with or without music, to charitable institutions was a tradition with a long history and firm roots in seventeenth- and eighteenth-century Europe; it seems almost as if a charitable end justified the questionable "morality" of all theaters, at least on an ethical and political level. Aside from the instances cited see the examples given in Bianconi and Walker, "Production, Consumption," 265–66 and 293–96. Curiously, Venice, the city in which impresarial theater was developed and from which it spread, seems not to have known this practice until the Jacobin age, when a manifesto of 1797 entitled *Per la istituzione d'un teatro civico* (signed by Ugo Foscolo, Pietro Buratti, Giacomo Colombina, Antonio and Francesco Psalidi, Giovanni Bianchi, and Giovanni and Pietro Comarolo) stated, as an argument in favor of the project, that it would combine "honest occupation during leisure hours, virtuous emulation, and a remedy for poverty . . . Everything taken in, after expenses, will be distributed to the poor." See Ugo Foscolo, *Scritti letterari e politici dal 1796 al 1808,* ed. Giovanni Gambarin (Florence: Le Monnier, 1972), 719.

founded on individual initiative and responsibility in its most explicitly professional and commercial form.[107] As we shall see, some of these—the Teatro Valle in Rome, the Nuovo in Naples, the Carignano in Turin, the Cocomero in Florence, and others—concentrated on a repertory of comic opera or spoken drama. The subordinate role of these "secondary" theaters is also clear from the fact that they often had to pay a tax to the municipal authorities or to the impresario of the city's principal theater (in Naples, for example, the Teatro Nuovo paid such a fee to the San Carlo).[108] Even in a city like Modena, where the tradition of "government" backing for operatic spectacles in the Teatro Ducale was fairly irregular, Count Nicolò Molza, who built a theater at his own expense in 1713, had to pay an annual tax and agree to maintain the premises and give over the locale, with no compensation, for such other uses as the billeting of troops when the governing authority required it.[109] In short, during the eighteenth century, the civic opera house seems to have taken over, with modifications and new interpretations, the prerogatives and privileges that had been typical of court theaters during the preceding century. It was an object of civic pride, the "flower in the city's buttonhole," and a manifest proof of economic prosperity and political stability. The function of providing a brilliant occasion for official entertainment that *opera in musica* had so magnificently offered in the courts of the seventeenth century now passed to the municipal opera house, the symbol and emblem of the prestige of civil society.[110]

7. Ballet and Its Mechanisms of Production

The large number of opera houses in Italy and the regularity and intensity of the operatic seasons was paralleled by more and more firmly established structures for the production of opera and by increasingly conscious cooperation among professional groups that prepared the way for the national and

107. For example, the Teatro Argentina in Rome was run by a shareholders' society around midcentury, whereas during the same period the Capranica, the Valle, the Tordinona, the Pace, and the Pallacorda were managed by single impresarios: see Rinaldi, *Due secoli di musica*, 1:129.

108. Felice De Filippis and Mario Mangini, *Il Teatro "Nuovo" di Napoli* (Naples: Berisio, 1967), 11.

109. See Alessandro Gandini, *Cronistoria dei teatri di Modena dal 1539 al 1871*, (1873; reprint, 3 vols in 2, Bologna: Arnaldo Forni, 1969), 1:43.

110. Both the tone and the contents of the 1761 charter for the society that administered the Teatro Argentina in Rome (see note 98) reflect this new function. During the eighteenth century a visit to the principal theater of the city was obligatory for the many illustrious persons who embarked on an "Italian tour," among them, Johann Friedrich Armand von Uffenbach, Montesquieu, Charles de Brosses, Gabriel-François Coyer, Joseph-Jérôme Le Français de Lalande, Samuel Sharp, Charles Burney, and Fragonard.

international theatrical circuits and agencies of the nineteenth century. One indication of these new circumstances is the publication of the first important theatrical periodical aimed at opera personnel, the annual *Indice de' teatrali spettacoli,* printed from 1764 to 1823, first in Milan, then in Venice, and later in Rome. This publication was of great help to producers and impresarios, and it gave the public accurate information about theatrical activities in Italy and abroad in the form of detailed listings of the programs and the casts of ballet and singing companies for the seasons just past, current, and to come. The *Indice,* which today serves as a witness to the intensity of theatrical activity in Italy during the latter eighteenth century, was at the time a useful tool that increased the efficiency and new professionalism of the impresarial system.[111]

This system also kept alive and even strengthened some of the mechanisms of production instituted in the seventeenth century. One of these was recourse to the national market (now an international market) for singers, dancers, composers, and scene designers—a process that, it goes without saying, was much facilitated by the *Indice.* The sheer number of opera houses, all functioning during the same periods (particularly in carnival season) led to an increased demand for singers and competition among the various impresarios to sign the best voices of the moment. In turn the leading singers were not timid about insisting on astronomical fees, which were disastrous for the theaters' budgets.[112] There was nothing new in this and, as we have seen, it could be argued that high singers' fees were justified by increased revenues. Earlier in the century the highest sums in the impresario's budget for singers went to castratos (Farinelli, Caffariello, Bernacchi, Crescentini, and others), but they also gradually spent increasing amounts for tenors—a sure reflection of the spectators' changing tastes. For example, the tenor Giacomo David was paid 131 testoni to sing at Lucca in 1777, about half the fee for the leading male singer, the castrato Gasparo Pacchiarotti (270 testoni). The anonymous writer of the ledger could not help commenting, "First time that so much has been

111. On the *Indice* see Roberto Verti, "The *Indice de' teatrali spettacoli,* Milan, Venice, Rome 1764–1823: Preliminary Research on a Source for the History of Italian Opera," *Periodica Musica* 3 (1985): 1–7.

112. One new element in this situation was the flourishing market for opera outside of Italy. Opera houses abroad paid high prices, and although they offered opera professionals an opportunity to work in theaters throughout Europe—from Vienna to London, from Madrid to Prague, from Copenhagen to St. Petersburg—the competition between the Italian and the international market also prompted a rise in fees. For many Italian singers and composers, a career launched in Italy might prove a springboard for work in foreign opera houses, where the best of them often found it easy to make enough money to return to Italy and enjoy the fruits of their labors. This was true of a number of the singers of opera seria (Nicola Grimaldi, Senesino, Faustina Bordoni, Farinelli) and opera buffa (Antonio Lottini, Anna Faini, Rosa Ungarelli, Antonio Ristorini) and of a number of composers (Jommelli, Sarti, Paisiello, and others).

given to the best tenors who have sung in the theater."[113] The singer—a male or female soprano, later a tenor—continued to be central to the success of operatic spectacles and to the public's enjoyment.

Even granting the gradual but continual spread of opera houses and their increasing importance in the life of cities, the opera-going public grew notably in numbers and developed a broader social base. Its principal component remained the aristocrats, but more and more commoners joined them. We have seen how "various noble gentlemen and citizens" came together to aid the construction of the new Teatro Comunale of Bologna in 1750–57. Elsewhere the presence of both groups is reflected in the records of the distribution of boxes: the first and second tiers were for nobles and patricians; the third and fourth for "citizens" and merchants. At Naples the first four of the six tiers of boxes in the Teatro San Carlo were declared "noble"; the others could be occupied by the less titled ranks of society. At Rome "the persons of quality rent boxes in the second, third, and even, if there is a crowd, fourth tiers; the higher ones are for the commoners."[114] Another French observer noted that in Italy "the artisan, the old-clothes peddler, and the coachman prefer to bring their money [to the opera house] rather than the tavern."[115] It was also true, however, that the worker class preferred to go to spectacles of the "popular" sort or to "comedies denominated 'of art,'" which "have no other audience than errand boys for the food sellers and barbers."[116] Still, the practices of selling reduced-price tickets to the last performances and of setting aside certain places (in the upper balconies and on the orchestra floor) for servants, for audiences not usually in attendance, and for the lower classes—along with the more "popular" prices for certain spectacles (a ticket for an opera buffa cost half as much as one for an opera seria)—hint at a broadening of the social spectrum among the public for operatic spectacles in the mid-eighteenth century.

---

113. Luigi Nerici, *Storia della musica in Lucca* (Lucca, 1880), 324. During the same period reviews of opera performance in a number of periodicals, journals, and gazettes testified to the tenors' success with the audience—often even greater than that of the castratos and the female sopranos. For example, *La gazzetta toscana* no. 38, 23 September 1775, 150, remarks of *Perseo e Andromeda* (by Vittorio Amedeo Cigna-Santi and Giuseppe Gazzaniga, given at the Teatro della Pergola of Florence) that "more than anything else, the prime object" was the "many excellent professionals who sung in it. Aside from the renowned Sig. Millico, soprano, we heard and still can hear a tenor of German nationality named Sig. Valentino Ademberger [Adamberger], whose equal in the grace of his recitation, his fine voice, and his bravura in singing we have not seen for some time."

114. Benedetto Croce, *I teatri di Napoli*, 164; de Brosses, *Lettres familières*, 2:989.

115. Gabriel-François Coyer, *Voyage d'Italie*, 2 vols. (Paris, 1776), 1:284.

116. This opinion of Agostino Paradisi's is quoted in Susi Davoli, "Agostino Paradisi uomo di teatro," in *Teatro a Reggio Emilia*, ed. Sergio Romagnoli and Elvira Garbero (Florence: Sansoni, 1980), 1:247–62, quotation 253.

Eighteenth-century theaters offered a composite repertory. Comic and balletic spectacles took their place beside heroic opera, which remained the most
prestigious and cultivated sort of work. Ballet figured prominently both in
the structure of the performances and in the operational strategies of the impresarios. The vicissitudes of theatrical dance in mid-eighteenth-century Italy
are described in detail in volume 5 of *The History of Italian Opera;* in our
present context of the production system up to 1780, a few brief remarks on
the increased diffusion of ballet in impresarial theaters and its increasingly
favorable reception will suffice.

The professional figure of the *inventore de' balli*—the choreographer and
often stage director of the ballets—took on increasing prominence within the
composite staff in the impresario's employ. The importance of this role within
the complex machinery of operatic production is clear from the appearance
of the choreographer's name in the librettos (where some of the more prominent names around the midcentury are Nicolò Levesque, Gaetano Grossatesta, Francesco Aquilanti, Pietro Gugliantini, François Sauveterre, and
"M. Lefèvre"—all men who were simultaneously dancers, choreographers,
and sometimes even composers),[117] from the high level of their activity and
diffusion of the works, and from their long and busy careers. The function
of the ballet was to provide an interlude between the acts of the opera, and
as such it initially competed with the comic sung intermezzo. As late as the
1730s, the two forms vied for predominance, but not long afterwards there
was a preference for dance, at times of an overriding nature. In Naples, for
instance, King Charles insisted on ballets rather than intermezzi at the new
Teatro San Carlo.[118]

Ballet's most glorious season came later, however. During the latter half of
the eighteenth century, dance changed, once and for all, from being an
ornamental interlude (the "material dance" that Gasparo Angiolini speaks
of, or the "insignificant agility" stigmatized by Stefano Arteaga)[119] to enjoying a narrative, emotional, spectacular, and dramatic autonomy that
would find full expression in the pantomime ballets of Jean-Georges Noverre

117. See the contract between Mariano Nicolini, impresario of the theater in Padua, and
Domenico Lefèvre concerning the latter's engagement to dance on the occasion of the fair of St.
Anthony in 1745: "With the obligation of the said Léfevr [*sic*], brother and sister, to dance three
padedu [pas de deux] and to compose the dances or concerts and to dance in both"; quoted in
Giovan Battista Cavalcaselle, *Tipi di scritture teatrali attraverso luoghi e tempi diversi: Contributo
storico-giuridico* (Rome: Athenaeum, 1919), section 3, 16.

118. See José Sasportes, "La danza: 1737–1900," in *Il Teatro di San Carlo di Napoli,* 2 vols.,
ed. Raffaele Ajello (Naples: Guida, 1987), 1:365–96.

119. Gasparo Angiolini, *Lettere a Monsieur Noverre sopra i balli pantomimi* (Milan, 1773),
78; Stefano Arteaga, *Le rivoluzioni del teatro musicale italiano dalla sua origine fino al presente,*
2d ed., 3 vols. (Venice, 1785), 3:182.

and Gasparo Angiolini and in the sweeping choreographic dramas of Francesco Clerico. No longer a minor art, ballet became the object of philosophical speculation and the subject of impassioned theoretical and polemical exchanges, as in Noverre's and Angiolini's letters and the interpretive essays of Matteo Borsa and Giovanni Rasori. Audiences were so fond of ballet that it soon became a principal and irreplaceable staple of both theatrical programming and the impresarios' operational strategies.[120] At the end of the eighteenth century, the ballets elicited even more interest and greater enthusiasm than *opera seria,* although they continued to be staged between the acts of the vocal works. Some people protested against the new and invasive presence of dance:

> The dancers have taken over the theater and the opera: instead of the ballets serving as an intermezzo for [the opera], the opera serves as an intermezzo for the ballets. No one who goes to the opera takes any interest in it any more: at best they will listen to the singing of an aria or a duet, but everyone's attention turns to the dances.[121]

This complaint seems to echo another expressed two hundred years earlier, when Antonfrancesco Grazzini had Comedy lament, "The wondrous show— alas!—of the intermedi" *(la meraviglia, ohimè! degli intermedi).*[122]

A number of things confirm that dance had an increasingly large function in spectacle and drama and accounted for an ever larger proportion of pro-

120. *La gazzetta toscana,* no. 43, 26 October 1776, 170, stated, "Sig. Giovanni Canziani, *primo ballerino* and director of the ballets at the Teatro di via della Pergola, has gone off to Venice, leaving the public with a great desire for his presence. Although well satisfied with seeing much in this genre, [the public] has not ceased applauding his ballets, full as they are of lovely [choreographic] figures, proper acting [*giusta espressione*], and scenic majesty." On the importance of the ballet in the impresarios' operational strategies, see Piperno, "Impresariato collettivo e strategie teatrali," 353–54.

121. "Lettera di un erudito Cavaliere ad un illustre giovinetto concernente l'istoria dell'opera seria italiana," *Giornale delle belle arti* 3 (1786): 228. See also the much earlier letters of Metastasio to Farinelli of 1 August 1750, to Anna Francesca Pignatelli of 16 December 1771, and to Saverio Mattei of 18 September 1774; Pietro Metastasio, *Tutte le opere,* ed. Bruno Brunelli, 5 vols. (Milan: Mondadori, 1947–54), 3: 555, 5:125, 308.

122. The complaint of the eighteenth-century writers finds numerical confirmation in the large number of dancers (many more than singers) who were active in the period. A list appended to the *Indice de' spettacoli* of 1776 gives some twelve hundred dancers, as opposed to nine hundred singers; *Elenco de' signori virtuosi di canto e di danza attualmente addetti alli Teatri con loro nome, cognome, e patria: Per servire d'aggiunta all'indice de' spettacoli* (Milan, 1776). We need to keep in mind, moreover, that this *Elenco* takes into account a good many minor theaters that had few ballet productions, hence it favors singers and fails to reflect the full extent of a much more pronounced imbalance in the larger theaters.

duction. One of these is the increasing number of notices and critiques in periodical literature and their greater length and detail.[123] Another was the increasingly detailed information printed in the librettos, which began to give ballet plots, descriptions of the scenery, and names of the dancers, the choreographer, and the composer. Still another was an increase in production costs and in the dancers' pay. For an example of the latter, the Teatro Regio of Turin in 1736–37 spent nearly three times as much for six singers as for the fourteen dancers (leads and corps de ballet), and Senesino alone was paid 9,975 lire, as opposed to the 2,992 lire paid jointly to the ballerinas, Barbara and Domitilla Campanini. The situation had changed as early as 1751–52, when the two principal dancers, Pietro Alovard and Caterina Anichini, who received 3,217 and 3,168 lire, respectively, were each paid more than a third of the fees of the first male singer, Angelo Maria Monticelli (8,312 lire), and the first female singer, Caterina Aschieri (7,312 lire), and more than any of the other singers in the cast.[124] Toward the end of the century, the lead singers were paid only slightly more than the lead dancers.

At the same time, the production and diffusion of ballet shifted from a system of organized traveling troupes to a lively market for individual dancers or couples. Stars emerged—dancers such as Charles Le Picq, Antoine Pitrot, Giovanni Canziani, Francesco Clerico, Vincent Saunier, Giustina Campioni, Jean Favier, and Onorato Viganò. At times these artists functioned as dancers, choreographers, and the composers (or arrangers) of the music, and at least one of them, Onorato Viganò, operated as an impresario as well. This particular professional versatility of the *inventore de' balli* undoubtedly arose out of the special demands for cohesion and coherence among the various ingredients of dance (rhythm, sound, choreographic movement, pantomimic narration), but, in the last analysis, one result was a certain homogeneity in the product. Dance became a formula, a sort of prefabricated product that

123. We can follow this increase in the attention paid to dance through the years. *Il diario ordinario di Roma,* a gazette that gave only minimal theatrical information, began in 1764 to note performances of opera seria "with ballet interludes." In 1771 it noted the presence of "new ballet intermezzi of excellent invention" (no. 8236, p. 10), and in 1772 it described their content. In 1778 it registered the presence of "two well-choreographed dances" (no. 316, p. 12); in 1785 that of "two amusing ballets of signor Viganò" (no. 1052, p. 22); and in 1786 that of "two most beautiful ballets composed by maestro Sig. Viganò" (no. 1152, p. 21). Even more frequent and explicit appreciations of dance appeared in *La gazzetta universale* (printed in Florence), in Gasparo Gozzi's *La gazzetta veneta,* and in *La gazzetta toscana.* The latter (no. 46, 14 November 1772, 181), for example, praised "the ability of Sig. Carlo Le Picq, who, in the added new ballet admirably performed by himself . . . merited universal applause, having shown himself to be one of the most talented dancers in Europe. He is so perfect in his movements and of such a gracious manner that he does some things with an agility that enchants the spectators, driving them to indiscretion in their clamor to see new and beautiful things from him."

124. Bouquet, *Il teatro di corte,* 146, 287.

traveled easily and could readily be packaged for replication in other theaters with other companies. For the most part, however, the choreographers collaborated with professional musicians, in certain places, at certain times, or out of necessity (Noverre, for instance, could not compose music). Some composers even specialized in ballet music: Vittorio Trento and Luigi Marescalchi in Venice, Luigi de Baillou in Milan, Alessio Razetti, Giuseppe Antonio Le Messier and Vittorio Amedeo Canavasso in Turin, and Pierre Dutillieu in Naples.

8. The Production and Diffusion of Opera Seria

During the eighteenth century the repertory of heroic opera was made up preponderantly of the dramatic works of Apostolo Zeno and, even more, Pietro Metastasio. Opera audiences never tired of seeing the histories of Lucius Aurelius Verus, Severus Alexander, Andromache, Dido, Artaxerxes, Hadrian, Demophon, or Titus portrayed over and over again. Throughout the century and even in the first decades of the following one, these and other ancient heroes were the pillars of Italian operatic programming. Even after Metastasio's early success in Italy had taken him to the court in Vienna, where he was imperial poet (a post he held from 1730 until his death in 1782), he dominated the Italian operatic stage. The dramas he wrote in Vienna in the 1730s appeared immediately in Italy and enjoyed a long life—a sign of an explicit interest in the author, his works, and the world of sentiments that he evoked. The popularity of his works was also due to a universality in his characters, his poetic and dramatic themes, and ideological structures that enabled them to be played even outside the confines of the Hapsburg court. (While true of Metastasio's dramas, this was not the case with the celebratory works that he wrote in praise of his employers.)[125]

Rome provides an example of how Metastasio's dramas were adapted, and, within certain limits, the data for Rome can be extended to the rest of Italy.[126] The first performances of five of the seven Metastasian serious operas

125. On the circulation of Metastasio's plays in Italy, see Klaus Hortschansky, "Die Rezeption der Wiener Dramen Metastasios in Italien," in Maria Teresa Muraro, ed., *Venezia e il melodramma nel Settecento*, 2 vols. (Florence: Olschki, 1978–81), 1:407–24. For Metastasio's plays in Venice and the Veneto see Anna Laura Bellina, "Metastasio in Venezia: Appunti per una *recensio*," *Italianistica* 13 (1984): 145–73.

126. The data that follow are taken from Claudio Sartori, *I libretti italiani a stampa dalle origini al 1800: Catalogo analitico con 16 indici*, 7 vols. (Cuneo: Bertola and Locatelli, 1990). For comparison with the situation in Rome summarized here, see (for Venice) Bellina, "Metastasio in Venezia," and (for Florence) Robert Weaver, "Metastasio in Firenze," in *Metastasio e il mondo musicale*, ed. Maria Teresa Muraro (Florence: Olschki, 1986), 199–206. See also various chronologies of theatrical spectacles: Bouquet, *Il teatro di corte* (for Turin); Biancamaria Brumana and

written in his Italian period took place at the Teatro delle Dame (*Catone in Utica* in 1728, *Ezio* and *Semiramide* in 1729, *Alessandro nell'Indie* and *Artaserse* in 1730), and the same theater produced Metastasio's other texts soon after. The Viennese operas arrived in Rome only a few months after their appearance in Vienna: *Demetrio* (autumn 1731 in Vienna and carnival 1732 in Rome) and *Issipile* (carnival 1732 in Vienna and spring 1732 in Rome). Other Viennese works of Metastasio took decades to reach Rome: *La Zenobia* (summer 1740 in Vienna and carnival 1762 in Rome; *Ipermestra* (carnival 1744 in Vienna and carnival 1766 in Rome). Other works were produced frequently on the Roman stages: *Artaserse* (eight productions), *L'Olimpiade* (six), *Ezio, Alessandro nell'Indie, Demofoonte,* and *Antigono* (five each). The librettos that Metastasio wrote after 1750 were seldom produced in Rome and infrequently in the rest of Italy and elsewhere (one exception was *La Nitteti,* Madrid, 1756): *Il re pastore, L'eroe cinese,* and *Il trionfo di Clelia* were given in Vienna in 1751, 1752, and 1762, respectively (though *Il trionfo di Clelia* was given to inaugurate the Teatro Comunale of Bologna, with music by Gluck, in 1763); *Romolo ed Ersilia* was given in Innsbruck in 1765; and *Il Ruggiero* was given in Milano in 1771. These five works have in common unpretentious scenic requirements and a celebratory and dynastic nature (in a period of stagnation in operatic production at the Hapsburg court), which may have made the Roman and other Italian impresarios less enthusiastic about them. The few productions of these operas in Italian theaters outside Rome were promoted and solicited by groups close to the Hapsburgs, as noted on the printed librettos, where we see notations such as "under the protection of His Imperial Majesty." [127] *La Nitteti,* on the other hand, was produced in Italy, Rome included, since its "changes of scene" offered spectacular possibilities that responded fully to the expectations of the Italian opera public. All in all there were no fewer than seventy-three productions of Metastasian operas in Rome between 1726 and 1792, an average of more than one per year, with high points of three in one year when Metastasio himself was present (in 1730, *Siface,* a revival of *La forza della virtù* with music by Domenico David, *Alessandro nell'Indie,* and *Artaserse*), or in the years following his death (*Artaserse, L'Olimpiade,* and *Antigono* in 1788). If we consider that these numbers were higher in cities with a more intense musical life than Rome's, we can see that they give tangible verification to the central importance of Metastasio in the theatrical life of eighteenth-century

---

Michelangelo Pascale, "Il teatro musicale a Perugia nel Settecento: Una cronologia dai libretti," *Esercizi: Arte, musica, spettacolo* 4 (1983): 71–134 (for Perugia); Carlo Marinelli Roscioni, *La cronologia 1737–1787,* vol. 2 of *Il Teatro di San Carlo di Napoli,* ed. Raffaele Ajello (Naples: Guida, 1987) (for Naples).

127. See Hortschansky, "Die Rezeption der Wiener Dramen," 411–12.

Italy, a popularity that was due to the proven commercial value of his works and to a complementary tendency in public taste toward stability and predictability. When the impresarios selected a libretto by Metastasio, they knew the product had been well tested and would be sure to be a success; it would also be a text in the public domain that would cost them little or nothing and was ready (or could be adapted with few changes) to meet the special demands of a their production.[128] Paolo Rolli observed that the temptation to reuse a Metastasio libretto (with a few variants, adaptations, and changes to bring it up to date) sprang from the opportunity to "spend nothing for the play"[129] and from the "money that can be made from the sale of the printed librettos," which might be as much as "the fee of a singer."[130]

Although opera librettos were reused frequently and had a long life (aided, in the cases of Zeno and Metastasio, by a number of literary editions as well), during the first half of the eighteenth century this was not true of the scores, rare exceptions aside. Copies of librettos could circulate freely, but the original manuscript score of the music remained the property of the impresario or the composer and was tied to that person's fortunes and movements. It was easier and more economical to procure a libretto that might then be reset to music than it was to acquire a score that would have to be adapted to the vocal needs of the cast available. The musicians themselves had little interest in soliciting the circulation of their scores: when the score passed out of their control and their sphere of activity, it would bring earnings to the local adapter alone. The composer's only sure means of generating new income was to write new operatic works and produce new scores, even when they made use of old materials or were written to librettos that had been set to music before.[131]

128. Charles de Brosses remarked, "A lyric poem, once written, is common property belonging to everyone; there is no lack of composers of music; whoever among them wishes to work takes a published poem already set to music by others and writes new music to the same words. Above all they use the operas of Metastasio; there are few of them on which maestros have not worked. The method is useful and convenient"; *Lettres familières*, 2: 991.

129. The remuneration of librettists seems always to have been modest. In 1762 in Turin, Vittorio Amedeo Cigna-Santi was paid 480 lire to write the libretto of *Ifigenia in Aulide* and to revise others, whereas Ferdinando Bertoni, who set *Ifigenia* to music, was paid 1,230 lire; see Bouquet, *Il teatro di corte*, 305–6.

130. Paolo Rolli, letter of 9 May 1750, to Princess Pignatelli, quoted in Sesto Fassini, *Il melodramma italiana a Londra nella prima metà del Settecento* (Turin: Bocca, 1914), 178–79. The wide diffusion of Metastasio's dramas could create marketing problems for the printers of librettos: in Turin the tax that the typesetter had to pay to print the librettos for the opera season at the Teatro Regio was cut in half for Metastasio's works, "since these remain well known to the public" and the printer "would suffer grave disadvantages in the sale of the books"; Bouquet, *Il teatro di corte*, 201.

131. A composer might even earn a modest sum by revising his own score. Johann Adolf Hasse, for example, revised his *L'Olimpiade* (Dresden, 1756) for a production in 1764 at the

Some scores had a wide diffusion during the first half of the eighteenth century, but they were the exception. To pick one significant example, printed librettos attest to at least eighteen productions in Italy of Metastasio's *Artaserse*, with music by Leonardo Vinci, between 1730 and 1754, and sixteen productions in Italy of Johann Adolf Hasse's setting of the same text between 1730 and 1765. These two musical settings of the same dramatic text, which circulated in the same period, clearly outran others by Gaetano Maria Schiassi, Giuseppe Ferdinando Brivio, Gluck, Niccolò Jommelli, Giuseppe Arena, and others for their unusual frequency and longevity—a success equaled only (and only in northern Italy) by the *Artaserse* set by Baldassare Galuppi for Vienna in 1749, which had almost a dozen productions between 1750 and 1761. The itineraries of the two 1730 versions of *Artaserse* permit the verification of certain other criteria for the diffusion of operatic repertory in Italy (see table 1).

Vinci's opera premiered in Rome; Hasse's in Venice. Both circulated widely in a well-defined geographical area: one might even say that these two scores divided up the map of Italian opera houses, Vinci's score circulating in the central-southern portions of the peninsula and Hasse's in the central-northern ones. It is significant that the two versions met in Ferrara, an ideal borderland between their respective zones of influence, in carnival 1745, when, as the printed librettos attest, a pastiche of *Artaserse* was mounted with music of both Vinci and Hasse. It is no less significant that although Hasse was known in Naples, having been active there between 1725 and 1735, he arrived there with a new version of *Artaserse* only in 1760 and 1762—that is, when Vinci's score had ceased circulating, leaving his turf (so to speak) unoccupied. The case presented here, although extreme, permits us to isolate a certain "logic" in the diffusion of opera: scores produced in the south had a central-southern distribution; scores produced in the north circulated in central-northern Italy. If such a "logic" existed, it depended on the spheres of influence of the respective centers of production and on the network of interests and relations that surrounded those centers. It did not depend on the singers, who were variously and differently distributed with each production; nor did it depend on the composers themselves, since Vinci died in 1730, the year in which both versions of *Artaserse* first appeared, and Hasse was active in Venice, but— precisely from 1730 on—his activities were centered in Dresden.

This case is in some ways exceptional, because opera seria scores of the first half of the eighteenth century usually had a much more limited circulation and a shorter life. The ease and rapidity with which librettos circulated

Teatro Regio of Turin not for the usual sort of fee but for "a gold tobacco case given to Sr. Hasse, 'the Saxon,' for having worked on the score in music of the opera *Olimpiade*"; quoted in Bouquet, *Il teatro di corte*, 314.

TABLE 1. Metastasio's *Artaserse;* Music by Vinci, Hasse, and Galuppi

YEAR/SEASON		VINCI	HASSE	GALUPPI
1730	carnival	Rome	Venice	
–	spring	Florence	Genoa	
–	summer		Bologna	
–	autumn		Turin; Lucca	
1731	carnival	Fano; Pesaro; Livorno	Milan	
–	spring	Rome		
–	autumn	Naples; Ferrara		
1732	carnival	Perugia		
1733	carnival	Naples; Camerino	Verona	
1734	carnival	Perugia	Venice	
1738	carnival	Naples	Bergamo	
–	summer		Vicenza; Treviso	
1739	carnival		Modena	
1740	carnival	Macerata; Florence		
1741	carnival		Bassano	
1743	carnival	Naples		
1747	carnival	Pistoia		
1750	summer			Sassuolo
1751	spring			Padua
1754	carnival	Parma		Venice
1755	carnival			Treviso
1756	carnival			Brescia
–	?			Vicenza
1757	?			Faenza
–	?			Ferrara
–	autumn			Lucca
1758	summer			Brescia
1760	carnival		Naples (new version)	
1761	carnival			Venice
1762	summer		Naples	
1765	carnival		Ferrara	

and the concentration on singers reduced the music to a "dressing" of the text—a mere, albeit indispensable, ornament. Thus impresarios tended, as we have seen, to have a new score written to fit the cast available. This practice seems to have been the rule even when the cast did not change or when it changed only in part in moving from one theater to another, a move that one might think would have permitted reusing the score more or less intact. To take an example from Metastasio's works, after the successful premiere of *Didone abbandonata,* with music by Domenico Sarro, in Naples at the Teatro San Bartolomeo during carnival, 1724, Marianna Benti-Bulgarelli and Nicola Grimaldi repeated their roles as Dido and Aeneas in Venice during carnival 1725, with a score by Tomaso Albinoni, and the following spring in Reggio

Emilia, with music by Nicola Porpora.[132] Although arias from the Neapolitan premiere were used in the later productions, the fact remains that these two singers—somewhat surprisingly—displayed closer ties to the dramatic text than the musical scores. This phenomenon was fairly frequent, particularly where "star" singers were concerned. A typical example was that of the soprano castrato Gioacchino Conti (called Gizziello), who played Arbace in Metastasio's *Artaserse* between 1749 and 1754 in settings by Jommelli (Rome, Teatro Argentina, 1749), Antonio Gaetano Pampani (Venice, San Giovanni Grisostomo, 1750), Galuppi (Padua, 1751, inauguration of the Teatro Nuovo), Giovanni Battista Pescetti (Milan, Teatro Regio Ducale, 1752), and Davide Perez (Lisbon, 1754).[133] This independence of movement on the part of both singers and scores can be confirmed by a look at how scores themselves circulated. For example, the librettos show that within the brief span of four years (1755–58), *Artaserse* was put on with Galuppi's music in six different theaters in northern Italy, each time with a different cast.

If singers or composers did not affect the circulation of scores, what did? Or, to expand the question, how can we explain or account for the mechanisms governing the impresarial theaters, the production of operatic seasons, and the actions of opera's prime movers? The reality of opera production seems too multiform to be reduced to a formula; still, if there is an answer, it needs to be sought in the mechanisms—which remain obscure and are difficult to investigate—of the impresarial system of production, in the contacts among the various impresarios, in the connections among different opera houses, and in the production requirements specific to each operatic center. Keeping in mind that there were many exceptions, as a general rule we can point to one standard practice: impresarios tended to engage the best singers available first; their next priority was novelty (in the cast, the text, the scenery, the music, or the ballet). Only then did they seek new music (a fact often noted in the libretto) for a drama that had already proven its drawing power elsewhere. The impresario of a smaller opera house ranking lower than those of the major centers would aim instead at winning a place for his theater in

132. Nor was this an isolated instance. The same singers, for example, sang the roles of Statira and Arsace in Antonio Salvi's *Arsace,* with music by Michelangelo Gasparini, in Venice during carnival 1718 and, with a score by Sarro, in Naples in autumn of the same year; see Michael F. Robinson, *Naples and Neapolitan Opera* (Oxford: Clarendon Press, 1972).

133. It is probable that a singer found it harder and more time-consuming to commit a text to memory (the recitatives in particular) than to memorize the music. When the text remained the same, it would help them to move easily from one musical version to another and to make a dramatic role their own. On this question see Reinhard Strohm, "Metastasios *Alessandro nell'Indie* und seine frühesten Vertonungen," in *Probleme der Händelschen Oper inbesondere am Beispiel "Poro,"* ed. Walther Siegmund-Schultze (Halle: Martin-Luther-Universität, 1982), 40–61, in English translation as "Metastasio's *Alessandro nell'Indie* and its Earliest Settings," in Strohm, *Essays on Handel and Italian Opera* (Cambridge: Cambridge University Press, 1985), 323–48.

circuits recycling a production, in whole or in part. Economic considerations came first in the impresarios' choices of personnel, their decisions, and their strategies of production; these were what determined the impresarios' moves and the use of both the human and the material resources that went into the definition and the construction of the operatic spectacle. In all cases the hierarchy of values concerning the spectacle itself, in the eyes of both the impresario and the public that conditioned his decisions, placed the singers first, even during the eighteenth century. After them there came, in order of importance, the libretto, the scenery and the set designers, and, much lower on the scale, the music and the composers. Although this was the case of the Vinci and Hasse settings of *Artaserse,* composers were rarely viewed, a priori, as the winning card that would guarantee the success of a spectacle. This scale of values was reflected in the remuneration that impresarios offered composers (and a composer could consider himself well paid if he managed to pocket half the amount given the lead singers).[134] It is also clear from the information found in the first pages of the printed librettos, where the singers' names are sure to be given, the name of the author and the set designer are often mentioned, but only sometimes is the composer's name printed.

Whereas the engagement of scenographers such as the Bibienas, the Mauros, Filippo Juvarra, or the Galliaris might represent a good investment for the theater and an additional attraction for the spectator, the impresario normally chose a composer for economic or other reasons of convenience. The young Handel probably owed his invitation to provide music for *Agrippina* — an anonymous drama plausibly attributed to Cardinal Vincenzo Grimani and pervaded by a vein of bitter anticlerical, antipapal satire that was put on at the Teatro San Giovanni Grisostomo during carnival 1710—to his frequenting of pro-Hapsburg circles in Rome (Cardinals Colonna and Grimani).[135] Their reputation was certainly the reason for Hasse's, Galuppi's, and Gluck's commissions to set to music the Metastasio operas that inaugurated the new theaters of Pesaro (1735), Padua (1751), and Bologna (1763). Inau-

---

134. Composers' fees varied according to whether their duties were limited to creating the score or whether they also directed performances, conducting from the keyboard for the first few evenings. The ratio of singers' fees to composers' fees was notably different outside Italy. At the Haymarket Theater in London in the 1712–1713 season, for instance, the highest fee paid to a singer was 296 pounds sterling, whereas Handel received 186 pounds, or about two-thirds the lead singer's earnings. In 1729 the budget for the next season of the Royal Academy, under the direction of John Jacob Heidegger and Handel, set aside 4,000 pounds for a cast of six singers and 1,000 pounds for Handel for his duties as composer; see Milhous, "Opera Finances in London," 576, 588. The composer had gained in both relative and absolute terms. (See also the remarks in note 112.)

135. Giovanni Morelli, "Handel alla scuola dei Cardinali: Ancora sul viaggio in Italia di G. F. Handel e per una nuova idea circa una poetica della committenza 'italiana' nei guadi dell'ultimo barocco" (1981), *Musica/Realtà* 4 (1985): 153–73.

gurations were of course exceptional occasions; if we look to more ordinary
levels of theatrical production, however, it is obvious that economic considerations came first in the choice and hiring of composers. Even Florence's prestigious Teatro della Pergola, in the person of its impresario, the academician
Luca Casimiro degli Albizzi, hired Vivaldi and not Porpora to compose the
music for *Ipermestra* (carnival 1727) for the sole reason that Vivaldi would
accept the 100 thaler that had been budgeted for the commission.[136] Where
the bottom line was concerned, in operatic production of the early eighteenth
century, the score, although indispensable, was viewed as an element whose
primary function was eminently ornamental and ephemeral; the score's "trade
mark"—that is, the composer's name—only occasionally determined the impresario's decision, and it did not always influence the success of the spectacle. Like the stage set, the music was made for a specific production, after
which the score, as a whole and in its original version, had exhausted its
functions and, if anything, was used again piece by piece in other later works.

The remainder of the eighteenth century brought a number of changes to
the mechanisms for the production and the diffusion of heroic opera repertory. Within the context of the firmly established traditions of the Italian opera houses, there was a gradual, discontinuous, episodic, but inevitable rise
in the importance of the composer (and in his remuneration),[137] and he began
to play a more decisive role in the success of the operatic spectacle. One indication of the composer's greater importance is his increased leverage when it
came to drawing up a contract. We have seen how Vivaldi was chosen over
Porpora in 1726 because Porpora refused the fee offered by the impresario
of the Pergola and was unable to impose his own demands. Only eighteen
years later Gluck negotiated at some length with the *Società dei Cavalieri*
managing Turin's Teatro Regio until he obtained the fee of 130 zecchini for
which he had asked.[138] In 1770 Niccolò Piccinni rejected an offer of 400
pounds sterling to go to England and write three operas, stating that he could
earn as much in Italy for only two operas. He added that he would not consider traveling for less than twice the sum offered him.[139] As composers became more central to the production and gained greater authority, the earlier
practice of resetting the same text began to disappear, and individual scores

136. Gino Conti, "Il Teatro la Pergola di Firenze e la stagione d'opera per il carnevale 1726–
1727: Lettere di Luca Casimiro degli Albizzi a Vivaldi, Porpora e altri," *Rivista italiana di musicologia* 15 (1980): 182–88.

137. See the table in the appendix to John Rosselli, "Verdi e la storia della retribuzione del
compositore italiano," *Studi verdiani* 2 (1983): 11–28, 28.

138. See Bouquet, *Il teatro di corte,* 276.

139. See Charles Burney, *An Eighteenth-Century Musical Tour in France and Italy,* vol. 1 of
Dr. Burney's Musical Tours in Europe, ed. Percy A. Scholes, 2 vols. (London: Oxford University
Press, 1959), 245–46.

began to circulate with greater frequency and over a longer period, both inside and outside Italy. Twelve productions of Galuppi's *Antigona* between
1751 and 1758 can be documented by librettos, nine of Tommaso Traetta's
Ifigenia in Tauride between 1763 and 1786, sixteen of Domenico Cimarosa's
L'Olimpiade between 1784 and 1798, twenty-three of Giuseppe Sarti's *Giulio
Sabino* between 1781 and 1792, thirty-one of Sarti's *Medonte re d'Epiro,*
eighteen of Giovanni Paisiello's *Pirro* between 1787 and 1798, and eight productions of Cimarosa's *Gli Orazi e i Curiazi* within the one year 1750. All of
these productions show that the situation had changed, and they point to
new demands and different listening expectations on the part of the public.

The composer tended to be lumped with the currently fashionable singer,
dancer, or set designer in their function of providing a special appeal that
could make or break a spectacle. One announcement in Rome during carnival
1770 stated, "The Teatro di Aliberti [Alibert] will open with great expectations, to the credit of *maestro di cappella* Monzino [Carlo Monza]"; another,
"On Monday the Argentina will open with music of Maestro Piccini [Pic-
cinni], who has urgently been called to Milan to stage his opera there." In
Turin during carnival 1777, it was announced that "the two dramas, *Calipso,*
set to music by Sig. Maestro Ottani, and *Gengiskam* [*Gengis-Kan*] of Sig.
Maestro Anfossi have brought forth the greatest applause from the public.
The magnificence of the scenery and the costumes, as well as the talent of
the singers enhanced the productions of such excellent composers." These
opinions, expressed in a periodical of the time, *La gazzetta universale,*
printed in Florence,[140] reflect the new and significant preeminence of the composer in the mechanisms of opera production and with it the eclipse of the
figure of the librettist.[141] Such notices reveal a change from those of thirty
years earlier, which paid more attention to the poet and at times did not
even mention the *maestro di cappella,* even when he was Niccolò Jommelli,
a musician of the first order: "Tuesday evening in the theater at Torre Argentina the second *dramma per musica, Artaserse,* of the famous Metastasio,
had its first performance."[142] The figure of the composer, his reputation, and
his contribution appear to have become increasingly important to the overall
structure of the spectacle: the music was no longer seen as the work of a
somewhat obscure technician specialized in putting together musical scores

140. *La gazzetta universale,* no. 4, 4 January 1770, 32, and no. 16, 25 February 1777, 125.
For further evidence see Piperno, "Impresariato collettivo e strategie teatrali."

141. There were negative as well as positive sides to the emergence of the composer: the same
periodical (no. 13, 15 February 1777, 103) reported, "The music of *maestro di cappella* Guglielmi
not having met with the least success in this second opera of the Teatro d'Argentina [*Artaserse*],
some arias of other composers who have set the drama of Artaxerxes on other occasions have
been put in."

142. *Il diario ordinario,* Rome, no. 4923, 8 February 1749, 7.

but of an established professional whose contribution was strongly personalized, individual, unique, and original.[143] One logical consequence was the gradual disappearance of the practice of the pasticcio, not only because it brought "neither honor nor profit" to those who practiced it,[144] but also for reasons inherent in the demand for internal coherence within a score and because the characteristics of musical language made it difficult to mix selections by different hands.[145]

Just as the custom of offering the "music of various excellent composers" in one evening declined, so did that of using the same dramatic text for a variety of musical settings.[146] Now a text circulated in the particular musical setting that had brought it success—often the first setting, composed when the libretto was new. We often can sense from how and when it circulated that the fortunes of a libretto during the later eighteenth century depended on the success of the score. A number of concomitant factors confirm this notion. On the one hand, as the century progressed the growing number of opera houses, in Italy and elsewhere, inevitably created an increased demand for scores; on the other hand, the fact that composers were busier, had more leverage in drawing up contracts, and were paid better induced some opera houses (and not just minor or provincial theaters) to renounce absolute novelty in favor of works new to their locale. When they used scores that had already been performed elsewhere, they saved on expenses, to the benefit of both the impresario who produced the work and the owner of the score. Reusing a score, perhaps with slight changes, was all the more possible because as early as the first half of the eighteenth century, the Metastasian tradition had established the typical opera cast in a standard mould, usually consisting of a lead man and a second man *(primo uomo; secondo uomo)*, a first and second woman *(prima donna; seconda donna)*, a tenor, and a "last part" *(ultima parte)*, often another woman. Finally, even when it was technically possible and economically advantageous for scores to circulate, there had to be some concrete reason for them to do so. Here the new role of the composer in the mechanisms of opera production profited from the public's increased

143. For example, it was the originality, the intrinsic interest, and the success of Gluck's *Alceste* that persuaded the impresarios of the Teatro Comunale of Bologna to produce the opera in 1778 (rather than have it reset by some other composer) in spite of the work's difficulties—vocal, instrumental, and scenic—and in spite of the composer's and the librettist's anxieties; see Ricci, *I teatri di Bologna,* 207–10, and appendix 3, 625–62.

144. According to Niccolò Piccinni, as reported by Charles Burney; see Burney, *Dr. Burney's Musical Tours,* 245.

145. The pasticcio seems to have survived above all in minor and provincial theaters or as a last-minute measure when an operatic score met with little success; see note 141.

146. Gasparo Gozzi's *La gazzetta veneta* offered interesting reflections on the inefficacy of such cobbled-together performances, and it suggested that what was needed was new music for new librettos; see *La gazzetta veneta,* ed. Antonio Zardo (Florence: Sansoni, 1915), 135.

interest in composers. This interest was expressed in a "taste" broadly shared in contemporary society and in a collective affect that may well have been prepared by opera's firm roots in eighteenth-century urban life and in Metastasian drama but that nonetheless encountered an eager, aware, and well-prepared public opinion in the late eighteenth century.

Although during the first two thirds of the century, debate on opera, leaving aside the erudite polemics of the literati, had not seemed to go much further than gossipy and scandal-mongering comment (for the most part in letters, satires, and conversation),[147] spectators of the late eighteenth century could measure their competence and awareness against a wealth of newspaper columns, chronicles, correspondence, and comments on theatrical subjects that appeared with increasing regularity in the journals, gazettes, and literary periodicals.[148] By then the journalist no longer reported events with neutrality; rather, he expressed judgments and kindled controversy, and he not only communicated information (on culture, politics, the sciences, literature, and the theater) but also discussed opinions and fanned debate. Critical reviews of theatrical offerings changed people's habits and their choices in reading matter, but they also effected changes in how and why people went to the theater. The success (or failure) of a production[149] or an evaluation of a composer or a singer[150] was news that aroused curiosity and determined demand. Discussions of aesthetic questions, which took up increasing amounts of space on the pages of the leading literary periodicals of the age, fed a public opinion, a critical awareness, and an intellectual curiosity that focused more and more on the musical component of the operatic spectacle. The music gained new importance, as we have seen, even in brief annotations

147. For examples of these see Alberto Cametti, "Critiche e satire teatrali romane del Settecento," *Rivista musicale italiana* 9 (1902): 1–35 (regarding the years 1761 and 1764), and Fabrizio della Seta, "Il relator sincero (Cronache teatrali romane, 1739–1756)," *Studi musicali* 9 (1980): 73–116.

148. Periodicals already mentioned include *La gazzetta universale, La gazzetta veneta, Il diario ordinario* of Rome; other periodicals that printed news about opera were *La gazzetta toscana,* the *Bologna,* the *Avvisi* from Naples, the *Memorie per le belle arti,* the *Giornale delle belle arti,* and others. Among those that specialized in chronicle and information but also mentioned opera were the *Mercure de France* and the *Pallade veneta.* For the musical news contained in the latter, see the edition, with commentary, by Eleanor Selfridge-Field, *Pallade Veneta: Writings on Music in Venetian Society 1650–1750* (Venice: Fondazione Levi, 1985).

149. *La gazzetta toscana,* no. 12, 22 March 1778, 46, announced that during the coming spring season at the Teatro della Pergola, the third opera "will be *Il Socrate Immaginario,* music by Sig. Giovanni Paisiello, which along with the libretto has created a great stir in the theaters of Naples, as can be read in the public papers."

150. *La gazzetta toscana,* no. 46, 16 November 1776, 181, wrote about the opera, *L'amore artigiano,* "The above-mentioned music of Sig. Floriano Gas[s]mann, formerly in the service of His Imperial Majesty, is well suited to the character of the libretto and loses only in comparison to the harmonies of the inimitable Paisiello, at present superior to all others."

in periodicals such as *La gazzetta universale,* the *Notizie del mondo,* and the *Diario ordinario*—papers whose chief stock in trade was political and administrative news but that nonetheless frequently mentioned the *maestro di cappella* as a figure in part responsible for operatic spectacle. Music, now the focus of interest and enthusiasm, acquired greater weight within the dynamics and the economics of opera production. In practical terms this gave the composer an increasingly central role in such matters. It gave him a greater share in the success of the opera, it assured the musical score a more intense and more lasting circulation, and it permitted a clearer definition of the composer's role and his artistic personality.[151]

9. The Production and Diffusion of Intermezzi and Comic Opera

Comic opera, which paralleled the more serious operatic genre and provided an alternative to it, came in two distinct but at times interrelated forms. During the last twenty years of the seventeenth century, it became customary in staging serious operas to introduce breaks (at the ends of each of the first two acts and before the last group of scenes in the third act) in which a pair of comic characters played sprightly interludes often involving comic quarrels. The stylistic autonomy (narrative, linguistic, and musical) of these scenes along with the professional independence of their interpreters combined to transform them into intermezzi—that is, into independent dramatic entities performed between the acts of opera seria. The simplicity of these two-character scenes, involving ordinary people of humble social extraction and the realism of the acting and singing changed them from merely amusing and episodic bits inserted into opera seria into a specific form of musical theater regulated by its own rules. There were librettists (among them Salvi, Bernardo Saddumene, and Gennaro Antonio Federico), composers (Giuseppe Maria Orlandini, Hasse, Giovanni Battista Pergolesi, and Giuseppe Sellitto), and singers who specialized in intermezzi, although without excluding their participation in other genres. The specialists in comic intermezzi had careers similar to those of their "serious" colleagues but totally separate from them.[152]

---

151. This new central position of the composer went along with a rehabilitation of the composer's figure and his intellectual dignity. True, questions such as "should the *maestro di cappella* be considered as an artisan?" (1785, Saverio Mattei) were still posed late in the eighteenth century and might still be answered affirmatively. Yet we cannot ignore Mattei's attestations of esteem and admiration for Jommelli in the same year (1785) nor the eulogies that appeared in the literary, artistic, and scientific journals of the time when a musician died. See, for example, the obituary for Antonio Sacchini in the *Giornale delle belle arti* 2 (1786): 288–89.

152. The independence of intermezzi from opera seria is confirmed by their use as an entr'acte by companies of prose actors (Giuseppe Imer, Girolamo Medebac, and Buonafede Vitali).

There were intermezzi whose text and music enjoyed a longevity unknown to most of the contemporary heroic operas. For example, there is the Pietro Pariati-Albinoni *Pimpinone,* whose circulation is documented at least from 1708 to 1731; Salvi's *Serpilla e Bacocco,* which was performed, usually with Orlandini's music, from 1719 to 1767; Saddumene's *La contadina,* which was played in a version with music by Hasse from 1728 to 1763; and the Federico-Pergolesi *La serva padrona,* a work written in 1733 and still being produced regularly at the end of the eighteenth century (Padua, 1791).[153] Texts and scores for the particular dramatic form of comic musical theater known as intermezzi thus had an intensive and long-lasting circulation right from the start—unlike opera seria, which, as we have seen, took hold only in the latter half of the eighteenth century. This success was determined by the greater "transportability" of the intermezzi and by the professional specialization of their interpreters.

Between 1710 and 1760, intermezzi were played everywhere—in court theaters, in public and private theaters, and in summer residences—including religious schools and academies of noble amateurs.[154] The success of these works is demonstrated by the large number of productions, the wide circulation of the repertory, the frequency of their performances, and the explicit evidence in periodicals and other documents reporting the fame of the interpreters and their audiences' appreciation of them. For example, a performance by Rosa Ungarelli and Antonio Ristorini at the Teatro dei Risvegliati of Pistoia in 1725 was described in enthusiastic terms by one eyewitness, the diarist Cosimo Rossi Melocchi. Charles de Brosses had an equally positive impression of a performance of *La serva padrona* given in San Giovanni in Persiceto, near Bologna, in 1739 (with Anna Castelli and Domenico Cricchi),

153. See Charles E. Troy, *The Comic Intermezzo: A Study in the History of Eighteenth-Century Italian Opera* (Ann Arbor, Mich.: UMI Research Press, 1979), 149–52. On the circulation of *Pimpinone* in particular, see the edition of the work by Michael Talbot (Madison, Wis.: A-R Editions, 1983), xxvi–xxx. On *La contadina* see Franco Piperno, "Note sulla diffusione degli intermezzi di J. A. Hasse (1726–1741)," *Analecta Musicologica* 25 (1987): 267–86, esp. 285–86. On *La serva padrona* see Piperno, "Gli interpreti buffi di Pergolesi: Note sulla diffusione de *La serva padrona,*" in *Studi pergolesiani/Pergolesi Studies,* ed. Francesco Degrada (Florence: La Nuova Italia, 1986), 1:166–77.

154. The simplicity of their staging and more limited vocal and instrumental requirements meant that intermezzi could be performed not only by comic opera troupes but also by amateurs and the pupils of religious schools. For example, in 1741 *La serva padrona* was performed by the "young students" of the Arcispedale of Siena between the acts of a prose tragedy, a practice fairly common in Rome among the students of the Seminario Romano, the Collegio Clementino, the Collegio Nazareno, and others. At Florence in 1766, on the other hand, *La serva padrona* was performed "to perfection by Vittoria Suares Carducci, lady of the court, and knight of the order of Malta Antonio degli Alessandri" between the acts of a prose drama, *La clemenza di Tito,* which was put on "by a brilliant company of noble subjects"; see *La gazzetta patria* (later *La gazzetta toscana*), 26 January 1766, 18.

as did Joseph-Jérôme Le Français de Lalande of a performance by Anna Tonelli in Paris in 1752.[155] Intermezzi were a success as an alternative to opera
seria thanks to their immediate dramatic impact as an entertaining, escapist
sort of musical theater, but the system of production and organization specific
to the genre also played a part in their popularity.[156] They made use of singers
who had chosen the buffo vocal style as their chief (though not exclusive)
professional specialization. Initially (around 1707) the individual theaters
usually had a duo of buffi singers, who constantly renewed their repertory
and served as permanent members of the company. In a second phase (after
about 1715) it became the custom to engage an itinerant minitroupe consisting of a pair of buffi singers who had their own limited repertory with
which they toured from one theater to another. After the 1730s the system
changed again: individual buffi sought engagements, collaborating for the occasion with a partner whose repertory coincided with theirs—a modus operandi that much resembled that of opera seria singers of the same period.
Thus the systems for producing the intermezzi, in their own way, paralleled
the development of the systems of seventeenth-century opera. Both genres
began by settling down to a routine, becoming institutionalized, and developing a stable personnel (opera at court, the buffi in the theater); both then
became organized with itinerant troupes; finally, the singers of both genres
operated as free agents in a free market.

The career of the most famous early-eighteenth-century buffo singer, Giovanni Battista Cavana, can stand as typical.[157] After specializing in comic
parts in Naples from 1696 to 1703, Cavana helped to create and establish
the first intermezzi, working together with Santa Marchesini, at the Teatro
San Cassiano in Venice between 1706 and 1709. With Marchesini and other
partners, Cavana traveled throughout Italy between 1711 and 1732. His repertory changed, but some titles recurred frequently (Albinoni's *Pimpinone*,
Francesco Gasparini's *Lisetta e Astrobolo*, Orlandini's *Madama Dulcinea e il
cuoco del marchese del Bosco*). Rosa Ungarelli and Antonio Ristorini provide
a good example of singers who traveled as a buffo couple. Their collaboration
lasted from 1715 to 1732, and they specialized in the musical intermezzi of
Orlandini, among them, *Serpilla e Bacocco* and *Monsieur de Porsugnacco*,

155. See Chiappelli, *Storia del teatro in Pistoia*, 195; de Brosses, *Lettres familières;* de Lalande, *Voyage en Italie*, 8:522.

156. On these questions, see Piperno, "Appunti sulla configurazione sociale e professionale
delle 'parti buffe' al tempo di Vivaldi," in *Antonio Vivaldi: Teatro musicale, cultura e società*, ed.
Lorenzo Bianconi and Giovanni Morelli, 2 vols., Studi di musica veneta: Quaderni vivaldiani, no.
2 (Florence: Olschki, 1982), 2:483–97; Piperno, "Buffe e buffi (considerazioni sulla professionalità degli interpreti di scene buffe ed intermezzi)," *Rivista italiana di musicologia* 17 (1982):
240–84; Piperno, "Note sulla diffusione degli intermezzi di J. A. Hasse."

157. See Piperno, "Buffe e buffi," 260–63; Pariati-Albinoni, *Pimpinone*, ed. Talbot,
xxvi–xxx.

after Molière.[158] Some of the outstanding singers of the third phase (who sang the comic repertory of Pergolesi, Hasse, and Sellitto) were Pietro Pertici, Caterina Brogi, Domenico Cricchi, Anna Isola, Rosa Ruvinetti, Ginevra Magagnoli, and Pellegrino Gaggiotti. One proof of their status as autonomous professionals who were prepared to collaborate, at short notice, with other artists who sang the same repertory can be seen in Cricchi's frequent engagements to perform Pergolesi's *La serva padrona* with Isola and Magagnoli but never with Rosa Ruvinetti, whereas the same Cricchi had engagements with Ruvinetti to sing the intermezzi of Hasse, which he never performed with Magagnoli.[159]

These modes of production and diffusion gave intermezzi widespread circulation. As a type of spectacle that was easy to put on, with modest orchestral requirements, little scenery, and a small budget, comic intermezzi were a highly marketable product. (Singers of intermezzi were paid notably less than opera seria singers, both because of an undervaluation of the buffo genre in general and because these short compositions were smaller in scope and had less demanding vocal requirements.)[160] It may not be exaggerated to see the intermezzi as one of the safest and most efficacious resources of theatrical ventures during the first half of the eighteenth century.

This is not the place for a full analysis of the historical relationship between the intermezzi and opera buffa (did one derive from the other? did they arise independently?). It is indisputable, however, that the massive presence of intermezzi on the programs of opera houses throughout Italy prepared the way for the vast acceptance of opera buffa. It was the intermezzi that acquainted audiences with comic musical theater of a bourgeois and (at least potentially) sentimental nature. One should not forget, however, that the *commedia per musica* of the early eighteenth century—a form of comic opera that, like a full-fledged opera, took up an entire evening at the theater—was a phenomenon of only very restricted circulation and of an exclusively local importance. Still, the poets who wrote intermezzi (Federico, Saddumene, Antonio Palomba, Goldoni), the composers of intermezzi (Orlandini, Sellitto, Pergolesi, Leonardo Leo, Rinaldo da Capua), and the singers of intermezzi were the same persons who were also actively involved in producing the repertory of *commedia per musica,* thus creating a vast osmosis between the two types of spectacle in their production techniques, their professional specialization, and their styles. Among the singers, Gioacchino Corrado, a basso buffo active in Naples between 1706 and 1744, dominated the market as a specialist in intermezzi at the Teatro San Bartolomeo—the theater for opera

---

158. See Piperno, "Buffe e buffi," 274–76.

159. See the tables in the appendix to Piperno, "Note sulla diffusione degli intermezzi di J. A. Hasse," and to Piperno, "Gli interpreti buffi di Pergolesi."

160. See Piperno, "Buffe e buffi," 249–50.

seria—working with Celeste Resse and other partners to present the first performances of comic scores by Hasse, Vinci, Pergolesi, and Sellitto. In 1735,
however, Corrado moved to the Teatro Nuovo—the theater for comic opera—where he appeared in a number of *commedie per musica* by Gaetano
Latilla, Pietro Auletta, Nicola Logroscino, Vincenzo Ciampi, Davide Perez,
and others. Among other roles, Corrado played Lamberto in the Palomba-
Auletta *Orazio,* one of the first great successes for a *commedia per musica*
on a national scale.[161] Antonio Lottini, Anna Faini, and Pietro Pertici, all
famous interpreters of intermezzi, had similar professional careers. We find
them playing together in 1730 at the Teatro in via del Cocomero in Florence
in the cast of *Lo speziale in villa* by Villifranchi (with music perhaps by Orlandini) and again the following year in the same theater, in Moniglia's *La
serva nobile,*[162] all genuine *drammi per musica* (according to the printed librettos) but with a comic subject. Many other singers, such as Pellegrino Gaggiotti, Caterina Brogi, Anna Tonelli, Ginevra Magagnoli, Filippo Laschi,
Anna Querzoli, and Giovanna Poli appeared in both intermezzi and opera
buffa.

Opera buffa gradually replaced intermezzi as an alternative form of musical theater to opera seria.[163] The rapid geographical spread of opera buffa
beginning in the 1740s coincided with an increased number of performances.
The genre had already existed but with a limited diffusion and an episodic
existence, and the impresarios launched it by using a mix of tried-and-true
stylistic conventions and professional devices borrowed from the intermezzi.
In turn, the intermezzi's function as interludes between the acts of an opera
seria was taken over by ballet, which conquered Italian audiences toward the
middle of the century. Opera buffa went through the same three phases of
specialization as had seventeenth-century *dramma per musica,* intermezzi,
and early-eighteenth-century ballet: it began within an institutional form of
production, it spread by organized cooperative efforts, and it ended up in a
free market of individual artists. We can see the institutional phase that gave
opera buffa its start not only in the intermezzi (a well-established form) but
also in the activities of a few theaters that had a stable company specializing
in the comic repertory (the Teatro Nuovo in Naples, the Teatro Valle in
Rome, and the Teatro in via del Cocomero in Florence). Opera buffa soon

161. Ibid., 264–67, to which the information on the *Orazio* given here should be added.

162. See Weaver and Weaver, *A Chronology,* 1:258, 261.

163. On the diffusion of opera buffa, see Helmut Hucke, "Die Entstehung der Opera buffa,"
in *Bericht über den Internationalen musikwissenschaftlichen Kongress Bayreuth 1981,* ed.
Christoph-Hellmut Mahling and Sigrid Wiesmann (Kassel and Basel: Bärenreiter, 1984), 78–85;
Piero Weiss, "La diffusione del repertorio operistico nell'Italia del Settecento: Il caso dell'opera
buffa," in *Civiltà teatrale e Settecento emiliano,* ed. Susi Davoli (Bologna: Il Mulino, 1986),
241–56.

moved, however, into the free-market phase in terms of its librettos, scores, performers, and composers, although some itinerant singing companies continued to perform the buffo repertory. One such company was the troupe of Pietro Pertici, a Florentine whose acting talents in spoken drama Goldoni admired.[164] The activities of these companies were interwoven in a variety of ways with those of the troupes of comic actors, echoing the overlapping itineraries and the competition between the seventeenth-century musical troupes of Febiarmonici and actors of the commedia dell'arte.

These companies launched a type of *commedia per musica* that never had more than a local appeal, even when it became a lively part of a city's theatrical tradition. And yet there was hardly a broader audience for the buffa operas put on at the Teatro Nuovo in Naples, the Cocomero in Florence, or the Malvezzi in Bologna during the 1730s—works often written in dialect and performed by musicians and singers of the company. As the printed librettos attest, after 1738, with the performances at the Teatro Valle in Rome of *La commedia in commedia* by Rinaldo da Capua and *La finta cameriera* of Latilla (a reworking of *Il Gismondo* by Federico and Latilla, first given at the Teatro Nuovo of Naples in 1737), this situation changed. One of the singers in both operas was the basso Francesco Baglioni, a Roman. Along with Pertici, Giuseppe Ristorini, Brogi, Eugenia Mellini, and others, Baglioni was one of the first singers to join with three or four others to form a traveling troupe (adding other singers as needed) for the purpose of performing *commedie per musica*. Although this new form of comic opera spread out from Rome (the Teatro Valle; the basso Baglioni), its singers came from Rome, Florence, and Bologna, its composers were almost without exception Neapolitan, and it played in theaters in Tuscany, Emilia, Lombardy, the Veneto, and Piedmont. This mixture would seem to eliminate all possibility of labeling it with some *appellation contrôlée* ("Neapolitan opera buffa," for instance), for when it became popular on a national and international scale, it was Italian in both its production and consumption.[165] Comic opera in Naples began to be diffused outside the immediate region after *La maestra* of Palomba-Gioacchino Cocchi, 1747; the same was true of Venetian comic opera by the duo Goldoni and Galuppi. Regional diffusion only became possible, however, after the itinerant companies had taken a number of *commedie per musica* out of the confines of their respective places of production, thus transforming a phenomenon of essentially local importance into a national one.

Baglioni, who played Marchionne in *La commedia in commedia* and Don

164. See Piperno, "Buffe e buffi," 255 n.48.

165. Piero Weiss, "La diffusione," points out an interesting fact: *La finta cameriera* was an adaptation of *Il Gismondo* in another sense as well, because the original text in Neapolitan dialect by Federico was translated into Italian (perhaps by Giovanni Gualberto Barlocci). This often occurred in Rome in the 1730s, and, according to Weiss, it first happened with *La costanza*, a

Calascione in *La finta cameriera,* and a Florentine, Pertici, were prominent
and energetic heads of such companies. They not only had a leading role in
the development of opera buffa in its first phase of rapidly circulating scores
but they also helped, in a second phase, to create a class of professional comic
singers outside the cooperative structure of the troupe. Baglioni, for example,
was an opera buffa singer who apparently acted as a free agent. His name
became attached to the success of *Arcifanfano re dei matti* by Goldoni and
Galuppi: between 1750 (Venice, San Moisè) and 1759, printed librettos attest
to performances of the opera in which he sang the leading role, working with
a number of partners.[166] Baglioni's and Pertici's professional reputations do
not mean, however, that the opera buffa singer of the latter half of the eighteenth century had the same general role, carried the same weight (in either
the mechanisms or the outcome of operatic production), or commanded as
high a fee as the singer of opera seria. In the heroic *dramma per musica,* the
vocal cast was always the central focus and the prime reason for its success
with the public, but that seems to have been less true of opera buffa. Perhaps
because it was felt that the comic repertory and its interpreters came from the
"lower" ethical, social, and dramatic echelons of seventeenth-century opera
(i.e., from comic scenes and comic characters in "serious" drama), or perhaps
because the eighteenth-century public (and eighteenth-century culture in general) accepted Aristotelian literary criteria that valued tragedy over comedy,
the opera buffa singer paid the price in the form of a considerably humbler
position in the structures of operatic spectacle and less influence on its production strategies.[167] In practice comic opera was immediately perceived as a

---

commedia per musica given at the Teatro Valle during carnival 1729 with a text by Saddumene
that was in fact an Italian translation of his *Li zite 'ngalera* of 1722.

166. The consolidation of a free market of individual professionals who sang in the opera
buffa style did not lead to the disappearance of the itinerant companies. Charles Burney mentions
"a burletta company under the direction of Signor Leopoldo Maria Scherli, *maestro di capella;*
the singers were Giovanni Simoni, Giuseppe Franceschini, Niccola Menichelli, Angiola Dotti, Geltrude Dotti, Teresa Menichelli, [and] Teresa Monti" that he had encountered in Brescia in 1770
(Burney, *An Eighteenth-Century Musical Tour,* 90). In July 1780 *La gazzetta toscana* mentioned
a "foreign company of singers" in Florence who were preparing to put on nine "of the best comic
music dramas, and the performances will continue for the whole month of August, and, if feasible,
for some days in September" (*La gazzetta toscana,* no. 26, 24 June 1780, 103). The *commedia
per musica* troupes occasionally even traveled to the far south: documentation is scarce, but one
company, headed by Matteo Benvenuto, was active in Cosenza and Rosano in 1778 (its librettos
were printed in Naples); see Ausilia Magaudda, "Feste e cerimonie con musica in Calabria nella
prima metà del Settecento," in *Musica e cultura a Napoli dal XV al XIX secolo,* ed. Lorenzo
Bianconi and Renato Bossa (Florence: Olschki, 1983), 165–206, esp. 175–76 n.

167. Whereas chronicles and journals abounded in praise for the *virtuosi* of opera seria and
for dancers, the opera buffa singers of the mid-eighteenth century rarely received better than a
simple mention. For example, in a review in *La gazzetta veneta* of a performance of the Goldoni-
Giovanni Battista Lampugnani *L'amore contadino* (Venice, Teatro Sant'Angelo, autumn 1760),

joint effort resulting from a collaboration among artistic equals, from the author to the set designer and from the composer to the singer. In particular, unlike opera seria its composer and score were immediately recognized as decisive to the success of the production. As early as midcentury—much earlier than for the composer of opera seria—the opera buffa composer had a determining role putting on a *commedia per musica* and in the subsequent fortunes of the production. He soon became its most prominent element and its winning card. In the 1770s (hence in the same period as the reports from theatrical correspondents in Rome and Turin examined above) *La gazzetta universale* printed a review of a buffo spectacle given in Rome that offered much more explicit praise of an otherwise unknown composer, Giuseppe Heiberger.

> One of the most brilliant and most applauded musical works to be heard in our leading theaters this last carnival was universally judged to be that of Signor Giuseppe Heiberger, Roman *maestro di cappella* and a member of the Accademia Filarmonica of Bologna. The merry drama that he set to music bears the title *Il colonello,* and it was performed amid the acclamations of all the nobility and the people at the Teatro delle Dame, called Aliberti. The worthiness of the eminent maestro is all the more admirable because he has exceeded all expectations in his young years and has been able to preserve his first fruits from the slanders and prejudices of the commonality.[168]

As early as the 1750s so many opera buffa productions were in circulation that they outnumbered those of opera seria. The figures speak for themselves: the catalogs of the collected works of single composers of the second half of the eighteenth century show a gradual rise in the numbers of comic produc-

---

the critic praised Goldoni for a libretto "full of the theatrical tricks that are that author's specialty" and admired the way Lampugnani had "clothed [the text] with harmonies pleasing to the public," but the singers, though complimented, were not mentioned by name; see Gasparo Gozzi, *La gazzetta veneta,* ed. Zardo, 344 n. 146, 427. Periodicals began to list the interpreters of opera buffa, often with words of praise, in the mid-1770s; for examples, see Piperno, "Impresariato collettivo e strategie teatrali," 355.

168. *La gazzetta universale,* no. 14, 18 February 1777, 115. Charles Burney had something to say on the appreciation of composers of opera buffa. About one performance in Naples in October 1770 he wrote, "Notwithstanding the court was at Portici, and a great number of families at their *Villeggiaturas* or country houses, so great is the reputation of Signor Piccini [sic] that every part of the house was crowded." In Burney's opinion, however, "this opera [*Gelosia per gelosia*] had nothing else but the merit and reputation of the composer to support it, as both the drama and singing were bad" (*Dr. Burney's Musical Tours,* 241). Composers could draw a crowd in Florence as well, as shown in April 1774: "The excellent music of the famous Sig. D[on] Giovanni Paisiello, Neapolitan *maestro di cappella,* performed in fine style by the singers, brings ever larger numbers to our Teatro di via del Cocomero, where many of the nobility, citizenry, and foreigners gather to enjoy this admirable spectacle"; *La gazzetta toscana,* no. 24, 11 April 1774, 94.

tions as compared to heroic operas, and librettos also indicate that opera buffa had a broader circulation. The major successes of Anfossi, Cimarosa, Vincenzo Fabrizi, Domenico Fischietti, Galuppi, Florian Leopold Gassmann, Giuseppe Gazzaniga, Pietro Alessandro Guglielmi, Vicente Martín y Soler, Paisiello, Piccinni, Antonio Sacchini, Antonio Salieri, and Sarti continued to be staged, in Italy and abroad, for fifteen to twenty years, at a rate, on average, of over one production per year. A few examples: *Il mercato di Malmantile* by Goldoni and Fischietti had thirty-six productions between 1758 and 1773; *Il filosofo di campagna* by Goldoni and Galuppi had thirty between 1754 and 1772; *La sposa fedele* by Pietro Chiari and Guglielmi had thirty-three between 1767 and 1779; *Il geloso in cimento* by Giovanni Bertati and Anfossi had thirty-eight between 1774 and 1793; *Una cosa rara* by Lorenzo da Ponte and Martín y Soler had forty-two between 1786 and 1796; *Giannina e Bernardone* by Filippo Livigni and Cimarosa had forty-one between 1781 and 1800, and so forth. These figures—misleading as they are, given that they are based on printed librettos alone in a period in which comic opera, especially in provincial areas, were often given without publishing a special edition of the libretto—are still notably higher than the figures for productions of opera seria by the same librettists and composers. Sarti's *Medonte re d'Epiro,* with its thirty-one productions, was the most frequently played opera seria of the second half of the eighteenth century, but some of the same composer's scores for comic operas saw even more performances: *Le gelosie villane,* with a libretto by Tommaso Grandi, had thirty-eight productions between 1776 and 1797. These figures were bettered by the most popular buffo operas of the century, Goldoni and Piccinni's *La buona figliuola* (with some fifty productions between 1760 and 1790) and *La Frascatana* by Livigni and Paisiello (about sixty productions between 1774 and 1799). A specific interest in comic opera's intrinsic musical qualities must have contributed to this widespread, continuing success. We have already mentioned the importance of the composer in the far-reaching success of opera buffa, an importance recognized and emphasized in periodicals of the time. The following excerpt illustrates the musical attraction of opera buffa for spectators in the second half of the eighteenth century.

> The impresarios of the theater of via del Cocomero, ever intent on satisfying the desires of the public, presented on Sunday evening a revival of the comedy *La Fraschetana* [sic], which, for its excellent music, can without exaggeration be called the acme of opera in the burlesque genre by the famous Paisiello. Although [the work] was heard over a lengthy period last year, it was received with great applause by the large audience that had come to hear it.[169]

169. *La gazzetta toscana,* no. 16, 20 April 1776, 61.

This massive diffusion of the repertory of the autonomous opera buffa—as distinguished from intermezzi, or at least from intermezzi when they were presented between the acts of a "serious" drama, since on occasion they were performed separately as comic operas—took place for the most part in the "secondary" theaters of the Italian cities. The principal theaters, for reasons of tradition and out of respect for their audience, remained faithful to the prestige and the more official character of opera seria.[170] The principal centers soon boasted theaters specializing in opera buffa, and in some cities they outnumbered those reserved for the serious genre. In Naples opera seria was the monopoly of the Teatro San Carlo, while *commedia per musica* was performed at the Fiorentini, the Nuovo, the Fondo, and others. In Rome opera seria was played at the Argentina and, in part, at the Dame, while the Valle, the Pace, the Granari, the Capranica, the Pallacorda, and the Rucellai all put on comic opera. In Florence comic opera appeared at the Cocomero, the Coletti, and the Tintori, while the repertory of opera seria was usually reserved for the Pergola but also appeared from time to time at the Cocomero. In Venice few theaters other than the prestigious San Giovanni Grisostomo and San Benedetto remained loyal to opera seria, which most of the city's other theaters abandoned in favor of opera buffa. A number of theaters were built for the purpose of putting on opera buffa (in Palermo the Santa Lucia, for one), and still others that had been active in the production of opera seria opted for the comic genre for economic reasons or because of keen competition (Turin, Carignano; Genoa, Sant'Agostino; Palermo, Santa Cecilia) or else they alternated between the two genres (Milan, Regio Ducale; Reggio Emilia, Pubblico; Fano, Fortuna, and others).

170. There were times when comic operas were performed in theaters that traditionally played opera seria, but these were exceptional instances, at least during the 1770s. The Teatro Argentina in Rome offered works from the comic repertory when financial problems beset the society that administered the theater. An opera buffa season was probably a way to economize temporarily with a less expensive type of spectacle; see Rinaldi, *Due secoli di musica*, 1:50, 130–40. A production of an opera buffa in September 1776 at the Teatro della Pergola in Florence (Paisiello's *Le due contesse*) was news because it was an exceptional event: *La gazzetta toscana* (no. 37, 14 September 1776, 145) noted the presence of "an infinite number of spectators attracted by the novelty of the spectacle because it has been almost half a century since anything but serious dramas were performed on that stage." At Turin comic operas were performed at the Teatro Regio on official, ceremonial occasions (see also note 175) when an appropriate celebratory "serious" work could not be produced. On such occasions the production was borrowed from a minor theater (the Carignano, for example) and transferred to the Regio. Such transfers necessarily implied transformations and improvements, however: in 1782, the plans for moving an opera buffa from the Carignano to the Regio (which fell though) involved the "addition of extras for the ballets and such other additions and variations as shall be deemed appropriate." There were also provisions for "further sums for expenditures to be incurred to that purpose, principally for the scenery, costumes, and orchestra"; see Bouquet, *Il teatro di corte*, 401 n.351.

The large number of theaters dedicated to opera buffa and the wide diffusion of the genre are evidence of a flourishing and profitable market. The
expansion and the success of comic opera does not imply a simultaneous
and complementary decline of opera seria, however: although opera buffa
outstripped the opera seria in terms of number of productions and popularity
with audiences, it never made a dent—nor did it attempt to do so—in the
prestige, fashionable cachet, or official character of the latter. The two varieties divided up the field: opera seria was refined, luxury entertainment ruled
by protocol and aimed at aristocratic and wealthy city dwellers;[171] opera
buffa was a genuinely escapist sort of spectacle, simple, economical, and
bourgeois, and aimed at a public that went to the theater for pleasure, not
for reasons of form.[172] The difference between the official character of opera
seria, with the prestige values it embodied, and the more common character
of opera buffa is reflected in their respective government subsidies. Opera
seria counted for more, and it cost more. Not only was it (at times) protected
by special legislation and by the so-called *ius prohibendi* that gave an opera
house a monopoly and limited other theatrical initiatives, it could also count
on more substantive and more dependable financial aid from the authorities
than opera buffa could. Consider one example of this sort of economic discrimination: in 1752 the Teatro Pubblico of Senigallia received a subsidy of
40 Roman scudi from the city government for the production of opera seria;
only in 1768 did the city extend the subsidy to opera buffa, and even then it
was in an attempt to revive a theater that was languishing.[173] Similarly the
Teatro Pubblico of Reggio Emilia received a subsidy of 25,000 lire from the
duke of Modena for the production of serious operas to be put on during
the spring fairs, the theater's major and most prestigious season. The same

171. In this connection see the charter (1761) for the *Società dei Cavalieri* that administered
the Teatro Argentina in Rome, given in Rinaldi, *Due secoli di musica,* 140. Other examples are
the aristocratic and exclusive association deputized for the construction and administration of the
Teatro Nuovo in Padua (see Brunelli, *I teatri di Padova,* 147) and the management of the Teatro
Nazari of Cremona (see Santoro, *Il teatro di Cremona,* 31, 66–72, and 95).

172. Were there different audiences for opera seria and opera buffa? Undoubtedly, where the
modes and motivations for going to the theater were concerned; less surely regarding the real
social composition of the audience. By its nature opera seria was the prerogative of the aristocratic
and wealthy classes, but the nobility did not scorn opera buffa and in fact contributed to its
success, as can be seen from contemporary chronicles and periodicals. It is less easy to prove that
non-noble, nonpatrician city dwellers assiduously frequented the theaters that gave heroic opera,
although de Brosses and Coyer suggest this was the case (see notes 114 and 115). Rather than the
difference between the two audiences, perhaps what we should look at is how and why people
went to the theater; that is, we should investigate the end results of the different types of operatic
spectacle that were offered to the same urban audience and ask what ends were being satisfied
(etiquette, official entertainment, and a fashionable occasion to see and be seen in the case of
opera seria and ballet; escapist pleasure and sheer entertainment for opera buffa).

173. Giuseppe Radiciotti, *Teatro, musica e musicisti in Sinigaglia* (Milan, 1893), 24.

theater received less than half that amount, 12,000 lire, for a carnival season of more local appeal that put on comic operas.[174] The difference between the financial aid given to opera seria as opposed to opera buffa reflected a corresponding ideological and social gap: in Milan the opening of the Teatro alla Scala was put off until August 1778 even though construction had been completed and the theater had been furnished by carnival time. In that way the theater could open with an opera seria rather than with less appropriate comic operas borrowed from the current productions for the carnival season of the Teatro Interinale.[175]

Although these instances of economic discrimination reflect the ideologically and socially more modest role of opera buffa, they must be seen in the context of the lower cost for producing comic operas. The sets for opera buffa were generic scenes—typically a middle-class interior, a shop, a marketplace, a city street or square—that could be used over and over; there were few set changes, and those few could be effected by a change of props. This simplicity contrasted strongly with the many imposing sets needed for serious opera: menacing prisons, temples, imperial palaces, arcades, infernal depths, dark forests, delightful gardens, and so forth. The size and composition of the orchestra required for opera buffa (mostly strings, two oboes, and two horns) were also modest in comparison to the extra woodwinds, brasses, and timpani called for in the scores of serious operas. Above all, the fees commanded by buffo singers were lower than for their "heroic" counterparts. The data are few but significant. In 1767 and 1768 at the Teatro Pubblico in Lucca, the singers hired for the *burlette*—comic operas—received fees ranging from 10 to 35 testoni each; the following year (1769) the singers in productions of opera seria were paid from 20 to 204 testoni. The best-paid opera buffa singer received only a little more than the most minor role in the opera seria cast and abysmally less than its star. In the same theater in the 1760s and 70s, the fees for the *buffi* ranged, in all cases, between 10 and 35 testoni, whereas serious singers earned from 20 to 270 testoni. The latter figure re-

---

174. See note 92.

175. Luigi Lorenzo Secchi, *1778–1978: Il Teatro alla Scala* (Milan: Electa, 1977), 42. This did not mean that the higher ranks of the aristocracy never attended opera buffa. For example, in April 1767 the grand duke and duchess of Tuscany attended several performances of *Le serve rivali* by Chiari and Traetta at Florence's Teatro del Cocomero (*La gazzetta toscana*, no. 17, 25 April 1767, 71). At Naples in 1768 several comic productions borrowed from the Teatro Nuovo and the Teatro Fiorentini were performed in the small court theater for the private entertainment of King Ferdinand, who also attended performances of *Dal finto il vero* by Zini and Paisiello: "By going to a public performance Ferdinando contributed further to the social acceptability of comic opera and also increased the prestige of the theatres where it was staged"; Robinson, *Naples and Neapolitan Opera,* 13. At Turin in 1773 and 1783, princely weddings and royal visits were celebrated with performances of comic works brought from the Teatro Carignano to the Teatro Regio for the occasion; see Bouquet, *Il teatro di corte,* 362 n, 407.

mained fairly stable, but the *buffi* were paid somewhat better toward the end of the century, reaching an upper limit of 55 testoni in the 1790s.[176] An analogous ratio between the pay scale of opera seria and opera buffa singers can be derived from data for Turinese theaters. In the spring of 1753, the fees for the singers hired for four comic operas to be performed at the Teatro Grondana (in use while the Carignano was being reconstructed) were as follows (in Turinese lire): Serafina Penni—2,437; Filippo Laschi and Giovanni Leonardi—536; Agata Ricci—1,170; Vittoria Querzoli—877, Domenica Lambertini—536; Ambrogio Ghezzi—487; Teresa Crespi—282. For the two serious operas produced at the Teatro Regio during carnival of the same year, the singers' fees ranged from 780 lire to 6,630 lire paid to Ferdinando Mazzanti and 6,650 lire to Teresa Pompeati.[177]

Not only was opera buffa more economical to produce, strong demand also made it possible to put it on at prices lower than those for opera seria. In 1766 the ticket price in Venice for a spoken comedy or an opera buffa was half what it was in a theater that played opera seria. At the Teatro Rangone of Modena in 1768, a box subscription for opera seria (120 to 150 Modenese lire) cost 30 lire more than one for opera buffa, while a single admission ticket cost 2 lire for a serious opera and 1.10 lire for a comic opera.[178] Relatively lower costs enabled a number of impresarios operating in the comic sector to get the better of their competition or to do without the supervision of an association (though this may have been true only of the Teatro Carignano of Turin, which was directed by the same *Società dei Cavalieri* who ran the Teatro Regio).[179] It may even have enabled them to do without government subsidies and pay the fee due to the impresario holding the monopoly on theatrical spectacles. This was the case for the Teatro Nuovo of Naples, which paid 90 ducats in fees, first to the impresario of the Teatro San Bartolomeo and later to the management of the Teatro San Carlo.[180]

These data show that the wider diffusion of comic opera in the Italian peninsula corresponded to a production system of greater economic solidity. Opera buffa did not generate the volume of business or require the massive capital outlay of opera seria, but neither did it bear the same ethical and ideological weight. Comic opera represented a reliable investment. On occa-

176. Nerici, *Storia della musica in Lucca,* 338–43.

177. Bouquet, *Il teatro di corte,* 291. As had been the case during carnival 1748, the lower cost of the opera buffa singers influenced the decisions of the directors of Turin's Teatro Regio when the War of Austrian Succession made it necessary to cut to the bone the budget for the opera seria season; see 280–81.

178. De Lalande, *Voyage en Italie,* 8:523; Gandini, *Cronistoria dei teatri di Modena,* 1:121–22.

179. For the situation in Rome, see note 107.

180. See note 108.

sion it was even used to compensate for losses from opera seria: in Turin a project was drawn up in the spring of 1782 "to find a way to increase the revenues of the theaters by combining two shows, one serious and one comic, during the course of the coming spring, in order to alleviate the greater expense of the serious opera with the comic opera. Budgeted for the opera seria: 66,500 lire; budgeted for the opera buffa: 25,840 lire."[181]

This examination of the production and consumption of serious opera and comic opera might seem to give the impression of two distinct entities, the one in competition with the other. In reality although each had its own specific production methods, financing, style, and aesthetics, they were two aspects of the same phenomenon—operatic theater as an organized, public, and civic form of social entertainment created by professional managers, specialized technicians, and performers. Moreover, opera seria and opera buffa had a number of points of contact, ranging from the more obvious case of librettists, composers, musicians, and singers who worked in both genres to the less obvious theatrical personnel (the impresarios included) who put their professional skills to the service of both genres. Where serious and comic opera differed was in their respective places on the scales of social and economic values: the first was more refined, aristocratic, and luxurious and the second more up-to-date, middle class, and economical. Everything pointed to the greater dignity and prestige of opera seria, from the external and internal aspects of the theaters to the magnificence of the productions, and from its high cost to its relatively select public. The great interpreters of opera seria became rich and famous; at best, opera buffa served a few of them as a way to make their debuts (as was the case with Venanzio Rauzzini, Anna Lucia De Amicis, Girolamo Crescentini, Giovanni Manzuoli, and others). Composers too probably put a higher value on their successes in opera seria than in opera buffa, despite the greater vitality and the more certain profits of the comic opera market.

BIBLIOGRAPHIC NOTE

The primary sources for studying the system of production and consumption developed by Italian opera during the seventeenth and eighteenth centuries are the administrative papers, account books, and balance sheets of the various city governments, theatrical institutions, single theater managements, and seasons. A good deal of this material has been lost: for instance, documentation is totally lacking, despite governmental sponsorship, for a theater as illustrious as the San Carlo in Naples. The documentation known and investigated to date is scarce, fragmentary, and discontinuous.

181. Bouquet, *Il teatro di corte*, 402 n. 353.

Its very nature has dictated studies that privilege the municipal point of view in research focused on the history of local theatrical institutions rather than a broader view.

For the seventeenth century in general, that broader view has at least begun to appear in Lorenzo Bianconi, *Il Seicento, Storia della musica,* vol. 4 (Turin: Edizioni di Torino/Musica, 1982), in English translation as *Music in the Seventeenth Century,* trans. David Bryant (Cambridge: Cambridge University Press, 1987), chapter 4 in particular; Lorenzo Bianconi and Thomas Walker, "Production, Consumption, and Political Function of Seventeenth-Century Opera," *Early Music History* 4 (1984): 209–96, an enlarged version of a paper read at a roundtable (chaired by Pierluigi Petrobelli and concerning the entire European picture) on "Seventeenth-Century Music Drama," for which see International Musicological Society, *Report of the Twelfth Congress, Berkeley 1977,* ed. Daniel Heartz and Bonnie Wade (Kassel and Basel: Bärenreiter, 1981), 680–711; Giovanni Morelli and Thomas Walker, "Tre controversie intorno al San Cassiano," in *Venezia e il melodramma nel Seicento,* ed. Maria Teresa Muraro (Florence: Olschki, 1976), 97–120, a study of the key cases of early impresarial theaters in Venice.

Questions on the production and consumption of opera in the eighteenth century in general are treated with some breadth of scope in Reinhard Strohm, *Italienische Opernarien des frühen Settecento (1720–1730),* Analecta musicologia, no. 16, 2 vols. (Cologne: Arno Volk, 1976), a work whose introduction is particularly important; Strohm, *Die italienische Oper im 18. Jahrhundert* (Wilhelmshaven: Heinrichshofen, 1979), in Italian translation as *Opera italiana nel Settecento* (Venice: Marsilio, 1991), which gives "readings" of some *drammi per musica* and comic operas; Strohm, "Aspetti sociali dell'opera italiana del primo Settecento," *Musica/Realtà* 2, no. 5 (August 1981): 117–41; Strohm, "Per una miglior comprensione dell'opera seria" (1979), *Musica/Realtà* 7, no. 21 (December 1986): 121–38, in English translation as "Towards an Understanding of the *opera seria,*" in Strohm, *Essays on Handel and Italian Opera* (Cambridge: Cambridge University Press, 1985), 93–105; Michael F. Robinson, *Naples and Neapolitan Opera* (Oxford: Clarendon Press, 1972), in Italian translation, updated, as *L'opera napoletana: Storia e geografia di un'idea musicale settecentesca,* ed. Giovanni Morelli (Venice: Marsilio, 1984); John Rosselli, *The Opera Industry in Italy from Cimarosa to Verdi: The Role of the Impresario* (Cambridge: Cambridge University Press, 1984), in Italian translation, amplified, as *L'impresario d'opera: Arte e affari nel teatro musicale italiano dell'Ottocento* (Turin: Edizioni di Torino/Musica, 1985), a work that, although it deals only with the end of the eighteenth century, amply covers preexistent tradition (as do the two complementary studies by John Rosselli cited in notes 102 and 137); Lorenzo Bianconi, "Condizione sociale e intellettuale del musicista di teatro ai tempi di Vivaldi," in *Antonio Vivaldi: Teatro musicale, cultura e società,* ed. Lorenzo Bianconi and Giovanni Morelli, Studi di musica veneta: Quaderni vivaldiani, 2 vols. (Florence: Olschki, 1982), 2:371–88; Franco Piperno, "Impresariato collettivo e strategie teatrali: Sul sistema produttivo dello spettacolo operistico settecentesco," in *Civiltà teatrale e Settecento emiliano,* ed. Susi Davoli (Bologna: Il Mulino, 1986), 345–56.

Periodicals provide a particularly rich secondary source of information on relations between opera houses and their public. There were few journals in the seventeenth century, but their numbers increased and they gave increasing notice of operatic events as the eighteenth century advanced. In addition to the *Pallade veneta* (brought to light by Eleanor Selfridge-Field; see note 148), there were various *Avvisi* in the larger cities in Italy: *Il diario ordinario* of Rome, *La gazzetta toscana, La gazzetta universale, La gazzetta veneta* of Gasparo Gozzi, the *Bologna,* the *Memorie per le belle arti, Il giornale per le belle arti,* and *L'indice de' teatrali spettacoli,* a specifically theatrical periodical (see note 111). Similarly, the many works on journeys to Italy are at times brimming with theatrical news and general observations on the theater. A useful (though geographically limited) recent critical bibliography can be found in Giorgio Cusatelli, ed., *Viaggi e viaggiatori del Settecento in Emilia e in Romagna,* 2 vols. (Bologna: Il Mulino, 1986). Travel accounts particularly worthy of note are those of Charles de Brosses, Charles Burney, Gabriel-François Coyer, and Joseph-Jérôme Le Français de Lalande (see notes 79, 139, 115, and 91, respectively). For two surveys of satirical publications, see note 147.

For historical-juridical, theoretical, and literary sources, which vary enormously in their scope and contents, especially regarding the eighteenth century, see Renato di Benedetto, "Poetics and Polemics," chapter 1 in volume 6 of the present *History of Italian Opera.*

For a more detailed grasp of the system of opera production in its early stages, see the collections of contemporary sources in Angelo Solerti, ed., *Le origini del melodramma: Testimonianze dei contemporanei* (Turin: Bocca, 1903; reprint, Bologna: Arnaldo Forni, 1969); Heinz Becker, ed., *Quellentexte zur Konzeption der europäischen Oper im 17. Jahrhundert* (Kassel and Basel: Bärenreiter, 1981); and the anonymous *Il Corago o vero Alcune osservazioni per metter bene in scena le composizioni drammatiche* (ca. 1630), ed. Paolo Fabbri and Angelo Pompilio (Florence: Olschki, 1983).

Recent studies of salient moments in court opera include Claude V. Palisca, "The First Performance of *Euridice,*" in *Queens College, Department of Music: Twenty-fifth Anniversary Festschrift (1937–1962),* ed. Albert Mell (New York: Queens College, 1964), 1–23; Iain Fenlon, "Monteverdi's Mantuan 'Orfeo': Some New Documentation," *Early Music* 12 (1984): 163–72; Tim Carter, "A Florentine Wedding of 1608," *Acta Musicologica* 55 (1983): 89–107. On the entire context of spectacles with music produced for a single dynastic event, none of which was, strictly speaking, an opera involving singing throughout, see Paolo Carpeggiani, "Le feste fiorentine del 1608," *Civiltà mantovana* 12 (1978): 14–56; Stuart Reiner, "Preparations in Parma—1618, 1627–28," *Music Review* 25 (1964): 273–310, on festivities with music; Pierluigi Petrobelli, "'L'Ermiona' di Pio Enea degli Obizzi ed i primi spettacoli d'opera veneziani," *Quaderno della rassegna musicale* 3 (1965): 125–41, on Padua; Thomas Walker, "Gli errori di *Minerva al tavolino,*" in *Venezia e il melodramma nel Seicento,* ed. Maria Teresa Muraro (Florence: Olschki, 1976), on spectacles in Ferrara in the mid-seventeenth century.

On models of production for "commercial" opera in its phase of expansion during the early seventeenth century, see Nino Pirrotta, "Commedia dell'arte e melodramma," *Santa Cecilia* 3, suppl. (1954): 23–37, in English translation as "Commedia dell'arte and Opera," *Musical Quarterly* 16 (1955): 305–24; Lorenzo Bianconi and Thomas Walker, "Dalla *Finta pazza* alla *Veremonda:* Storie di Febiarmonici," *Rivista italiana di musicologia* 10 (1975): 379–454.

On Venetian opera houses, see Maria Teresa Muraro, ed., *Venezia e il melodramma nel Seicento* (Florence: Olschki, 1976); Ludovico Zorzi, preface to the exhibition catalog, *I teatri pubblici di Venezia (secoli XVII–XVIII)* (Venice: Teatro La Fenice-La Biennale, 1971), 9–50, a study of the broader social and ideological picture that also appears as "Venezia: La Repubblica a teatro," chap. 3 in Zorzi, *Il teatro e la città: Saggi sulla scena italiana* (Turin: Einaudi, 1977), 235–91.

For primary sources on Venice, see Cristoforo Ivanovich, "Memorie teatrali di Venezia," in *Minerva al tavolino* (Venice, 1681), excerpts from which are in English translation in Lorenzo Bianconi, *Music in the Seventeenth Century,* source readings, "The Impresarial Organization of Venetian Theatres: Cristoforo Ivanovich," (Cambridge: Cambridge University Press, 1987), 303–11; Nicola Mangini, *I teatri di Venezia* (Milan: Mursia, 1974).

On individual episodes of theatrical life in seventeenth-century Venice, see Bruno Brunelli, "L'impresario in angustie," *Rivista italiana del dramma* 5 (1941): 311–41; Remo Giazotto, "La guerra dei palchi: Documenti per servire alla storia del teatro musicale a Venezia come istituto sociale e iniziativa privata nei secoli XVII e XVIII," *Nuova rivista musicale italiana* 1 (1967): 245–86; 465–508; Carl B. Schmidt, "An Episode in the History of Venetian Opera: The *Tito* Commission (1665–66)," *Journal of the American Musicological Society* 31 (1978): 442–66; Nino Pirrotta, "Il caval zoppo e il vetturino: Cronache di Parnaso 1642," Collectanea Historiae Musicae, (Florence: Olschki, 1966), 4:215–26; prefaces to the various volumes of the series Drammaturgia musicale veneta (Milan: Ricordi, 1983–). See also Beth L. Glixon and Jonathan E. Glixon, "Marco Faustini and Venetian Opera Production in the 1650s: Recent Archival Discoveries," *Journal of Musicology* 10 (1992): 48–73.

For the role of librettos and librettists in Venice in the seventeenth century, see Nino Pirrotta, "Early Venetian Libretti at Los Angeles," in *Essays in Musicology in Honor of Dragan Plamenac,* ed. Gustave Reese and Robert J. Snow (Pittsburgh: University of Pittsburgh Press, 1969), 233–43; in Italian (with other essays on seventeenth-century opera theater) in Pirrotta, *Scelte poetiche di musicisti* (Venice: Marsilio, 1987), 243–54; Ellen Rosand, "In Defense of the Venetian Libretto," *Studi musicali* 9 (1980): 271–85.

There are extensive but uneven bibliographies for seventeenth-century opera houses elsewhere than in Venice, often covering two or more centuries. For an ample listing see Alfredo Giovine, *Bibliografia di teatri musicali italiani* (Bari: Fratelli Laterza, 1982). Recent works and some of the "classics" on the subject include the following.

For Genoa see Armando Fabio Ivaldi, "Gli Adorno e l'hostaria-teatro del Falcone di Genova (1600–1680)," *Rivista italiana di musicologia* 15 (1980): 87–152.

For Florence see Françoise Decroisette, "Un Exemple d'administration des théâtres au XVIIème siècle: Le théâtre de la Pergola à Florence (1652–1662)," in *Arts du spectacle et histoire des idées: Recueil offert en hommage à Jean Jacquot* (Tours: Centre d'études supérieures de la Renaissance, 1984), 73–90; John Walter Hill, "Le relazioni di Antonio Cesti con la corte e i teatri di Firenze," *Rivista italiana di musicologia* 11 (1976): 27–47; Robert Lamar Weaver and Norma Wright Weaver, *A Chronology of Music in the Florentine Theater,* Detroit Studies in Musical Bibliography, nos. 30 and 70 (Detroit: Information Coordinators; Harmonie Park Press, 1978, 1993); William

C. Holmes, *Opera Observed: Views of a Florentine Impresario in the Early Eighteenth Century* (Chicago: University of Chicago Press, 1993).

For Naples see Benedetto Croce, *I teatri di Napoli dal rinascimento alla fine del secolo decimottavo,* 4th ed., rev. and enl. (Bari: Laterza, 1947), critical edition of the 1891 edition, ed. Giuseppe Galasso (Milan: Adelphi, 1992); Ulisse Prota-Giurleo, "Breve storia del teatro di corte e della musica a Napoli nei secoli XVII–XVIII," in *Il teatro di Corte del Palazzo reale di Napoli* (Naples, 1952), 19–158; Prota-Giurleo, *I teatri di Napoli nel '600: La commedia e le maschere* (Naples: Fiorentino, 1962); Lorenzo Bianconi, "Funktionen des Operntheaters in Neapel bis 1700 und die Rolle Alessandro Scarlattis," in *Colloquium Alessandro Scarlatti, Würzburg 1975,* ed. Wolfgang Osthoff and Jutta Ruile-Dronke (Tutzing: Schneider, 1979): 13–111, 220–27; Domenico Antonio d'Alessandro, "L'opera in musica a Napoli dal 1650 al 1670," in *Seicento napoletano: Arte, costume e ambiente,* ed. Roberto Pane (Milan: Edizioni di Comunità, 1984). 409–30, 543–49.

For Rome see Alberto Cametti, *Il Teatro di Tordinona poi di Apollo* (Tivoli: Chicca, 1938); Per Bjurström, *Feast and Theatre in Queen Christina's Rome* (Stockholm: Nationalmuseum, 1966); Margaret Murata, "Il carnevale a Roma sotto Clemente IX Rospigliosi," *Rivista italiana di musicologia* 12 (1977): 83–99; Murata, "The Church and the Stage in Seicento Rome," (paper read at the national meeting of the American Musicological Society, Philadelphia, October 1984).

For Bologna see Corrado Ricci, *I teatri di Bologna nei secoli XVII e XVIII* (1888; reprint, Bologna: Arnaldo Forni, 1965).

For Turin see Marie-Thérèse Bouquet, *Il teatro di corte: Dalle origini al 1788;* and Mercedes Viale Ferrero, *La scenografia: Dalle origini al 1936,* vols. 1 and 3, *Storia del Teatro Regio di Torino,* ed. Alberto Basso (Turin: Cassa di Risparmio di Torino, 1976–83).

For Modena and Reggio Emilia see Graziella Martinelli Braglia, "Il Teatro Fontanelli: Note su impresari e artisti nella Modena di Francesco II e Rinaldo I," and Paolo Fabbri, "Il municipio e la corte: Il teatro per musica tra Reggio e Modena nel secondo Seicento," in *Alessandro Stradella e Modena,* ed. Carolyn Gianturco (Modena: Teatro Comunale, 1985), 139–59, 160–84.

For the eighteenth century, one notable study on an eminent musician-impresario by Reinhard Strohm should be added to the list of Strohm's studies above: "Vivaldi's Career as an Opera Producer," in *Antonio Vivaldi: Teatro musicale, cultura e società,* ed. Lorenzo Bianconi and Giovanni Morelli, Studi di musica veneta: Quaderni vivaldiani, no. 2 (2 vols.) (Florence: Olschki, 1982), 11–63, and in Strohm, *Essays on Handel* (Cambridge: Cambridge University Press, 1985), 122–63.

Aside from the titles already mentioned concerning the seventeenth century, works on individual cities, opera houses, and theatrical managements include Gino Conti, "Il Teatro La Pergola di Firenze e la stagione d'opera per il carnevale 1726–1727: Lettere di Luca Casimiro degli Albizzi a Vivaldi, Porpora e altri," *Rivista italiana di musicologia* 15 (1980): 182–88. The wealth of impresarial materials in the Archivio Albizzi of Florence is also exploited in William C. Holmes, "Quindici lettere inedite su Alessandro Scarlatti," in *La musica a Napoli durante il Seicento, ,* ed. Domenico Antonio d'Alessandro e Agostino Ziino (Rome: Torre d'Orfeo, 1987), 369–78, and

Opera Observed: Views of a Florentine Impresario in the Early Eighteenth Century (Chicago: University of Chicago Press, 1993).

On the Teatro Argentina in Rome, see Raimondo Guarino, "Il Teatro dell'indifferenza: Questioni storiche e storiografiche sullo spettacolo inaugurale del Teatro Argentina," in *Il teatro a Roma nel Settecento,* 2 vols. (Rome: Istituto della Enciclopedia Italiana, 1989), 1:421–44; Mario Rinaldi, *Due secoli di musica al Teatro Argentina,* 3 vols. (Florence: Olschki, 1978)

For Padua see Bruno Brunelli, *I teatri di Padova dalle origini alla fine del secolo XIX* (Padua: Angelo Draghi, 1921).

For Cremona see Elia Santoro, *Il teatro di Cremona,* 4 vols. (Cremona: Pizzoni, 1969–72).

For Pavia see Elena Ferrari Barassi, "Osservazioni e commenti intorno agli spettacoli in musica nella Pavia settecentesca," *Bollettino della Società pavese di storia patria* 70/71 (1970–71): 99–130.

For Piacenza see Francesco Bussi, "I teatri d'opera a Piacenza prima della costruzione del Teatro municipal," *Nuova rivista musicale italiana* 24 (1990): 457–64.

For Genoa see Armando Fabio Ivaldi, "L'impresa dei teatri di Genova (1772): Per una gestione sociale della cultura," *Studi musicali* 7 (1978): 215–36.

For Perugia see Biancamaria Brumana and Michelangelo Pascale, "Il teatro musicale a Perugia nel Settecento: Una cronologia dai libretti," *Esercizi: Arte, musica, spettacolo* 6 (1983): 71–134.

For Lugo see Paolo Fabbri, "Teatri settecenteschi della Romagna estense: Lugo," *Romagna, arte e storia* 8 (1983): 55–76.

For Mantua see Luigi Cataldi, "I rapporti di Vivaldi con il 'Teatro detto Il Comico' di Mantova," *Informazioni e studi vivaldiani* 6 (1985): 88–110.

Volumes containing studies by various authors include Maria Teresa Muraro, ed., *Venezia e il melodramma nel Settecento,* 2 vols. (Florence: Olschki, 1978–81); Sergio Romagnoli and Elvira Garbero, eds., *Teatro a Reggio Emilia,* 2 vols. (Florence: Sansoni, 1980); Susi Davoli, ed., *Civiltà teatrale e Settecento emiliano* (Bologna: Il Mulino, 1986), which contains an important study on Reggio by Paolo Fabbri and Roberto Verti, "Struttura del repertorio operistico reggiano nel Settecento," 257–75, 277–99, and another on Parma by Giuliana Ferrari, Paola Mecarelli, and Paola Melloni, "L'organizzazione teatrale parmense all'epoca del Du Tillot: I rapporti fra la corte e gli impresari," 357–80.

Thus far the institutional and artistic history of several of the largest theaters, those of Milan among them, is inadequately known or has not been studied in depth. For the Teatro San Carlo of Naples there is now Raffaele Ajello, ed., *Il teatro di San Carlo di Napoli,* 2 vols. (Naples: Guida, 1987), and *Il teatro di San Carlo, 1737–1987,* ed. Franco Mancini, Bruno Cagli, and Agostino Ziino, 3 vols. (Naples: Electra, 1987), published on the occasion of the two hundred fiftieth anniversary of the theater.

Given the separation of genres into opera seria, comic opera, intermezzi, and ballet that occurred in eighteenth-century operatic productions, the bibliographies also tend to specialize.

For dance see the bibliography given in Kathleen Kuzmick Hansell, "Theatrical Dance and Italian Opera," chapter 3, volume 5 of the present *History of Italian Opera.*

For operatic theater in general see Lorenzo Bianconi and Thomas Walker, "Production, Consumption, and Political Function of Seventeenth-Century Opera," *Early Music History* 4 (1984): 209–96; Michele Timotei, *Il cortegiano, nel quale si tratta di tutti gli offizii della corte* (Rome, 1614).

For opera seria see Klaus Hortschansky, "Die Rezeption der Wiener Dramen Metastasios in Italien," in *Venezia e il melodramma nel Settecento*, ed. Maria Teresa Muraro, 2 vols. (Florence: Olschki, 1978–81); Anna Laura Bellina, "Metastasio in Venezia: Appunti per una *recensio*," *Italianistica* 13 (1984): 145–73; Reinhard Strohm, "Metastasios *Alessandro nell'Indie* und seine frühesten Vertonungen," in Walther Seigmund-Schultze, ed., *Probleme der Händelschen Oper inbesondere am Beispiel "Poro"*) (Halle: Martin-Luther-Universität, 1982), 40–61, in Italian translation in *La drammaturgia musicale*, ed. Lorenzo Bianconi (Bologna: Il Mulino, 1986), 157–76, and in English as "Metastasio's *Alessandro nell'Indie* and its Earliest Settings," in *Essays on Handel* (Cambridge: Cambridge University Press, 1985), 232–48. See also Costantino Maeder, *Metastasio, l'"Olimpiade" e l'opera del Settecento* (Bologna: Il Mulino, 1993).

For comic opera and the intermezzi, see Charles E. Troy, *The Comic Intermezzo: A Study in the History of Eighteenth-Century Italian Opera* (Ann Arbor, Mich.: UMI Research Press, 1979); Pietro Pariati and Tomaso Albinoni, *Pimpinone*, ed. Michael Talbot (Madison, Wis.: A-R Editions, 1983); Franco Piperno, "Note sulla diffusione degli intermezzi di J. A. Hasse (1726–1741)," *Analecta Musicologica* 25 (1987): 267–86; Piperno, "Gli interpreti buffi di Pergolesi: Note sulla diffusione de *La serva padrona*," in *Studi pergolesiani/Pergolesi Studies*, ed. Francesco Degrada, 2 vols. (Florence: La Nuova Italia, 1986), 1:166–77; Piperno, "Appunti sulla configurazione sociale e professionale delle 'parti buffe' al tempo di Vivaldi," in *Antonio Vivaldi: Teatro musicale, cultura e società*, ed. Lorenzo Bianconi and Giovanni Morelli, Studi di musica veneta: Quaderni vivaldiani, vol. 2 (2 vols.) (Florence: Olschki, 1982); Piperno, "Buffe e buffi (considerazioni sulla professionalità degli interpreti di scene buffe ed intermezzi)," *Rivista italiana di musicologia* 17 (1982): 240–84; Helmut Hucke, "Die Entstehung der Opera buffa," in *Bericht über den Internationalen musikwissenschaftlichen Kongress Bayreuth 1981*, ed. Christoph-Hellmut Mahling and Sigrid Weismann (Kassel and Basel: Bärenreiter, 1984), 78–85; Piero Weiss, "La diffusione del repertorio operistico nell'Italia del Settecento: Il caso dell'opera buffa, in *Civiltà teatrale e Settecento emiliano*, ed. Davoli (Bologna: Il Mulino, 1986, 241–56).

Finally, for studies on the truly decisive role of singers in opera, see the bibliography in Sergio Durante, "The Singer," chapter 6.

— 2 —

Opera Production, 1780–1880

JOHN ROSSELLI

1. Opera as the Expression of a Hierarchical and Conservative Society

Opera was an industry. Yet it was also a means of displaying the hierarchical structure of Italian society and the ascendancy within it of the upper classes. These two elements—business and hierarchy—continued to be typical of opera from the late eighteenth century through most of the nineteenth century.

Shortly before his death Cavour was to define opera as "a great industry with ramifications all over the world." At least as early as 1780, and from time to time throughout the nineteenth century, the argument was put forward that opera stimulated trade, tourism, and the circulation of money; it gave employment not only to theater people (said to number some three thousand people in Milan alone by 1889) but to ancillary trades; it provided invisible exports reckoned in the 1880s at over 5 million French francs a year.[1]

For libraries and archives, see the list of abbreviations in the front matter. The abbreviation Dep. Pub. Sp. (Deputazione dei Pubblici Spettacoli), used with several libraries, follows the library siglum after a comma. The following abbreviations indicate theatrical seasons: C = Carnival; Q = Quaresima (Lent); P = Primavera (spring); E = Estate (summer); A = Autunno (autumn); F = Fiera (annual fair) (C season usually started on 26 or 27 December of the previous year; C1837 started on 26 December 1836.) References to certain theater histories that are arranged chronologically year by year do not give page numbers if the year referred to is obvious.

1. Pompeo Cambiasi, *La Scala*, 4th ed. (Milan, 1889), xii–xviii; prospectus for a joint-stock *impresa*, 1780, I-Bas Assunteria di Camera, Diversorum, tomo 128; Paolo Emilio Ferrari, *Spettacoli drammatico-musicali e coreografici in Parma* (Parma, 1884), 89–90.; Count Künigl to the Nobile Associazione del Teatro alla Scala, 26 March 1788, I-Mas, Sp. P. 28; Angelo Petracchi,

Opera gradually shifted from being conceived of as a royal or noble entertainment to being seen as an industry. Although it was partially commercialized from the founding of the first public theaters in Venice in the 1630s,
opera nonetheless continued to center around the well-off, which meant that
in the cities of late eighteenth-century Italy (the commercial ports of Livorno
and Trieste excepted), it was almost totally dependent upon the aristocracy.
From the earliest days of public theater, the impresarios who carried on this
great industry went some way to bear out the description by referring to
themselves as tradesmen *(commercianti; negozianti)*, but, as we shall see,
not even at the height of "industrial" opera in the nineteenth century did they
become entrepreneurs risking their own capital or that of others on the open
market. Around 1780 management by an impresario continued to exist side
by side with administration by nobles (an individual theater owner or an
association), who might have supervisory powers over the impresario, and
even when the impresario ran the opera season singlehandedly, he usually
received both his contract *(appalto)* and—more importantly—funds to meet
almost certain losses from patrons who were nearly always from the upper
classes.

The Italian opera house of the nineteenth century has commonly been spoken of as a meeting place of all classes. The Austrian government of
Lombardy-Venetia went so far as to call La Scala the only such meeting
place.[2] What this conventional view ignored was the acute sense of hierarchy
that ran through the theater in Italy and was recognized by everyone involved.
There was no single meeting place and no single mixture of classes. On the
contrary, there was a well-understood hierarchy of theaters, of areas within
the theater, of audiences, of seasons, and of genres. On every count, opera
seria—the old eighteenth-century heroic opera on mythological or historical
subjects, gradually evolving into the mid-nineteenth-century historical or domestic tragedy of Verdi—stood at the top. What is more, throughout most
of the first half of the nineteenth century, when it began to absorb musical
influences from other genres, opera seria continued to be socio-economically
distinct from opera buffa and opera semiseria.

The superior status of opera seria was demonstrated in the most practical

---

Sul reggimento de' pubblici teatri (Milan, 1821), 17–21; Enrico Rosmini, *La legislazione e la
giurisprudenza dei teatri*, 2 vols. (Milan, 1872), 1:171 n; Francesco D'Arcais, "L'industria musicale in Italia," *Nuova antologia di scienze, lettere ed arti*, 2d ser., 15 (15 May 1879): 133–48.

    2. Giuseppe Radiciotti, *Gioacchino Rossini: Vita documentata opere ed influenza su l'arte*, 3
vols. (Tivoli: Majella, 1927–29), 3:55–56; Alberto Asor Rosa, *La cultura*, pt. 2, vol. 2, *Dall'Unità
a oggi*, in *Storia d'Italia*, ed. Ruggiero Romano and Corrado Vivanti (Turin: Einaudi, 1972–
76), 964ff.; Government of Lombardy-Venetia to I. R. Chancellery, 20 March 1820, I-Mt, Sp. P.
60/3.

way: it cost more. It cost more to put on than the sentimental opera semiseria (an invention of the late eighteenth century), which in turn cost more than the straightforwardly comic opera buffa. This was because opera seria was understood to demand lavish and historically accurate sets and costumes, the most expensive singers, a larger chorus, and more extras. It also cost more to get into: only in 1838 did La Scala, as a rule the pioneer in making changes of this kind, start charging the same price of admission for serious and for comic opera.[3] Finally, if the impresario got a subsidy, it was usually higher for serious opera. Theory dictated (as is so often the case, at a moment when the old hierarchical order was disintegrating) that the "grandiose spectacles" of opera seria were better suited to the well-off, whereas the less well-off preferred opera buffa. This might well have been true enough in 1750, when opera buffa was still fairly new. In 1850, when the statement was made, it was at best doubtful: its real point was to maintain old distinctions. Indeed, the government agency that emitted this opinion, the Deputazione dei Pubblici Spettacoli of Bologna, was soon obliged to include opera seria in the off-season program of the Teatro Comunale, "(1) because these days there are practically no comic operas worthy of the great Teatro Comunale; (2) because these days artists of true merit will not do buffo roles."[4] According to these distinctions, not only did the three kinds of opera form a hierarchy, they all (unless the comic opera was of a low form often called *farsa*) stood a little higher than spoken plays, which in turn stood higher than equestrian spectacle, acrobats, demonstrations of animal magnetism, and so on down to performing monkeys.

The most aristocratic audience was to be found at the opera seria in the leading theater of the town during the most fashionable season. This was usually carnival, although in Bologna it was autumn and in some cities (Reggio Emilia, Padua, and Bergamo) it was the season of the spring or summer fairs. Furthermore, in order to guarantee its predominance, the leading theater usually had a monopoly, or *privativa,* of opera seria during the high season. This explains the observations of one Modenese noble who visited Venice in 1835 and thought at first that the secondary theaters offered "spectacles good for the people, which the better society does not frequent." He soon discovered that the performances at the Teatro San Giovanni Grisostomo (a mixed evening of the Duse theatrical troupe, circus riders, acrobats, and *balletto pantomimico*) were, "all in all, good popular entertainment, and

---

3. Giovanni Valle, *Cenni teorico-pratici sulle aziende teatrali* (Milan, 1823), 8–10; [Carlo Ritorni], *Consigli sull'arte di dirigere gli spettacoli* (Bologna, 1825), 31–32.; Cambiasi, *La Scala.*

4. Deputazione dei Pubblici Spettacoli, Bologna, to Commissione Comunale, 12 January 1850, and Count Filippo Agucchi, conservatore delegato, to the senator of Bologna, 28 February 1852, I-Bas, Comune, Dep. Pub. Sp., tit. I, rub. 1, 1850, 1852.

I am sure that many of the upper classes will go as well."[5] That is, nobles might have gone to such theaters once, for amusement, but the better part of their social life took place at the opera, where they went nearly every evening, accompanied by servants, to eat, drink, gamble, and chat in their own boxes or in the foyer, and even to listen intermittently to the music.

The sense of hierarchy in the theater depended only in part on who owned the building. Some Italian theaters belonged to monarchs, some to municipalities, some to individuals (in the eighteenth century these were generally noble), and some to associations of boxholders. Often there was mixed ownership: the building might belong to the government or to a noble family, while most of the boxes were the property of boxholders who, in many theaters, could sell, mortgage, or let them (within limits, which the period of revolutionary and Napoleonic rule tended to break down). The boxholders of the Teatro Municipale of Reggio Emilia had originally been forbidden to sell out to noncitizens of the town, to "mechanics," or to Jews, but in 1814 Jews were allowed, perhaps in conformity with a Napoleonic decree, to buy boxes in the third tier.[6] The reason for mixed ownership was either that the sale of boxes had originally helped to finance the building of the theater or that an existing owner had resorted to it to raise capital. By the late eighteenth century individual property in boxes was common, and boxholders (often represented by an elected committee) had a good deal of say in the running of the theater even where they were not full owners.

There were exceptions. Some theaters remained under direct government control, particularly in those monarchies (Piedmont, Naples) that had never known the ascendancy of the medieval and Renaissance city state, and (in the hereditary lands of Austria) Trieste. In the Teatro Regio in Turin and the San Carlo in Naples, both of which were attached to the royal palace, the question of which families should be allowed to rent a box (or for that matter to give it up) was an affair of state. In Turin the king saw to it himself each year; at the restoration Vittorio Emanuele I insisted on allocating the first three tiers to the aristocracy, thereby angering the Turin bourgeoisie, which through nearly twenty years of French rule had grown used to living on an equal footing with nobles.[7] In both Turin and Naples the king could reallocate boxes if

5. Count Giuseppe Rangone to Count Francesco Rangone, Venice 21, 24 December 1835, Archiginnasio Carte Rangone B2827. See also Lady Morgan [Sydney Owenson], *Italy,* 2 vols. (London, 1821), 1:102.

6. Giovanni Crocioni, *I teatri di Reggio nell'Emilia* (Reggio Emilia: Cooperativa Lavoranti Tipografi, 1907), 66, 115, 117.

7. Michael F. Robinson, *Naples and Neapolitan Opera* (Oxford: Clarendon Press, 1972), 9; Mme de Boigne, *Mémoires de la Comtesse de Boigne née d'Osmond,* ed. Jean-Claude Berchet, 2 vols. (Paris: Mercure de France, 1971), 1:291f., quoted in Alberto Basso, *Il teatro della città dal 1788 al 1936,* vol. 2 of *Storia del Teatro Regio di Torino,* ed. Alberto Basso, 5 vols. (Turin: Cassa di Risparmio di Torino, 1976–83), 148–49.

tenants fell into arrears (a common problem, worse than ever in times of economic slump), or if they sublet, or even, in Turin, if they failed to turn up often enough. In practice noble boxholders were treated gingerly: after repeated pleas from the impresario Domenico Barbaja, the Naples government agreed to take away defaulters' boxes in the Teatro San Carlo, but it did so slowly and reluctantly.[8]

In Trieste, a virtual creation of the Austrian monarchy and a city of newly rich merchants from many countries, the opera house in the late eighteenth century was municipally owned, but the music-loving governor and chief of police between them controlled it at least as tightly as the kings of Piedmont and Naples did theirs. One boxholder had his box taken away for having sold it without authority to an unsuitable person—the young son of an apothecary—and for anyhow being himself too poor. Not until 1847 was control effectively transferred to the municipal council and the boxholders.[9]

In Rome, where ownership of theaters by individual noble families prevailed well into the nineteenth century, the Teatro Valle in the 1820s appears to have had no boxholder-proprietors. But because ambassadors to the Holy See had a history of quarrels over precedence in the opera house almost as long as that of opera itself, the papal government controlled the seasonal letting of boxes in the "noble" tiers even of second-rank theaters like the Valle and even as late as 1846: the declared aim was a proper hierarchical arrangement to assure "proper placement of preference to royal personages, to the most excellent diplomatic corps, and to the Roman nobility, relative to rank."[10]

There was no doubt in any leading theater, whatever its structure of ownership, which were the "noble" areas. The seating arrangements were hierarchical in the most visible way. The second tier of boxes (out of four, five, or six) was always the most aristocratic: except in commercial ports like Trieste and Livorno, it was largely or wholly occupied by nobles, at least in the fashionable season. The first and third tier in some theaters enjoyed equal standing with the second. More often both were a little lower in esteem and price; in leading or second-rank theaters boxholders' lists show a mixture of nobles

8. Marie-Thérèse Bouquet, *Il teatro di corte: Dalle origini al 1788*, vol. 1 of *Storia del Teatro Regio di Torino*, ed. Alberto Basso (Turin: Cassa di Risparmio di Torino, 1976), 211–14; I-Nas Teatri, fol. 98, Domenico Barbaja to Soprintendente, 18 November 1819, Min. Interno II inv., fol. 4355, Barbaja petitions, 1822–23.

9. Carlo L. Curiel, *Il Teatro San Pietro di Trieste* (Milan: Archetipografia, 1937), 21–25, 142–43.; Giuseppe Carlo Bottura, *Storia . . . del Teatro Comunale di Trieste* (Trieste, 1885), 119, 107–8 n, 293.

10. Contracts, 24 December 1823, 31 October 1829, Paterni-Capranica correspondence, I-Rasc, Archivio Capranica, busta 469; Notificazioni della Deputazione dei Pubblici Spettacoli, Teatri Valle e Metastasio, 16 March 1842 and 4 December 1846, Biblioteca dell'Istituto di Storia dell'Arte e Archeologia, Rome, Manifesti teatrali.

and professional men—lawyers, doctors, civil servants, and bankers. The status of the tier or tiers above the third was lower still but varied with the theater. It was not unknown to find the odd (presumably impoverished) noble in a top-tier box. Taking out the partitions in this top tier to make a gallery was a signal that the lower classes—however defined—were being let in. Two leading theaters most heavily dominated by aristocratic boxholders were late in making this change: the Carolino, Palermo, did so about 1830, and La Fenice, Venice, not until 1878.[11]

So conscious were boxholders of belonging to a particular tier that, in the statutes proposed for a boxholders' association that owned one of the Lucca theaters, the executive body was to be made up of eight men, two of them elected by each of the four tiers; for meetings to be valid at least one from each tier must be present. A refinement in the small town of Recanati gave boxholders in the top tier only half a vote.[12] Nor did the dominance of the nobility end in the boxes or in the passages and dressing rooms behind them. Part of the stalls area at La Scala was filled with black capes *(cappe nere)*— upper servants of the nobility, who were admitted at a special price. There and in many other theaters, employees of a noble household (such as major-domos, secretaries, and liveried servants) accompanying their masters had free entry. In some theaters they had free or specially cheap entry to the gallery: at Padua the Teatro Nuovo had its top tier wholly reserved for them until 1786.

Where French rule from 1796 to 1814 brought about substantial social change, as in Milan with its emerging middle class, these practices came to an end and did not return. At the other extreme, the Carolino, Palermo, had the servants of the nobility filling the back of the stalls area well into the nineteenth century. Other places fell somewhere in between. At the Piacenza municipal theater, servants' virtually free entry to the gallery was dropped sometime after 1812; by 1850 their masters had to pay for them to get into the building, though at a special low rate. But at Bologna two years later, servants still had free entry to the building, and their masters needed reminding that servants had to pay full price to get into the gallery.[13] From

11. Ottavio Tiby, *Il Real Teatro Carolino e l'Ottocento musicale palermitano* (Florence: Olschki, 1957), 21–22; Mario Nani Mocenigo, *La Fenice* (Venice: Industrie Poligrafiche Venete, 1926), 24–25; lists of box subscribers at the Teatro Apollo, Rome, C1848, Biblioteca dell'Istituto di Storia dell'Arte e Archeologia, Rome, Manifesti teatrali; list of box subscribers at the Teatro Valle, 1824, 1831–32, 1835, 1838, I-Rasc, Archivio Capranica, busta 469 (causa Paterni), and I-Rburcardo, Fondo Capranica, borderò, bilanci 8–12.

12. I-Las, Segreteria di Stato e di Gabinetto, fol. 87, no. 432, capitolato del Teatro Castiglioncelli (early nineteenth century); Giuseppe Radiciotti, *Teatro, musica e musicisti in Recanati* (Recanati: Simboli, 1904), 12–21 (1823 plan for a new theater, by Monaldo Leopardi).

13. Cambiasi, *La Scala;* Tiby, *Il Real Teatro Carolino,* 21–22; I-Bas, Dep. Pub. Sp., tit. I, rub. 2, 1852; Egidio Papi, *Il Teatro Municipale di Piacenza* (Piacenza: Bosi, 1912).

about 1800 the arrangements that gave noble households visible privileges all over the theater were in silent retreat, but it was a piecemeal retreat, and in some places it dragged on all the way to the unification of Italy.

This was true of other forms of hierarchical pricing. It had been common in the late eighteenth century to charge men more than women, and nobles and "foreigners" (from outside the state or the city) more than citizens. These distinctions had vanished, again piecemeal, from leading theaters by the early 1830s, though as late as 1839 a minor Florence theater owned by an academy of no doubt conservative-minded nobles—the Alfieri—still maintained a full set of price differentials. It even had a special price for bankers, who were deemed to stand halfway between nobles and citizens.[14]

Even when these particular differentials were done away with, there remained in many theaters the distinction between the military and civilians. This too was in part a price differential: by government decree, military officers (and, in Lombardy-Venetia, civil servants) enjoyed a discount. But the most visible distinction, found in Naples and Bologna as well as in Milan and other garrison towns, was the reservation for military officers of the first row or rows of stalls. This did not just show up the white tunics of Austrian officers in the tense years after the 1848 revolutions. Italian officers—of the papal army—could choose to stand instead of sit, and so prevent the rest of the audience from seeing the stage. This happened at the leading Bologna theater in the fashionable season, and all the impresario could do was to appeal to the military command by way of the government supervisory body, the Deputazione dei Pubblici Spettacoli.[15] After 1859–60 the new Italian state kept on the discount for military men and civil servants but dropped the reservation of the front rows.

Who else was in the stalls or in the next-to-last tier of boxes in those theaters provided with a gallery? The answer varied from time to time and from theater to theater. It is hazardous to speak of a bourgeois audience everywhere. True, at La Scala in 1821 habitual attenders at the back of the stalls and in the (presumably upper) boxes were described as "well-bred men and women" *(galantuomini e donne di garbo)* who did not dress elegantly, had no carriage, and might arrive dusty or muddy from the Milan streets.[16] These

---

14. La Scala stopped discriminating against "foreigners" in 1797, Modena in 1820, Parma in 1830, Cesena in 1831: see Cambiasi, *La Scala;* Alessandro Gandini, *Cronistoria dei teatri di Modena,* 3 vols. (Modena, 1873; reprint, Bologna: Arnaldo Forni, 1969); Werklein to Sanvitale, 19 December 1829, I-PAt, carteggi 1829; Alessandro Raggi and Luigi Raggi, *Il Teatro Comunale di Cesena* (Cesena: Vignuzzi, 1906), 26–27.; Antonio Gazzuoli to Alessandro Lanari, 1838–39, I-Fn, CV, 365/51, 58 (on the Alfieri in Florence).

15. Comando 3.a Divisione Militare to the Deputazione, 24 November 1852, I-Bas, Dep. Pub. Sp., tit. I, rub. 1, 1852.

16. Anonymous pamphlet quoted in Cambiasi, *La Scala,* 83–85.

well-bred people were probably lawyers and doctors of the less fashionable kind, civil servants, engineers, pharmacists, and the better-off tradesmen and shopkeepers. In university towns like Padua and Bologna, the stalls audience included many students; in tourist towns like Venice, Florence, Rome, and Naples, many non-Italians; almost anywhere, a number of out-of-town Italians passing through. On a night of pouring rain in Florence, "foreigners" were almost the only people to turn up at La Pergola.[17]

When in Rome the Apollo and the Argentina gave opera on the same night, the people who went to the second-best Argentina were mainly shopkeepers, many of them grocers or otherwise engaged in food trades.[18] In the provincial town of Cremona, the stallholders were so little "well-bred" that by treading with muddy boots all over the seats of the new theater (to get from row to row in a hurry), they made it necessary to reupholster the benches within two years of the theater's opening in 1809.[19] As one went down the hierarchy of theaters, seasons, genres, and seating areas, the audience in a preindustrial country tended to consist more and more of shopkeepers and artisans. That was what a visitor observed at a decidedly minor Naples theater, the San Carlino, that never put on anything "higher" than comic opera: many boxes were occupied by families "of the lower cittadini [citizen] class, even to the livery-boy and the baby."[20]

Still further down the hierarchy, the audience in the gallery at La Scala in 1820 was defined by a civil servant as the "lesser people" *(minuto popolo)*.[21] This too meant artisans, though not of a kind likely to keep livery boys, and other providers of petty services. A celebrated dialect poem about misadventures and near riot in the La Scala gallery in 1813 involved a fireman, a lamplighter, several soldiers, and a tailor employed as assistant to an old-clothes dealer.[22] What the La Scala gallery did not contain was a representation of the lower classes as a whole—of laborers, let alone peasants—when admission cost about as much as a construction worker could earn in a day.[23] Those humbler members of society could be found outside the theater rather than inside it: a member of the audience who slipped out early might have seen standing outside the stage door a knot of people without the price even of a

---

17. I-Fn, CV, 344/41.

18. Giovanni Pacini, *Le mie memorie artistiche* (Florence, 1875), 20.

19. Elia Santoro, *Il Teatro di Cremona*, 4 vols. (Cremona: Pizzorni, 1969–72), 2:114.

20. Lady Morgan, *Italy,* 2:411.

21. I. R. Ufficale Fiscale to Government of Lombardy-Venetia, 3 July 1820, I-Mt, Sp. P. 60/3.

22. Carlo Porta, "Olter desgrazzi de Giovannin Bongee," in *Poesie scelte di Carlo Porta,* ed. Piero Gallardo, 3d ed., 2 vols. (Turin: Unione Tipografico-Editrice Torinese, 1971), 1:48–67.

23. Admission to the La Scala gallery in carnival seasons from 1823 to 1831 varied from 0.65 francs to 0.87 francs; the daily wage of a construction worker in those years was 0.77 francs; see Cambiasi, *La Scala,* and Aldo De Maddalena, *Prezzi e mercedi a Milano dal 1701 al 1860* (Milan: Banca Commerciale Italiana, 1974), 420.

gallery ticket. They were listening to what they could catch of the sounds wafting from the stage and the orchestra pit, and some were singing the tunes.[24]

2. *The Economic Vicissitudes of the Opera Industry*

The hierarchical disposition of audiences, attendants, and custodians of opera theater was accompanied by an equally hierarchical array of methods of payment.

A theater, one might think, is a piece of capital equipment; its owners can do no better than to run it themselves at maximum profit without letting in middlemen. Yet that is not how any Italian theater was run or thought of; it is not even how many theaters are run today.

For the owners to run the opera season themselves was not unknown. But this *amministrazione economica* (from the old sense of *economy* as "household management") was generally acknowledged to be the reverse of economical. Governments or boxholder-proprietors might have to resort to it in difficult times when no impresario would contract for the season. This happened at La Scala in 1815–16 and again in 1821–24, and at La Fenice in 1823. On these occasions there was plenty of "splendor": La Fenice put on a lavish Rossini season that included the first performance of *Semiramide*. But the losses were alarming. Nor did they improve when a professional impresario was put in charge, not this time at his own risk but answerable to a committee of the owners. The upper classes were expected to be lavish. The point was made by a leading agent to a bass who wanted an impresario to pay him a fee as high as another bass had been paid by the board of directors *(presidenza)* of La Fenice in a season under direct management. The bass was told, "The case is very different when an artist is engaged by a *presidenza* rather than by an impresario," and that he must now be content with less.[25] This kind of reasoning had led some eighteenth-century governments to farm out tax collection. Such governments lacked the necessary administrative apparatus to do the job themselves without running into wasteful loss. In the opera house too the impresario's first task was to stand between the ruling groups and the extravagance expected of them. At the same time he was supposed to be accessible and answerable to his superiors.

The same habits of mind that farmed out tax revenues occasionally granted an impresario a so-called monopoly of theaters—that is, of theatrical management in a particular city. As with other monopolies this could amount

24. Ferrari, *Spettacoli drammatico-musicali*, 208; Hippolyte Taine, *Voyage en Italie*, 5th ed., 2 vols. (Paris, 1884), 1:100.
25. Giovanni Battista Bonola to Lanari, 10 October 1844, I-Fn, CV, 349/72.

in practice to a mere power of licensing competitors and getting a rake-off. In this form the impresarios of La Scala enjoyed such a monopoly between 1790 and 1814 together with a guarantee that no new theaters would be permitted to open, but the guarantee was breached in 1814 and the system appears not to have gone on.[26] A more literal monopoly of theater management survived in backward Rome down to the early 1830s.

Opera management, then, was a concession, potentially a monopoly. But what was temporarily handed over to the impresario was not the opera house as a whole. It was not thought of as a single economic entity that he could exploit to greatest advantage. Just as the boxes were physically and socially distinct from the rest, so they—or some of them—might not figure in the theater takings at all.

Italian opera house takings were made up in a fairly complex manner. Anyone entering the theater—except, sometimes, those who owned or rented boxes—paid admission to enter the building *(ingresso)*, and you could buy a season's subscription for this purpose. Since the opera house was the center of social life, you might pay the *ingresso* merely to visit friends or gamble in the foyer. In some eighteenth-century theaters (and occasionally in those of the nineteenth century) one therefore paid separately to enter the orchestra or stalls area and again separately for one of a small number of fixed seats that an attendant unlocked. In other theaters—at La Scala the arrangement dated from the return of the French in 1800[27]—the *ingresso* let you into the stalls area as well, which, in most theaters, had a good deal of standing room at the back (the Teatro San Carlo, which had its stalls area filled with seats, was an exception) as well as unnumbered bench seats and the usual locked seats to be paid for separately. In some theaters (the Comunale in Bologna around 1850, for one) you might pay extra for any kind of seat, in which case the number of benches provided varied with the impresario's judgment of what the traffic would bear.[28] The general movement during the nineteenth century was toward filling the stalls with fixed and numbered seats, called *poltrone* and *poltroncine*. The gallery, if there was one, had a separate entrance. It was often sublet for a fixed sum. Carlo Porta's poem in Milanese dialect describes the two subcontractor impresarios of the La Scala gallery making their way through the waiting crowd with a lantern and a key to let loose a free-for-all scramble up the stairs.

What happened about the boxes varied according to the ownership pat-

26. Maldonati contract, 1789, I-Mt, Sp. P. 28; Ricci contract, 1811, and correspondence, 1814, I-Mt, Sp. P. 20.

27. Correspondence of Ricci and Lonati with the Commissione Governativa, 1801, I-Mt, Sp. P. 29.

28. Promemoria serale, Teatro Comunale, Bologna, A1852, Conservatore Delegato to the Deputazione, A1854, I-Bas, Comune, Dep. Pub. Sp., tit. I, rub. 1, 1853, 1854.

tern and the management contract. Boxholder-proprietors were not ordinary customers. In many theaters they could sublet their boxes at a profit, thus in effect competing with the impresario for custom; this was something that impresarios at La Scala tried in vain to stop.[29] On the other hand they could contribute a levy *(canone* or *tratta)* either by voting one as a corporate body or else by agreeing individually to use their boxes on payment of the levy set by the impresario. A boxholder who disliked the terms could give up his box for the season.[30] The levy might be in lieu of a seasonal subscription or might supplement it; there were intermediate arrangements under which the levy was fixed for a term of years as the normal subscription. In theaters where there was no property in boxes, those renting them merely paid a subscription. In all theaters any boxes not subscribed for could be turned over to the impresario to be let nightly.

Before Italian unification all prices were controlled both by the theater owners and by the government superintending body, which had to agree to changes. When boxholders paid a levy this was usually shown in the accounts not as part of the takings but as part of the "endowment" *(dote;* in practice, a subsidy). Where this happened the boxholders were by implication acting not as undifferentiated consumers but as a privileged group who—perhaps with government help—provided a service, with the impresario as their intermediary. They appeared partly as consumers, since they got the benefit of the opera season in return for their money, but also as producer-patrons; their contribution to the endowment can be thought of as a management charge.

As the matter was understood in Italy at the turn of the eighteenth and nineteenth centuries, all theater seasons run by impresarios had an endowment. This could consist of a cash sum, of privileges (generally for running some form of gambling or lottery), or of rights in boxes. The cash sum could consist of the boxholders' levy, a subsidy allowed by the government or the municipality, or both together, the whole supplemented by the rent of the refreshment rooms and other ancillary services of the theater. The gambling privilege could be highly profitable in Napoleonic times, when it meant the monopoly of games of chance; after 1814 (in Naples after 1820) it meant at best a few evenings of tombola, a tame lottery with prizes in kind.[31] Endowment in boxes for nightly letting remained common, but where we can follow the relations between owners and impresarios over several decades, we notice

29. Macchi and Maldonati progetti d'appalto, 1788, 1789, I-Mt, Sp. P. 28; Government of Lombardy-Venetia to Marchese Cagnola, 1 February 1820, I-Mt, Sp. P. 60/3.

30. These were the contrasting arrangements in Venice at La Fenice (owned by the boxholders) at all times and at the San Luca (owned by the Vendramin family, with boxes owned by others) for an opera seria season in P1816: Venice, Museo Civico Correr, MSS PD, buste C 1419.

31. Valle, *Cenni teorico-pratici,* 5–6, 189; I-Fas, Prefettura di Firenze, 1869, fol. 164; 1870, fol. 145. Lotteries with cash prizes were allowed under a law of 1836.

a change, with some backslidings, from endowment chiefly in boxes in the later eighteenth century to endowment chiefly in cash in the nineteenth.[32]

Regular government or municipal subsidy in cash seems, in eighteenth-century Italy, to have been uncommon away from the Turin and Naples royal theaters. Elsewhere a municipality like that of Senigallia on the east coast would contribute a small sum to encourage an opera seria season during the important summer trade fair, or a duke of Modena would give a "present" to make up part of the loss on a opera season in a privately owned theater.[33] These were stopgap measures. The official gambling monopoly, until its temporary suppression in the later eighteenth century, probably yielded at most times and in most places a good deal less than it would when revived in the hectic wartime conditions of Napoleonic Italy.

None of these endowments, subsidies, or privileges could guarantee an impresario against loss. We might expect that with only marginal help from the government, impresarios in most seasons would balance the costs of production against the theater takings and the endowment from the boxholders, and perhaps manage a small profit besides. If we find impresarios going bankrupt in the early nineteenth century, we might be led to think that some change must have intervened to upset the old balance. This is exactly what some nineteenth-century impresarios did assert, and with them some of the officials concerned with the theater. A full list of their complaints was drawn up in 1823: singers were demanding more money; good ones were becoming scarce; the public wanted ever more complex productions, with more singers and dancers, more extras, more musicians, more lavish sets and costumes. On the other hand resources were finite or shrinking: men with capital were not coming forward and management was falling into unsuitable hands.[34] In twentieth-century language this meant that production costs were outstripping consumers' purchasing power, and the industrial product, opera, was pricing itself out of the market.

The trouble with this diagnosis is that most elements in it can be found asserted at intervals all the way from the 1680s to the 1880s.[35] Just one new

32. Contracts for *impresa* of the Teatro del Cocomero, Florence, 1764–1806, I-Fcomune, fol. 8374; Ugo Morini, *La R. Accademia degli Immobili e il suo Teatro "La Pergola" (1649–1925)* (Pisa: Simoncini, 1926), 29–31, 60–61, 103–6.

33. Giuseppe Radiciotti, *Teatro, musica e musicisti in Sinigaglia* (Milan, 1893), 21ff.; Gandini, *Cronistoria dei teatri di Modena,* 1:82–83.

34. Valle, *Cenni teorico-pratici,* iii–vi, 180–91.

35. Cristoforo Ivanovich, *Minerva al tavolino* (Venice, 1681), 407–8, also in part in Lorenzo Bianconi, *Il Seicento,* Storia della musica, vol. 4 (Turin: Edizioni di Torino/Musica, 1982), 304, in English translation as "The Impresarial Organization of Venetian Theaters: Cristoforo Ivanovich," in Bianconi, *Music in the Seventeenth Century,* trans. David Bryant (Cambridge: Cambridge University Press, 1987), 302–11. See also official statements of 1755 in Mario Rinaldi, *Due secoli di musica al Teatro Argentina,* 3 vols. (Florence: Olschki, 1978), 1:91, and of 1827, I-Ras, Cam-

element entered the catalog in the early post–Napoleonic period: impresarios started blaming the increased fees demanded by singers on offers from abroad higher than Italian theaters could safely meet.[36] There was some truth in all this, but an analysis of imbalance in the economics of opera made at intervals over two centuries cannot be taken at face value.

An investigation of the costs of opera production throughout the period 1700–1880 leads, if not to definitive conclusions, at least to some suggestive and fairly convincing data.[37] We know that absolute costs went up throughout the period from the early eighteenth century to the 1860s, especially during the inflation of the Napoleonic period (at its height in 1810–12) and again, for reasons we shall see, from around 1825–30 and after. But given the slow inflation that went on (with an occasional respite) throughout the period, it is more important first to observe fluctuations in the relative cost of the various elements of an opera season and then the changes in absolute costs of an unusual magnitude.

Throughout this period there are surprisingly few wide fluctuations in the relative cost of performers, and remuneration for soloists (singers and dancers) usually accounted for between 45 and 55 percent of these costs and was the greatest single expense. In spite of complaints renewed over two centuries, soloists' fees rose in the long term no faster than other costs, though there may have been short periods when they fell behind or raced ahead. Other relative costs as well showed little significant change, although composers' fees went up, thanks to the Austro-Sardinian copyright treaty of 1840 and to changes in the ways in which composers were remunerated: up to that time the composer was paid a fee for writing a new opera; afterwards, he could count on royalties from all performances and from the sale of printed piano-vocal scores. In any event the cost of the music was less than 10 percent of total costs. Orchestral costs are more difficult to establish. Even if, as seems possible, the relative cost of the orchestra changed little between the early eighteenth century and the 1870s, its size increased steadily, with a first in-

erale III, Teatri, busta 2131, Teatro Capranica/24; Gazzuoli to Lanari, 23 February 1837, I-Fas, CV 364/118; Francesco Regli, *Dizionario biografico dei più celebri poeti ed artisti melodrammatici . . . che fiorirono in Italia dal 1800 al 1860* (Turin, 1860), xii–xiv; *Il Liuto*, 7 November 1874, quoted in Rinaldi, *Due secoli di musica*, 2:1069; D'Arcais, "L'industria musicale."

36. Andrea Bandini to Sanvitale, 23 September 1819, I-PAt, carteggi 1819. See also Alberto Cametti, *Il Teatro di Tordinona poi di Apollo*, 2 vols. (Tivoli: Chicca, 1938), 1:255; Alessandro Lanari, *Memoria . . . ai signori componenti la Nobile Accademia del . . . Teatro degli Immobili*, 2 vols. (Florence: Giunta Regionale Tostana/La Nuova Italia, 1982), 2:265ff.

37. For a detailed analysis of what follows, see John Rosselli, *The Opera Industry in Italy from Cimarosa to Verdi: The Role of the Impresario* (Cambridge: Cambridge University Press, 1984), 51–78, 178–81, in Italian translation in an amplified version, as *L'impresario d'opera: Arte e affari nel teatro musicale italiano dell'Ottocento* (Turin: Edizioni di Torino/Musica, 1985), 49–77, 177–80.

crease toward the early nineteenth century and a second toward midcentury, under the influence of the spectacular sort of grand opera typified by the works of Meyerbeer. If orchestral numbers were rising but their relative cost was not, some players' real wages must have been falling, as perhaps was quality. There are indications of a loss of quality in the Teatro Regio in Turin after the restoration, and Roman theater orchestras, which were neither permanent nor subsidized, had a poor reputation.

Of all expenses production costs are unfortunately the most elusive. There were some technological changes, especially in lighting: in the eighteenth century the stage and the auditorium were lit by wax candles, but in the first half of the nineteenth century, until gas came in, all parts of the theater—dressing rooms, stage, auditorium, foyers, the lot—had to be lit by now unimaginable quantities of pure olive oil. Such changes may have meant a saving in relative costs. At the same time, however, the budgets of the leading opera theaters had suffered a bitter blow with a rise in the absolute cost of singers' fees that occurred around 1825–30.

The change in commercial relations between singers and their employers was extremely gradual, like everything else in opera. Although the leading singers of the early eighteenth century may still have had the patronage of a sovereign, a noble, or a group of nobles (which is also attested by the custom of paying them in jewels, gold snuffboxes, or even in chocolate and other foodstuffs), soloists in a first-rank theater such as the Regio of Turin were paid in cash, and at the highest their fees were about equal to the annual salary of the Piedmontese prime minister. Around 1830, however, their fees represented the working of a market. Alessandro Lanari wrote that when it came to judging a singer's quality, "the price must be the thermometer [of quality]," and somewhat later the *prima donna* Marianna Barbieri-Nini wrote to an agent, "The first who offers me more is the one I shall accept."[38] The fee paid by one impresario to another to secure a singer's release was—like a transfer fee in soccer today—directly proportionate to the singer's recent performance. Artists' fees undeniably doubled and even tripled in comparison to the fees paid in the eighteenth century, a phenomenon that was not limited to the extraordinary fees paid to the two singers reckoned each to be unique, Giuditta Pasta and Maria Malibran, but that can be verified for other front-rank singers such as Amalia Schütz, Carolina Ungher, Giuseppina Ronzi, Domenico Donzelli, and Henriette Méric-Lalande. The standard of payment reached in these years seems in general to have been kept up, with a temporary lowering of fees following the scarcity and depression of 1848

---

38. Lanari to Ercole Marzi, 15 April 1849, I-Fas, CV 393/58; Marianna Barbieri-Nini to Luigi Ronzi, 11 January 1853, I-Ms, Coll. Casati 45.

(from which some, perhaps most, theaters did not fully recover until the mid-1850s), at least until the longer crisis of the 1870s.

Although contemporaries were probably right in attributing the rise in singers' fees to competition from abroad, its real cause was not so much competition (Madrid and London, for example, had already consistently been paying more for singers than any Italian theater) as it was the spread of the "many Italian theaters that are opening in Europe."[39] It was Italian opera's success not only in Europe but throughout the world (at first largely due to the popularity of Rossini)—in commercial cities such as Manchester and Odessa, in Greek and Turkish cities like Patras and Constantinople, and in cities of the Americas like Havana, Caracas, and New York—that commercialized Italian opera and imposed international cost levels on the best Italian theaters.

How was the rise in fees paid for? Not, for the most part, by raising prices of admission. All the evidence points either to formidable resistance to price increases or to government reluctance to authorize them, or both. In Italy in the first half of the century, even leading theaters—other than La Scala, the San Carlo, and La Fenice—could not manage much more than an average of 1,000 francs a night and often fell below that. Not even the three most prominent theaters could count on takings equal to those of the Paris Opéra, where, what is more, the basic price of admission after 1830 was higher than theirs by one-third. In Italy the nightly admission price was more resistant to increase than all other prices, and it remained unchanged in a number of theaters from the restoration to Italian unification. Even then the price for a single evening admission increased much more slowly than did subscription prices. Moreover, even a modest increase in admission price could set off a disturbance, as at the Teatro Valle, Rome, where the first increase (from about 1.08 francs to 1.60 francs) "raised a shout throughout the town" and could only be made to stick for a few scattered seasons. The same happened in Modena after Italian unification, when an increase in the admission price from 1 franc to 1.20 francs set off whistling in the theater.[40] The policy of fixed prices for entrance to the theater seems to have favored people, especially young men, with little money but with professional aspirations—students, military officers, minor civil servants, struggling doctors, lawyers, and pharmacists; the stuff of political agitation in the Risorgimento period and also of theatrical faction fights and disturbances. Such was the fear of offending this section of the public that when Giuditta Pasta was engaged for

39. Said by the Roman impresario Vincenzo Jacovacci, quoted in Cametti, *Il Teatro di Tordinona,* 1:155.

40. Rinaldi, *Due secoli,* 1:487; Gandini, *Cronistoria dei teatri di Modena.*

the 1833 carnival season at La Fenice for an unprecedented fee of 1,000 francs a performance, a proposal to raise the *ingresso* price barely got through the association of boxholder-proprietors; Pasta herself then took fright and insisted that there must be no increase lest she should be blamed.[41] Even after unification the relatively slow rise in the nightly *ingresso* price suggests that the stalls audience were still seen as allowing little flexibility, whether from poverty or from their potential for making trouble.

Since prices could not be raised, or not enough, subsidies were needed. Opera had probably been subsidized at most times since its birth in the early seventeenth century, though in ways not always obvious. One arrangement, in force at Trieste and Turin, was for other theaters to pay 10 percent or 20 percent of their takings to the leading opera house. This was highly unpopular and was abolished in those cities in 1841 and 1852.[42] The main form of subsidy, in force through much of the eighteenth century and again during the Napoleonic years, was the gambling monopoly granted to the impresario of the opera house. When this was abolished at La Scala in 1788, the only way that the authorities could persuade an impresario to risk involving himself in opera management was to allow him to economize: new operas need no longer have been expressly composed for Milan, in short carnival seasons only one new opera need be put on instead of two, artists need not be star attractions *(di cartello)*, costumes need not be quite new. In contemporary eyes all these changes seriously detracted from the "splendor" of La Scala seasons.[43]

When the gambling monopoly was again abolished in 1814 all over northern Italy (and in 1820 in Naples and Palermo), matters were no longer so simple. Audiences had had a decade and a half to get used to the unexampled "splendor" typified in Milan by the grandiose mythological ballets of Salvatore Viganò and in Naples by such opere serie of Rossini as *La donna del lago* and *Mosè in Egitto*. The authorities in Milan deemed it unthinkable to cut down on standards that dressed all the chorus and extras playing medieval Scots in Simon Mayr's *Ginevra di Scozia* (La Scala, carnival 1816) in satin. A few years later the official committee that was trying (in vain) to attract impresarios to La Scala gave its opinion that "in a city where there are many other theaters and which is used to continual new and grand productions, to cut down even though minimally on their splendor would be the same as to destroy them and to drive away the public."[44]

41. I-Vt, Processi verbali convocazioni, busta 5, Spettacoli, busta 3.

42. Bottura, *Storia . . . del Teatro Comunale di Trieste*, 251, 254; Basso, *Il teatro della città*, vol. 2 of *Storia del Teatro Regio di Torino*, ed. Alberto Basso (Turin: Cassa di Risparmio di Torino, 1976–83), 266–77.

43. Contract with Gaetano Maldonati, 31 July 1789, and preceding correspondence, I-Mt, Sp. P. 28.

44. Commissione Governativa per i Teatri, verbale seduta 20 February 1821, I-Mt, Sp. P. 60.

The conclusion was obvious: "Unfortunately, experience has shown," Carlo Ritorni wrote in 1825, that performances of opera seria "cannot be supported without [cash] endowments."[45] Some years passed, however, before the governments reconciled themselves to conceding them. Detailed study of the affairs of La Scala, the San Carlo, and La Fenice in 1815–26 shows a recurrent struggle between impresarios and theater controllers over the terms of proposed contracts. At La Scala and La Fenice the upshot was, in several of those years, expensive direct management, or else impresarios once again agreed to take on a season or seasons with no more precise obligation than that their productions would "suit the decorum of a leading theater." Eventually governments brought themselves (or compelled municipalities) to pay subsidies at a rate that would attract impresarios. The result was a general rise in subsidies between the 1820s and 1840, sustained in some theaters up to 1848; then, after the 1848–53 slump, a standstill or a further rise until unification. The two major exceptions are Naples, where the financial outlay of the Rossini period could not be kept up, and Turin, where an early result of the granting of a parliamentary constitution in 1848 (the *Statuto*) was the cutting off of the government subsidy.

Were the subsidies granted in the best years (from about 1830 to 1860) sufficient? Even if we leave out variations from one city to another, the question is not a simple one. It seems that when the subsidy was roughly equal to the season's revenues, the management might hope to break even or even show a profit. This did not often happen, even in the best-subsidized theaters (La Scala, the San Carlo, and La Fenice), where subsidies never went over one-third or one-half those of the Paris opera houses of the time. Not that there could be any question in Italy of subsidy anywhere near the Paris scale. France's relatively developed economy made possible Paris subsidies and Paris prices. Italy remained a poor country. As it was, opera subsidies were paid for largely by municipal taxes on food.

This explains the outcry against subsidy after unification. The old eighteenth-century opera seria had been disliked by the republicans of the Jacobin period (1796–99) as a genre bound up with absolutist courts and sung by extravagantly rewarded castratos; *melodramma* was denounced in the same terms (even though the castratos had disappeared from the stage) by some Milanese democrats of 1848 who wanted to keep La Scala closed, arguing that "the people who then slumbered to the sound of lascivious harmonies have now awakened to the thunder of cannon."[46] Even within the government (the austere and reform-minded government of Joseph II) a high-

---

45. [Ritorni], *Consigli*, 14–15. For fuller discussion of the topic, see Rosselli, *The Opera Industry*, 71–76 (*L'impresario d'opera*, 68–73).

46. Poster dated 10 April 1848, quoted in Rosmini, *La legislazione*, 2:38 n.

placed official had pointed out as far back as 1788 the injustice of making the public at large subsidize the enjoyment of a few privileged persons.[47] The moment there were elected persons in national and local government—even though elected on a narrow franchise—opera subsidies came into question.

At the first major financial crisis of the new Kingdom of Italy in 1867, the Chamber of Deputies insisted on abolishing all central government subsidies inherited from the old Italian states. It then went one better and imposed a tax of 10 percent on all theater takings.[48] Opera subsidies were at first mostly taken over by municipalities, but the new middle class that was moving into power kept gunning for them, and from the 1880s, so did the new socialists. The result was a brief spurt here and there after 1860 but then a general decline, rapid in the former capitals (Venice, Naples, Florence, Parma, Modena), longer delayed in prosperous Milan and Turin and in some smaller provincial towns. Whether or not subsidies had fully bridged the "income gap" in the old despotic states, they were certainly now failing to do so. At the same time two other changes came together to damage the opera industry. One was the economic crisis that started in 1873 and that created recurrent depressions to the end of the century. The other big change—also helped along by the coming of new and rapid means of transportation—was a decisive rise in the fees some singers could command abroad, not only in European cities but in such cities as Cairo, Rio de Janeiro, and San Francisco.

By the 1870s the Italian opera industry was going through a phase of simultaneous expansion and disintegration. Within Italy it was expanding through the appearance—from the 1840s and especially the 1850s—of large new "popular" theaters as well as of new seasons in parts of the south previously unregarded and in small towns everywhere. Yet this very expansion was breaking down the old system of regular seasons. In former capitals now deprived of their courts, it took a special financial effort to attempt a short season with singers of the front rank: the San Carlo was closed for three seasons in the 1870s, La Fenice for eleven seasons between 1873 and 1897, and after 1877, La Pergola in Florence put on opera only fitfully.

In the rest of the world the export of Italian opera had been a fast-growing business since the 1840s, but as with other exports volume had been achieved partly by expanding production at the cheaper end and by multiplying outlets. Thus Adelina Patti might earn over 20,000 francs per performance in a United States tour in 1882–23, but the second or third-rank Italian principals who went out to Athens, Malta, and the Azores in the 1870s got 600, 800, or 900 francs a month—more or less what they might have gotten in Italy.

47. Count Künigl to the Nobile Associazione del Teatro alla Scala, 26 March 1788, I-Mas, Sp. P. 28.
48. Rosmini, *La legislazione*, 1:162–72.

Within Italy itself an even wider range of fees prevailed. Patti could get 10,000 francs for each of two Turin appearances in 1879 (ten times Giuditta Pasta's honorarium), and the internationally famous tenor Roberto Stagno got 5,000 francs an evening for some performances (also in Turin) six years later. A principal tenor at Assisi in 1889, on the other hand, was being offered 6 francs a night—and that was in the carnival season, when most singers were employed. In other seasons struggling artists in minor theaters might have to perform when driven to the edge of starvation.[49]

A few artists with offers from two or three continents could command unprecedented fees—three, four, or five times, performance for performance, those of the 1830s—but good singers without an international reputation did little better than before, and possibly worse. It may well be that the rise in singers' fees had less to do with bringing opera into crisis than had depression (which hit some of the boxholders), the end of the court hierarchies in former capital cities, and the cutting down or withdrawal of subsidy. In such conditions, Verdi wrote,

> The unfortunate impresarios can no longer meet the requirements of artist and public. Instead of worthily serving art they are often compelled, after having struggled in vain against a thousand odds, to flee, to go bankrupt, and, what is worse, to degrade that art with productions that certainly do no good either to its splendor or to public morals![50]

Verdi's answer was to call for renewed government subsidy—something that would come about only in the twentieth century when control of opera houses had passed to public bodies. The coming of a centralized state with liberal representative institutions and a growing middle class meant that the lyric theater, like other realms but a generation later, required new systems that no longer depended on local hierarchies.

3. The Strong Arm of Authority

The Italian states before unification were all despotisms. The one exception was Piedmont after 1848. There were in practice gradations and differences,

49. Harold Rosenthal,. ed., *The Mapleson Memoirs* (London: Putnam, 1966), 172–73; I-Ms, Coll. Casati 1082 (contracts of the agent Ippolito Canedi with Antonio Padovani and Italo Giovannetti, 1872–73, 1875); Giuseppe Depanis, *I Concerti Popolari e il Teatro Regio di Torino: Quindici anni di vita musicale; appunti-ricordi* (Turin: Società Tipografico-Editrice Nazionale, 1914–15), 2:40–41; Alberto Scalaberni to Giovanni Marchetti, November 1889, Piancastelli Autografi, s. v. "Marchetti"; Charles Santley, *Student and Singer* (London, 1892), 89–90.

50. To the Minister Guido Baccelli, 4 February 1883, in Giuseppe Verdi, *I copialettere di Giuseppe Verdi*, ed. Gaetano Cesari and Alessandro Luzio (Milan: Stucchi Ceretti, 1913; reprint,

but in principle the opera house was an object of high policy in all of them. In order to make sure than an opera season went well, governments were ready to apply what contracts sometimes called the "strong arm" of the authority and bring it to bear, for instance, on a *prima donna* who failed to turn up, on an undisciplined corps de ballet, or on orchestral players who demanded higher wages or urinated in the backstage corridors.[51] Several considerations entered into both the importance granted opera and the authoritarian measures for its regulation.

One of the most important of these was the opera theater's function as a place in which to demonstrate both the hierarchy of the local society and the relations between subjects and governments. There were also police considerations (in the larger sense) that had little to do with the ruler's personal tastes. King Charles of Naples was bored by music; he nonetheless built and attended the San Carlo to keep his nobles under his eye.[52] By the restoration period the chief minister of Lombardy-Venetia was anxious that La Scala should be kept open in the usual seasons because it "attracts to a place open to observation during the hours of darkness a large part of the educated population."[53] It was possible to see even wider advantages: mindful of the perils of liberalism and revolution, the government supervisory body in Rome advised the pope that the theater was the best means of keeping the people quiet and contented with the rulers set over them, hence "the most salutary antidote to those plagues that have been growing almost throughout the world."[54]

The interference of the authorities touched all aspects of opera theater. Censorship of the libretto was one means of control but, at least until 1848, it was perhaps not even the most important one. Intervention worked at various levels of a complex hierarchical structure. At the top was the ruler, who, unlike King Charles, might take an intense interest in opera. Besides screening the boxholders, King Carlo Felice of Sardinia chose subjects, approved librettos, and even demanded fewer arias and more concerted pieces. He made

Bologna: Arnaldo Forni, 1968), 321–22, translated here from the version in Giuseppe Verdi, *Autobiografia dalle lettere,* ed. Marcello Conati (Milan: Rizzoli, 1981), 430–31.

51. Contract for the RR. Teatri di Napoli with the impresario and composer Gaetano Andreozzi, 11 March 1806, Duke of Noja to the Minister of the Interior, 30 April 1821, in I-Nas, Teatri, fol. 98; Min. Interno II inv., fol. 4355; Giuseppe Janni, *Gioacchino Belli* (Milan: Mondadori, 1962), 657; Cambiasi, *La Scala,* 59–63; Maldonati petition, 22 December 1789, I-Mt, Sp. P. 28.

52. Robinson, *Naples and Neapolitan Opera,* 7–8.

53. Count Strassoldo, President of the Government of Lombardy-Venetia, to the Viceroy Archduke Ranieri, 1 August 1825, I-Mt, Sp. P. 56. For analogous sentiments, see [Ritorni], *Consigli,* 11.

54. Deputazione degli Spettacoli to Pope Gregory XVI, 1834, quoted in Cametti, *Il Teatro di Tordinona,* 1:244–45.

himself so at home in the theater that he could be seen nibbling bread sticks.[55] The ruler's ministers were also likely to be involved in many decisions, especially the ministers of the interior, of police, and of finance. Below them there was usually in each city a government body known as the Deputazione (or Soprintendenza, or Direzione) degli Spettacoli (or dei Teatri). This was in one sense a government body in that it was appointed by the ruler; in another sense it was an emanation of the local nobility who generally made it up (with the usual exceptions of Trieste and Livorno). In some cities the supervisory board would have one member assigned to each theater, with a paid inspector of much lowlier status under him to do the day-to-day work. There might also be a small executive committee or board of directors with a civil servant as secretary. On the next tier down, a theater owned or part owned by box-holders was likely to have an association of proprietors. In Tuscany and Umbria this was usually called an academy, even though it had been formed for the specific purpose of running a theater. The association as a rule had an elected or appointed executive committee, generally also called *deputazione, direzione,* or *presidenza,* and might have a professional secretary and other employees.

There were variations in this three-tier model of ruler, supervisory body, and owners' association. In a monarchical opera house like the Ducale, Parma, the ruler's great chamberlain at first supervised everything, with a noble inspector and plebeian subinspector under him but without a board. By the 1830s, however, he was flanked by a mixed body of government and boxholders' representatives. In Rome until 1801 the cardinal-governor of the city had been in charge of supervising theaters; even after a lay supervisory body was set up, he often took a close interest in opera. So did Cardinal Ercole Consalvi, the secretary of state in 1814–23 (a passionate admirer of Cimarosa's music), and, at various dates, some of the cardinal-legates in other parts of the Papal States. In Tuscany there was no official supervisory board; the academies were allowed to supervise their own theaters under the general guidance of the minister of police.[56]

The seeming clarity of a three-tier model was further complicated by the intervention of parallel hierarchies. The minister of police and the officer commanding the garrison were involved through the presence in the theater of their subordinates: at La Scala in 1802 responsibility for order was divided among the official supervisory board (in charge of the stage and backstage

55. Giulio Vaccai, *Vita di Nicola Vaccaj* (Bologna, 1882), 80–81.

56. Ferrari, *Spettacoli drammatico-musicali,* 175; ordinance of General Menou, 8 September 1808, Mayor of Florence to Accademia degli Infuocati, 16 September 1808, I-Fas, fol. 8278, no. 84; Morini, *La R. Accademia degli Immobili,* 110–11; Ercole Consalvi, *Memorie,* ed. Mario Nasalli Rocca di Corneliano (Rome: Signorelli, 1950), 149–51.

areas and of the licensing of cabs outside), the civil police (in charge of the auditorium and foyers and of traffic outside), and the military guard (in charge of the approaches)—a fairly standard arrangement.[57] The municipality was also involved if it paid a subsidy or maintained the orchestra.

The government might choose to be involved even when it owned no part of the theater. La Fenice was wholly owned by a boxholders' association, but the mayor of Venice and a representative of the government attended the association's meetings ex officio. The government representative virtually imposed on the association the expensive Rossini season of 1823 (at a bad time when nobody wished to serve on the board of directors); at different moments of his term as mayor *(podestà),* Count Giacomo Correr deleted from the season contract Carlo Coccia's name as a possible composer, tried to insist on a particular singer (the expensive Giuditta Pasta, by then in decline), and established the right to pass on all productions, down to costume designs. On the other hand the owners' association resisted all government efforts to make it open the theater in the last period of Austrian rule in 1860–66; it did so on economic grounds that were afterward explained as—and no doubt were in part—patriotic.[58]

The same largely aristocratic group staffed nearly all these institutions. This could mean an extraordinary concentration of functions in one man. Marquis Bartolomeo Capranica was in 1826 virtual impresario of the Teatro Valle in Rome, owner of the theater, secretary-general of the supervisory board, and secretary-general of the ministry of police. To keep a company of actors in order, he could threaten to appeal to himself.[59] On the other hand it was common for institutions to differ. In the early 1850s, after the taste of autonomy that Pius IX's early reforms had given municipalities, the Bologna local government and supervisory body carried on a continual tug-of-war over the terms of management contracts and the choice of singers. The municipality seems to have won, since it came to approve theater prices and programs and even to authorize the lighting of stoves in a cold snap.[60]

Each of the two or three authorities that had an interest in the opera house might claim a right at least to be informed of what was going on during the season and possibly to dictate what was to go on. The bureaucracy was at its worst in monarchical theaters. At Naples in the 1820s requests usually went from impresario Barbaja to the supervisory board, then to the minister of the interior, then to the council of ministers, and finally to the king, on such

57. Cambiasi, *La Scala,* 63–64.

58. I-Vt, Sandro Dalla Libera, "La Presidenza del Teatro La Fenice" (typescript), Processi verbali convocazioni, busta 5; Sussidio comunale, buste 1–3.

59. Marchese Bartolomeo Capranica to Aniceto Pistoni, 19 September 1826, other correspondence from 1826, I-Rburcardo, Fondo Capranica.

60. I-Bas, Comune, Dep. Pub. Sp., tit. I, rub. 1, 1850–54.

questions as whether a dancer should be given his passport, whether to go on trying out a weak tenor, whether new seats should be made of wood or iron, whether artists should be fined or allowed to hold a benefit. When the king was in Vienna the government insisted on getting his consent to the slightest change in a gala program that he had previously approved: it took fifteen days each way.[61] Even in a theater away from capital cities, a high-ranking official with a strong interest in opera would have his say: in an attempt to get the contract for the 1834 season at the Senigallia fair, Alessandro Lanari had to correspond not only with the chief city official, the *gonfalo-niere*, whose municipality was subsidizing the season, but with the cardinal-legate of Pesaro, who questioned his proposed choice of singers and objected to their singing less often than had been usual. Lanari appealed to Rome and tried to bring in another cardinal as reinforcement.[62]

Except in theaters directly dependent on the monarch, rulers and high-ranking officials were by and large concerned less with day-to-day operations than with the terms of the impresario's contract; these they looked into and discussed in extraordinary detail, especially the provision made for a suitable level of "splendor." The Austrian authorities of Lombardy-Venetia tried again and again, with ponderous legalism, to achieve the terms they wanted by putting the concession up to auction, generally in vain: impresarios either did not bid or set up collusive "rings." But auctions were required by the imperial government in Vienna, to which everything of importance had to be referred.

A manual of 1823 set out the supervisory board's functions. It was to reinforce discipline at rehearsals; settle from the start any questions of relative status among soloists (a frequent source of trouble); see that soloists were punctual; regulate access to the stage and behavior on it; enforce fire precautions; ensure the cleanliness, decency, and historical accuracy of the costumes; require certificates for any absence on medical grounds; fight off sloppiness in performances; look out for immoral conduct; approve all posters and printed announcements; and call on the government's armed forces to arrest any theater personnel who were insubordinate during the performance.[63] These were typical activities for the more diligent executives of the boxholder-proprietors' associations as well. The documents show that the system did make for duplication. Quite often the supervisory authority, owners, and impresario seem to have all been dealing with the same matter and writing to one another about it. The system also encouraged buck-passing. At one point in 1857, the Milan supervisory board, the two impresarios of La Scala, and the chief *répétiteur* of the orchestra were all trying to get one of the other

61. I-Nas, Min. Interno inv., fol. 4355, passim.
62. Correspondence between Lanari, Count Amici-Pasquini, and Cardinal Albani, February 1834, I-Fn, CV 343/10.
63. Valle, *Cenni teorico-pratici,* 11–24.

parties to decide which orchestral players should be got rid of for "incapacity and negligence."[64]

This suggests a continuing ambiguity in the relations between the supervisory authority and the theater owners on the one hand and the impresarios on the other. By granting an endowment (and dangling before the impresario's eyes the possibility of further financing in case of unexpected losses) the supervisory bodies acquired the right to intervene in management. These bodies often saw themselves as upholding standards against the slackness of impresarios and fending off perilous discontent among operagoers. Unless the supervisory authority in Parma laid down requirements for costumes, one official noted, "absurdities will never be got rid of that are now remarked all too often and with all too much scandal, such as seeing a [Native] American dressed like a Turk, or a Parisian like a Roman." The members of the Bologna supervisory board thought that if they did not order an impresario to get rid of bad singers before the first night they would "all expose [themselves] to the just animadversions of the public." According to Carlo Ritorni it was up to the supervisory authority to do away with the bad custom of arriving at the dress rehearsal, the very day of the opening performance, with "the actors hoarse and tired, the orchestra exhausted, the costumes held together with pins, the paint still fresh on the scenery, and the carpenters still driving nails, while a Babel and an intolerable Chaos forms, amid the trilling of the musicians, that then ripens and matures with successive performances!"[65]

Thanks in great part to the increasingly frantic pace of seasons in an industry in full expansion, difficulties of that sort often did occur. They explain such phenomena as the near fiasco on the opening night of *Norma*. Impresarios, for their part, were sometimes scornful of the "ignorance" of supervisory authorities and owners, particularly of their insistence on established names, the result, no doubt, of their wishing to play safe in an age when no one could know for sure what a singer sounded like until he or she turned up, and when bad singers could cause a riot.

Supervisory boards generally asserted the right to dismiss singers who turned out badly when they opened their mouths at rehearsal; careful impresarios put a clause into contracts exempting them from paying singers thus dismissed, and in 1861 the clause was upheld by the courts.[66] On similar grounds supervisory boards at times required new works to be put on earlier than impresario and composer had planned (because intervening operas had

64. Eugenio Cavallini, *maestro direttore,* to Direzione, 9 April 1857, I-Ms, CA 1063.

65. Anonymous "Riflessioni intorno al quaderno de' patti compilato da S. E. il sig. Presidente delle Finanze," I-PAt, carteggi 1830; Deputazione dei pubblici spettacoli di Bologna to Cesare Aria, *maestro direttore* of the Teatro Contavalli, 29 December 1853, I-Bas, Comune, Dep. Pub. Sp., tit. I, rub. 3, 1853; [Ritorni], *Consigli,* 27–29.

66. Rosmini, *La legislazione,* 1:138–39, 140–42.

failed and the public might grow impatient), and they could threaten to with-hold part of the endowment if this was not done.[67]

How arbitrarily a supervisory board might act seems to have varied with time and circumstance and no doubt also with persons. Probably the worst irritants were picayune, as when one deputy inspector altered on his own authority the time the impresario had set for a rehearsal. The impresario in this particular case demanded that the man should be admonished; whether he was or not we do not know, but the system with its tiers of authority lent itself to petty annoyances of this kind.[68] They were probably harder to take than were the effects of sexual intrigue between upper-class members of the supervisory authority or the boxholders and artists in the impresario's com-pany. Barbaja and Lanari at any rate felt strong enough to refuse to employ or promote an artist "protected" by the head of the supervisory authority.[69] The question is of necessity ill documented, but in a country where no singer could get by on only a minimum of voice and a maximum of sexual attrac-tiveness—there were famously ugly but successful prima donnas like Ros-munda Pisaroni and Barbieri-Nini—it probably mattered little among leading soloists. Things were no doubt different among beginners and minor artists, not to mention the ballerinas.

Similar variations can be found in the dealings between impresarios and theater owners. Lanari got some of the provincial Tuscan academies and some town councils in neighboring regions to accept what would now be called "package deals"; one Livorno academy complained only of not having been told about the program for the coming season before it appeared in a newspaper. A generation later Lanari's son Antonio told the Cesena town council, in effect, they could "take it or leave it."[70] These minor authorities presumably took it because it was a way of securing better performances than they could have gotten from smaller, more amenable local impresarios. On the other hand the executives of the academies in charge of the two main Florentine theaters can be found rebuking the impresario twice in one night for letting the stage remain too dark and the performance run too late, or else carefully checking over the costumes for a new ballet (the executives in question here bore the fabled Renaissance names Guicciardini and Pazzi).[71]

At La Fenice the upper-class directors *(presidenti)* were as a rule extremely

67. Luigi Alberti to Pacini, 8 December 1855, Fondo Pacini 1139 (about *Margherita Pusterla,* Naples, San Carlo C1856).

68. Claudio Musi to the Direttore, Parma, 17 December 1844, I-PAt, carteggi 1844.

69. Vaccai, *Vita di Nicola Vaccaj,* 112; I-Fn, CV 343/139.

70. Gazzuoli to Lanari, 27 May 1837, I-Fn, CV 364/143; to Pacini from Antonio Lanari, 28 March, and from Angelo Ghini, 28 April 1857, Fondo Pacini 968–69, 1000.

71. Direttori of the Accademia degli Infuocati to Giorgio Frilli, 3 January 1802, Copialettere, I-Fcomune, fol. 8364; Gazzuoli to Lanari, April 1837, I-Fn, CV 364/129.

active: from 1843 their secretary, Guglielmo Brenna, acted as a kind of resident manager. For some years the directors of La Fenice, not content with vetoing some names on the list of possible soloists submitted by the impresario, also gave explicit approval of certain soloists whom the impresario would then have to hire at any cost, a system that of course hemmed in his bargaining power in contract negotiations. In the early 1820s, when the endowment for La Fenice was clearly inadequate, the old gambling concessionaires Carlo Balochino, Giuseppe Crivelli, and Barbaja probably got together to cut down the directors' claims. They all bid for the management concession or showed interest. Balochino offered the directors only the negative right to turn down certain names out of a list; when this was rejected, Crivelli got the contract, which allowed the directors positive approval of soloists but which was without the usual provision that the leading singers should be established names.[72]

"There's no trifling with those *illustrissimi* on the board of directors": so Alessandro Lanari concluded fifteen years later.[73] Lanari ran seasons at La Fenice in 1832–33 and from 1837 to 1840, but both times, irritated by the directors' demands, he either provoked them to break the contract or attempted to repeat Barbaja, Balochino, and Crivelli's game by operating in collusion with Bartolomeo Merelli, another major impresario. On both occasions the directors brought in the more accommodating local impresario Natale Fabrici, but in other years they had to fall back on direct management.[74] Similar tension seems to have been the norm in other theaters whose noble directors had high pretensions, as in La Pergola in Florence.

Three questions regarding the management of opera seasons were of particular interest to the authorities: first, the make-up of the free list and the problem of bilkers in the theater; then, censorship; finally, the maintenance of discipline during performances, perhaps through arbitrary arrest.

A free list was normal in eighteenth- and nineteenth-century theaters, not only in Italy. Theaters were not expected to be full on other than special occasions. In most Italian theaters until the late nineteenth century, there was a good deal of standing room: free entrance tickets given out to stagehands and other theater personnel might be a way of piecing out low wages without keeping out paying customers or taking up seats. The free list was nonetheless a problem to opera impresarios for three main reasons. First, governments based on hierarchy and personal dependence used the free list to make a pub-

72. I-Vt, Processi verbali convocazioni, busta 3 (1823).

73. To Donizetti, 25 September 1837, quoted in Jeremy Commons, "Una corrispondenza tra Alessandro Lanari e Donizetti," *Studi donizettiani* 3 (1978): 60.

74. I-Vt, Processi verbali convocazioni, busta 5; Spettacoli, busta 3; Bartolomeo Merelli to Lanari, 15 January 1839, I-Fn, CV 396/87.

lic show of their own dignity while at the same time rewarding their servants. Second, endowment gave them some sort of quid pro quo. Finally, part of the population in each town was straitened in their circumstances, keen to hear opera, and persuaded that they were somehow entitled to get in free. These pressures could easily take up far more than the slack left in a half-full theater. Governments, what is more, claimed not just entrance passes but boxes.

The free lists were a state affair. The only government we know of that tried to abolish them or whittle them down to almost nothing was the weak and idealistic Roman republic of 1798–99, which lasted only a few months.[75] Even then it is doubtful whether the officers of the French army of occupation took much notice. Other governments worked on one of two principles, the hierarchical and the functional, to draw up their free lists.

The papal territories, the most conservative of the Italian states, showed the hierarchical free list in full bloom. For the opening season of a fairly small opera house at Faenza in 1788, an official free list was drawn up of 105 people—exclusive of the cardinal-legate and vice-legate and their "families," if they chose to come over from neighboring Ravenna. On the list were, among others, the bishop's chancery (eleven people), the Holy Office (thirteen people, including four monks and a cook), and the governor's greengrocer. This was very like earlier lists at Bologna and Senigallia, which if anything had gone further in giving free entrance and free boxes to a number of judges and their dependents, and some later lists, as in Parma in 1829 (153 persons, plus an unknown number of the supervisory authority's "families," down to an apothecary and a smith).[76]

True, when the cardinal-legate saw the Faenza list, he thought it "exorbitant," had it cut down to sixty-six, and took steps to guard against people stockpiling free tickets. His action speaks for an enlightened rationalism common at that particular time. It heralded a change to a functional free list— that is, one limited to those functionaries who had a clear connection with the theater. We can see this criterion being applied at La Scala in 1790, under pressure from an impresario who had to do without the old gambling privilege, recently rescinded.[77] From then on the shift seems to have taken place in the same scattered manner as the cutting down of free space for boxholders' liveried servants. Impresarios who complained of excessive free lists were

75. I-Ras, *Collezione di carte pubbliche, proclami, editti . . . della rigenerata Repubblica Romana* (Rome, [1799]), 2:532–35.

76. Lista esentati, Faenza, and correspondence, Piancastelli 130, 184, 200; Piano degli esenti . . . nel Pubblico Teatro Nuovo, 1763, contract with Giuseppe Mienci, 1769, I-Bas, Assunteria di Camera, Diversorum, tomo 128; Radiciotti, *Teatro, musica e musicisti in Sinigaglia,* 192; Stato nominativo dei signori esenti, I-PAt, carteggi 1829.

77. Maldonati contract, I-Mt, Sp. P. 28. See also [Ritorni], *Consigli,* 44–45.

sometimes granted an extra subsidy.[78] Governments found it easier to do this than to curb their officials, many of whom considered either that they had a prescriptive right to free entry or that if others had it so should they.

The problem abated somewhat after the early years of the nineteenth century. One no longer hears of riots such as those at Bologna in 1770–71, when government retainers forced their way into theaters without paying, or at Rimini in 1806, when some French dragoons tried to do the same, an occasion on which several people were killed and wounded.[79] Associations of boxholder-proprietors, some of recent date, stood out as best they could against government interference and made even governors pay for their boxes. The owners of La Fenice boasted in 1854 that they had never allowed the chief of police a free box, though this was not strictly true: a French chief of police in Napoleonic times had truculently refused to pay for his box either there or, later, in Florence at La Pergola. In this he followed the example of some French generals, one of whose first acts on taking over an Italian town was to demand half-price entry for their soldiers and a number of free boxes for themselves.[80] As municipalities came to subsidize opera, they too wanted boxes, but, it seems, in fewer numbers. Things did not change much after unification: a potentially damaging provision at the San Carlo, Naples, late in the century allowed municipal employees designated by the mayor to pay half price.[81] This was in tune with a general Italian assumption that people connected, however indirectly, with government should pay less than others for public services.

Administering a large free list raised the problem of being sure of who was who. In 1794 people at the old Teatro Regio Ducale in Parma (attached to the ducal palace) would sail through the linking door "announcing titles before which the impresario had to bow" and failing to pay.[82] But the problem

78. For example, the impresarios of the three main Florence theaters after an increase in the free list in 1806: I-Fas, Segreteria di Stato 292, prot. 1, no. 2, 305, prot. 81, no. 4.

79. Giuseppe Cosentino, *Il Teatro Marsigli-Rossi* (Bologna: Garagnani, 1900), 143–47; Alfredo Comandini, *L'Italia nei 100 anni del secolo XIX giorno per giorno illustrata . . .*, 4 vols. (Milan: Vallardi, 1901–2), 29 January 1806.

80. Correspondence of the Presidenza of La Fenice and the Prefect, 24 September, 22, 26 December, 1806, I-Vas, Prefettura dell'Adriatico, busta 26; the Presidenza to the Direzione of Teatro Grande, Brescia, 1854, I-Vt, Autografi diversi; Bruno Brunelli, *I teatri di Padova, dalle origini alla fine del secolo XIX* (Padua: Draghi, 1921), 379; the Prefect of the Arno to Minister of Police, 9 January 1812, F-Pan, F⁷ 3655; Bulletin de police, Turin 7 nivose XIV (27 December 1805), F-Pan, F⁷ 3817; Basso, *Il teatro della città,* 69 n, 112–13; Proclamation of Gen. Reille, Florence 6 April 1801, I-Fas, Leggi e bandi.

81. Municipio di Napoli, *Concessione d'esercizio per le stagioni teatrali 1889–90 e 1890–91, Quaderno di oneri per la concessione del Teatro San Carlo,* in the Biblioteca Lucchesi-Palli, Naples.

82. Ferrari, *Spettacoli drammatico-musicali,* 91.

1. Opera, a type of spectacle aimed more than any other at the general public, made early use of modern forms of publicity. Like all propagandistic messages, theatrical posters throughout opera history tell us much about the products they advertise, but above all they tell us about theatergoers' expectations and the promoters' interests. This poster for the season of the spring fair in Reggio Emilia, one of the earliest that have come down to us (Reggio Emilia, Biblioteca Municipale, Curti collection) is laconic and concise. It fails to mention the names of the librettist, the composer, or the singers, and it does not even tell us that the title, according to a custom frequent in the latter seventeenth century, is an alternate one for the work, which was *Il carceriere di se medesimo*, to a text by Lodovico Adimari, composed by Alessandro Melani (Florence, 1681).

NEL TEATRO FONTANELLI
IN MODONA
SI RAPPRESENTARA'
IL MAVRITIO
OPERA DEL MORSELLI, MVSICA DEL SIG. DOMENICO GABRIELLI

VIRTVOSO DI SVA ALTEZZA SERENISSIMA,

E SI DARA' PRINCIPIO LI SEGVENTI GIORNI

Li 29. Ottobre 1589.
30.
5. Nouembre.
6.
8.
9.

12.
13.
15.
15.
19.
20.

NOMI DE'SIGNORI MVSICI, CHE RECITANO NELL'OPERA.

Sig. Dom.co Zecchi da Cortona Mufico del Ser.mo di Mantoua.
Sig. Antonio Cottini Mufico del Serenifs. di Modona.
Sig. Gio: Francefco Grofsi detto Siface, Mufico di S. A. S.
Signora Francefca Saru Cottini Virtuofa di S. A. S.

Signora Angiola Paris Venetiana.
Signora Angiola Cocchi Virtuofa del Serenifs. di Mantoua.
Sig. Gio: Battifta Nini Mufico del Sig. March. Guido Rangoni.
Sig. Gio: Battifta Vergelli Mufico di S. A. S.

2, 3, 4. Compared to the preceding poster, the announcement for a production of *Maurizio* in Modena (Modena, Archivio di Stato, aut. 1948/V.9) is extraordinarily informative. It tells us the names of the librettist, the composer, the singers, and the singers' protectors. In general, theatrical posters tended to include more and more information. Although in the late seventeenth century the dances inserted between the acts of the opera were not even mentioned, by the eighteenth century indications of the singers of the intermezzi (given separately from the other singers, since they were specialists and not an integral part of the *dramma per musica*) and of the dancers in the ballets that soon took the place of the intermezzi became standard. The music for the operas given in Modena in 1719 (plate 2) was composed by Michelangelo Gasparini and Andrea Paulati. The poster for Reggio Emilia in 1741 (Reggio Emilia, Archivio di Stato, aut. n. 3; photo: Studio Clic) mentions gambling and masks as further attractions.

IN MODENA

L'AUTUNNO 1719.

NEL TEATRO MOLZA

SI RAPPRESENTERANNO

L'ARSACE,

et

I VERI AMICI

DRAMI PER MUSICA.

NOMI DE' SIGNORI VIRTUOSI.

Signora Anna Guglielmini Bolognese.
Signora Girolama Valsecchi Veneziana.
Signora Cammilla Zoboli Modenese.

Signor Paolo Mariani da Urbino.
Signor Antonio Barbieri Reggiano.
Signor Luciano Lenzi Bolognese.

NE GL' INTERMEZZI.

Signora Margarita Dolfini.

Signor Cosimo Erminj Fiorentino.

Le Scene, & apparenze sono di nuova, e bizzara idea del Sig. Andrea Galluzzi Allievo del Sig. Francesco Bibiena, e Servitore familiare del Sereniſsimo Sig. Principe Antonio di Parma.
Li Veſtiarj sono di vaga invenzione del Sig Natale Canciani Veneziano.

Le Recite del primo Drama comincieranno li 14. Ottobre, e proſ-
seguiranno sino li 5. Novembre.
Le Recite del secondo Drama principieranno li 7. Novembre, e termineranno all'Avvento.

3

APRENDOSI LA PRIMA VOLTA IL NUOVO TEATRO
DELL' ILLUSTRISSIMO PUBBLICO DI REGGIO

In occasione della Fiera nell' Anno corrente 1741.,

Ideato dal Sig. Antonio Cugini Reggiano, Architetto, e Servitore attuale di S. A. S.
il Sig. Duca di Modena; ed eretto sotto la Direzione di esso:

VI SI RAPPRESENTERÀ IL DRAMMA PER MUSICA INTITOLATO

VOLOGESO RE DE' PARTI.

SIGNORI VIRTUOSI.

Sig. Vittoria Tesi Tramontini Virtuosa di S. A. S.
Sig. Antonia Rafaelli, detta la Falegnamina.
Sig. Giovanni Carestini Virtuoso di S. A. E. di Baviera.

Sig. Felice Salimbeni.
Sig. Angelo Amorevoli.
Sig. Niccola Giovanetti Virtuoso di S. M. Sarda.

La Musica farà nuova del Sig. Pietro Pulli Napolitano, Virtuoso della Real Cappella di S. M. il Re delle due Sicilie.

I Balli saranno eseguiti da Undici Persone, e d' Invenzione di Monsieur Sauvterre.

Sig. Orsola Collucci.
Madamoiselle Groeznet Virtuosa delle
Serenis Principesse Sorelle di S. A. S.
il Sig. Duca.
Sig. Anna Maria Bresciani.
Sig. Maria Vigano.

Monsieur Sauvterre.
Sig. Giacomo Brignenti,
Sig. Pietro Gugliangini.
Sig. Andrea Cattraco.

Madamoisselle Roland.
Monsieur Poirier.
Monsieur Carlo Poitier.

Le Scene saranno di vaga Invenzione del Sig. Giovanni Paglia Reggiano, Pittore, Architetto, e Servitore
attuale di Sua Altezza Serenissima di Modena.
Il Vestiario farà di ricca, bizzara, e tutta nuova Invenzione del Sig. Hermano Compstoff di Firenze.

I giorni delle Recite saranno li 29. 30. Aprile. In Maggio 1. 3. 4. 6. 7. 8. 10. 11.
13. 14. 15. 17. 18. 21. 22. 23. 25. 27. 28. 30. In Giugno 1. 3. 4.

Dalla prima all' ultima Recita vi sarà pubblico Ridotto di Giuoco, e Maschera.

IN MODENA
NEL TEATRO RANGONE
NEL PROSSIMO CARNEVALE MDCCLXIV.

Si rappresenteranno due Opere Giocose per Musica, la prima delle quali sarà:

LE CONTADINE BIZZARRE.

GLI ATTORI SONO:

PARTI SERIE.

Signora Angela Guadagni. ❋ *Signora Maria Maddalena Valli.*

PARTI BUFFE.

Sig. Cesare Malinari. ❋ *Sig. Lodovico Felloni.*

Signora Margarita Caldinelli.
Signora Anna Giorgi. ❋ *Sig. Massimo Giuliani.*
Signora Luigia Manozzi.

I Balli sono di vaga, e bizzarra invenzione del Sig. Giuseppe Rubini, ed eseguiti da' seguenti:

Signora Veronica Cocchi. ❋ *Sig. Antonio Rubini.*
Signora Angela Lazzari. ❋ *Sig. Giuseppe Rubini suddetto.*
Signora Anna Ferraresi. ❋ *Sig. Giovanni Ferraresi.*
Signora Anna Zoccoli. ❋ *Sig. N. N.*

La Musica è del Sig. Niccola Piccini Maestro di Cappella Napolitano. Le Recite comincieranno li 26. Dicembre 1763, e proseguiranno a tutto il Carnevale, come gl'Anni scorsi.
Tutte le sere vi sarà Maschera, e Ridotto. La nota delle Feste da Ballo si darà a parte.

Restano avvisati tutti i Signori, che sono soliti a prendere in affitto li Palchi per tutto il corso delle Recite di presentarsi al solito luogo, per levare le Chiavi de' medesimi, e per denunziare i loro nomi, mentre spirato il giorno 25. resteranno in libertà dell' Impresario.

I PREZZI DE' PALCHI SONO:

In Ordine Primo Palco doppio Lir. 240. Detto sempio Lir. 150. In Ordine Secondo Palco doppio Lir. 240. Detto sempio Lir. 150. In Ordine Terzo, e Peppiano Palco doppio Lir. 150. Detti sempi Lir. 75. Quelli che vorranno affittarsi per ambedue le Porte pagheranno Lir. 60., e quelli poi, che vorranno affittarsi per la prima sola Lir. 45.

1772. a' 4. Dicembre
PREZZI
DE' BIGLIETTI E PALCHI
Per le diverfe Rapprefentazioni Teatrali

Stabiliti di concerto con li MM. Incombenzati

DAGLI ECCELLENTISSIMI

NICCOLO'-ALESSANDRO GIOVO, E LUCA DE FORNARI

A ciò deftinati dal Sereniffimo Senato.

Per le Opere Serie in Mufica.

Biglietti ferali di Portagrande	con fefta di ballo .. lir. 4.
	fenza fefta di ballo .. l. 3.
Biglietti perpetui di Portagrande	per Dame ...... l. 50.
	per Cavalieri ..... l. 72.
	per l'ordine non afcritto l. 52.
Palchi ferali di prima e feconda fila	con fefta di ballo ... l. 24.
	fenza fefta di ballo ... l. 16.
Palchi perpetui di prima e feconda fila	1.240.
Palchi ferali di terza fila	con fefta di ballo ... l. 14.
	fenza fefta di ballo .. l. 9.
Palchi perpetui di terza fila	1 130.
Palchi ferali di quarta fila	con fefta di ballo ... l. 10.
	fenza fefta di ballo .. l. 7.
Palchi perpetui di quarta fila	1.100.
Biglietti ferali di Portapiccola	fenza fefta di ballo . , l. 1. 4
Biglietti perpetui di Portapiccola	per Signore ...... l. 32.
	per Uomini ...... l. 40.

Per le Opere buffe in Mufica.

Biglietti ferali di Portagrande	con fefta di ballo : . . l. 2.
	fenza fefta di ballo .. l. 1. 10.
Biglietti perpetui di Portagrande	per Dame .... l. 32.
	per Cavalieri .... l. 40.
	per l'ordine non afcritto l. 34.
Palchi ferali di prima, e feconda fila	con fefta di ballo ... l. 13.
	fenza fefta di ballo .. l. 10.
Palchi perpetui di prima, e feconda fila	1.150.
Palchi ferali di terza fila	con fefta di ballo ... l. 9.
	fenza fefta di ballo .. l. 6.
Palchi perpetui di terza fila	1.100.
Palchi ferali di quarta fila	con fefta di ballo ... l. 6.
	fenza fefta di ballo .. l. 4.
Palchi perpetui di quarta fila	l. 80.
Biglietti ferali di Portapiccola	fenza fefta di ballo .. l. 00. 16.
Biglietti perpetui di Portapiccola	per Signore .... l. 24.
	per Uomini .... l. 28.

DISTRIBUZIONE
DE' DIVERTIMENTI PUBBLICI
Nel Carnevale dell' Anno 1791.

DICEMBRE.
26 Domenica Opera Seria.
27 Lunedì Opera.
28 Martedì Opera.
29 Mercoledì Opera.
30 Giovedì Opera.

GENNAJO.
1 Sabbato Opera.
2 Domenica Opera.
3 Lunedì Opera.
5 Mercoledì Opera.
6 Giovedì Opera.
8 Sabbato Opera.
9 Domenica Opera.
11 Martedì Opera.
12 Mercoledì Opera.
15 Sabbato Opera Buffa.
16 Domenica Opera.
17 Lunedì Opera.
18 Martedì Festa di Ballo in Teatro, che
   comincierà alle ore 7. in punto.
19 Mercoledì Opera.
20 Giovedì Opera.
22 Sabbato Opera.
23 Domenica Opera.
25 Martedì Festa in Teatro alle ore 7.
26 Mercoledì Opera.
27 Giovedì Opera.
29 Sabbato Opera.
31 Lunedì Opera.

FEBBRAJO.
1 Martedì Opera.

2 Mercoledì Opera.
3 Giovedì Festa in Teatro alle ore 7.
5 Sabbato Opera.
6 Domenica Opera.
7 Lunedì Opera.
8 Martedì Festa in Teatro alle ore 7.
9 Mercoledì Opera.
12 Sabbato Opera.
13 Domenica Opera.
14 Lunedì Opera.
15 Martedì Festa in Teatro alle ore 7.
16 Mercoledì Opera.
19 Sabbato Opera Buffa nuova.
20 Domenica Opera.
21 Lunedì Festa in Teatro alle ore 7.
22 Martedì Opera.
23 Mercoledì Opera.
24 Giovedì Festa in Teatro alle ore 7.
26 Sabbato Opera.
27 Domenica Opera.
28 Lunedì Opera.

MARZO.
1 Martedì Festa in Teatro alle ore 7.
2 Mercoledì Opera.
3 Giovedì Opera e Festa.
5 Sabbato Opera.
6 Domenica Opera, e Festa.
7 Lunedì Opera, e Festa.
8 Martedì Opera, e Festa.
12 Sabbato Opera.
13 Domenica Opera.

LE Opere Serie, e Buffe non s' individuano; ma si daranno alternativamente secondo le circostan-
ze, e l' altrui piacimento, e se ne darà opportunamente preventivo Avviso, quando il tempo
lo permetterà, o la necessità non obbligasse a cambiamento.

SI avvisa il Pubblico, che ne' Giorni 28. di Febbrajo, 1. 2. 3. 5. 6. 7. 8. di Marzo lungo il
nuovo Portico grande della Strada Maestra si farà adunanza di Maschere ad uso del volgarmen-
te chiamato Listone. A tal effetto però si terrà pulito il nominato Portico, e le Strade ad-
jacenti, e ne sarà impedito l' ingresso ai Contadini, e alla Gente rozza, e malvestita. Non potranno passare davanti al Portico della Strada Maestra Vetture improprie, Bovi, Carri, Bestie con
Some, quando non debbano portarsi alla Ducale Dogana. Sarà bensì permesso alle Carrozze di
passarvi, ma non già di restarvi ferme, e si permetterà l' ingresso alle Maschere, e alle Persone
smascherate ancora di ogni Sesso, purchè sieno decentemente vestite. Si desidera che le Botteghe
del Portico grande sieno tenute nella migliore veduta, e vien concesso a qualunque Mercante della Città di mettere ne' vacui, che sono tra di esse, de' Banchi colle Merci convenienti a tal Luogo, e saranno collocati dei Sedili sotto gli Archi di rimpetto.
Avvertasi, che nella Domenica 6. Marzo non si dovranno aprire le Botteghe, nè si permetteranno
le Maschere che dopo il Mezzogiorno, secondo il costume.

Modena 22. Dicembre 1790.

ANDREA MARCHESE CORTESE
SOPRANTENDENTE DEGLI SPETTACOLI.

In MODENA, per gli Eredi di Bartolomeo Soliani Stampatori Ducali.)(1790.)(

7, 8. Some messages publicized social customs of the opera house rather than the spectacles themselves. In Genoa in 1772 "li MM. Incombenzati" (those in charge) published a highly detailed list
of prices, which differed according to the cost of the various productions rather than for ideological reasons. The document goes on to list *Opere Pastorali in Musica, Commedie Italiane,* and
Commedie Francesi (Genoa, collection E. Ivaldi di Campolongo. This and the following reproduc-
tions of material from this collection are published here with the special and exclusive authorization of the owner). In Modena in 1791, on the other hand, the calendar of festivities and spectacles was given along with certain restrictions; for instance, the exclusion even of the momentary
presence of "peasants . . . rough, ill-dressed persons . . . [and] inappropriate vehicles" on the most
popular days.

9, 10. This very detailed poster from Turin in 1782 (Turin, Archivio storico della Città) not only lists in great detail the singers, the dancers, and the titles of the operas and ballets but also gives information relating to the city's two opera theaters (under the same management), the Teatro Regio, which staged opera seria—here, an extraordinary, post-season production put on at the king's command to honor northern counts who were visiting Turin—and the Teatro Carignano, which staged opera buffa. In that same year (1782) a decree specified that theater posters showing the program of the performances must be put up in three places in the city rather than the two places that had been customary. The 1796 poster from Genoa shows just as much information as the poster in plate 9, but it is distinguished by the elegance of its design. It also mentions the leading musicians in the orchestra. (Genoa, collection E. Ivaldi di Campolongo)

IN GENOVA
Nel Carnovale del 1796.
NEL TEATRO DA S. AGOSTINO
SI RAPPRESENTERANNO DUE DRAMMI SERJ PER MUSICA
IL PRIMO DE QUALI SARA'
ENEA E LAVINIA
MUSICA DEL CELEBRE SIGNOR MAESTRO GUGLIELMI
IL SECONDO DA DESTINARSI.

ATTORI

Primo Soprano	Prima Donna	Primo Tenore
Sig. Vitale Damiani.	Sig. Elena Cantoni.	Sig. Matteo Babini.
Secondo Soprano	Seconda Donna	Secondo Tenore
Sig. Raimondo del Moro.	Sig. Antonia Boffi.	Sig. Luigi Moriconi.

LI BALLI
Saranno composti e diretti dal Sig. Luigi Dupen primo Ballerino.

Primo Ballo Serio	Secondo Ballo Comico
LA DISTRUZIONE D'AQUILEJA	LA NINA PAZZA
fatta da Attila Re degli Unni.	per amore.

La Musica di detti Balli è composta dal Sig. Giovanni Scannavino
Primi Ballerini Serj assoluti.
Sig. Giuseppe Rossi.   Sig. Luigia Accerbi.
Primi Grotteschi a perfetta vicenda estratti a forte

Sig. Domenico Magni.	Sig. Lorenzo Monati.	Sig Domenico Turchi.
Sig. Rosa Dupen.	Sig Giuditta Pontiggia.	Sig. Teresa Brunetti.

Ballerini per le Parti

Sig. Steffano Paccini.	Sig. Salvator La Ros.
Sig. Massimiglia Pontiggia.	Sig. Angela Pirovani.

Con Num. 16. Ballerini di concerto.

Maestro al Cembalo Sig. Gaetano Isola.
Primo Violino dell' Opera Sig. Giambatista Serra.   Primo Controbasso Sig. Giuseppe Saetone detto Bona.
Primo de' secondi Sig. Gio. Ocello.   Primo Violino dei Balli Sig. Giovanni Scannavino.
Violoncello Sig. Domenico Suardi.   Primo Oboe Sig. Giambatista Gallo.
Lo Scenario farà dipinto ed inventato dal celebre pittore Sig. Pasquale Canna Milanese.
Le Decorazioni, e Machinismo de' Balli. e dell' Opera d'invenzione, ed esecuzione del
Sig. Giambatista Tagliafico.
Il Vestiario di ricca, e vaga invenzione del Sig. Carlo Songia Milanese.

PREZZI

Biglietti serali di Porta Grande con festa di Ballo . . . lir. 3. 10.	Biglietti serali di Porta Piccola senza festa di Ballo . . . . lir. 1. 4.	
Senza festa di Ballo . . . lir. 2. 10.	Biglietti perpetui di Porta Piccola per Signore . . . . . lir. 32.	
Biglietti perpetui di Porta Grande per Dame . . . . . lir. 30.	Per Uomini . . . . . lir. 40.	
Per Cavalieri . . . . lir. 72.	Palchi perpetui di terza fila . . lir. 130.	
Per l' ordine non ascritto. . lir. 52.	Detti di quarta, quinta e sesta . lir. 100.	
Palchi perpetui di prima e seconda fila lir. 240.		

Biglietto annuale per Cavalieri . . lir. 120.
Per Dame . . lir. 90.
Biglietto annuale per l' ordine non ascritto lir. 100.
Per Signore . . . . lir. 70.

L'Impresa Generale fa noto che gli Abbonamenti annui non si faranno, che dentro al termine del corrente mese di Dicembre, e col previo pagamento. Spirato questo tempo ognuno dovrà pagare l'abbonamento a tenore della Tariffa emanata dal Serenissimo Governo.
Li Biglietti per detto Abbonamento si potranno avere dal Sig. Vincenzo Molinari primo portinaro del Teatro, alla sua Bottega dalla cattena del Ponte Reale.

Libertà	Eguaglianza	Liberté	Egalité

AVVISO
PER IL TEATRO ALLA SCALA.
LA continuata indifposizione della prima Donna, e la riftrettezza del tempo, che non permette di abilitare la Parte di Supplemento, impedifce di mettere in iscena domani l' Opera Buffa , per la quale farà indicato un altro giorno.
Dal Teatro li 15. Febbrajo 1799. v. s.

AVIS
POUR LE THÉATRE À LA SCALA.
POur la maladie continuée de la premiere Actrice, & pour ne pouvoir pas autrement fupléer, il eft differé à un autre jour l' Opera Boufton qu' on avoit indiqué pour demain.
Au Théatre le 27. Pluviose an VII. Républicain.

11, 12. Theater posters were quick to reflect changes in government: during the Napoleonic regime in 1799 La Scala announced the indisposition of a *prima donna* in French as well as Italian (Milan, Archivio Storico Civico). In Genoa only a few years after the serious opera *Enea e Lavinia* in 1796 (see plate 10), the Teatro Sant'Agostino was staging comic operas in the form of *drammi giocosi* and *farse veneziane* (the latter a new genre that proved highly successful up to the time of the young Rossini, here sung by "citizens" rather than by *virtuosi*. (The same Genoese private collection contains the manuscript draft for a wall poster of 1804 changing all the republican phraseology to conform with Napoleonic directives.)

IN GENOVA
AL TEATRO DA S. AGOSTINO
NEL DECORSO DELLA CORRENTE PRIMAVERA 1802.
SI RAPPRESENTERANNO DIVERSI DRAMMI GIOCOSI PER MUSICA
IL PRIMO DE QUALI HA PER TITOLO

IL PODESTÀ DI CHIOGGIA
MUSICA DEL MAESTRO FERDINANDO ORLAND
IL SECONDO

Due Nuovissime Farse scritte a Venezia, la prima dal Maestro GIUSEPPE MOSCA Napolitano che porta per titolo

IL FILOSOFO
La Seconda del Maestro SIMONE MAYER che porta per titolo

CHE ORIGINALI
IL TERZO DA DESTINARSI

ED ESEGUITI DAI SEGUENTI ARTISTI CANTANTI

Cittadino Luigi Pacini

Cittadina Annunziata Berni

Cittadina Elisabetta Gafforini

Cittadino Nicola De Grecis

Cittadino Francesco Gafforini

Cittadino Gio: Battista Viscardi

Cittadino Luigi Bonfanti

Cittadina Antonia Sevesi

Li Balli saranno composti e diretti dal Cittadino GIACOMO GENTILI

Primo Ballo serio Pantomimo
VARBEK D'INERES
Cittadino Giacomo Gentili suddetto

Cittadino Giuseppe Pappini

Cittadina Vittoria Paris

Cittadino Andrea Massai
Cittadino Pietro Palladini

Ed eseguiti dai seguenti Artisti Ballerini

Cittadino Giovanni Francolini

Con N.° 24. Artisti di Concerto

Secondo Ballo Mezzo Carattere
DIVERTIMENTO CAMPESTRE
Cittadina Antonia Tarappatoni

Cittadino Paolo Mersi

Cittadina Maria Pappini

Cittadina Rachelle Paganetti
Cittadino Gaspare Cenni

Le Scene saranno inventate, e dipinte dal Cittadino Carlo Baratta Genovese.
Direttore del Palco Scenico, e Macchinista il Cittadino Gio: Battista Tagliafico Genovese.
Il Vestiario tutto nuovo, d'invenzione e direzione del Cittadino Carlo Songia Milanese.

PREZZI STABILITI

Abbonamento di Porta grande per Uomini . lir. 54.	} lir. 57. 8.	Abbonamento di Porta piccola per uomini . lir. 28.	} lir. 30. 16.		
Aumento per l'Ospedale . . . . " 3. 8.		Aumento per l'Ospedale . . . . " 2. 16.			
Abbonamento di Porta grande per Donne . " 52.	} " 55. 4.	Abbonamento di Porta piccola per Donne " 24.	} " 26. 8.		
Aumento per l'Ospedale . . . . " 3. 4.		Aumento per l'Ospedale . . . . " 2. 8.			
Biglietto Serale di Porta grande . . . . " 3. 4.	} " 1. 14.	Biglietto Serale di Porta piccola . . . . " 16.	} " 1.		
Aumento per l'Ospedale . . . . " 4.		Aumento per l'Ospedale . . . . " 2.			
Palchi perpetui di Prima, e Seconda fila " 150.	} " 187. 10.	Palchi perpetui di Terza fila . . . . . . " 100.	} " 125.		
Aumento per l'Ospedale . . . . " 37. 10.		Aumento per l'Ospedale . . . . " 25.			
Palchi perpetui di Quarta, Quinta, e Sesta fila " 80.	} " 100.	Palchi serali di Prima fila . . . . " 12.	} " 15.		
Aumento per l'Ospedale . . . . " 20.		Aumento per l'Ospedale . . . . " 3.			
Palchi serali di Quarta, Quinta, e Sesta fila " 8.	} " 10.	Palchi serali di Prima, e 2.da fila con festa di Ballo " 16.	} " 20.		
Aumento per l'Ospedale . . . . " 2.		Aumento per l'Ospedale . . . . " 4.			
		Palchi serali di Sesta fila con festa di Ballo " 10.	} " 12.		
		Aumento per l'Ospedale . . . . " 2.			

Si avverte che si anderà in Scena col primo Ballo solamente, mentre per mancanza di tempo non si è potuto ultimare il Secondo, quale anderà in Scena dopo qualche giorno.

Si previene in tempo, che alla porta del Teatro non si scrive Biglietto alcuno, e a chi non avrà soddisfatto al debito del Teatro sarà negato l'ingresso.

Le Recite per gli Abbonati, e per i Palchi perpetui saranno N. 40., e principieranno Domenica giorno 18. corrente Aprile 1802.

STAMPERIA DELLA LIBERTA IN SCURRERIA LA VECCHIA N. 84.

REAL TEATRO DEL FONDO

SABBATO 6. Giugno 1818. – Recita 6.ª

SI RAPPRESENTA IL DRAMMA

C E N E R E N T O L A

Musica del Signor Maestro ROSSINI.

INDI

Z E F F I R O

Ballo di Composizione del Sig. DUPORT.

ATTORI DEL DRAMMA

Signore Festa, Checcherini, e Manzi seconda — Signori Rubini, Pellegrini, Casaccia, e Pace,

PERSONAGGI DEL BALLO.

Sig. Duport. Signore Taglioni, Mersi, Ronzi, Sichera, Vitolo, Aquino, Sica, de Luca, Oliva, Ricci 1., Pompei, Porta, Talma, e Ricci 2. con gli Allievi della Real Scuola di Ballo.

P R E Z Z I.

PALCHI		PLATEA	
Prima Fila	D.⁵ 5	Viglietti numerati	Gr. 50
Seconda	" 6	Detti di quinta fila	" 15
Terza	" 4		
Quarta	" 3		
Quinta	" 1 20		

ALLA PORTA NON SI PRENDONO DENARI.

Si comincia ad un'ora di notte in punto.

DALLA TIPOGRAFIA FLAUTINA.

13, 14. The posters of the period of Austrian Restoration do not show any great graphic quality or elegance in their format. The information is generally stripped to the essentials (composer, singers, choreographer, dancers, prices, hours). This poster (from the private collection of Sergio Ragni, Naples; photo: Luciano Romano) dates from the era of Rossini's predominance in Naples, but it refers to the Teatro del Fondo rather than the Teatro San Carlo. The royal administration of the theaters of the city can be seen even in the police regulations that take care to prescribe that "money will not be taken at the door." During the nineteenth century the poster became more and more a vehicle for the impresario, who used the walls of the city to appeal to an "indulgent and magnanimous public" and to the "Illustrious Garrison." (Imola, Comune di Imola, Archivio Tozzoni)

Visto pel Bollo di Dimensione a Imola li   Agosto 1836. come al N   e pagati quatt.
IL PREPOSTO

TEATRO DE' SIGNORI SOCJ
IN IMOLA

AVVISO

Pieno di quei profondi sentimenti di tenera riconoscenza che ispira un Pubblico indulgente, e magnanimo, ardisce il rispettoso SALVATORE PARADISI di presentare un invito per la sera di Mercoledì 17 del corrente Agosto 1836 il di cui introito viene devoluto dall' Impresa a suo totale beneficio.

Il fortunato incontro delle sue deboli fatiche, e le non dubbie testimonianze di parziale bontà e di gradimento, con cui questo Pubblico Illustre, non che questa Inclita Guarnigione, si sono degnati d' accogliere, gli hanno imposto il dolce dovere di approfittare della circostanza, per esternare in qualche modo la sua gratitudine; ed è perciò che ha determinato lo Spettacolo nel modo seguente. Il primo atto

DELLA NORMA
INDI IL BALLO

LA SCIMIA   RICONOSCENTE

Nella fine del detto Ballo terminato il Terzetto delli Primi Ballerini il *Paradisi* ballerà un A SOLO DI CARATTERE INGLESE. Indi verrà Cantato il Duetto della NINA PAZZA, Musica del celebre Maestro Coppola eseguito dal Signor ZILIOLI primo Tenore che graziosamente si presta, e dalla Signora TERESA GUERRIERI PARADISI.

Si avverte che questa recita non è compresa nell' abbonamento e che la prima Donna Signora SERAFINA RUBINI DE SANCTIS cessando in detta sera il suo contratto, cessano pure anche le recite della NORMA. Sabbato prossimo la Signora CLEMENTINA MAZZONI farà la sua prima comparsa coll' Opera Seria intitolata I CAPULETI ED I MONTECCHJ del *Bellini*.

Generoso Pubblico, accorrete e siate utili ad un Artista, che vi consacra le sue fatiche; e che in prevenzione vi anticipa i sentimenti della sua indelebile riconoscenza.
Imola li 16. Agosto 1836.

Imola per Ignazio Galeati.

TEATRO DE' SIGNORI SOCJ IN IMOLA

AVVISO

L' Impresa si fa un dovere di prevenire il rispettabile Pubblico, ed inclita Guarnigione che con la sera di Domenica 10. corrente Febbrajo avranno termine le Teatrali Rappresentazioni, e sarà esposto il secondo Atto

DEL NUOVO FIGARO

ed il primo Atto

DELL' FURIOSO.

Fra mezzo dei suddetti Atti per favorire l' Impresa verranno gentilmente ripetuti i seguenti pezzi, e cioè

Momenti lugubri di M. Malibran : *Gran Duo per Piano e Violoncello*, eseguito dalla Sig. ALBINA FERRARINI, e dal Sig. Professore PARISINI. | *Duetto nell' Atto Secondo della NORMA* cantato dalla Sig. ANNUNCIATA FANTI, e dalla Sig. CARLOTTA FERRARINI.

Nel Lunedì poi avrà luogo nel Teatro medesimo il

VEGLIONE

CON MASCHERA.

Non ommetterà l' Impresa premura, o diligenza, perchè la maggior possibile proprietà, e decenza concorrano ad appagare il desiderio dei Concorrenti che spera numerosissimi.
Imola dal Camerino del Teatro li 9 Febbrajo 1839.

IMOLA PER IGNAZIO GALEATI.

15, 16. The theater administration addressed its "respectable Public" to announce its program and "anticipate" and "satisfy the desire of the Audience" (Imola, Comune di Imola, Archivio Tozzoni). On other occasions, as at the Venetian premiere of Verdi's *Ernani,* the theater management had to admit that old sets had been used in order not to "delay the production." The occurrence was common; admitting it was absolutely unheard of. This unaccustomed sincerity was probably due to complaints from Verdi, who, with Piave, the opera's librettist, sent the directors of the Teatro La Fenice a letter cautioning them against putting on *Ernani* "before the scenery and the costumes are completely finished, in order to avoid scandalous talk harmful to both the interests of the management and the effect of the spectacle."

GRAN TEATRO
LA FENICE

Oggi 9 Marzo 1844.   Recita 44 dell'Abbonamento.

Prima rappresentazione del Dramma Lirico in quattro Parti

ERNANI

Parole di Francesco Maria Piave.   Musica del Maestro Giuseppe Verdi.

PERSONAGGI	ATTORI	PERSONAGGI	ATTORI
ERNANI, il Bandito.	Sig. Guasco Carlo.	ELVIRA, sua nipote e fidanzata,	Sign. Loewe Sofia.
D. CARLO, re di Spagna.	Sig. Superchi Antonio.	GIOVANNA, di lei nutrice,	Sign. Sani Laura.
D. RUY GOMEZ DE SILVA, grande		D. RICCARDO, scudiere del re.	Sig. Lanner Giovanni.
di Spagna.	Sig. Selva Antonio.	JAGO, scudiero di D. Ruy.	Sig. Bellini Andrea.

Coro. Montanari ribelli e banditi - Cavalieri, famigliari di Silva - Ancelle di Elvira - Cavalieri del re - Personaggi della Lega - Nobili
spagnoli e alemanni - Dame spagnole e alemanne. Comparse. Montanari e banditi - Elettori e grandi della corte
imperiale - Paggi dell'impero - Soldati alemanni - Dame e famigliari d'ambo i sessi. Epoca, l'anno 1519.
La Scena ha luogo: P.e I. Nelle montagne d'Aragona e nel castello di D. Ruy Gomez De Silva. II. Nello stesso castello.
III. In Aquisgrana. IV. In Saragozza.

Dopo la Seconda Parte il Gran Ballo Fantastico

NADIR SCIÀ DI PERSIA

Nel Primo Atto vi sarà un Terzetto composto dal Primo Ballerino Sig. BORRI PASQUALE
eseguito dallo stesso, e dalle Sign. POLIN ADELE, e SCRIBANY DELLA CELLA AMAL

Prezzo del Viglietto d'ingresso Aust. L. 3.   Pei piccoli Fanciulli Aust. L. 4.

Pei Sigg. Militari in Uniforme Aust. L. 1 50

Gli Scanni, riservata la prima pei Sigg. Militari, sono tutti vendibili ad Aust. L. 3.
al Cancello di Marco Marangoni.   Si alza la tela alle ore 8 precise.

Dal Camerino del Teatro il 9 Marzo 1844.   Tipografia Molinari.

Non essendo ultimate le due scene ultima della Parte Prima, e Prima della Parte Seconda,
per non ritardare la produzione dell'Opera, se ne sostituiscono due di ripiego fino a che
sieno compiute le tele appositamente dipinte.

Oggi si distribuiranno i Libretti della nuova Opera ai Sigg. Abbonati
nel solito locale del Teatro dalle ore 1 alle 5 pom.

I.R.P.L. Bogi   Barozzi

REGIO TEATRO DELLA SCALA

L'Impresa per aderire al desiderio di una parte del Pubblico ha creduto di provvedere meglio all'andamento dello spettacolo, lasciando luogo al Ballo e dividendo l'Opera in due sere, senza alterare l'integrità dello spartito il **MEFISTOFELE**. Perchè la divisione corrisponda al concetto poetico dell'Opera si darà una sera il prologo, il primo, secondo e terzo atto, che costituiscono la prima parte del Poèma di Goethe; l'altra sera si darà oltre il prologo, il quarto atto, l'intermezzo sinfonico ed il quinto atto che costituiscono la seconda parte dello stesso Poèma.

ORDINE DELLO SPETTACOLO

Prologo, primo, secondo e terzo atto dell'Opera indi il Ballo BRAHMA colla sig.ª *Ferraris*.
Domani si darà la Seconda parte dell'Opera suddetta, cioè:
il prologo, quarto atto, intermezzo sinfonico e quinto atto dell'Opera ed il Ballo.

Prezzo del Biglietto serale L. 5 – Pei signori Militari (in uniforme) L. 5 – Pel Loggione L. 1. 50
Per una Sedia distinta a bracciuoli L. 10 (oltre il biglietto serale) – Per una Sedia chiusa comune L. 3.
Si aprirà la porta del Teatro alle ore 7

Milano, 7 Marzo 1868.   Tip. Pirola.   L'Impresa BONOLA e COMP.

17. After the disastrous premiere of Arrigo Boito's *Mefistofele* at La Scala, the management sought to salvage what they could by dividing the opera into two evenings, "leaving room for the ballet" (*Brahma*) in order to satisfy at least "some of the public."

existed as well in theaters not connected with a court, and impresarios were always trying to fend off people who got in by pretending to be extras or journalists, using someone else's season ticket, or getting themselves smuggled in by a friendly usher,[83] phenomena of a poor country.

Preventive censorship was the norm in Italy. It went on before, during, and after the period of revolutionary and Napoleonic rule (but for a very short outburst of free expression in 1796–97) and before and after unification, though the practice of censorship in united Italy was much more liberal. Studies of the censorship have fastened on its political aspects—the ban on regicide, for instance, that gave Verdi such trouble over *Rigoletto* and *Un ballo in maschera*—though a recent study by Mario Lavagetto has shown how much censorship was concerned to uphold a timorous morality and avoid anything unpleasantly specific.[84] Even when librettos passed through the censorship, unsuspected dangers might spring up in performance.

Because the opera house was the center of social life, few things went down so well as local allusions—not, heaven forfend, allusions to the authorities but to a well-known noble cuckold or an eccentric literary man. For the same reason there were few things the paternal authorities of old Italy detested more. Allusions might cause murmurs, gossip, disorder; they must be stopped. So a comic opera by Giovanni Pacini making fun of the poet Vincenzo Monti was forbidden after the third performance. La Fenice refused *I due Foscari* as a new opera because the noble Venetian families of Loredan and Barbarigo might have been upset at seeing their fifteenth-century ancestors in a poor light; it did put on the work after a Roman theater had taken responsibility for the first performance—a nice distinction.[85]

The danger was that local allusions not in the text might be worked in by a singer, particularly in opera buffa. Severer vigilance after the restoration may indeed go some way to explain the decay of comic opera: it killed improvisation. A kindred peril was that "obscenities" might creep in. It is seldom easy to know what these were. Mostly they seem to have had to do with ballet dancers showing too much leg. The Imperial Royal Provincial Delegation at Padua was only one of several authorities to express indignation on this score (pointing to the number of university students in the audience); at such times

83. Gazzuoli to Lanari, February 1837, January 1839, I-Fn, CV 364/111, 365/63; Vittorio Frajese, *Dal Costanzi all'Opera*, 4 vols. (Rome: Capitolium, 1977–78), 1:37.

84. Mario Lavagetto, *Un caso di censura: Il "Rigoletto"* (Milan: Il Formichiere, 1979). See also Rosmini, *La legislazione*, vol. 1, chap. 5, 2:249.

85. Pacini, *Le mie memorie*, 11; the Presidenza of La Fenice to Verdi, 26 July 1843, I-Vt, Sandro Dalla Libera, "*Ernani*-Cronologia" (typescript), and Marcello Conati, *La bottega della musica: Verdi e la Fenice* (Milan: Il Saggiatore, 1983), 62–63. See also Radiciotti, *Gioacchino Rossini*, 1:138, 269–70.

the impresario might be ordered to have the dancers' skirts lengthened by the evening performance.[86] Worse trouble hit the impresario of the Teatro Regio Ducale, Parma, just before the opening of the carnival season of 1837. The director-general of police came backstage with the censor and the supervisory board to demand immediate changes in costumes: some costumes for the ballet were "indecent," and those of the female chorus in *Lucia di Lammermoor* had red and green ribbons on a white background—the tricolor of the Napoleonic Kingdom of Italy. The allusion was quite unintended by the designer, but the chief of police "threatened like a madman that the fortress stood ready for anyone reported to have deviated in the slightest [from his orders]." The man in charge of costumes had the green ribbons hurriedly taken off, but the impresario was so frightened that he insisted on substituting black ribbons at his own expense. The whole breakneck change cost over 1,000 francs.[87] When the Parma chief of police threatened to send people to the fortress he meant business. To such men arrest came easy. The old Italian states nevertheless tried in the first place to control the people involved in the opera season by more bureaucratic means—the company through their passports and the audience through elaborate regulations published and posted at intervals.

Italy was a part of Europe where passports were always needed, not just to go from one petty state to another but to go from one town to another within the same state. This was in itself a problem for itinerant theater people. When Verdi was in Venice preparing *Ernani,* his passport had to be applied for before he could go to Verona (still within the province of Venetia) to hear a possible tenor.[88] In anxious times, as after the 1831 risings at Bologna and Modena, artists might need to produce documentary evidence of an engagement elsewhere if they were to leave town without going through "infinite petitions and applications."[89] Once they reached the *piazza*—the town putting on the opera season—their passports were impounded as a matter of course until the end of the season. In general the point was to stop artists from bolting if they were offered a better engagement elsewhere.

Regulations governing audience behavior were largely uniform across the Italian states. It made little difference whether the government was republican or monarchical, Hapsburg, Bourbon, or Napoleonic, or was operating in the eighteenth century or the nineteenth. Their main points were: to forbid applause in the presence of the ruler (unless he gave the lead); to forbid curtain calls before the end of an act and encores at any time; to forbid whistling (the Italian equivalent of hissing) and excessive noise, including excessive ap-

86. Brunelli, *I teatri di Padova,* 422–23; Ferrari, *Spettacoli drammatico-musicali,* 116.
87. Gazzuoli to Lanari, December 1836, I-Fn, CV 364/104–7.
88. Dalla Libera, "Ernani-Cronologia"; Conati, *La bottega della musica,* 115.
89. Angelo Tinti to Lanari, Bologna, 22 November 1833, I-Fn, CV 411/177.

plause.[90] There are two main explanations of such regulations, which obviously ran counter to the public's inclinations. Governments had a not unjustified fear of riot in the theater; this shifted somewhat from fear of rowdiness in the eighteenth century to fear of political trouble after the French Revolution. At the same time, however, the rules look like another manifestation of the parent-child relationship so many Italians saw as the model for dealings between ruler and subject. This was shown by the way monarchs would deliberately refrain from applauding during a first performance—which was therefore heard in disconcerting silence—but would allow some applause at later performances: they displayed first their paternal power, then their indulgence.[91]

As in many parent-child relationships, however, it was not always clear that prohibitions would stick. A Padua audience in 1794 got the representative of the Venetian Republic to allow an encore of the overture in spite of large placards forbidding such things; when he refused them an encore of a duet, they booed and whistled for half an hour, the performance was suspended, and soldiers were brought in. It was not unknown for a Neapolitan audience to call out to the king in dialect, "Se tu non batti, battimo nui" (If you don't applaud, we will), and for a Milanese audience to defeat an archduke's ban on applause or whistling by all coughing or blowing their noses at once.[92] Faced with this kind of demonstration, governments might threaten: the papal government, which believed in old-fashioned remedies, in 1824 put up a flogging block outside the Teatro Valle as a warning against excessive applause by a *prima donna's* supporters. Or they might retreat: the authorities at Parma changed their regulations in 1833 and 1850, as did those at Bologna in 1852, to allow some encores and curtain calls.[93]

The authorities might also move in and arrest. This was a well-tried procedure. The best-known example of it was the arrest of a singer who had feigned illness or who was alleged to have otherwise broken his or her con-

90. Many sets of regulations are printed in theater histories, such as Ferrari, *Spettacoli drammatico-musicali,* 86, 94–95, 103; Cambiasi, *La Scala,* passim; Radiciotti, *Teatro, musica e musicisti in Sinigaglia,* 190–97. For the Napoleonic period, see also I-Mt, Gride 6/123; I-Ms, CA 244.

91. Pacini, *Le mie memorie,* 34–38 (concerning *Alessandro nell'Indie,* Naples, San Carlo, 1824); Vincenzo Bellini, *Epistolario,* ed. Luisa Cambi (Milan: Mondadori, 1943), 79 (concerning *Bianca e Fernando,* Genoa, Carlo Felice, 1828).

92. Brunelli, *I teatri di Padova,* 327–28; Pacini, *Le mie memorie,* 46–47; Francesco Melzi d'Eril, *Carteggi,* ed. Carlo Zaghi, 9 vols. (Milan: Museo del Risorgimento e Raccolte storiche del Comune di Milano, 1959), 3:239.

93. Alberto Cametti, *Un poeta melodrammatico romano: Appunti e notizie in gran parte inedite sopra Jacopo Ferretti e i musicisti del suo tempo* (Milan, [1898]), 212; Ferrari, *Spettacoli drammatico-musicali,* 174, 229; C. Masini to Deputazione, 30 October 1853, Notificazione, 29 September 1854, I-Bas, ASCB, Dep. Pub. Sp., tit. I, rub. 3, 1853; tit. II, rub. 2, 1854.

tract; the singer was then kept either in prison or under house arrest and was each night brought to the opera house under guard to perform. This happened from time to time to eminent singers and dancers all through the eighteenth century and right up to the 1850s. In a bad case, as when the tenor Alberico Curioni—already arrested once for "insults" to the public—at the end of the season whistled back at the Parma audience, the singer went to the fortress for eight days and was then expelled from the duchy.[94] But supervisory bodies also used arbitrary arrest to punish minor dancers for slanging each other backstage, orchestral players for refusing to play in certain intermezzi, and stagehands for arriving late or for allowing a backcloth to descend in mid scene, recalling the climax of the Marx Brothers' *A Night at the Opera*.[95] Arrest was used as a means of labor discipline.

Yet this was not unmitigated oppression. The arrests lasted as a rule for a few days, sometimes for twenty-four hours or merely overnight. Those arrested were often released as an "act of grace," or on their expressing contrition, or when their friends asked for mercy on their behalf. What was being displayed was, once again, a power relationship between superior and inferior. Nor was the strength all on one side, at least at the level of virtuoso singers and dancers rather than of stagehands. Star performers were aware that their rarity value might more than counterbalance the ruler's will. An English soprano, Clara Novello, for example, was singing at Modena in 1842 during the festivities that attended the marriage of the duke's heir. At one point she refused to sing on her rest day. "They sent down two dragoons to take me off to prison, but I only laughed and said, 'You can put me into prison but who then will sing for the princess?' . . . Only fancy them trying to frighten me like that." Novello's position was different from that of a refractory dancer and first violinist at Faenza in 1788: they—it was pointed out to the authorities—could be dealt with by force because they were not irreplaceable.[96] Arrest was also commonly used to keep order in the audito-

94. Barbaja to Soprintendenza, 8, 12 April 1822, I-Nas, Teatri, fol. 98 (arrest of minor singer for refusing to sing in the chorus); Deputazione to Minister, 10 June 1825, I-Nas, Min. Interno II inv., fol. 4356 (arrest of choreographer Henry and leading dancers Samengo and Brugnoli over failure to dance a pas de deux that had been announced); Gandini, *Cronistoria dei teatri di Modena*, 1:149; Crocioni, *I teatri di Reggio*, 71; Giuseppe Pasolini-Zanelli, *Il Teatro di Faenza* (Faenza, 1888), 67 (arrest of Giorgio Ronconi for giving an encore without permission); Brunelli, *I teatri di Padova*, 432–33; Santley, *Student and Singer*, 79–81; Ferrari, *Spettacoli drammatico-musicali*, 102.

95. Promemoria serale per lo spettacolo autunnale 1852, Teatro Comunale, Bologna, I-Bas, ASCB, Dep. Pub. Sp., tit. I, rub. 1, 1853; Soprintendente to Minister, 14 December 1817, I-Nas, Min. Interno II inv., fol. 4353; Vaccai, *Vita di Nicola Vaccaj*, 110–11.

96. Averil Mackenzie-Grieve, *Clara Novello* (London: Bles, 1955), 119; Gioanni Tacconi to Count Francesco Conti, 5 April 1788, I-FOc, Piancastelli 130.13.

rium. It was a means used alongside rather than in place of institutional justice. Criminal prosecution still dealt with serious offenses, and civil jurisdiction was not ignored: a singer who was made to perform under threat of arrest, like Luigia Boccabadati at Naples in 1831, could still take the issue under dispute before the courts and win.[97] The rule of status and the rule of contract went on side by side.

Not even impresarios were immune from arrest when a first night angered the audience or, occasionally, when a company was left unpaid or a nobleman in authority thought he had been insulted.[98] The examples we have all date from before 1820. Impresarios were anyhow the first to ask the authorities for help in organizing their seasons and sometimes in keeping discipline. Barbaja's and Lanari's notion of how to get defaulting singers and musicians to turn up or composers to finish their work on time was to go to the police. Balochino, more subtly, hinted that a singer who did not honor his contract to sing in a government theater might in future have trouble getting a passport.[99]

It made sense to turn to the governments, who wanted to see the best possible season and were prepared to exert themselves to get it. The brother of the king of Naples interceded on Barbaja's behalf with the ruling duke of Lucca to have a tenor released from his contract there, the papal nuncio in Vienna several times persuaded leading singers and dancers to appear at the Senigallia fair, and the cardinal secretary of state—the nearest thing in Rome to a prime minister—was at one time trying to remedy a shortage of bassoon players. Diplomats or chiefs of police in other states could be asked to report on a new singer or inquire whether it was true that a dancer was pregnant.[100]

Control of opera seasons and of discipline in the theater was one matter where Italian unification made a difference. The prefect—the representative of central authority in each province—and the police still had wide powers to keep order; seasons could not begin without police permission. But it was no longer their business to enforce private obligations through arbitrary ar-

97. Gaetano Badolisani, *Per la signora Donna Luigia Boccabadati* (Naples, 1832), a printed brief of an argument in the Biblioteca della Società Napoletana di Storia Patria; I-Nas, Giustizia, Decisioni civili, fol. 95, 27 March 1832.

98. Cambiasi, *La Scala*, 49; Beniamino Gutierrez, *Il Teatro Carcano (1803–1914)* (Milan: Sonzogno, 1914), 41–43; Crocioni, *I teatri di Reggio*, 51–54; I-Mt, Sp. P. 56, correspondence on the arrest of Angelo Petracchi, 1819.

99. Noja to the Minister, 30 April 1821, I-Nas, Min. Interno II inv., fol. 4355; Pacini, *Le mie memorie*, 58–59; Lanari to the Presidenza of La Fenice, 16 December 1831, I-Vt, Spettacoli, busta 3; Carlo Balochino to Giorgio Ronconi, 18 November 1839, Wiener Stadtbibliothek.

100. Barbaja to Lorenzo Panzieri, 12 July 1827, I-Fn, CV 344/118; Radiciotti, *Teatro, musica e musicisti in Sinigaglia*, 92–93; Rinaldi, *Due secoli di musica*, 1:363–65; I-Rburcardo, Fondo Capranica, correspondence 1826–27; Basso, *Il teatro della città*, 294; I-Vt, Autografi diversi, s. v. "Fanny Cerrito."

rest or to demand that impresarios should provide financial guarantees. The army by 1870 no longer mounted a military guard in the theater.[101] Liberal individualism had come to power, and with it the belief in the primacy of contract and the rule of law. It became easier for impresarios and artists to default; disputes now ended more often in court.

For the opera world the change was at first disconcerting. The police in Bologna in the first months after unification were still being asked to compel a ballet dancer to perform or to make a financial guarantor pay up; they appear to have swung between trying informal persuasion and referring petitioners to the courts.[102] Storms of booing and whistling, of the kind that stopped performances or even cut short a season, seem in later years to have become more frequent in some of the towns of Emilia-Romagna, a region that combined political radicalism with headlong partisanship in operatic matters. This happened at Modena in 1862, 1866, and 1869, and at Cesena in 1870. At Parma, where there had already been one suspension in 1857, serious trouble recurred in 1865, 1870, 1872, 1878, 1879, and 1882. In most of those years performances had to be stopped, sometimes before the end of the first act, and on two occasions the booing was such that *prime donne* fainted on stage.[103]

Even before unification, opera audiences in Emilia-Romagna had the reputation of being hard to please, but it was in those years that Parma especially came to be known (it still is) as a place where a stentorian tenor might set off avalanches of applause but other singers might feel that they were lucky to get away unhurt. Declining standards in a former capital had something to do with it, but so had the withdrawal of the strong arm that had formerly kept the lid down on the passions the human voice can rouse.

4. *The Profession of the Impresario*

Opera houses of the eighteenth and early nineteenth centuries were still organized and run on a family basis. People who made a success brought in fathers, brothers, and nephews, some to do jobs of work and others as hangers-on. It comes as no surprise that a good many impresarios were the sons of impresarios or of other theater people. They might also be themselves artists,

101. Rosmini, *La legislazione*, vol. 1, chap. 4, 2:13–15, 336–37; correspondence of the Prefect and the Direzione of the Teatro Comunale, Parma, March 1870, I-PAt, carteggi 1870.

102. I-Bas, ASCB, Dep. Pub. Sp., tit. I, rub. 1, 3, 1860, passim.

103. Gandini, *Cronistoria dei teatri di Modena*, vol. 2; Raggi and Raggi, *Il Teatro Comunale di Cesena*, 132; Ferrari, *Spettacoli drammatico-musicali*, 246, 252, 257–58, 267, 271, 290, 295, 312.

in general former singers (for the most part who had failed or who had undistinguished careers) or choreographers. The latter were more apt to go on with their old line of work. The organizing skills needed to devise the ballets of the time, with their elaborate plots and scene changes and their crowds of extras, were after all akin to those of management in general, and we find some well-known choreographers among the impresarios—Onorato Viganò, Lorenzo Panzieri, Livio Morosini, Domenico Ronzani. For similar reasons the owner of a costume workshop (they were often described as *capitalisti di vestiario*) found it easy to become an impresario, both because of the importance given to "splendor" in the season's offerings (the contracts in leading theaters stipulated that everything had to be new if possible and that leading singers' costumes must be made entirely of silk and velvet) and because it was convenient for them to take on a season as a means of getting a return on their stock. Less often impresarios were musicians who took on the running of a season, usually as a last resort when a professional impresario had failed part way through and as a way of keeping the orchestra employed.

Theater management by an association of nobles declined but never totally disappeared. After the Napoleonic period it was generally recognized that management by an association of nobles (normal practice in some leading theaters during the eighteenth century, Turin, Milan, and Bologna in particular) was extravagant and expensive, a notion confirmed by an attempt to revive it in the Turin royal theaters between 1824 and 1833.[104] On the same grounds associations of boxholder-proprietors like those of La Fenice, Venice, did their best to attract professional impresarios. In Venice and other cities—with Rome a notable exception—family owners had mostly given way to boxholders' associations or to professionals in controlling and running seasons. Some members of the upper classes who took an active interest in an opera *impresa* had singers or ballerinas as their mistresses or wives. One of these was an expatriate member of the English gentry, Joseph Glossop, whose fling as an impresario ended in failure in two houses at once, La Scala and San Carlo, in 1824–25. Others seem to have been speculators, such as Duke Carlo Visconti di Modrone, the impresario of La Scala from 1833 until his death in 1836.

What we hardly find in Italy is the kind of bourgeois impresario who flourished in Paris in the middle decades of the nineteenth century—men with professional or journalistic backgrounds and aptitudes for speculative ventures, such as Louis Véron and his successors at the Paris Opéra. The few bourgeois impresarios we do find were tradesmen, such as Andrea Campigli, a jeweller (at La Pergola from 1775 to 1789), the Neapolitan typographer Vincenzio Flauto, the Roman grocer *(droghiere)* Pietro Cartoni (1776–1848),

104. Basso, *Il teatro della città*, 178–204.

and his rivals, first Giovanni Paterni (1779–1837), a distiller, then Vincenzo Jacovacci (1811–81), a fishmonger. In Rome this type of impresario continued to run seasons until after Italian unification, in close dependence on the small number of noble families who owned theaters (first the Capranica and the Sforza-Cesarini families, later the Torlonia family). Cartoni, who put on the first performance of Rossini's *La Cenerentola* at the Teatro Valle in 1816, had his flat and shop in the Marchese Capranica's palace and supplied Capranica's household with chocolate and candles besides running some of his theater seasons. Jacovacci was famous for his shopkeeper's outlook and his penny-pinching, but the low level of subsidies in papal Rome also played a part in his economies. When Verdi complained that the women singers for the first performance of *Un ballo in maschera* (1859) were all mediocre, Jacovacci replied that the house was full anyhow, adding, "Next year I'll get hold of some good women singers, so the opera will still be new for the audience. This year half—later the other half." [105] Like old-style traders, Paterni and Cartoni attempted to outbid one another for the monopoly of theatrical production in Rome by competing to see which one could offer the papal government more Etruscan vases and other antiquities for the Vatican Museum. [106]

Another way of gaining entry to the running of opera seasons was gambling promotion, in particular during and immediately after the Napoleonic period. From the early eighteenth century on, the opera house, as the center of social life, was usually the place where the upper classes gambled: that was the purpose of the spacious foyers in Italian opera houses of the age. The old Italian governments sometimes permitted games of chance, sometimes not, but even when faro and roulette were forbidden, operagoers were allowed to bet small sums on milder games such as backgammon. In the eighteenth century the normal practice was to forbid games of chance everywhere else but to grant a monopoly concession to the impresario of the opera house. This monopoly was abolished at various dates between 1753 and 1788 as "enlightened" principles spread through the Italian states, but from 1802 the new states of Napoleonic Italy revived it as a means of raising badly needed revenue. Large garrisons, free-spending governments, and wartime upheaval between them made Milan, Naples, and the spa of Bagni di Lucca centers of gambling on an unexampled scale: between 1802 and 1810 those impresarios who had the gambling concession enjoyed a bonanza. But the restoration governments once again suppressed the monopoly, in north and central Italy from 1814 and in Naples and Sicily from 1820. Only the tiny Duchy of Lucca went on upholding the monopoly—and financing opera sea-

105. Franco Abbiati, *Giuseppe Verdi*, vol. 4 (Milan: Ricordi, 1959), 2:529; Giuseppe Verdi, *I copialettere*, 570–71, 575–76.

106. I-Rs, Camerale III, Teatri, busta 2138, nos. 22–23, 30–31.

sons at Lucca of unusual quality for so small a place—until it too was taken away in 1847.[107]

Eighteenth-century impresarios as a matter of course organized gambling, provided cards and dice, and collected profits of which part had to be paid to the state or to a charity. That did not make the impresarios crooks, though there were crooks among them, such as the Neapolitan Giuseppe Affligio (1722–88), who began as a cardsharp around army camps and managed to become a colonel, a rich man, and the impresario of the Vienna court theaters from 1767 to 1769, and who, in the latter year, was arrested for forgery and sentenced to the galleys. The impresarios who came up with the Napoleonic gambling monopoly were not like that. They were a close-knit group that dominated opera in Milan for a quarter century (in Naples and Vienna for longer still): men such as Francesco Benedetto Ricci, who ran La Scala throughout the Napoleonic years (one of the theater's most splendid periods, at least in ballet and scene design), Crivelli, who started in Turin but moved on to Milan and Venice before his death in 1831, and, above all, Balochino (1770–1850) and Barbaja (1778–1841). Barbaja, a Milanese and a former café waiter, made his first success with the new game of roulette. He joined forces with Balochino to create a gambling syndicate with a monopoly on gambling throughout much of Italy, following in the wake of the French armies; at the same time (in 1809) he began his nearly thirty-year career as the quasi-permanent impresario of the royal theaters of Naples (working in some years in Milan and Vienna as well).

As a pair, Balochino and Barbaja tell us much about the way the Italian theater functioned. Balochino was stubborn but controlled and wrote educated Italian in correspondence; Barbaja was exuberant, scarcely literate, and such letters as he wrote in his own hand were spelled phonetically in Milanese Italian (he wrote "Lugharesia Borgia," and rendered *L'assedio di Calais* as "Lasedio dicale") and bespattered not only with vigorous multiple dashes and underlinings but also with swearwords. There was no doubt of who was boss. Barbaja became a millionaire and lived like one. His millions came not just from the gambling monopoly but from army contracts in the Napoleonic period and then from large-scale building contracts employing thousands of men (the new Teatro San Carlo, rebuilt after a fire in 1816, was among his firm's projects). He quickly developed the tastes of a millionaire: diamonds, racehorses, a picture collection, not to mention his mistress, the famous soprano Isabella Colbran, who later became Rossini's wife. Despite his rough exterior, his naïveté, and his irritability (he was quick to call others "murderers" and himself an ass—*coglione*), Barbaja had considerable organizing ge-

---

107. For a detailed account of gambling, see John Rosselli, "Governi, appaltatori e giuochi d'azzardo nell'Italia napoleonica," *Rivista storica italiana* 93 (1981): 346–83.

nius (which he applied to gaming rooms), and governments appreciated him because he paid on the nail. When he applied his considerable talents to the opera stage, he not only showed himself capable of putting on grandiose productions but demonstrated uncommon dramatic and musical taste: he seems to have contributed to assuring Mozart's success in Italy, and he put on all of Rossini's Neapolitan serious operas from *Elisabetta regina d'Inghilterra* to *Zelmira* and may have marked them with his influence, particularly in the great ensemble and choral scenes, such as the introduction to *Mosè in Egitto*.

Another and more modern model for the impresario came from a theatrical agency—not the more questionable sort of agency akin to venal journalism discussed below, but of the relatively more solid and trustworthy sort. The figure who represented the agent or journalist type of impresario at its most successful was Bartolomeo Merelli (1794–1879). The son of a steward to a noble family of Bergamo, Merelli was destined for the law, but he showed talent early on as an agent and librettist (for his young fellow townsman Donizetti, among other composers). After an awkward episode when he was eighteen in which he was accused of attempted theft from the house of a noblewoman, Merelli made his way to Milan, where he became a busy theatrical agent: at the height of his activities, he wrote some eight thousand letters a year. He was one of the few agents to develop a system of giving artists long-term contracts and then trying to make a profit by selling their services. When he became an impresario himself, he placed his own artists at La Scala (above all) and its sister theater, the Canobbiana (where he ran seasons for much of the twenty-year period from 1828 to 1848), at the Kärntnertortheater, Vienna, (1836–59, which he ran with a partner, Balochino, until 1848) and in many other cities and towns in northern Italy. Merelli became a rich man, kept English horses, and accumulated a collection of paintings by old masters, but he also spent years trying to prove his aristocratic origins and seems to have deliberately behaved like a gentleman and to have been treated like one. This mania for gentility may have had something to do with the lack of professionalism for which both Verdi and Donizetti reproached him. Verdi, who owed Merelli a great deal—it was Merelli who launched him and who got him out of his depression after the deaths of his wife and children and into the composition of *Nabucco*—nevertheless refused to let La Scala put on any more of his works after experiencing Merelli's shabby productions. Donizetti, who may also have owed Merelli something, complained of careless staging and cavalier treatment of his music.[108] His real failing was probably glibness; he remained the agent who assumes that all is well when the right "package" has been put together and does not follow through.

---

108. Abbiati, *Giuseppe Verdi*, 1:539, 546, 604–5, 673; Guido Zavadini, *Donizetti: Vita, musiche, epistolario* (Bergamo: Istituto Italiano d'Arti Grafiche, 1948), 696, 815.

Yet an ideal of the professional impresario did exist. So far as it was embodied in any one man, that man was Alessandro Lanari (1787–1852). The virtues of Lanari's that struck contemporaries were his knowledge and competence in all branches of his business and his care for what are now called production values, especially the finish and historical authenticity of sets and costumes. It was for good reason that Verdi trusted him with the premiere of *Macbeth*, well aware that it needed careful production. Fairly soon in Lanari's career, which ran from at least as early as 1819 until his death, an observer stressed his talent as a producer: "Costumes, scenery, even part of the ballet are directed by him, and he is expert in all of them. I see him on stage in the evening doing what few people could manage, always coolly and without getting upset."[109] A creature of the theater in all things, Lanari married a successful singer, and when they separated he lived with another (but minor) singer. The two main influences that shaped his career were theatrical as well—that is, the costume workshop in Florence that he took over in 1823 and the agency that he founded during the 1820s in which he, much like Merelli, gave promising singers long-term contracts and then tried to place them at a profit. Workshop and agency both led Lanari to form circuits where his costumes and his singers could be exploited with the fewest possible gaps. One circuit took in Florence, Lucca, and the secondary towns of Tuscany and Umbria, particularly Pisa, Livorno, Siena, Perugia, and Foligno, a region in which Lanari, despite some competition over the running of La Pergola in Florence, enjoyed a near monopoly. The larger circuit on which Lanari operated took in almost the whole of operatic Italy except for Turin, Genoa, and Trieste. He had long runs of seasons at La Fenice, Venice, and at the Senigallia fair; he also worked at various times in other cities, often in partnership with others. During his busy career he launched two of Bellini's operas, two of Verdi's, and five of Donizetti's.[110] He also helped to launch some of the finest singers of the day, in particular the French tenor Gilbert-Louis Duprez, who, under the guidance in Italy of Lanari and Pietro Romani, chief *répétiteur* at the Pergola, became a first-rate singer and was credited with the discovery of the "chest-voice high C" that changed the development of the tenor voice.

All this was done with the impresario constantly on the move, firing off

109. G. Caroselli to Marchese Capranica, Ancona 5 June 1827, I-Rburcardo, Fondo Capranica. See also Marcello Conati, "Aspetti della messinscena del *Macbeth* di Verdi," *Nuova rivista musicale italiana* 15 (1981): 374–404.

110. The nine operas were: *I Capuleti e i Montecchi, Beatrice di Tenda, Attila, Macbeth, La Parisina, Rosmonda d'Inghilterra, Lucia di Lammermoor, Pia de' Tolomei,* and *Maria di Rudenz.* This account of Lanari's career is based on a large amount of correspondence in I-Fn, CV, and elsewhere. See also Regli, *Dizionario biografico;* Marcello de Angelis, *Le carte dell'impresario: Melodramma e costume teatrale nell'Ottocento* (Florence: Sansoni, 1982), which is based on the Fondo Lanari, Biblioteca Nazionale di Firenze, a catalog of which De Angelis has published in his *Le cifre del melodramma.*

letters to partners and subordinates elsewhere while he rehearsed new works for the season he had chosen to run himself. While Lanari was away his widowed sister, a semiliterate woman, ran the costume workshop; a nephew accompanied him as secretary; other relatives and retainers, among them a couple of broken-down former impresarios, did various jobs at his Florence headquarters. Despite the broad scope of his affairs and his thorough knowledge of his craft, Lanari was narrow in his dealings with all these people and a hard taskmaster. When his common-law wife Carlotta Corazza exclaimed with pleasure on first hearing Duprez's voice at rehearsal, Lanari slapped her—her praise might drive up the young tenor's price.[111] Nothing was too small for him to scrutinize. When away from Florence he insisted on trying to control the number of sequins bought for the workshop and the price paid for cloth. If the price seemed too high, he complained that he was being "assassinated." Because he was suspicious he did not delegate authority clearly, and the people he left in charge quarreled among themselves. He snapped at his subordinates when they failed to consult him ("I ought to be everywhere"); he snapped at them just as much when they pestered him with detail ("I don't know how you expect me to deal with such matters from here").[112] Yet Lanari had every reason to drive and be driven. His finances were precarious. He depended on a complex traffic in credit notes that might or might not keep him solvent; at several points in his career he was in serious difficulties. Probably it was his tireless attention to the price of sequins, as well as to the detail of costumes and scenery, that kept him going. After withdrawing as impresario in the financial disasters of 1848–49, Lanari made up his mind to take on running seasons in Bologna (though not under his own name), but he died in 1852 before he could recover fully, and his son Antonio, trained as a lawyer, took over but went bankrupt ten years later.

Alessandro Lanari had shown that a hard-working impresario could make a career on a national scale—indeed international, for Lanari's agency had a branch in Paris, run in partnership with Achille Lorini, and at various times he supplied singers for European cities and for the fast developing American market, especially Havana and New York. For all his being a product of the theater world who had learned his craft from the bottom up, he also stood at the apex of respectability in opera management and bourgeois morality. Lanari had been haunted by the fear of cutting a poor figure *(sfigurare)* in a world where bankruptcy had been equated with "civil death."[113]

In this still largely artisanal climate, the unit of management in opera—the firm—was essentially an individual even though that individual might

111. Gilbert-Louis Duprez, *Souvenirs d'un chanteur* (Paris, 1880), 79.
112. To Basetti, 14 January 1837, to Bonini, March 1845, I-Fn, CV 345/94, 348/141.
113. Gazzuoli to Niccola Dottori, 31 July 1836, I-Fn, CV 364/91.

move about surrounded by a group of dependent relatives and assistants. Collective management was difficult when secrecy was considered of the greatest importance. Jacovacci, for example, did not like people to know even the date on which he was to set out on a journey.[114] Indeed, the attempts that were made to run opera seasons collectively all ended badly.

The noblemen's joint-stock association of the eighteenth century was by and large a thing of the past; in the nineteenth century noblemen might still join with citizens (among whom there might be a professional impresario), but this kind of collective effort was generally found in small towns and for special occasions such as the opening of a new theater. It was not the way opera management was normally carried on.[115] Collective management by artists, musicians, and perhaps stage staff was as a rule limited to one season and was intended to make the best of a bad job when a professional impresario could not be had or went bankrupt part way through his contract. This sort of management also had variants: the Teatro del Corso, Bologna, was managed in 1853 by an association based on twenty-six shares of about 105 francs each, four of which shares were held jointly by members of the municipal orchestra, two by the lessee and sometime impresario of the Corso, and others by non-noble citizens of the town, with an agent as nominee. This too was said to be a means of keeping musicians and theater people in work for a season, even though at an almost certain loss.[116] Collective management on something like this mixed pattern was to become common in the difficult last years of the century. It is best understood as a mixture of self-help and patronage, intended as a stopgap rather than as a substitute for commercial management.

Joint managements *(imprese sociali)* involving professional impresarios seem to have been of two main types. One was the partnership or series of interlocking partnerships with unlimited liability, at least for certain purposes. The other was the limited liability company *(società anonima)* whose shares might be promoted and sold to members of the public. Partnerships were fairly common, and they sometimes went on for a number of years, but the examples that can be studied seem all to have been unstable. Limited liability companies had about them more than a touch of wishful thinking; two that were launched in Naples promptly fell apart.

A partnership might bring together a well-known singer who invested his savings and an impresario who needed capital for a deposit of caution money; a more disreputable form involved giving a young singer a share in the man-

114. Jacovacci to Pippo [Cencetti], 1850, Piancastelli Autografi, s. v. "Jacovacci."

115. The new theater at Faenza was managed in its opening season in 1788 by an association of forty-six shareholders, both nobles and citizens, including Osea Francia and Vincenzo Caldesi: Papers of Faenza *impresa*, I-FOc, Piancastelli 130.1–14, 39–79, 119, 180, 184, 212.

116. I-Bas, Comune, Dep. Pub. Sp., tit. I, rub. 2, 1853.

agement instead of a fee.[117] Partnerships among impresarios that aimed at a run of several seasons, occasionally in more than one city, were more complex. They were meant to unite complementary interests: one man's holding of costumes, another man's contracts with artists, a third man's local connections or expertise. Such partnerships as are documented all involved Alessandro Lanari and at least one other impresario. They were all based on Lanari's costume workshop, and most if not all of them on his long-term contract artists as well. Their exact legal form is not known, but it involved unlimited liability within the limited purposes of the partnerships, which were all aimed at running specific seasons or series of seasons. The experience of such associations, which were perhaps not typical of others for which there is less documentation, was not encouraging. After a first arrangement to run seasons at La Pergola, Florence, 1823–28, in partnership with the choreographer Lorenzo Panzieri and the tenor Nicola Tacchinardi—a relatively harmonious venture—Lanari was involved in other attempts that ended badly, first with Merelli and Crivelli for the management of La Scala and La Fenice in 1828–31, and second in a complex set of interlocking arrangements with various other impresarios for seasons at Florence, Parma, Bologna, and Venice in 1836–38. They failed in part because the interests at play were not truly compatible, because of difficulties inherent in running a partnership by post when complex decisions regarding a number of cities had to be taken, and because each man was used to trusting only in continuous personal control. "We spend all our time," Lanari's representative reported, "with the partnership contract in our hands."[118] Partnerships, even so, were a fairly normal way of running seasons. Limited liability companies were, in opera management, a freak. Not that they differed greatly in this from other companies that were floated in Naples in the 1830s, often by the same mixed group of noble reformers, foreign merchants, and monopoly concessionaires.

The problem of financing opera management through a limited liability company was that although shareholders were protected from having to meet losses beyond the amount of their stake, there was little hope of attracting them through regular cash dividends. Promoters accordingly devised schemes whereby shareholders would be rewarded in free entry tickets to the opera house or free seats: what they proposed was a kind of opera consumer cooperative.

117. Examples of the first kind proposed to the baritone Giovanni Marchetti by the impresario Federico Radicchi (for Chieti, P1886) and Filippo Moreno (for somewhere in Tuscany or Romagna, P1887), I-FOc, Piancastelli, Autografi s. v. "Marchetti"; of the second kind, between the debutante soprano Zaira Tamburini and the (ultimately defaulting) impresario Salani, Teatro Contavalli, Bologna, P1860, I-Bas, ASCB, Dep. Pub. Sp., tit. I, rub. 3, 1860.

118. Gazzuoli to Lanari, February 1837, I-Fn, CV 364/119.

One program of this sort, perhaps among the first but never put into effect, proposed a "new form of association" to manage the Teatro Comunale in Bologna in 1780 that was to have no fewer than eight hundred shareholders.[119] A much bigger venture was the Compagnia d'Industria e Belle Arti, which actually ran the 1834–35 season in the Naples royal theaters before foundering. The association offered its shareholders the prospect of cash dividends as well as of benefits in theater seats, to be distributed daily. The nobles, merchants, and bankers who ran it enjoyed the services of the ubiquitous Alessandro Lanari, in the threefold capacity of shareholder, salaried manager, and provider of artists under contract. The season was lavish, and by the summer of 1835 the company was in deep trouble. It just managed to put on the first performance of *Lucia di Lammermoor*, with Lanari's prize contract artist Duprez, before going out of business.[120] In 1836–40 a new limited liability company succeeded the Compagnia d'Industria e Belli Arte, a more restricted affair without any attempt at a consumer cooperative that involved the aging Barbaja, Prince Ottajano (a central figure in Naples business ventures of those years), and the rising impresario Vincenzio Flauto. The company lost money and finally split up, in particular because of a sustained campaign on the part of Flauto and Ottajano aimed at putting Barbaja in the wrong.[121] In spite of this record, proposals for yet another limited liability company to run the theaters as a consumer cooperative were being put forward in 1850; by 1858 a joint venture by nobles and non-nobles was running them (under what arrangements is not clear) but was once again deeply divided.[122]

Why did these Naples companies run into such trouble? We do not know their affairs in enough detail to be sure. The principle of a consumer cooperative need not have been absurd, but it was fatally optimistic to link it with a

119. "Foglio di associazione per un dramma serio in musica da rappresentarsi nel nuovo Pubblico Teatro la primavera dell'anno 1780" (printed prospectus), I-Bas, Assunteria di Camera, Diversorum, tomo 128.

120. *Proposta di una società commerciale in anonimo per la intrapresa dei RR. Teatri* (Naples, 1834); *Progetto di statuto della Compagnia d'Industria e Belle Arti* (Naples, 1834); Antonio Larussa, *Sulle cagioni del decadimento delli spettacoli nelli teatri in Napoli* (Naples, 1850), 7–9; *Almanacco de' Teatri Reali San Carlo e Fondo dell'annata teatrale 1834* (Naples, 1835). The first two pamphlets are in the British Library; the second two in Biblioteca Lucchesi-Palli, Naples. See also Zavadini, *Donizetti*, 373–83; Lanari's correspondence with the prince of Torella and with Francesco Capecelatro and Salvatore Taglioni, I-Fn, CV 352/175, 411/108.

121. Marchese Domenico Andreotti to Lanari, 28 October 1837, I-Fn, VC 343/35; [Antonio Starace], *Per alcuni socii nella impresa de' RR. Teatri contro il signor Domenico Barbaja socio impresario* (Naples, 1839).

122. Antonio Larussa, *Poche idee spontanee in rapporto alli teatri* (Naples, 1850), in the Biblioteca Lucchesi-Palli; Vincenzo Torelli to Pacini, 2 February 1858, I-PEA, Pacini 1080.

hope of cash profits, all the more so when government subsidy was falling. The companies, besides, operated in an economy where capital was short; such trade as went on was often in the hands of foreigners, and even they depended largely on the government. These enterprises are best seen as an aspect of the short-lived 1830s boom during the early years of the reign of Ferdinando II, a period in which illusions abounded.[123] The Società Impresaria Romandiolo-Picena, launched in 1856 as another attempt to create a consumers' cooperative, lasted somewhat longer, running seasons in the Marches and in Romagna before it disappeared.[124]

This is not to say that individual impresarios did not at times cooperate. They did, at arm's length. They sometimes cashed each other's bills of exchange and gave each other credit in a sort of rudimentary banking system, at least when they trusted each other enough. They exchanged information, within limits. They very occasionally attempted to create operatic cartels or to divide Italy into spheres of influence. In the bad years of 1848–49, Lanari, with his costume workshop based in Florence, and Pietro Camuri and Antonio Ghelli, owners of the leading Bologna workshop, agreed to divide Italy between Rome and the river Po and not to hire out costumes on each other's territory, or at least to do so only by consent and on payment of a commission—a far cry from the late 1830s when Lanari had tried to corner the costume market in the whole of this area.[125] They formed rings when authorities in control of theaters sought to put the management up to auction, either sending in more or less identical bids or collectively staying away, though this probably did not happen quite so often as a Milan official thought: "These people," he wrote, "are generally united in their interests while pretending [to compete]."[126] Rings and cartels seem to have been formed most often when times were bad. When there was a hope of profit, an outsider was likely to come in and spoil the game.

The outlook that led to the formation of rings was at bottom monopolistic. It assumed that resources were limited and that the ideal arrangement was for a single impresario or group of impresarios to deal with a single theater controller. This assumption was probably sound, up to the mid-nineteenth century at any rate. Not only did the hierarchical array of Italian

123. John A. Davis, *Società e imprenditori nel Regno Borbonico 1815–1860* (Bari: Laterza, 1979), 148–69.

124. Prospectus of the Società Impresaria Romandiolo-Picena, I-Bas, Comune, Dep. Pub. Sp., tit. IV, rub. 2, 1855; *Teatri, arti e letteratura* 74, no. 38 (1860–61): 94–95; 75, no. 39 (1861–62): 29–30.

125. Correspondence of Lanari, Camuri, Ghelli, and Agostino Marchesi, I-Fn, CV 365/120, 123–24, 132.

126. Paolo De' Capitani, marginal note on minute on Government of Lombardy to I. R. Chancellery, 2 June 1828, I-Mt, Sp. P. 56.

society make opera a privileged genre; the restricted size of the upper-class opera audience in most Italian towns might well make competition ruinous.

The same monopolistic outlook helps to explain the recurrent "wars" between theaters giving opera seasons. These might occur even between neighboring towns. For an opera season at Vicenza in 1787 to coincide with one at Padua was regarded by Paduans as an outrage. In 1791–92 Padua itself was split between parties supporting rival theaters until the government stepped in and forced a compromise agreement to divide up their seasons.[127] There the initiative came from noble theater owners. Elsewhere the impresarios carried on the struggle themselves. Lanari's Livorno agent regarded it as self-evidently outrageous for another impresario to send a company to that city when he knew that Lanari was about to put on the opening season at a new opera house: such behavior warranted taking steps to spoil the other man's business or force him out altogether. In Bologna, where the regulations allowed only two theaters to open during the spring season, another agent advised contracting to put on a season of plays at a minor theater alongside the opera season at the Comunale for the sole purpose of keeping out a rival opera season at a third house. It did not matter whether or not the prose season materialized: it would pay to engage a theater company and then keep it idle if this would guarantee monopoly of opera.[128] Even after the mid-century expansion of audiences and theaters, the impresario of the Teatro del Corso, Bologna, claimed in 1879 to have been ruined because the rival Teatro Brunetti had unexpectedly prolonged its opera season into Lent.[129] Although some of these rivalries seem to have been dictated by spite—Jacovacci was advised to sign up two promising young singers mostly so as to deny them to Lanari[130]—a more consistent explanation lay in a widespread and monopolistic outlook in preindustrial societies, where secrecy, close-fistedness, perhaps deceit were prime commercial virtues.

Yet in other ways theatrical business dealings had a modern aspect. This was shown first in the impresario's reliance on contract and second in their eagerness to work a free labor market, especially when it was likely to favor them. Opera contracts went back to the Venetian public theaters of the early seventeenth century. At that time they were simple agreements by performers to appear at a certain theater for a given fee. By the first half of the eighteenth century, they had grown far more elaborate. By 1780 such a wealth of practice had built up that printed forms began to come in; impresarios went on revising them throughout the nineteenth century to keep up with court judgments

127. Brunelli, *I teatri di Padova*, 211–12, 271ff.

128. To Lanari from Costantino Brendoli, Livorno, June 1841, from Gazzuoli, Bologna, December 1836, I-Fn, CV 350/43–44, 364/98, 100.

129. Angelo Vitti to Marchetti, I-FOc, Piancastelli, Autografi, s. v. "Marchetti."

130. Antonio Tassinari to Jacovacci, 6 June 1841, I-FOc, Piancastelli 690.69.

and if possible to tighten them up in their own favor.[131] The rule of contract, though, went hand in hand with the rule of custom. The many recognized customs governing theatrical affairs seem not to have been written down systematically until the appearance in 1823 of Giovanni Valle's manual—itself a sign that a more cash-bound and impersonal outlook was coming. Contracts, Valle wrote, should be as specific as possible, but various points were so well understood that they need not be spelled out. For example, leading performers must not appear in the season preceding the one they were contracted for anywhere within sixty miles (minor performers not within thirty miles); "within the first days of the month" meant "up to the 10th"; an obligation on singers to perform whatever they were given did not mean that they must undertake roles damaging to their voices, and so on.[132]

As the nineteenth century wore on, these customs were increasingly written down in contracts; after unification the sixty-mile rule was simply turned into a sixty-kilometer rule. Points that Valle had thought well understood were tested in the courts. In the early years of the century the administrative office *(camerino)* of La Scala had by custom settled disputed points among impresarios and artists throughout Italy, but by 1823 Valle thought its authority obsolete.[133] If this suggests an increased readiness to go to law—and there was plenty of litigation throughout the remainder of the century—that too points to a slow shift away from reliance on custom and personal ties and toward more strictly contractual relationships.

Such a shift took place in the contracts that gave impresarios their seasonal concessions. A form still in use at the Comunale, Bologna, in 1782, but probably obsolescent, said nothing at all about the program, the artists, or the seat prices apart from stating that there would be two operas—presumably because the Bologna authorities intended to settle these matters themselves. What the form did talk about was the theater building, scenery and scenic equipment, safety regulations, boxholders' rights, theater employees to be kept on, the free list, and the impresario's rent payment and caution money.[134] At the other extreme the form of contract for La Scala in 1887 took up seven closely printed pages and dealt even with the material the corps de ballet's shoes were to be made of (only the front two rows got satin). This complexity was much more typical of late eighteenth- and nineteenth-century contracts,

131. See Giovan Battista Cavalcaselle, *Tipi di scritture teatrali attraverso luoghi e tempi diversi* (Rome: Athenaeum, 1919); Rosmini, *La legislazione,* 1:417.

132. Valle, *Cenni teorico-pratici,* 24–34, 85–88, 91.

133. Barbaja maintained in 1837 that the writ of the Milan *camerino* still ran, but he had been out of north-central Italy for many years and was probably mistaken (or else was prevaricating): to Lanari, 6 August, 1837, I-Fn, CV 344/167.

134. Draft contract, 1782, identical with actual contract of 1769 with Giuseppe Mienci, I-Bas, Assunteria di Camera, Diversorum, tomo 128.

which included all the main headings of the Bologna contract except rent but also provided elaborately for the number and kinds of operas and ballets to be given, the number and frequency of performances, and the dates by which every aspect of every production was to be submitted to the supervisory board for approval. One missing feature that had been common earlier in the century was the requirement in leading theaters that soloists should be already successful *(di cartello)*. This requirement had been resisted by impresarios in bad times; it faded out in the 1860s and 1870s with the general crisis of the old opera system, and it was deliberately abolished in Naples in 1884.[135]

Impresarios on the whole tried to carry out the terms of their contracts or else asked the controlling authority to exempt them. Though charges of bad faith were common, only seldom do we find evidence of impresarios deliberately flouting their obligations—and then not without some excuse. To meet the demand of the conservative Turin audience for both an opera and a separate ballet, even when the opera was as long as *Don Carlos* or *Aida* and already included a ballet, the late nineteenth-century impresario of the Regio faked an illness or an accident so as to cut out part of the program. Turin society, it seems, preferred its ballet ration to *Aida* in full.[136]

What was much more common than a violation of the terms of the contract was a dispute over the arrangements for ending it prematurely. Since the early eighteenth century at least, contracts had provided that the season could be stopped because of fire, war, epidemics, the death of the ruler, or some other overriding government act *(fatto di principe)*.

In an age when theaters were made wholly or partially of wood, were heated (if at all) by wood-burning stoves, and were full of lighted candles and oil lamps, theater owners tried to insert into contracts a clause making the impresario liable for fire damage while impresarios—especially after the San Carlo fire of 1816, which led to Barbaja's being sued for alleged breach of contract—at times successfully insisted on narrowing down their responsibility to matters of immediate and culpable negligence.[137]

Of the other causes that might stop a season, only government acts were thought to warrant compensation; after 1814, so as to cut short possible arguments over the terms, Milan contracts generally stated that when a season was stopped impresarios should receive subsidy, endowment, or subscription money only in proportion to the number of performances already given. The

135. See Cambiasi, *La Scala*, 234–40; contracts for the *impresa* of the Cocomero, Florence, 1775–95, I-Fcomune, fol. 8374; *Prospetti di appalto per lo R. Teatro S. Carlo*, in the Biblioteca Lucchesi-Palli, Naples; Consiglio comunale, Naples, deliberazione 20 May 1884, I-Nas, Prefettura di Napoli, fol. 3487.

136. Depanis, *I Concerti Popolari*, 1:171–72, 2:66–67.

137. Balochino-Crivelli contract for II. RR. Teatri, Milan, 1820, I-Mt, Sp. P. 60/3; Edoardo Guillaume contract for RR. Teatri, Naples, 1846, I-Nas, Min, Interno II inv., fol. 4359; Carlo De

contracts between impresarios and artists dealt similarly with artists' fees; a weak impresario on occasion pressed the government to close the theaters when times were bad so that he in turn could stop paying his artists.[138]

The crucial question was what should happen if the season went badly, the audience was hostile, or the impresario ran out of money or was unable to carry out the advertised program—all common situations. The theater owners could release the impresario from his contract—and impresarios in a tight corner often pressed for this—but they did not necessarily choose to do so, particularly if they considered that the impresario was at fault or if he had found a pretext for claiming compensation. In such a case the owners might play a waiting game in the hope that the impresario would go bankrupt. If the owners did agree to break the contract, and if they wished the season to go on, they had either to make a contract with someone else or to take over themselves. What happened depended a good deal on the will of a few upper-class personages.

Here too we see a movement toward greater contract-mindedness. When the former king of Sardinia, Vittorio Emanuele I, died near the start of the 1824 carnival season and the theaters were closed, the impresario and company of the Regio, Turin, implored the authorities to compensate them beyond the terms of their contracts, on the usual grounds that they were "almost all heads of families" reduced to "a state of destitution." But by the 1850s and 1860s, the courts were ruling that a Genoa impresario whose season had been cut short must give the subscribers a refund; whatever the municipality might have decreed, the contractual tie with the subscribers overrode everything. They also ruled that when theater owners took over an impresario's contract instead of canceling it, they must take over his contractual obligations to the artists.[139] So far did this shift toward stressing contractual rather than personal ties go that in 1871 a lawyer with much theatrical experience gave his opinion that no composer or artist could back out of a contract made with one impresario if the seasonal concession was then transferred to another impresario: he or she still had to perform for the new man what had been promised the old, on the grounds that "a change of impresario as a rule matters little to the conduct and execution of performances."[140] Such an opinion, given a generation earlier, would have startled the contemporaries of Barbaja and Lanari. It reflected not only a new legalism but the decline of the impresario as an individual creative force.

Nicola, "Diario napoletano," *Archivio storico per le province napoletane* 26–29 (1901–4): diary entries for 16–28 February 1816, appendix, 60–61.

138. Valle, *Cenni teorico-pratici*, 107ff.; Rinaldi, *Due secoli di musica*, 1:474, 476; Francesco Montignani to Sanvitale, June–July 1819, I-PAt, carteggi 1819.

139. Basso, *Il teatro della città*, 173–75; Rosmini, *La legislazione*, 1:147–52, 265–71.

140. Rosmini, *La legislazione*, 2:43–44, 364–65.

When an impresario could not meet his commitments, the old governments were inclined to arrest him, seize his assets, and give the opera company and the theater suppliers a preferential claim on them before other creditors could take their chances in the courts. Formal bankruptcies of impresarios seem to have been rare. Jacovacci did go bankrupt in 1848 (paying off his creditors three years later at 6 percent); Antonio Lanari in 1862 reached a settlement with his creditors, apparently out of court.[141] But these were respectable men. Between 1858 and 1867 the Marzi brothers, the busiest impresarios of the day, failed five times over in different cities, so far as we know without going through the bankruptcy courts or paying off anybody. In the troubled years of the 1870s and 1880s, we hear of impresarios who fled without paying their companies and singers who demanded payment in installments before every performance. The Rome impresario Costantino Boccacci was said to have given his creditors an appointment at the box office after the last performance, stuffed the takings into his clothes, and made his escape over the rooftops.[142] If such men did not land in court, it was presumably because everyone knew there was nothing to be got out of them. But this, once again, showed how far the profession had declined toward the very end of the century.

5. The Labor Market

The labor market in opera theater was by no means homogeneous. The humbler sections of the work force—orchestral players, chorus singers, production and front-of-house staff—were those where corporate privilege and customary rights were more common, though levels of pay were generally lower. From about 1820 in particular, impresarios made repeated efforts to break down these pockets of privilege and to establish a free labor market. They met with resistance, often effective. In their dealings with soloists whose earnings were potentially far greater, the impresarios enjoyed something closer to a free market but one in which the other party was keenly aware of his or her own value.

Italy was a poor country; not only was the lyric theater one of the few means to a living but people who managed to get a job in the opera house did their best to hang on to it for themselves and for their families. Govern-

141. Cametti, *Il Teatro di Tordinona*, 1:252–57; Antonio Lanari to Pacini, 20 April 1862, I-PEA, Pacini 1322. See also the Notificazione by the Reggente di Giustizia e Polizia di Roma e Giudice Privativo dei Teatri, 27 February 1800, in Rome, Biblioteca Casanatense, Editti, and Gutierrez, *Il Teatro Carcano*, 41–43.

142. Gino Monaldi, *Impresari celebri del secolo XIX* (Rocca San Casciano: Cappelli, 1918), 190; D'Arcais, "L'industria musicale."

ments before unification (and some elected municipalities after it) tended to protect these jobs and keep "foreigners" from out of town at bay, though the old governments also wished to put down "insubordination."

For an orchestra player or theater employee, the ideal was to work for a royal or municipal theater with a fixed roll of salaried staff who must be taken on by the impresario. We can see this system at work in Bologna. There Napoleonic rule shook the old corporate order when the famous Accademia Filarmonica lost its control of orchestras; this allowed impresarios, as hostile witnesses complained, to hire cheap, incompetent players. At the restoration, however, the best musicians banded together in what has been described as a trade union but was probably more like a labor monopoly run by a permanent contractor. At any rate the municipal orchestra by the 1850s was paid and run by the first violin and leader of the orchestra *(maestro direttore)* under regulations enforced by the supervisory board. It consisted of an inner core of officially appointed lifetime members (some of whom also taught in Bologna's well-known music school, the Conservatorio), a surrounding ring of officially temporary but often long-serving players who hoped to be taken on one day as permanent, and an outer ring of students who played for nothing. There was an intricate system of officially approved substitutes: a permanent member could hire out his instrument and make over part of his salary to a deputy of his own choice while he himself took leave, with the permission of the supervisory board, sometimes for years at a time. A homemade pension system allowed a member too old or ill to go on playing to draw half his salary until his death while his replacement drew the other half. There were also "customs practiced from time immemorial" whereby established players had special rights *(polizze e permessi)* to extra payment for attending certain rehearsals or else could send deputies to them. Players in theaters other than the Comunale keenly aspired to join the municipal orchestra and meanwhile tried to establish similar rights in other jobs (even though without official sanction).[143]

This system shows exactly the kind of entrenched group whose privileges impresarios wished to break down, even though the impresario Mauro Corticelli's attempt to do away with "immemorial" abuses brought a threat of a strike that had to be settled by a compromise.[144] The opera season at the Senigallia fair shows the free market in musicians fully at work. Here was a brief but important season held during a generally slack season (July–August) in a town where otherwise there was no permanent orchestra. "Arrange to get me an excellent orchestra . . . for little money," Lanari wrote in 1836 to

143. Filippo Bosdari, "La vita musicale a Bologna nel periodo napoleonico," *L'Archiginnasio* 9, no. 4 (July–August 1914): 213–38, esp. 226–27; I-Bas, Comune, Dep. Pub. Sp., tit. I, rub. 7, 1850–60, passim.

144. I-Bas, Comune, Dep. Pub. Sp., tit. I, rub. 1, 1854, rub. 7, 1855.

his local agent, "and I will thank you much and think highly of you." In order to do this, the man at least once openly recruited a second-best player for the sake of cheapness, but in general he asserted that he had gotten some of the best available; he even claimed to have found a bassoonist better than the one who had played the year before but costing little more than half as much. The labor market this Senigallia agent drew on spread as far as Bologna, Perugia, and Ascoli—a good slice of east-central Italy, presumably overstocked with musicians at that time of year. Since the impresario did want a good orchestra, however, the bargaining power was not all on one side. Some players refused to come down below a certain figure. Some took engagements still farther afield, in Padua or Viterbo or even Cadiz, rather than accept Lanari's terms.[145] The players' readiness to move about did something to counter the impresario's ability to tap a wide pool of labor. By the 1850s some Bologna musicians were able to get regular engagements in Athens and even Constantinople and then get back home for the important autumn season. But players of no more than average skill clearly had a thin time. In a crowded profession, some managed to find a place in a traditional, protected environment; far more were enabled by expanding demand to get some kind of work but were unprotected. Yet we also have to recognize that when impresarios tried to crack down on the use of deputies or attempted to get rid of mediocre players from protected orchestras, they were acting not unlike the young Toscanini, who so upset the custom-bound opera orchestras of Genoa and Pisa in the early 1890s by his insistence on using only the best musicians that he caused a strike.[146]

What was true of orchestra players was true of many theater staff members: the head of stage staff *(macchinista)* and the stagehands, the scene painter, the stage manager, the box-office manager *(bollettinaro),* and their staffs. In each department the man in charge was often a labor contractor, and in each there was the same contrast between protected and unprotected theaters, the same official privilege accorded only to certain jobs, and the same general expectation of tenure or a place on the permanent roll. Cosimo Canovetti, head of stage staff at La Pergola, Florence, had dealings with Lanari over two decades, and so did his son Cesare. Father and son complained several times that Lanari was "assassinating" them by seeking to cut estimates or had failed to advance money they needed to build sets. On the one hand the Canovettis felt themselves protected, not by having any officially fixed post but by the fact of working in a theater owned by a leading academy under the patronage of the grand duke. On the other hand they worked for

145. Correspondence between Lanari and Pacifico Balducci, 1836, I-Fn, CV 346/42–56.
146. Harvey Sachs, *Toscanini* (London: Weidenfeld and Nicolson; Philadelphia: J. B. Lippincott, 1978), 34, 46–47.

the impresario, and on one occasion tried to borrow money from him. The head of stage staff and the leading Florence impresario were bound in uneasy symbiosis.[147] In the second-rank Teatro del Corso, Bologna, on the other hand, the supervisory board, faced with similar disputes between impresario and head of stage staff over a bill and between impresario and stage manager over a 25 percent wage cut, could do no more than attempt conciliation. The impresario Corticelli's retort to the stage manager—"He answered that I might do whatever I pleased, and we would be friends none the less"— shows the confidence of a man aware of working in a free labor market.[148] Such a free market could also be encouraged by the spread of economic liberalism and by the financial weakness of governments and other theater controllers. With some exceptions—Tuscany in the days of Pietro Leopoldo (1765–90) was one—uninhibited freedom of contract would have to wait until unification and even then would meet with constraints from newly elective municipal authorities.

What happened in the Naples royal theaters is revealing. There the government first gave way in the 1820s, after the highly lucrative gambling monopoly had been abolished. In an attempt at compensation, it allowed the impresario to dismiss any theater employee (1822) and to bargain with orchestral players and members of the corps de ballet over wages (1824), which in practice meant that he could get rid of them if they refused to take a wage cut. Free bargaining, however, seems to have been thought troublesome, and later contracts went back to a fixed wage scale. But in 1843, after the impresario had endured a cut in subsidy, he was allowed to take on at fixed salaries only half the *masse* (orchestra, chorus, corps de ballet); the other half were to be offered contracts, but at much lower pay. In 1848, under a (briefly) constitutional government, the impresario had once again to take everyone on at a fixed tariff, and this arrangement was still in force in the early 1860s. With the removal of the strong arm of Bourbon authority, the chief problem came to be the defaulting impresario who left the *masse* unpaid. The Naples municipality therefore started holding back over half the subsidy, to be either paid to the *masse* directly or kept in reserve for them and for the theater staff. The impresario kept a right to turn down individual members as too old or unfit, but one who tried to do this in 1892 got into a dispute with most of the orchestra and had to go back on nearly all his demands.[149]

147. Correspondence of Lanari with Antonio Bonini and with the Canovettis, 1833, 1841, 1845, I-Fn, CV 348/137, 352/150.

148. I-Bas, ASCB, Dep. Pub. Sp., tit. I, rub. 2, 1852, 1853.

149. Contracts with Barbaja, 1822, 1824, with Guillaume, 1840, 1843, with Berardo Calveri Winter, 1848, with Alfredo Prestreau, 1861, Commissione Amministrativa dei RR. Teatri di Napoli, "Condizioni generali . . . alla concessione . . . ," I-Nas, Teatri, fols. 98, 105; Min. Interno II inv., fol. 4359; *Quaderno di oneri per la concessione del Teatro San Carlo, 1889–91* (Naples,

As the Naples story suggests, low-paid members of an opera company were not wholly defenseless, at least at certain times. Chorus singers appear to have been, as one official put it with some exaggeration, "always troublesome in all seasons and in all theaters."[150] Italian chorus singers were notoriously cooks, street vendors, minor artisans, and the like who sang part-time; few could read music. Their inability to look like ladies and gentlemen was given by the directors of La Fenice as the reason for putting *La traviata* into the fashions of about 1700: "The shoemaker, the printer, the fisherman, the common women who make up the chorus disappear beneath the costumes of ages past, but put them in today's evening clothes and they remain caricatures embarrassed by pretending to belong to good society." Members of the chorus were paid laborers' wages, were apt to smoke, drink, and gamble in the dressing rooms, and were altogether "the pariahs of art."[151] Yet chorus strikes recurred throughout the nineteenth century, and impresarios reacted to them by hiring scabs to break them. Like orchestral players, many chorus members were mobile; it was not difficult to import them. Under the old governments, entire choruses that had gone on strike were arrested at Lucca in 1836 and at Piacenza in 1844; a Parma chorus rioted in 1829, and its self-proclaimed leader was arrested by an officer who feared that any more trouble might lead the impresario to bring in "foreigners."[152] Methods of discipline might be crude: Lanari's deputy, faced with an unruly chorus, slapped one of its members. He later reported, "I said that I would pack them off to the Bargello [police headquarters]. In fact, opening night I had a number of policemen put in plain sight on the stage. All went well, however."[153]

Choruses took advantage of uncertain times when the old despotic governments had been overthrown and no new order had as yet firmly taken their place, notably the 1848–49 revolutions and the turbulent period of unifica-

---

1892), and *Impresa Teatro San Carlo e masse orchestrali* (Naples, 1892), both in the Biblioteca Lucchesi-Palli.

150. Dr. Paolo Cantoni, inspector of the Teatro del Corso, to Deputazione, 29 March 1855, I-Bas, Comune, Dep. Pub. Sp., tit. I, rub. 2, 1855.

151. Alessandro Carcano, "Progetto d'ordinamento delle masse corali e d'orchestra del Teatro Comunale di Roma," 28 November 1872, I-Rasc, tit. XV; Lady Morgan, *Italy*, 1: 269; Rosenthal, *The Mapleson Memoirs*, 262; Giuseppe Rossi-Gallicno, *Saggio di economia teatrale* (Milan, 1839), 49–50; chorus regulations, Bologna 1852, Ravenna 1855, in I-Bas, Comune, Dep. Pub. Sp., tit. I, rub. 1, 1853 (Promemoria serale A1852); rub. 2, 1855; Sandro dalla Libera, "L'archivio del Teatro La Fenice," *Ateneo veneto*, n. s. 6 (1968): 135–46, esp. 143.

152. Cesare Sardi, *Lucca e il suo Ducato* (Florence: Rassegna Nazionale, 1912), 118; Papi, *Il Teatro Municipale di Piacenza*, 136; Proni, comandante dei Ducali Dragoni, to Sanvitale, 19 May 1829, I-PAt, carteggi 1829.

153. Gazzuoli to Lanari, 12, 31 January 1839, I-Fn, CV 365/64, 66 (Teatro Alfieri, Florence, C1839).

tion in 1859–60. A Lucca impresario in carnival 1849 doubted whether he could stand out against the chorus if they used "force"; the issue, a recurrent one, was a convention that sometimes allowed chorus members to wear their stage costumes in the street during carnival masquerades. In 1849 the Lucca chorus threatened to ruin the costumes if they could not wear them; there was no question just then of carting everyone off to jail.[154] At Bologna the chorus of the Comunale won a wage increase in 1859. The following year they demanded not only a further increase of 31 percent overall (including payment for rehearsal time) but a tenure system on a par with the orchestra's and the right to choose their own chorus master. They referred to themselves as "this corps which has given honorable service for twenty-eight years." The impresario Ercole Tinti protested against "mutinies unheard of in the theater world." He offered to break the strike by bringing in scabs from outside if the municipality would pay him an extra subsidy, but clearly the moment was not right and the dispute was settled by a compromise. Tinti paid 23 percent more overall while the chorus dropped their other demands, that for rehearsal pay included.[155] The impresario Luigi Piontelli, however, had no difficulty in breaking a chorus strike for higher pay at the Carlo Felice, Genoa, in 1891. By then the state was firmly reestablished and if anything was on the employer's side.[156]

In a highly seasonal business like opera, not only revolution but the rush of the carnival season could give lowly employees a chance to assert themselves. That was the time when music copyists went on strike if they were not paid daily.[157] It was also the time when tailors and seamstresses employed in costume workshops—among the worst paid of urban craftsmen—formed shadowy "combinations" *(leghe),* and employers dared not sack anybody; the right time to sack was late spring, when activity was at a minimum. To pick one example, in the period between 1836 and 1839, Lanari's costume workshop next to La Pergola in Florence employed at peak periods forty, fifty, or sixty men and women, some in the workshop, some working at home, with women who specialized in embroidery, braid and tassel making, and dyeing. By carnival 1837 the workshop was producing costumes for three operas and two ballets at La Pergola, two operas at La Fenice, Venice, two operas and a ballet at Parma, and two operas at Pisa. Most of these were new, and the two main ballets at Florence and Parma (one Chinese, one Turkish) required 255 and 211 costumes, respectively. Everyone was working fifteen to seventeen

154. Correspondence of Gaetano Coccetti and Lanari, January 1849, I-Fn, CV 353/173–74.

155. Correspondence of Tinti, Deputazione, and chorus, June–July 1860, I-Bas, ASCB, Dep. Pub. Sp., tit. I, rub. 1, 1860.

156. Monaldi, *Impresarios celebri,* 201–2. See also Alberto Mazzucato to Giraldoni, 5 March 1867, I-Ms, CA 2904 (chorus strike at La Scala).

157. Cencetti to Capranica, 1836, I-Rburcardo, Fondo Capranica.

hours a day, Sundays and holidays included. Carnival 1839 was much the same; by 1840 costumes were being made for Havana. "All we need," Lanari's deputy wrote in desperation, "is one more order . . . and we can all go and jump in the Arno." [158]

The labor force was for the most part casual and flexible; it was paid not only poorly but often late, which meant that workers might have to pawn their household goods to keep going. Lanari, a difficult, demanding man, relied heavily on his able, (indeed indispensable) but cantankerous chief tailor, Vincenzo Battistini, a man suspected not only of stealing but of taking bribes from singers to make their costumes more splendid and perhaps of egging on the workforce to go slow at peak periods. The entire costume business was at once complex and precarious. Designs had to be sent to other towns for approval, many kinds of material had to be bought, and costumes had to be cleaned, adjusted, checked, and dispatched in good time to get through customs, all this to a famously high standard and to the tightest of schedules. Yet money was often short; an undercapitalized business was being run from hand to mouth. Hence Lanari's angry complaints at every setback that it was leading to his "total ruin" led to his attempts to control everything from a distance.

Composers and first-rank singers were in a quite different situation. What made this section of the market so open was the eagerness of nearly all concerned to move—not just within Italy but abroad as well. Here and there we can find a minor singer who sang secondary parts in the same theater year after year, no doubt giving lessons on the side. Composers whose operatic careers were failing or were only moderately successful settled down as cathedral organists (as Stefano Pavesi did in Crema and Carlo Coccia and Saverio Mercadante did in Novara) or as heads of conservatories (like Nicola Vaccai). Others failed altogether and vanished from sight. But their goal was first the circuit of leading Italian opera houses, then Madrid, Paris, London, and ultimately, from the 1840s, New York.

By the late eighteenth century, cash payment was the standard that measured achievement and artistic status. There was still some payment in kind— as late as around 1840, leading singers and composers were sometimes found lodgings, on occasion in the impresario's house—but the custom was dying out fast and no longer counted for much. Cash was, in Lanari's words, "the thermometer" of quality. [159] Artists who were paid the same were reckoned to enjoy the same standing, and leading singers frequently refused to sing for less than had been paid to a rival. These pretensions, and with them the entire

158. Gazzuoli to Lanari, 5 January 1839, I-Fn, CV 365/62. For other correspondence on the Sartoria with Baldisseri, Gazzuoli, and Panzieri, see I-Fn, CV 365/62, 343–44, 364–65, 400.

159. Lanari to Ercole Marzi, 15 April 1849, I-Fn, CV 393/58.

array of *convenienze*—an untranslatable term conveying the requirements both of status and of individual vocal aptitudes—were often ridiculed and satirized throughout the history of opera. To take two examples among many, singers demanded elaborate and steadily inflated titles indicating status. *Altra prima donna* (other leading lady) came to be a euphemism for *seconda donna;* the term *assoluto,* originally applicable to one person only, came to be demanded by all leading performers, and two performers' names sometimes had to be printed diagonally across each other to avoid giving one of them precedence.[160] There were economic reasons for such claims: like disputes about star billing in the Hollywood of the 1930s—a world in some ways not unlike the one we are dealing with—the fuss about parity of fees and *convenienze* is best understood as a means of establishing a market quotation.

We can see the negative side of this by looking at what happened to two men who failed to make their quotations stick. Nicola Vaccai achieved some success as an opera composer in 1824–27; although his fee was never more than two-thirds of Bellini's, the publisher Giovanni Ricordi was begging him "with joined hands" for songs. Vaccai's career then faltered and he made a living chiefly as a fashionable singing teacher in Paris and London. When a late opera, *Virginia,* had a moderate success in 1845, Ricordi found excuses for not paying him any kind of fee to publish it. He could have free copies—that was all.[161] Stefano Pavesi was a prolific opera composer who by 1830 was aged sixty-one, out of fashion, and knew it. Merelli got him to write an opera for a second-rank Milan theater, the Canobbiana, at a low fee. Pavesi was irked to begin with, then agreed on condition the fee was kept secret. He went to Milan, but Merelli kept him waiting, then, late in the evening told him, "You're an honest man and you won't fail me on account of the fee. If you like, you can take advantage of the moment; you can make your own terms." Pavesi reported, "Well, by dint of telling me I was an honest man, he got me to sign the contract for 2,400 Austrian lire," or 2,088 francs—more than 300 francs less than Pavesi had expected to settle for.[162]

If Bellini, Donizetti, and Verdi dealt at times sharply, even fiercely with impresarios, that was because they did not want to suffer the fate of Vaccai and Pavesi. If singers fussed about dressing rooms, lodgings, and the order in which the impresario's carriages picked them up, that was partly because they did not want to end like one *seconda donna* given a precontract at La Fenice who railed and wept when she found that she was not, after all, to get a

160. Valle, *Cenni teorico-pratici,* 35–45; [Ritorni], *Consigli,* 58.
161. Giovanni Ricordi to Vaccai, 9 February 1825, 7 February 1827, 17 February, 9 March 1845, in Tolentino, Biblioteca Comunale, Archivio Vaccai.
162. Pavesi to Count Gaetano Melzi, 1, 4, 6 July 1830, I-Ms, CA 4793–5 (the opera was *La donna bianca d'Avenello,* Teatro della Canobbiana A1830).

modest engagement, or the minor bass who was willing to do anything, even sing in the chorus, for the mere cost of his food.[163] In a profession that depended on public favor, anxiety could strike even the great Giuditta Pasta; so worked up was she during rehearsals of the first *Norma* that she declared that if her performance did not go down well she would quit the stage.[164]

From the impresario's point of view, the ideal market was one overstocked with good performers. Goldoni once again put it in a nutshell when he made his noble impresario play off one singer against another, saying each time, "Take it or leave it—there are ten more who are begging me to take them on."[165] Reality was often like that among minor singers and in minor theaters, particularly outside the carnival season. The baritone Charles Santley, who started in Italy in the 1850s, remembered it as a deadly struggle for survival.[166] But things were different when the impresario had to mount a season of some importance. Then he had to engage in prolonged, intricate sessions of bazaar bargaining.

Singers mattered most. The impresario might approach a number of artists and ask them to state their demands. This opening demand was often referred to as the singer's "opening shot" *(sparata* or *cannonata),* and it was usually turned down as impossibly high. Sometimes the impresario made an opening offer, and it was up to the singer to reject it as absurdly low. Then, (often though not always) the parties edged toward agreement in a series of steps. Singers and impresarios became expert in devising elegant formulas for talking fees up or down, for expressing agreements that must not be allowed to set a precedent, and for breaking off negotiations while remaining on cordial terms. When the Genoa impresario Francesco Sanguineti asked Marianna Barbieri-Nini to appear at his theater, she said she would "restrict" her fee to 20,000 francs "for the sake of the pleasure of singing at the Teatro Carlo Felice, and also in order to enjoy the beautiful views of Genoa." Sanguineti replied that he could not meet her "limited" request, but that he would be delighted to send her a postcard of the view.[167] Terminology was important: a singer who for one reason or another agreed to take less than the usual fee was said to be getting a "present" *(regalo)* rather than a "fee" *(paga* or *compenso);* an impresario might even coax a singer to take, as an intermediate arrangement, a "little fee" *(paghetta).*[168]

---

163. Gazzuoli to Lanari, 1836, 1837, I-Fn, CV 364/99, 144. See also Depanis, *I Concerti Popolari,* 1:118–21.

164. Merelli to Lanari, 8 December 1831, I-Fn, CV 396/2.

165. Carlo Goldoni, *L'impresario delle Smirne,* 1759, act 4, scene 4.

166. Santley, *Student and Singer,* 89–90.

167. Francesco Sanguineti to Lanari, 8 January 1849, I-Fn, CV 409/77.

168. Lanari to Luigi Pacini, 12 October 1830, I-Bca, Collezione Autografi LXXXVI; correspondence between Capranica and Giuseppina Ronzi, 1836, I-Rburcardo, Fondo Capranica.

Because bargains generally had to be sealed in a hurry, intricate points arose of professional ethics and of law. A common Italian arrangement was to make a precontract *(compromesso)*, which was binding for a time (perhaps only for a few days) but which either party could get out of on certain conditions. An impresario and a singer often made a precontract while each still carried on a crisscross of negotiations with other singers and impresarios. When (as happened to an Italian tenor at Barcelona in 1830) the singer was negotiating with two Spanish impresarios and one Italian, while the Italian impresario to whom he was precontracted was himself negotiating with another tenor—all this by slow post—the singer could end up without an engagement even though no one was legally at fault.[169] On the other hand a letter of acceptance or an oral undertaking from a singer—without a legal contract or even a precontract—was sometimes asserted by impresarios to be binding; one claim based on an oral undertaking was thrown out by the courts, but only because the witnesses were interested parties.[170]

Like much else in the dealings between singers and impresarios, how far this kind of claim could be pressed depended on their relative power in the market. Balochino in Vienna tried to make out that Fanny Tacchinardi-Persiani was "in some way under contract with the most excellent ministers of state" of Austria, his official employers, but she used her prerogative as the leading light soprano of the day and kept him pleading for another eight years before consenting to come to Vienna.[171] Now and then a singer signed two contracts for the same date, usually because a more appetizing contract had come along after signing the first. In such a case the impresario who had been ditched could not compel the singer to perform, but he could sue for damages or try to reach an agreed settlement.[172] The telegraph and the railways speeded up negotiations but did not quite do away with all these hazards.

Apart from the amount of the fee, the questions uppermost in singers' minds were whether they could be sure of collecting it, how often they could be required to sing, and how well particular roles would suit their voices. There were also more indefinite questions of mood and confidence.

When they worked for the most successful impresarios, artists could be nearly sure of being paid punctually. When working for minor impresarios, singers might reasonably fear that they would be paid late, perhaps not at all. Some got around this by demanding a guaranteed fee: this usually meant that

169. Nicola Tacchinardi to Lanari, 29 January 1830, I-Ms, Collezione Casati 1128.

170. Alessandro Magotti to Giordani, 1880, I-Bca, Collezione Autografi XLI 11.119; Rosmini, *La legislazione,* 2:86–89.

171. Correspondence of Carlo Balochino and Fanny Tacchinardi-Persiani, 1837–45, Vienna, Stadtbibliothek.

172. Rosmini, *La legislazione,* 1:433–34, 436–44.

they would have first call on the government's or the patrons' endowment, a device frowned upon by many supervisory authorities because it was unfair to lesser artists and stage staff who had no such assurance. Leading artists got it none the less; the tenor Luigi Mari, knowing that the impresario in Modena in 1826 was running out of money, successfully held out for a guarantee even at the cost of a spell in jail. Nothing, however, exempted artists from performing if they were left unpaid part way through the season—unless, exceptionally, they had a clause in their contracts to that effect. Sing first, sue later was the rule.[173]

Another hazard was that a singer, on first being heard at rehearsal, might be turned down by the impresario or by the supervisory board as unfit; or he or she might rouse such hostility in the first-night audience as to have to be speedily replaced. This problem seems to have gotten worse as the nineteenth century went on and seasons multiplied. Law and custom were unclear, except on one point—beginners could have their contracts canceled if they did badly at the first performance.[174]

How many performances a singer would give each week was another difficult problem. Until the late nineteenth century it was still the norm in Italy for opera singers to sing leading parts four or five times a week, and six times a week was not unknown. Most opera companies gave four or five performances a week; unless there was a "double company" (with two lots of soloists) all the leading singers would have to appear at each performance. Double companies were rare outside La Scala and the San Carlo, and could not always be afforded even there. Until the early nineteenth century this frequency seems to have been regarded as normal. The tenor Andrea Nozzari was described in 1809 as "capricious" because he refused to sing more than three or four times a week.[175] But by the 1820s and the 1830s the most successful singers were imposing the same limitation. Others no less successful, however, can be found doing things that would now be thought crazy: Giuseppina Strepponi, Verdi's future companion and wife, sang Norma, of all parts, five times in six days when in the early stages of pregnancy (and at one point six times in one week); the tenor Duprez sang in *Lucia* five times a week, at one point six times; as late as 1866 Antonietta Fricci, one of the foremost singers of the day, sang five times a week at La Scala in *Norma* and *L'Ebrea* (as *La Juive* was known in Italy), another heavy part.[176]

173. Valle, *Cenni teorico-pratici*, 58–63; Gandini, *Cronistoria dei teatri di Modena*, 1:288; contract with Maria Lafon, La Scala CQ1860 (exemption clause), I-Mt, Sp. P. 112/1.

174. Rosmini, *La legislazione*, 1: 500–501, 519–20, 2:11–18.

175. Rinaldi, *Due secoli di musica*, 1:408.

176. Gazzuoli to Lanari, February 1837 (Ducale, Parma C1837, with Duprez), October 1838 (Alfieri, Florence, A1838, with Strepponi), I-Fn, CV 364/106, 111, 365/51–54; Santley, *Student and Singer*, 233.

This was exploitation, but it was the singers who exploited themselves. The reasons why they came to prefer three or at most four performances a week are clear: from the early-nineteenth-century singers faced heightened technical demands in the withering away of recitative, heavier instrumentation, larger orchestras, and heavier vocal writing.[177] What needs explaining is why they so often agreed to give four, five, or six weekly performances. With the "single company" system, to do so was simply professional behavior, and if to some extent singers were helping the impresario they were also pressing forward their own careers in the hope of one day being able to demand more favorable conditions. When she refused to sing more than four times a week, Teresa Brambilla, the first Gilda, explained, "In the past I have played havoc with my voice in all sorts of operas in order to make a name; now that I have done so I would be imprudent if I could not profit from it reasonably."[178] Another reason was to make as much money as possible, or at least to balance money against status. Eugenia Tadolini wanted to sing no more than three times a week at La Fenice in 1847 but was prepared to sing four times a week for more money; Erminia Frezzolini, shortly afterwards, was also prepared to sing four times a week, "on her word of honor," provided her contract read "three times a week."[179]

Impresarios and supervisory boards were well aware of the risks to voices and health. Duprez's six *Lucia*s in one week were made possible only by announcing (falsely) that the baritone was ill, thus making it possible for Duprez to cut out the Wolf's Crag duet. But the reason for the six *Lucia*s in one week was that the management was contractually obliged to give thirty-six performances that season, had missed two earlier ones because of Duprez's own illness, and was bound by the calendar: if the management fell short, it would have to pay compensation.

When time pressed as it did in Italian opera seasons, illness was a troublesome matter. Custom said that leading singers were entitled to up to eight consecutive days' illness without loss of pay; this was generally embodied in contracts, especially after the Milan and Rome courts in 1826–29 had given perverse and contradictory rulings. An illness or a pregnancy that developed between signature of a contract and the start of the season could cancel the contract (but if it had been concealed at the time of signing it could be grounds for an action for damages). Medical certificates were essential; impresarios who, as we have seen, could do a bit of faking of their own when it suited them were frequently suspicious. A more normal cause of dispute

177. Already noted in 1821 by Petracchi, *Sul reggimento,* 82–83.

178. Teresa Brambilla to Lanari, 19 September 1849, in Jarro [Giulio Piccini], *Memorie d'un impresario fiorentino* (Florence, 1892), 73.

179. Eugenia Tadolini to Alberto Torri, 17 February 1846, I-Vt, Autografi diversi; Charles Rigatti to Lanari, 10 September 1851, I-Fn, CV 405/55.

was a singer's feeling off color without being clinically ill. The impresario would then plead, coax, and press; star singers made a big difference to the box-office takings, and it looks as though—at a time when replacements of equal standing could not be quickly found—they were often induced to perform below their best. At the same time a singer in a strong position on the opera market could get away with an occasional caprice.[180]

The logic of the market indeed ruled here as in most things. Leading singers could defend themselves. Minor artists who appeared in places like Malta or Bari in the 1870s, or in a third-rank Milan theater, not only had to perform five times a week as a matter of course but some of them were allowed no sick pay at all, could have their contracts revoked at any time on vague grounds of "imperfect performance" or on no grounds at all, and had to pay heavy damages in circumstances (such as failure to turn up on time) that for a leading performer would have led to no more than cancellation of the contract.[181]

Though impresarios had often begun as singers or dancers, they were apt among themselves to speak contemptuously of "the performing rabble" *(la virtuosa canaglia)* or, as Barbaja called artists, "these scoundrels and ingrates." One side or the other, it seemed, must "lay down the law": from time to time there was talk of a managers' cartel to keep down "exorbitant" fees, but then as now such talk got nowhere—impresarios were aware that with London and Paris as well as Italian cities eager to hear the best singers, there was no real hope of drawing a line.[182]

What was true of singers was largely true of composers as well. The one novelty in the nineteenth century was the emergence of the composer who could not only dictate terms but could impose himself as an autonomous artist, entitled to his privacy and able to create away from the world of the theater—in a word, the emergence of Verdi. That was in fact the difference between the young Rossini, who stayed at his impresario's house and composed with the opera company laughing, talking, and singing around him, and Verdi, who not only insisted on staying at a hotel but was the first well-known composer to receive a commission for an Italian opera (*Il corsaro,* 1848) without having a specific theater or company of singers in mind.[183]

Composers who had made a decided hit could pretty well control the

180. Valle, *Cenni teorico-pratici,* 126–28; Rosmini, *La legislazione,* 1:468–70, 509, 2:27; Merelli to Lanari, 9 October 1826, I-Fn, CV 395/115; I-Bas, ASCB, Dep. Pub. Sp., tit. I, rub. 1, 1855 (correspondence with Mauro Corticelli on the "indisposition" of Augusta Albertini Baucardé).

181. Contracts, I-Ms, Collezione Casati 1427, 1448; I-Bca, Collezione Autografi XLI 11.107.

182. Correspondence of Lanari with Barbaja, Merelli, and Giovanni Battista Villa, 1836–37, I-Fn, CV 344/128–32, 152, 415/180; Balochino to Filippo Taglioni, 23 January 1836, Vienna, Stadtbibliothek; Bouquet, *Il teatro di corte,* 231.

183. See John Rosselli, "Verdi e la storia della retribuzione del compositore italiano," *Studi verdiani* 2 (1983): 11–28.

choice of singers for their later operas. It was again Verdi who was first able to demand that his works should be performed as written, without the transpositions and interpolations that had been common form, although even then he remained willing to make changes so long as he could control them. Verdi was also the first composer to permit himself (after *Un ballo in maschera,* 1859) the luxury of having virtually no direct dealings with the impresario. His unchallengeable position, backed as it was by a publisher who could enforce his copyright, was by then a sign that the old helter-skelter opera business with its "journalistic" methods (see below) was drawing to an end.

On the opera market as it worked in the late eighteenth century and for much of the nineteenth century, composers' reputations went by their current fees in much the same way as singers'. On occasion someone, usually a young man with a modest local reputation and high-placed relatives or friends, would make an unpaid debut or would even pay for the privilege of having his work put on. None of the best-known composers ever had to do this except the visiting German, Otto Nicolai, who wrote a cantata unpaid.[184] Meyerbeer was an unusual figure, disconcerting to impresarios. His early Italian operas (1817–25) were successful, but as a rich banker's son he refused a fee. At the same time he made unusual demands for control of the production and, after his earliest experiences, for sole ownership of the score.[185]

Meyerbeer had a point. Scores were by then salable. In the days before effective copyright but at a time when opera houses no longer insisted on putting on new works—roughly from the late eighteenth century to the 1850s—composer and impresario were in some circumstances able to make money from letting out the score of a successful work and from allowing publishers to print a vocal or piano score. The change in temper that these new commercial resources brought can be seen by comparing Simon Mayr's gentle complaint in 1808 about an unauthorized vocal score with the angry denunciations of Bellini and Donizetti some twenty years later.[186] Mayr seemed unprepared to do anything; Bellini was all for setting the police on the trail of the pirates.

In the first half of the nineteenth century, the usual arrangement was for the impresario either to buy the full score outright or to divide the rights in it with the composer. Either way this meant an iron watch on copyists and, if possible, on fellow impresarios to whom the score was hired out. These

---

184. Lanari to Dr. E. Basevi, 1834 (rejecting a subsidized opera by the young Abramo Basevi), I-Fn, CV 345/107. See also Rosmini, *La legislazione,* 2:346–4, 355–56.

185. Giacomo Meyerbeer, *Briefwechsel und Tagebücher,* ed. Heinz Becker and Gudrun Becker, 4 vols. (Berlin: De Gruyter, 1960), 1:324–26, 387, 396, 399, 426–27, 466, 514.

186. Simon Mayr to Giovanni Morandi, 1808, in Giuseppe Radiciotti, *Lettere inedite di celebri musicisti* (Milan, 1892), 79 (about the piano score of *Adelasia e Aleramo,* published by Ricordi).

safeguards generally failed, and the correspondence of the time is full of complaints about pirated scores, often orchestrated by a hack composer from the printed vocal score but sometimes stolen.

Double standards prevailed. Impresarios complained bitterly about others' piracy, but even Barbaja and Lanari were willing on occasion to buy a pirated score cheap. Even Bellini, so indignant on his own behalf, tried to make a secret deal for the Naples rights to *I puritani* so as to cheat out of their legal share the Paris impresarios who had first staged it. A common negotiating ploy was for one impresario to write to another that he could get a score locally very cheap but that he would hire the authentic version if the price were reasonable.[187] Occasionally a vigilant impresario managed to do good business out of secondary rights in scores, as Lanari did out of some of "his" Donizetti and Mercadante operas, but this meant generally either putting on the works himself in one city after another or else a straight exchange with an impresario who had an equally valuable score to offer. Dealings between impresarios over rights could be stretched out, one is tempted to say luxuriously, over many months. Barbaja and Lanari carried on one such set of negotiations (over a proposed hiring out to Naples of Donizetti operas) that continued for over a year; even then they came to an agreement only because the Naples censorship had unexpectedly forbidden Donizetti's newest opera, *Poliuto,* and Barbaja had to find a substitute in a hurry. In the end Lanari took 725 francs instead of the 1,000 francs he had originally demanded.[188]

The step-by-step procedure followed in this bazaar bargaining can best be observed in a relatively simple and amiable exchange between Lanari and Sanguineti. Sanguineti wished to hire the tenor Eugenio Musich for Genoa's spring season of 1843, but he did not want to pay more than he had the previous year: Musich, he wrote, could not have made so much progress in a year as to deserve more. Lanari (acting as Musich's agent because he had him under long-term contract) replied that he had in fact progressed a lot, but as a concession the fee would be unchanged. Sanguineti then objected to providing lodgings for the singer—it was an "immense nuisance" and a certain expense—and he proposed to pay an extra 200 francs instead. Lanari pointed out that by the terms of the contract, Sanguineti was obliged to provide lodgings but, as another concession, he was willing to settle for 270 francs extra plus Musich's traveling expenses. Sanguineti then brought up as reinforcement the fact that this year, unlike the previous one, Lanari was not having to pay commission to an agent in Genoa and was therefore saving 250 francs:

187. Lanari to Giovanni and Rosa Morandi, 3 March 1820, I-FOc, Piancastelli 407.182; Lanari-Barbaja correspondence, 1836–38, I-Fn, CV 344/132, 345/31, 37, 44; Gazzuoli to Lanari, 1837, I-Fn, CV 364/120; Bellini, *Epistolario,* 451–52; Tito Ricordi to Verdi, 7 November 1848, I-P.

188. I-Fn, CV 344/168, 345/19, 29,31, 37, 44.

let him therefore bear the cost of travel while, to show that he was not stubborn, he, Sanguineti, would provide lodgings after all. Lanari agreed, but he
added that since he now had to pay traveling costs, Musich would not travel
by post and would therefore arrive a little later than planned. It is this master
stroke (in which Sanguineti acquiesced) that reveals the master bargainer.[189]

It was the theatrical agents who carried the free market to its highest point.
The professional agent, as that figure emerged toward the late eighteenth century out of occasional or amateur "mediation," was an individual backed by
no corporative structure and who might at times even have no fixed place of
business.[190] In the early nineteenth century the larger part of the market gradually shifted from Bologna, the center of theatrical exchange in the eighteenth
century, to Milan, both in terms of numbers of people and numbers of exchanges. In July 1861 Milan had 427 available singers (including seventy-
eight leading sopranos); during the second half of the century, a second-rank
baritone had dealt with at least forty-four agencies during his career of over
thirty years. It was not unusual for an agent to write twenty or thirty letters,
one after the other, in pursuit of his 5 percent on a contract that later
eluded him.

In a profession that demanded nothing but a pen, ink, industry, and tenacity (or nerve), a constant oversupply of agents put them in a particularly weak
position with impresarios and theater owners. There were a few exceptions:
Giovanni Battista Bonola, a Milanese agent who described himself as "the
least scoundrelly" of all the agents; Antonio and Alessandro Magotti, a father
and son team in Bologna who specialized in bringing together opera companies for towns in Emilia and Umbria, in Puglia, or in Greece; even more exceptional were the agent-impresarios Merelli and Lanari, who exploited their
system of long-term contracts with artists by employing them in their own
many theatrical ventures or by "peddling" them elsewhere. Most agents,
however, were men of all work, ready not only to engage well-known singers but chorus singers, orchestral players, stagehands, and prompters, and
equally ready to act as a forwarding agent, to sell sheet music and musical
instruments, and, above all, to function as a journalist. The better part of the
musical journalism that arose along with a renewed passion for opera between 1820 and 1848 was venal in the most literal sense: journals were
mouthpieces for agents. These parasitical publications did not hesitate to
stoop to blackmail, and the opera profession paid for what they printed.
Agents were also at the mercy of theater owners and impresarios who made
them compete to be the first to submit a signed contract with a given artist

189. I-Fn, CV 409/61–64.
190. On theatrical agents see John Rosselli, "Agenti teatrali nel mondo dell'opera lirica italiana dell'Ottocento," *Rivista italiana di musicologia* 17 (1982): 134–54.

but who felt they had incurred no obligation toward the agent. This led to fierce competition among agents and to their attempts to turn things to their advantage by approaching both artists and impresarios with proposals not authorized by any contract. One agent would readily describe another as a "scoundrel" and "intriguer," and worse. "He is eaten up with rage," the agent Filippo Burcardi wrote of his rival Merelli, "because I have taken a couple of good theaters away from him, and if God grants me life I want to show him a thing or two."[191]

This was an extreme case of the competitive attitude of the entire opera market. The principle underlying nearly all these negotiations was that either party should at all times put forward its maximum merits and grievances and should use the areas of uncertainty in existing or proposed contracts as a means of maneuver to get the upper hand, sometimes beyond the obvious needs of the case. How strong the ritual element was in these dealings may be seen from the language used by members of the opera world in their business correspondence. It was so stereotyped that the letters of singers or impresarios often seem almost interchangeable. Certain key terms recurred. The most important were "friendship" *(amicizia)*, "condescension" *(condiscendenza,* in the sense of "helpfulness"), "interest" *(interesse)*, "sacrifice" *(sacrificio)*, and "self-esteem" *(amor proprio)*.

Barbaja, first coaxing Pacini to come to Naples to see his new opera on the stage and then upbraiding him for being late with the score, wrote, "If you are my friend, as I believe, you will find a way," and later, "Never would I have believed that you could act like that toward a friend." Asking Lanari to pay him 10,000 francs to write a new opera, Donizetti wrote, "You [are] not returning the friendship I profess for you."[192] "Friendship" could be attributed to someone you had not even met.[193] A "friend" was someone who did what you wanted ("condescended"); hence the many calls on the other party in a bargain to "demonstrate friendship," for instance by putting business your way or by knocking something off the hire of costumes. "Interest" of course meant financial interest. It could be opposed to friendship: "You are looking after your interest and I praise you for it," a minor Florence impresario wrote to Lanari (who was refusing him a discount on costume hire); but by so doing Lanari was failing to show himself a "great friend" *(amicone)*. Another line of argument was that the other party was neglecting both friendship and his true interest: this might well go with a dispassionate-sounding remark that, after all, both parties could do each other a bit of

191. Burcardi to Lanari, 1833, I-Fn, CV 350/143.

192. Barbaja to Pacini, 19 June, 3 August 1841, I-PEA, Pacini 1148, 1151; Lanari to Donizetti, 30 June 1836, in Commons, "Una corrispondenza," 33.

193. Giovanni Battista Lasina to Giovanni Marchetti, 29 November 1865, I-FOc, Piancastelli, Autografi, s. v. "Marchetti"; Bonola to Lanari, 1838, I-Fn, CV 349/41.

good. A minor Naples impresario who had just been angrily denounced by a baritone as a "trader in human flesh" (another cliché) offered a financial compromise and added that if the baritone refused this it would mean "not only . . . that you are not my friend, but that you are not at all good at looking after your own interest, since . . . I could later on propose to you some better deals."[194] This reciprocity was often stressed: a man who had just said that he would make a "sacrifice" in favor of the other party would then spell out that he expected similar favorable treatment at some future date. What was perhaps more deeply felt was the need to safeguard one's "self-esteem" and to avoid cutting a bad figure *(sfigurare)*. This was bound up with status. Merelli declared that his self-esteem had suffered because the *prima donna* Carolina Ungher had demanded more money from him than she had been content to get from Lanari. Ungher, for her part, said she had raised her demand because she wanted to be paid as much as Giulia Grisi had been, hence her self-esteem (and status) were also involved.[195]

The Italian opera world was a great bazaar; an art that dealt in utmost contrivance was grounded in a poor society's understanding of the need to scrabble for every penny. In such a world, not even the impresario, according to the famous baritone Achille de Bassini, should think himself indispensable or even necessary: "The only necessary man I know is the cashier."[196]

6. The Impresario and the Public

Like sports fans, the majority of Italian opera spectators in the early nineteenth century were conservative when it came to the rules of the game but were capable of wild enthusiasm over a first-rate display of skill. Berlioz understood this (though his remark was meant to be disparaging) when he called Italian operagoers *routiniers et fanatiques* untouched by innovation or the poetic aspect of art: all they wanted was "scores whose substance they can assimilate immediately, without reflection, even without attention, as they would a plate of macaroni."[197] In this sense Berlioz's observation does not contradict Verdi's later statement that the Italian audience was impatient, capable of tiring even of Giovanni Battista Rubini, Antonio Tamburini, and

---

194. Achille Batelli to Lanari, 1847, I-Fn, CV 345/126–71; G. Trisolini to Marchetti, 1866, I-FOc, Piancastelli, Autografi, s. v. "Marchetti."

195. Merelli to Lanari, 1837, I-Fn, CV 396/33.

196. Achille De Bassini to Francesco Lucca, 4 January 1851, I-Ms, Collezione Casati 319.

197. Hector Berlioz, *Voyage musical en Allemagne et en Italie* (Paris, 1844), 218–20, in English translation as *The Memoirs of Hector Berlioz . . . Including His Travels in Italy, Germany, and England, 1803–1865*, ed. and trans. David Cairns (New York: Norton, 1975).

Luigi Lablache.[198] Like the opera public then, sports fans today may tire of the star players but resist change in the game.

Though the old Italy was fragmented into petty states, the opera audience seems to have struck foreign visitors as much the same from one town to another. Italians themselves, especially members of the opera world, saw differences. Rome audiences were supposed to need something out of the ordinary to rouse them; failing that, they would not bother to turn up. Until the early nineteenth century the opera public in Rome was largely made up of clerics; Stendhal describes fanatical abbés holding rush lights to make out the libretto and trading insults with the composer whenever they disliked the music. Florence operagoers, in contrast—at least those who went to the most fashionable theater, La Pergola—were supposed to be restrained and highly cultivated. Yet a little further north, in Emilia-Romagna, audiences were feared as highly partisan and unpredictable.[199] Cities such as Bologna, Modena, Reggio, and Parma do seem to have had a high incidence of riot in the theater. Yet just as Italian opera spoke the same musical language from Palermo and Naples to Turin and Trieste, so its audiences seem to have shared much the same expectations and to have behaved in much the same way.

What is most striking is the central importance, especially before the 1848 revolutions, of the opera season in the course of city life. The arrival of the company at the start of rehearsals was news on the street corners, and the season was likely to keep the town in gossip. With luck it might arouse *furore*, *fanatismo*, and *entusiasmo* that might well attain a pitch seldom known elsewhere. In 1849 a letter of the dead Bellini was cut up and sold piece by piece like a saint's relics.[200] On the other hand the failure of a season could mean danger to life and limb. At the Pagliano, a Florence theater of a more popular kind than La Pergola—it flourished in the latter half of the century—a bench thrown from the fifth tier once narrowly missed the impresario; after that a dried cod's head thrown at the baritone was a trifle.[201] The relationship between the opera company and the public was a personal one. In Italian cities before the great urbanization from 1870 to 1900, the townspeople who might attend opera were not an anonymous mass. They knew one another

198. Verdi to Opprandino Arrivabene, 5 February 1876, *I copialettere*, 687–89 (and in Verdi, *Autobiografia dalle lettere*, 440–42).

199. To Lanari from Pietro Cartoni and from Pietro Camuri, 1841, I-Fn, CV 352, 353/84; Stendhal, *Quelques promenades dans Rome, suivi de Les Cenci* (Lausanne: Guide du Livre, 1942), 132–33 (16 June 1828), in English translation as *A Roman Journal*, ed. and trans. Haakon Chevalier (New York: Orion Press, 1957; distributed by Crown Publishers); Alberto Manzi, "I teatri di musica," in *Firenze d'oggi* (Florence, 1896), 61–62; to Pacini from Antonio Lanari, 27 April 1857, from Luigi Fioravanti, 24 April 1862, I-PEA, Pacini 950, 1001.

200. Bellini, *Epistolario*, 172 n.

201. Manzi, "I teatri di musica," 65–69.

and many of them, in the boxes especially, were known to the impresario. Up to the first night or even beyond, the question might be whether they would choose to take the plunge and subscribe.

In these conditions an impresario could hope for a personal reward: not just profit but a curtain call and a round of applause for himself. Sonnets might be addressed to him such as the mordant topical sonnets that the great dialect poet Giuseppe Gioachino Belli addressed to the various impresarios of Rome theaters commenting on the theatrical news of the day. When things went wrong the punishment was just as personal, and the cry of *impresario in galera!* (send the impresario to jail) might go up—not an empty threat in the early nineteenth century, and one that was carried out on occasion. There was reason for the impresario's eagerness to present himself as the humble servant of the public. One minor impresario ran into trouble in 1829 with the audience at a second-rank Venice theater, the San Luca, when he had to replace the *prima donna* and the comic bass (both of whom had received catcalls), and when the new *prima donna* fell seriously ill:

> The unfortunate impresario, after having made so many sacrifices, is unable to remedy this unforeseen new mishap. He begs of you Venetians, his patrons, that you should not impute to him the ending of the season through any lack of the regard he owes you on so many counts, but rather to a fatal consequence of that destiny which sometimes persecutes those who are most respectful toward you and most intent on doing you good service.

Presumably in order to put himself in the clear and to hope to get away undisturbed and perhaps come back to a good reception one or two seasons later, the impresario added that he would give subscribers their money back in proportion to the number of performances missed, and that he had reached an accommodation with the singers over the remaining portion of their fees.[202] We can understand the annoyance of one impresario of the Carlo Felice, Genoa, who wrote that the public "is the sworn enemy of all impresarios [and] is always waiting for the management to leave a weak flank uncovered so that it may plunge into it the dagger of malice and calumny."[203]

The first thing an impresario could do to forestall a battle with the audience was to avoid any seeming offense to local patriotism. When we keep in mind how split up Italy was before unification and how intense local pride *(campanilismo)* was in each town, it is surprising how few impresarios got into trouble through being foreigners. On occasion, though, an impresario crossed local feeling. One Bologna impresario putting on a season at Reggio

202. "Avviso al rispettabile pubblico veneto" of Clemente Riesch, impresario at the Teatro San Luca, spring 1829, Venice, Museo Civico Correr, MS PD, buste C 1419.
203. Michele Novaro to Pacini, 22 January 1862, I-PEA, Pacini 1026.

Emilia in 1791 was rumored to have spoken ill of the townspeople; this led to such riot in and out of the theater that soldiers were brought in, the officer in command (another "outsider"—from Modena) was murdered, the government arrested the impresario and promised to put him on trial, and singers and dancers had to be escorted to the theater under armed guard through a city in a virtual state of siege. The same circumstances—an impresario's supposed insults to civic pride—caused disturbances at Piacenza in 1846 that were less serious but still led the government to close the theater. Both these episodes took place in times of general political tension, but another episode at Modena—the well-known singers Erminia Frezzolini and Antonio Poggi had stones thrown at them for being reluctant to appear in a work by a local composer—suggests that injured civic pride was explanation enough.[204]

Another danger the impresario had to watch for before the season opened was overselling of tickets. The combination of unnumbered seats and tickets giving entry to the theater meant, on those rare occasions when the house was full, a recipe for a scramble when the doors were opened, with hats and scarves lost in the crush and some people squeezing in ticketless.[205] This probably happened every evening on the gallery stairs without anyone's noticing, but when it happened in the nineteenth century to the ladies and gentlemen who frequented the lower parts of the house, the trouble was much more serious. It was worse still if more tickets had been sold than there were places: on one notorious occasion, the first night of Donizetti's *Adelia* at the Apollo, Rome, in 1841, the performance came to a halt and the impresario Jacovacci was arrested and heavily fined.[206]

Jacovacci was almost certainly not the culprit. All through the eighteenth and early nineteenth centuries, governments and impresarios tried to guard against the sale of scalped tickets, the resale of used tickets part way through the performance, and the printing of fake tickets. The crucial figure was the *bollettinaio*, a kind of box-office manager (usually a native of the town), and the ticket takers and ushers (*maschere*, for in the eighteenth century they were sometimes masked to give them some clout in their dealings with their social superiors in the audience). Manuals of theater management warned impresarios to watch these men closely and ward off their tricks by marking and checking tickets daily.[207] Impresarios tried to follow their advice, but with

204. Crocioni, *I teatri di Reggio,* 51–54; Papi, *Il Teatro Municipale,* 140–41; Gandini, *Cronistoria dei teatri di Modena,* 2:279–83.

205. For example, to Donizetti's *Marino Faliero,* Parma, Teatro Ducale, P1838: see Ferrari, *Spettacoli drammatico-musicali,* 193.

206. Herbert Weinstock, *Donizetti* (London: Methuen, 1963), 165–66.

207. Rinaldi, *Due secoli di musica,* 1:58–59, 88–89, 200; Benedetto Marcello, *Il teatro alla moda* (Venice, 1720), modern edition, ed. A. Marianni (Milan: Rizzoli, 1959), 64–65; in English translation by Reinhard G. Pauly, *Musical Quarterly* 34 (1948): 371–403; 35 (1949): 85–

little success. The problem may have become easier to cope with in the late nineteenth century with the spread of numbered seats.

Another thing that made the job of the *bollettinaio* and his staff particularly tricky was the habit among operagoers of asking for and expecting credit. Most announcements of opera seasons stated that no credit would be given, but it is clear that in the poverty-stricken Italy of the eighteenth century, credit had to be given to some boxholders and townspeople as they signed up for subscription tickets and even to some members of the audience at the doors. The practice went on into the nineteenth century but was probably on the wane: one woman of the merchant class at Livorno pledged her wedding ring in exchange for a box in 1823.[208] Credit meant troublesome extra bookkeeping and repeated applications for payment, but clerical labor was cheap.

Other employees who made a difference to the impresario's relations with the public were the secretary who dealt with boxholders, the stage manager (*buttafuori* or *butta in scena,* literally "thrower onto the stage"—a thought-provoking title), the porter who defended the stage door against intruders, and the callboy whose manifold duties might include finding lodgings for the company, bringing them to the theater in hierarchical order, and acting as a go-between, at times as a pimp. It was often the stage manager who had to face the audience when there was an awkward announcement to be made, unless the impresario did it himself. Even he might be borne down by the sheer noise from an unruly audience.

A means well known in Paris for ensuring at least the appearance of success in the opera house was a claque hired out on set terms. No such body existed in Italy: we have Verdi's word for it and that of the tenor Adolphe Nourrit, from the Paris Opéra but active at the San Carlo, Naples, as well.[209] We hear occasionally of support groups organized by a singer, but we hear much more often of what might be called an anticlaque—a group organized to hiss and to bring about the failure of an opera, usually inspired by a rival impresario or singer or by their supporters in the town. The Italian opera house, with its passionate clientele, was subject to cabal and faction rather than to the straightforward commercial performance of the claque.[210] We can

---

105. Barbaja to Deputazione, 31 May 1882, I-Nas, Teatri, fol. 98; Valle, *Cenni teorico-pratici,* 171–74; [Joseph-Jérôme Le Français de Lalande], *Voyage d'un françois en Italie,* 9 vols. (Paris, 1769), 5:189.

208. Cambiasi, *La Scala,* 36; Edict of Direttore generale de' regio-ducali teatri, Piacenza, 1754, I-Mt, Gride 6/123; L. Bruni to Lanari, 1823, I-Fn, CV 350/113.

209. Giuseppe Verdi, *I copialettere,* 541; Louis Quicherat, *Adolphe Nourrit: Sa vie, son talent, son caractère, sa correspondance,* 3 vols. (Paris, 1867), 3:203–4.

210. Basso, *Il teatro della città,* 292–93, 304; Alessandro Maragliano, *I teatri di Voghera* (Casteggio: Cerri, 1901), 169–71; Giovacchino Forzano, *Come li ho conosciuti* (Turin: Edizioni RAI Radiotelevisione Italiana, 1957), 11.

see them at work in so-called spontaneous demonstrations. A refrain of Italian opera chronicles is the torchlight procession after the triumphal first performance, ending beneath the composer's windows, sometimes with a serenade by the theater orchestra, all to tremendous cheers. On one occasion at least this torchlight procession had been planned in advance; we know this because the place was Rome in the troubled period just before the 1848 revolutions and because a friend of the composer who was to be honored advised Pacini to call off the demonstration for fear that the demonstrators would be taken for the low-class radicals whose riots had been disturbing the city.[211] How many more such demonstrations were similarly arranged? At least it can be said, once again, that partisanship rather than sheer commercial promotion was likely to be the motive. Certainly this was true of the young Bolognese supporters who accompanied their fellow citizen Stefano Gobatti to neighboring towns and organized curtain calls and yet more torchlight processions. Gobatti was a composer whose *I Goti* had a flash-in-the-pan success in the 1870s, but the enthusiasm of the Bolognese, though misplaced, was real.[212]

Who organized hostile demonstrations? A man of much experience has left us a list:

> A tenor or a ballerina without a contract, a hanger-on of an unemployed *prima donna*, an author who has been hissed and who longs to ensure for a brother artist successes similar to his own, impresarios or would-be impresarios who aspire to the theater concession in the following year and who begin by bringing down the current impresario, journalists in search of subscribers who want to punish an artist for having dared to return their paper, now and then ill-advised champions among the public who seek to make themselves arbiters of domestic and private questions, avenging on the stage a betrayed lover or a disappointed hope.[213]

All these might set up a deliberate barrage of whistling and overbear the general feeling even of a well-disposed audience.

Sometimes a rival management might do this: at least the management of the Teatro Carcano, Milan, in carnival 1831 (an ambitious season that launched Bellini's *La sonnambula*) was accused of having planted troublemakers at La Scala.[214] At other times we hear more vaguely about "individuals known for their restless temper" or "an ill-disposed party" *(partitaccio)* from a rival theater doing their best to make a new opera fail. This was al-

211. Luigi Dall'Olio to Pacini, 15 December 1847, I-PEA, Pacini 1245. See also Pacini, *Le mie memorie*, 82, 87.

212. Ferrari, *Spettacoli drammatico-musicali*, 279, 285, 312.

213. Rosmini, *La legislazione*, 1:328.

214. Luigi Prividali to Giuseppe Berti, 9 February 1831, I-Vt, Spettacoli b. 3.

leged of the first nights of Rossini's *Il barbiere di Siviglia* (1816) and Bellini's *Beatrice di Tenda* (1833),[215] and something of the kind was to happen much later, in 1904, at the notorious first night of *Madama Butterfly*. We cannot now, however, make out how far these theatrical storms were organized.

More often disorders in the opera house centered on factions that supported rival *prime donne* or dancers, on occasion rival actresses or first violinists. Here too it is not always clear whether these factions were riotous fan clubs or whether they reflected preexisting divisions among local notables and their families, with the two singers or dancers affording a pretext. Disturbances might also be political. In the Napoleonic period opera factions at Turin and Parma reflected struggles between radicals and moderates, or else between the followers of the military governor-general of Parma (who supported Freemasonry) and those of the civilian prefect (who seems to have been a Catholic conservative).[216] Conflicts between anticlerical liberals and clerical conservatives lay behind the extraordinarily bitter struggles in the small town of Busseto over the appointment of a music master—struggles involving first the young Verdi and then, nearly twenty years later, his pupil Emanuele Muzio—though no doubt personal animosities within a little group of notables came into it too.[217] In how many other towns did such struggles go on about less well-known artists? At Lucca in 1841 fights in the two main theaters had something to do with resentment among local democrats of a lavish opera performance put on by rich amateurs, members of the princely Poniatowski family; they countered by supporting a tragedy by a local poet of peasant origin.[218]

No such explanation has come down to us for the violence of other struggles over rival performers—at Padua in 1788, 1825, and 1829, at Piacenza in 1824, at Parma in 1843 and 1866, at Voghera in 1820, 1851, and 1867, at Palermo in 1838–40 and 1844. But their intensity is not in doubt. At Reggio Emilia in 1841 tempers ran so high that the authorities temporarily expelled some of the nobles, local people beat up a *prima donna*'s lover, and demonstrations in the theater were such that a performance had to be stopped and the season cut short. At Cesena in 1858 the *prima donna* had to be changed four times in twenty performances: "Not one evening went by without hissing or without the various factions throwing eggplants, tomatoes, and

215. Rinaldi, *Due secoli di musica,* 1:503; Bellini, *Epistolario,* 343, 345–46.

216. General Menou to Minister of the Interior, I complémentaire XII (18 September 1804), F-Pan, F¹ᵉ 79; correspondence between Nardon and Minister, June–July 1807, F-Pan, F¹ᵉ 88.

217. Frank Walker, *The Man Verdi* (London: Dent, 1962), 14–20, 117–18, 127–28, 153–55.

218. Sardi, *Lucca e il suo Ducato,* 146–49 (*Lucrezia Borgia* by Donizetti at the Teatro del Giglio; *Eleonora di Toledo* by Pietro Pacini at the Teatro Pantera).

the like at one another."[219] One is again left wondering when a leading figure in recurrent faction fights between supporters of rival *prime donne* at the Carolino, Palermo, turns out to have been the Mazzinian democrat Rosolino Pilo: in 1844, as a gesture of derision at once heavily symbolic and in poor taste, he threw at the singer he opposed (from the fourth tier of boxes) a wreath of esparto grass with a live owl attached,[220] a futile gesture that in the tense political climate before 1848 may have served to let off steam about complaints that could not yet be expressed openly.

Impresarios by and large clung to the authorities, taking no part in these semipolitical faction fights. This failed to shield them from all danger, as Pietro Rovaglia, the owner of a Milan costume workshop who ran seasons at the two main Modena theaters, discovered. Relying on the protection of the all-powerful minister of the aging duke of Modena, Francesco IV, Rovaglia thought it safe to economize on production costs and on singers, but this earned him the "diabolical hatred" of the Modenese public, which expected performances worthy of a capital city at rock-bottom prices. When some in the theater overhead a critical remark by the heir to the throne, they spread it around the house. This was enough to set the audience to whistling and to set Rovaglia to flight, pursued by a howling mob. The episode, which occurred shortly before the death of Francesco IV, followed by the fall of the minister, shows that opera could set fire to widely shared political resentments.[221] After unification, as we have seen from the example of Parma, riots became more frequent and more unmanageable, but perhaps less political.

The opera impresario catered to a minority public throughout much of the nineteenth century. This was obvious inside the theater, filled largely with the well-to-do, with perhaps a gallery occupied by artisans. It was also well understood by contemporaries, who took it as a matter of course.[222] The wider diffusion of opera through the population in the late nineteenth century seems to have come about through workers' choral societies, amateur bands, and even itinerant puppeteers and to have owed little to the traditional system of production—a system that was already shaken and in decline.

The revolutions and wars of 1848–49 and the serious economic slump that preceded them in 1847 marked a decisive turning point in the opera world. Wars going on at a distance could mean prosperity for theaters thanks

219. Crocioni, *I teatri di Reggio*, 69–70; Raggi and Raggi, *Il Teatro Comunale di Cesena*, 121 n.

220. Tiby, *Il Real Teatro Carolino*, 182–92.

221. Gandini, *Cronistoria dei Teatri di Modena*, 2:116ff., 301, 336–39; Bonola to Lanari, November 1844, I-Fn CV 349/74.

222. Rossi-Gallieno, *Saggio di economia teatrale*, 56; Cametti, *Il Teatro di Tordinona*, 1:297–98.

to the presence of large garrisons with money to spend, as in Milan after 1802. In 1848–49 everyone did badly. With occasional shots fired in the streets, no one would go out after nightfall; there was so little money about that Malibran or Pasta herself could have made no difference to the takings. In such times not even a new score by God Himself would be worth paying for—so ran the correspondence of impresarios and publishers.[223] Seasons were cut short, pay scales were reduced, some of the weaker impresarios failed, and even the "Napoleons" of the profession such as Merelli and Lanari were badly shaken. The opera industry did not completely recover from the revolutionary years until 1854.

Until around 1843 the opera world—according to one reliable witness, Antonio Ghislanzoni, active at the time in Milan—had shown little nationalistic ardor either in the hall or on the stage.[224] Attitudes varied, but the commonest seems to have been that expressed by the agent Giovanni Battista Benelli: "If they would only get it over with, one way or another, and let the poor artists breathe!"[225] Many performers took engagements abroad, in countries like Spain and Cuba, which were on a different revolutionary timetable. But even when calm returned after 1849, the strength of the reaction itself showed that the 1848 upheaval had shaken beyond repair the old local hierarchies on which the theaters had depended and with them the unquestioning loyalty to the old governments of the various states. In the world of opera this questioning of assumptions within the upper classes coincided with other changes that had been under way even before 1848, such as the rise of journals and scientific clubs and the habit of reading novels. In Piedmont after 1848 and in the rest of Italy after unification, opportunities for political pursuits opened up on both the national and the municipal level. All of these things undermined the old opera industry even as it seemed to be entering its period of greatest expansion.

The old masked balls that had been the high spot of the social year gradually faded away. By 1869 the author of a popular work of moral uplift found it necessary to say that "no one who has not lived in Italy before 1848 can realize what the theater meant in those days. . . . The success of a new opera was a capital event that stirred to its depths the city lucky enough to have witnessed it, and word of it ran all over Italy."[226] In short, in a long process

223. Carlo Gagliani to Agostino Marchesi, Faenza 11 January 1849, Berardo Winter to Lanari, Naples 25 September 1849, BNF CV 364/36, 416/179; Giovanni Ricordi to Rosa Morandi, 14 June 1848, in Radiciotti, *Lettere inedite*, 105; Giovanni Ricordi to Verdi, 21 February 1849, I-PA; (quoting Sanguineti, impresario of the Teatro Carlo Felice, Genoa).

224. Antonio Ghislanzoni, *Storia di Milano dal 1836 al 1848*, in *In chiave di baritono* (Milan, 1882), 159–60.

225. Giovanni Battista Benelli to Lanari, 6 April 1849, I-Fn, CV 346/142.

226. Michele Lessona, *Volere è potere* (Florence, 1869), 298.

that varied from one place and one generation to another, the lyric theater was losing its central place in town life.

The opera industry was also becoming less creative. It was producing more and more performances of fewer and fewer works. The modern notion of opera as a museum art was wholly foreign to Italy up to the late eighteenth century: operas were by definition new works. That notion remained largely foreign to Italy until the 1830s, though the habit began to spread of putting on operas that had had their first performance in another town, usually no more than a few years back. The whole outlook of the people who created operas was still much more akin to that of Hollywood in the 1930s than to anything that goes on in opera houses today; so many new works were constantly being turned out that Meyerbeer, for instance, feared his librettist might let a rival composer get in first with some striking "situations" he was counting on for his own new opera.[227]

The notion of repertory opera began to come in during the 1840s. The term itself was used in correspondence of 1845 between the impresario Balochino and the soprano Tacchinardi-Persiani, who was to start a Vienna season in "a repertory opera best suited to her and to the company." The term came up at the Regio, Turin, from 1849, and it was officially embodied in the contract for the management of the Naples royal theaters from 1851.[228]

This was the time when the rhythm of production of new works began to slacken. If we allow for comic operas, one-act *farse,* and pasticcios (operas cobbled together from bits of existing works), it seems likely that more new works were produced in some of the years between 1750 and 1814 than at any time before or after. At La Scala (founded in 1778) the decade with the highest number of new creations was 1831–40, with thirty-eight. By the 1860s new creations were down to one or two a year. The San Carlo in the late 1830s was still expected to put on five operas a year that had not previously been heard there, three of them expressly written for Naples, but in the 1840s no more than one or two of these bespoke jobs were asked for each year.[229] By the mid-1850s, when the industry had fully recovered from the upheaval of 1848–49, repertory opera was becoming established. By the 1870s it was the norm. A leading singer had his or her repertory of perhaps twenty parts: star singers could ask for the right to choose which operas they would appear in and could in turn be asked to appear in "their" parts at short notice. This made for frequent disputes and for scamped productions.

227. Meyerbeer, *Briefwechsel,* 1:525, 529 (about *Il crociato in Egitto,* 1824).

228. Carlo Balochino to Fanny Tacchinardi-Persiani, 12 February 1845, Vienna, Stadtbibliothek; Basso, *Il teatro della città,* 263–65; *Prospetti di appalto per lo R. Teatro di San Carlo.*

229. Carlo Gatti, *Il Teatro alla Scala nella storia e nell'arte (1778–1963),* 2 vols. (Milan: Ricordi, 1964), chronology by Giampiero Tintori; *Prospetti di appalto per lo R. Teatro di San Carlo.*

If this was the rule even at La Scala, one hardly likes to imagine what the Constantinople season of that same year can have been like: the leading bass was expected, though under protest, to sing up to eighteen parts.[230]

The slackening of creativity had something to do with the spread of a new kind of opera house, a large, unsubsidized house that brought low-priced opera and ballet to a wider public. The history of theater construction in Italy in the years from 1750 to 1850 saw, on the one hand, wooden theaters replaced with theaters of masonry construction, often after a fire or other disaster, and on the other hand, the construction of many new theaters, some next to the old ones but others in towns that had not previously had a permanent opera house. In the first category are the principal theaters of Florence (La Pergola, reconstructed in masonry in 1755), Rome (Tordinona, later Apollo, 1796, and Argentina, 1837), Bergamo (Cerri, later Sociale, 1807), and Palermo (Carolino, 1809), among others. In the second category there were opera houses built in cities that already had a number of theaters, such as La Fenice, Venice (1792), and the Carlo Felice, Genoa (1828); there were also cities with new theaters, such as Faenza (1788), Pesaro (1818), and Forlimpopoli (1825), among many others. All of these theaters, however, still represented the traditional hierarchical scheme for an opera house centered on the aristocracy. The new large opera houses built in the 1850s and the 1860s, to the contrary, brought on, as Marcello Conati has written, a new commercialization of opera through private investment on an "epic and adventurous" scale, but also a "hardening of models and formulas" and therefore an impoverishment.[231]

Large theaters offering some kind of entertainment at low prices were not new. In the early nineteenth century several open-air arenas were built to give daytime as well as evening performances. Performances in the daytime or early evening were generally understood to appeal to a lower social class than late evening performances: the Naples authorities more than once forbade matinees at the royal theater of San Carlo in order to avoid "putting it on the same level as theaters of the third rank."[232] The arenas, however, seem at first not to have given opera, though some were run by impresarios who at the same time put on opera in fashionable indoor theaters. The Anfiteatro Corea, Rome (built 1803), did well enough out of bullbaiting, bareback riding, and

230. Santley, *Student and Singer,* 234; Rosmini, *La legislazione,* 1:527; Luigi Parmeggiani to Marchetti, 1866, I-FOc, Piancastelli, Autografi, s. v. "Marchetti."

231. Marcello Conati, "La musica a Reggio nel secondo Ottocento," in *Teatro a Reggio Emilia,* ed. Sergio Romagnoli and Elvira Garbero, 2 vols. (Florence: Sansoni, 1980), 2:127–60, esp. 127–28.

232. *Storia di Napoli,* 10 vols. (Naples: Edizioni Scientifiche Italiane, 1967–74), 8:773; Deputazione degli Spettacoli to Minister of the Interior, 29 July 1823, I-Nas, Min. Interno II inv., fol. 4355; Larussa, *Sulle cagioni del decadimento,* 22–26.

fireworks displays to be contended for over several decades by Paterni and the Cartoni family.[233] There were also minor theaters of no great size where cheap opera performances were given: in Naples the Teatro La Fenice as early as 1817 was putting on daytime and evening performances, with two companies singing alternately, and by 1839 it was giving twice-daily *Norma*s, no less.[234]

Around midcentury the new style of theater building and the new repertory opera came together. Very large theaters were now built for the specific purpose of giving operas, though they might also put on equestrian or acrobatic displays or, from the 1870s, the new French- or German-inspired operetta. Of a number of such theaters built in the 1850s, two (at Bari and Salerno) were in the south, a region where, until then, theaters outside the capital cities had been few and had in the main been used fitfully by comic opera companies touring a southern circuit. From the 1830s on, the social customs of north-central Italy spread gradually to the southern provinces: the first permanent theater was built in Foggia in 1828, in Taranto, and in Lecce and other towns between 1830 and 1850. Still, as late as 1871, of the 940 Italian theaters on the official list, only 170 were in the former Kingdom of the Two Sicilies, and many of these were small.[235] Other theaters, such as the Pagliano in Florence (built in 1853 by an eccentric who had made a fortune out of an herbal elixir), the Vittorio Emanuele in Turin (1857), and the Dal Verme in Milan (1864), at times played an important part in the operatic life of those cities.

Because these theaters were built by private enterprise and were unsubsidized, we know far less about the way they were run than we do about those older theaters with which governments concerned themselves. Most were expected to pay their way, and some—the Politeama in Rome (1862–83) for one—did not last long. The Marzi brothers, exceptionally busy but financially unreliable impresarios, behaved no worse, it would seem, in the cheap theaters than at La Scala: if anything the pretensions of the old leading theaters may have brought disaster closer once resources failed and governments ceased to care.

Admission prices in the new large theaters—to judge from the little we know of them—were lower than those of the old leading theaters by about one-half or two-thirds in the cheaper parts of the house. It says something about the audience that in 1868 the Pagliano in Florence gave commercial

---

233. I-Ras, Camerale III, Teatri, busta 2137, nos. 6, 7, 19.

234. Rossini to Pietro Cartoni, 26 October 1817, I-FOc, Piancastelli 405.39; *Cronache del giorno,* 1839 (broadsheet put out by Deputazione degli Spettacoli, Naples, in the private collection of Franco Mancini).

235. See the original version of Benedetto Croce, *I teatri di Napoli, secolo XV–XVIII* (Naples, 1891), appendix 10; I-Nas, Min. Interno II inv., fol. 706; Rosmini, *La legislazione,* 2:581–97.

travelers a discount, while in 1885 a large new opera house at Lecce had a special price for children under seven.[236] Audiences such as these, with a strong contingent of shopkeepers, minor civil servants and other clerical employees, and artisans and their families, had existed since the mid-eighteenth century. But until the mid-nineteenth century they had not been expected to appear (elsewhere than in the gallery) at the opera seria, especially not in the fashionable season; if they did, that was because the upper-class audience was at another theater that evening.[237] Now the hierarchical array shifted somewhat. Opera seria invaded far more theaters that once specialized in "minor" genres; at the same time the shopkeeping, clerical, and artisan audiences no doubt expanded, but chiefly into the better parts of the large new "popular" theaters. In the old leading theaters, generally dominated by the boxholders, the traditional hierarchy died hard. This we may deduce from the way they closed down (presumably rather than put on something cheaper) when times were bad and subsidies were cut and from the near boycott with which the Rome aristocracy greeted the Teatro Costanzi in 1880: the new opera house had two open galleries and only three tiers of boxes—proof in their eyes that it was a "popular" theater.[238] Things were changing even in the old fashionable theaters—after the first years the Costanzi established itself as the leading Rome opera house—but the process was slow. The nominal impresario of the first season at the Costanzi was the old Vincenzo Jacovacci, then at the end of a forty-year career; he died immediately afterwards. In practice he had done little beyond supplying a company. Whether in new popular theaters or old royal ones, the initiative by the 1870s had slipped out of the hands of the impresarios.

Barbaja had made an undeniable difference to the career of the young Rossini, and Merelli and Lanari to that of the young Verdi. But the composers whose first works appeared in these decades—Ponchielli, Catalani, Puccini—were launched by publishers. Not only that, publishers decided where operas were to be done, controlled casting, supplied set and costume designs, and often directed the production, if not in person then through the issue of detailed production books.

This change too had come about gradually. Italian music publishers developed out of music copying, engraving, and printing, thanks in large part to the spread of the piano. The firms of Artaria and Ricordi—both founded in Milan by Italians with previous German experience—made a modest start in 1805 and 1808; the firm of Lucca was a breakaway from Ricordi in 1825. There were other music publishers, especially in Naples, but those who mat-

236. I-Fas, Prefettura di Firenze, 1868, fol. 164, no. 11802; manifesto of Politeama Principe di Napoli, Lecce, E1885, I-FOc, Piancastelli, Autografi, s. v. "Marchetti."

237. Pacini, *Le mie memorie,* 20 (on opening night at the Teatro Argentina, Rome, C1821).

238. Frajese, *Dal Costanzi all'Opera,* 1:25, 45–46.

tered by the 1870s were Ricordi, Lucca (to be merged with Ricordi again in 1888), and Sonzogno, an existing firm of publisher-printers who branched out into opera.[239]

What brought the publishers into opera production was first, the gradual trend toward repertory opera, which meant an increasing demand for the hire of orchestral scores, and second, the establishment of copyright protection. In 1836 a publisher in Naples could still be described by a rival as eccentric and mad for wanting to know where a score let out on hire was to be performed and by which singers.[240] Within a few years not only were publishers beginning to exercise this kind of "quality control"; they were beginning to commission scores and act as go-betweens to composers and impresarios.

Francesco Lucca and his wife were something of pioneers in this. In 1845 the Lucca firm commissioned Verdi to write an opera (which later became *Il corsaro*) without at that time having any particular theater in mind; the same firm attempted to commission a libretto for the composer Lauro Rossi to set to music for Madrid; in the following year Lucca dealt on Verdi's behalf with the London manager who was to put on the first production of *I masnadieri*. In 1853 he influenced Mercadante's choice of subject for an opera for Naples, and he seems to have been determinant in working out the contract with the impresario. Verdi had meanwhile taken a dislike to Lucca and signed (in 1847) his first long-term contract with Ricordi.[241] From then on Ricordi acted on Verdi's behalf in dealings with impresarios.

During the 1850s publishers began to supply designs and sometimes production books.[242] The key influence here was the example of the Paris Opéra, with its elaborate and historically accurate productions, an influence that worked on Italy through Verdi—by then a Paris composer some of the time— and through the requirements of Meyerbeer's Paris operas. At the same time publishers started insisting that scores should not be altered without their consent and that any changes should be made by the composer. Somewhat later publishers started dictating casting. In 1865 Lucca laid down who

239. Gatti, *Il Teatro alla Scala*, 1:49–52, 141–42, 154–55, 164–65; *Dizionario biografico degli italiani*, s.v. "Artaria," 4:348–51; Rosmini, *La legislazione*, 2:228–81.

240. Giuseppe Viceconta to Capranica, 18 February 1836, I-Rburcardo, Fondo Capranica.

241. Julian Budden, *The Operas of Verdi*, 3 vols. (London: Cassell, 1973–81; rev. ed., Oxford: Clarendon Press, 1991), 1:245, 364–65 (volume and page number citations are to the original edition); Cametti, *Un poeta melodrammatico romano*, 245; Verdi, *I copialettere*, 26–34, 37–40; Saverio Mercadante to Francesco Lucca, 29 July 1853, I-Ms, CA 3735. See also contracts between the Marzi brothers on one side and Lucca and the composer Errico Petrella on the other, for Petrella's *Il Duca di Scilla*, 30 March 1858, I-Mt, Sp. P. 112/1.

242. For example, for *Simon Boccanegra* at Reggio Emilia, F1857: Tito Ricordi to Verdi, 6 May 1857, I-PAi. For a detailed account of these productions, see Marcello Conati, *Il "Simon Boccanegra" di Verdi a Reggio Emilia (1857): Storia documentata: Alcune varianti alla prima edizione dell'opera* (Reggio Emilia: Teatro Municipale "Romolo Valli," 1984).

should sing in Meyerbeer's *L'Africaine* at La Scala; by the 1870s it was the general practice for the publisher "to propose, accept, or refuse artists."[243]

By the last third of the century the publisher controlled the composer and much of the production and casting, so much so that the Turin impresario who had successfully introduced Massenet to Italy (with *Le roi de Lahore,* 1878), and to whom the composer had promised his next opera *(Hérodiade),* could not get that work because of disagreements with the publisher over casting. In the next decade Catalani would not contemplate dealing with an impresario directly even when the publisher was too busy to attend to him or gave Catalani other grounds for dissatisfaction.[244]

What was new in all this was not so much the publishers' control over opera seasons: Ricordi and Sonzogno alternated, acting in substance as managers of La Scala through most of the 1890s, which put them in a position in Milan akin to that of the old noble proprietors of Venice and Rome theaters who had virtually run their own opera seasons, though with an impresario nominally in charge. What was new was their ability to dictate to professional impresarios in hundreds of theaters scattered throughout Italy. It was, in short, the arrival of modern mechanisms of publicity and administration and the rise of demands that those mechanisms could meet that made the old system of opera production meaningless and antiquated.

BIBLIOGRAPHIC NOTE

Only recently has the subject of this chapter begun to be studied in detail, which means that the reader must necessarily be referred to the only systematic attempt to deal with Italian opera on the whole as a business, John Rosselli, *The Opera Industry in Italy from Cimarosa to Verdi: The Role of the Impresario* (Cambridge: Cambridge University Press, 1984), in Italian translation in an amplified verstion as *L'impresario d'opera: Arte e affari nel teatro musicale italiano dell'Ottocento* (Turin: Edizioni di Torino/ Musica, 1985). For a more recent study of an individual impresario, Luca Casimiro degli Albizzi, see William C. Holmes, *Opera Observed: Views of a Florentine Impresario in the Early Eighteenth Century* (Chicago: University of Chicago Press, 1993). Other overall views can be found in works dedicated to a variety of topics: for the eighteenth century, Michael F. Robinson, *Naples and Neapolitan Opera* (Oxford: Clarendon Press, 1972); for the nineteenth century, general information can be found in several works on Verdi by two authors with a profound knowledge of Italian musi-

---

243. Mazzucato to Giraldoni, 1865, I-Ms, CA 2905; Gomes to Cattaneo, 2 July 1874, in Antônio Carlos Gomes, *Carteggi italiani,* ed. Gaspare Nello Vetro (Milan: Nuove Edizioni, 1979), 101.

244. Depanis, *I Concerti Popolari,* 1:187–88; Alfredo Catalani, *Lettere di Alfredo Catalani a Giuseppe Depanis,* ed. Carlo Gatti (Milan: Istituto di Alta Cultura, 1946), 83, 115.

cal culture: Bruno Cagli, "Verdi and the Business of Writing Operas," and Julian Budden, "Verdi and the Contemporary Italian Operatic Scene," both in *The Verdi Companion,* ed. William Weaver and Martin Chusid (New York: Norton, 1979), 106–20 and 67–105, respectively. There are also important chapters of a general nature in each of the three volumes of Julian Budden, *The Operas of Verdi,* 3 vols. (London: Cassell, 1973–81; rev. ed., Oxford: Clarendon Press, 1991). For an analogous attempt to provide background for Donizetti's opera production, see Alexander L. Ringer, "Aspetti socio-economici dell'opera italiana nel periodo donizettiano," in *Atti del primo convegno internazionale di studi donizettiani, 22–28 settembre 1975* (Bergamo: Azienda Autonoma di Turismo, 1983), 943–58.

In the current state of scholarship it is still essential to consult the manuscript documentation that is conserved in abundance, although not always in complete series, in many state and municipal archives and in a number of special collections, especially those of the Museo Teatrale alla Scala, Milan, the Biblioteca Teatrale del Burcardo, Rome, and the Collezione Piancastelli of the Biblioteca Comunale, Forlì. There is material in a limited number of theater archives, especially those of La Fenice (Venice) (in the Fondazione Olga e Ugo Levi, Venice), Teatro Regio Ducal (Parma), and in the archives of some composers, Verdi in particular. There are many Verdi letters in photocopy or transcription at the Istituto Nazionale di Studi Verdiani, Parma; the large microfilm collection of its U.S. sister institution, the American Institute for Verdi Studies at New York University, contains in addition to many of the same materials the entire collection of the composer's correspondence and other documents preserved at his villa at Sant'Agata, near Parma; up to now scholars have had only very limited access to the actual archive at Sant'Agata, which is undoubtedly very rich. Another important resource for the correspondence of Verdi, Puccini, and many other nineteenth-century composers is the Archivio Storico of the publisher Ricordi in Milan. The archives of Casa Ricordi also contain many kinds of documents on opera production; those pertaining to Verdi are also available on microfilm at the American Institute for Verdi Studies. The Biblioteca Comunale, Pescia, has an important collection of Pacini materials, and there are Nicola Vaccai papers in the Biblioteca Comunale, Tolentino.

Persons directly involved in the production system of opera have left very little archival material: two important exceptions are the collection of portions of the papers of the impresarios Luca Casimiro degli Albizzi (some 3,500 documents) in the private collection of the Palazzo Guicciardini, Florence, and of Alessandro Lanari (some 15,000 letters) in the Carteggi Vari of the Biblioteca Nazionale, Florence. On the Albizzi papers see the study by William Holmes cited above. Another important portion of the Lanari archives in the same library is labeled as the Fondo Lanari and has been cataloged in Marcello de Angelis, ed., *Le cifre del melodramma: L'archivio inedito dell'impresario teatrale Alessandro Lanari nella Biblioteca nazionale centrale di Firenze (1815–1870),* 2 vols. (Florence: Giunta Regionale Toscana/La Nuova Italia, 1982). De Angelis discusses the activities of Lanari in his *Le carte dell'impresario: Melodramma e costume teatrale nell'Ottocento* (Florence: Sansoni, 1982). The papers of the impresario Carlo Balochino in the Stadtbibliothek of Vienna and those of the agent Giovanni Battista Benelli in the Biblioteca Braidense of Milan are also worthy of note. On them see Bruno Cagli, "Rossini a Londra e al Théâtre Italien di Parigi: Con documenti inediti dell'impresario G. B. Benelli," *Bollettino del Centro rossiniano di studi* 1–3 (1981): 5–53.

The best contemporaneous guides are two manuals by and for practitioners: Giovanni Valle, *Cenni teorico — pratici sulle aziende teatrali* (Milan, 1823), and Enrico Rosmini, *La legislazione e la giurisprudenza dei teatri,* 2 vols. (Milan, 1872–73). Of interest even if inspired by more propagandistic ends are Angelo Petracchi, *Sul reggimento de' pubblici teatri* (Milan, 1821); [Carlo Ritorni], *Consigli sull'arte di dirigere gli spettacoli* (Bologna, 1825); Francesco D'Arcais, "L'industria musicale in Italia," *Nuova antologia di scienze, lettere ed arti,* 2d ser., 15 (15 May 1879): 133–48. In a class of their own are the writings of Stendhal, whose direct reports offer a startling mixture of inside knowledge and wild misstatement, particularly in his *Vie de Rossini* (Paris, 1824), in English translation as *Life of Rossini,* trans. and ed. Richard N. Coe, new and rev. ed. (London: J. Calder; New York: Orion Press, 1970; reprint, New York: Riverrun Press, 1985), his *Rome, Naples et Florence,* 3d ed., 2 vols. (Paris, 1826), in English translation as *Rome, Naples, and Florence,* trans. Richard N. Coe (London: J. Calder, 1959), and his *Correspondance,* ed. Henri Martineau and Vittorio Del Litto, 2 vols. (Paris: Gallimard/Bibliothèque de la Pléiade, 1962–67).

The attentive reader will find a good deal of material about the opera business (often not exploited except on the level of anecdote) in the biographies, autobiographies, and correspondence of the leading figures in opera, composers first among them. An exhaustive critical edition of Rossini's correspondence has now been inaugurated with the first volume of Giochino Rossini, *Lettere e documenti (dal 29 febbraio al 17 marzo 1822),* ed. Bruno Cagli and Sergio Ragni (Pesaro: Fondazione Rossini, 1992); see also Giuseppe Radiciotti, *Gioacchino Rossini: Vita documentata, opere ed influenza su l'arte,* 3 vols. (Tivoli: Majella, 1927–29). The correspondence of Bellini—*Epistolario,* ed. Luisa Cambi (Milan: Mondadori, 1943)—is a rich source, as is Donizetti's correspondence—Guido Zavadini, *Donizetti: Vita, musiche, epistolario* (Bergamo: Istituto Italiano d'Arti Grafiche, 1948). Verdi's published letter books, *I copialettere di Giuseppe Verdi,* ed. Gaetano Cesari and Alessandro Luzio (Milan: Stucchi Ceretti, 1913; reprint, Bologna, Arnaldo Forni, 1968), are the most useful of several collections; all of them will ultimately be superseded by the edition of Verdi's complete correspondence now being prepared by the Istituto di Studi Verdiani at Parma. In the meantime there is an important study on Verdi's relations with his favorite theater that presents a large number of documents: Marcello Conati, *La bottega della musica: Verdi e la Fenice* (Milan: Il Saggiatore, 1983). See also *Carteggio Verdi-Boito,* ed. Mario Medici and Marcello Conati, in English translation as *The Verdi-Boito Correspondence,* trans. William Weaver (Chicago: University of Chicago Press, 1994). See also Hans Busch, ed. and trans., *Verdi's "Aida": The History of an Opera in Letters and Documents* (Minneapolis: University of Minnesota Press, 1978), and *Verdi's "Othello" and "Simon Boccanegra" (Revised Version) in Letters and Documents,* 2 vols. (Oxford: Clarendon Press, 1988). The careers of once well-known but now forgotten composers can be revealing: witness the *Vita di Nicola Vaccaj* by his son, Giulio Vaccai (Bologna, 1882) and the lively though inaccurate *Le mie memorie artistiche* by Giovanni Pacini (Florence 1875; reprint Lucca: Maria Pacini Fazzi, 1981).

The correspondence and journals of foreign composers trying their hand in Italy can be illuminating, especially the colorful *Mémoires* . . . *comprenant ses voyages in Italie, en Allemagne, en Russie, et en Angleterre, 1803–1865* of Hector Berlioz (Paris, 1870), in English translation as *The Memoirs of Hector Berlioz* . . . *Including His Travels in Italy, Germany, Russia, and England, 1803–1865,* ed. and trans. David Cairns (New York: Norton, 1975); Giacomo Meyerbeer, *Briefwechsel und Tagebücher,* ed. Heinz and Gudrun Becker, 4 vols. (Berlin: De Gruyter, 1960–85); Antônio Carlos Gomes, *Carteggi italiani,* ed. Gaspare Nello Vetro (Milan: Nuove Edizioni, 1979); Otto Nicolai, *Tagebücher,* ed. B. Schröder (Leipzig: Breitkopf und Härtel, 1892), and *Briefe an seinen Vater,* ed. Wilhelm Altmann (Regensburg: Bosse, 1924).

Biographies and autobiographies of singers are generally of an unpromising, self-congratulatory genre, but two stand out for their information on the production system: Gilbert-Louis Duprez, *Souvenirs d'un chanteur* (Paris, 1880), and Charles Santley, *Student and Singer* (London, 1892), to which we might add the biography of a singer who moved to Italy, Louis Quicherat, *Adolphe Nourrit: Sa vie, son talent, son caractère, sa correspondance,* 3 vols. (Paris, 1867). See also John Rosselli, *Singers of Italian Opera: The History of a Profession* (Cambridge: Cambridge University Press, 1992).

Biographical studies on individual impresarios or others in the production system of opera are almost totally lacking. Two exceptions are Marcello de Angelis, *Le carte dell'impresario: Melodramma e costume teatrale nell'Ottocento* (Florence: Sansoni: 1982), on Alessandro Lanari, and Giovanni Azzaroni and Paola Bignami, *Corticelli Mauro impresario* (Bologna: Nuova Alfa, 1990). Useful for the later nineteenth century is Giuseppe Depanis, *I Concerti Popolari e il Teatro Regio di Torino: Quindici anni di vita musicale; appunti-ricordi,* 2 vols. (Turin: Società Tipografico-Editrice Nazionale, 1914–15). Gino Monaldi, *Impresari celebri del secolo XIX* (Rocca San Casciano: Cappelli, 1918) is so inaccurate as to be of only questionable value. More reliable is the *Dizionario biografico dei più celebri poeti ed artisti melodrammatici* . . . *che fiorirono in Italia dal 1800 at 1860* (Turin, 1860), whose author, the agent Francesco Regli, lists impresarios and agents as well as artists (with some inaccuracy, however) and gives, somewhat incidentally, a picture of the overall operatic scene in the early nineteenth century. I have myself followed Regli's lead to compile a directory; see John Rosselli, *Elenco degli impresarios e agenti teatrali italiani,* a computer printout that can be consulted in a number of libraries: Music Library, Senate House Library, London; American Institute for Verdi Studies, New York University; Museo Teatrale alla Scala, Milan; Istituto di Studi Verdiani, Parma; Società Italiana di Musicologia, Bologna; Istituto di Bibliografia Musicale, Rome. See also Rosselli, "Agenti teatrali nel mondo dell'opera lirica italiana dell'Ottocento," *Rivista italiana di musicologia* 17 (1982): 134–54.

Another type of source, and one so uneven as to require patient scrutiny, is the many histories of individual theaters, on which see the copious listing in Alfredo Giovine, *Bibliografia di teatri musicali italiani* (Bari: Fratelli Laterza, 1982). These histories divide into older works written in the late nineteenth and early twentieth centuries, often by people directly involved in the theatrical activities they describe, and more recent works. Some of the first group are particularly useful, thanks to their positivistic belief in the value of accurate facts: Alessandro Gandini, *Cronistoria dei teatri di Modena*, 3 vols. (Modena, 1873; reprint, Bologna: Arnaldo Forni, 1969); Paolo Emilio Ferrari, *Spettacoli drammatico-musicali e coreografici in Parma* (Parma, 1884); Pompeo Cambiasi, *La Scala*, 4th ed. (Milan, 1889); various works by Giuseppe Radiciotti, in particular, *Teatro, musica e musicisti in Sinigaglia* (Milan, 1893); Carlo L. Curiel, *Il Teatro San Pietro di Trieste* (Milan: Archetipografia, 1937); Alberto Cametti, *Il Teatro di Tordinona poi di Apollo*, 2 vols. (Tivoli: Chicca, 1938). Some more recent histories have sumptuous illustrations but, unfortunately, somewhat imprecise texts. However, notable exceptions exist among them: Alberto Basso, ed., *Storia del Teatro Regio di Torino*, 5 vols. (Turin: Cassa di Risparmio di Torino, 1976–83); Nicola Mangini, *I teatri di Venezia* (Milan: Mursia, 1974); Michele Girardi and Franco Rossi, *Il Teatro La Fenice di Venezia: Cronologia degli spettacoli 1792–1936* (Venice: Albrizzi Editori, 1989); Thomas Bauman, "The Society of La Fenice and its First Impresarios," *Journal of the American Musicological Society* 39 (1986): 332–54; Paolo Fabbri and Roberto Verti, *Due secoli di teatro per musica a Reggio Emilia: Repertorio cronologico delle opere e dei balli, 1645–1857* (Reggio Emilia: Teatro Edizioni del Municipale Valle, 1987); Marcello Conati, "La musica a Reggio nel secondo Ottocento," in *Teatro a Reggio Emilia*, ed. Sergio Romagnoli and Elvira Garbero, 2 vols. (Florence: Sansoni, 1980), 127–60, an essay that ranges far beyond its geographically restricted topic; and various articles on individual cities and theaters in *Enciclopedia dello spettacolo*, ed. Sandro d'Amico, 9 vols. (Rome: Le Maschere, 1954–62). For La Scala there is the excellent chronology of Giampiero Tintori in appendix to Carlo Gatti, *Il Teatro alla Scala nella storia e nell'arte (1778–1963)*, 2 vols. (Milan: Ricordi, 1964), a work written according to now outdated criteria. Until very recently there was no adequate history of the San Carlo, Naples. The theater's 250th anniversary produced two large celebratory sets, of which the most important historical studies are found in *Il Teatro di San Carlo, 1737–1987*, ed. Franco Mancini, Bruno Cagli, and Agostino Ziino, 3 vols. (Naples: Electa, 1987); Carlo Marinelli Roscioni's chronology and articles by others are found in *Il Teatro di San Carlo di Napoli*, 2 vols. (Naples: Guida, 1987). We need more comparative studies like Elvidio Surian, "Organizzazione, gestione, politica teatrale e repertori operistici a Napoli e in Italia, 1800–1820," in *Musica e cultura a Napoli dal XV al XIX secolo*, ed. Lorenzo Bianconi and Renato Bossa (Florence: Olschki, 1983), 317–67.

A bibliographical review of these and other problems connected with the full panorama of a bibliography *raisonnée* can be found in Roberto Verti, "Dieci anni di studi sulle fonti per la storia materiale dell'opera italiana nell'Ottocento," *Rivista italiana di musicologia* 20 (1985): 124–63.

Opera Production from Italian Unification to the Present

FIAMMA NICOLODI

1. Opera in the New Italy: Municipal Theaters and Impresarial Management

In June 1867 the Italian government ceded the opera houses to the governing bodies of their respective cities. This was no enlightened program of decentralization; rather, it was a choice dictated by urgent economic demands. Since the city governments—the *comuni*—had the authority (but not the obligation) to provide financing, many theaters went without their help. There were many complex reasons for the cities' decision (which constituted a real deterrent for the impresario). Among these were flaming quarrels, at times reaching the point of litigation, between the town councils and the boxholders; the cuts that the national government imposed on municipal budgets; the city's more urgent need to allocate money for public expenditures that had absolute priority—roads, water mains, hospitals, and schools. There was also political and social discussion concerning an institution—opera—that was still thought, generally and not always inappropriately, to benefit only the few.

Opera houses that had formerly flourished declined for a number of rea-

The following abbreviations are used in the notes: ACS = Archivio Centrale dello Stato; Div. = Divisione; B. = Busta; MinCulPop = Ministero della Cultura Popolare; Min. P. I. = Ministero della Pubblica Istruzione; Ord. = Carteggio Ordinario; PCM = Presidenza del Consiglio dei Ministri; RAI = Radio-Audizione Italiana; SIAE = Società Italiana degli Autori e Editori; SPD = Segreteria Particolare del Duce.

sons. The new nation lacked a clear cultural program (or, to put it differently, its policy was the nonintervention typical of liberal nations). There were recurrent economic downturns that hit agriculture particularly hard during the 1880s, bringing on crises of adjustment in a nation whose structure was predominantly agricultural as it evolved toward a new, industrial dimension. Not the least, there were changed artistic trends in the 1870s that increased the inherent risks of all aspects of opera production and made costs rise precipitously. Tastes had changed, and a higher artistic level was expected (this was the period of grand opera in four acts with ballets, huge choruses, and elaborate scenic effects). The chorus and the orchestra had grown in size, and productions had become more historically accurate. These, in short, are some of the factors that served to undermine the flourishing state of the theaters of the past.

La Pergola in Florence faced a difficult future after 1877, when the mayor of the city adamantly refused to continue the usual subsidies to the theater's owners (the members of the Accademia degli Immobili); from 1879 to 1883 the Teatro Carlo Felice of Genoa was inactive after a long quarrel between the boxholders and the city council had led to dissolving the civic orchestra, which had been led in its best days by Angelo Mariani; in 1884 the Teatro Apollo in Rome was closed (prompting a petition of protest to the municipal government signed by three hundred shopkeepers from the center of the city who claimed that its closing would hurt their businesses); in 1891 the Teatro Comunale of Bologna only presented concerts; in Venice La Fenice offered a carnival season only twelve times between 1872 and 1897 and was in a precarious financial state; in 1898 La Scala closed its doors because of a decision by the Milan city council that stated it was inopportune to contribute public funds to the entertainment "of the rich." On the traditional opening night at La Scala, 26 December 1897, an anonymous Milanese posted a black-bordered notice: "Closed due to the death of art, civic honor, and common sense."[1] There was increasing criticism of a state that provided for the education of its citizenry by financing schools, universities, libraries, and music conservatories, but that ignored the entire theatrical sector, in striking contrast, many objected, to other, culturally more evolved European countries.

    1. Ugo Morini, *La R. Accademia degli Immobili ed il suo Teatro "La Pergola" (1649–1925)* (Pisa: Simoncini, 1926), 133–34; Giovanni Battista Vallebona, *Il Teatro Carlo Felice: Cronistoria di un secolo 1828–1928* (Genoa: Cooperativa Fascista Poligrafici, 1928), 182; Alberto Cametti, *Il Teatro di Tordinona, poi di Apollo* (Tivoli: Chicca, 1938), 2:584; Lamberto Trezzini, ed., *Due secoli di vita musicale: Storia del Teatro Comunale di Bologna*, rev. ed., 3 vols. (Bologna: Nuova Alfa, 1987), 2:118; Nicola Mangini, *I teatri di Venezia* (Milan: Mursia, 1974), 227 (more accurately, La Fenice remained closed in the years 1872–73, 1877–78, 1880–81, 1882–83, 1883–84, 1887–88, 1890–91, and from 1892–93 to 1896–97); Giampiero Tintori, *Duecento anni di Teatro alla Scala: Cronologia* (Gorle: Grafica Gutenberg, 1979), 53.

Others pointed out that despite the dire economic problems that had resulted from the Franco-Prussian War (1870–71), France had never failed to grant its major theatrical institution, the Paris Opéra (which was, however, a state theater), a subsidy of 800,000 francs per year.[2]

Laws governing theatrical affairs were few and erratic. There were provisions for copyright protection (law of 25 June 1865, no. 2337); a surtax (much protested) of 10 percent on the gross earnings of theatrical spectacles (19 July 1868, no. 4480); and a law on censorship, enforcement of which was the task of the prefects (who were expected to defend morality, good conduct, the family, and public order). In 1883 *La gazzetta musicale di Milano*, a periodical owned by the Ricordi firm, complained, "Since the constitution of the Kingdom of Italy, nothing has been done for music." Its complaint was echoed by *La nuova antologia*, which, in contrast to Verdi's high opinion of the illustrious statesman, blamed Cavour for a major share in the government's lack of interest in the arts.[3]

In a nation that did not view musical education as part of society's cultural patrimony, the function of the theater as an institution was inevitably seen as hedonistic and recreational rather than educational or formative. One commentator observed:

> We cannot hope for a revival of the art of music in Italy if the nation does not promote education in the arts. The admirable system of theaters, concerts, and conservatories in Germany is based in the musical culture of the people, [a culture] that reaches the lowest social strata, thanks to obligatory instruction in choral singing from kindergarten and elementary school all the way to the university.[4]

Music went unmentioned in the law on obligatory, free elementary schools (Legge Coppino, 1877), and it was confined among optional activities (along with shop, gymnastics, and drawing) in decrees on the school system in 1888 (Boselli) and 1894 (Baccelli). It was recognized as an official and obligatory school subject only in the twentieth century—in 1923—with a program, in effect for little more than a year, worked out for Giovanni Gentile (then Minister of Public Instruction) by Giuseppe Lombardo Radice, and again, permanently, with the middle-school reform of 1962 (the provisions of which were inadequate, however). During the second half of the nineteenth century, some

2. Salvatore Farina, "La sovvenzione ai teatri," *La gazzetta musicale di Milano* 27 (31 March 1872): 103.

3. R. [Giulio Ricordi], "Musica e politica," *La gazzetta musicale di Milano* 38 (13 May 1883): 181; Francesco D'Arcais, "Il teatro musicale in Italia," *Nuova antologia di scienze, lettere ed arti* 1 (January 1866): 114–30, esp. 120.

4. Francesco D'Arcais, "Rassegna musicale e drammatica," *La nuova antologia* 25 (16 September 1889): 369–78, esp. 374.

individual cities acted to correct the negligence of the ministry of public education. This was true in Milan (initially, only in Milan), a city that had benefited from the school reforms of the Hapsburgs when it was under Austrian domination and where choral singing ("based on the study and the exercise of the cardinal principles of music") was part of school programs drawn up in 1867. The Milan city authorities stated, "Only when the principles of musical education are extended to all classes of the people will we have in the theaters and the other places where works of the [musical] arts are produced an intelligent public capable of a just evaluation of beauty."[5]

The unification of Italy produced a new theatrical map. In the 1890s official sources listed 1,055 theaters (prose theaters and opera houses) in 775 municipalities, only eleven of which were first-rank theaters offering opera only. These eleven were the Teatro Comunale in Bologna (autumn season only), the Bellini in Catania, La Pergola in Florence, the Carlo Felice in Genoa, La Scala in Milan, the San Carlo in Naples, the Bellini in Palermo, the Argentina and the Costanzi in Rome, the Regio in Turin, and La Fenice in Venice.[6]

The most interesting productions were concentrated in the "bourgeois capitals"; the provincial theaters, whose activity was notably less regular, offered productions limited for the most part to the existing repertory, not always put on in the best of taste but serving young singers and composers as a proving ground for their talents. One indication that times had changed and opportunities had shrunk is that beginning artists had to pay for their "self-promotion" when they moved up from a secondary theater to a more prestigious one.

Such payments were a clandestine practice that can be attested with certainty as early as the beginning of the twentieth century but that went back to around the mid-nineteenth century—to a time, that is, when repertory opera became the rule, the "consumer" attitude toward new works shifted to appreciation of a "museum" art, and beginners could no longer hope for support from an impresario acting as a talent scout. One proposal to aid young artists was drawn up in 1868 by Lauro Rossi, at the time director of the Milan Conservatory and a musician whose personal experience made him sympathetic to the problems of beginners (after the failure of a work of his in Naples in 1834, he headed an opera company in Mexico, then became impresario of theaters in New Orleans and Havana). Criticizing the exaggerated demands of the first-rank theaters (to which a composer gained entry "either because the maestro can pay the impresario a half-dozen thousands of

5. Antonio Ghislanzoni, "Del canto corale," *La gazzetta musicale di Milano* 22 (12 May 1867): 145–47 (quote, 147).

6. Enrico Rosmini, *Legislazione e giurisprudenza dei teatri,* 3d ed. (Milan, 1893), 843–65.

lire or thanks to protection"), Rossi proposed the founding of "experimental theaters" in every city in Italy. This, he argued, was "the most suitable way—because it is the most practical way—to encourage beginners and get the public to know them."

The Minister of Public Instruction, Emilio Broglio, seemed covertly to justify the operations of the larger theaters instead. Grand opera was popular everywhere and costs had risen: why, Broglio asked, should opera house managements sinking under the "Mephistophelian presumptions" (a reference to Boito's recent opera) of the "musical mastodons" then in vogue take on "such enormous expenses, with a high degree of probability that [the money] would be tossed away in an opening night greeted with catcalls?" Girolamo Alessandro Biaggi agreed with Broglio. Writing in 1876 he stated that in order to do away with the immoral custom of composers' having to pay to have their works performed (which discriminated against impoverished musicians and favored those who, "having money to spend in inverse proportion to their talent, try the patience of the public"), management contracts should stipulate that new works "be written by composers already known for other works that have met with success in some of the leading theaters of the realm."[7]

The end of the century saw the decline of a number of opera houses in small agricultural centers (such as Senigallia, Rimini, Pesaro, and Forlì), where during the summer or autumn fairs, the theater had once been able to offer operas of the highest quality, fully equal to those given in the capital cities. In the 1840s the impresario Alessandro Lanari had been able to put on the same operas, with the same company, throughout his customary circuit: the Teatro Comunale of Faenza, the Teatro della Comune in Forlì, La Fenice in Senigallia, the Apollo in Rome, or La Pergola in Florence. Fairs changed along with new trends in Italy's economic development: national expositions and world's fairs took the place of the old regional and local fairs, differing from them in both character (they tended to become more commercial and touristic) and in frequency (they were no longer annual).

Opera seasons tended to become more homogeneous, and in the subsidized theaters the summer and autumn seasons gradually died out. There

---

7. See D'Arcais, "Il teatro musicale," 123; Lauro Rossi, "Lettera ad un amico," *La gazzetta musicale di Milano* 23 (5 April 1868): 106; Salvatore Farina, "Cose della Scala," *La gazzetta musicale di Milano* 29 (4 October 1874): 323; C. M., "Torino," *La gazetta musicale di Milano* 26 (5 March 1871): 88; Piero Nardi, *Vita di Arrigo Boito* (Milan: Mondadori, 1942), 314ff. "The impresarios, hard, greedy, *inhuman, immoral* (as people say), demand to be paid to put on the works of beginners! But let's be fair: why would we want this to be different? . . . Once beginners used to start with farces, with brief opere buffe in two acts, and . . . now they all want to begin with tragic opera—with the so-called opera-ballo in four and five acts. And by choosing a grand opera for their first work, the young composers demonstrate and prove . . . that they don't really know what music is, what drama is, what theater is"; Girolamo Alessandro Biaggi, "Rassegna musicale," *La nuova antologia* 11 (February 1876): 431–32.

were several reasons for these changes: on the one hand the social condition of the petit bourgeois and middle classes had changed (their political dominance would be confirmed by the electoral reform of 1882); on the other hand the development of new means of communication (steamships, improved roads, railways) favored the exodus of the best artists, who left in search of new worlds to conquer and deprived Italy of a sizable number of voices. One journalist commented in 1889,

> From July or even June well into September, if not halfway through October, the big cities are deserted. The wealthy and those who want to be thought wealthy emigrate, and no major theatrical venture is possible during that period.[8]

Rio de Janeiro, Buenos Aires, Havana, Lima, Caracas, Santiago de Chile, New York, Chicago, Philadelphia, and San Francisco—cities that impresarios of the 1840s had already tested out in pioneering tours—became the most desirable destinations not only for the most highly acclaimed singers, whose fees reached dizzying sums,[9] but also for entire companies, including orchestral musicians, directorial personnel, chorus members, and corps de ballet.

In 1889 some twelve hundred persons took advantage of the different dates for opera seasons in the two hemispheres and left Italy (or, more precisely, left Milan, the city that had the greatest concentration of resources, with its eleven agencies, nine theatrical journals, four costume workshops, etc.) for South America.[10] In the five-year period between 1880 and 1885, the total spent by opera houses in Montevideo, New York, Caracas, Santiago, Buenos Aires, and Rio de Janeiro to pay the Milanese managements for principals, choruses, orchestras, costumes, sets, equipment, and shoes has been calculated at about 15 million lire.[11] As one commentator pointed out,

> Artists go to Buenos Aires and to Montevideo with the same nonchalance with which they once went from Rome to Bologna or from Milan to Venice. The steamships of the companies Navigazione Generale or Veloce companies are a good deal more comfortable than the dilapidated stagecoaches of old, the sea captains are more civil and nicer than the coachmen, and if at sea one runs the risk of having an accident, there is little chance of meeting with the brigands who, fifty years ago and even more recently, awaited travelers on the narrow mountain passes of the Apennines.[12]

---

8. D'Arcais, "Rassegna musicale e drammatica," 369.

9. See Giulio Ricordi, "L'arte musicale italiana," *La gazzetta musicale di Milano* 44 (30 June 1889): 411.

10. Ibid.

11. "Bonna nott ai sonador!" *La gazzetta musicale di Milano* 52 (15 July 1897): 403.

12. D'Arcais, "Rassegna musicale e drammatica," 371.

This great migration at the beginning of the twentieth century, which involved such Italian impresarios as Angelo Ferrari, Cesare Ciacchi, Walter Mocchi, and Ottavio Scotto, declined after World War I. In the early years of the twentieth century, America continued to attract not only composers of the "young school" (Puccini, Mascagni, Leoncavallo), whose visits were heralded in elaborate publicity campaigns, but also singers lured by the high fees paid by the opera houses and new phonograph companies (fees that Italian periodicals called "a real insult to the poverty . . . of the vocal cords").[13]

The chief victim of these changes was the impresario. If in the early nineteenth century the impresarios bore such nicknames as "emperor," "Napoleon," "dictator," "prince," these anachronisms were soon replaced by other, less noble but perhaps more pertinent sobriquets such as "stony-broke" *(spiantato)* or "left-overs cook" *(rimestatore).*" "Government protection— that is, endowments to the theaters—not taxes!" was what Verdi proposed to Guido Baccelli, the Minister of Public Instruction in 1883: "Given the condition of all sorts of theaters today, the poor impresarios cannot meet the demands of the artists and the public."

With or without subsidies to add to revenues from box rentals, seat subscriptions, and box-office ticket sales, the life of the impresario in post-unification Italy was more precarious and beset by worries than it had been in the past. Gone were paternalistic relations with the staff and artists' contracts that covered one or more seasons; the transatlantic voyages of the Strakosches, father and son, or Schürmann were still a thing of the future: "The impresario on tour always has an air about him of a man who gambles at Montecarlo, hence is always feverish, now rich, now poor."[14]

Marquis Gino Monaldi, a prolific chronicler of theatrical life whose career as impresario of the Argentina and the Costanzi in Rome ended, toward the end of the century, with balance sheets in the red, later recalled (in 1918) that

13. "Il teatro d'opera e i nostri artisti negli Stati Uniti d'America," *Il mondo artistico* 41 (1 April 1907): 4–5.

14. Alessandro Fiaschi, "L'impresario," *Il mondo artistico* 36 (11 January 1902): 2. For a complete account of the impresario, see John Rosselli, *The Opera Industry in Italy from Cimarosa to Verdi: The Role of the Impresario* (Cambridge: Cambridge University Press, 1984), in Italian translation, in an amplified version, as *L'impresario d'opera: Arte e affari nel teatro musicale italiano dell'Ottocento* (Turin: Edizioni di Torino/Musica, 1985). For a study totally devoted to the impresario Alessandro Lanari, see Marcello de Angelis, *Le carte dell'impresario: Melodramma e costume teatrale nell'Ottocento* (Florence: Sansoni, 1982), and De Angelis, ed., *Le cifre del melodramma: L'archivio inedito dell'impresario teatrale Alessandro Lanari nella Biblioteca nazionale centrale di Firenze (1815–1870),* 2 vols. (Florence: Giunta Regionale Toscana/La Nuova Italia, 1982). Although what they have to say is not always reliable, see also Maurice Strakosch, "Souvenirs d'un impresario" and Joseph Johan Schürmann, "Les étoiles en voyage" (1893), in Italian translation in Eugenio Gara, ed., *L'impresario in angustie: Adelina Patti e altre stelle fuori della leggenda (1886–1893)* (Milan: Bompiani, 1940).

only two or three of the fifty-odd impresarios he had known had made any money: "All the others either were completely ruined, became ushers, street-corner agents, doorkeepers, or clerks earning fifty or sixty lire a month (sometimes in the same theater where they had commanded, lording it over everyone), or they died in harness."[15] Guglielmo Canori, a journalist and impresario who succeeded Monaldi in Rome, "ended up hastening [the end of] his days in poverty and suffering."[16] At the peak of his fame, Canori had been responsible for organizing the "*Otello* train" in April 1888—that is, for transporting the Milan production of Verdi's *Otello* (singers, orchestra, chorus, and scenery) to Rome from Milan, where the production had just been put on at La Scala. For Anna Stolzmann, a renowned mezzo-soprano who became an impresario in Rome, the end of the road came in January 1895, a time when the city was shaken by a building crisis and bank scandals, with a summons to appear in court. At the same time, news reached her from Naples, where she held the contract for the San Carlo, that her management had been declared bankrupt.[17]

The impresarios faced serious problems. They were hemmed in by music publishers, who, as we shall see, had taken over opera house ownership as their special fief and were demanding higher and higher rents.[18] They had to pay a surtax of 10 percent on the gross receipts—a tax that not only the impresarios of opera houses but musicians, managers of prose theaters, playwrights, and critics did their utmost to combat.[19] They were at the mercy of the city councils, which might or might not provide subsidies and seldom delivered them on time. They had to deal with administrative commissions and city governments that dictated harsh contract terms, made heavy demands, and gave them little margin for individual initiative. As a result the impresarios lost autonomy and were universally regarded with mistrust.

During the last thirty years of the century, the theatrical press was filled with news of contracts unfilled, of impresarios in flight (Costantino Boccacci hid in a chimney flue to escape lynching), or of impresarios who had been caught trying to cut costs in dubious ways. Confrontations with mayors and theater owners were daily occurrences, as were orchestras and choruses in revolt because they had not been paid or having to find money from other

---

15. Gino Monaldi, *Impresari celebri del secolo XIX* (Rocca San Casciano: Cappelli, 1918), 5–6.

16. Ibid., 200.

17. Vittorio Frajese, *Dal Costanzi all'Opera*, 4 vols. (Rome: Capitolium, 1977–78), 1:135; Mario Rinaldi, *Due secoli di musica al Teatro Argentina*, 3 vols (Florence: Olschki, 1978), 2:1224ff.

18. Giovanni Ferrero, "Crisi teatrale: Appunti sul Teatro Regio di Torino," *La rivista musicale italiana* 6 (1899): 604–34, esp. 610.

19. Salvatore Farina, "La tassa sui teatri," *La gazzetta musicale di Milano* 24 (15 June 1869): 211–12; "La tassa teatrale," *Il teatro illustrato* 3 (30 June 1883): 94.

sources than the budget for hiring scabs. The Teatro La Fenice in Venice went through particularly turbulent times in the 1870s. It was already difficult to find someone willing to take on the contract to run the *gran teatro* because the contract terms stated that all revenues were to be handled by the board of directors (the *presidenza*), which would also pay the theater's creditors. This precaution was thought necessary "so that it will no longer happen, as in the past, that in spite of revenues from subscriptions and installment payments from the endowment, the impresario runs out of money after a few performances, making it necessary to tamper with the security [deposit]."[20] When the city council promised 79,000 lire, the board of directors declared its willingness, in the name of the owners' association, to finance the season. (The entire grant—*dote,* or "endowment"—amounted to 200,000 lire a year.) In return, however, it demanded that the impresario sign up a company of "first-rank artists" and "good singers for secondary parts" as important as those contracted in the past. In that particular year (1870) the roster of singers included Teresa Stolz (engaged for 36,000 lire for the season), Antonio Cotogni (18,000 lire), Giuseppe Fancelli (25,000 lire), Angelini (14,000 lire), and others. Dancers included the prima ballerina Gérod (10,000 lire), and Rossi-Brighenti (4,000 lire). After making their calculations the three candidates for the post of impresario withdrew, because "even if all the performances were successful and the receipts were as good as predicted," the expenses would still be exorbitant.[21] In 1872 the Venice city council, driven by the more vigilant democratic spirit demanded by the new times, proposed reducing the subsidy to 50,000 lire because La Fenice, which had no gallery, "cannot be frequented by all levels of the population." The top tier of boxes was made into a gallery in 1878.[22]

The Teatro Carlo Felice in Genoa went through difficult times as well, even before the tempestuous troubles that led to the theater's closing in 1879–83. In 1871 the impresario Alessandro Lavaggi fled the city without making the final quarterly payments *(quartali)* to his personnel, performances were suspended, and creditors stormed the city hall.[23] The contract to run seasons in Genoa's main opera house was offered competitively and ran for three years. It stipulated that each year five serious operas had to be given (one of them a premiere for the city), along with one "grand opera with ballet" *(grande opera-ballo)* and two full-scale ballets. The new works (as civic pride dictated

20. E. P., "Carteggi," *La gazzetta musicale di Milano* 25 (1 May 1870): 147.

21. *La gazzetta musicale di Milano* 25 (12 June 1870): 195.

22. *La gazzetta musicale di Milano* 25 (12 June 1870): 195; *La gazzetta musicale di Milano* 28 (16 March 1873): 87. See also Mangini, *I teatri di Venezia,* 227–28.

23. Vallebona, *Il Teatro Carlo Felice,* 172. For the Teatro Carlo Felice, see also Edilio Frassoni, *Due secoli di lirica a Genova,* 2 vols. (Genoa: Cassa di Risparmio di Genova e Imperia, 1980).

here and elsewhere) were to be "preferably by Genoese composers." The city council offered 55,000 lire, the use of nineteen boxes that it owned, and the services of the civic orchestra of sixty-three professional musicians; the impresario agreed to pay a security deposit of 30,000 lire.[24]

The vicissitudes of the Teatro San Carlo in Naples were just as picturesque as the city itself. From its founding in 1737 to the early nineteenth century, when Domenico Barbaja reigned supreme as its impresario, the San Carlo was the center of musical life in Naples. With the decline of subsidies— 250,000 francs in 1869–73, 214,243 francs in 1889–91—the theater's activities became erratic, productions were dropped before the end of the season, quarrels broke out between the impresarios and the political authorities, and the *masse* (orchestra, chorus, stage staff) went on strike.[25]

In the 1870s the San Carlo was directed by "Don" Antonio Musella, a figure always at the center of debate and worthy of the theater's colorful history. Verdi remembered him with bitterness despite the enormous success of the Neapolitan premiere of *Aida* in the spring of 1873, when Musella was impresario. By 1871 Musella had already earned a poor reputation for not fulfilling his obligations to artists, for his rough manners, and for a nasty habit of cutting short the scheduled program of performances. He closed the 1871 season "forgetting" (the press's ironic euphemism) to pay the last quarterly installment of Gabrielle Krauss's fee, and the following year he sent a letter to Teresa Stolz (who would later sing Aida in Naples) treating her with no more regard than an ordinary second-lead singer, thus provoking the indignation of both the famous soprano and Verdi.[26] In the summer of 1872, when the musicians in the orchestra (who had not been paid) refused to play,[27] Musella quarreled bitterly with the mayor, who had dared to order the curtain brought down on a particularly riotous performance. This dispute, in which the city council at first sided with the mayor,[28] ended with the latter's clamorous retirement from office and the rehiring of the impresario, who may

---

24. "Genova: Progetto d'appalto del teatro 'Carlo Felice,'" *La gazzetta musicale di Milano* 27 (19 May 1872): 170.

25. John Rosselli, "Materiali per la storia socio-economica del San Carlo nell'Ottocento," in *Musica e cultura a Napoli dal XV al XIX secoli,* ed. Lorenzo Bianconi and Renato Bossa (Florence: Olschki, 1983), 369–81, esp. 274.

26. Acuto, "Napoli," *La gazzetta musicale di Milano* 27 (20 May 1872): 178. Verdi reported that Musella "has written an extremely discourteous letter to Stolz saying, 'if you come I will pay your meals in the inn for fifteen days, etc. etc.' Just picture Stolz's blue eyes! I think she answered him that she had no need of anyone to pay for her food, and that she would be in Naples on the date stated in the contract" (letter from Verdi to Tito Ricordi, 24 October 1872); see Franco Abbiati, *Giuseppe Verdi* (Milan: Ricordi, 1959), 3:607.

27. Acuto, "Napoli," *La gazzetta musicale di Milano* 27 (20 May 1872).

28. Acuto, "Napoli," *La gazzetta musicale di Milano* 27 (2 June 1872): 186.

have been the blackguard *(briccone)* that Verdi called him,[29] but who was also a man of considerable parts. He displayed his skill in his training of the orchestra and preparation of the production of *Aida:* even Verdi had to admit that the "orchestral forces" were "much better than those in Milan," and on another occasion Verdi remarked, "I do not know what the mise en scène will be like . . . but I believe that it will fulfill my expectations."[30]

The Naples correspondent of *Il pungolo* gave further information on the Teatro San Carlo in 1878:

> The theater was open yesterday only for a daytime performance . . . (the performance for children and their nurses) of *Don Pasquale,* sung by second-rank artists. And in all this week there have been only two performances, one of *Il trovatore* and the other of *Norma,* with *no subscription seats* and *lowered prices!* Today there is no performance, tomorrow the same. . . . The management of the San Carlo should hang a permanent sign by the entrance to the theater: "No performance today; come back tomorrow." It would be more economical and more honest.[31]

During the 1880s, in spite of the usual delays in receiving the subsidy from the city and competition with other theaters—among them, the Teatro Bellini, which opened in 1877 under the control of the Sonzogno publishing firm and, two years later, gave the Italian premiere of Bizet's *Carmen*—the Teatro San Carlo put on several major productions, including a performance of Meyerbeer's *L'étoile du nord (La stella del Nord),* which opened the season in 1880, and the Neapolitan premiere of *Lohengrin* in February 1881. However, it had become almost normal procedure for performances to be "cut short because of public dissatisfaction."[32]

It must be borne in mind that the listener was the final judge and the court of last appeal regarding opera productions in the nineteenth century. This was a convention in open opposition (as has been remarked) with workers' rights, but it was a notion commonly accepted and even codified in theatrical legislation up to the early twentieth century. In respect of that custom, contracts were considered valid only after an artist had survived the so-called *debutto trino,* a trial period of three performances. If these went well the singer would

29. "Musella has the reputation of being a cheat and a blackguard. This is a usurped reputation! He's merely an ass! *[un gran coglione]*" (letter from Verdi to Giulio Ricordi 26 December 1872); see Abbiati, *Giuseppe Verdi,* 3:619.

30. Letters from Verdi to Giulio Ricordi, 12 December 1872, and to Léon Escudier, 20 March 1873; see Abbiati, *Giuseppe Verdi,* 3:618, 622.

31. Reprinted in *La gazzetta musicale di Milano* 33 (3 March 1878): 75.

32. Francesco D'Arcais, "Rassegna musicale," *La nuova antologia* 15 (15 April 1880): 756–64, esp. 757.

be paid according to the contract, but if they "resulted in a more or less total fiasco, the written contract was as null and void as if it had never existed."[33] When an opera (or a ballet) was a flop, it had to be replaced at the expense of the management. But since the system of subscriptions for an entire cycle of performances of the same work obliged the subscriber to attend it several times, a "thumbs down" often served not only to get rid of works not to the subscribers' taste but also to avoid the boredom of repeat performances of overly familiar works. For example, when the management of the Teatro Apollo in Rome was obliged to drop a performance of *Don Carlo* in 1881 because several of the lead singers were indisposed, it announced a nineteenth performance of *Aida* (an opera that had already been produced four times in recent years): "the subscribers would have none of it, and they stopped the performance by shouting so much that [the management] had to give the public its money back."[34]

Some commentators claimed that theater managements still enjoyed a margin of earnings realized by reducing production costs (fewer precious stuffs for the costumes, fewer chorus members, a smaller orchestra) or by making special arrangements with the music publishers to cut rental fees for scores and parts. Luigi Scalaberni did just that in 1876 when he persuaded the Lucca publishing firm to lower the rental fees for the three theaters he managed, La Pergola and the Pagliano in Florence, and the Comunale in Bologna.[35] Another way to cut costs was to sign less famous singers: Bianca Blume, the first Italian Elsa in *Lohengrin,* earned 5,000 lire for the 1871 season in Bologna, whereas Teresa Stolz, in the same year, was paid 42,000 lire to sing at La Scala. In 1879 Francesco D'Arcais reacted to such practices by noting that the choice was between a policy that was antiartistic and one that was antieconomic.[36] To demonstrate his theory D'Arcais examined the finances of a hypothetical first-rank opera house with a subsidy of 150,000 lire, a sum roughly equivalent to the average subsidy granted by the various cities, either wholly in cash or partly in cash and partly in direct payment of the orchestra, the chorus, and the corps de ballet. Leaving aside the minimal and "laughable" aid to the theater in Barbara, in the province of Ancona, for *Il trovatore* (75 lire) and the 30 lire to the theater in Anghiari, in the province

33. Cesare Molinari, *L'attrice divina: Eleonora Duse nel teatro italiano fra i due secoli* (Rome: Bulzoni, 1985), 49. The quotation is taken from Nicola Tabanelli, *Il codice del teatro* (Milan: Hoepli, 1901), 99. See also Alberto Musatti, "Della consuetudine dei tre debutti," *Rivista di diritto commerciale* 7, no. 2 (1909): 338–44.

34. Cametti, *Il Teatro di Tordinona,* 2:576.

35. *La gazzetta musicale di Milano* 31 (10 September 1876): 312–13.

36. Francesco D'Arcais, "L'industria musicale in Italia," *La nuova antologia* 15 (1 May 1879): 133–48.

of Arezzo,[37] D'Arcais's calculations seem plausible. In the 1870s La Scala received a subsidy of 200,000 lire, La Pergola in Florence, 100,000 lire, the Apollo in Rome, 140,000 lire, and the Regio in Turin, 80,000 lire (plus the services of the orchestra and the ballet, an indirect subsidy of 36,000 lire and 20,000 lire, respectively), and the Teatro Comunale in Trieste, 62,000 florins.[38] By adding revenues from subscriptions (150,000 lire) and box-office receipts (150,000 lire), D'Arcais reached a total of 450,000 lire in global revenues. But what were the expenses?

D'Arcais continued: when an opera house had to offer four new productions *(opere d'obbligo)* and two revivals *(opere di ripiego)* during the major season of carnival and Lent, it needed to budget 150,000 lire for a double company of singers—something of a rarity and a luxury reserved for privileged theaters. A first rank soprano could demand 25,000 to 35,000 lire; a tenor, 40,000 to 50,000 lire; a mezzo-soprano or a contralto, 10,000 to 15,000 lire; a baritone or a prima ballerina, an equal figure; a bass, 8,000 lire to 10,000 lire. Adding 10,000 lire for the second lead singers, 100,000 lire for the chorus and the orchestra, 40,000 lire for rental of scores, 50,000 lire for production costs, he arrived at a total for expenses of around 350,000 lire, which did not include the ballet company and its scenery, lighting, stagehands, or front-of-house staff, which would come to at least another 100,000 lire. If by following this hypothetical but plausible budget, "the predicted expenses are equal to the predicted entrance receipts," the situation was less rosy in theaters that had no subsidy, where trust in luck was elevated to a system, and where "performances are at times mediocre and more often bad."[39]

2. The Role of Singers, Joint Stock Companies, and Publishers

The biggest budget item continued to be singers, who customarily relied on agents to seek contracts for them in opera houses in Italy and abroad. According to a hierarchy that had existed from time immemorial, singers divided into two categories. The first included the stars, the singers *di cartello,* who added to their fame by going abroad, by not deigning to attend rehearsals of operatic revivals (usually consulting privately with the conductor to set tem-

37. *La gazzetta musical di Milano* 25 (12 June 1870): 194.
38. See the bibliographical references given in note 1, above. See also Alberto Basso, *Il teatro della città dal 1788 al 1936,* vol. 2 of *Storia del Teatro Regio di Torino,* ed. Alberto Basso (Turin: Cassa di Risparmio di Torino, 1976–83), 340; *La gazzetta musicale di Milano* 27 (7 April 1872): 120.
39. D'Arcais, "L'industria musicale," 135.

pos), by refusing to wear their stage costumes at the dress rehearsal, and by cultivating the outbursts of temperament and the superstitious rituals that had become traditional. Singers of secondary roles made up the second category. The dividing line between the two groups was as clear "as it ever had been between baron and vassal; between a minister and an antechamber sweep."[40]

As far as we can tell from the available figures, Adelina Patti was one of the highest-paid singers of the later nineteenth century. Born in Madrid of Italian parents, in Italy Patti reached the unheard-of peak of 10,000 francs a performance in the decade from 1875 to 1885, but if we can believe her former agent, Roberto Strakosch, elsewhere in the world she was paid 25,000 francs. The Tuscan tenor Giuseppe Fancelli, a singer who had a limpid, accurate voice but was a dreadful actor (Jules Massenet recalled that he was nicknamed "five and five make ten" because he sang with both hands spread wide), was paid 40,000 lire in gold for the 1877–78 season at the Teatro Regio in Turin; the tenor Angelo Masini, famous for the firmness of sound of his mezza voce passages, was paid between 80,000 and 100,000 lire for carnival and Lent seasons in the 1880s; Francesco Tamagno, after a resounding success in the title role in Verdi's *Otello* in 1887, demanded 10,000 lire per performance; Enrico Caruso was paid 50,000 lire for three months at La Scala in 1900.[41]

A star's fee was obviously a sacrifice for the impresario, but he could turn it into a profitable investment if it would guarantee "standing room only" at higher prices. At the Teatro Pagliano in Florence, where an admission ticket never cost more than 3 lire in the 1870s, Scalaberni raised the ticket price to 10 lire when Patti sang: "The result was excellent . . . and his audacity . . . generously rewarded."[42] Gino Monaldi, who had pointed to 1830 as a time when singers' honoraria rose strikingly in proportion to overall expenses, stated in 1910 that "singers' fees of yesteryear" were not much different "from those of today," though he was speaking of global expenses for singers in the opera house budget.[43] Some commentators attributed this rise to acceptance of a pay scale imported from abroad (from America, but also from London, Cairo, Lisbon, and elsewhere); others have pointed to a difference

40. Antonio Ghislanzoni, *Gli artisti da teatro* (Milan, 1896), 60.

41. *La gazzetta musicale di Milano* 33 (3 March 1878): 77; Jules Massenet, *Mes souvenirs (1848–1912)* (Paris: Lafitte, 1912), 113; Giuseppe Depanis, *I Concerti Popolari e il Teatro Regio di Torino: Quindici anni di vita musicale; appunti-ricordi* (Turin: Società Tipografico-Editrice Nazionale, 1914–15), 1:186–87, 2:41; Rinaldi, *Due secoli di musica,* 2:1166; D'Arcais, "Rassegna musicale," *La nuova antologia* 20 (16 September 1885): 343–52; *La nazione,* 25 April 1888; Giuseppe Barigazzi, *La Scala racconta* (Milan: Rizzoli, 1984), 390.

42. Monaldi, *Impresari celebri,* 168.

43. Gino Monaldi, *Cantanti celebri del secolo XIX* (Rome: Nuova Antologia, 1910), 309.

in professional status and levels of remuneration between Italian singers and foreign artists. The Austro-German singer, for instance, had a different outlook and training ("nearly always cultivated, well-mannered . . . he dislikes the errant life"); the German singer "is content with a fair remuneration, with modest prosperity, [and] with a secure position in some subsidized theater." Just as a good German singer earned in a year what an Italian singer could earn in a month,[44] the two differed in their sense of civic responsibility and their fiscal status, given that the Italian, obliged to "move constantly from one place to another," was "not a voter, not a civil employee, not a taxpayer."[45]

———

In 1898, the year in which General Fiorenzo Bava Beccaris savagely repressed a popular insurrection in Milan that had grown out of a riot to protest high prices and a time when La Scala, assailed by unending disputes between the boxholders and the city government, had been shut down for a year, citizens of Milan, boxholders, and the city set up a joint stock company—*società anonima*—with a capital of 300,000 lire that took over the management of the theater for three years. The executive board (a group with high musical qualifications that included Arrigo Boito as vice president and Giuseppe Gallignani, the head of the Milan Conservatory) was presided by Duke Guido Visconti di Modrone, a patron of the arts and a cotton manufacturer who had inherited his passion for the theater from his uncle Carlo (the impresario of La Scala in 1834–36). Giulio Gatti-Casazza was named general director, sharing responsibilities in the artistic sector with a thirty-one-year-old conductor, Arturo Toscanini, who was fresh from a triumphant success at the Teatro Regio in Turin. Toscanini proved capable of imposing his own conditions, operating like an artistic director before the fact, and his contract gave him maximum freedom to choose operas, singers, musicians, chorus members, and set designers and to set the number of rehearsals and performances.[46] Toscanini made a number of changes at La Scala: he introduced a more varied repertory, including many more Wagner operas than had been the rule (in the sacred temple of Italian *melodramma!*); he insisted on polished productions, perfect down to the least bit of stage business; if the opera was long, he eliminated the ballet that usually ended the evening; later, he championed a "critical" interpretation of *Il trovatore*, a work that had been

---

44. D'Arcais, "Rassegna musicale," *La nuova antologia* 20 (16 September 1885): 349.

45. D'Arcais, "Il teatro musicale," 128. For singers' contracts see Giovan Battista Cavalcaselle, *Tipi di scritture teatrali attraverso luoghi e tempi diversi: Contributo storico-giuridico* (Rome: Athenaeum, 1919).

46. *La gazzetta musicale di Milano* 23 (31 March, 28 April, 5 May, 2 and 30 June 1898); Barigazzi, *La Scala racconta*, 37ff.

manhandled in current operatic practice; he ordered the hall darkened during performances; he abolished encores ("no encores" was a rule in existence at La Scala since 1793, but it was usually ignored). An enthusiastic minority hailed the young conductor's innovations, which also aroused perplexity in some quarters and created unspoken friction with the publisher Giulio Ricordi.[47]

The contract for the three-year experiment ended in 1902 with a loss of 78,000 lire, made good by Visconti personally. The agreement between the city and the boxholders was then renewed for five years, and a new stock corporation was formed, enlarging the number of shareholders to include industrialists in cotton manufacturing, pharmaceuticals (Luigi Erba), and cosmetics. Gatti-Casazza and Toscanini, who both moved to the Metropolitan Opera House in New York in 1908, again shared responsibility for artistic direction. In the meantime, however, the city had reduced its grant to 60,000 lire rather than the previous 150,000 lire, in part as a result of a referendum on the subsidy put to the voters of Milan in December 1901 in which the "no"s had a clear majority. (Fewer than one-third of registered voters went to the polls; of these, 11,460 voted against subsidies for La Scala and only 7,214 voted for them.)[48]

At the end of the first three years of this new and artistically outstanding administration, the theater was already operating in the red with a large deficit of 138,000 lire. Once again the board of directors made up the deficit, and, as always, the largest budget item was for singers, followed, in descending order, by the orchestra and the conductors, the corps de ballet and the school connected with it, the costumes, and the chorus.[49] Every time the "La Scala question" was discussed in the city council it aroused bitter controversy. "The private consortium's administration . . . has cost us 394,000 lire in eight years," one irate city council member pointed out. "This cannot, must not go on, also because that loss brings a profit to the box owners, who rent out their boxes rather than use them themselves and draw . . . revenues from [rental]." Carlo Porro, a Radical attentive to the popular vote, called for a theater open to a "much larger number of citizens." He also pointed out that the juridical relationship between the municipality and the boxholders should be changed: if the latter could be persuaded to "give their boxes" rather than

47. Harvey Sachs, *Toscanini* (London: Weidenfeld and Nicolson; Philadelphia: J. B. Lippincott, 1978); on La Scala, see esp. 60–102.

48. See "Torna sul tappeto la questione della Scala," *Il mondo artistico* 40 (11 and 21 February, 21 March 1906); Giampiero Tintori, *Palco di proscenio: Il melodramma: autori, cantanti, teatri, impresari* (Milan: Feltrinelli, 1980), 167; Barigazzi, *La Scala racconta*, 386.

49. "Torna sul tappeto la questione della Scala," *Il mondo artistico* 40 (11 February 1906). The bill for singers was 789,500 lire; for the orchestra and conductors, 410,000 lire; for the corps de ballet, 244,500 lire.

be paid for them, "the artistic and economic question would be resolved, thanks to them." A Liberal opponent countered that all theaters administered under criteria of high quality "inevitably" operated at a loss and that it was only right that the municipality made good the loss.[50] Other administrative contracts followed, the city's contributions fell still further, and La Scala's administrations continued to operate in the red.[51] Finally, in 1910, a commission appointed to study the future of the opera house declared unequivocally that it must be set up as a self-governing, not-for-profit institution—an *ente autonomo* (autonomous agency). The leading opera house of Milan—which had been kept going by private patrons, at their financial loss, in the interest of protecting privileges and a social image that they felt called upon to defend—closed its doors during the years immediately following the First World War (1918–21). It was reborn, out of the ashes of the old institution, as the first *ente autonomo* in Italy.[52]

In 1908, ten years after the owner of the Teatro Costanzi in Rome, the building constructor Domenico Costanzi, had died, that theater also passed into the hands of a corporation—the STIN (Società Teatrale Internazionale), which had bought the building. In association with another corporation, the STIA (Società Teatrale Italo-Argentina), a South American industrial trust with headquarters in Buenos Aires, the STIN engaged Walter Mocchi (in younger days an active supporter of radical syndicalism) to act as "general agent" for the dual organization. The master plan involved sending the Costanzi's company on an annual tour to South America and controlling the management of a number of other theaters (the Regio in Turin, the Carlo Felice in Genoa, the Petruzzelli in Bari) with the intent—at least on paper—of preventing competition among singers and keeping fees low. Toscanini expressed his firm disapproval when he had wind of a projected link between Milan and Buenos Aires.[53]

In its early years the Teatro Costanzi had tried (as had Rossini at the San Carlo in Naples as far back as 1815) to combine the roles of the composer and the artistic director. The first to take on that dual role at the Costanzi was Giacomo Orefice in 1908–9, but he met with little success, either financially or with the public. The resounding failure of Claude Debussy's *Pelléas et Mélisande* at its Rome premiere on 28 March 1909 occurred under his

50. *Il mondo artistico* 40 (21 March 1906).

51. *La nuova musica* 15 (20 February 1910): 23.

52. See Lamberto Trezzini and Angelo Curtolo, *Oltre le quinte: Idee, cultura e organizzazione del teatro musicale in Italia* (Venice: Marsilio, 1983), 26–27.

53. Frajese, *Dal Costanzi all'Opera*, vols. 1 and 2, passim; Augusto Carelli, *Emma Carelli: Trent'anni di vita del teatro lirico* (Rome: Maglione, 1932); letter of Arturo Toscanini to Uberto Visconti di Modrone, n.d. [1916]. My sincere thanks to Harvey Sachs for providing me with a photocopy of this document, conserved in the Archivio Gaetano Cesari.

management. In 1909–10 Pietro Mascagni, who also took on duties as conductor, met with somewhat better success.[54] After a number of vicissitudes
that eventually led to the disappearance of the STIA, the Società La Teatral
was created in 1910 with Mocchi as director of the Agenzia Italo-Sudamerica
of Milan and administrator of a number of opera houses (the Coliseo in Buenos Aires, the Municipal in Rio de Janeiro and in São Paolo, the leading
theater in Santiago de Chile, the Solis in Montevideo, the Opera in Rosario,
and the Costanzi in Rome). The STIN (Mocchi had become its major stock-
holder) drew up a contract for a limited partnership, the Impresa del Teatro
Costanzi, which continued operations until 1926 and was administered by
the noted soprano (and Mocchi's wife) Emma Carelli.

———

Beginning in the early nineteenth century, music publishers seconded the activities of the opera houses and worked to make opera both more "popular"
and "contemporary."

Publishers sought proprietary rights to musical manuscripts, buying up
the musical holdings in the archives of the opera houses, buying back scores
owned by impresarios, or drawing up contracts directly with composers. Such
contracts not only specified the lump sum to be paid a composer at the
premiere of a work but also contained clauses regarding the publisher's and
composer's earnings, applicable if the work should prove a success, and on
publishing rights and royalties on the sale and rental of orchestral scores,
orchestral and vocal parts, and piano-vocal scores. Around 1850, when repertory opera became the rule (the Verdi "trilogy" was symptomatic of this),
publishers played a determining role as mediators for public taste, focusing
on a limited range of operas destined to last and making full use of the sizable
store of works that they themselves owned.

The protection of earnings from artistic and literary works was a principle
that had already been introduced in Italy with a convention drawn up 26
June 1840 between the Austrian government and the Kingdom of Sardinia,
to which other states had adhered (Rome, Modena, Lucca, Parma, Tuscany).
Application of these norms was hampered, however, by the political fragmen-
tation of Italy.

The first law on copyright to be passed in the newly unified Italy (Verdi
participated in its making, both as a musician and as a deputy) dates from
1865 (law of 25 June 1865, no. 2337). It was followed ten years later by law
number 2652 of 10 August 1875, which eliminated all distinction between
printed and manuscript works and assigned equal protection to performance

54. *La nuova musica* 15 (5 May 1910): 54.

and the printed score (an important acquisition: even today theatrical works are often published after their first performance, which gives their creators an opportunity to make changes). These two measures were combined in royal decree number 1012 of 19 September 1882, the "Testo unico delle leggi sui diritti spettanti agli autori delle opere dell'ingegno" (the sole text of laws on the rights due the authors of works of the intellect). This was a long-awaited recognition of the "products of the intelligence and talent"; it guaranteed "freedom and dignity to intellectual-workers," as the jurist Enrico Rosmini stated, in much the same way as the "democratic movement" in Italian society of the later nineteenth century was working to reshape social institutions in favor of the "workers of thousands of industries."[55] Musicians' desperate appeals to the authorities in defense of their interests, material and moral, were finally backed by law; they no longer had to depend so entirely on stratagems to conceal original manuscript scores that were easy prey for counterfeiters (pirating publishers and copyists) or for impresarios who acquired inaccurate, low-priced copies and gave them to musical hacks to be orchestrated. Even so, differences in laws between the various countries of Europe and the Americas and ingenious ways to cheat cut into their earnings.

Vincenzo Bellini, a musician who wrote no more than one opera a year (at a time when his contemporaries were turning out an average of three annually) and who was perfectly aware of what his works were worth, declared that composers ought to be able to make a living from their works. His wish came true, but only a decade or so after his death. "In Italy," Bellini wrote in 1835 to the chief of police of Naples, in an attempt to persuade him to put a stop to the circulation of a pirated copy of *I puritani*, "people make a *Piracy* of everything that should be the most respected and backed by the laws, as is true in France and in England—that is, the *author's right to his property*. . . . An author's domains . . . are the offspring of his intellect, and if the first sort of ownership is sacred, the second should be equally so."[56]

In April 1882, five months before the "testo unico" became law, a private association of writers, playwrights, scholars, publishers, and musicians was founded under the name of Società Italiana degli Autori (it became a public corporation in 1941). Its members included Giosue Carducci, Francesco De Sanctis, Felice Cavallotti, Giovanni Verga, Cesare Cantù, Edoardo Sonzogno, Verdi, Boito, and many others. This organization consulted with a number

55. Enrico Rosmini, *Legislazione e giurisprudenza sui diritti d'autore* (Milan, 1890), 7. See also Bruno Cagli, "Organizzazione economica e gestione teatrale nell'800," in *Per un "progetto Verdi" anni '80: Seminario internazionale di studi, Parma-Busseto 3–4 aprile 1980* (Reggio Emilia: Regione Emilia Romagna, Assessorato per la cultura, n.d.), 63–85, in English translation as Bruno Cagli, "Verdi and the Business of Writing Operas," in *The Verdi Companion*, ed. William Weaver and Martin Chusid (New York: Norton, 1979), 106–20.

56. Vincenzo Bellini, *Epistolario*, ed. Luisa Cambi (Milan: Mondadori, 1943), 579–80.

of prominent jurists with a view to drawing up efficacious juridical mechanisms for pursuing violations of the copyright laws, and in 1887 the Ricordi
firm was to make available some of its representations to serve as a first nucleus of investigative agents. Music publishers—Lucca, Sonzogno, Ricordi,
Giudici e Strada in Turin, Pigna e Rovida in Milan, Genesio Venturini in
Florence, Buffa and Company in Turin, Teodoro Cottrau in Naples—empow-
ered the society to represent them and collect their copyright fees. Finally, it
was thanks to the society's efforts that Italy participated in 1887 in the creation of the Berne Union, the first international copyright convention (the
other original participants were France, Germany, England, Spain, Belgium,
Switzerland, Tunisia, Haiti, Liberia, and Luxembourg).

Verdi was the first composer to emancipate himself from the trammels
of tradition, demanding what his predecessors had never dreamed of even
requesting. As early as the 1850s he insisted that his contracts with publishers
contain a clause stating that his scores must be played in full. Verdi's contracts
later contained a crescendo of demands: he would have the right to choose
the conductor and the singers for his works; he would have to approve a
production; he would decide whether a production had had sufficient rehearsal to go into performance. Within the limits of the possible, Verdi sought
to save his works from a dreadful fate in revivals, which were notorious for
their laxity. "La Fricci . . . saw nothing wrong in plucking several pieces out
of her role and replacing them with an act of *Gli Ugonotti* [*Les Huguenots*]
or an act of *Macbeth*! . . . Yet there is a contract that says '*Don Carlos* must
be performed intact'! . . . What have the Ricordi people done about it?" This
was Verdi, complaining in 1874 about a performance of *Don Carlos* (as *Don
Carlo*) in Reggio Emilia.[57] In practice there were (and continued to be) hundreds of ways to infringe on the integrity of a score. Force majeure veiled
infringements with impunity.[58]

When it came to a show of force between an opera and a ballet, it was
almost always the opera that gave way, particularly if it was a revival of a
standard work. In 1882–83 the Teatro Apollo in Rome offered "*centoni* [pot-
pourri] of operas, barbarously mutilating *Il profeta* [*Le Prophète*] and forcing
it to serve as a prologue to the ballet." (The ballet in question was the Rome
premiere of the famous *Excelsior* of Luigi Manzotti and Romualdo Marenco,
which, faithful to its theme—an apologia of "progress"—inaugurated the
new electrical system in the theater.) Another work used as a prelude to the
same ballet (in a second triumphal production) was *Il Guarany* by the Brazil-

57. Letter from Verdi to Eugenio Tornaghi, 8 September 1874, in Giuseppe Verdi, *I copialettere di Giuseppe Verdi,* ed. Gaetano Cesari and Alessandro Luzio (Milan: Stucchi Ceretti, 1913;
reprint, Bologna: Arnaldo Forni, 1968), 295. "La Fricci" was the famous mezzo-soprano Antonietta Fricci.

58. Depanis, *I Concerti Popolari,* 1:171–72, 2:66–67.

ian composer Carlos Gomes, a score owned by the Lucca publishing firm.[59] The following year at the Teatro Argentina in Rome, Halévy's *La reine de Chypre* (as *La regina di Cipro*), a work then forty years old, was mangled "with unheard-of cruelty" and its finale was rewritten by Pietro Platania so as to make it more "acceptable to the public."[60] There were also frequent cases of contemporary works that were pirated in countries that had no copyright laws. The journals *Il trovatore* and *Il teatro illustrato* noted in 1891 that a counterfeit version of Mascagni's *Cavalleria rusticana* was about to be put on in Buenos Aires, orchestrated by an unknown hand. The management of the Buenos Aires opera house had acquired a cheap copy of the score and had given it to "an unscrupulous maestro" to orchestrate, presumably in order to avoid the cost of renting the score and paying the royalties.[61]

The 1882 copyright law gave the author exclusive rights to his work for forty years from the date of publication or from its first performance, or up to his date of death; for another forty years anyone might put on or publish the work on payment to the composer's heirs of 5 percent of the gross price. If the composer had ceded his copyright (in whole or in part) to the publisher, it was the latter who took on the task of dealing with theaters, demanding the right to supervise productions and approve set and costume designs, requesting additional rehearsals or additional personnel when necessary, and vetoing the engagement of certain performers and demanding contracts for others.

With the exception of Verdi (who was one of a kind in his business dealings as well as his art, and whose contracts with his publishers anticipated modern arrangements and gave him notable financial advantages) the successful composer of the 1870s usually sold his rights to a score for a sum that ranged from 20,000 to 40,000 lire, retaining his share of from 30 to 40 percent of the income from the sale and rental of scores and parts. Calculating on the basis of Filippo Marchetti's earnings from *Ruy Blas* (1869), a successful opera might bring its author something like 100,000 lire.[62] Except for new operas, when tradition dictated that the composer be invited to conduct at the rehearsals and the first three performances or to accompany the singers "at the keyboard," which gave him a direct opportunity to offer suggestions and directions, it was now the responsibility of the publishing house to supervise the production in agreement with the composer (in some cases with the conductor), but no longer with the librettist.

Thus the role and the duties of the publisher, who also took over from the

59. D'Arcais, "Rassegna musicale," *La nuova antologia* 27 (15 February 1883): 755.

60. D'Arcais, "Rassegna musicale," *La nuova antologia* 19 (1 January 1884): 136.

61. "Piraterie," *Il teatro illustrato* 11 (May 1891): 79.

62. D'Arcais, "L'industria musicale," 145; John Rosselli, "Verdi e la storia della retribuzione del compositore italiano," *Studi verdiani* 2 (1983): 11–28.

impresario the choice of librettist, grew ever larger. The impresarios reacted
to this change with ill-concealed annoyance, and they accused the publishers
of "despotism" and "tyranny." Giulio Ricordi and Vincenzo Jacovacci quarreled in 1872 when Jacovacci was denied permission to stage the first Roman
production of *Aida* at the Teatro Apollo (a premiere that did not take place
until February 1875). The reason Ricordi gave for his refusal made the proud
inhabitants of the city tremble with indignation: "The publisher, who owns
the rights . . . thinks it impossible to obtain a good performance in Rome and
cannot bear the thought of permitting Verdi's latest masterpiece to be mas-
sacred."[63]

The press, which had become receptive to questions of cultural policy and
was ready to launch its attacks from a variety of political points of view,
waved the specter of "monopoly." Writing in *La rivista musicale italiana* in
1899, Giovanni Ferrero, a political conservative, put the blame on the publishers, who had "taken over all the major theaters as fiefs and exploit them,
in collusion with the impresarios," by scheduling operas for which the publisher holds the rights, thus shutting out competition.[64] The vice president of
the Società Italiana degli Autori, Tommaso Montefiore, returned in 1907 to
the problems that young composers faced when they were excluded from
publishing circuits and forced to "pay tens of thousands of lire" to have their
works performed (often in mediocre productions). Montefiore proposed a
modification of the 1882 copyright law to limit exclusive performing rights
to ten years (for the succeeding seventy years anyone would be able to produce an opera, without the author's consent, on payment of a royalty based
on a percentage of gross receipts).[65] The most clamorous contribution to the
debate (because it was the first on this topic in the annals of Italian parliamentary government) came from the Socialist deputy Guido Podrecca, who denounced the misdeeds—real or presumed—of the major "monopolistic"
publishing houses in a speech before the Chamber of Deputies in 1907. According to Podrecca Italian musical culture suffered enormous harm because
orchestral scores (which could be had easily and at a reasonable price in other
countries) were not published in Italy. His list of grievances continued: costly
rental fees were charged for works in the public domain; theater managements were forced to put on "very out-of-date" operas lest the publishers
deny them the ones they wanted; no publicity was given composers who once
had been famous (among them, Antonio Smareglia); the "commercial" interest of the publishing houses dictated artistic choices to better qualified judges
(conductors). Tito Ricordi responded to Podrecca in *Il giornale d'Italia*, offer-

63. "Cose Romane," *La gazzetta musicale di Milano* 27 (14 July 1872): 231.

64. Ferrero, "Crisi teatrale," 610.

65. "Ancora i diritti d'autore," *Il mondo artistico* 41 (1 July 1907); "Un opuscolo di T. Montefiore," *La nuova musica* 12 (June–July 1907): 195.

ing technical arguments to counter the deputy's accusations, which he judged obviously demagogic.[66]

This state of affairs had come about because the weaker publishing firms had in fact not survived the shift to the industrial phase in publishing. The general picture had changed considerably from the early nineteenth century, when there had been a varied array of companies, each able to carve out its own special niche and offer a good-sized catalog. At that time in Rome Giovanni Battista Cencetti and Leopoldo Ratti (1821–74) had pioneered the publication of full orchestral scores (something unusual in Italy in their day, as earlier) with the works of Rossini; in Florence Giovanni Gualberto Guidi had been the first to print miniature scores (1854–83); in Turin the firm of Giudici e Strada had a list that included many "minor" composers in vogue at the time (Errico Petrella, Antonio Cagnoni, Lauro Rossi, Friedrich von Flotow); in Naples Cottrau in partnership with Bernardo Girard specialized in Neapolitan music; Francesco Lucca and his wife, Giovannina Strazza, published both Italian and non-Italian music (Saverio Mercadante, Marchetti, Alfredo Catalani, Meyerbeer, Charles Gounod, Karl Goldmark). With happy perspicuity Lucca championed Wagnerian opera. Formerly an engraver for Ricordi, in 1868 Lucca had bought from Wagner, for the sum of 10,000 gold francs, the Italian rights (including Trieste) to the composer's published and unpublished works.[67] By the end of the century, however, only two giants were left to divide up the field, Ricordi and Sonzogno.

The Ricordi publishing firm, founded in 1808, held the copyright to the most important Italian operatic works (Rossini, Bellini, Donizetti, Verdi). It had acquired those rights initially by negotiating with impresarios and the boards of directors of opera houses and later by commissioning operas from the composers themselves. Through the *Gazzetta musicale di Milano,* a journal founded in 1842 that soon became the best informed and culturally most advanced periodical in Italy, Ricordi actively promoted its own stable of com-

---

66. This dispute was printed in part in "Il monopolio delle opere musicali e la Camera italiana," *Il mondo artistico* 43 (1 June 1909), and ("Intorno al monopolio musicale," *Il mondo artistico* 43 (21 July 1909).

67. See Claudio Sartori, *Dizionario degli editori italiani* (Florence: Olschki, 1958); Sartori, *Casa Ricordi 1808–1958* (Milan: Ricordi, 1958); Emilia Zanetti, "L'editoria musicale a Roma nel secolo XIX: Avvio di una ricerca," *Nuova rivista musicale italiana* 18 (1984): 191–99; Bruno Cagli, "L'Ottocento: dal notturno ai Monumenta," in the exposition catalog, *Cinque secoli di stampa musicale in Europa,* Rome 1985 (Naples: Electa, 1985), 141–43; Anna Pasquinelli, "Contributo per la storia di Casa Lucca," *Nuova rivista musicale italiana* 16 (1982): 568–81, and "La proprietà delle opere di Wagner," *Il teatro illustrato* 3 (June 1883): 95; Francesco Degrada, "Il segno e il suono: Storia di un editore musicale e del suo mondo," in *Musica musicisti editoria: 175 anni di Casa Ricordi 1808–1983* (Milan: Ricordi, 1983), 11ff.; Mario Morini, Nandi Ostali, and Piero Ostali Jr., *Casa musicale Sonzogno: Cronologia, saggi, testimonianze,* 2 vols. (Milan: Sonzogno, 1995).

posers. Beginning in the 1870s, however, the review showed some prejudice against foreign works: Wagner was one of the victims of this attitude, particularly when *Lohengrin* failed at La Scala in 1873. At the same time the Ricordi firm worked indefatigably in support of the new legislation on copyright protection, and the firm expanded its activities, investing in new fields and taking over publishing houses in decline (among many others, Guidi in 1887 and Lucca in 1888).

Edoardo Sonzogno, the scion of a dynasty of printer-publishers active as early as the eighteenth century, was known for his series of popular works and for the publication of a number of journals and periodicals (among them *Il secolo* of Milan, a daily of radical leanings that had the highest circulation in Italy). He began his musical activities in 1874 with the publication of popularly priced piano reductions of opera scores. He was responsible for the diffusion of operetta in Italy (Hervé, Alexandre-Charles Lecocq, Jacques Offenbach) and for introducing the French opera repertory (Bizet, Ambroise Thomas, Massenet, Léo Delibes, Camille Saint-Saëns). He also operated as an impresario. In 1875 he took over management of the Teatro Santa Radegonda in Milan; in 1888–92, that of the Costanzi in Rome; in 1894–97, that of La Scala. In 1894 he inaugurated the new Teatro Lirico Internazionale in what had formerly been the Canobbiana in Milan. The organizer of renowned tours of Italian companies (in 1889 to Paris, in 1892 and 1893 to Vienna, in 1895 to various Germany cities), in 1883 Sonzogno instituted a competition to encourage original works. The success of the 1889 prizewinner, Pietro Mascagni (with *Cavalleria rusticana*), influenced the firm's subsequent preference for operas of the verismo school.

3. The Giolitti Era: From the Politeama to the First Ente Autonomo

When industrialization took off in Italy, it brought many changes, notably the rise of an urban proletariat, the development of class consciousness, an improved salary scale for workers and state employees, and, later, negotiation as a method for reconciling social conflict, a technique introduced by Giovanni Giolitti. All these created conditions favorable to new and more popular currents in Italian politics and culture. The organization and modes of leisure changed, and new fashions and new meeting places sprang up, from the nascent cinema to automobile racing, from soccer to bicycle races. Theaters changed as well.

One sort of theater that came to be highly popular was the *politeama* or all-purpose house—a theater building with socially undifferentiated seating, capable of holding a large number of people (usually two to five thousand), which offered a broad range of entertainment including prose drama, opera, musical reviews, variety shows, and circus acts. These locales were already in use in the 1850s. For the most part they were privately owned and run by an impresario, and their popular repertory and low ticket prices (made possible by lower management and upkeep costs) offered serious competition to the historic opera houses.

In 1880 the Teatro Costanzi was inaugurated in Rome. Its hall had a seating capacity of four thousand; above the third tier of boxes there was a large balcony with numbered seats and above that a gallery with unnumbered places. The Politeama Vittorio Emanuele II in Florence (later the Teatro Comunale), built as an arena in 1862, was given a roof in 1882–83 but retained its seating capacity of over six thousand places ("a truly vast building, unique of its kind," the press announced). The most prestigious opera houses sought to catch up with the times. In 1891 La Scala did away with the fifth tier of boxes in order to make room for a first balcony: Boito commented, "It frees the theater of a part of the audience that by age-old tradition was distracted, bored, and unruly, and puts in its place a great gallery of middle-class spectators who will pay very little and, once the opportunity arises, will enjoy themselves very much." The Teatro Regio in Turin, where projects for a "democratic" renovation of the building continued to encounter strong resistance, instituted a special lower-priced subscription series. Ferrero reported on this initiative in 1899 with aristocratic disdain:

> How merry they were, those cooks and greengrocers with their colored kerchiefs on their heads, and those ladies of the petite bourgeoisie smiling from the boxes in their summer dress; excellent persons, proud to play the grand lords for an evening, and utterly persuaded that they had displayed to one another that they, too, could permit themselves the luxury of paying 3 lire for an orchestra seat or 40 lire for a box.[68]

In 1892 the management's contract for La Scala stipulated for the first time that "two popular performances" would be part of the obligations of the Piontelli administration. The experiment was launched with the world premiere of Catalani's last opera, *La Wally,* and popular performances became more frequent in the years to come, spreading to many other, formerly more exclusive theaters. The press reported that the traditional public and the new

---

68. Ferrero, "Crisi teatrale," 623. See also Marcello Conati, "La musica a Reggio nel secondo Ottocento," in *Dalla restaurazione al secondo Novecento,* vol. 2 of *Teatro a Reggio Emilia,* ed. Sergio Romagnoli and Elvira Garbero, 2 vols. (Florence: Sansoni, 1980), 127–60, esp. 148; *La gazzetta musicale di Milano* 24 (11 July 1869): 246; Piero Roselli, Giuseppina Carlo Romby, and Osanna Fantozzi Micali, *I teatri di Firenze* (Florence: Bonechi, 1978), 220ff.; letters of Boito to Verdi and Verdi to Boito, 29 April and 1 May 1891, in *Verdi-Boito Correspondence,* ed. Mario Medici and Marcello Conati, trans. William Weaver (Chicago: University of Chicago Press, 1994), 178.

public, on different evenings, had enjoyed *La Wally* in equal measure. Giulio Ricordi wrote:

> Popular performances, by bringing to La Scala a very large class of citizens that would not otherwise have the means to enter the leading Milanese theater, accomplished the task of true, high artistic education: they refined the taste of the masses with productions that, even when not totally perfect, will nonetheless always be superior to those to be seen in the lesser theaters of the city.[69]

The conservative forces feared the advance of the Left—in particular, that of the Socialist Party, which supported the union movement and the rights and demands of the lower classes. That, along with the anxieties prompted by social tension and strikes, led the press to harshly reactionary statements in 1902. From the pages of the *Gazzetta musicale di Milano,* Carlo Arner wondered "What on earth might a Socialist opera be?"

> Perhaps the musical notes would change place or there would be more of them? Or subjects for librettos would be furnished exclusively by the state? Or perhaps the music, the orchestration, etc., would have to bear the stamp of approval of a Socialist commission? Or the singers would be free to sing off-key with impunity?[70]

Although the librettist Giuseppe Giacosa was affected by the literary ferment of a social and democratic bohemianism and declared himself in favor of cautious renewal in the subject matter of theatrical works, many critics imputed the decline of music to recent social conquests in Italy: "Study the events of the last twenty years—it was, precisely, twenty years ago that Socialist agitation and economic struggle by means of strikes began—and you can readily see a greater and greater artistic decadence, particularly in opera."[71]

The conservatives' and the reactionaries' execration of social progress in Italy combined with a general defeatism in the post-unification years in statements deploring the laxity of the state, the current pall of mediocrity, and the fall of the heroic ideals of the Risorgimento. To be fair, however, and to avoid the danger of abstract Manichaeism in the matter of ideological disagreements, I might add that as long as the Left remained in the opposition, it was openly critical of "bourgeois" institutions, the "elitist" consumption of music, and spending public money to subsidize municipal theaters. It was only later—with the first victories of the Left in administrative elections (in

---

69. Giulio Ricordi, "Arte? . . . Democrazia?" *La gazzetta musicale di Milano* 47 (31 January 1892): 70.

70. Carlo Arner, "L'arte lirica e gli scioperi," *La gazzetta musicale di Milano* 57 (14 August 1902): 452.

71. Ibid.

Milan the first leftist city council, headed by a Radical, was formed in 1899)—that it had first-hand, intimate experience with problems, artistic and otherwise. When that happened the theater changed from being an ideological topic of debate to a concrete problem—a terrain for government action and projects for education and reform. The Teatro Municipale of Reggio Emilia, for example, formerly a target for bitter condemnation from the democratic press, had the active support of the Socialists when the Socialist Party came into power in the city in 1899, and they and the trade unions worked together to encourage larger popular audiences by offering reduced prices for members of the Camera del Lavoro.[72] Furthermore, in 1911 it was a Socialist, Podrecca, who argued before the municipal council of Rome in favor of a subsidy for the Teatro Costanzi and who the following year proposed legislation to encourage young composers. "Theater subsidy," Podrecca declared, "avoids the bankruptcy of art. That's the way things are today: our only hope is that the gradual spread of well-being and culture, which we Socialists ardently desire, will broaden what is still the privilege of the minorities."[73]

In 1918, as we have seen, La Scala interrupted its activities. Among its most pressing problems was the rebuilding and modernization of the stage and backstage area. The Socialist mayor of Milan, Emilio Caldara, who had been a fierce adversary of La Scala in the days of the 1901 referendum and was now a determined advocate of the "public function" of theaters, found an invaluable ally in the newspaper *Il corriere della sera* and its director, Luigi Albertini, for a campaign to collect funds. The appeal produced the notable sum of 6 million lire in contributions from the citizenry. In November 1920 the city council and the boxholders signed an agreement for fixing a trial period of nine years. This was the birth in Italy of the *ente autonomo* in the current sense of a not-for-profit corporation under public law, with its own juridical status, and supported by funds from the community. Among its aims, as the statutes declared, was the organization of theatrical performances and concerts "for the musical culture of the people." In 1921 La Scala was officially recognized as an *ente morale* (a not-for-profit corporation for the public good) by virtue of its "ends of a public nature and of public interest" (royal decree of 23 December 1921). The city of Milan agreed to provide an annual contribution of 350,000 lire; the boxholders ceded the right to rent out their boxes in exchange for an annual payment equal to 4 percent of the value of their holdings, and they promised to cede the box itself at some future time and at a price to be determined by an appropriate appraisal. Toscanini, called in as artistic director, reorganized the orchestra from top to

---

72. Giuseppe Armani, "Teatro e vita politica dal 1848 al 1915," in *Dalla restaurazione al secondo Novecento,* vol. 2 of *Teatro a Reggio Emilia,* ed. Sergio Romagnoli and Elvira Garbero (Florence: Sansoni, 1980), 225–41, esp. 237ff.

73. Quoted in Frajese, *Dal Costanzi all'Opera,* 2:60.

bottom, searching throughout Italy for the best players, who were offered a renewable three-year contract. He also launched experimental performances of "repertory theater" (with reprises of the same operas in succeeding years). In May 1920 the first indirect state aid to opera occurred in the form of an article, backed by a group of influential Milanese, that was introduced into a governmental decree on a surtax on tickets sold. This article added 2 percent to the surtax on theater tickets, to be applied to theaters in "provinces whose capital city has a population of more than 300,000 inhabitants, in which there exists an opera house of national importance administered not for profit by an *ente autonomo* or by an association of citizens." Only one institution— La Scala—fit the conditions set down in the law, hence only La Scala benefited from the provision: in the first year (1921–22) it received 1,580,000 lire.

The Italian government took other timid steps in support of music during those same years. In 1921 it budgeted 100,000 lire and delegated the task of studying ways to use the money most efficaciously to a permanent commission set up for the purpose. The members of the commission—Marco Enrico Bossi, Pietro Mascagni, Giacomo Puccini, and Nicola D'Atri—at first considered and then rejected the idea of helping young composers by subsidizing the publishing houses (which were usually not overly generous, as Mascagni reminded the commission during the plenary session). They eventually decided to set up a competition among the impresarios. Two prizes of 50,000 lire were offered, to be given to the opera managements that had presented the two best works by living Italian composers. (The operas thus chosen had to have had at least three performances.) In spite of the fact that none of the twenty operas (on average) that were submitted each year during the next five years stood out as particularly brilliant (though at the time the 1921 prize winners, Giuseppe Mulè's *La monacella della fontana* and Primo Riccitelli's *I compagnacci,* were well received), the first group of judges (Mascagni, Francesco Cilea, Puccini, D'Atri, and Bernardino Molinari) nonetheless praised the initiative, "which has served to discredit the unfortunate legend of the state's lack of interest in our operatic art."[74]

4. *The Fascist Regime: Tradition and Transformation*

In October 1922, while Italy was struggling with nagging postwar problems (veterans' demands, the "mutilated victory," social unrest, unemployment, poverty) and popular sentiment against the governing class made the future of the country uncertain, Benito Mussolini used the tactic of his March on

---

74. Minutes of the Commissione Permanente sent to the Under Secretary of State for Antiquities and the Fine Arts, Rome, 20 April 1922 (ACS Min.P.I.Div.XIII B.118).

Rome to become head of government, and he was soon invested by the king with full constitutional powers.

The new prime minister (who was portrayed in the incipient mythology in the dual—and usurped—guise of a musical connoisseur and a skilled violinist) had intentions regarding music. They were on the one hand to bring the state's influence to bear on institutions (theaters, conservatories, and concert societies), sweeping away the "laxity" of the preceding Liberal governments, and on the other hand to weave a dense network of personal relations and ties with musicians that would seem to reinforce the cult of "the chief" *(Il Capo)*. Flattery and blandishments made it less traumatic for independent artists to shift to playing the bureaucratic role of functionary that was theirs in the new state. Music and politics were to progress together, not following parallel or separate courses but integrated. At first Giuseppe Bottai, the Minister of Public Education, pursued a more flexible, elastic, and open-minded policy than the retrograde line of Roberto Farinacci, the Fascist Party secretary, and Bottai recognized that experiment, individual autonomy, and even criticism had their place as long as the overall framework of totalitarianism was left intact. "I love discussion," Bottai admonished, "but we must discuss and judge within the limits of Fascism, not against Fascism; within the Party, not against the Party; within the Fascist State, not against the Fascist State." [75] Every musician was free to cultivate a personal style of composition (and the modernist current had as good a right to do so as the more traditional one) on the condition that musicians conform to—or at any rate not work against—the ideological and political directives imparted from on high. In the 1930s both composers and institutions were required to pursue a more uniform course, in conformity with the regime's more radically demagogic line (these were the years of Mussolini's admonition to "go toward the people"). Cultural power was concentrated in one organization, the office of the Under Secretary, later the Ministry, of Press and Propaganda (and still later the Ministry of Popular Culture). Repressive measures, often in tune with foreign policy (the war with Ethiopia, the formation of the Rome-Berlin Axis), soon followed. [76]

While the majority of the leading Italian opera houses were the property of their municipalities, in Rome the most active theater, the Costanzi, belonged, as we have seen, to a private corporation (the STIN) headed by Mocchi and managed by Carelli. In 1926, after rejecting as too costly the idea of constructing a new theater, the government of Rome, with the prime minis-

75. Giuseppe Bottai, *Esperienza corporativa, 1929–1934* (Florence: Vallecchi, 1934), quoted in Emilio Gentile, *Il mito dello Stato nuovo dall'antigiolittismo al fascismo* (Bari: Laterza, 1982), 213ff.

76. For more detailed documentation and bibliography, see Fiamma Nicolodi, *Musica e musicisti nel ventennio fascista* (Fiesole: Discanto, 1984).

ter's approval, took over a majority of the shares of the STIN corporation and fired Carelli. After the renovation of the auditorium (Marcello Piacentini, architect) and extensive changes in the stage area, Romans boasted that the theater was the most modern in the world. Renamed the Teatro Reale dell'Opera, it was inaugurated in February 1928 with a performance of Boito's *Nerone*. The following year the theater was given *ente autonomo* status.[77] Government involvement was focused at first on the theaters of Milan and Rome, but provisions to foster the public nature of these institutions were made only intermittently, and a clear vision of the means to more direct political control was lacking. Despite the lip service that the "higher-ups" gave to innovation, the opera houses themselves continued the administrative policies of the past and produced the traditional museum operatic repertory.

The situation was even more stagnant outside the largest cities. In 1926 a heartfelt appeal to the government from the opera workers' trade union, the Sindacato artisti lirici, called attention to the unemployment crisis that had struck "thousands of families." The only result of the appeal, however, was that the central government shifted the problem out of its own hands and into those of the prefects, who could do little about it. (A government circular advised the prefects, "With the aim of alleviating such a painful state of affairs . . . you will meet the desires of the aforementioned artists, giving encouragement of the most efficacious sort to initiatives concerning performances.")[78] The reply came back that many theaters had closed or failed to reopen because of insufficient subsidies, the singers' high fees, the "antiquated conditions in some buildings," and (despite attempts to do away with them) the "anachronistic rights of the boxholders." A poll taken in 1934 by the Società Italiana degli Autori, or SIA (soon, with the addition of publishers—Società Italiana degli Autori e Editori—the SIAE), showed, however, that during the decade just past, the theater (both prose and opera) had been outstripped by other forms of public entertainment, with the cinema at the top of the list. In 1924 the gross revenues for opera amounted to 50 million lire and those for the cinema to 150 million lire; in 1933 opera's revenues had fallen to 23 million lire, while the silver screen's takings had risen to 329 million lire.[79]

Only after the Fascist regime was firmly established did it return with renewed energy to its role in the life of theatrical institutions and to working

77. Enrico di San Martino Valperga, "Il Teatro Reale dell'Opera," *La nuova antologia* 66 (16 April 1931): 486–99.

78. Memoriale of the Sindacato Italiano Fascista Artisti Lirici to Presidenza del Consiglio dei Ministri, 18 December 1926, ACS PCM (1931–33), 3.25.206; circular no. 4721/3–25 of the Presidenza del Consiglio dei Ministri to Prefetti del Regno, signed by the Under Secretary of State Francesco Giunta, 10 January 1927.

79. *La vita dello spettacolo 1924–33* (Rome: Società Italiana Autori ed Editori, 1934).

toward "rationalizing" (or "fascistizing"—*fascistizzare,* as the term went) the work of musicians, singers, and composers within the framework of state assistance as benefactor and patron.[80] The result was twofold. In 1931 La Scala was restructured in a more political direction, a move that was designed to serve as a model for other theaters: the members of its administrative council were named by the ministries of National Education and of Corporations, and the council's president was chosen by the prime minister. The government also strove to better the working conditions, the pay scale, and the benefits of people in the performing arts.[81] In 1935 three separate ministries were merged into one in the Ispettorato del Teatro (Theater Inspectorate), which after 1941 became the Direzione Generale per il Teatro e la Musica (General Directorate for Theater and Music), an organization that operated first under the Ministry of Press and Propaganda and later (in 1937) under the Ministry of Popular Culture. In presenting the program of the new agency, the inspector, Nicola de Pirro, stated that it was "necessary to give a discipline to the great opera houses—that is, to liberate them from the parliamentarianism that still, here and there, impedes their movements."[82] The agency worked to satisfy the tastes of the masses, who demanded accessible and popular works, but also to encourage modern composers, who, as state "functionaries," came under state protection and demanded the aid of the state. (The musicians wrote, "We must demand of the state that the number of new operas to be performed in the subsidized theaters be proportionate to the amount of their subsidies.")[83] This forced opera managements to operate on two levels, and instead of uniting audiences it established an even more radical break between "cultivated" music and "ultracultivated" music, and between occasions for hearing the two. This in turn led to renewed efforts to provide "theater for the masses": the "thespians" of the Carro di Tespi, an opera group that toured rural areas in the summer of 1930, or after 1937 the Saturday Theater (Sabato teatrale) run by the MinCulPop (the familiar designation for the Ministry of Popular Culture), a venture aimed at students, soldiers, and office workers that offered special performances in some of the major opera houses at "political" prices ranging from 2 lire to 50 centesimi. Also beginning in 1937 the Estate Musicale Italiana presented summer open-air operas and concerts at picturesque spots.[84] In accordance with the protectionist policies of those years, the works presented were "mostly by Italian authors."

80. Luigi Pestalozza, "Lo Stato dell'organizzazione musicale: La svolta del fascismo e la sua lunga durata," *Musica/Realtà* 2, no. 5 (August 1981): 143–60.

81. Trezzini and Curtolo, *Oltre le quinte,* 45–46.

82. Nicola de Pirro, "L'Ispettorato del Teatro," *Scenario* 4, no. 8 (August 1935): 403–4.

83. Mario Labroca, "Il teatro lirico," *Bollettino dei musicisti* 3, no. 12 (September–October 1936): 39.

84. Nicola de Pirro, *Teatro per il popolo* (Rome: Tipografia Novissima, 1938).

The Novecentista wing of the Fascist Party (from the review, *Novecento*) joined with some of the leading political figures to oppose the more conservative Fascists and support a variety of initiatives aimed at an elite audience. With the exception of the International Festival of Contemporary Music, created in Venice in 1930, which concentrated on instrumental music (and in 1932 launched "chamber opera," a genre little cultivated in Italy at that time), the musical initiatives that prompted the most interest were the Maggio Musicale in Florence, the Teatro delle Arti in Rome, the Teatro delle Novità in Bergamo, the Settimana Musicale Senese in Siena, and the Ciclo di Opere Contemporanee (which despite its name and its hopes was a one-time affair).

The Maggio Musicale, which started in 1933 as a biennial festival (and later became annual), took place in the Teatro Politeama Vittorio Emanuele II, which had been granted *ente autonomo* status in 1931. The Maggio Musicale earned an international reputation for the quality of its performances, the modernity of its stage resources (which were put to good use by noted directors, such as Jacques Copeau and Max Reinhardt, and by scenic designers who were famous artists, such as Giorgio De Chirico, Felice Casorati, and Mario Sironi), the prestige of its singers and musicians, and the professionalism of its stage staff. The Maggio concentrated on revivals of neglected but worthwhile Italian works from the seventeenth to the nineteenth century (Monteverdi's *Il ritorno di Ulisse in patria*, Gaspare Spontini's *La vestale*, Rossini's *Mosè*, and Bellini's *I puritani*) and contemporary Italian operas (by Ildebrando Pizzetti, Ottorino Respighi, Alfredo Casella, Gian Francesco Malipiero, and Luigi Dallapiccola). Vittorio Gui and Guido M. Gatti, who came to the Maggio from the pioneering venture of the Teatro di Torino, a private theater, directed the Maggio from 1925 to 1931; from 1936 on, superintendent Mario Labroca gave the Maggio added impetus. The administrative expenses of this festival, the pride and joy of the Fascist regime's cultural policies, were covered by ticket sales, by the additional 2 percent special surtax (a privilege accorded to the theater in 1932, on the example of La Scala), and by contributions from the national government, local agencies, and banks.

The Teatro delle Arti in Rome, which had put on prose works under Anton Giulio Bragaglia since 1937, began in 1941 to offer such refined musical curiosities as Luigi Cherubini's *L'hôtellerie portugaise (La locanda portoghese)* and Modest Mussorgsky's *The Marriage* as well as works new to Italy such as Malipiero's *Torneo notturno,* Igor Stravinsky's *Apollon Musagète,* and Paul Hindemith's *Hin und zurück.* The Teatro delle Arti had a small budget, but it boasted famous names, even among its set designers (Filippo de Pisis, Mino Maccari, Orfeo Tamburi, Enrico Prampolini). It was subsidized by the Confederazione dei Professionisti e Artisti and by the MinCulPop.

The Teatro delle Novità in Bergamo, founded in 1937 by the MinCulPop, specialized in world premieres of Italian works (such as Giorgio Federico

Ghedini's *Maria d'Alessandria* in 1937); in 1939 the Settimana Musicale Senese, founded by the Accademia Chigiana in Siena, launched a series of revivals of operas by Antonio Vivaldi, Alessandro Scarlatti, and Giovanni Battista Pergolesi.

The Ciclo di Opere Contemporanee was founded in 1942, in the middle of World War II. The venture was backed and entirely financed by the Min-CulPop on the initiative of De Pirro, and it was worked out with the help of Enrico di San Martino, who served as the Ciclo's president; Mario Labroca and Vincenzo Tommasini, who functioned as consultants; and Carlo Gatti and Tullio Serafin, the artistic directors of La Scala and the Teatro Reale, Rome, respectively. Ignoring Nazi directives regarding "degenerate art," the Ciclo operated autonomously, sponsoring productions in theaters in Milan and Rome of Alban Berg's *Wozzeck* (with Serafin as conductor, Aurel M. Milloss as director, and István Pekáry as scene designer), Béla Bartók's *Miraculous Mandarin* (choreography by Milloss, scene design by Enrico Prampolini), and works by Malipiero, Respighi, Casella, Ferruccio Busoni, Dallapiccola, and Goffredo Petrassi.

These somewhat elitist initiatives were accompanied by more usual theatrical activities, which the Fascist regime regulated by promulgating two separate laws in February 1936. The first regarded the so-called minor opera theaters; the second, the major public theaters that were run as *enti autonomi*. In January 1936, even before these provisions became law, the Federazione degli Industriali dello Spettacolo (Federation of Performing Arts Administrators) attempted to aid theater managements in the preparation of operas and to coordinate opera seasons nationwide by creating a bureau of technical assistance, known as the Centro Lirico Italiano (Italian Opera Center), with offices in Rome and Milan. This agency made available to impresarios and theater administrators statistics on productions that had been put on in recent years and a list of the "modern operas" (defined as those from 1918 on) that were obligatory if they sought state funding. The center announced that "The upper Hierarchies desire the frequent performance of such works with the aim of arriving at the desired renewal of the repertory through the gradual education of the public."

The law on minor opera houses was aimed at "having provincial theaters return to their function of forming new artists and diffusing new works." The state, which indirectly subsidized these institutions with a contribution of 6.17 percent of the revenues from the levies on radio subscriptions, rounded out funds contributed by the municipalities, local institutions, and even private individuals. To hire singers these theaters had to go through the Ufficio di Collocamento (placement bureau) that had been instituted when theatrical agencies were abolished in 1932, and the Ministry of Press and Propaganda arrogated to itself the right to dictate policy concerning programming, to fix the calendars for the season, to set the amounts of the subsidy (which was not given until the end of the season), and in practice to supervise all activities in the opera houses. The hoped-for "renewal of the repertory" was never achieved, thanks not only to the "conservative tendencies" of provincial Italy (as Ottavio Tiby noted) and to the resistance of theater managements (who tended to pick from among the "modern operas of the last twenty years" that were obligatory for their subsidies those operas that they knew would be popular—*Turandot, Il piccolo Marat,* and others), but also, as Labroca pointed out, because artists, chorus members, and orchestras found it difficult to rehearse when rehearsal venues were scattered all over Italy.[85]

The need to standardize the administrations of the major theatrical institutions (in the interests of achieving more efficacious political control and artistic quality more "worthy of the Italian tradition"), to eliminate agents (Fascism's bête noire), and to promote "the musical and theatrical education of the people" led to the law of February 1936 regarding opera houses. All municipalities and private entities that ran opera seasons of one month or more were obliged to create a new organization with its own juridical status and autonomous administration. After La Scala, the Teatro Reale in Rome, and the Teatro Comunale in Florence, other *enti autonomi* were created for the opera houses of Turin, Venice, Trieste, Verona (the Amphitheater), Genoa, Bologna, Naples, and Palermo. The map of Italian opera houses began to resemble that of today. Working funds were to come from the season's revenues, subsidies from the municipalities, the provincial governments, the provincial councils for the economy, and other organizations, public and private. The state, which did not appear explicitly in these arrangements, stood ready to cover losses by means of ordinary and extraordinary grants of funds. The governing bodies of these new *enti* included a president (usually the *podestà,* or mayor, of the city; for Rome, the governor), a superintendent (named by the ministry), representatives of the Sindacato musicisti (musicians' union), and the Federazione degli Industriali e Lavoratori dello Spettacolo (Association of Administrators and Workers in the Performing Arts). The inspectorate had the right to change programs, switch calendar dates, and mandate the hiring of young singers. This was what the law said, but in practice the duties of the inspector, who was assisted by a plethora of other officials of the ministry of press and propaganda, were a good deal broader, including the sending of press bulletins *(veline)* on government directives, vetoing or recommending

85. Ottavio Tiby, "Il teatro lirico e il concerto," in *Musica* (Florence: Sansoni, 1942), 1:257–63; Giuseppe Savagnone, "Valorizzazione della produzione lirica," and Gaspare Scuderi, "Il Teatro lirico in provincia," *Il musicista* 5, nos. 1–3 (October-December 1937): 14–16; 16–17, respectively; Mario Labroca, "Enti autonomi o Teatri di Stato?" *Scenario* 11, no. 11 (November 1942): 389–91, esp. 391,and "I giovani nel teatro lirico," in *Musica* (Florence: Sansoni, 1942), 1:243–48.

composers, librettists, and performers, fixing pay-scale limits for singers and conductors, allocating subsidies, censoring texts, and standardizing decisions with bureaucratic impartiality. "From the way all new and contemporary operas are treated alike, without distinction, you might think that [you could pick] one or another of them, this one or that one. . . . They all have the same value and merit equal attention—that is, they all are worth almost nothing"; this remark came from the composer Pizzetti, deploring the indiscriminate "protectionism" of the MinCulPop.[86] Thanks to that policy the *enti autonomi* performed more works by living Italian musicians than by dead ones (320 to 315, respectively) during the years 1935 to 1943.

The line they followed was a compromise. The glorious old works were to be revived, but the more recent generations were not to be forgotten; a good deal of room was left for maneuvering among conformist and client-pleasing solutions (such as operas composed by music critics, by distinguished dilettantes, by members of the Italian academy better versed in other disciplines, or by winners of the competitions put on by the secretary of the musicians' union, Giuseppe Mulè). The contemporary composers most performed by the state-supported opera houses were the *veristi* (realists) and musicians of traditional leanings—the same composers who dominated the popular radio stations founded by the Dopolavoro (afterwork), the Fascist regime's program for workers' leisure time, and by the National Fascist Party. Mascagni led the list of composers played, followed by Umberto Giordano, Respighi, Riccardo Zandonai, Cilea, and Ermanno Wolf-Ferrari (see table 1).

The state-subsidized opera houses, still working under the aegis of the MinCulPop, also put on a large number of works by earlier composers between 1935 and 1943, among them works by Donizetti (thirty-four productions), Rossini (twenty-seven productions of comic operas and opere serie), Bellini (twelve productions), and Monteverdi (six productions). Works of Monteverdi and other composers that returned to the stage after centuries of neglect (such as Scarlatti, Vivaldi, and Niccolò Piccinni) were produced in "creative" transcriptions by composers of repute (Respighi, Dallapiccola, Vito Frazzi, and Alceo Toni). These productions made no attempt to be faithful to the original and were not motivated by scholarly interests (see table 2). The cult of purely Italian opera, energetically asserted during the 1930s, inspired a number of celebrations that reached out beyond theatrical performance into a variety of cultural, didactic, and popularizing initiatives (set-design competitions, exhibits of the memorabilia of famous figures, scholarly studies, lectures on works and composers, radio programs). Among these celebrations were the centenary of the death of Bellini (1935), the fortieth anni-

---

86. Ildebrando Pizzetti, "Osservazioni e appunti sul nostro teatro in musica," *La nuova antologia* 73 (1 July 1938): 18–19. For data on performances see Nicolodi, *Musica e musicisti,* 20ff.

TABLE 1. Operas and Ballets by Living Composers Performed in Major Italian Opera Houses 1935–36 to 1942–43

COMPOSER	1935–6 O	1935–6 B	1936–7 O	1936–7 B	1937–8 O	1937–8 B	1938–9 O	1938–9 B	1939–40 O	1939–40 B	1940–1 O	1940–1 B	1941–2 O	1941–2 B	1942–3 O	1942–3 B	Total Prod.
1. Alfano	1		1		2		1		2		1		3			1	12
2. Allegra	1																1
3. Barbieri			1														1
4. Barilli							1						1				2
5. Bianchi			1										1				2
6. Bizzelli	1																1
7. Caetani													1				1
8. Camussi			1														1
9. Canonica			1														1
10. Carabella		1									1						2
11. Casavola			1														1
12. Casella			2		1		1		1		2		1		1	2	11
13. Cicogna	1																1
14. Cilea	3		1		2		3		3		4		1		2		19
15. Dallapiccola									1				1				2
16. Ferrari Trecate									1				1				2
17. Ferro											1		1		1		3
18. Filiasi										1							1
19. Frazzi						1											1
20. Garau	1																1
21. Gerelli														1			1
22. Ghedini							2		1				1				4
23. Ghislanzoni			1														1
24. Giordano	4		5		4		3		5		4		6		2		33
25. Gnecchi													1				1
26. Gui							1										1
27. Laccetti	1																1
28. Lattuada					1				1				1				3
29. Lualdi				1	2		1				1				2		7
30. Malipiero	1				1		1				1				1		5
31. Marinuzzi			1				1								1		3
32. Mascagni	4		6		5		4		11		5		5		2		42
33. Menotti							1										1
34. Montemezzi	1		1				2										4
35. Mulè			2		1		4				1		3		1		12
36. Napoli					1						1						2
37. Pannain									1		1		1		1		4
38. Pedrollo					1												1
39. Peragallo			1								1		1				3
40. Persico	1				1		1				1						4
41. Petrassi																1	1
42. Piccioli														1			1
43. Pick-Mangiagalli	1		2		1		2				1		1		1	1	10
44. Pietri									1								1

TABLE 1. *Continued*

COMPOSER	1935-6		1936-7		1937-8		1938-9		1939-40		1940-1		1941-2		1942-3		Total Prod.
	O	B	O	B	O	B	O	B	O	B	O	B	O	B	O	B	
45. Pizzetti	2		1		2		4				1		3		2		15
46. Porrino											1		1				2
47. Ragni																1	1
48. Refice	2				1		1						1				5
49. Respighi	1		8	3	1	1	1	1	3	1	1	2	2	1	1		27
50. Riccitelli							1										1
51. Rocca	1		2		2		1		1				1				8
52. Scuderi					1		1		1				1				4
53. Sonzogno			1	1													2
54. Tommasini										1							1
55. Vittadini					1												1
56. Wolf-Ferrari	1		3		3		3		4		2		3				19
57. Zandonai	2		3		2		4		4		3		2		1		21
58. Zanella									1								1

Total productions 320

Note: Theaters include the Maggio Musicale Fiorentino and the Ciclo di Opere Contemporanee of Rome and Milan. Performances of a more popular character are excluded.
O = opera;　　B = ballet

TABLE 2. Operas and Ballets by Earlier Italian Composers Performed in Major Italian Opera Houses from 1935–36 to 1942–43

COMPOSER	1935-6		1936-7		1937-8		1938-9		1939-40		1940-1		1941-2		1942-3		Total Prod.
	O	B	O	B	O	B	O	B	O	B	O	B	O	B	O	B	
1. Bellini							2		1		2		4		3		12
2. Boito	2		1		2		1		1		1		1				9
3. Busoni									2				2				4
4. Catalani	1				1		1		3				1				7
5. Cherubini													1				1
6. Cimarosa	2		1		1		1										5
7. Donizetti	6		5		5		3		6		4		3		2		34
8. Leoncavallo							1		1				3		1		6
9. Monteverdi			2						1				1		2		6
10. Paisiello							1		1								2
11. Piccinni													1				1
12. Ponchielli	3				1								1		1		6
13. Puccini	10		10		11		13		14		12		12		5		87
14. Rossini	3		5		5		2		4		3		5				27
15. Spontini															1		1
16. Vecchi					1		1										2
17. Verdi	12		13		14		14		13		15		12		12		105

Total productions 315

Note: Theaters include the Maggio Musicale Fiorentino and the Ciclo di Opere Contemporanee of Rome and Milan. Performances of a more popular character are excluded.

versary of Verdi's death (in 1941, by Mussolini's special command), the sesquicentennial of Rossini's birth (Pesaro 1942), and the tricentenary of the death of Monteverdi (coordinated by Minister Farinacci, Cremona 1943).

Among the inspectorate's first decisions were measures passed in 1935 (at the time of the Italian war in Ethiopia) prohibiting the production of works from countries that were members of the League of Nations—France and Russia in particular.[87] Although the Italian hierarchy spoke of Italy's "act of generosity" when these measures were abrogated a year later in reaction to the League of Nations' sanctions (leaving theaters free to return to producing works formerly prohibited), the Italian laws were no less an act of political opportunism than the League of Nations' own revocation of its sanctions, voted at the Congress of Geneva 4 July 1936. By then, though, Italian autocracy had become an irreversible reality.[88]

In 1937 the Italian government prohibited Italian opera companies from participating in the Paris International Exhibition. Enrico di San Martino, the head of the organizing committee, lamented, "The news that the scheduled performances of the Teatro alla Scala, the Rome Opera, and the Maggio [Musicale] Fiorentino will not take place has produced a very poor impression, not only among the French public but among the international public, not to mention the Italian colony." In the same year Italy's closer ties with Nazi Germany with the Rome-Berlin Axis, sealed in 1939 by the treaty of military alliance known as the Pact of Steel, established a privileged channel for musical accords and exchanges. In August 1937 *Il musicista,* the official organ of the musicians' union, echoed the speech Hitler had given in Munich a month earlier against "degenerate," "Bolshevik," and "Hebrew" art. As a result, any enthusiasm shown for "foreign" art or even for Italian forms of modernism was severely repressed. ("Art . . . must be the object of vigilant and constant attention on the part of . . . those regimes that fundamentally repudiate all agnosticism. . . . It is thus logical to intervene to make selections and purify it from those toxic agents and those spiritual and technical tendencies counter to the ethical and social ends of the regime.")[89]

Soon after—in 1938—racial laws were to shake the operatic world as well as the rest of Italian society.

> It is decreed and absolutely forbidden for those of the Hebrew race, even if exculpated, and no matter of what nationality, to engage in any form of activity in the theatrical field. . . . Included [in this prohibition] are composers, librettists, transla-

---

87. "Notizie," *Musica d'oggi* 17, no. 12 (December 1935): 441–42.

88. See the paper by Giuseppe Mulè to the Second National Congress of Musicians, *Bollettino dei musicisti,* 3, no. 12 (September–October 1936): 21.

89. For Alberto Ghislanzoni's glosses on Hitler's speech, see Ghislanzoni, "Il discorso del Cancelliere Hitler sull'arte moderna," *Il musicista* 4, no. 8 (August 1937): 125–29. On the Paris

tors, scriptwriters, set designers, singers of whatsoever level, directors, extras, chorus members, orchestral conductors and musicians, corps de ballet . . .

Soon after, the prohibition was enlarged to include not only works composed by Jewish composers or librettists after 1938 but also works written before that date. It was only by virtue of "superior authorization" that the operas composed by Respighi to librettos by Claudio Guastalla could be produced. (Ennio Porrino's *Gli Orazi,* with a libretto by Guastalla, was produced in 1941 without listing the librettist's name.) Still later all it took was a biblical or Jewish subject to have a work censored, a fate suffered by Pizzetti's *Dèbora e Jaéle* (1922) and Lodovico Rocca's *Il Dibuk* (1934), among others.[90]

In 1939 the MinCulPop cut off financial aid to the Italian section of the International Society for Contemporary Music (ISCM), a move that deprived Italy of the prestigious support of the English musicologist Edward J. Dent, the Italian section's spiritual guide. (The reasons put forward by the ministry, all of which were expressed in strongly revanchist tones, concerned the lack of sufficient Italian representation in recent seasons of the festival sponsored by that organization.) When war broke out, the MinCulPop further rationed foreign contemporary music by forbidding the playing of works by English, Russian, and French composers ("the classics" were tolerated).[91] German composers were shown special favor, among them Richard Strauss and younger composers such as Werner Egk, Carl Orff, and Norbert Schultze (who wrote the celebrated *Schwarzer Peter*), but also some composers of minimal importance to the annals of opera. The ministry recommended to the opera houses that they give preference to performers of Italy's ally: "The superintendents, in presenting . . . the draft program . . . will indicate which among the operas they propose will be performed with German conductors and German singers, and they will express their desires concerning the name of the conductor." Among the few, involuntary bright notes in those years of sinister torpor was the greater diffusion of Mozart's operas, which were still not well known in Italy (see tables 3 and 4).

Italians operated with circumspection, using a host of small tricks, as had become the rule in a country by now totally under the thumb of Germany and where an admiration for German efficiency and organization in cultural

International Exhibition, see Enrico di San Martino, letter to Mussolini from Paris, 12 July 1937, ACS PCM (1937–39) 14.2.2200.

90. For the "superior" authorization for the Respighi-Guastalla operas, see the circular of the Ministero della Cultura Popolare, Direzione Generale per il Teatro, Div. II, Sez. I, no. 8687, 3 May 1942, signed by Alessandro Pavolini and Ottavio Tiby and addressed to all managements of the major opera houses. See also Leopoldo Zurlo, *Memorie inutili: La censura teatrale nel ventennio* (Rome: Edizioni dell'Ateneo, 1952), 241–44.

91. "Comunicazioni del Sindacato," *Il musicista* 9, no. 2 (November 1941): 17.

TABLE 3. Operas and Ballets by Living Non-Italian Composers Performed in Major Italian Opera Houses from 1935 to 1943

COMPOSER	1935-6		1936-7		1937-8		1938-9		1939-40		1940-1		1941-2		1942-3		Total
	O	B	O	B	O	B	O	B	O	B	O	B	O	B	O	B	Prod.
1. Bartók					1										1		2
2. Berg															1		1
3. Bloch					1												1
4. Donisch											1						1
5. Egk															1		1
6. de Falla					2		1						1				4
7. Gerster													1				1
8. Gotovac													2				2
9. Honegger			1												1		2
10. Honegger/ Ibert							1										1
11. Janáček											1						1
12. Kempff											1						1
13. Kodály					1		1										2
14. Orff															1		1
15. Prokofiev													1				1
16. Rabaud							1										1
17. Ravel							2		1								3
18. Roussel			1														1
19. Schultze									1								1
20. Strauss	2		2		2		2		4		3		6		3		24
21. Stravinsky			1				1		2		2		1		2	1	10

Total productions   62

Note: Theaters include the Maggio Musicale Fiorentino and the Ciclo di Opere Contemporanee of Rome and Milan. Performances of a more popular character are excluded.

matters mixed with a lingering ambition for autonomy. Italians learned to keep within the laws without seconding Nazi rules and vetos in everything or in every way. This attitude explains the welcome given to the music of Hindemith, Berg, and Bartók (in instrumental music in particular, but also in opera)—composers detested by the Hitler regime but ones whose "arianism," loudly proclaimed by any Italian management that opted to include their works in its program, was beyond reproach. A quite different fate awaited composers who had not been particularly popular in past times and whom no one had an interest in defending: "As the Ministry [of Popular Culture] has ruled, performance . . . of the compositions of Shostakovich is forbidden," the General Directorate for the Theater warned in 1939.[92]

Aside from its duties in enforcing respect for laws dictated by Italy's foreign policy, the inspectorate had a well-defined role as censor. In 1931, with

92. Circular of the Ministero della Cultura Popolare, Direzione Generale per il Teatro, Div. II, Sez. I, no. 21134/Cr 110, 9 November 1939, to all state-supported opera theaters.

TABLE 4. Operas and Ballets of Non-Living, Non-Italian Composers Performed in Major Italian Opera Houses 1935–36 to 1942–43

COMPOSER	1935–6		1936–7		1937–8		1938–9		1939–40		1940–1		1941–2		1942–3		Total Prod.
	O	B	O	B	O	B	O	B	O	B	O	B	O	B	O	B	
1. Beethoven				1			1		1		1	2	1				7
2. Berlioz	1		1						1								3
3. Bizet			2		3		4						2		1		12
4. Borodin									1								1
5. Debussy			1														1
6. Delibes				1													1
7. Flotow					1												1
8. Gluck			2								3		1		1		7
9. Gomez			2														2
10. Gounod							2		1								3
11. Granados					1												1
12. Handel									1								1
13. Haydn					1												1
14. Humperdinck			1		1		2		1		2		1				8
15. Liszt														1		1	2
16. Massenet	1		4		3		1		1				1		3		14
17. Meyerbeer					1												1
18. Mozart	1		2		1		1		4		5		1				15
19. Mussorgsky			1		3		1		3		1		2		1		12
20. Offenbach					1												1
21. Purcell									1								1
22. Rimsky-Korsakov				1	1				1		1						4
23. Saint-Saëns	1		1		1												3
24. Tchaikovsky							1				1						2
25. Thomas	1		1														2
26. Wagner	4		7		14		14		8		8		8		10		73
27. Weber							2		2								4

Total productions 183

Note: Theaters include the Maggio Musicale Fiorentino and the Ciclo di Opera Contemporanee of Rome and Milan. Performances of a more popular character are excluded.

the promulgation of the Unified Law on Public Security, responsibility for censorship was taken away from the various prefects and put into the hands of the chief of police, Arturo Bocchini, who worked under the aegis of the Ministry of the Interior. Bocchini felt himself unequal to the task, and he assigned the responsibility to Leopoldo Zurlo, a former prefect under the Giolitti government who dabbled in literature. The provision in the enabling legislation of the unified law prohibited

> works contrary to morality, good conduct, public order, the law, the constituting principles of the family, religious sentiment; [works] promoting vice and crime,

perturbing international relations, inspiring aversion among the social classes; [works] offensive to the king, the holy pontiff, the head of the government, sovereigns of foreign states, the decorum and prestige of the authorities, the ministers, the agents of public security, the private life of persons; [or works] relating to the nefarious events that may have impressed public opinion.

In 1935 Zurlo's office, which had been transferred under the Ministry of Press and Propaganda, acted to eliminate texts that failed to reflect the themes and the values of Fascism.[93] Operas from the past were "corrected" on the basis of the latest political events. During the war years inopportune passages in Antonio Somma's libretto for Verdi's *Un ballo in maschera* were modified (with total disregard of rhyme): "O figlio d'Inghilterra, / amor di questa terra!" became "O figlio della patria . . ." *Madama Butterfly* completely disappeared from opera programs, thanks to the "Star-Spangled Banner."

Before censorship ever reached the level of being embodied in a specific governmental institution, however, it operated (consciously or unconsciously) within individual authors and composers, inducing them to avoid possible infractions of rules explicitly codified by the regime or implicit in its attitudes. Operatic productions were such costly events (for the theaters that put them on), and the artists involved so keenly wanted their works to be performed (both for the fame they brought and the earnings) that no one was eager to run risks. In practice the censor's scissors, which regarded the librettos rather than the stylistic and formal components of the music, were used only rarely. When a work was censored it was often because its creator had been ingenuous or guilty of political naïveté. The Austrian composer Franz Lehár, an enthusiastic admirer (as he himself declared) of the "land and the race" of Italy, had exchanged correspondence with Mussolini as early as 1924 (when Lehár sent Mussolini several compositions in homage), and in 1933 he dedicated his most recent operetta, *Giuditta,* to Il Duce. Because the plot hinged on the adventures of an Italian army captain who deserts his regiment for love of an adventuress, the composer was asked to transfer the setting to Portugal. As the censorship office explained, the protagonist was "not shown in a light appropriate to encouraging self-respect, nor is [the work] sensitive to the military sentiments of possible comrades-in-arms who might be present, in uniform, among the spectators."[94] Zurlo's office was not the only source of decisions: Mussolini himself responded to works that composers had sent

93. See Philip V. Cannistraro, *La fabbrica del consenso: Fascismo e mass media* (Bari: Laterza, 1975), 113, a revision of the author's thesis, "The Organization of Totalitarian Culture: Cultural Policy and the Mass Media in Fascist Italy 1922–1945" (1971).

94. An undated summary of the plot of the *Giuditta* libretto written by the Ufficio censura (censor's office) can be found in the file headed "Franz Lehár" in ACS SPD Ord. 16818.

to him, either as a gift or to read. In 1925 he opposed the withdrawal of an operetta, Carlo Lombardo and Virgilio Ranzato's *Cin-ci-là*, which had made "a disgusting impression" on the citizenry of Crema, who urged its removal from the bill; in 1932, after reading the libretto of *Orsèolo* that had been sent to him by the composer, Pizzetti, Mussolini invited the librettist to find another expression to replace "giustizia e libertà" (justice and liberty) because it was too directly reminiscent of the slogan of the anti-Fascist movement of the Rosselli brothers.[95]

An opera could be performed only when it had received the censor's seal of approval. There was one case, however, of a work that was stopped after the premiere, even though all the proper bureaucratic procedures had been fulfilled. The opera was *La favola del figlio cambiato* by Francesco Malipiero, with a libretto by Luigi Pirandello. Zurlo had authorized performance of the work pursuant to the deletion of a few lines that he found too irreverent toward the monarchy.[96] Il Duce, present at the Italian premiere (Rome, Teatro Reale, 24 March 1934), had been lukewarm about the text ("The protestors would love it, since it gives them an excuse to whistle"), and he ordered its removal from the bill. The work never appeared again during the Fascist regime and was revived only in 1952. Malipiero's later (and unsuccessful) attempts to revise the opera clearly show self-censorship put to the task of correcting moral standards and values of the institution of monarchy that were presumed to be endangered. Not only were phrases dropped that referred indirectly to authority (ministers, rulers, etc.); all more daring expressions were adjusted as well. As the composer explained to the librettist, he was acting "in order to avoid the ignoble grimaces used to express hypocritical indignation by a bourgeoisie that is capable of all manner of vileness but is easily scandalized."[97]

95. For Lombardo and Ranzato see ACS SPD Ord. 220 alphanumerical series D/PSE 19; for Pizzetti see ACS SPD Ord. 538707.

96. Zurlo, *Memorie inutili*, 130–31. The lines that were removed were "Non importa che sia / questa o quella persona: / importa la corona! / Cangiate questa di carta e vetraglia / in una d'oro e di gemme di vaglia, / il mantelletto in un manto / e il re da burla diventa sul serio / a cui voi vi inchinate" (It does not matter whether it is this person or that: it's the crown that is important! Change this one of paper and glass into one of gold and precious gems, the little cape into a robe, and the comic king becomes a real king to whom you bow down). See also Gigi Livio, "I testi e le forme del teatro malipieriano: *La favola del figlio cambiato*" (1982), in G. F. *Malipiero e le nuove forme della musica europea*, ed. Luigi Pestalozza (Milan: Unicopli, 1984), 112–36, esp. 129–35.

97. Silvio D'Amico, *Il teatro non deve morire* (Rome: Eden, 1945), 50–51. For the vicissitudes of *La favola del figlio cambiato*, according to someone who attended the premiere, see Fedele D'Amico, "La farsa degli equivoci nella *Favola del figlio cambiato*," *Vie nuove* (17 August 1952); for an amplified version see *Cinquant'anni del Teatro dell'Opera*, ed. Jole Tognelli (Rome:

5. The New Republic: Reconstruction and the "Consumer Society"

In 1945, when Vittorio Gui compared the postwar situation in Italy to the period immediately after World War I, he noted that World War II had brought incalculably more harm to musical life in Italy than the earlier one. He blamed that state of affairs on psychological reactions to Italy's defeat and on a particularly bitter civil war. Italy lacked moral glue. The economic situation was grim as well, thanks to widespread destruction from bombardments and air raids, to lowered agricultural productivity, and to the losses suffered by Italian industry.

The leading opera houses had been destroyed. La Scala, transformed into "a sad, dusty, open cavern," had lost its famous acoustics along with its roof; the Teatro Comunale in Florence was unusable; in Turin, where a fire had badly damaged the Teatro Regio back in 1936, performances continued wearily in the Teatro Vittorio Emanuele (renamed Teatro Lirico in 1945); Genoa was left with not one theater standing, and ad hoc "mini" opera seasons were put on in movie theaters. Only Venice, which became the seat of the Ministry of Popular Culture in 1943, had survived: the subsidies for La Fenice had been voted and paid promptly by the Salò government, and the players of the La Fenice orchestra enjoyed special privileges as well as full-year contracts. In other places orchestral musicians had a much harder time. Often organized into cooperatives, they accepted difficult transfers to cities that had theaters, or they were ceded to other institutions that could offer them better opportunities for work: the musical personnel of Rome's Santa Cecilia, for example, who specialized in the symphonic repertory, moved to the Teatro Adriano in 1945 for a brief cycle of operas.

The Ministry of Popular Culture, accused of favoritism and of wasting public funds, was abolished in 1944. Sentiment ran so high concerning the "abuses" and "cabals" of Fascism that some exacerbated observers declared (with little historical veracity) that it would be better to return to the old system of the municipal administration of theaters rather than be further subjected to the despotic intrusion of the state.[98] But in 1948, when the new climate of democracy signaled that the time had come to put some order back into the theatrical sector and the president of the Council of Ministers set up

Bestetti, 1979), 207–29. For a different point of view, see Nicolodi, *Musica e musicisti*, 221–9, which quotes Malipiero's letter to Pirandello of 9 August 1934.

98. Vittorio Gui, "Roma 1919–Roma 1945," *Il mondo* (21 July 1945): 12; Beniamino Dal Fabbro, *Musica e verità* (Milan: Feltrinelli, 1967), 22; Louis Cortese, "La Società Filarmonica di Genova," *Il mondo* (18 May 1946); Guido Piamonte, "La vita musicale a Venezia," *Il mondo* (15 December 1945); Guido M. Gatti, "Organizzazione del nostro teatro lirico," *Il mondo* (2 June 1945); Vittorio Gui, "Per la vita musicale italiana di domani," *Il ponte* 1, no. 4 (July 1945): 308–14.

a Direzione Generale dello Spettacolo (General Directorate of the Performing Arts), some of the "technicians" of the previous inspectorate were necessarily called back into service, including De Pirro, who continued to serve as director of the General Directorate until 1963.

Italians set to work catching up as soon as the war was over, and opera houses were no exception. By 1945 the stage of the Teatro Comunale in Florence had been reconstructed, and two years later the city inaugurated its first postwar Maggio Musicale with a program of symphonic music; opera had to wait until 1948. La Scala, which had been seriously damaged by bombs in 1943, reopened its doors three years later, completely refurbished. On 11 May 1946 Toscanini inaugurated the new auditorium with a memorable concert, and the first postwar opera season opened on 26 December of that year with *Nabucco*. Fascist cultural policies had regarded "the people" as an inert mass to be indoctrinated with propaganda and wooed with easily digested fare (the "factory concerts" inaugurated toward the end of the Fascist regime, for example, treated music as purely recreational), but now a number of new ventures sprang up to try new ways of combining "progress" with "contemporaneity." In Turin in 1945 the Unione Culturale organized a concert for workers in the auditorium of the RAI (the Italian broadcasting corporation) with an all-modern program of works by Darius Milhaud, Bartók, Busoni, and Hindemith. One observer of this experiment commented that the audience showed "not even a shadow of the bourgeois mad fear of being mocked the minute they don't understand something; no prideful condemnation, no hasty rejection."[99] Admittedly some ideas were blatantly demagogic, to the point that Dallapiccola, a composer fully aware of the connotations of the word *impegno* (commitment) and the ambiguity of the term *popolare* (popular), advised his colleagues to avoid being caught up by the ideological slogans of the moment.

> Humanity, social values . . . are all beautiful words. But today artists worthy of the name use them as little as possible. Because in spite of appearances our times have taught artists the harsh lesson—harsher than is generally known—of what modesty is.[100]

In another about-face from the previous regime, exchanges with other countries were renewed with particular fervor, a move aided by the return of the Italian section to the International Society for Contemporary Music and the abrogation of the nationalistic and protectionist laws of the Fascist regime. The International Festival of Contemporary Music in Venice produced some of the major twentieth-century European works: Berg's *Lulu* in 1949,

99. Massimo Mila, "A musica nuova, pubblico nuovo," *Il mondo* (20 October 1945).
100. Luigi Dallapiccola, "La musica fra le due guerre," *Radiocorriere* (21–27 April 1946).

Stravinsky's *The Rake's Progress* in its world premiere in 1951, Hindemith's *Cardillac* in 1948, the Italian premiere of Kurt Weill's "Songspiel," *Mahagonny*, in 1949, and Benjamin Britten's *The Turn of the Screw* in its world premiere in 1954.

In 1946, the year in which Italians responded to the institutional referendum that created the Republic, the so-called Scoccimarro law (from the name of the Communist Minister of Finance) was approved on 30 May 1946. Although this law left the 1936 provisions unchanged, by official decree it sanctioned the role of the state as the direct sponsor of the opera industry. The *enti autonomi*, the Accademia di Santa Cecilia, and, in general terms, "other not-for-profit theatrical and musical bodies and institutions" would receive 12 percent of the state's fiscal revenues from theatrical spectacles and betting. State funding was to be granted on the basis of an examination of each institution's account books, artistic programs, and past activities, and financing was contingent on the favorable opinion of a committee, chaired by the Under Secretary of State for the Treasury, which included among its members a "musical expert" named by the president of the Council of Ministers. It was immediately clear that the sums allocated were inadequate, and in fact the rates were adjusted in the following years. The law also provided funds for the maintenance of "permanent" artistic organizations—something that was as yet a totally abstract entity and in practice nonexistent, given that the activities of the orchestras, the choruses, and the singers were seasonal. Still, in the new climate of social values that had been ushered in by the Resistance, the unions were strong enough to impose an interpretation that gave theatrical workers *(lavoratori dello spettacolo)* the same rights as employees in the private sector.

In 1946 some observers came out in favor of these provisions: they were an attempt to remedy the problem of unemployment; they aimed at greater harmony among opera personnel, which would lead to better-prepared performances. Others felt instead that by "unproductively gulping down the state's payments," theatrical institutions, unable to fulfill their artistic mandates, would end up in a "permanent state of bankruptcy."[101] In 1950 the total cost for employees of the *enti autonomi* and the concert organizations that enjoyed similar status (the orchestras Santa Cecilia in Rome and the G. P. da Palestrina in Cagliari) was 2,178,441,000 lire. By 1980 this figure had risen to over 113 billion lire.. The superintendents, who served as both general directors and artistic directors of these institutions and who worked as hard as ever to balance their budgets, had other grievances, first among them

101. Paolo Salviucci, *La musica e lo Stato* (Milan and Rome: Bocca, 1953), 120–21; Pietro Righini, "La 'virtuosa canaglia' (Orchestre italiane e orchestrali, dalle lotte sindacali degli anni Venti all'attuale professionalità)," *Nuova rivista musicale italiana* 14 (1980): 240–54, esp. 250ff.

the exorbitant cost of overtime ("a sort of cost-of-living allowance for incompetence" was how Paolo Salviucci, the superintendent of the Rome Opera, defined it) and the high fees of the star singers. In the mid-1950s tenors and sopranos commanded fees of from 500,000 to 1 million lire a performance; baritones and bases from 200,000 to 300,000 lire. The superintendents also had to contend with a precarious financial situation: the state repeatedly threatened to reduce its contributions, and payment was always delayed—often as much as sixteen months—which meant that the superintendents had to take out loans and pay interest on them. No wonder the opera world was in constant turmoil. In January 1950 the staff of the Rome Opera threatened to cancel performances of *Tosca,* the work chosen to celebrate the fiftieth anniversary of the opening of the Teatro Costanzi, unless the promised state subsidies were paid. Only after exhausting negotiations involving representatives of the Rome city government and the General Director for the Performing Arts were funds found and the danger averted. In 1951 a legislative measure intended to reduce expenditures for opera and concerts (which also effected a sweeping decentralization of theater administration and closer coordination with the RAI) brought a reaction of alarm from the press and from the union, the Federazione Italiana dei Lavoratori dello Spettacolo.[102]

At first the state's efforts were focused on the opera houses and orchestras with *ente autonomo* status, and the other institutions—municipal theaters and provincial theaters—led a highly unstable existence and were often managed by incompetent impresarios. In 1948 some in the Italian music world rose to the defense of these "minor" institutions and pointed out that government intervention was urgently needed if they were to serve larger numbers.[103] The appeal fell on deaf ears, however, and anarchy continued to spread. At the same time, operatic ventures proliferated, and opera cooperatives and other projects sprang up with no coordination and no plan to distribute them better between northern and southern Italy or between large and small towns.

In the bigger cities opera remained a manifestation of the city's prestige, and its main audience comprised the upper and upper-middle class (not to mention the nouveaux riches of the black-market economy), a segment of Italian society that had taken heart at the results of the political elections of 1948, the defeat of the Left, and the coming to power of the four-party centrist coalition guided by the Christian Democrats. Opera premieres once again became opulent, fashionable social events. "Splendid automobiles" brought the audience that came to see Rossini's *Mosè* in Rome in 1948, an occasion on which the foyers of the Rome Opera house were crowded with

---

102. Salviucci, *La musica e lo Stato,* 63; Frajese, *Dal Costanzi all'Opera,* 3:231.

103. Remo Giazotto, "Teatro di provincia e sovvenzioni," in *Atti del Quinto Congresso di Musica* (1948) (Florence: Barbera, 1948), 135.

"signore e signorine sunk into the softness of furs" who displayed "innumerable varieties of hairstyles . . . with plumes, artificial flowers, shimmering diadems, bird of paradise feathers, feathered sprays, veils."[104]

The mid-fifties were the high point of the star system and its corollary, displays of *prima donna* temperament and tension between superstars. Stargazing was a habit that audiences were unable to outgrow, and mired in a state of "musical illiteracy," as one observer noted, they took "the means for the ends, considering operatic masterpieces as springboards for the exhibition of virtuoso singing."[105] This was the shoddy end result, in the "land of *melodramma*," of a tradition in which "fans" had always flocked around singers. Admittedly those years brought a particularly fine harvest of vocal talents that further encouraged the fans' exaggerations. To name only Italians (and including Maria Callas, a Greek artist whom Italy adopted as early as 1947), those were the years of sopranos Renata Tebaldi, Rosanna Carteri, Antonietta Stella, Anita Cerquetti; mezzo-sopranos Fedora Barbieri, Giulietta Simionato; tenors Mario Del Monaco, Giuseppe Di Stefano, Giacinto Prandelli, Ferruccio Tagliavini; baritones Ettore Bastianini, Carlo Tagliabue, Tito Gobbi, Giuseppe Taddei; and basses Mario Petri and Cesare Siepi.

Composers, critics, and conductors raised the specter of the "death of opera." They investigated the possible causes of opera's demise, scrutinized the effects of popular disaffection with opera, proposed a variety of solutions, economic, organizational, and artistic (funding permanent companies, putting on simplified productions with a return to painted backdrops, paying greater attention to the dramatic component in opera, producing chamber opera, attempting to modify—we are in 1950—"union regulations that set rigid limits to the needs of art"). According to Giorgio Graziosi, who saw the survival of opera as connected to its willingness to adapt to "the *visual* society of modern times," the problem lay not in the quality or the quantity of operas but in their mode of production. The real culprit was the cinema, not only because it was a type of entertainment "within the reach of all minds and all pockets" but because it was capable of taking over, "like a parasite," the "narrative and typological techniques of the operatic world . . . with, in addition . . . a truth and an immediacy in its effects impossible on the stage."[106]

104. Quoted in Frajese, *Dal Costanzi all'Opera,* 3:201.

105. Massimo Mila, "I divi alla riscossa," *L'espresso* (27 July 1958), now in Mila, *Cronache musicali 1955–1959* (Turin: Einaudi, 1959), 486.

106. Fernando Previtali, "Sulla crisi del teatro d'opera," *La rassegna musicale* 20, no. 1 (January 1950): 23–31; Virgilio Mortari, "Il parere di un indipendente," *Ulisse* 5, no. 14 (April 1951): 144–45; Emilia Zanetti, "La polemica delle piccole opere," *Ulisse* 5, no. 14 (April 1951): 160ff.; Giorgio Graziosi, "Un diverso teatro musicale," *Il mondo* (4 August 1945); Graziosi, "Il melodramma è morto?" *Ulisse* 5, no. 14 (April 1951): 154–59.

In the 1950s the programs of the major opera houses (the *enti autonomi*) abounded with repertory operas, but they also contained contemporary works, both Italian and non-Italian, particularly those of more moderate musical tendencies. Modern works were less warmly received in the same houses thirty years later: in 1982 the composers' and publishers' association, the SIAE, complained that this dearth came just when "Italian composers are establishing themselves abroad as leaders in a new creative movement."[107] One of the works in a post-Puccini vein that premiered in the 1950s was Renzo Rossellini's *La guerra* (Naples, 1956). Some of the surviving composers of the "generation of the 1880s" remained faithful to their aesthetic concepts in new works, among them *Il dottor Antonio* by Franco Alfano (Rome, 1949), *Vanna Lupa* (Florence, 1949) and *Assassinio nella cattedrale* (Milan, 1958) by Pizzetti, *Venere prigioniera* by Malipiero (Florence, 1957), and *L'uragano* by Rocca (Milan, 1952, composed in 1942–51). In the 1960s, while the composers of the young avant-garde were honing their weapons and getting ready to take the opera houses by storm, the middle-aged generation of composers offered a broad variety of works that, while not denying the functions of "classical" drama, used abstract, epic, and symbolic themes that brought them closer to the musical scene elsewhere in Europe. Among these works were Dallapiccola's *Il prigioniero* (Florence, 1950, composed in 1944–48) and his *sacra rappresentazione, Job* (Rome, 1950), and Petrassi's two one-act operas, *Il cordovano* (Milan, 1949) and *La morte dell'aria* (Rome, 1950). Other works returned to the form and style of opera buffa in a neo-Rossinian vein, as in Nino Rota's *Il cappello di paglia di Firenze* (Palermo, 1955, but composed in 1946), or they followed the tradition of comic realism, as in Mario Peregallo's *La gita in campagna* (Milan, 1954), or preferred a more "grotesque" style, as in Valentino Bucchi's *Il contrabbasso* (Florence, 1954). There were repeated performances of the works of Gian Carlo Menotti, an operatic composer trained in the United States, whose discursive and "theatrical" style was hailed in the immediate postwar period as a possible panacea for Italian opera, and who founded (in 1958) the Festival of the Two Worlds at Spoleto, one of the most cosmopolitan and refined operatic venues of the time. The leading opera houses also mounted new works by non-Italian composers: the Italian premieres of Britten's *The Rape of Lucretia* (Rome, 1949), Sergei Prokofiev's *War and Peace* (Florence, 1953), Milhaud's *David* (Milan, 1955), and the world premiere of Francis Poulenc's *Les dialogues des carmélites* (Milan, 1957).

The 1950s were also the years of the cold war, a time of violent antago-

---

107. Luigi Conte, "Recessione economica e consumo dello spettacolo in Italia nel 1981," *Lo spettacolo* 32 (1982): 192.

nism in Italy between the political parties of the Left and the Right. Music, an ephemeral art with a diversity of meanings and one that can absorb terms such as *reactionary* or *progressive* only in general terms and with multiple time lags, was nonetheless the center of a good deal of ideological and rigidly schematic debate. Dallapiccola's *Il prigioniero* offended the sensibilities of the church, which found its purported criticism of the Spanish Inquisition inopportune during the Holy Year; the work irritated the Marxists as well, who interpreted it as a protest against Stalinism and Soviet prisons. When Rossini's *Stabat Mater* was performed in 1952 at the Conference for Peace and Christian Civilization sponsored by Giorgio La Pira, the Christian Democrat mayor of Florence, the Communist newspaper *Unità* complained bitterly about the use of "spiritual music"; the Socialist newspaper *Avanti!* branded Menotti's *Amahl and the Night Visitors,* which had its Italian premiere in Florence in 1953, a "bourgeois opera." Mario Scelba, the Christian Democrat President of the Council, Minister of the Interior, and a man who nurtured little esteem for art and the intellectual world (which he referred to, somewhat haughtily, with the collective noun *culturame*—"cultural stuff") red-penciled a tour of Soviet artists in Italy. In Florence in 1953 it was rumored that Luchino Visconti, who was known for having leftist political ideas, was denied the post of director of the Teatro Comunale out of fear that his success might negatively affect an electoral campaign that hinged on the *legge truffa* (swindle law).[108]

Critics valued *impegno* (commitment) in political life and dedication to "social reality": Fedele D'Amico wrote, "An advance in culture, a development, an evolution, are conceivable only within total contact with the contemporary world; the future is built only by working on the entire man, that is, the entirely committed man, within society." On a less abstract level, however, the critics' suggestions covered a broad range of possibilities: according to Enzo Borrelli, the music critic for *Unità*, although there was room for twelve-tone composers because they were linked to the historicity of language and its expressive potential, the neoclassical composers had no rights to musical citizenship because they were overly given to "uncommitted self-games" *(autogiochi disimpegnati)*. The composer Mario Zafred, also a critic for *Unità,* took an even more rigid and obviously Zhdanovist position: "formalism," he announced, included atonality and polytonality, dodecaphonic music, and all types of linguistic experimentation. These were expressions of "decadent," "escapist," and "elitist" art and of a sort of music that was "the most implacable and the most deceitful enemy of art of today." The true avant-garde,

108. Dietrich Kämper, *Luigi Dallapiccola* (Cologne: n. p., 1984), in Italian translation (Florence: Sansoni, 1985), 123–24; Leonardo Pinzauti, *Il Maggio musicale fiorentino dalla prima alla trentesima edizione* (Florence: Vallecchi, 1967), 129ff.; Fedele D'Amico, *I casi della musica* (Milan: Il Saggiatore, 1962), 74.

Zafred continued, was "in the lands of Socialism": true art was Soviet realism.[109]

The expanding awareness that arose from exchanges with other European cultures in the period after World War II was a phenomenon of much broader scope. Italian musicians came back into contact with a vast store of experiences—theoretical, aesthetic, historiographic, and compositional. The solid conceptual nucleus of idealism that had been the gravitational pole for musical aesthetics and music criticism from the 1920s to the 1940s disintegrated, leaving room for original second thoughts and new proposals to filter through (Massimo Mila coined a term for this artistic notion: "unawareness"—*inconsapevolezza*). Newly refurbished critical means and interpretive categories were needed if critics were to have a better grip on the contemporary social and cultural scene (one that included Marxism, phenomenology, and structuralism). The works and the poetics of the Vienna school received a broad hearing (Luigi Rognoni's *Espressionismo e dodecafonia* was published in 1954; Roman Vlad's *Storia della dodecafonia* appeared in 1958). Italian criticism also became aware of the thought of Theodor Adorno (much earlier than in the English- and French-speaking worlds): the Italian translation of his *Minima moralia* dates from 1954; that of his *Philosophie der neuer Musik* and his *Dissonanzen* from 1959.[110]

In 1959 the youngest generation of Italian musicians—Bruno Maderna, Luciano Berio, Luigi Nono, and Sylvano Bussotti—began their summer exodus to Germany for the Internationale Ferienkurse für Neue Musik, founded in Darmstadt in 1946. There a number of cults were celebrated in a radical avant-garde spirit: post-Webern structuralist pointillism, "aleatory composition," "open composition," neo-Dada "gestuality," and "happenings." In 1955, on the model of a similar initiative in Cologne, Alberto Mantelli and Rognoni founded the first Studio of Musical Phonology at the RAI in Milan, with Maderna and Berio as its directors. The humanistic canons of unity, uniqueness, and expression were out; the traditional categories of form, language, and sonic space were transformed, and the old musical notation was no longer adequate to the task.

109. Fedele D'Amico, "Il compositore e il languaggio musicale," *Atti del Quinto Congresso*, 16; Enzo Borrelli, "Dal Neoclassicismo alla Dodecafonia," in *Atti del Quinto Congresso*, 146–52; Mario Zafred, "Contributo ad una critica di alcune posizioni formalistiche," in *Atti del sesto congresso internazionale di musica* (1949) (Florence: Barbera, 1950), 87–93; Zafred, "Ragioni dell'anti-formalismo," *Ulisse* 5, no. 14 (April 1951): 138–43.

110. Massimo Mila, "Sul carattere inconsapevole dell'espressione artistica," in *Atti del Sesto Congresso*, 97–103; reprinted, with some changes, as "L'equivoco dell'oggettivismo e il suo senso positivo," in Mila, *L'esperienza musicale e l'estetica* (Turin: Einaudi, 1956), 113–25. For a clear reconstruction of critical and aesthetic thought during these years, see Enrico Fubini, "La cultura musicale dall'unità a oggi," in *Storia della società italiana*, ed. Giovanni Cherubini (Milan: Teti, 1980–82), 16:273–313, esp. 291ff.

TABLE 5. Attendance Statistics, 1936–1965

YEAR	NUMBER OF PERFORMANCES	TICKETS SOLD
1936	2,233	2,312,100
1940	2,434	2,293,930
1951	2,054	2,154,696
1955	1,984	2,097,930
1960	1,549	1,374,665
1963	1,338	1,399,917
1965	1,487	1,445,620

Note: Figures are taken from statistics furnished by the SIAE (Società degli Autori e Editori) and the AGIS (Associazione Generale Italiana dello Spettacolo). See also Riccardo Allorto, "Il consumo musicale in Italia (II: L'opera e il concerto)," *Nuova rivista musicale italiana* 1 (1967): 534–58, esp. 548.

The "official" opera houses stood apart, for the moment indifferent to the stimuli, the provocations, and the discoveries of the new generation of composers, continuing instead to satisfy the average in public taste. The government limited its efforts to "adjusting" *(ritoccare)* the amounts of its subsidies (in bureaucratic jargon, *provvidenze,* or "acts of providence"), delivering them with its customary delays. In 1959 the General Directorate for the Performing Arts was transferred from the presidency of the Council of Ministers to the newly established Ministry of Tourism and the Performing Arts (Ministero del Turismo e dello Spettacolo). The following year the leading opera houses were given authorization to contract for loans to meet their budget requirements with the Istituto di Credito of the combined Casse di Risparmio (savings banks) of Italy. The most eloquent results of these lazy administrative methods lay in a decline in the number of opera and ballet productions that was paralleled by a decline in the number of paying spectators (see table 5). Cinema attendance rose continually over the same thirty-year period, reaching its peak in 1955. Film is still Italians' favorite form of entertainment, although in the early 1950s they continued to spend more (in proportion to the gross national product) for musical and theatrical performances than they did in later years.

Radical social and economic changes toward the end of the 1950s soon modified the life, habits, and traditions of the Italian population. In those years Italy's economic structure was roughly that of all industrial countries, albeit with some contradictions and imbalances. Investments and employment were up and salaries rose (less than in other European countries, however, which gave Italy a competitive edge on the international market); the massive exodus of workers out of rural areas toward the large cities and of the population of the south toward the north changed the demographic map; the extraordinary development of private means of transportation and the superhighways reduced distances; the lower classes became a more integral part of Italian society by "coming into contact with and becoming familiar with the objects of daily use of capitalistic mass production."[111]

With the advent of the "affluent society," the economic boom, and rising incomes, essential expenditures took up less of the Italian family's budget, which means that cultural demands changed. The proportion of income devoted to "goods and services for recreation" (entertainment, books, newspapers, radio and television sets, various kinds of private instruction) declined, to be replaced by other, more opulent models of consumption (cars, motorcycles and scooters, home furnishings, domestic appliances, etc.).[112] One commentator noted: "Out of an overall total of more than 16 trillion lire that Italians set aside for personal consumption in 1963 . . . the categories that have shown the greatest increase in recent years are new luxury expenditures, whereas theatrical spectacles and public entertainment are in last place in percentage terms."[113]

Faced with declining attendance figures and growing production costs, the state continued to aim only at simple survival for the opera houses and passed a series of minor, stopgap financial measures. It was up to the individual institutions to make up the shortfalls in their budgets and deal with late delivery of state subsidies. They did so by launching a campaign to broaden their audience, by offering new works, and by instituting long-deferred educational initiatives. The La Scala audience—the audience always cited as the most open-minded and the most up-to-date—continued to be mired in its usual adoration of the diva of the moment and its preference for the established repertory. Operagoers in Milan much resembled their counterparts in the 1950s who were shocked to see an automobile appear on stage (in Peregallo's *La gita in campagna*) and greeted *Wozzeck,* Dimitri Mitropoulos conducting, with salvos of whistles (1952). Opera audiences seemed stagnant, totally separated from the young, who sought their own musical identity in jazz, rock, and popular music. At the same time there were early signs of a dissatisfaction that was to come to a head in bitter confrontations in 1968. On the opening night of the 1968–69 season (with *Don Carlo,* under the baton of Claudio Abbado), a crowd of demonstrators pelted the ladies' elegant evening clothes with eggs and paint, and the protesters carried signs reading, "Rich people, enjoy yourselves! This is the last time!" For the next few years opening night at La Scala was a more somber affair, and in the early 1970s a superintendent mindful of the theater's "social" problems,

111. Ernesto Galli della Loggia, "Crescita neo-capitalistica e 'civiltà' dei consumi," in *Novecento: I contemporanei,* ed. Gianni Grana, 10 vols. (Milan: Marzorati, 1979), 9:8770–76.

112. Mary Fraire, "La spesa per spettacoli in rapporto al reddito ed ai consumi privati in Italia dal 1951 al 1976," *Lo spettacolo* 28 (1978): 55–70.

113. Antonio Ciampi, *Il tempo libero in Italia* (Milan: Bompiani, 1965), 22.

Paolo Grassi, worked to change its cultural policy (among other ways, by offering more performances for workers and students).[114]

6. *The Corona Act and the Current Situation*

The first overall legislative provisions covering opera houses and concert halls came in 1967. The project was presented, after laborious discussion, by the Minister of Tourism and the Performing Arts, Achille Corona, and it became law, known as the Legge Corona, or Corona Act, on 14 August 1967. Operatic and concert activities were recognized as being "of notable general interest, in that they encourage the musical, cultural, and social education of the general public." The law was subdivided into fifty-four articles, some of which had a rich potential for innovation, for the most part never realized (coordination between opera and radio and television; connections among the leading opera houses and concert groups to facilitate the exchange of productions, sets, and artists; centers for professional training, and more). It reinforced the discrepancy between the leading opera houses—the *enti autonomi*—and the minor houses, solidifying the geographical imbalance between a privileged central-northern Italy and the south—the "two Italies," in the jargon of the SIAE's musical statistics.[115] The major opera houses and concert institutions that enjoyed *ente autonomo* status received a subsidy of a fixed sum (adjusted biennially; 12 billion lire in 1967—a sum that was immediately declared insufficient); all other theatrical ventures (other opera companies and concert groups, choruses, ballet companies) were allotted a more uncertain sum, contingent on the revenues and subscriptions of the RAI and on the surtax collected on theater admissions and betting. A consultative organization, the central commission, was set up under the Ministry of Tourism and the Performing Arts. Its thirty-two members (many of whom were superintendents or representatives of opera houses and concert societies) had the task of examining problems "concerning musical activities" and of working out the allotments stipulated in the law. The commission later came in for harsh criticism for being "too corporate-minded" and for having an insufficiently dynamic notion of culture.[116]

One entire section of the Corona Act (thick with detailed dispositions) was devoted to the thirteen *enti autonomi*, whose legal nature was defined as "of

114. Barigazzi, *La Scala racconta,* 515, 529.

115. Luigi Conte, "Attività spettacolistiche ed evoluzione delle preferenze del pubblico," *Lo spettacolo* 31 (1981): 154.

116. See the declarations of Luigi Pestalozza, Carlo Fontana, Massimo Bogianckino, Italo Gomez, and others in the investigation on "Musica, istituzione e legislazione," supplement to *Laboratorio musica* (February 1980): 8–31.

public law." The law listed the thirteen opera houses and concert societies, giving particular prominence to the Rome Opera and La Scala, the first "for [the] function of representation that it fulfills in the nation's capital," the second because it was "of particular national interest." The other opera houses were the Comunale of Bologna, the Comunale of Florence, the Comunale of Genoa, the San Carlo of Naples, the Massimo of Palermo, the Regio of Turin, the Verdi of Trieste, La Fenice of Venice, and the Amphitheater of Verona, as well as the Accademia di Santa Cecilia in Rome and the Palestrina concert society of Cagliari. The law also specified the structure and the duties of their management teams, which were to be composed of a president (or the mayor of the city), the superintendent of the theater, its artistic director, its administrative council (which included representatives from local sponsoring institutions and the various trade unions and professional associations), and the auditors. The law also prescribed sources of financing, public and private; it stipulated how the balance sheets and the annual programs should be set up; it specified that reduced-price performances should be given; it suggested various "incentives to encourage new national production." The law recognized seventeen lesser opera houses "of long-standing tradition" (a number that was later extended to twenty-four). These were the opera houses of Bari, Brescia, Catania, Como, Cremona, Ferrara, Livorno, Mantua, Modena, Novara, Parma, Piacenza, Pisa, Reggio Emilia, Rovigo, Sassari, and Treviso, with the later addition of Bergamo, Cosenza, Jesi, Lecce, Lucca, Macerata, and Ravenna. Some orchestral societies and festivals were covered by the same section of the law; it also covered impresarial activities and included the same protectionist provisions (for Italian artists and Italian operas) that applied for the *enti autonomi*.

The last section of the Corona Act regarded the "placement of artistic personnel" (concert soloists, singers, conductors, stage directors, set designers, choreographers, plus such "permanent" personnel as the stage and technical staff and members of the orchestra, the chorus, and the ballet). The drafter of the law, sensitive to widespread complaints about the function of agents and other middlemen (who were accused of cutting into the performers' earnings and affecting artistic decisions), dictated norms of an anachronistic severity: organizers who failed to turn to the "contract service of the special office for the placement of theatrical workers" in order to hire personnel were threatened with criminal action.[117] Since that placement service was never instituted, however, by 1978 the situation had become confused enough to inspire the American weekly *Newsweek* (12 June) to compare the situation to an opera buffa plot. The Italian courts received formal complaints from

117. Riccardo Allorto, "La Legge Corona ha compiuto due anni," *Nuova rivista musicale italiana* 3 (1969): 708–20, esp. 714ff.

several singers who had been obliged to pay a kickback to an agency in order to work, and the courts sent out summonses to the top directors of several theaters for failing to conform to the terms of a measure that forced them to choose between paralysis and infraction of the law. This episode, which aroused a good deal of fuss, was resolved with the issuing of a new law (on 8 January 1979) to modify the articles of the Corona Act that had caused the problem, thus adding to the operatic scene the figure of the "artist's representative."

The Corona Act did achieve some of its objectives, if we can disregard the government's failure to pass enabling legislation and the law's unfulfilled proposals, inadequate financial provisions, and ambiguous wording (in particular, article 12 on the artistic director, a relatively new institutional figure, who was to be chosen from among the "most renowned musicians and [be] of proven theatrical competence"). It undeniably led to a higher degree of coherence in state aid and to the broader diffusion of music.[118] Results were already noticeable in the early 1970s, and they paralleled a general rise in cultural level in Italy, the advent of new and more "cultured" modes of entertainment (precisely, opera performances and concerts), more widespread musical instruction (after the middle school reform of 1962), and an improvement in the quality of opera productions. Neither the rise in Italy's population (from 50 million in 1970 to 57 million in 1985) nor increased affluence, nor the somewhat high price of opera tickets had any significant influence on the demand for opera performances.[119] After 1970, according to one recent investigation, what Italians spent for recreational activities, entertainment, instruction, and culture rose notably (in real terms), but only a small proportion of Italians' leisure-time expenditures went for traditional opera performances. In other words, what the Italian population spent on music and the theater became a very small sum indeed, in comparison to their "notable expenditures for tourism and vacations [and] for audiovisual devices, old and new." Even considering all theatrical spectacles and musical performances together, these made up a minimal proportion of the family budget (1.09 percent in 1970; 0.71 percent in 1983).[120]

The discrepancy between demand and supply for opera and ballet from 1970 to 1983 is shown in table 6. In 1984 at the head of the list of *attività spettacolistiche* (to use the terminology of the SIAE) came *trattenimenti vari*

118. See Piero Rattalino, report (1983) in *Enti lirici tra crisi e riforma,* ed. Paolo Barile and Stefano Merlini (Florence: Passigli, 1984), 30–40, esp. 33.

119. See "Spettacolo come industria," typescript, edited by Pietro Gennaro, Massimo Teoldi, Silvia Biffignandi, Pia Cillario, Milan, "Strategia e organizzazione," February 1986, 21–22. See also Stefano Jacini, "Molti spettacoli in vendita," *Il giornale della musica* 1, no. 5 (April 1986): 11; Lorenzo Arruga, "Spettacolo e profitto," *Musica viva* 7–8 (July–August 1986): 70–73.

120. Luigi Conte, *Lo spettacolo* 34 (1984): 133–63, esp. 136–37.

TABLE 6. Attendance Statistics, 1970–1985

YEAR	NUMBER OF PERFORMANCES	TICKETS SOLD
1970	1,739	1,678,815
1975	2,001	1,937,828
1980	3,351	2,769,435
1985	4,013	2,874,927

Note: Figures are from the annual publications of the SIAE (see note to table 5).

(various entertainments): discotheques, billiards, admission to museums and art expositions, fairs, circuses, as well as pinball machines and the like. Close behind these came television; in third place came the cinema; fourth, sports matches; fifth and last, as usual, came theatrical and musical activities (prose theater, opera, ballet, concerts of classical music and popular music, reviews and musical comedies, and so forth). But although offerings in opera and ballet more than doubled in fifteen years and audiences grew notably (from 1970 to 1984 audiences for all theatrical and musical offerings grew 66.45 percent; audiences for classical music, 118.29 percent), a clear imbalance still remained between the audience for opera and for concerts, with opera attendance in decline. Or perhaps the opera houses—the major public ones, that is—were producing more music than audiences could appreciate. Music required more practical management: new consumers had to be found, or, as one commentator theorized, marketing strategies needed to be shifted to take into account the product, the price, the modes, and the channels of sale.[121]

It was pointed out that among the positive results of the Corona Act were new promotional (as distinct from strictly educational) activities, in the form of special performances for school groups and direct subsidies to schools. Indeed, one of the aims of the law, as article 5 stated, was "the musical education of all."[122] The decentralization that it tried to foster met with negative reactions, however, and decentralization was in fact achieved only in the 1970s with the establishment of the regions (more than twenty years after the 1948 Constitution had prescribed their creation), which brought a new role to the various local authorities. In the 1960s, although a more equal distribution of theatrical resources throughout Italy was still invoked as a panacea that would encourage the development of democracy, attempts to spread theatrical initiatives more broadly were governed by the logic of "punitive expeditions" with no continuity and no coordinated program, while in some cases the *enti autonomi* operating within one or another of the new regions fictitiously inflated the volume of their activities in order to obtain higher subsi-

121. See "Spettacolo come industria," 24.

122. Rattalino, report (1983) in *Enti lirici tra crisi e riforma*, ed. Paolo Barile and Stefano Merlini (Florence: Passigli, 1984), 34.

dies.[123] With the gradual transfer of supervisory powers from the state to local authorities (and with the passage of the necessary laws), decentralization became better organized, regional orchestras were created or strengthened, and theatrical circuits were expanded, especially where permanent, professional structures for production already existed. One forerunner of these circuits was the Associazione Teatri Emilia Romagna (ATER), an organization set up in 1964 to coordinate opera production among the Teatro Comunale of Bologna and the six "theaters of long-standing tradition" in the province of Emilia.[124]

The major opera theaters and concert organizations continued to face perennial problems. One of the knottiest of these was a built-in (that is, a permanent and ongoing) deficit resulting from budget items that could not be cut. In the period from 1976 to 1984, 59.49 percent (on the average) of the total budgets of the *enti autonomi* was absorbed by personnel (8,000 regular, full-time employees, a figure that rose to 12,000 with extras, ushers and other house personnel, and other part-time employees); 14.07 percent was tied up in interest payments on the loans taken out to cover the gap in cash flow when state and local subsidies were delayed; 13.04 percent went for general expenses; 13.40 percent for the artists under contract (singers, conductors, stage directors).[125] This means that only a small portion of the billions of lire allocated to opera houses went into expenses directly related to production, and that an opera house was a costly affair even when it remained closed. On the income side of the ledger, the largest item was the state subsidy (80 percent of total income, or 191 billion lire in 1983, 226 billion lire in 1984, and 308 billion lire in 1985); next came subsidies from local sources, which varied from one opera house to another but averaged some 10 percent of total income; finally, revenues from box-office receipts, subscriptions, rental income, and sponsorships. On paper the state might seem a munificent patron, but the real situation was less rosy: scarcely 0.12 percent of the national budget was earmarked for theatrical endeavors; in France this figure was 1 percent and in the Federal Republic of Germany it was later even higher.[126]

123. Leonardo Pinzauti, "La musica in Italia dopo la 'Legge Corona,'" *Nuova rivista musicale italiana* 6 (1972): 218–27, esp. 224–26.

124. Carlo Smuraglia, "Le Regioni per la musica," *Musica/Realtà* 1, no. 1 (April 1980): 15–18; Pestalozza, "Lo Stato dell'organizzazione musicale," 154; Carla Bodo, "Regioni, promozione culturale e spettacolo," *Musica/Realtà* 2, no. 6 (September–December 1981): 166–80.

125. These figures are taken from "Spettacolo come industria," 44. "General expenses" usually included lighting, programs, posters and publicity, legal fees, cleaning staff, etc. In the figures given here this item also includes production costs (costumes, sets, stage staff, stage director, etc.).

126. See Lamberto Trezzini, in *Enti lirici tra crisi e riforma,* ed. Paolo Barile and Stefano Merlini (Florence: Passigli, 1984), 11–12. On the problems of the income and expenditures of opera houses, their legal status, their sources of financing, and their administrative boards, see the contributions of Stefano Merlini, Cosimo Mazzoni, and Stefano Passigli in *Enti lirici tra crisi e*

A gap between costs and revenues was nothing new for opera. As early as 1966 an American economist, William J. Baumol, pointed out in a study on theatrical activity in the United States from the nineteenth century to the present that the income gap could only increase, given that live performances have no way to increase productivity (roughly the same number of hours have always been needed to produce an opera without sacrificing quality). The same is not true in other sectors of the economy (industry, for example), which can increase productivity and reduce work hours by the use of improved technology.[127]

In 1979 the superintendent of La Scala attempted to do something about his perennial deficit, and he suggested that private individuals could be asked for contributions. This was done for sports events in Italy and for artistic ventures elsewhere (in the United States, for instance, where the performing arts have corporate sponsors who receive in exchange publicity and tax deductions).[128] At first this proposal met with bitter criticism: the major objections were that the government might be led to renege on the principle of its obligation to finance artistic ventures and withdraw its subsidies, but also that if sponsorship were guided by precise commercial interests, they might end up influencing decisions concerning the artistic program, the standard repertory and the star system might be overemphasized, and sponsorship might be concentrated in the most prestigious institutions. In recent years sponsorship has become a part of the production system of the performing arts, and since no specific legislation has yet been provided, it is up to the opera houses themselves to negotiate proposals, modes of participation, and their choice of partners.[129]

With the law of 30 April 1985, "Nuova disciplina degli interventi dello Stato a favore dello spettacolo" (new rules for state initiatives in the performing arts), the problem of interest payments on stopgap loans was resolved. Government financial aid to all the various institutions, associations, and enterprises operating in the field of the performing arts was doubled, and a *fondo triennale* was set up to be divided among the various sectors, enabling

---

riforma. For a comparison with state financing of opera houses in other European countries, see the data presented in the course of a meeting among the thirteen Italian opera organizations and the press that took place in the offices of the AGIS on 17 April 1986, reported by Landa Ketoff in *La repubblica* (19 April 1986).

127. William J. Baumol and William G. Bowen, *Performing Arts: The Economic Dilemma: A Study of Problems Common to Theater, Opera, Music, and Dance,* a Twentieth Century Fund Study (Cambridge: Massachusetts Institute of Technology Press, 1966; reprint, Millwood, N.Y.: Kraus Reprints, 1978); Trezzini and Curtolo, *Oltre le quinte,* 123.

128. See the interview with Carlo Maria Badini in *Panorama* (13 August 1979): 58–59.

129. Paolo Barile, "Sponsorship ed Enti lirico-sinfonici," *Musica/Realtà* 3, no. 8 (August 1982): 5–7.

them to operate in a climate of greater stability. (Forty-two percent of total funds was assigned to the major opera houses and concert organizations, 13 percent to the "traditional" opera houses, concert organizations, festivals, and foreign tours, 25 percent to the cinema, 15 percent to prose theater, and 1.5 percent to circuses and other traveling shows.) The problem remains of how to replace the old Corona Act with a law more appropriate for current needs. The government and the political parties have put forth a number of suggestions, many of them already outdated.

Only if the theater is considered as providing a public service and music accepted as an irreplaceable component of culture and a source of true growth in democracy[130] can Italy block extremist demands (to close all unproductive and expensive ventures), remedy the defects of the current administrative system, and help some of the proposed solutions to be put into effect. Much remains to be done: administrative structures need to be modernized to halt runaway overtime expenses; more revivals and more productions of contemporary works should be put on (the *enti autonomi,* which are publicly funded, should stand out for their daring and original choices of works); greater efforts need to be put into creating high-quality productions. Performances should be diffused through the modern media and telecommunications systems: admittedly a surrogate for live performance, the media have a potential for extending the range of the opera audience at the highest level, if opera can withstand the blandishments of the multinational corporations. The major state-supported opera houses need to show a more efficacious and dynamic spirit of enterprise (which would also require a change in their legal definition). Courses to train musical technicians and to develop professionalism need to be instituted. Dividing contracts among the various political parties *(lottizzazione)* has to stop; local bureaucracies need to operate with greater efficiency; the trade unions need to broaden their corporative attitude.

BIBLIOGRAPHIC NOTE

The point of departure for a general examination of Italian opera theater in its productive aspects remains John Rosselli, *The Opera Industry in Italy from Cimarosa to Verdi: The Role of the Impresario* (Cambridge: Cambridge University Press, 1984), in Italian translation, in an amplified version, as *L'impresario d'opera: Arte e affari nel teatro musicale italiano dell'Ottocento* (Turin: Edizioni di Torino/Musica, 1985). See also John Rosselli, *Music and Musicians in Nineteenth-Century Italy* (Portland, Oreg.: Amadeus Press, 1991), and *Singers of Italian Opera: The History of a Profession* (Cambridge: Cambridge University Press, 1992). For the impresario and his role, see

130. See Andrea Mascagni, in *Enti lirici tra crisi e riforma,* 209ff.

Gino Monaldi, *Impresari celebri del secolo XIX* (Rocca San Casciano: Cappelli, 1918), a work largely made up of anecdotes and firsthand remembrances. For a study based on archival research on the impresarial activities of Alessandro Lanari (which also covers the period after Lanari's death), see Marcello de Angelis, ed., *Le cifre del melodramma: L'archivio inedito dell'impresario teatrale Alessandro Lanari nella Biblioteca nazionale centrale di Firenze (1815–1870)*, 2 vols. (Florence: Giunta Regionale Toscana/La Nuova Italia, 1982). Also on Lanari, see also De Angelis, *Le carte dell'impresario: Melodramma e costume teatrale nell'Ottocento* (Florence: Sansoni, 1982).

On the social and cultural atmosphere in which various artists operated, see the historical reconstructions in Julian Budden, *The Operas of Verdi*, 3 vols. (London: Cassell, 1973–81; rev. ed., Oxford: Clarendon Press, 1991), and "Primi rapporti fra Leoncavallo e la casa Ricordi: Dieci missive finora sconosciute," in *Ruggero Leoncavallo nel suo tempo,* ed. Jürgen Maehder and Lorenza Guiot, Atti del I Convegno internazionale di studi su Ruggero Leoncavallo (Milan: Sonzogno, 1993), 49–60. See also Carlo Piccardi, "'L'artista è un uom e . . . per gli uomini scrivere ei deve': Opera e pubblico agli albori della società di massa," in *Letteratura, musica e teatro al tempo di Ruggero Leoncavallo,* ed. Jürgen Maehder and Lorenza Guiot, Atti del II Convegno internazionale di studi su Ruggero Leoncavallo (Milan: Sonzogno, 1995), 215–67. See also Marcello Conati, "Teatri e orchestre al tempo di Verdi," in *Giuseppe Verdi: Vicende, problemi e mito di un artista e del suo tempo,* exhibition catalog for Palazzo Ducale di Colorno, 31 August–8 December 1985 (Colorno: Edizioni "Una città costruisce una mostra," 1985), 47–78; Giovanni Morelli, "Suicidio e Pazza Gioia: Ponchielli e la poetica dell'Opera Italiana neo-nazional-popolare," in *Amilcare Ponchielli 1834–1886: Saggi e ricerche nel 150° anniversario della nascita* (Casalmorano: Cassa Rurale ed Artigiana, 1984), 171–231, and Morelli, "'Quelle lor belle incognite borghesi': Sulla popolarità nazionale dell'opera lirica italiana, da 'Rigoletto' alla 'Fanciulla' attraverso 'Cavalleria-Pagliacci,'" in *L'Europa musicale,* ed. Anna Laura Bellina and Giovanni Morelli (Florence: Vallecchi, 1988), 245–96.

Other information on the sociocultural setting of the late nineteenth century and the early twentieth century can be found in collections of letters, among them, Giuseppe Verdi, *I copialettere di Giuseppe Verdi,* ed. Gaetano Cesari and Alessandro Luzio (Milan: Stucchi Ceretti, 1913; reprinted, Bologna: Arnaldo Forni, 1968); *Carteggio Verdi-Boito,* ed. Mario Medici and Marcello Conati (Parma: Istituto di Studi Verdiani, 1978), in English translation as *The Verdi-Boito Correspondence,* trans. William Weaver (Chicago: University of Chicago Press, 1994); Antônio Carlos Gomes, *Carteggi italiani,* ed. Gaspare Nello Vetro (Milan: Nuove Edizioni, 1979); Alfredo Catalani, *Lettere di Alfredo Catalani a Giuseppe Depanis,* ed. Carlo Gatti (Milan: Istituto di Alta Cultura, 1946); *Carteggi pucciniani,* ed. Eugenio Gara (Milan: Ricordi, 1958); Mario Morini, Nandi Ostali, and Piero Ostali, Jr., *Casa musicale Sonzogno: Cronologie, saggi, testimonianze,* 2 vols. (Milan: Sonzogno, 1995). There is also information in studies such as Michelangelo Zurletti, *Catalani* (Turin: Edizioni di Torino/Musica , 1982); *Pietro Mascagni,* ed. Mario Morini (Milan: Sonzogno, 1964); *Umberto Giordano,* ed. Mario Morini (Milan: Sonzogno, 1968); Mosco Carner, *Puccini: A Critical Biography,* 3d ed. (New York: Holmes and Meier, 1992).

Contracts, receipt statements, and commercial correspondence with artists, agents, impresarios, and others are still for the most part available only in manuscript in civic archives, Italian state archives, or the archives of the various theaters. On one impresario see Giovanni Azzaroni and Paola Bignami, *Corticelli Mauro impresario* (Bologna: Nuova Alfa, 1990). The conditions for the concession of a contract between the owners of a theater and the impresario were often given in the press. They were reported, for example, in the *Gazzetta musicale di Milano* (with details on the length of the contract, the amount of subsidies, the number of operas to be put on, the caution the impresario had to deposit, and so forth). On these questions and more in general on the legislative aspects of theater management, see Enrico Rosmini, *Legislazione e giurisprudenza dei teatri,* 3d ed., 2 vols. (Milan, 1893); Giovan Battista Cavalcaselle, *Tipi di scritture teatrali attraverso luoghi e tempi diversi: contributo storico-giuridico* (Rome: Athenaeum, 1919); Nicola Tabanelli, *Il codice del teatro* (Milan: Hoepli, 1901).

There are a great many chronologies and performance lists for the various opera houses. Among those worth mentioning concerning "first-rank theaters" (written recently or in the past) are Giampiero Tintori, *Duecento anni di Teatro alla Scala: Cronologia* (Gorle: Grafica Gutenberg, 1979); Alberto Basso, *Il teatro della città dal 1788 at 1936,* vol. 2 of *Storia del Teatro Regio di Torino,* ed. Alberto Basso (Turin: Cassa di Risparmio di Torino, 1976–83); Lamberto Trezzini, ed., *Due secoli di vita musicale: Storia del Teatro Comunale di Bologna,* rev. ed., 3 vols. (Bologna: Nuova Alfa, 1987); Edilio Frassoni, *Due secoli di lirica a Genova,* 2 vols. (Genoa: Cassa di Risparmio di Genova e Imperia, 1980); Nicola Mangini, *I teatri di Venezia* (Milan: Mursia, 1974); Michele Girardi and Franco Rossi, *Il Teatro La Fenice: Cronologia degli spettacoli, 1792–1936* (Venice: Albrizzi, 1989) and *Il Teatro La Fenice: Cronologia degli spettacoli, 1938–1991* (Venice: Albrizzi, 1992). Ugo Morini, *La R. Accademia degli Immobili ed il suo Teatro "La Pergola" (1649–1925)* (Pisa: Simoncini, 1926); Piero Rosselli, Giuseppina Carla Romby, and Osanna Fantozzi Micali, *I teatri di Firenze* (Florence: Bonechi, 1978); Vittorio Frajese, *Dal Costanzi all'Opera,* 4 vols. (Rome: Capitolium, 1977–78); Mario Rinaldi, *Due secoli di musica al Teatro Argentina,* 3 vols. (Florence: Olschki, 1978); Raffaele Ajello et al., eds., *Il Teatro di San Carlo di Napoli,* 2 vols. (Naples: Guida, 1987); Franco Mancini, Bruno Cagli, and Agostino Ziino, *Il Teatro di San Carlo 1737–1987,* 3 vols. (Naples: Electa, 1987); Luigi Maniscalco Basile, *Storia del Teatro Massimo di Palermo* (Florence: Olschki, 1984).

On theaters classified as "of the second rank" in the late nineteenth century, see, among other works, Paolo Emilio Ferrari, *Spettacoli drammatico-musicali e coreografici in Parma* (Parma, 1884); Sergio Romagnoli and Elvira Garbero, eds., *Dalla restaurazione al secondo Novecento;* vol. 2 of *Teatro a Reggio Emilia* (Florence: Sansoni, 1980); Paolo Fabbri and Roberto Verti, *Due secoli di musica a Reggio Emilia: Repertorio cronologico delle opere e dei balli, 1645–1857* (Reggio Emilia: Teatro Edizioni del Municipale Valli, 1987); Alberto Cametti, *Il Teatro di Tordinona, poi di Apollo,* 2 vols. (Tivoli: Chicca, 1938); Michele Raffaelli, *Il Teatro Comunale di Forlì (1766–1944)* (Forlì: STC, 1982); and, for Trieste, Vito Levi, Guido Botteri, and Ireneo Bremini, *Il Comunale di Trieste (dal 1801 al 1961)* (Udine: Del Bianco, n.d.). Useful information on the activities of opera houses can also be found in Giuseppe Depanis, *I Concerti Popolari e il Teatro Regio di Torino: Quindici anni di vita musicale; appuntiricordi,* 2 vols. (Turin: Società Tipografico-Editrice Nazionale, 1914–15); Alberto de

Angelis, *La musica a Roma nel secolo XIX* (Rome: Bardi, 1935); Leonardo Pinzauti, *Il Maggio musicale fiorentino dalla prima alla trentesima edizione* (Florence: Vallecchi, 1967); Giuseppe Barigazzi, *La Scala racconta* (Milan: Rizzoli, 1984); Laura Zingarelli, "Il sistema theatrale in Puglia fra storia e sviluppo," in *Puglia: L'organizzazione musicale,* ed. P. Moliterni (Rome: CIDIM, 1986), 218–331; Guido Leone, *L'opera a Palermo dal 1865 al 1987,* 2 vols. (Palermo: Publisicula, 1988). For purely economic information, see John Rosselli, "Materiali per la storia socio-economica del San Carlo nell'Ottocento," in *Musica e cultura a Napoli dal XV al XIX secolo,* ed. Lorenzo Bianconi and Renato Bossa (Florence: Olschki, 1983), 369–81. For an updated bibliography see Alfredo Giovine, *Bibliografia di teatri musicali italiani* (Bari: Fratelli Laterza, 1982).

On the problem of copyright in the late nineteenth century and its implications for music, see Enrico Rosmini, *Legislazione e giurisprudenza sui diritti d'autore,* 3d ed. (Milan, 1893); an excellent study that treats these questions indirectly is Bruno Cagli, "Organizzazione economica e gestione teatrale nell'800," in *Per un "progetto Verdi" anni '80: Seminario internazionale di studi, Parma-Busseto 3–4 aprile 1980* (Reggio Emilia: Regione Emilia Romagna, Assessorato per la Cultura, n.d.), 63–85, in English translation as Bruno Cagli, "Verdi and the Business of Writing Operas," in *The Verdi Companion,* ed. William Weaver and Martin Chusid (New York: Norton, 1979), 106–20.

For music publishing and the various publishers, see note 67 above. For information on broadening taste and the musical orientation of the public and for the debate on theatrical activities at the turn of the twentieth century, the appendixes and reviews of the more highly qualified critics are essential. Serial consultation of the *Gazzetta musicale di Milano, Il pungolo, La perseveranza, Nuova antologia di scienze, lettere ed arti, Il teatro illustrato, Il mondo artistico, Rivista musicale italiana,* and other periodicals of the day is indispensable. For a useful reconstruction of critical culture and thought, see Enrico Fubini, "La cultura musicale dall'unità a oggi," in *Storia della società italiana* (Milan: Teti, 1982), 16:273–313; Marcello Conati, "'L'oltracotata turba che s'indraca': Inforestieramento dell'opera italiana nel secondo Ottocento," in *Musica senz'aggettivi: Studi per Fedele D'Amico,* ed. Agostino Ziino (Florence: Olschki, 1991); Marco Capra, "La musica e il tempo libero: Domande e riflessioni sulla fruizione musicale nel Ottocento," in *Il tempo libero nell'Italia unita,* ed. Fiorenza Tozzi and Angelo Varni (Bologna: CLUEB, 1992); Fiamma Nicolodi, "Il teatro lirico e il suo pubblico," in *Fare gli italiani: Scuole e cultura nell'Italia contemporanea,* ed. Simonetta Soldani and Gabriele Turi, 2 vols. (Bologna: Il Mulino, 1993), 1:257–304.

For opera in the twentieth century and its organizational and legislative aspects, see Lamberto Trezzini and Angelo Curtolo, *Oltre le quinte: Idee, cultura e organizzazione del teatro musicale in Italia* (Venice: Marsilio, 1983). Documentation (unfortunately with many gaps) on the theaters active during the twenty years of Fascism can be found in the Archivio Centrale dello Stato in Rome. For an overall view of the cultural policies of Fascism and its institutions, see Philip V. Cannistraro, *La fabbrica del consenso: Fascismo e mass media* (Bari: Laterza, 1975). For a work more specifically focused on the musical sector, see Luigi Pestalozza, "Lo Stato dell'organizzazione musicale: La svolta del fascismo e la sua lunga durata," *Musica/Realtà* 2, no. 5 (August 1981): 143–60. See also Fiamma Nicolodi, *Musica e musicisti nel ventennio fascista* (Fiesole: Discanto, 1984); Harvey Sachs, *Music in Fascist Italy* (London: Weidenfeld and Nicolson, 1987). A comparison with the more rigid cultural policies of Nazism can be found in Fred K. Prieberg, *Musik im NS-Staat* (Frankfurt am Main: Fischer, 1982); Hanns-Werner Heister and Hans-Günter Klein, eds., *Musik und Musikpolitik im faschistischen Deutschland* (Frankfurt am Main: Fischer, 1984).

For the immediate post–World War II period, see Paolo Salviucci, *La musica e lo Stato* (Milan and Rome: Bocca, 1953). For current legislation see Barbara Bianchini, *La disciplina degli Enti Lirici e Istituzioni Concertistiche assimilate* (Milan: Amici della Scala, 1986). See also Piero Rattalino, *L'ente lirico va in trasferta* (Milan: Il Saggiatore, 1983), a lively treatment of the current situation. The annual publications of the AGIS (Associazione Generale Italiana dello Spettacolo) and *Lo Spettacolo* provide statistical data elaborated by the SIAE. Among the musical journals most interested in problems of legislation and production are *Laboratorio musica* and *Nuova rivista musicale italiana* (for the 1970s) and *Musica/Realtà* (for the 1980s). For a detailed examination, especially from the juridical point of view, see the acts of the conference promoted by the Ente Teatro Romano di Fiesole (December 1983), *Enti lirici tra crisi e riforma,* ed. Paolo Barile and Stefano Merlini (Fiesole: Passigli, 1984). For an interesting economic analysis of the performing arts that refutes a number of commonplaces, see the report of "Strategia e Organizzazione," Milan, February 1986 (see note 119 above). For a comparison between public institutions in Italy and private institutions in the United States and a discussion of the problem of sponsorship, see Carlo Bodo, ed., *Pubblico o privato: Un falso dilemma: La politica culturale negli Stati Uniti* (Naples: Guida, 1986); Lamberto Trezzini and Angelo Curtolo, *L'Europa della musica: I teatri d'opera nei paesi del CEE* (Bologna: Il Mulino, 1987).

There are two noteworthy studies on orchestras, the first historical, the second economic and institutional: Marcello Conati and Marcello Pavarani, eds., *Orchestre in Emilia-Romagna nell'Ottocento e Novecento* (Parma: Orchestra Sinfonica dell'Emilia Romagna, 1982), *Orchestre e teatri nelle regioni: Strumenti di un nuovo sviluppo musicale* (Parma: Orchestra Sinfonica dell'Emilia Romagna, 1986).

4

The Librettist

FABRIZIO DELLA SETA

> In general, within this link between music and poetry the preponderance
> of one art damages the other. . . . If the musician is to have free scope, the poet
> must not try to be admired as a poet. In this respect it is the Italians, like
> Metastasio, e.g., and others, who have displayed great skill.
> HEGEL, *Aesthetics* (Knox translation)

1. A Problem of Conscience

There is an essential question touching on the very purpose of our inquiry
that needs to be raised at the start of any consideration of the librettist over
nearly four centuries of the history of Italian opera. Can we even speak of a
"librettist" throughout that period? Can he be defined, even summarily, as
an entity? Is there an "ideal type" that will enable us to see beyond the variety
of particular cases and identify consistent traits—traits that will permit historical discourse? Only then will we get beyond the tautological statement
that the topic of the present chapter is a series of persons who have in common that they all wrote librettos.

The problem becomes clearer if we think for a moment of the operatic
composer and the singer, for whom we can readily define a professional figure
who has maintained many of the same characteristics throughout history. We
can consider figures long before our own day or in the more recent past—
Francesco Cavalli, Johann Adolph Hasse, Gaetano Donizetti, and Pietro
Mascagni, for example, or Francesco Pistocchi, Carlo Broschi (Farinelli),

Giuditta Pasta, and Renata Tebaldi—and find analogies in such things as their social background, training, career development, and recognition.

This is not true of the librettist. If we compare the careers of two men who could unhesitatingly be called "professional librettists," Pietro Metastasio and Francesco Maria Piave, it would be difficult to find any other significant analogies. It might even be perplexing to define the writing of librettos as a profession, given that only in very exceptional cases—those two men, for example—was writing opera librettos an ongoing activity and a predominant source of income.

There is at least one constant in the history of the librettist: he invariably was a person who fit into the historical category of a man of letters. Writing librettos has always been an activity that went along with writing poetry, plays, novels, historical studies, or journalism. This is not the tautology it might seem, as it does not mean that writing librettos was one of the fields of endeavor that a man of letters might pursue. A recent study of Italian literature with the stated intention of conducting a historical and sociological investigation of the condition of the man (or woman) of letters does not consider libretto writing as a category apart—a late but telling symptom of how difficult it has always been for Italian literati to accept the writing of librettos as among their normal activities.[1] The subject of the present chapter. therefore, is the Italian man of letters and his crisis of conscience concerning opera—his tormented relations with a world that he tolerated, mocked, at times cursed and hated, but a world to which he was tied, both because librettos provided a modest but sure source of income and because other opportunities for gaining a hearing were shrinking. Thus we will need to look at his relations with the other people who operated in that world—impresarios, singers, and composers.

In order to understand the true scope of this crisis of conscience, we need to take a brief backward glance at the history of changes in the hierarchy of activities connected with the arts. In a tradition rooted in classical antiquity, the concept of the lettered person (in the broadest sense and in the many variations) coincided with the concept of the intellectual—the person who pursues an activity that is rational and free in that it is linked with the word, humankind's least material means of expression. Literature was held worthy of pursuit, for pure enjoyment, by persons who might have been ashamed to

---

1. See *Il letterato e le istituzioni* and *Produzione e consumo*, vols. 1 and 2 of *Letteratura italiana*, ed. Alberto Asor Rosa, 8 vols. (Turin: Einaudi, 1982, 1983). This critical neglect is partially remedied by Renato di Benedetto, "Il Settecento e l'Ottocento," in *Teatro, musica, tradizione dei classici*, vol. 6 of *Letteratura italiana*, ed. Alberto Asor Rosa (Turin: Einaudi, 1986), 365–410. The fact that librettists are discussed only in the context of narrowly focused remarks on the relations between music and literature simply confirms the intellectuals' exclusion of the libretto from the literary fields that they recognize.

paint or sculpt.[2] Even when the pursuit of literature was a profession, it was clearly distinguished from craftsmanship; the man of letters made his living by means of activities of high social prestige—as a courtier, government official, administrator, secretary, diplomat, or teacher—that in some sense ennobled letters by giving them the dignity of a disinterested activity. Such duties also made the man of letters the delegated administrator and mediator for the real political and economic power that he served—a position of privilege that he naturally tended to safeguard.

Renaissance figurative artists were the first to proclaim the artist's intellectual dignity, and it is significant that one of their favorite arguments was that the image is rational because it is like speech.[3] In contrast the social condition of the musician from the sixteenth to the seventeenth centuries seems to have been stagnant, if not to have declined in inverse proportion to the expanding role of music in cultural life.

This is precisely where the new phenomenon of opera (and, particularly after 1640, the phenomenon of public opera) came into the picture. Whether the man or letters was aware of it or not, he became involved in a cultural operation that soon challenged his own social and intellectual prestige. There were several reasons for this. First, the man of letters discovered that he was only one part of a production mechanism that he had not created and for which he did not hold prime responsibility. Second, the literary contribution to opera was put on the same plane as (and soon became subordinate to) the musical and even the spectacular components of opera. Third, the preferences of the opera audience gave the financial advantage to others who contributed to the production of opera. Financial figures spoke just as eloquently to the man of letters of the seventeenth and eighteenth centuries as they do to historians today. By far the highest place on the earnings scale went to the singer, followed, at some distance, by the composer and the set designer. It was up to the librettist to find other sources of income to safeguard his dignity and hide the fact that invariably his pay was ludicrously small in proportion to total expenses. In the nineteenth century, when composers' remuneration improved their relative position and other opportunities dried up for operatic poets, the librettists' situation became almost humiliating.

The reader should be warned that because we shall be speaking more about the librettist's awareness of his role than about his material rewards, we will be largely concerned with sources that express that awareness—letters, autobiographies, memoirs, and polemical declarations—and the fact that

2. On the artistic vocation of Michelangelo, for example, see Peter Burke, "The Italian Artist and His Roles," in *History of Italian Art,* trans. Ellen Bianchini and Clare Dorey, 2 vols. (Cambridge: Polity Press/Blackwell, 1994), 1–28.

3. Rensselaer W. Lee, *Ut pictura poesis: A Humanistic Theory of Painting* (New York: Norton, 1967).

such sources often distort historical reality must be accepted as such, since the distortion reveals precisely the sort of information that we are seeking.

2. The Seventeenth Century

Opera, that is, a drama in which the actors and actresses sing some or all of their parts, was "born under the sign of discord." This aphorism, which origi- nally referred to the bitter struggle for precedence that arose in connection with the theatrical spectacles in Florence in 1600, could be extended to cover the multiple elements that went into the creation of those spectacles, their antecedents, and their immediate successors.[4] There were at least three such elements: the spoken text, the music to which that text was set, and the visual realization of text and music on the stage. That triad of poetry, music, and spectacle recurred in all later reflection on opera. From the viewpoint of the poet who wrote the texts for these experiments, however, it was difficult to imagine that those multiple components could give rise to discord. Ottavio Rinuccini would have seen obvious truth in another definition—that opera was born "out of the spirit of poetry."[5] Rinuccini was just as firmly persuaded that he was principally responsible for the new sort of spectacle, but his dedi- cation to the libretto of *L'Euridice* gave Emilio de' Cavalieri cause to com- plain that he had been ignored while Rinuccini took full credit for having invented the new manner of representing dramatic actions in music.[6]

We do not know much about Rinuccini's opinion of the composers who collaborated with him. *La Dafne,* he tells us, was written at the request of Jacopo Corsi. Rinuccini himself had no great faith in the expressive possibili- ties of "modern" music; it was only the "grace" with which Jacopo Peri ful- filled his assignment—and, above all, the demonstrable enjoyment of a select public—that persuaded him to repeat the experiment on a larger scale with *L'Euridice.*[7] We do not even know how Rinuccini reacted to Giulio Caccini's

4. See Nino Pirrotta, "Inizio dell'opera e aria," in *Li due Orfei: Da Poliziano a Monteverdi,* 2d ed. (Turin: Einaudi, 1975), 276–333, esp. 277, in English translation as "Early Opera and Aria," in Nino Pirrotta and Elena Povoledo, *Music and Theatre from Poliziano to Monteverdi,* trans. Karen Eales (Cambridge: Cambridge University Press, 1982), 237–80.

5. Luigi Ronga, "La nascita del melodramma dallo spirito della poesia," in *Teatro del Sei- cento,* ed. Luigi Fassò (Milan: Ricciardi, 1956), xxvii–liii.

6. Claude V. Palisca, "Musical Asides in the Diplomatic Correspondence of Emilio de' Cava- lieri," *Musical Quarterly* 49 (1963): 339–55, esp. 353–54.

7. Ottavio Rinuccini, dedication to *L'Euridice* (Florence, 1600), reprinted in Angelo Solerti, *Le origini del melodramma* (Turin: Bocca, 1903; reprint, Bologna: Arnaldo Forni, 1969), 40–43, in English translation in Oliver Strunk, *Source Readings in Music History from Classical Antiq- uity through the Romantic Era* (New York: Norton, 1950), 367–69. The dedication is also re- printed in Heinz Becker, ed., *Quellentexte zur Konzeption der europäischen Oper im 17. Jahr- hundert* (Kassel and Basel: Bärenreiter, 1981), 16–17.

heavy-handed interference when he imposed his own music for some "airs" and choruses "sung by persons under his direction." He probably thought this quarrel was between the two composers, and he probably saw the function of music as one aspect of the staging and nothing more. He must have been a good deal more disturbed by Caccini's arrogance when the work was published with the title, *L'Euridice composta in musica in stile rappresentativo da Giulio Caccini detto Romano*, with no mention of Rinuccini's name.[8] He may have been mollified by Jacopo Peri's much more obsequious attitude when Peri published his music. Peri, who was quite conscious of his own merits, stated in his preface that his music was "proportionate to the perfections of this new poem, in which signor Ottavio Rinuccini . . . has shown himself to be a poet admirable in all parts and equal to the most famous ancient [poets]."[9]

Rinuccini's major satisfaction, however, was that he was soon recognized as a specialist in the new type of spectacle. In 1608 he was invited to Mantua, which was not to be outdone by Florence, to put on three different musical spectacles: *La Dafne* during carnival; *L'Arianna* in May, and *Il ballo delle ingrate* in June. This time Rinuccini had little reason to complain of the composers, if we can believe Marco da Gagliano's declaration that he "was very conscientious and satisfied the poet's exquisite taste."[10] Rather, Rinuccini must have experienced how the new genre was by its very nature subject to local whims that were more powerful than the ones the court poet usually faced. Even though in Mantua there was no Caccini to impose his pretensions, the fable of Daphne was presented "enlarged and embellished" with choral scenes, stage wizardry (for instance, in the scenic effects of the combat between Apollo and Python, the serpent), choruses and songs to "display the grace and the disposition" of the singers of the Gonzaga court, and even pieces of music composed by "one of our principal academicians, a great protector of music, and one of its great connoisseurs," who was none other than Cardinal Ferdinando Gonzaga himself.[11] *L'Arianna* was subjected to even greater alterations. It was a work that aspired to the dignity of tragedy, but the duchess of Mantua ordered "signor Ottavio" to "enrich [it] with

8. Florence, 1600.

9. Jacopo Peri, dedication to *Le musiche . . . sopra l'Euridice* (Florence, 1600; *ab incarnatione* [1601]), quoted in Solerti, *Le origini*, 43–44, in English translation in Oliver Strunk, *Source Readings in Music History from Classical Antiquity through the Romantic Era* (New York: Norton, 1950), 373–76.

10. Marco da Gagliano, preface to *La Dafne* (Florence, 1608), given in Solerti, *Le origini*, 78, in English translation in Piero Weiss and Richard Taruskin, *Music in the Western World: A History in Documents* (New York: Schirmer Books; London: Collier Macmillian, 1984), 174–77.

11. See Solerti, *Le origini*, 78–89, and Becker, *Quellentexte*, 23–26, as well as the comparison of the two versions of the drama in Solerti, *Gli albori del melodramma*, 3 vols. (Milan: Sandron, 1904; reprint, Bologna: Arnaldo Forni, 1976), 2:66–99.

some action, being somewhat dry":[12] music (more for the fascination of the singing than for its composition) and spectacle both claimed equal rights with poetry.

As the new genre became better established, writing a poetic text to be set to music began to be an activity with its own demands and its own rules. It is a pleasing thought that Rinuccini's son Pierfrancesco may have been the author of an anonymous treatise, written after 1628, entitled *Il corago, o vero Alcune osservazioni per metter bene in scena le composizioni drammatiche*.[13] Not only did this treatise accept *teatro in musica* as a natural alternative to spoken drama and pantomime, it even tended to prefer it. *Il corago* offered advice, in a robustly practical spirit, to the "poet-dramatist, so that his composition will be better adapted for setting to music in the recitative style."[14] The anonymous author refused to allow himself to be swayed by classical aesthetic prejudices: he invited the poet to accept the notion that *teatro in musica* was primarily entertainment and to sacrifice poetry on the altar of music. The work is a genuine catalog of the faults that eighteenth-century polemicists later imputed to opera, except that *Il corago* presents them as available expedients inherent in the craft; far from holding those expedients blameworthy, it does not even grudgingly accept them as an inevitable evil.

The librettist could still accept such compromises without taxing his conscience as an intellectual. Beyond all latent tension among the poet, the composer, the singer, and the scene designer, the court acted as a supreme guarantor and regulator of the traditional hierarchy of values, and it was within a court that all operatic experiments took place during the first forty years of the seventeenth century.

The privileged position that the man of letters felt he still enjoyed in that hierarchy was confirmed by the prestigious figure of Giulio Rospigliosi. A man whose brilliant ecclesiastical career took him to the papacy (1667–69), Rospigliosi was a living demonstration of a man of letters-librettist at the highest social level who gave concrete form to his own social class's desire for artistic opulence. Between 1631 and 1656 Rospigliosi was principally responsible for ten or more *opere in musica;* he personally supervised their production, carefully choosing musical and scenographic collaborators but keeping the best and noblest task for himself—writing the text—which he clearly considered on the same plane as the texts of traditional spoken dramas.

Rospigliosi's example continued to be followed into the next century. Nonetheless, toward the beginning of his years of operatic activity, something happened that was to upset the precarious equilibrium between the poet and

---

12. Letter of Carlo Rossi, Mantua 27 February 1608, quoted in Solerti, *Gli albori*, 1:92.
13. *Il corago . . .* , ed. Paolo Fabbri and Angelo Pompilio (Florence: Olschki, 1983).
14. Ibid., 63–79.

the world of opera: public theaters came into being in Venice. As a consequence opera shifted to an impresarial system of production that signaled the end of court patronage and a move toward an economic system based on competition.

Obviously that change did not happen overnight. The earliest librettists in Venice—Giacomo Badoaro, Maiolino Bisaccioni, Giovanni Francesco Busenello, Giacinto Andrea Cicognini, Giulio Strozzi, and Paolo Vendramin (one of the few instances of a group of librettists with nearly homogeneous characteristics)—played a dual role, combining something of the patron and something of the impresario. Nearly all these men were from patrician or wealthy families; they were men of the law or public officials, and they tended to be members of elitist academies of libertine leanings. In practical terms they could be considered among the promoters of the first public operas, whose librettos they wrote as dilettantes making literary use of their leisure. In the still fluid world of the opera between 1630 and 1640, roles were not fixed: Benedetto Ferrari and Francesco Manelli were at the same time composers, librettists, and impresarios; Giovanni Faustini was both a librettist and an impresario; Cavalli combined the roles of composer and impresario (although Cavalli and Faustini already began to show increased specialization). Faustini might in fact be considered the first professional librettist: he had eleven librettos (written between 1642 and 1651) to his credit, and his example was followed—to note only the most obvious instances—by Nicolò Minato, a nobleman and a lawyer who wrote eleven librettos for Venetian theaters, and Aurelio Aureli and Matteo Noris, each of whom wrote some thirty librettos.

These men bring us to the threshold of the eighteenth century, when "the opera business" shifted out of the hands of the man of letters. Not coincidentally the first signs of the librettist's discontent began to be felt, and a note of protest crept into libretto prefaces, along with an unfortunate penchant for repeating commonplaces. Ferrari, who was conscious of his own worth as a practitioner, was an exception to this rule. It was, he stated, "more out of a pleasure in serving those who had the power to command me than out of a whim to poetize [that] I wrote five works to be set to music. . . . I care little for being a poet, but I claim to be a good musician and to know what poetry is best suited to the music."[15] Busenello's need for self-justification is more typical: noting that even the greatest poets were subjected to criticisms, he wrote, "I cannot hope that everyone will pardon my poor and enervated style. Because I write and have written poetry that must be sung (and because the meter, the endings, and the assonances regard the music), the strophes, antis-

15. From the foreword to *Il pastor regio* (Venice, 1640), quoted in Francesco Vatielli, "Operisti-librettisti dei sec. XVII–XVIII," *Rivista musicale italiana* 47 (1939): 1–17, 315–32, 605–20, esp. 323.

trophes, and epodes of the Greeks have no place in it." He added, "It must be admitted that poetry on the stage is somewhat different from the other sorts."[16] Complaint became the fashion, and in 1672 Aureli stated,

> I present to you my *Claudius,* which is richer in songs and little arias than in incidents. It is enough to say that it is a music drama. What can one do? Since today Venice's whims want it that way, I try to meet their taste. . . . I sympathize with [librettists] today for the difficulty they encounter in trying to satisfy not only the many bizarre whims of this city but also the extravagant humors of the singers.[17]

An obscure librettist named Francesco Melosio complained in verse when the impresario (Cavalli) was late in paying the fee they had agreed upon:

> Deh, se pure un Orfeo non mi stimate,
> Non vogliate, Signor, che a' versi miei,
> Invece di danar, corran sassate

> (So, even if you do not think me an Orpheus, please, sir, do not wish for stones to greet my verse rather than coins.)

Poetry, even of modest worth, was to be respected:

> Già son privato del furor divino,
> Ché, a gir dietro un Cavallo per denari,
> Son fatto, di poeta, un vetturino

> (Already I have been stripped of my divine fury because, having to run after a Cavallo [horse/Cavalli] for money, from a poet, I've become a coachman.)[18]

Melosio hit the economic nub of the question, but the librettist who contracted for his fee with the impresario seems to have been an exception (or a transitory situation) in Venice. Quite soon Venetian theaters developed a form of remuneration that was advantageous for the impresario (who no longer had any out-of-pocket expense) and morally satisfying for the poet. Cristoforo Ivanovich, a Dalmatian man of letters and librettist who became a historian of Venetian theaters, tells us how it worked.[19] According to Iva-

---

16. Giovanni Francesco Busenello, manuscript letter on *La satira* quoted in Arthur Livingston, *La vita veneziana e le opere di Gian Francesco Busenello* (Venice: Callegari, 1913), 376–77.

17. Preface to *Claudio Cesare,* quoted in Simon Towneley Worsthorne, *Venetian Opera in the Seventeenth Century* (Oxford: Clarendon Press, 1954, 1968), 122.

18. Quoted in Nino Pirrotta, "Il caval zoppo e il vetturino: Cronache di Parnaso 1642," *Collectanea Historiae Musicae,* vol. 4 (Florence: Olschki, 1966), 215–26, esp. 223–24.

19. Cristoforo Ivanovich, "Memorie teatrali di Venezia," in *Minerva al tavolino* (Venice, 1681; 2d ed. 1688), 361–453 (page citations are to the 2d edition).

novich, "the principal object of a good [poet] must be glory; the second object, the reward," which meant that "whoever writes should therefore seek
praise first, and second, the reward." Ivanovich noted, however, that "such
felicity rarely occurs, particularly in theatrical compositions, [which are] subject to censure, spiteful comments, and to chance. From the beginning, when
music drama first appeared in the theaters of Venice, the author has been
content with what glory he got from his applause."[20]

However, Ivanovich continues, now that it is increasingly difficult to elicit
that applause,

> the custom has been introduced, and is still practiced, of leaving to the author of
> the drama, as a reward for his labors, all that can be gotten from the sale of the
> librettos, printed at his expense, and from the dedicatory letter that he is at liberty
> to write—revenues that depend upon the success of the drama. Furthermore, the
> author has free admission to the theater every evening, the option to bring friends
> with him, and the use of a box put at his disposal.[21]

This form of compensation maintained a connection with the courtly tradition of the Renaissance man of letters; it freed the poet from the humiliation
of having to negotiate a contract (which composers and singers had to do);
and it guaranteed that the poetic text would have a life of its own over and
above the circumstances that had occasioned it. The system had disadvantages as well, however, given that the sale of librettos was tied to the success
of the performances, hence dependent upon things that were beyond the librettist's control.

As the saying went, If you cannot save your purse, at least save your honor.
In the final chapter of his *Memorie teatrali di Venezia,* Ivanovich stated:

> The drama reaches the stage after a variety of events and extraordinary accidents,
> each one of which is enough to grant the author applause or deny it . . . all [of
> which are] circumstances beyond the author's control but can prejudice success. . . .
> In short it seems that for the most part fate works to favor the least meritorious.
> Thus it may prove true that when the dramas (cited in the catalog of the present
> memoirs) of these virtuoso authors who have labored nobly with their minds are
> read, they can hope for the praise they merit from the dispassionate judgment of
> future ages.[22]

Ivanovich's chronological catalog of Venetian *drammi per musica* from
1637 to 1681 (and 1688) was thus a monument to the librettist, and given

20. Ibid., 413.
21. Ibid., 414.
22. Ibid., 425–26.

the strategic location of this statement in the work, it is perhaps not an exaggeration to say that his *Memorie teatrali* should be understood as a grandiose attempt at self-justification on the part of a man of letters and librettist. The work closes with Ivanovich's response to Marquis Pio Enea degli Obizzi, who had recommended to him a young poet interested in breaking into theatrical circles.[23] As he advises the young man against making any such move, Ivanovich expresses all his own disgust for a world in which the poet leaves himself open to extortionate demands a thousand times just to have his work heard by powerful persons incompetent to judge its merits, then suffers when his work is rejected and the best bits are stolen from it. In his response to Obizzi, Ivanovich unhesitatingly puts his finger on the underlying cause of such a rotten state of affairs: "Unlike princes, who with gifts and magnificence support poetic decorum in their theaters, here everything has become a commerce of interests in which a thousand roads are open to the ills introduced by putrid haggling."[24]

The court was the promised land of the librettist, the place where the ignorance of the common public could not overwhelm the refined understanding that always went with august origins. Italy was not lacking in rulers who loved the theater, even in rulers who sought to reconcile their own traditions of splendor with the less costly new forms of production. This was particularly true of the Florence-Rome axis: the city of the Medicis, which could boast of the patronage of Cardinal Giancarlo de' Medici and of princes such as Mattias and Ferdinando de' Medici, had a thriving tradition of literary librettists. That tradition began with Cicognini, as we have seen, and continued with a number of men, such as Giovanni Andrea Moniglia, Giovanni Cosimo Villifranchi, and Antonio Salvi, who mixed the writing of librettos with their role as court physician or natural philosopher, in the tradition of Galileo. Public theaters failed to take hold in Rome, but there were a number of small courts in the city, whose librettists included Francesco Buti, secretary to Cardinal Antonio Barberini (whom Buti followed to Paris, where he helped to introduce Italian opera), and Giovanni Filippo Apolloni, a Tuscan who had entered the service of Cardinal Flavio Chigi in 1660. Finally, there was the fascinating figure of Filippo Acciaiuoli, a knight, a traveler, and a genuine factotum in Roman theater, where he operated as an impresario (in the uncertain vicissitudes of the Teatro Tordinona between 1670 and 1672), a genial inventor of scenic effects and "machines," perhaps a composer of music, and (not surprisingly) a librettist in the service of such patrons as the Colonna family, the Chigi family, and Queen Christina of Sweden, a figure of near-mythical proportions.

23. Ibid., 427–32.
24. Ibid., 429.

All librettists dreamed, however, of going to Vienna, Leopold I's capital and a city that had already been conquered by Italian opera. Aurelio Aureli went there in 1659, and Ivanovich in 1665. In 1667 Francesco Sbarra, a patrician from Lucca who had been active in Venice, was introduced by the composer Antonio Cesti into theatrical circles in Vienna, where he composed texts to celebrate the marriage of Leopold I and Margaret of Spain. Count Nicolò Minato went from experiences as an impresario in Venice to become the first official court poet in Vienna; in his thirty years or so in the post, he produced roughly 170 secular works and 40 sacred works—a pace that bears the mark of workman-like production.

Even the post of poet laureate of the imperial court had its unpleasant aspects. We have witness from an outsider, the famous Carlo de' Dottori. When Dottori returned to Padua after a stay in Vienna during which he had served the court writing verse, he had only two thoughts: to obtain the emperor's recognition of his title, count, which the duke of Mantua had conferred on him, and to obtain a permanent passport. Between 1666 and 1667 he spoke of little else in his correspondence with Domenico Federici (also a poet at court),[25] who acted as a go-between for Dottori with the imperial chancery, held responsible for the delay. Dottori complained, "I have written two plays to serve His Majesty. The first was better than it needed to be, and perhaps better than the music, which garbed it with what clothes I cannot say." The second work, which was not performed in Vienna, was now being requested for theaters in Venice. Dottori reported:

> I let things take their course, but I have not lost my affection for the play, which has been asked of me several times for the stages of this country, [a request] that I have always denied because it has become a sacred thing and must not be profaned. Besides which, to tell the truth, I do not want other stages than the imperial one to mount any of the works in a similar vein that might chance to slip from my pen.[26]

What was Dottori's reward for his loyalty? His passport was denied, while, as he complained, "you can see similar ordinary passports every day in the hands of singers and like performers who cross the Alps."[27] Dottori strove to avoid descending to their level; when he sought a gift for his son's wedding, he wrote that he would be happy to receive "a testimony of Caesar's benevolence, but not one to be begged for; not a plebeian one—that is, common among musicians."[28]

25. Carlo de' Dottori, *Lettere a Domenico Federici*, ed. Giorgio Cerboni Baiardi (Urbino: Argalìa, 1971).

26. Ibid., 40–41.

27. Ibid., 48.

28. Ibid., 120–2.

Dottori treated his artistic colleagues to double-edged compliments, especially when they were composers who dabbled in poetry.

> I hear that an opera of Sbarra's is being performed, and another by Draghi, the composer and librettist. Oh! How many poets! But who would not become a poet for Caesar? Draghi has talent and handles the stage well; it's a pity that he doesn't know certain things. Still, where verse for music is concerned, he does acrobat's flip-flops. If Tasso were to come back to life, he would watch the show along with the others, and he would say, "Oh, wonderful!" You have to flow with the times.[29]

The librettist also had to learn to resign himself to seeing others get more recognition than he. For Dottori one of those others was the physician Girolamo Frigimelica, the uncle of the future librettist with the same name.

> Three years ago . . . Cardinal Carafa brought a superb and magnificent imperial document to Count Girolamo Frigimelica, our gentleman and physician (do not be astonished: here medicine is no derogation to nobility), gratis. . . . I am no physician, nor is anyone of my house; all I know how to do is merrily sing the praises of Caesar to a guitar, [which I have done] for some years now.[30]

Both composers and physicians were included in the man of letters's ancient scorn of the plebeian arts. Even the arrival of the passport he had yearned for could not eliminate the disagreeable sensation that such men stood closer to the imperial heart than Dottori, the prideful author of *Aristodemo*. The century that had begun under the sign of a brilliant victory for letters came to its end with a foretaste of a melancholy decline.

3. The Eighteenth Century

In a hypothesis aimed directly at the nineteenth-century historian and literary critic Francesco De Sanctis (which is suggestive but open to debate), Alberto Asor Rosa has stated that there are two Italian literatures—the first and greatest until the mid-seventeenth century, the second after that time. When we note that his watershed moment coincides with the explosion of the phenomenon of opera, the question arises as to what extent *opera in musica* can be considered the true heir of "that gigantic system of forms, that fascinating proposal of life by means of signs that winds through its most productive phase from the Trecento to the Seicento, advancing through, and in spite of, acute social and political crisis."[31] Opera was like that great literature, whose

29. Ibid., 104.
30. Ibid., 98.
31. Alberto Asor Rosa, "Letteratura, testo, società," in *Letteratura italiana,* 1:5–29, quotation 23.

fundamental skepticism opened the way to all manner of compromises with power; also like that great literature, opera was a system of formal codes that furnished a stylistic model for all of Europe. If this parallel could be demonstrated, it might perhaps help to explain another coincidence: the same persons who began to reflect on Italy's literary past—from Ludovico Antonio Muratori, Giovanni Mario Crescimbeni, and Gian Vincenzo Gravina to Francesco Saverio Quadro and GirolamoTiraboschi—also treated opera to close criticism.

What they had to say is examined elsewhere in this *History of Italian Opera*. What is important to note here is that this criticism arose in the context of a vast revolt on the part of Italian literati that reached its fullest expression in the founding and the broad diffusion of the concepts of Arcadia. If the academy was by definition the place where intellectual life was organized, Arcadia was the sublimation of the academic experience, no longer on a local scale but throughout Italy, under the sign of an ideological unity of Roman Catholic inspiration. Even people who remained outside this movement nonetheless yearned for "an alliance of all the most prominent literati of Italy, of whatever condition and rank, and professing whichever of the liberal arts or sciences, whose object would be the reform of those arts and sciences for the benefit of the Catholic religion, for the glory of Italy, and for public and private profit." [32]

Both baroque literature and opera came in for accusations of being suspect in their morals, unworthy in their form, and insufficiently "Italian." Muratori's opinions on Carlo Maria Maggi's activities as a librettist are an even better illustration of his thoughts on poetry for music than the famous passages in his treatise *La perfetta poesia italiana*. Maggi, who held a post as secretary in Milan, was a harbinger of the decline of baroque taste. He was obliged, against his better judgment and to satisfy requests from powerful persons, to write librettos of his own and rewrite those of others, a labor that he later mocked. According to Muratori,

In tragic and comic compositions, although he did not arrive at winning the princely crown, which in Italy perhaps still awaits someone to conquer it, he came close in many ways. If he did not fully achieve it, it was the fault of the times, not of any defect in his talent. This is because the theaters of Italy are turned over to the performers, who believe they cannot entertain their hearers unless they rouse them from their slumbers with less-than-honest pleasantries, or it is because tragedy and comedy, made effeminate so to speak, by over-use of music, cannot ever

32. Ludovico Antonio Muratori, *Primi disegni della Repubblica letteraria d'Italia*, in *Opere*, ed. Giorgio Falco and Fiorenzo Forti, 2 vols. (Milan: Ricciardi, 1964), 1:182. It is worth noting that Muratori does not place music among the liberal arts.

reach their perfection. In truth, now both the subject matter and the poetry are constrained to serve the music, when the opposite should be the case.[33]

The man of letters in the Arcadian age regarded opera with a profound suspicion rooted in an aesthetic conception that still relegated music to the domain of the irrational. But the Italian man of letters in the early eighteenth century lived in a world permeated with music, a world in which public theaters were springing up everywhere and in which the aristocracy adored music and worked, above and beyond factions, to effect the social promotion of composers. A strategy of compromise was more successful than frontal resistance; it led, for example, to welcoming into the Arcadian academy one musician who had shown signs of interest in a new type of good taste and whose muse

> d'ogni merto ignuda e pellegrina,
> spera ben di fugar suoi foschi errori
> al sol che splende in voi d'alta dottrina.
>
> (totally without merit and wandering, hopes to flee from his murky errors into the sunshine of high doctrine that shines in you.)[34]

The greatest victory in this jockeying for position was the establishment of a new custom in the art of writing librettos (later consecrated as a "reform") by poets who had left Arcadian circles, three of whom succeeded one another in the prestigious position of imperial poet in Vienna: Silvio Stampiglia (1706–14), Apostolo Zeno (1718–29), and Pietro Metastasio (1729–82).[35]

The collected letters of Zeno, a major figure in eighteenth-century musical theater, give a good deal of information about his attitude toward opera.[36] Even the selection of his letters for publication that his editors made after his death, but which probably reflects the range of his own interests, tells us that for him, writing librettos was a marginal activity in a life dedicated in large part to erudition of a more literary, historical, and antiquarian sort. His attitudes changed through the various phases of his life.

During the first period, 1697–1717, Zeno makes only sporadic reference to his own theatrical writings. Yet it was during those years that he built his

33. Ludovico Antonio Muratori, *Vita di Carlo Maria Maggi* (Milan, 1700), 91–92.

34. From a sonnet by Alessandro Scarlatti written for his admission to the Arcadian Academy (1706) and quoted in Fabrizio Della Seta, "La musica in Arcadia al tempo di Corelli," in *Nuovissimi studi corelliani,* ed. Sergio Durante and Pierluigi Petrobelli (Florence: Olschki, 1982), 123–48, quotation 143.

35. Between 1714 and 1718 the post was occupied by Pietro Pariati, who continued to maintain it even after the arrival of Zeno.

36. *Lettere di Apostolo Zeno, cittadino veneziano,* 3 vols. (Venice, 1752).

fame as a librettist, and he was well aware that the musical theater was one of the few sure sources of income for a scholar. He wrote to a Milanese impresario who was late in sending a payment to his colleague, Pietro Pariati: "All you have to know is that he is a man of letters to know he is not wealthy."[37]

Zeno's heart and mind were occupied, however, with his relations to persons of high intellectual level, such as Muratori, Antonio Magliabechi, Antonfrancesco Marmi, Antonio Vallisnieri, and Scipione Maffei (the last two of whom collaborated with him to found the literary journal *Il giornale de' letterati d'Italia*). It was to Muratori that Zeno admitted his impatience with the librettist's craft in a letter that Muratori saw fit to quote in *La perfetta poesia italiana:*

> Furthermore, I don't wonder that this custom of dramas does not meet with your approval. I myself, to tell you my feelings sincerely, though I have composed many of them, am the first to give them my vote of condemnation. Long exercise has taught me that [even] when they are not given to many abuses they lose the prime objective of such compositions, which is delight. . . . Music is much at fault for this, since it weakens the best scenes, thanks to the composers' lack of intelligence. The singers are at fault as well: not understanding [those scenes], they do not know how to perform them.[38]

Can we take this list of grievances as perfectly sincere? There is some truth to them, but we also need to take into account that the psychological aspects of an author's relationship to his own work and to the environment in which he operates can be more subtle and varied than we, with our desire to rationalize, are willing to grasp. Zeno's few references to his own dramas show a certain affection for them, an interest in following their vicissitudes, and even, despite his declarations of principle, a certain tolerance toward theatrical practices.[39]

Early in 1718 Zeno accepted the invitation to go to Vienna to take on the position of dramatic poet at the court of Charles VI. Remarks made in confidence to friends show that it was a difficult decision, but they also show that Zeno was determined to accept a position that guaranteed him economic independence and a chance to devote himself to his beloved studies. Moreover his reputation enabled him to obtain extremely favorable conditions: a stipend of 4,000 florins a year, the help of Pariati (his collaborator from earlier

37. To Federico Piantanida, March 1707, in ibid., 1:181.

38. To Muratori, August 1701, in ibid., 1:56.

39. See, for example, Zeno's letter to Antonfrancesco Marmi, 24 February 1702, in ibid, 1:66, where (speaking of *Griselda*) Zeno praises "the insignificant touches that sig. Gigli has so skillfully added to it," "the excellence of the music made by sig. Albinoni," and even "the talent of the actors."

times), the privilege of not having to write comic pieces and lightweight dramatic works, and the title of imperial historian as well as that of imperial poet. The last was his greatest satisfaction, as he makes clear in his account of his first meeting with the emperor.

> He then spoke of my person, telling me that he had been persuaded to call me to his royal service not by the recommendation of others but by a reading of my works. . . . Twice he said to me that it was not his intention to make use of me only for poetry, stating to me that he was persuaded that such was the smaller part of my studies. He spoke to me of the *Giornale;* asked me for literary news; wanted to know whether Italy is now blooming with excellent talents; and he indicated his desire to have literary meetings held in this city, in the form of a public academy of which he would be the protector and the head.[40]

Zeno seems to be reviving the humanistic dream of the prince as restorer of letters. Even before this encounter, however, he must have learned that court theater lays traps for the poet not unlike those of the public theaters.[41] In Zeno's letters from his Viennese period there are increasingly frequent references to his own poetic works (not only his labors at court but also revivals of his works in Italy). There are also increasing signs of his discontent for a workload that was proving to be just as onerous as in Venice: "Oh! How much more willingly would I attend to my primary concerns rather than to these dramatic trifles! But I must take patience, adjust to the times and to needs, as it pleases God."[42] On another occasion he wrote,

> I screw up my courage and forge ahead with the hope, in particular, that very soon I shall be free from this sort of labor, in which I have lost pleasure and in which I find only tedium. Other more substantial studies call me to them on this downward slope on which I find myself, and I must now put my thoughts to other developments than pastorals and dramas.[43]

Zeno had to wait until 1729, when Metastasio was "established in the service with an annual stipend of 3,000 florins, not to replace me but rather to aid and assist me."[44] It was only in 1731 that Zeno could return to Italy. His jubilation was short lived, however.[45] His theatrical career was over, and Zeno's letters of the last twenty years of his life make little reference to it, except for a backward glance or two.

40. To Pier Caterino Zeno, 10 December 1718, in ibid., 2:21.
41. See the letter to Pier Caterino Zeno, 5 November 1718, in ibid., 2:14–15.
42. To Pier Caterino Zeno, 24 December 1719, in ibid., 2:93.
43. To Luisa Bergalli, 26 May 1725, ibid., 2:373. See also the letter to Andrea Cornaro, 21 December 1726, in ibid., 2:461–62.
44. To Pier Caterino Zeno, 19 December 1729, in ibid., 2:531.
45. See the letter to Andrea Cornaro, 8 September 1731, in ibid., 2:551–52.

Of my dramatic things I now make so little account that rather than drawing satisfaction from having written them I feel repentance and scorn, to the point that I would almost feel more obliged to someone who set about criticizing them and saying bad things about them than to someone who might defend them and praise them to the skies. With the exception of a few, I consider them botched and aborted works.[46]

Barely five years earlier, however, Zeno had written to the same correspondent about his attitude toward his own work.

I will tell you only that in general, no matter how much I might condemn musical dramas as irregular tragedies, I cannot bring myself to call them, as does Muratori, "monsters and unions of a thousand unbelievable things"—at least in the considered form in which they have been treated by a number of fine men in recent times. And I would be too unjust if I fiercely attacked a sort of composition in which I have acquired some reputation, both in Italy and in Germany, and much profit, not to mention the appreciation with which my works have been greeted by the major monarch on earth, by his most brilliant court, and generally by all the princes of Italy.[47]

Once again one cannot demand too much coherence in declarations made with no claim to being systematic, at different times, in different states of mind, and, above all, to different correspondents. (Except as a deliberate mystification, would Zeno ever have confessed to the severe Muratori his affection for his own dramas for the income they brought him?) If Zeno's letters present contradictions, these apply less to him personally than to the historical condition of the man of letters in Italy, who saw with increasing clarity that opera was his only possible channel of communication with a real public, either bourgeois or aristocratic. Only those who (like Muratori and Gravina) totally abstained from commerce with that world and paid the price of isolation could permit themselves the luxury of condemning it completely. Others—Zeno among them—had little choice but to practice a double standard of truth, one which the first Venetian librettists had learned in the religious sphere from the teachings of Cesare Cremonini.

Only one person in the long history of the Italian libretto succeeded in realizing a perfect compromise between an ideal and a real situation. That man was Pietro Metastasio. At first glance his career seems fairly similar to Zeno's: after less than a decade of experience in the world of commercial opera, he received his invitation to go to Vienna, where he served three emperors. There was one fundamental difference, however, between the two poets

---

46. To Giuseppe Gravisi, 27 September 1735, in ibid., 3:89.
47. To Giuseppe Gravisi, 3 November 1730 in ibid., 2:538–39.

laureate: Metastasio never had any other vocation than the theater, and although that vocation was rooted in a reaffirmation of the central importance of the text, it could be realized only in musical drama.

Metastasio's early training destined him for a quite different career. His teacher and Pygmalion, Gravina, hoped that Metastasio would carry on his own work with a career in law and, in the poetic sphere, realize his own classical ideals of tragedy. Metastasio's actions after Gravina's death bear all the signs of gleeful betrayal masked by an appearance of gratitude. First, he displayed an open veneration of Torquato Tasso, Battista Guarini, and Giambattista Marino, the most affected and most "musical" of the classical Italian writers and authors forbidden him by his master's moral rigidity. Second, he proposed marriage to the daughter of a famous musician, a move that some interpreters have seen as a deliberate attempt to gain entry to the theatrical world in Rome.[48] When that came to naught, he did his best to break into theatrical circles in Naples, both in the public theaters and in aristocratic salons. His determination is attested, if not in the very few letters from that period, in the success of his attempts: his name is indissolubly linked with an entire generation of composers (Nicola Porpora, Leonardo Leo, Leonardo Vinci, Hasse) and singers (Farinelli)—a generation that marked an epoch in European opera.

Metastasio dreamed of being called to the imperial court as early as 1719, when he made inquiries about a possible post in Turin and contemplated moving to Vienna. In 1729, when his name echoed from Naples to Rome and Venice, his dream came true when he was appointed assistant and then successor to Zeno.

Metastasio, never a modest man, held himself at least the equal of his illustrious predecessor, and on that basis "humbly restricted" his salary request to 4,000 florins a year, a sum that he thought barely sufficient to maintain his family, "which has no other support than what, fortunately, my weak efforts produce in Italy." He added, persuasively, that a lesser sum would certainly mean "that I could apply myself only poorly to the task entrusted to me, distracted as I would be by the continuously painful thought of the discomforts and requirements of fatherhood."[49] Even for a poet with an established reputation, the sum requested was too high, as his correspondent reminded him.

> It is true that signor Zeno obtained the stipend of 4,000 florins, but it is also true that he had them as both historian and poet. . . . I do not doubt that as time passes,

48. Enrico Celani, "Il primo amore di Pietro Metastasio," *Rivista musicale italiana* 11 (1904): 228–64.

49. To Luigi Pio di Savoia, 28 September 1729, in Pietro Metastasio, *Tutte le opere,* ed. Bruno Brunelli (Milan: Mondadori, 1947–54), 3:46–47.

you will arrive at the enjoyment of such a sum. Abbé Pariati had . . . only 2,600 florins. For all these reasons, and in recognition of your merit, His Majesty will grant 3,000 florins a year and 100 ungheri for the trip.[50]

The son of a merchant, Metastasio had probably built in a margin for negotiation, for he hastened to accept the offer.

> I would not be so much an enemy to myself as to fail to embrace eagerly the greatest of honors that my studies could lead me to hope for; and, although to know one's self is difficult, I know myself well enough to confess that what has been accorded to me is wholly the effect of imperial beneficence, which is accustomed to measuring itself against its own grandeur, not against the merit of others.[51]

Metastasio's summation of his first audience with the emperor contrasts with the analogous report made by Zeno in several significant ways. Zeno focused on His Majesty's interest in his—Zeno's—literary and historical activities; with Metastasio the emphasis was more on the courtier's role and on the generosity of the imperial goodwill.

> I spoke with a voice that I fear was not too firm, expressing these sentiments: "I do not know whether it is my contentment or my confusion that is greater on finding myself at the feet of Your Imperial Majesty. This is a moment I have sighed for from my earliest days, and now I find myself not only before the greatest monarch on earth but here in the glorious title of his present servant. . . . I know that no matter how great my weakness, it will always be less than Your Majesty's infinite clemency, and I hope that the role of Caesar's poet will confer on me a worth for which I cannot hope from my talent."
>
> As I was speaking I saw the face of my most august patron soften, and he finally responded quite clearly: "I was already persuaded of your worth, but now I am further informed of your good manners, and I do not doubt that you will content me in everything to be done in my imperial service; even more, you will oblige me to be content with you."[52]

Although Francesco De Sanctis's negative opinion of Metastasio sprang from his own liberal tendencies and his Risorgimento enthusiasms, we must admit that there was some truth to it.[53] Metastasio was the last successful incarnation of the Italian man of letters who aspired to carve out a niche in

50. Letter of Luigi Pio di Savoia to Metastasio, 19 September 1729, in ibid., 3:1184–45.

51. Letter to Luigi Pio di Savoia, 3 November 1729, in ibid., 3:47–48.

52. To a friend in Rome, 25 July 1730, in ibid., 3:50–51.

53. "His life was an idyll. And if this be happiness, then he lived in happiness till the advanced age of eighty-four," Francesco De Sanctis, *Storia della letteratura italiana,* ed. Gianfranco Contini (Turin: Unione Tipografica-Editrice Torinese, 1968), 753, quoted from *History of Italian Literature,* trans. Joan Redfern, 2 vols. (New York: Harcourt, Brace, 1931), 2:838.

which to work in tranquillity under the protection of the supreme political authority (an aspiration that one scholar has dubbed a "lust for servitude").[54] From this point of view, Metastasio could indeed call his ambitions satisfied—even more than Zeno, who came from the wealthy upper-middle class of the Venetian Republic, whereas Metastasio came from a modest Roman shop. Even more than the success of his dramatic works, Metastasio's greatest satisfaction must have been to find himself surrounded by well-known people (women, in particular) from the aristocracy of all Europe.

The "idyll" was not as rosy as De Sanctis thought: a growing sense of dissatisfaction and bitterness veils the unfailingly affable tone of Metastasio's letters. They show proof of a hypochondriac depression that tormented him but that he hid under an appearance of jovial well-being; they also show the tedium of painstaking and difficult work, masked for the public at large by the flowing, singing quality of the finished product. And they clearly show that Metastasio was keenly aware of the insuperable limits that contemporary society put to the aspirations of a man of letters who was not born into the world of privilege.

> Are the advantages truly great that one gets from having ruined one's body and sacrificed the best years of one's life either wandering deliriously among the ravings of famous ancient madmen or scribbling useless pages to serve as a boring distraction for the idle and as savory fodder for the ill-intentioned? Is it possible that you have not yet realized how little the world appreciates such ideal and abstract merits? Anyone in search of pleasures and fortune, my lady countess, should apply himself totally to the physical, to the solid, to the real. . . . Oh! If I were to be born again, I would like to see whether that good man, my father, could make me learn to read a second time.[55]

We cannot imagine that the mind of Metastasio—a mind perfectly in tune with the social structure of the ancien régime—could have harbored any explicit challenge to the aristocracy, the beneficiaries of all privilege. Rather, his bitter remarks were aimed no further than the economic well-being enjoyed by the singers with whom he had always had close contacts. He must not have been able to resist comparing his own respectable prosperity with the brilliant position that his "dear twin" Farinelli had managed to win at the Spanish court at the other end of Europe.

Metastasio's relations with the practical aspects of musical theater in his time were no less problematic and tormented than Zeno's. But Metastasio

---

54. Gino Benzoni, *Gli affanni della cultura: Intellettuali e potere nell'Italia della Controriforma e barocca* (Milan: Feltrinelli, 1978), 78–143.

55. To Francesca Maria Torres Orzoni, 28 February 1758, in Metastasio, *Tutte le opere,* 4:41–42.

had an advantage over Zeno in that unlike Zeno, for whom opera was a parenthesis in a life devoted to other occupations, he had an intimate and vital interest in things theatrical. Metastasio had a second advantage in his sensitivity to music, which enabled him to enter (at least in part) into the composers' way of thinking and which led him (again, unlike Zeno) to count among his acquaintances many composers, singers, and others from the world of the theater. Nonetheless Metastasio remained persuaded of the literary autonomy of his works: the care that he took throughout his life to see his works through all their many editions reveals a desire to remove his dramas from the ephemeral life of the stage and present them to the intellectual world as definitive and self-contained works. In 1733 he admonished his first publisher, "Take care not to print the names of the designers of scenic effects, the ballet masters, composers, etc.,"[56] and in his later days he wrote to Antonio Eximeno to express his skepticism about the need for a new edition of his dramas accompanied by the scores of the best music composed for them.[57]

Metastasio's concept of the theater remained tenaciously rooted in a rationalistic ideal. Arcadian to the end he put the text above all the other components of the operatic spectacle. He did not hide the fact that he not only saw those other components as auxiliary to the poetry but considered them concessions to the mental laziness of intellectually retarded spectators.

> Those parts of opera that require only the spectators' eyes and ears to plead for them always garner more votes than the other parts, whose merits can be measured only with intelligence and ratiocination. Everyone can see, everyone can hear, but not everyone understands and not everyone reasons. It is true that when the first and second parts are well-suited to one another, even a lowbrow spectator feels a greater pleasure without understanding why: it is just as true that the difficulty and rarity of such accord obliges, so to speak, the commercial theaters to put their trust more in those arts everyone can judge.[58]

Metastasio touches here on several recurrent themes in literary criticism of opera that persistently claimed authority over theatrical spectacles.[59] Un-

56. To Giuseppe Bettinelli, 14 November 1733, in ibid., 3: 97.

57. Letter of 22 August 1776, in ibid., 5:399–402.

58. To Francesco Algarotti, 9 February 1756, in ibid., 3:1092. See also the important letters to Francesco Giovanni di Chastellux of 15 July 1765, in ibid. 5:397–99, and 29 January 1766, in ibid., 5:435–40.

59. See, for example, Francesco Algarotti, *Saggio sopra l'opera in musica,* 2d ed. (Livorno, 1763), in Algarotti, *Saggi,* ed. Giovanni da Pozzo (Bari: Laterza, 1963), 150–51; translated into English in 1767 (London) and 1768 (Glasgow); excerpts from the 1768 translation appear in Strunk, *Source Readings,* 657–72; other excerpts are available in Enrico Fubini, *Music and Culture in Eighteenth-Century Europe: A Source Book,* ed. Bonnie J. Blackburn (Chicago: University of Chicago Press, 1994), 233–40; Antonio Planelli, *Dell'opera in musica,* ed. Francesco Degrada (Fiesole: Discanto, 1981), 126; for excerpts in English see Fubini, 240–51.

derlying the differentiation between arts of the mind and arts of the senses was the extremely old distinction between the intellectual and the artisan.[60] Here the criterion of differentiation was not the intrinsic value of the work but whether it was created for money (as in the case of the *maestro di cappella*) or by disinterested participation (as in the aristocratic condition to which the man of letters aspired, albeit in the mitigated form of a post bearing a fixed stipend that freed him from competition in which he might risk coming out second best).

On closer inspection, however, the hope of refurbishing the privileged role of the poet by removing opera from its commercial routine and offering it to a public of elect connoisseurs (and the various "reforms" of the eighteenth century were attempts to put that idea into practice) proved illusory, as Dottori, Zeno, and even Metastasio discovered. Even at court the poet's labors were tiresome and ungrateful, and although he avoided the constraints to which singers subjected him, he still felt the full weight of demands that powerful patrons put on him. This was grudgingly admitted by the anonymous biographer of the Parma court librettist, Carlo Innocenzo Frugoni (probably echoing the dead poet's own opinion).

> It pains me to say that Frugoni, who was most successful in lyric [poetry], could not be so in the dramatic, and this was through the fault of others. . . . He did not lack the grace or the robustness to weave a drama to equal the immortal Metastasio's, but his genius had to bend to the will of others, and he formed no plan [of his own] for dramatic works but exactly followed the outline and distribution indicated to him by the one who was in power. He complained to his friends of this slavery, however much he made a show (for excellent reasons) of honoring it.[61]

Frugoni's biographer points with admiration and envy to Metastasio as the incarnation of an ideal to which all librettists aspired. If this was what Metastasio represented for a court poet like Frugoni, it must have been all the more true for people in the world of commercial theater—that is, for the overwhelming majority of librettists, men whose activities and personalities are, for the most part, unknown. Not famous enough to merit publication of their collected letters, these men have not even left traces in documents concerning the composers, as would happen in the nineteenth century.

Although Zeno's and Metastasio's prestige could offer librettists intellec-

60. That distinction still appeared in the late eighteenth century, as demonstrated by the quarrel that raged in Naples in 1785 between Saverio Mattei and Ferdinando Galiani, the high points of which are reported in Vanda Monaco, *Giambattista Lorenzi e la commedia per musica* (Naples: Berisio, 1968), 97–101.

61. *Memorie storiche e letterarie della vita e delle opere del signor abate Frugoni,* in Carlo Innocenzo Frugoni, *Opere poetiche,* 9 vols. (Parma, 1779), 1:xiii.

tual satisfaction, there was less satisfaction for their pocketbooks: the innumerable revivals of librettos by Zeno and Metastasio were precisely so many opportunities lost to local librettists, who were forced into the more obscure and less remunerative labor of adaptation.[62] Information on the remuneration for writing and adapting librettos is scarce and fragmentary. It is probable that the model Ivanovich had described in the seventeenth century was true only for Venice, although it persisted there.[63] In other cities the librettist was most probably engaged in much the same way as the others involved in opera: as we have seen, even Zeno had to negotiate with a Milanese impresario.

The following data, chosen among the few indications available but covering nearly a century, will have to suffice as evidence of the librettist's remuneration and his place in overall theatrical budgets.

1. Reggio Emilia 1697. For a performance of *L'Oreste in Sparta*, a new opera by Pompeo Luchesi and Carlo Francesco Pollarolo, the poet Luchesi was paid 20 doppie, the composer Pollarolo 25 doppie; the *prima donna*, Margherita Salicola, received 200 doppie plus 40 doppie for living expenses, and the other singers received fees that ranged between 50 and 17 doppie.[64]

2. Turin 1772. For the performances of *Demetrio*, by Metastasio and Giuseppe Ponzo, and of *Ifigenia in Aulide*, a new work by Vittorio Amedeo Cigna-Santi and Ferdinando Bertoni, Cigna-Santi was paid 480 lire for the new work and his adaptation of the older one, the soprano castrato Giuseppe Aprile was paid 7,573 lire, the soprano Caterina Gabrielli was paid 9,466 lire, and the other singers between 2,840 lire and 426 lire. Ponzo's fee was 1,420 lire and Bertoni's about 1,240 lire.[65]

3. Naples 1775. For a performance of *Il Socrate immaginario*, a new work by Giambattista Lorenzi and Giovanni Paisiello, the poet was paid 115 ducats, and the composer was paid 190 ducats. The singers' fees are not known, but the total expenditures amounted to 1,129 ducats.[66]

62. See Paolo Rolli, letter to Princess Pignatelli, 9 May 1750, quoted in Sesto Fassini, *Il melodramma italiano a Londra nella prima metà del Settecento* (Turin: Bocca, 1914), 178–79. See also the document quoted in Marie-Thérèse Bouquet, *Il teatro di corte: Dalle origini al 1788*, vol. 1 of *Storia del Teatro Regio di Torino*, ed. Alberto Basso, 5 vols. (Turin: Cassa di Risparmio di Torino, 1976–83), 201, and the opinion of Pietro Napoli-Signorelli quoted in Michael F. Robinson, *Naples and Neapolitan Opera* (Oxford: Clarendon Press, 1972), 37.

63. Goldoni said of the 1730s, "Adaptations in those days had declined from the fortune that they had enjoyed in past times; they still had a certain reputation, however: Lalli realized some profits from adaptations of old librettos when they reappeared on the stage"; preface to vol. 13 of the Pasquali edition, in Carlo Goldoni, *Tutte le opere*, ed. Giuseppe Ortolani, 14 vols. (Milan: Mondadori, 1935–56), 721.

64. Reggio Emilia, Archivio di Stato, Teatro e feste pubbliche, no. 1, 1697 (my thanks to Paolo Fabbri for communicating this information).

65. Bouquet, *Il teatro di corte*, 305–6.

66. Monaco, *Giambattista Lorenzi*, 124–25.

As these data show, the level of the librettist's compensation was somewhat lower than the composer's, and both were abysmally lower than the fees offered to the more famous singers. This means that we can believe Benedetto Marcello when he states that "poets of little credit will take on, within the year, legal work, stewardships, economic superintendencies; they will copy handbills, correct printed proofs, speak ill of one another, and so forth."[67]

The librettist could only react to this situation with the weapons of ironic resignation (on the model of Pier Jacopo Martello's dialogue, *Della tragedia*) or satire (on the model of Marcello's *Il teatro alla Moda*). This led to the development of the genre of the "opera within an opera," which mocks the impresario, the singer, or the composer, according to the work. Even the librettist was satirized, although he was more apt to be shown sympathetically, as the victim.[68]

It is hardly surprising that librettists, who operated in an atmosphere of constant frustration, often had a spirit of adventure, rebellion, irregularity, and libertinism characteristic of other broad segments of eighteenth-century culture. A certain restlessness shows through in the work of Girolamo Gigli, who was a member of the aristocratic and academic world in Tuscany and Rome but was expelled from the Accademia della Crusca and from the Arcadian Academy for his penchant for writing anti-Jesuit and antipedantic satire. These same attitudes were amplified in the case of the Neapolitan lawyer, Pietro Trinchera, who committed suicide in 1755 in the jail cell to which he had been committed (for the second time) for the extremely scabrous eroticism and the religious satire of his librettos in Neapolitan dialect.

One forerunner of the eighteenth-century adventurer was Sebastiano Biancardi, a Neapolitan in flight from Naples after a bankruptcy. He went all over Italy under the false name of Domenico Lalli, exploiting the favor shown him by powerful persons and in the company of another odd personality, the baron and musician Emanuele d'Astorga. When Lalli got to Venice, he gained entry into theatrical circles thanks to his friendship with Zeno (who later lost patience with him), and he ended a fairly promising career in poverty, subcontracting to Carlo Goldoni the post of poet for the Grimani theaters (keeping the writing of the adaptations for himself, however).

Even Goldoni's biography shows traits that are picaresque if not downright adventurous (his travels with a commedia dell'arte troupe; his unsettled, vagabond life), but other authors were genuine adventurers. Ranieri de' Calzabigi

---

67. Benedetto Marcello, *Il teatro alla moda* (Venice, 1720), modern edition, ed. A. Marianni (Milan: Rizzoli, 1959), 28; in English translation by Reinhard G. Pauly, *Musical Quarterly* 34 (1948): 371–403; 35 (1949): 85–105.

68. The most characteristic examples of this subgenre are: Goldoni, *La bella verità* (1762; in *Tutte le opere,* 12:109–59); Giambattista Casti, *Prima la musica, poi le parole* (1768; in appendix to Pietro Metastasio, *Opere,* ed. Mario Fubini [Milan and Naples: Ricciardi, 1968], 1039–69).

was involved in dubious lotteries in Paris, along with Giovanni Giacomo Casanova and Madame de Pompadour; Giovanni de Gamerra was first an abbé, then a soldier, and later imperial poet in Vienna and a colleague of Calzabigi's in Naples; Giovanni Battista Casti was also an abbé, and he was equally famous for his librettos and for the satirical and often obscene verse that earned him expulsion from both Rome and Vienna, where he nonetheless managed to return as imperial poet in 1790. To end the list there was Lorenzo da Ponte, the quintessential librettist and a writer of memoirs second only to Goldoni in that flourishing eighteenth-century genre. Such memoirs did not arise from any desire to leave an objective report of one's own life but to present a deliberately distorted, reassuring, and even justificatory version of the protagonist's life.

Goldoni wrote his own memoirs twice: the first time, as a preface to the Pasquali edition of his works; the second, in his late and less trustworthy *Mémoires* written for a French audience.[69] Even the first version, now considered somewhat closer to the truth, is obviously shaped by the author's desire to show his career as moving steadfastly and without digression toward the reform of the comic theater.[70] Goldoni presents his activity as a librettist as a momentary expedient, and the two episodes that develop that theme most fully—the first, an attempt to write an opera seria in which he clashed, head on, with the implacable unwritten laws of the singers, despots of the stage, and second, his meeting with Antonio Vivaldi to rework Zeno's *Griselda*[71]— are quite obviously influenced by the satirical model of Marcello's *Il teatro alla moda*. In reality Goldoni's activities as an author of opera seria, and particularly as a rewriter of other people's librettos, continued for a decade and were anything but a marginal amusement.[72]

Da Ponte's self-serving memoirs are of a quite different sort. Da Ponte felt he had to justify himself to the world and to himself for less-than-perfect conduct in his life, a task that he accomplished by brazenly eliminating everything he wished to conceal (his birth in a family of converted Jews, his ordina-

---

69. The prefaces to the Pasquali edition (including the Italian memoirs) appear in Goldoni, *Tutte le opere,* 1:621–757; the French *Mémoires* appear in the same volume, 1–605; for an English translation of the French, see *Memoirs of Carlo Goldoni, written by himself,* trans. John Black, ed. William A. Drake, with an introduction by William A. Drake (New York: A. A. Knopf, 1926).

70. In the preface to vol. 13 in the Pasquali edition, given in Goldoni, *Tutte le opere,* 1:717, Goldoni says, "I was dying to turn my hand to true characters and to attempt the reform that I had in mind; but the time had not yet come, and I had to be satisfied with working as best I could on intermezzi and making some of those stage works that I let the actors call tragedies, but that I knew in all good conscience could not pass for the same."

71. See the prefaces to vols. 11 and 13 in the Pasquali edition, given in Goldoni, *Tutte le opere,* 1:685–86; 1:721–23, respectively.

72. See Piero Weiss, "Goldoni poeta d'opere serie per musica," *Studi goldoniani* 3 (1973): 7–40.

tion as a priest, his seduction of a married woman), by attributing his every disgrace to bad luck, his own ingenuousness, and envious enemies, and finally by offering testimony to his virtues from illustrious persons who had helped him (in particular, dead persons), beginning with Emperor Joseph II. Da Ponte's supreme ambition was to be poet laureate at the imperial court, to the point that his hatred for Casti was motivated purely by the latter's having won those laurels.

As far as his own writings were concerned, however, Da Ponte was a pure librettist and a writer totally free of literary preconceptions. If at times we find him laughing at certain theatrical practices, "in the face of reason, good sense, Aristotle, and all the powers of heaven or earth,"[73] we should not forget that three pages earlier he had stated that the emperor's goodwill had been "of greater help to me than all the precepts and all the rules of Aristotle— little read by me and studied less."[74] Da Ponte's conception of the theater was empirical to an almost scandalous degree.

> I realized then that it was not sufficient to be a great poet (Casti was that, beyond question) to write a good drama; that no end of tricks had to be learned—the singers, for instance, had to be studied individually [so] that their parts might fit; that one had to watch actual performances on the stage to note the mistakes of others and one's own, and then, after two or three thousand booings, find some way to correct them; these things, however necessary, are nevertheless very difficult to attain, for they are hindered now by the pressure of time or money, now by the niggardliness of the impresario, now by the author's own vanity.[75]

Da Ponte's opinion regarding composers also differed from the most widespread eighteenth-century evaluation. On the one hand he remained faithful to a low opinion of the intellectual level of musicians.

> To the disgraceful decline of this wonderful art in Italy there also contributed the unsurpassable ignorance of almost all our *maestri di cappella,* who generally would set the most beautiful music to the indecent and trivial words of Neapolitan street people quite as readily, or perhaps more so, as they would to the sweetest ditties of Metastasio.[76]

Da Ponte handed Antonio Salieri a double-edged compliment, calling him "cultivated," even though a *maestro di cappella,* "and fond of men of let-

73. Lorenzo da Ponte, *Memorie* (New York, 1823–27; 2d ed.1829–30), in the edition *Memorie: Libretti mozartiani* (Milan: Garzanti, 1976), 93, and quoted from Da Ponte, *Memoirs of Lorenzo da Ponte* (1929), trans. Elisabeth Abbott, ed. Arthur Livingston, reprinted a with new preface by Stanley Sadie (New York: Da Capo Press, 1988), 133.

74. Da Ponte, *Memorie,* 90; *Memoirs,* 130.

75. Da Ponte, *Memorie,* 94–95; *Memoirs,* 136, edited.

76. Da Ponte, *Memorie,* 74–75; *Memoirs,* 116, edited.

ters."[77] On the other hand Da Ponte's evaluation of Mozart showed quite a different attitude.

> Though gifted with talents superior perhaps to those of any other composer in the world, past, present, or future, Mozart had, thanks to the intrigues of his rivals, never been able to exercise his divine genius in Vienna and was living there unknown and obscure, like a priceless jewel buried in the bowels of the earth and hiding the refulgent excellence of its splendors. I can never remember without exultation and complacency that it was to my perseverance and firmness alone that Europe and the world in great part owe the exquisite vocal compositions of that admirable genius. The unfairness and envy of journalists, gazetteers, and especially of biographers of Mozart have never permitted them to concede such glory to an Italian; but all Vienna, all those who knew him and me in Germany, Bohemia, and Saxony . . . must bear me witness to the truth which I now reveal.[78]

There was a precise reason behind Da Ponte's praise of Mozart, however: Da Ponte was writing his memoirs during the 1820s, when Mozart's name was already legendary and a new concept of music was taking hold. By attributing to himself the merit of having discovered a genius, Da Ponte was launching a theme recurrent in librettists' memoirs during the nineteenth century.

4. The Nineteenth Century

The period of Italian opera's greatest splendor signaled the lowest point on the declining parabola of the librettist's social and intellectual status. Although the librettist could still call himself a member of the literary family in Italy, he was now a poor relation, to be hidden from view when company came. Indeed, literary histories devote an entire chapter to Metastasio and a page or two to his predecessors and imitators, but they usually do not even list the names of heroic artisans such as Francesco Maria Piave or poets of some worth such as Felice Romani.

Although seventeenth-and eighteenth-century librettos had been criticized (even ferociously), it was always on the plane of literary debate; when the nineteenth-century libretto was mentioned, it was now fated to receive only ironic witticisms, smiles of sympathy, or—as its greatest honor—the inclusion of a couplet or two in the everyday oral folklore of the bourgeoisie. What caused this collapse? The determining factor, in a system of production that showed substantial continuity with the eighteenth-century model (the disappearance of court opera aside), was undeniably the irresistible rise of the composer on the scale of social and cultural prestige.

77. Da Ponte, *Memorie*, 87; *Memoirs*, 126.
78. Da Ponte, *Memorie*, 104; *Memoirs*, 148, edited.

In seventeenth-and eighteenth-century opera, the declared rival of the librettist was the singer, who was seen as responsible for all infringements on a literary work's artistic integrity and as the major financial beneficiary of the "opera industry." The singer's preeminence was ephemeral, however, because it was limited to the single performance. Afterward, the poet was at liberty to publish his work as he had conceived it, and publication endowed it with artistic autonomy.

The rise of the composer, to the contrary, took the librettist's work out of his own hands, because now the text was a purely functional part of an artistic product whose spiritual paternity the musician claimed. It is thanks to this turnabout that we speak of *L'Olimpiade* as a drama by Metastasio, only rarely recalling the various composers who set it to music, but we unhesitatingly speak of *Il trovatore* as an opera by Giuseppe Verdi, forgetting, more often than not, to mention the author of the libretto.[79]

When the composer moved ahead of the librettist on the social scale, that new status was of course reflected on the economic scale. Once the custom of leaving to the librettist both the risks and the profits of printing the libretto disappeared forever, this cost might be assumed by the theater management, but a new system was gaining ground in which the composer, who paid the librettist for composing the libretto, took ownership of it himself. Now more than ever the libretto lost its status as an intellectual work and became mere merchandise: to cite one example, in 1843 Verdi paid Piave for a libretto that he never set to music, and later Piave had to buy back his own work in order to resell it to Giovanni Pacini.

For the nineteenth century (as for other centuries) there is still no exhaustive study quantifying the exact economic relationship between the composer and the librettist, and archival documents often say nothing about the question, probably because most agreements were amicable arrangements made directly between the interested parties. We can say, however, that in the majority of cases the librettist lived in genteel poverty, and that he attained a certain well-being, without luxury, only when his name was regularly coupled with that of a successful composer. The librettist almost always had other employment of a middle-class sort, and he rounded out his income by doing literary odd jobs.[80] Jacopo Ferretti was an employee in a tobacco factory in Rome,

---

79. This situation was sanctioned by the law on copyright of 25 June 1865 (confirmed in 1875), which stated, "The writer of a libretto or any sort of composition set to music cannot dispose of the right to reproduce the music along with it or offer it for sale; but the composer of the musical work can have it reproduced and offered for sale along with the words to which the music is applied"; quoted in Anna Laura Bellina, *L'ingegnosa congiunzione: Melos e immagine nella "favola" per musica* (Florence: Olschki, 1984), 141–42.

80. One exception to this rule was Luigi Romanelli, professor of declamation and letters at the conservatory in Milan from 1816 to 1831 and the poet-in-residence of La Scala. Romanelli

which was a very provincial city at the time of Gregory XVI, but he also wrote epithalamia, sermons, and encomiastic sonnets. Giuseppe Maria Foppa was a specialist in cadastral estimates and became the keeper of records for the Venice lawcourts.

Felice Romani, the leading librettist of his generation (but who wrote librettos "not so much by his free inclination as because he was often constrained to it by his meagre income"),[81] was an exceptional case. He fell into a permanent position in 1834 (when he was already forty-six years old) when King Carlo Alberto called him to Turin to the well-paying post of director of *La gazzetta ufficiale piemontese*.[82] In the turbulent times of 1848–49, a series of intrigues forced Romani to give up this post and return to Milan, where, according to his wife, he had the strength of character to refuse the lucrative position of imperial poet in Vienna.

Not all librettists were so fortunate. Relations between Gaetano Rossi (whose librettos included highly successful works such as *Tancredi* and *Semiramide*) and Giacomo Meyerbeer reached a pathetic point when Rossi, riddled with debts, was obliged to ask Meyerbeer for a loan of 300 francs or a gift of some used clothing for himself and his four children.[83] Rossi confided to his friend and benefactor,

> Yesterday—Oh how much!—I envied your independence! Miserable, thrice miserable is the artist who fatally finds himself in need of work! Yesterday I wanted to tear up the text for the second opera, and I wanted not even to respond to a very bitter letter from Morlacchi. . . . If he continues to be suspicious of me, if he attacks me with prejudiced statements, my artist's delicacy will take offense with the same bitter feelings. . . . Whatever happens . . . there is a Providence for my children. I will withdraw my libretto: I dare say that it is good enough to find its price. At least he will know that I withdrew the libretto, before he rejected it, on the pretext of [its] being unappreciated.[84]

If we want to leave the realm of anecdotes and work with concrete data, we need to turn to the rich store of documents concerning Verdi. The negotiations between Verdi and Piave regarding their first collaboration provide im-

---

was perhaps also the only nineteenth-century librettist who lived to see his dramatic works collected and published (in 8 volumes, Milan, 1832).

81. Emilia Branca, *Felice Romani ed i più riputati maestri di musica del suo tempo* (Turin, 1882), 25.

82. Ibid., 60.

83. Letter of 24 October 1823; letters of 30 September and 8 October 1826, in Giacomo Meyerbeer, *Briefwechsel und Tagebücher*, ed. Heinz Becker and Gudrun Becker, 4 vols. (Berlin: De Gruyter, 1960–70), 1:562, 2:39–40.

84. Letter to Meyerbeer of 29 July 1823 in ibid., 1:529.

portant information that goes beyond the particular matter under discussion.[85]

Verdi had signed a contract with the Teatro La Fenice for a new opera to be produced during carnival 1844. He was paid 12,000 Austrian lire to cede all rights to the score (as compared to Alessandro Nini's asking price of 7,500 lire for similar rights, Pacini's 10,000 lire, and Donizetti's 30,000 lire). The cost of the libretto was included in Verdi's compensation, as were a revival of his opera *I Lombardi alla prima crociata* and his lodgings in Venice, but the fee was still high for a composer who, at the time, had only two successes to his credit (Bellini had been paid the same sum for *Norma*).

For the libretto (which was to be called *Cromvello*), the secretary of the theater, Guglielmo Brenna, recommended Piave, whom he described in glowing terms.

> Piave is a man of letters, and although this is the first libretto for a serious opera that he has set about writing, he is extremely well known as a lyric poet and has no equal in the grace of his concepts and his spontaneity.
>
> As for his fee, Piave is asking 300 florins [the equivalent of 900 Austrian lire]. . . . If not [acceptable], tell me what you would find it reasonable to spend, and I do not doubt that I can make Piave bend to your every desire, if for no other reason, for the pleasure of writing for the maestro who today fills all Italy with his brilliant fame.[86]

Naturally, Verdi found the request excessive. His reply gives us valuable information on the remuneration of librettists who were more firmly established than Piave.

> Regarding the price that you have asked of me, may I point out that Solera, after he had written two or three librettos, was paid 500 Austrian lire for *Nabucodonosor* and, later, 700 Austrian lire for *I Lombardi;* that Romani, the great Romani, after having written one or two hundred librettos and becoming the leading poet in opera, was paid 800 francs for *Norma*. These observations made, I leave it to you to adjust things and to set the amount, half of which will be paid on delivery of the libretto, the other half after the first performance.[87]

Brenna, as Verdi had predicted, managed to bring down Piave's price, but Piave insisted on defending his dignity as a poet. Brenna reported,

> The reflections that . . . you made it my duty to pass on to him led him to limit his asking price to 600 Austrian lire, but I absolutely could not bring him down more.

85. The data that follow are taken from Marcello Conati, *La bottega della musica: Verdi e La Fenice* (Milan: Il Saggiatore, 1983), 33ff.

86. Letter of 1 August 1843 in ibid., 64.

87. Letter of 8 August 1843, ibid., 66.

He is a man of letters who draws a stipend from several printers. A whim to write for the theater and the pleasure of knowing that his verse will be set to music by you have induced him to tear himself away from more serious pursuits for a while, but they have not induced him to renounce his hoped-for recompense.[88]

When the parties had come to an agreement, Piave set to work, and he soon sent Verdi his *Cromvello,* which, in the meantime had become *Allan Cameron.* An unpleasant surprise awaited Piave: Verdi had become disaffected with the topic and wanted instead to set Victor Hugo's *Hernani.* With great dignity Piave bowed to the maestro's desires, but he insisted that he be paid for the work he had already done, that he be given a further 400 lire for the new libretto, and that Verdi promise to commission another libretto from him within a year—"another drama on a subject of his choosing, and the price of which cannot be less than that agreed upon for *Alan Cameron.*"[89]

This led to new negotiations: Verdi found Piave's first condition acceptable, but the additional 400 lire seemed to him "a sum somewhat out of line,"[90] and he managed to get it reduced to 300 lire. He then had this to say about Piave's third request.

I accept all the conditions except the obligation to have [him] write a third libretto. I do not find it just or proper to ask this of me for many reasons. . . . Besides, if signor Piave is to do a libretto (which I do not doubt) that will satisfy the demands of the public, may he be assured that, in the current scarcity of good poets, I will have every interest in seeking him out and paying him even more than he asks of me.[91]

In the end Piave was paid 900 lire. Calculating that Verdi had 9,000 lire left when he had paid all his expenses, the ratio between the payment for the labor to produce two librettos and the labor to produce one score was 1:10. Verdi spoke sincerely in his reaction to Piave's third condition: Piave became his most loyal collaborator (not to mention the tens of librettos he wrote for other composers), and he obtained satisfactions that he could not have hoped for from his poetic gifts alone.

Unfortunately for us the two men became friends, and from that date on almost all mention of Piave's fees disappears from the Verdi correspondence. We know, however, that Piave's fee for *Rigoletto* amounted to 1,000 lire, charged against the 6,000 lire paid to Verdi for rights to score rentals (Verdi

88. Letter of 11 August 1843, ibid., 67.

89. Piave, memorandum to Brenna, undated [September 1843], in ibid., 75.

90. Letter to Brenna, 19 September, and contract dated 23 September 1843, in ibid., 78 and 86, respectively.

91. Letter to Brenna, 25 September 1843, in ibid., 87.

had asked 30,000 lire for the full ownership rights).[92] Piave's remuneration
for the libretto of *La traviata,* for which Verdi got 8,000 lire (again, for score
rentals) had increased proportionally, but added to this fee was an annual
stipend of 600 Austrian lire for a three-year contract as stage director *(direttore di scena)* of La Fenice,[93] a position that Piave most probably owed to
Verdi's recommendation.

When Piave and his family left Venice for Milan in 1860, it was again
Verdi who got him an analogous position at La Scala. On 17 March of that
year, Piave wrote a memorandum to the then governor of the city, Massimo
d'Azeglio, in which he described himself as a "poet of *melodrammi,* author
of many poems set to music by the illustrious cavalier, Giuseppe Verdi." He
recalled his long service at La Fenice and stated that he was certain that D'A-
zeglio would not fail "to satisfy the desire of a person who has dedicated his
entire life to letters and who has thus far drawn the sole support of his honored existence primarily from the theater.[94]

Three months later Piave applied to have his nomination made effective,
adding to his letter some notes on the stage director's responsibilities.

> The duties of the poet in the theaters concerning the operas:
>   1. Compile the notes and orders for costume sketches or costumes from the
> costume designer; for the quantity and quality of the costumes from the costume
> shop; for the props from the head of props.
>   2. Commission the scenery and give the description of the scenery to the scene
> painter, reaching an agreement with him and with the head of stage staff to decide
> on and note the placement of the lights, the moveable stage pieces, and the stage
> machinery required.
>   3. Decide on the number of extras, dancers, etc.
>   4. Hold the rehearsals necessary to stage the entire opera, according to the de-
> mands of the drama, assisted, as needed, by the *maestro al cembalo* [vocal coach].
> Partial rehearsals will be held with the individual artists, explaining to them the
> import of the action and the way of representing it to the spectators; then rehears-
> ing with the *masse* [chorus, corps de ballet]; finally, [rehearsing] with everyone to-
> gether.
>   5. The poet is personally obliged to be present on stage on opening night.
>
> Concerning the librettos and the inspection of same:
>   1. Review the scenarios of the librettos and report on the effects they may pro-
> duce; also, arrange for them to be easily read.

92. Ibid., 191.
93. Ibid., 278 and 291.
94. A photograph of this document, which, like the one in the next note, is in the museum of
the Teatro alla Scala, Milan, is reproduced in Antonio Cassi Ramelli, *Libretti e librettisti* (Milan:
Ceschina, 1973), fig. 16.

2. Correct the printed proofs.

3. Alter [the librettos] when requested.

For such services there used to be a fixed stipend, but when this task was given to persons who either were not sufficiently familiar with its practical aspects, were too occupied with other matters, or were in poor health and thus unable to do the whole job, then the tasks were divided up, and with them the honoraria.

The poet reserved to himself correction of the ballet scenarios, [writing] the variants of the operas, and arranging for the publicity, leaving the other tasks to others.

Since the undersigned has benefited from long experience gained by the composition of over fifty opera librettos and by handling the direction of operas at the Gran Teatro La Fenice at Venice, and since, thank God, he enjoys excellent health, he is disposed to take on, as was the custom in the past, all the obligations belonging to the position to which he aspires, hence, to receive the entire compensation for them.

This he begs to do, and with no fear of bringing harm to a third party, since the person who now fulfills these functions is already the legal counsel of the management and as such enjoys another stipend, nor can he legally combine two positions of such contrary nature.

The poet, in fact, must concern himself with the greatest decorum and perfect decoration of the operas in all that is not music (which is the exclusive province of the *maestro concertatore* [violin director]), while the representative of the management has as his special mandate the finances and payments, things too often contrary to the overall success of the spectacles.

This leads to a new and powerful reason for the poet's independence from the management concerning the exercise of his functions. Therefore the right to name him is of increasingly critical importance. As stated above, that right is held by the royal government: in Naples, in fact, the poet is nominated, on a permanent basis, by the government; in Venice, by the noble administration [of the theater].[95]

Piave's conclusion is basically a late echo of the eighteenth-century utopian ideal of a theater placed under the supreme control of a political authority, with the tacit conviction that such a power could restore the dignity of the librettist—almost as if the old habits could be maintained intact simply by changing the absolutist ideology to a Risorgimento ideology. It should be unnecessary to point out how out of date this utopia was in the age of political liberalism and a competitive free-market economy. Even Verdi had understood that the market economy (rather than a state stipend), together with an increasing acceptance of copyrights backed by laws, would bring the librettists a fair share of earnings. In 1861 Verdi wrote of Solera (a late example of the eighteenth-century adventurer, who was reduced to poverty),

95. Transcript in ibid., 310–11.

It is his fault if he has not had a brilliant career and become the leading operatic poet of our times. Nor can he tell himself that he would not have earned money. If he had chosen to put his mind to it and become *necessary,* he could have gotten himself paid three or four thousand francs for every libretto, plus he could have had a share in the publication of the librettos in every country where the opera was given. I myself sought some time ago to get these earnings for the poets, but I did not succeed. I did not succeed because the librettos were not worth the trouble, but if I could instead have presented a libretto not imitated but of [the author's] invention and with everything it needed to command admiration, it would have been easy to get what we wanted and make the fortunes of the poets. Imagine, for example, if in all countries in which *Trovatore, Traviata,* etc., etc., have been given the poet had gotten even one third on the sale of the librettos! . . . They wouldn't have come off too badly.[96]

Between the eighteenth and the nineteenth centuries, the librettist's work methods changed profoundly, and in ways that reflected his loss of autonomy. The principal interlocutor for the common sort of librettist in the eighteenth century was the impresario more than the composer: it was to the impresario that the poet normally gave the finished libretto (either an original work or a reworking of an older text). Should he be called upon to make changes, it was usually to touch up an individual aria rather than to recast the entire dramatic fabric of the work. Metastasio's suggesting to Hasse how one of his scenes should be set to music was just as exceptional as Metastasio's prestige.[97] A librettist who acted in that manner would have been unthinkable in the nineteenth century, when the composer took the principal responsibility for the opera and it was the composer who advised the librettist or demanded changes in the text and the relocation of lines, stanzas, or entire scenes.

One sign of that tendency in Rossini's day, in a situation substantially similar to that of the eighteenth century, is illustrated in a series of letters written in 1816 by Carlo Porta to his friend Vincenzo Lancetti, a fairly well-known man of letters.[98] Porta was acting as a go-between for the management of the Teatro alla Scala, which, as he stated,

96. Letter to Clarina Maffei of 3 April 1861, quoted from Giuseppe Verdi, *Autobiografia dalle lettere,* ed. Marcello Conati (Milan: Rizzoli, 1981): 315.

97. Letter of 20 October 1749, in Metastasio, *Tutte le opere,* 3:427–36. A few nineteenth-century librettists did make suggestions to composers, however, and one example is Gaetano Rossi; see Maria Giovanna Miggiani, "Di alcuni termini e concetti prescrittivi in Gaetano Rossi," in *Le parole della musica, I: Studi sulla lingua della letteratura musicale in onore di Gianfranco Folena,* ed. Fiamma Nicolodi and Paolo Trovato (Florence: Olschki, 1994), 225–58. In this case Rossi was working with a composer, Alberto Guillion, who was at the start of his career.

98. Letters of September 1816, published in *Le lettere di Carlo Porta e degli amici della cameretta,* ed. Dante Isella (Milan: Ricciardi, 1967), 214–21.

would like to turn your rural leisure to your profit by asking you, through me, to mold the libretto that you are writing according to the norms I have indicated to you on the paper included here. . . . The music is to be composed by Soliva, who will not accept the commission unless he can write it for two female voices. If the subject of the Amazons doesn't give you enough stuff to tailor, think about choosing another appropriate one.

It is thanks to Carlo Soliva—an opera composer who, at the age of twenty-four, had just made a successful debut at La Scala with *La testa di bronzo* (Felice Romani librettist)—that we have the "norms" that Porta enclosed with his letter. Their chief concern was optimum use of the roster of singers at hand.

The book must be adapted for five leading parts, that is

One *prima donna*	la sig.ra Forti
One contralto [a breeches role]	la sig.ra Bassi
One tenor	il s.r Donzelli
Two first basses	li s.ri Galli and Remorini

A good number of ensemble pieces is desired, following the norms of the libretto for *La testa di bronzo,* among these, a duet for the *prima donna* and the contralto and a quintet for the five leading roles.

Avoid having a duet for the two basses.

Work it out so that, as custom dictates, the number of duets, trios, etc., are equal among the five leading parts.

The contralto does not want a cavatina; she likes an entrance duet.

Be as sparing as possible with the secondary roles.

Only three arias each for the contralto, the *prima donna,* and the tenor.

Not too many choruses.

Note that one of the two basses, Galli, is a great actor; the other, Remorini, less of an actor, predominantly a singer.

Brevity is recommended, on the model of *La testa di bronzo.*

The greatest possible speed is recommended for the composition of the libretto, which is to be used for the next carnival season.

Lancetti, promised a generous remuneration, promptly accepted, and if he did not agree to transform his drama into a libretto, at least he agreed to stop writing it to devote his time to a work for La Scala. A few days later Porta, still speaking in the name of the theater management, communicated another of Soliva's desires: "And that you take care, when you write for Bassi, to give her a vibrant character and a good deal of action, since she is extremely touchy, both on principle and by temperament." It is clear that here the composer is not so much the poet's partner as he is a mediator for the demands of the theater management, which are, in the last analysis, the singers' demands. (It is interesting that contrary to what is usually presumed, the singers put pressure on the librettist to give them an opportunity to display their qualities as actors rather than stressing their singing, and that they requested ensembles and action rather than solo arias.) The tendency to make the composer the organizer and coordinator of the various components of the operatic spectacle is also clear. These were the first steps along the road that led to the composer-playwright.

Surviving collections of composers' letters (another indication of their higher place in society) permit a fairly precise idea of their working methods. The genesis of an opera (if not all operas, at least a reasonable number of them) can be summarized as follows: the first phase was the choice of subject, which involved the composer, the theater management, and, only later, the librettist; a prose outline *(selva)* was written up and submitted to the censor's office for approval; then the outline was given to the poet, who worked out the scenes and did the versification, all in close collaboration with the composer. The last phase was the one in which disagreement between the librettist and the composer was most likely to arise, and disagreement was inevitable if the poet obstinately followed his own ideas without taking into account the demands of musical logic.

Few librettists were as submissive and as sincerely devoted to a composer as Gaetano Rossi was to Meyerbeer. When he was getting ready to write the libretto for an opera that was to be called *Malek Adel* (but was never completed), Rossi promised Meyerbeer, "As soon as I receive 'Matilde,' I will read it and make my scene division and my outline [*ossatura*], which I will immediately submit to you so that you can make the opportune observations and exceptions, can pass on the layout, and give your approval." [99] Very soon, however, despite the enthusiasm with which he had set to work, and despite his sensitivity to Meyerbeer's musical demands, Rossi was treated to Meyerbeer's rebukes when his outline was late to arrive. Rossi defended himself:

> You wrongly reproach me of laziness and slowness. . . . A job of this scope, of this difficulty, requires that everything mature fully; it demands careful study in the choice and connection between events [in the action]—sometimes detached from one another, very often opposed to one another, and all so interesting; it demands a free mind. [This is] a task that interests me more than any other, and one to which I attach more of my amour propre. I cannot—I do not know how to—hurry it along in a few days. I must not do so, for you, and for me. [100]

Rossi felt the pride of creation and of artistic paternity, to the point that he wrote, "'Matilde,' that interesting daughter of our hearts, belongs to me too." [101]

99. Letter of 8 April 1823, in Meyerbeer, *Briefwechsel und Tagebücher,* 1:469–70.
100. Letter of 18 April, in ibid., 478.
101. Letter of 6 July 1823, in ibid., 510.

The artistic partnership between Romani and Bellini was one of the most fertile and long lasting in all of opera history. Few traces remain of this relationship in Bellini's letters, but those few do not show any excessive deference on the young composer's part toward a poet who had already made his reputation.

> Romani has not yet arrived, which disturbs me. Still, I hope everything will go well, because I have already sketched out the music—that is, the cabalettas and the andantes—and all I have to do is write them out. . . . Yesterday evening with [Adelaide] Tosi we worked out all the bravura passages (few as they are) in those two pieces, and all that is left is to put them together, whenever Romani—that blessed Romani—gives me the stretta for the scene and rewrites for me the poetry of the cavatina, which I have already composed on another [text but] whose expression of sentiment I did not like.[102]

It is true that after *Norma* Bellini deigned to call Romani "my worthy and favorite poet,"[103] but two years later he wrote, "I hope not to find myself at the end of my tether, as it always happens with Romani, the prince of sluggards."[104] This remark referred to the opera that Bellini was to write for Paris (and that later became *I puritani*), but a quarrel with Romani obliged Bellini to turn to Count Carlo Pepoli, a political exile and a friend of Leopardi's, about whom Bellini wrote, "I hope he will succeed, and perhaps very well, because he is capable of making fine verse and has a facility for it."[105]

The count's first drafts seem to have dispersed fears that Bellini may really have held deep in his heart.[106] Several days later the idyll had already ended, however, and Pepoli received a lesson in elementary operatic poetics.

> Do not forget to bring with you the piece already sketched out so that we can talk definitively about the first act, which, if you arm yourself with a healthy dose of philosophical patience, will turn out to be interesting, magnificent, and worthy poetry for music, in spite of you and all your absurd rules. . . . If my music turns out to be beautiful and the opera is well liked, you can write a million letters against

---

102. Io Francesco Florimo, [March 1828] and 24 March 1828, in Vincenzo Bellini, *Epistolario,* ed. Luisa Cambi (Milan: Mondadori, 1943), 60, 68.

103. To Giuseppe Ruggieri, 6 October 1832, in ibid., 324.

104. To Filippo Santocanale, 14 February 1834, in ibid., 387.

105. To Francesco Florimo, 11 March 1834, in ibid., 391. In the same letter Bellini wrote of Romani, "Tell me now why the administration [of the Teatro San Carlo] or the association does not sign up Romani, not for one libretto only but by the year, calculating a thousand francs per libretto, on the understanding that he come to live in Naples. In that way he would write the libretto for me, as the sole poet belonging to the theater, and if they want to negotiate this they can give me the commission. I should like to render good for ill to that person with a bad head but much talent."

106. See the letter to Carlo Pepoli, 30 May 1834, in ibid., 402–3.

composers' abuse of poetry, etc., and you will not have proven anything. Facts, not chitchat. . . . It is a defect to want to treat all the pieces equally; but it is a necessity that they all be in some way fashioned so as to render the music intelligible with the clarity of their expression, [which must be] as concise as it is striking. Musical artifices kill the effect of the plot; poetic artifices in a libretto are even worse. . . . Do you know why I told you that a good drama is one that does not make good sense? Because I know full well what an intractable beast a man of letters is, and how absurd his rules of good sense are: what I say about the fine arts is proven in practice, because the better part of your celebrities have been trapped by effect. Mamiani said as much of Alfieri the other evening.[107]

A month later Bellini was nostalgic for his former librettist: "Tell my dear Romani that, cruel as he is, I love him still. . . . There is another poet here who is enamored of me, but Count Pepoli cannot ever hope to replace Romani; that would be impossible."[108] That did not mean that Bellini thought that Romani's verse could be credited with illuminating his inspiration: to the contrary, as he confided to his friend Francesco Florimo, "Romani is worth nothing away from me; what is more, he was born to jeopardize all unwitting composers."[109] With Pepoli, however, things were going from bad to worse.

If you only knew what I have suffered and am suffering to get Pepoli to move along! It is incredible; his character is curious. He puts all his effort into the play of poetic combinations—or, to put it better, into a certain kind of repartee—that makes me lose patience. Between us, I think him totally dry of expressions that have any real consistency, and of sentiments. For that reason he struggles along as best he can, not in making verses the way he wants but in making verses in my fashion, which are those that depict the passions more from life.[110]

Donizetti also complained on several occasions of Romani's slowness, but, a milder man than Bellini, he avoided ripping into him.

The fault must be mine if Romani has not produced, for not having known how to kindle enough friendship in him. . . . And if Romani still has not given me the libretto for Paris by the beginning of July, please tell him, in a friendly way, that I do not hold it against him—but at least I will be calm and turn my ideas elsewhere.[111]

107. To Carlo Pepoli, undated, in ibid., 399–400. This letter is published in the Cambi edition of Bellini's letters before the one cited in the preceding note, but its contents suggest that it was written later. The letters are published in that order in *Le lettere di Bellini*, ed. Francesco Pastura (Catania: Totalità, 1935), 158–59.

108. Letter to an unknown person, 11 July 1834, in Bellini, *Epistolario*, 411.

109. To Francesco Florimo, 4 August 1834, in ibid., 422.

110. Ibid., 421–22.

111. Letter to Giovanni Ricordi, 23 May 1834, in Guido Zavadini, *Donizetti: Vita, musiche, epistolario* (Bergamo: Istituto Italiano d'Arti Grafiche, 1948), 352.

The fact is that Donizetti caught his poets up in his own frantic pace, and at least once Romani had to read him a lesson of his own on serious professional behavior.

> As for the *reminders* you honor me with, I thought that they had been consigned to oblivion. Nonetheless, if I remember well a good many recriminations would be in order, and they always will until *maestri di musica* can be persuaded that the time they need to do a good job is equally—and perhaps more—necessary to the poets. To the good poets, that is, not the scribblers who, to our misfortune, are sprouting up all over Italy like weeds.[112]

One cannot say that Romani was wrong, but it is true that librettists, in pursuing their own poetic aspirations, forgot the concrete, petty demands of everyday theatrical practice, to the point that Donizetti was persuaded that "whoever drinks from the spring of Hippocrene swears eternal hatred of pecuniary matters." This time the object of his desperation was Jacopo Ferretti, one of the most prolific and expert libretto writers of the time.

> Good lord! What nonsense has our friend Ferretti come up with now? Five pieces? And what kind of pieces? He comes along merrily with *Latinum grossum,* while I answer him in *Italianum picculum* that we will really have a long job of it with all this stuff, and that if we did, it would give me the greatest displeasure. This miserable Ferretti comes dancing along with a chorus and cavatina, a chorus and aria, a chorus and duet, a chorus and *introduzione,* and a choral chorus, when we don't have any *choruses.*[113]

It would be wasted effort to retrace once more Verdi's working relations with his librettists; his recommendations for clarity and stripped-down dramatic intensity are so well known that they have become almost proverbial. They are summed up in a sentence he wrote to Antonio Ghislanzoni: "Unfortunately for the theater, poets and composers sometimes need to have the talent not to make either poetry or music."[114] Throughout his life Verdi sought librettists willing to execute his dramatic will blindly. His masterpiece in this sense was of course Piave. When Verdi wrote, "I have the weakness to think . . . that *Rigoletto* is one of the finest librettos in existence—except for the poetry," he was praising himself.[115]

112. Letter of 23 November 1841, in ibid., 890.

113. To Antonio Vasselli, 7 October 1823, in ibid., 239.

114. Letter of 17 August 1870, in Giuseppe Verdi, *I copialettere di Giuseppe Verdi,* ed. Gaetano Cesari and Alessandro Luzio (Milan: Stucchi, Ceretti, 1913; reprint, Bologna: Arnaldo Forni, 1968), 641.

115. To Cesare de Sanctis, 7 February 1856, in *Carteggi verdiani,* ed. Alessandro Luzio (Rome: Reale Accademia d'Italia, 1935), 1:32.

Still, as we have seen, Piave liked to be presented as a "man of letters," and he had written serious literary studies in Rome in the late 1830s. During his first, tormented collaboration with Verdi, Piave wrote to his friend Ferretti:

> Oh! Why aren't you here? Your theatrical experience and your friendship would be balm to this poor novice poet. In seventy days I have had to write two opera seria librettos. The first, *Cromvello,* was found not sufficiently spectacular; this obliged me to write the second, which is entitled *Ernani..* . . . I think I have finished, but when my maestro Verdi (I only know him by name) arrives in town, I foresee that there will be the usual annoyances of changes, cuts, etc. etc. etc. Patience! I will be paid 100 florins apiece for these two dramas; it's in my contract. For a beginner that's not bad.[116]

Piave then added a transcription of the first version of the "Chorus of the Spanish Conspirators." He concluded, "I hope that the maestro of *Nabucco* and *I Lombardi* will find some *inspiration* in this verse."

Immediately after the premiere, Piave was totally (or nearly totally) converted to seeing things as "his" maestro saw them: "I am still moved by the great success obtained by these scenes of my poor *Ernani;* garbed, however, by the divine Verdi with such musical richness that even I, their own poor father, would suspect that I have a wealthy son." However, Piave's admiration for Verdi did not totally eliminate his fundamentally eighteenth-century concept of operatic creation (as in "my" *Ernani* and his reference to its being "garbed" with music).

Nearly all of Verdi's librettists (Salvadore Cammarano and Antonio Somma in particular) fostered literary ambitions, but probably the only librettist whose literary prestige gave pause to Verdi, and the only one unable, or unwilling, to bend to the composer's orders, was Andrea Maffei. The result was the libretto least in tune with Verdi's dramatic ideals, *I masnadieri.* The two men did not quarrel and they remained friends, but Verdi did not ask Maffei to work with him again, with the exception of a few verses that he used in *La forza del destino.*

In this examination of the relationship between librettists and composers in the nineteenth century, we have heard the composer often, but only a few timid protests or bursts of wounded pride from the librettist. This does not mean that librettists, particularly those of the generation closest to the eighteenth century, never made public statements of self-justification, self-pity, or self-reassurance, or that they never retraced the history of opera as the history

---

116. Letter of 13 November 1843. This and the following quotations are taken from a group of Piave's unpublished letters to Ferretti in Bruno Cagli, "'Questo povero poeta exordiente': Piave a Roma, un carteggio con Ferretti, la genesi di *Ernani,*" *Bollettino dell'Istituto di Studi Verdiani,* no. 10, *Ernani* (Parma: Istituto di Studi Verdiani, 1987).

18. The opulent caryatids flanking and framing the poster for the world premiere of Ponchielli's *La Gioconda* signal the period of transition from the opera poster as an informative message to an image with great power of suggestion and seduction.

19. Pictures have an informative function of their own. Under the archaeological motifs of the framing frieze and the title, at the lower right, this poster for Verdi's *Aida* shows one of the sets for the opera, the Temple of Isis in the third act. (Venice, Archivio del Teatro La Fenice)

20. Accumulated written information, informative images, and decoration could produce an effect of *horror vacui,* as in this crowded poster for the season's offerings in Ferrara in 1884–85. (Ferrara, Biblioteca Ariostea; photo: Sergio Guerra)

21. Opera seasons were offered increasingly as celebrations of patriotic occasions and anniversaries connected with Italy's glorious past. In this case it is noteworthy that below the portrait of Christopher Columbus, the personality being celebrated, appears not his name but that of the theater's managers, Piontelli and Co. (Genoa, Archivio Sagep Editrice)

22. Superabundant decoration was often combined with the truly physical opulence of the figures portrayed: here Music and pudgy musician cherubs seem to promise the spectators an Eden of earthly rather than spiritual pleasures. (By gracious permission, Edizioni LINT, Trieste)

23. In a poster that displays a clear preference for innovation in typography and conception, the elegant, spare design nonetheless carries a wealth of references and symbolic allusions. In this production at the Teatro Comunale of Trieste, Wagner's *Tristan* was given in Italian, as it always was in Italy until World War II. (By gracious permission, Edizioni LINT, Trieste)

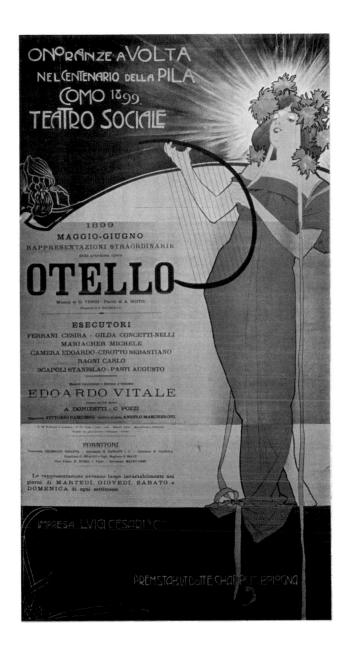

24. Another poster of extraordinary elegance, which shows Music almost in a priestly attitude (but is she a druidess? a vestal?) in an image borrowed from the pictorial tradition of opera.

25. In this poster for the celebration of the centenary of Verdi's birth held at Parma in 1913, the density of printed information has an equally busy pictorial accompaniment of theatrical and propagandistic commonplaces: the city, the theater, the public, the appeal of tradition, the fascination with progress. And, naturally, the effigy of the composer in a medallion (Verdi almost seems to have a halo) surrounded by a symbolic assemblage of laurel, horns, a lyre, and the Italian flag. The poster seems to have borrowed its effects and celebratory intent from one of those *macchine di gloria*—elaborate stage machines—so typical of seventeenth-century stage design. (Busseto, Collection Stefanini; photo: Studio Tosi, Parma)

26. In this poster for the celebrations of the Verdi centenary in Busseto, his home town, the composer is presented in what appears to be a faithful and nearly photographic portrait. The exaggerated scale makes his figure tower over the city in the background and makes him seem its patron saint. (Milan, Archivio Ricordi)

27. The "seasons" at the Amphitheater of Verona were inaugurated with this exciting image of Radamès, who "returns triumphant." The style of the poster reflects operatic gesture and transmits not so much information as an emotional state. (By gracious permission, Edizioni LINT, Trieste)

28. The 1913 Radamès in plate 27 belonged to the Belle Epoque; this 1924 Parsifal, again, at the Amphitheater of Verona, comes from the iconoclastic climate of the 1920s. Still, like Radamès, he raises his armed hand in sign of victory: conventional operatic gestures seem to have persisted, indifferent to passing time and changing composers, operas, and themes. (By gracious permission, Edizioni LINT, Trieste)

ANFITEATRO
DI VERONA

STAGIONE LIRICA 1924
DAL FINE LUGLIO
A METÀ AGOSTO
GRANDIOSE
ESECUZIONI

PARSIFAL

M.° SERGIO FAILONI

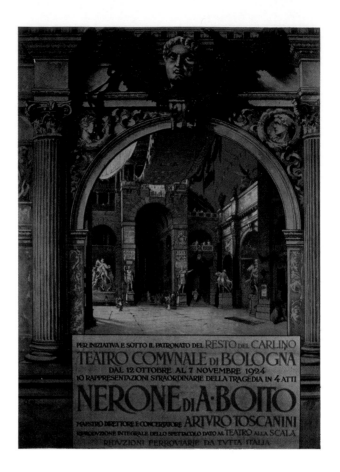

29, 30. The architecture of the stage set is integrated here into the architecture of the poster for Boito's *Nerone,* creating a singular mixture of truth and fiction. The scene (act 4, the Oppidum of ancient Rome) shows an imaginary—or at least reinvented—city as it was actually staged in a real theater (the Teatro Comunale of Bologna). Looking at this poster the viewers would have the illusion of being seated in the theater but also of being drawn under the arch to enter the "real" city. (By gracious permission, Edizioni LINT, Trieste.) Unlike the "impresario's" poster, which announced to the public the production of one or more works at a specific place and time, the "publisher's" poster displayed and publicized a work in itself, independent of the place, time, and circumstances of its production. The latter had obvious economic advantages, as the same poster could be widely circulated, used, and reused. This format was also particularly prestigious and gratifying for the publisher, as his name appeared beside those of the "poet" and the composer, forming a perfect theatrical trinity. At the same time, publicity posters moved from a crowded layout of printed information, images, and decorative elements to concentrate on one emblematic figure. In this poster for Franchetti's *La figlia di Iorio,* the artist—Alfredo de Carolis—has pictured Mila in flight against a whirling background of the harvest, visually anticipating her destiny of passion and death. (Milan, Archivio Ricordi)

31. Here, in a poster for Montemezzi's *Héllera*, is another image of a title figure in an extenuated, floral, and languorous rapture. The gesture, lighting effects, and even the furnishings pictured recall images from silent film, at the time in its infancy. However, it was the cinema that took over operatic images and used them for its own purposes, not vice versa (there are famous images of the Italian film star Pina Menichelli with her head thrown back in much the same way as this). (Milan, Archivio Ricordi)

32. This poster by Adolfo Hohenstein, isolating the key scene of Puccini's *Tosca* and heightening (if that is possible) its dramatic expression with telling communicative force, illustrates the "publisher's" poster at its best and most concise. Rarely if ever in the history of this quite particular sort of publicity has there been such total identity between image and message. (Milan, Archivio Ricordi)

33. The anonymous designer of this "publisher's" poster has chosen to stress the exotic and decorative aspects of Puccini's *Turandot*. This enigmatic image is something of a point of arrival in the long tradition of Chinese themes in opera: that land had been shown at times as a place of fantastic, bizarre happenings; at times a place of elite intellectual egalitarianism; at times a somber mixture of exquisite refinement and equally exquisite tortures. Here the problem is solved with an individualistic concentration on the personage, closed within a cocoon of frigidity, but seeming about to burst into lyrical effusions of sentiment. (Milan, Archivio Ricordi)

of operatic poetry. That view was, of course, a way to shore up an identity that was fast dissolving and to reinforce such mythical commonplaces of a privileged condition as the Florentine Camerata and, above all, Metastasio, the admired and envied paragon for writers who were by then far removed from his stylistic model.

What these librettists' writing lacked was the eighteenth-century polemic verve, which had given way to a diffused sense of resignation. In the face of the irresistible ascendancy of the composer, the librettist's greatest glory was now to have favored, or even inspired, that success with his verse.

Giuseppe Foppa, born in Venice in 1760, wrote his memoirs in 1840.[117] From his youth Foppa had been in contact with musical circles in Venice, where he knew Baldassare Galuppi in his old age and Ferdinando Bertoni, and where, as he put it, he was given an "opportunity to second my innate talent for music."[118] He studied singing, after which he began "to sniff out opera as a theatrical poet."[119] Taking up poetry did not mean that he gave up displaying his "talent for music"; when he wrote his first libretto he noted,

> While the composer was setting the libretto to music, some difficulties arose with the aria for the *seconda donna,* who was his "friend," and he wanted me to change it. When I held my ground [insisting] that my poetry would give any composer musical ideas, he responded resentfully, annoyed by my insistence, . . . "Set it to music yourself, signor maestro." Begging him to calm down and offering to change it, I sang my own music to those words. Such was the astonishment and acceptance of this maestro that he deigned to seize upon the musical ideas I had put forth by writing a lovely arietta, and he offered to teach me counterpoint, maintaining that from what I had sung to him, improvising, I would turn out to be a good composer with study.[120]

With such a start it is hardly surprising that Foppa declared himself principally responsible for the success of a number of famous composers.

> And here it is opportune to note that the glory of having introduced to the world a *maestro di cappella* who has brought great honor to Italy and continues to do so, and who can rightfully be called a *first-class composer* was all mine. This composer is signor Simon Mayr.[121]

Rossini, now justly honored with the title of *cavaliere,* who lords it over the

---

117. *Memorie storiche della vita di Giuseppe M.ᵃ Foppa viniziano già primo protocollista di consiglio di questo I. R. Tribunale criminale scritte da lui medesimo* (Venice, 1840). The *Memorie storiche* were followed by an *Appendice alle memorie storiche* (Venice, 1842).
118. *Memorie storiche,* 18.
119. Ibid., 21.
120. Ibid., 26–27.
121. Ibid., 22.

music profession, for which he earns the admiration and the delight of all the theaters of Europe, had in his early days composed for the theater of San Moisè . . . a farce entitled (if memory serves me) *Una cambiale di matrimonio* that met with little success. [When I was] called to write for that same theater the following year, he set to music my farce, *L'inganno felice*, a clamorous success that is still remembered, that later brought him to the eminence he still enjoys, and that will never decline. Since he has risen to such great glory on words I have written, I am proud to have taken part in some way in an event that created and will continue to create a luminous era for *teatro in musica*.[122]

Ferretti left in manuscript a lecture on the history of poetry in Roman opera that he read in 1834 before the Accademia Tiberina.[123] Ferretti, the librettist of *La Cenerentola*, regarded the contemporary scene as an advance over the profound decadence of the last twenty years of the eighteenth century and the early years of the nineteenth century. As custom dictated in eighteenth-century journalism, he saw the causes of that decline "in the goodness of the public, which was a bit too indulgent, in the tyranny of the eunuchs, which was nauseating; in the lack of culture in the old theatrical versifiers, which was deplorable."[124]

The proliferating brood of mediocre and worse poets, Ferretti continued, obliterated the example of the great librettists of the past: the first of these was Zeno, who, just as "Descartes was the blow of steel that put sparks to the mind of Newton," had prepared the way for the inimitable Metastasio.

In his earliest works Metastasio did not strive to emancipate himself completely from the taste that was in fashion in those days, yet as soon as his first footprint was seen, everyone was moved to cry out, "He is a giant." You should give heartfelt thanks to those stupid people who unfairly attacked him in his own country, because if he had been able to earn ten scudi a month, perhaps instead of first dramatic poet he would have remained next to last among jurists or last among bookkeepers. . . . He appeared and envy burst out against him; he appeared and was whisked away to the Ister [the Danube]. Most happy abduction, which gave Italy a poet without equal among the ancients and who still awaits his equal among the moderns. He flew to the Ister, and the mediocre returned to the field; and then they butchered his dramas, either to serve the fantasies of *virtuosi* in name only or to

122. Ibid., 25. Foppa was not alone in claiming this sort of glory for himself. Gaetano Rossi, in a "Pagina autobiografica," calls himself "the hardest-working librettist of our times. . . . Rossini was born, and he began with words by Rossi in a farce in San Moisè. . . . He became immortal with *Semiramide,* also by Rossi. The great Maestro always drew advantages and honors from his high priest of words"; quoted in Daniela Goldin, *La vera fenice: Librettisti e libretti tra Sette e Ottocento* (Turin: Einaudi, 1985), 208.

123. Jacopo Ferretti, "Sulla storia della poesia melodrammatica romana," unpublished lecture, with notes by Alberto Cametti, extracted in *Cronaca musicale,* 1, nos. 6–7 (1896).

124. Ibid., 10.

shorten the recitatives. . . . Roccaforte, Casini, Pizzi, Mallio, Carminati—all mediocre talents—extinguished (or at least attempted to extinguish) the sacred flame lit
by Metastasio.[125]

Now, Ferretti continued, the situation was better, thanks to a new generation
of poets, first among them the learned Cesare Sterbini, who "immediately
was able to make use of the new pacts established between the audience and
the poets."

> He emerged in an epoch in which the *musici* [castratos] had undergone a second
> operation; their belated exile from our stages . . . one in which scenic designers
> began to be dependent on the instructions of the librettists . . . and the name of
> dramatic poet was not synonymous with cobbler. . . . And Bertati, Da Ponte,
> Cencelli, Giambattista da Montefiascone, Calzabigi, and Berio ennobled that art
> with the eloquence of their example and showed the world that they could be pro-
> foundly literate and reputed writers and, at the same time, theatrical poets.[126]

Despite all this, Ferretti lamented, operatic poetry in Rome "even in our days
is far—alas!—from enjoying the luminous fortune with which it was ennobled by sublime concepts of the Thyrtaeus, the Anacreon, the Pindar of Ligu-
ria, my venerated master [Felice Romani], the writer of *Norma, La parisina,
Ismalia,* and *Caterina di Guisa.*"[127]

Felice Romani was, in fact, the only nineteenth-century librettist who was
admired both in his lifetime and after his death and whose works could aspire
to the dignity of being considered classics. He left an apologia in the form of
a funeral monument to his honor, for such is the biography produced by his
wife, Emilia Branca (who was much younger than he), some twenty years
after his death. This work, which is written with such bias as to require extreme caution when used as a source of information, undoubtedly reflects a
good many of Romani's own ideas and opinions.

Indeed, Branca used Romani's own words to present a brief history of
opera that fits the mold of eighteenth-century criticism to perfection, including opera's mythical origins in Greece and a stigmatization of seventeenth-
century decadence. Afterward,

> Lyric poetry languished and wilted to such an extent that it would have died and
> been buried if Apostolo Zeno had not rescued it in its death throes and so to speak
> cured it in order then to transmit it into the hands of Pietro Metastasio, whose task
> it was to rejuvenate it and return it, splendid and beautiful, to its former royal
> throne.[128]

125. Ibid, 25–26.
126. Ibid., 30–31.
127. Ibid., 10.
128. Branca, *Felice Romani,* 110–11.

A recurrent idea in Branca's book is that Romani was the nineteenth-century Metastasio. The court in Vienna was simply giving him his due when, "appreciating the dignity and the sweetness of his poetry, it invited him there to occupy the position of imperial poet, the same in which Metastasio had shone . . . and lived, wealthy and blessed, and whose genius all recognized in Romani, his heir."[129] Although Romani was enough of a patriot to refuse the offer, the myth of the court poet undeniably still warmed his heart.

With the opinions of Vittorio Bersezio and Pacini to back her up,[130] Branca asserted,

> [in Romani] one saw Metastasio's lyrical form united with Zeno's tragic [form]; one saw music and poetry come together again in the firmest brotherhood; [one saw] elegant verse, sweet, melodic [poetry] overflowing with sentiment, inspire composers to melody. Zeno and Metastasio, united in one, gave complete drama.[131]

Branca's portrait of her late husband dwelled almost obsessively on another idea: an entire generation of composers added new gems to the faded splendor of Italian opera because they were inspired by Romani's verse, for it already contained their music. Leaving aside what Romani's biographer had to say about his relations with Donizetti, Saverio Mercadante, Meyerbeer, and many others, the composer that Romani considered almost his creature was Bellini. It was Romani who had counseled Bellini in his first, uncertain moves and who, intuiting his talent, had recommended him to the leading theaters. Romani is quoted as saying,

> I alone penetrated that poetic soul, that impassioned heart, that mind desirous of flying above the sphere to which both school rules and servile imitation constrained him, and it was then that I wrote for Bellini *Il pirata*, a subject that seemed to me apt to touch, so to speak, the most responsive chord in his heart, nor was I mistaken.[132]

We have already seen what Bellini thought of Romani. Nonetheless, from the poet's viewpoint Bellini, "more than any other, protested, with his characteristic candor and ingenuousness, that *his glory could not be separated from Romani's poetry.*"[133] Moreover, Bellini felt the "need to have Romani's dra-

129. Ibid., 27.
130. For Bersezio, ibid., 25–26; for Pacini, ibid., 100–101.
131. Ibid., 118.
132. Ibid., 128–29.
133. Ibid., 134–35.

mas, and he needed to find himself at the side of his friend the poet, from whom he drew wise counsel, strength, and inspiration."[134]

Romani's biography mentions Giuseppe Verdi only incidentally and with forced courtesy as it discusses the "most reputed masters of music" of the day. Similarly Piave's name does not figure among the librettists, good or bad, who were Romani's contemporaries, except for one acid comment on hearing *Ernani,* when Romani, thinking of the aborted project of the same title with Bellini, purportedly exclaimed, "Oh, what a pity, what a pity! . . . Such a fine subject, and so badly handled!"[135] Admittedly a poet who was still dreaming of an ideal beauty would have seen Verdian opera as the epitome of the new romantic fury that he deplored in the generation following his own. Still, we cannot exclude the possibility that the coupling of Verdi's and Piave's names brought home to Romani the more disagreeable reality that opera had left behind it, once and for all, any illusion of being "born of the spirit of poetry."

5. From the Nineteenth to the Twentieth Century

Antonio Ghislanzoni, the librettist of *Aida* and many other operas, wrote *L'arte di far libretti* in the form of a libretto that was perhaps the last descendant of the eighteenth-century satirical tradition.[136] The premiere of *Aida* (1871) can well serve as the starting point for the high season of Italian opera as it had developed since the 1640s—the years of Verdi's last works and the operas of the "young school"—with the premiere of *Turandot* (1926) marking its end point. Within the same period the opera house changed from a place of living, ongoing, regularly renewed production to a museum, a place in which to find the great monuments of the past, some ghosts of those monuments, and now and then experiments in musical theater of varying quality that have little in common with operatic tradition.

During this same time span, the parabola of the librettist's rise and fall traced in these pages reached its end. It was not an inglorious end; to the contrary, it showed signs of a decided recovery from the decline of previous decades.

The long-standing war between the man of letters and the world of opera

---

134. Ibid., 182. Romani had managed to plant the same notion in the minds of his circle, as seen in the verse of Andrea Maffei (ibid., 41) and Francesco Regli (ibid., 57): "Oh! di Bellini il vate / colui che lo ispirò . . ." (Oh! Bellini's bard, who inspired him).

135. Ibid., 157.

136. Antonio Ghislanzoni, *L'arte di far libretti,* an "opera serio-buffa" in three acts, in Ghislanzoni, *Libro allegro* (Milan: Tipografia Editrice Lombarda, 1878), 73–111. See also the series of "Conversazioni musicali" by Ghislanzoni that appeared serially in *La gazzetta musicale di Milano* in 1866.

ended with a truce honorable for both sides. One of the reasons for this truce was opera's return to an ideal of literary dignity that had been almost entirely lost during the nineteenth century. Before 1925 the lack of interest in Verdi's early works on the part of critics was due, among other things, to the fact that "modern taste" found the style of Piave and Cammarano's librettos unacceptable; Arrigo Boito's librettos, to the contrary, seemed artistic productions worthy of full respect. Moreover, the composer, now definitively removed from the workman category and given a role approaching that of the intellectual, had become cultivated, and he demanded librettos not only guaranteed to work well on the stage but also ennobled by literary diction. Whatever one might think about the supposed corruption of taste that Boito caused in Verdi, it is certain that in 1887 Verdi would never have accepted an *Otello* in the style of *Rigoletto* ("one of the finest librettos in existence—except for the poetry"). One critic, who saw *I puritani* as an Italian example of modern musical drama, added, "Certainly, if Bellini were still alive today, we would begin by rejecting that absurd libretto . . . in which you do not know which is worse, the awkward form or the puerile action."[137]

The increasing diffusion not only of Wagner's operas but also of his ideas and tastes counted for much in that change in taste. After experiencing the Wagnerian music drama (albeit if only in the Italian versions of Pietro Floridia and Angelo Zanardini, which still bear traces of the traditional libretto styles), there remained little doubt among composers of the need for a literary text with full and autonomous validity—even among those who were far from subscribing to the "music of the future."

The Wagner phenomenon was an event in the literary world as well: for the first time in history, a composer in his own right had not only been welcomed into the sacred precincts of culture but shaped an entire phase of European literary taste. With Wagner opera officially became a work of art—better, the work of art of the future—in which the man of letters could participate with no harm to his conscience as an intellectual.

Relations between literature and music had changed, but Wagner's influence was neither the decisive nor the earliest factor. When "modern music drama" was debated in some circles, the phrase referred to the French operas of Meyerbeer. Not all of the group of artists who were conveniently grouped under the label *scapigliati* ("longhairs"; bohemians) were Wagnerians. Giuseppe Rovani, a tenacious champion of Rossinian taste and a man who distrusted Verdi's "ultramontanism," was no Wagnerian, nor was Ghislanzoni. Even Boito's relations with Wagner were ambiguous, with suspicion decidedly prevailing over persuasion.

Something deeper was on foot in which Wagner entered later as a catalyz-

137. Leone Fortis (Dottor Veritas), *Conversazioni della domenica* (Milan, 1877), 170.

ing element: lyric opera was dominated by the indisputable and overpowering cultural presence of the canonical "quartet"—Rossini, Bellini, Donizetti, and Verdi. It was that presence that enabled Rovani to assert,

> What proves the mental superiority of Vincenzo Bellini is his having contributed . . . to putting his art on the same road as the sister arts. No one can aspire to first place in an art unless he can make himself the evident and concrete expression of the century's and the nation's vague aspirations, which are sedimented in confusion in the great reservoir of the multitude.[138]

The parallel progress of the various arts was a recurrent theme in Rovani's criticism; it repeated a commonplace of eighteenth-century debate, but even in 1830 it would have been unthinkable to write a comparative history of the arts in Italy in which Rossini was explicitly compared to Alessandro Manzoni.[139]

This picture was, however, not only too simplistic but excessively optimistic. It spoke of intent; in reality the truce between the man of letters and the composer was neither immediate nor free of doubts, suspicions, and on occasion renewed hostilities. This was, of course, because opera as practiced by Verdi in his last years and by Mascagni, Giacomo Puccini, and Umberto Giordano—for all its more or less legitimate aspirations to artistic dignity— had not yet given up trying to communicate with a broad public, nor had it ceased to be a good source of income: to the contrary, it was at the peak of its profitability. Occasions for conflict multiplied when, in search of literary ennoblement, a composer turned to a prestigious writer—even more so when the latter had his own coherent vision of the dramatic art. It is not by accident that Gabriele D'Annunzio collaborated more successfully with Mascagni than with Puccini,[140] even though we might instinctively think that Puccini would have been better disposed toward D'Annunzio's decadent preciosity or even have had a certain affinity for it.

Arrigo Boito is emblematic of the aspirations and contradictions of this period. Both poet and composer, he personified the new ideal of the total artist, the creator of a new, unified form of musical drama. In his younger, more bellicose years, he proclaimed,

---

138. Giuseppe Rovani, *Le tre arti considerate in alcuni illustri italiani contemporanei*, 2 vols. (Milan, 1874), 2:42.

139. Ibid., 31.

140. Not that Mascagni was completely bereft of perceptive notions of dramatic art: on his clear view of the difficulties in setting to music Giovanni Verga's *La lupa*, see his letter to Giulio Ricordi of 1895 cited by Mario Morini during a roundtable on opera librettos reported in *Teatro dell'Italia unita, Atti dei convegni, Firenze, 10–11 decembre 1977, 4–6 novembre 1978*, ed. Siro Ferrone (Milan: Il Saggiatore, 1980), 299–300.

The time for a change of style has arrived, and the form that the other arts have achieved on a large scale must also take place in our discipline; the time of its virility is ripe; let it remove its praetexta and be covered with the toga; let it change name and shape, and instead of saying *libretto*, a belittling term of conventional art, may we call it and may we write *tragedy*, as with the Greeks. . . . Today it is not to be taken for granted that beautiful or good music can be made not only on a bad *libretto* but on any libretto at all.[141]

What emerges from Boito's words is a danger that lurked for all of his generation—dilettantism; the lack of an energizing and commercial daily routine and of practical experience in the theater. This was what had provided the traditional opera composer (including Wagner) with his most profound doctrine, and it was something that could not be replaced with good intentions. In Boito's case a personal weakness in musical inspiration combined with dilettantism.

Things came to a head with the clamorous failure in 1868 of his *Mefistofele*, a work whose musical structure was perhaps ill suited to a text that aimed at being the operatic equivalent of Goethe's poem. In 1875 the opera had its second baptism in the version that would enter into the repertory— not surprisingly, since Boito's changes reduced the philosophical dimension of the text and made it more like a conventional libretto. It was not in vain that he had spent years writing librettos (and other works) under the pseudonym of Tobia Gorrio (an anagram of Arrigo Boito).

Still, Boito never resolved the dualism inherent in his conceptions of the libretto and the opera. His friend Leone Fortis—himself a librettist, a stage manager at La Scala for many years, a dramatist, and a critic—realized as much. In his review of Boito's libretto for *La Gioconda* (1876), Fortis first praised the poetry, then stated reservations about the text "as lyric drama; as a libretto for music."[142] He thought the libretto contained "too much confusion, too much and too anxious a search for variety, for spectacle, for grandiosity, at the expense of truth, clarity, simplicity. . . . Perhaps the stage will prove me wrong. . . . So much the better! The libretto will still have a poetic form to its credit, which I wish for its musical setting."[143]

Fortis concluded his review with an invitation "to Tobia Gorrio to stop writing for others, and to think about getting his friend Arrigo Boito to work for himself."[144] Fortis touched on a sore point here: writing librettos for other composers, oscillating indecisively between music and literature, continually

---

141. Arrigo Boito, "Cronaca musicale," *La perseveranza* (13 September 1863), now in his *Opere*, ed. Mario Lavagetto (Milan: Garzanti, 1979), 126–27.

142. Fortis, *Conversazioni*, 213–26, esp. 219.

143. Ibid., 221–25.

144. Ibid., 225.

putting off and never completing the gigantic task of his opera *Nerone,* all bore the signs of a crisis of creativity bordering on impotence. Boito was perfectly aware of this; the letter that he wrote to Verdi in April 1884, as Verdi was hard at work on *Otello,* was a bitter but extremely lucid confession on the part of an artist who felt himself incapable of translating his own imaginary world into reality and who, not unlike the modest Piave, entrusted the future memory of his own name to a collaboration with a composer whom he had scorned when he was a younger man.

> My great wish . . . is to hear your music to a libretto I wrote only for the joy of seeing you pick up your pen again *through my efforts,* for the glory of being your working companion, for the ambition of hearing my name linked with yours, and our names with that of Shakespeare. . . . You alone can compose *Otello;* all the theater that you have given us affirms this truth. If I have been able to sense the powerful musical possiblilities of the Shakespearian tragedy, which I did not feel before, and if I have been able to prove it in deed with my libretto, it is because I worked from the point of view of Verdian art.

A journalistic misunderstanding had attributed to Boito a regret that he himself could not set *Otello* to music, and Verdi, in one of his typically theatrical gestures, declared himself willing to give back the libretto. When the misunderstanding had been cleared up, Boito commented,

> Maestro, what you cannot suspect is the irony I felt in that offer, through no fault of yours. You see, for seven or eight years now perhaps I have been working on *Nerone* (put the "perhaps" where you like, next to the word "years" or the word "working"). I am oppressed by that incubus: on the days when I do not work I spend hours calling myself lazy; on the days when I do work I call myself an ass; and so my life flows on and I continue existing, slowly asphyxiated by an Ideal too lofty for me. . . . I will finish *Nerone* or I will not finish it, but it is certain that I will never abandon it for another work; and if I do not have the strength to finish it I will not complain, and I will spend my life, neither sad nor happy, with that dream in my mind. . . . But for God's sake do not abandon *Othello.* . . . You are healthier than I, stronger than I. We have pitted the strength of our arms against one another, and mine bent beneath yours. Your life is tranquil and serene; take up your pen again and write me soon, "Dear Boito, do me the favor of changing these verses," etc., etc., and I will change them at once, joyfully, and I will be able to work for you, I who am unable to work for myself, because you live in the true and real life of Art, and I in the world of hallucinations.[145]

We do not have to be experts in biological adaptation or physiological kinetics to decipher the symbolic and ritual meaning of this test of strength

145. *Verdi-Boito Correspondence,* ed. Mario Medici and Marcello Conati, trans. William Weaver (Chicago: University of Chicago Press, 1994), 71–72.

between the seventy-year-old maestro and the forty-one-year-old poet; Thomas Mann could have used the episode to write a short story on his favorite theme of the weak intellectual crushed by overwhelming life forces. I do not mean to credit the opposing theory (also based on a priori reasoning) that Verdi in his later years felt culturally inferior to Boito. Verdi worked with Boito in substantially the same way that he had with Piave and Ghislanzoni; if their relationship was more one of equals, it was thanks to the combined effect of the aging Verdi's spiritual serenity and Boito's intelligent openness as he fulfilled his own need for renewed inspiration in his collaboration with Verdi.

Their contemporaries understood perfectly that the result of their collaboration differed from older practice. Luigi Illica, for example, at the time deeply involved in a stormy collaboration with Puccini, let off steam in a letter to the publisher Giulio Ricordi.

> Permit me to say to you that I do not feel I have the strength to go back to paraphrasing the music—and permit me to express to you all the ill that I think of this system—now that since Verdi, since Boito, the great artistic endeavor is to give music the most complete truth and efficacy of the spoken word, which is the [special] characteristic of the theater.[146]

These are words that recall eighteenth-century disputes, and in fact Puccini's system was not very far from that of Casti's *Prima la musica, poi le parole* (First the music, then the words): Puccini often asked his librettists to write verse according to a predetermined meter patterned on a melody he had already composed.

Puccini reasoned like a composer from the past, but unfortunately for him there were no longer librettists as submissive as the ones Verdi had found. Throughout his operatic career Puccini was engaged in a frantic search for collaborators, often in pairs so that they might remedy one another's limitations. *Manon Lescaut* went as far as one could go in that direction, with so many authors to its libretto that historians lose count, but there were also the teams of Illica and Giuseppe Giacosa, Guelfo Civinini and Carlo Zangarini, Giuseppe Adami and Renato Simoni. The librettists who best fit the traditional role of a writer who carried out orders were perhaps Adami and Giovacchino Forzano. Forzano, a true man of the theater of the old style, claimed to have approached Puccini motivated by the sole ambition to write an original libretto for him.[147]

146. Letter of January 1893, in *Carteggi pucciniani,* ed. Eugenio Gara (Milan: Ricordi, 1958), 78.

147. Giovacchino Forzano, *Come li ho conosciuti* (Turin: Edizione RAI Radiotelevisione Italiana, 1957), 12–13.

These two exceptions aside, all of Puccini's collaborations with librettists were troubled and often stormy, in particular his relations with Illica and Giacosa. The two librettists had joined forces, working together much as Zeno and Pariati had done: Illica did the dramatic outline and Giacosa touched up the verse. Both of them struggled to contain Puccini's continual requests for changes, and Giulio Ricordi watched over all three of them as coordinator and peacemaker but also as dispenser of advice and criticism to librettists and composer alike. (It was a sign of the times that opera had become a carefully programmed long-term investment.) The three operas produced by that quartet were born under the auspices of a friendly collaboration, but they weathered crises that threatened to sink them, and the working agreement that brought them safely into port left deep-felt aftereffects and lasting quarrels.

Giacosa was always ready to sing his own praises: for him, as an author of successful plays, hence a "true writer," doing a libretto could not be compared with genuine literary activity, either from the viewpoint of artistic satisfaction or, as he wrote Ricordi, of remuneration.

> The trouble is that what I am doing as regards that libretto is not a work of art but of painstaking, indispensable, and extremely laborious pedantry. It is work that absolutely must be done; it is work that demands an artist. But it is work with no stimuli and no inner warmth. The work of art has its difficult and laborious hours, but in recompense it has its hours of pure inspiration in which the hand is slow to follow the thought. Here there is nothing to raise the spirit. I assure you that I will never again agree to take on such an endeavor (and do it conscientiously) at any price.
>
> Out of courtesy you have assigned to me a raise of 200 lire, but I beg you to reflect that . . . in the time devoted to these patch-ups I could easily have written four articles for *La nuova antologia* for which I would have been paid 300 lire per printed page.[148]

Furthermore, the moment always came when the poet had to deal with theatrical conventions.

> I yield, and I will send you the verses that with considerable effort I have managed to write. . . . I have not given thought to the dramatic moment, or to the personality of the characters, or to the psychology of "il signor tenore," as you call him (because it seems that for you and for Puccini, Mario Cavaradossi is nothing but "il signor tenore"); I have not even given thought to common sense. You wanted a "lyric piece," and obviously a "lyric piece" is something that has nothing to do with psychology or dramatics. Let there be the lyric piece! And also to please you

148. Giacosa to Giulio Ricordi, 2 October 1893 and 25 June 1895, in *Carteggi pucciniani*, 88–89 and 115, respectively.

I have faithfully followed the metric pattern that you had sent me. The prosody will not be very satisfactory, but the lyric piece cares not a fig for prosody. . . . And that "non tradirmi" that rhymes with nothing is ghastly and will make the poet look like a fool. But that is the last thing to worry about in an opera.[149]

When the work on *Tosca* was finally completed, Giacosa found that his text had been expropriated from him and reduced to little more than a support to Puccini's music, as he complained to Ricordi.

My dearest Sor Giulio, I insist with all the strength I have left that the entire text of the libretto be printed. This mutilation may suit the maestro, but it offends the poet profoundly. I cannot give my approval to print a scene without rhythms, without syntax, and without common sense. . . . But must I abandon the libretto to the scorn and the delight of all those who know something about prosody? . . . Believe in me, dear Sor Giulio, and let us print a libretto that is not too obvious an offense against literary and dramatic reason. Let the maestro set to music whatever part he likes. . . . I do not want to enter into the musical task which is the maestro's. I have expressed my doubts and my fears in all good conscience, and I will be utterly happy if the outcome proves me wrong. But the responsibility for the libretto is mine, and I cannot let it be stripped to a skeleton in this manner.[150]

Illica was more sensitive to the specific demands of opera, and to Puccini he declared himself convinced that "the form of a libretto is made by the music, only the music, and nothing but the music! It alone, Puccini, is form! A libretto is nothing but its general outline."[151] That did not keep Illica from fiercely defending the spiritual paternity of his librettos against anyone who attributed their merits to Giacosa, or against Giacosa himself when, now and then, Giacosa permitted himself the liberty of publishing extracts under his name alone. Still, Illica noted a clear difference between the task of the librettist and the poet's conscience.

It used to be true—when Metastasio was writing librettos—that "words by so-and-so" was written at the top of a libretto. This custom reflected a profound factual truth. Libretto verse is nothing but a habit that has become common practice, a mode that has passed into the repertory, just like calling those who write librettos "poets." What has true value in the libretto is the word. Let the words correspond to the truth of the moment (the situation) and of the passion (the character)! Everything is there; the rest is *blague* [bunkum].[152]

It is certainly odd that the name of Metastasio (who surely never considered himself the author of simple "words") be evoked in support of theorizing

149. To Giulio Ricordi, 9 September 1898, in ibid., 170.
150. To Giulio Ricordi, 1 January 1904, in ibid., 250.
151. Letter to Puccini, reported in a letter to Giulio Ricordi, October 1907, in ibid., 358.
152. Ibid.

what amounted to Verdi's *parola scenica*. It is also a sign of lucidity that Illica saw the causes of decline in the immediate present and in the intellectualism that was undermining the healthy principles of operatic tradition.

> Today, instead, decadentism and D'Annunzianism, by corrupting the simplicity and the naturalness of language, threaten (in the theater) truth and logic (the two guardian angels that sit by your side when you write music), especially when decadentism and D'Annunzianism denature the word, trying to impose their martingale on the stage.[153]

The moment had in fact come for the meeting between Puccini and D'Annunzio, the *imaginifico* (image maker). Their encounter was predestined if it is true that as early as 1894 Puccini stated that he had wished "for years and years to possess something sweetly original from the leading mind of Italy."[154] He had to wait until 1906, however, for his wish to come true (under the auspices of Marco Praga).

At first everything seemed idyllic. Puccini reported, "I have just . . . finished a conversation with D'A[nnunzio]. His ideas harmonize with mine regarding opera."[155] D'Annunzio echoed Puccini: "Concerning the conception of musical drama we are already in perfect agreement. And I hope to be able to offer him a poem in which the most ardent human breath infuses the visions of the most unusual poetry." While Puccini's friend Praga was more interested in seeing to it "that they reach an agreement" with Ricordi, "with all due respect to 'Saint Poetry' and 'Madonna Equity,'" "D'Annunzio was looking forward "to writing a poem in which a *note* can be heard under every *syllable*."[156]

Several months later Puccini announced that "the extraordinary libretto" had almost been completed (although he had not yet seen a line of it);[157] while D'Annunzio was asking Tito Ricordi's help to "overcome the *usual laziness*" that, according to D'Annunzio, would make its appearance when it came time to look over the text and revise it. There would be no serious problems, however: "From the most beautiful verse springs the most beautiful music. Music has a need to twist and mistreat the strophe; it cannot have anything false in it." Furthermore, he added, "I am composing, with a finely tuned ear, a *singable* [*cantabile*] poem."[158]

As is well known, D'Annunzio had exquisite taste in music, and he com-

153. Ibid.
154. Puccini to Carlo Clausetti, 18 July 1894, in ibid., 104.
155. To Carlo Clausetti, 13 February 1906, in ibid., 317–18.
156. D'Annunzio to Tito Ricordi, 16 and 21 February 1906, in ibid., 318–19.
157. Puccini to Alfredo Vandini, 3 May 1906, in ibid., 321.
158. D'Annunzio to Tito Ricordi, August 1906, in ibid., 324.

bined that taste with a penetrating critical intelligence. Still, his claim to inspire Puccini's music with his verse (need we recall Foppa and Romani?) must
have disconcerted the composer when he received the outline for a morning
prelude, half mystical, half descriptive, rife with cocks' crows and church
bells, that D'Annunzio had imagined as he lay between sleep and wakening,
listening to two roosters.[159] Above all, when Puccini read D'Annunzio's text,
it was clear to him how remote the poet's world was from his own idea of
theater. D'Annunzio exhorted him to abandon "the somewhat patched-up
romanticism" of his old librettos[160] and the "dramatic *realism* to which I
could bend only with difficulty."[161] Puccini responded that it was not realism
that he wanted "but a *quid medium* that takes possession of the hearers
through painful and amorous events, which live and palpitate, logically, in an
aura of poetry more of life than of dreams."[162]

The two eventually became resigned to the inevitable, and each one gave
the other his liberty with ample protestations of friendship. To another
friend, however, D'Annunzio (who had seen in the projected collaboration a
chance for earnings that would have come in handy in reducing his mounting
debts) spoke his mind.

> My contacts with the maestro from Lucca were without result. He becomes bewil-
> dered before the force of poetry. He found two excellent ideas . . . too grandiose
> for his tastes. He reached the point of admitting to me that he needed "a light little
> thing to set to music in a few months, between one trip and another." And for that
> he had come to the poet of *Francesca da Rimini!*
>
> The disappointment has been very sad. Not art but commerce, it seems. Ah
> well![163]

A few years later Puccini and D'Annunzio made another attempt to work
together, which came to naught for the same reasons. Puccini turned for comfort to his faithful old collaborator Illica, to whom he confessed:

> I believe that the opera libretto is a plant extinct on this earth. I look around me
> and I am convinced of it. . . . The poverty of librettos is so real and so evident that
> in desperation I grab whatever comes along that is least bad.[164]

The figure of the librettist was indeed on its way to extinction, perhaps
because the production of operas, its reason for being, drastically declined.

159. Letter from D'Annunzio to Puccini, 7 August 1906, in ibid., 325.
160. Letter of 9 August 1906, in ibid., 326.
161. Letter of 12 August 1906, in ibid., 327.
162. Letter of 16 August 1906, in ibid., 328.
163. To Camillo Bondi, 31 August 1906, quoted in Arnaldo Marchetti, "Carezze e graffi di
D'Annunzio a Puccini," *Nuova rivista musicale italiana* 8 (1974): 536–39, quotation 539.
164. Letters of 24 and 28 January 1913, in *Carteggi pucciniani*, 408–9.

We could stop here if our curiosity were not piqued to see whether the problems that for some centuries had continually besieged librettists were still applicable in new theatrical productions to which the concept of libretto hardly fits—for example, in the operas of composers of the so-called generation of the 1880s, whose works began to appear on stage in the 1920s.

In his search for an indissoluble unity of music and drama, Ildebrando Pizzetti was obliged to write the texts for his operas himself. The only exception was his first opera, *Fedra* (1915), for which he preferred to collaborate with D'Annunzio rather than bring to completion a dramatic idea that he himself had worked out. It seems that the two men got along well together: D'Annunzio was evidently much more in harmony with a composer of a generation whose tastes he had helped to form than with Puccini. In spite of this harmony one critic (who was a declared admirer of Pizzetti's) could not help noting in the opera some "rare moments of collapse in which the collaboration with D'Annunzio ends in strident collision: for example, the luxuriant vocal quality of the text makes the music wander and lose color." According to the same critic those moments were marginal, and the general conception of the opera provided a "verbal richness [that] was immediately subjected by the maestro to the logic of his own expression by pruning and accepting only what was sufficient to establish an atmosphere and sculpt a character without insistence or useless abundance." This was done so successfully, the critic added, that "Pizzetti's *Fedra* managed, at least in part, to be as little D'Annunzian as possible."[165] In other words Pizzetti had reorganized D'Annunzio's text to the order of ideas that he himself had expressed in an essay written a few years earlier.

That ideal *dramma per musica* can only be realized by the poet if he molds the action [to include] only the episodes necessary to its development, . . . reducing the verbal expressions of the characters to the words needed to manifest their hidden sentiments intelligibly—that is, removing from their discourse all trace of psychological self-analysis. . . . All that a superabundance of words succeeds in doing is hinder the free development of the music and lessen its effectiveness. . . . Lyricism can offer no argument that justifies the verbosity of a character who in order to express his own sentiments has to analyze them subtly and completely.[166]

Gian Francesco Malipiero was another composer who nearly always wrote his own texts, beginning with his trial ventures in a musical theater of a totally new and by definition antilibrettist sort, in works such as *L'Orfeide* and

165. Adelmo Damerini, "Ildebrando Pizzetti: L'uomo e l'artista," *L'approdo musicale* 21 (1966): 8–81, esp. 26–27.

166. Ildebrando Pizzetti, "*Ariane et Barbebleu* . . . de Paul Dukas," *Rivista musicale italiana* 15 (1908): 73–111, quotation 88.

Torneo notturno. Only once did Malipiero write an opera on a text by someone else, *La favola del figlio cambiato*, with a libretto by Luigi Pirandello. This was a work unique in the entire history of opera: it was not the composer who commissioned a text from a dramatist who was at the height of his fame; rather, Pirandello, at the urging of Mario Labroca, offered to adapt a one-act play that he had written to make a three-act opera with music by Malipiero.[167] As far as is known, Pirandello showed a genuine interest in opera,[168] and he displayed keen intelligence in his understanding of the specific requirements of musical theater. When he sent the first act to Malipiero, he wrote to him,

> I fully understand . . . your requirements, and as I told you, I leave you full liberty to add, remove, adapt; what counts is that the spirit of the work be respected, and I cannot have the least fear in that regard, having entrusted it to an artist like yourself.[169]

Not long after, when he sent the second and third acts, Pirandello wrote,

> Regarding the musical needs, let me say again that you are to be the absolute judge. Poetic drama, which must satisfy the laws of its organic aesthetic unity and has laws of its own, is another affair. . . . For that reason I do not think that our direct collaboration—aside from the collaboration that resides in the very fact that in offering you my work I have offered pure and simple *material* to be used for the opera as a whole—can turn out to be useful, because you have to remain alone and free in the face of your task just as I have been in the face of mine.[170]

One might even say that here for the first time a relationship of perfect autonomy and equilibrium had been established between the librettist and the composer. Rather than with the Piave-Verdi collaboration, the relationship between Pirandello and Malipiero might be compared with the one between Victor Hugo or Schiller and Verdi, with the added advantage of needing no intermediary. Still, it is possible that Malipiero never totally espoused the text that he set to music, since many years later he was still mulling it over. He wrote, with some perplexity,

> Italian literary critics' stinging attacks on the third act of *La favola del figlio cambiato* have always made me suffer, because they always make me wonder whether

167. Fedele D'Amico, "La favola della favola," in *Teatro dell'Opera* [of Rome] *Stagione 1981–82* [program booklet], 587–607, esp. 588.

168. Mario Labroca, *L'usignolo di Boboli (Cinquant' anni di vita musicale)* (Venice: Pozza, 1959), 70–73.

169. Letter of 3 April 1932, given in *Teatro dell'Opera Stagione 1981–82*, 648.

170. Letter of unknown date, quoted in Gian Francesco Malipiero, "Luigi Pirandello mio librettista," in Malipiero, *Il filo d'Arianna: Saggi e fantasie* (Turin: Einaudi, 1966), 156–58, quotation 156–57.

I should admit that they were right, given that I myself had to overcome a few doubts before I could fully enter into the spirit of the [opera's] very Pirandellian ending. And that doubt has pursued me, in spite of the fact that many operas have absurd librettos and are held together by the music alone.[171]

Luigi Dallapiccola also chose to write his own texts. Nor could it have been otherwise for an artist whose every opera gave a condensed version of his own life experience filtered by memory. Text and music necessarily had to spring from the same mind as aspects of one creative process. The libretto could, in turn, become an occasion for an excavation of memory and a meditation on the reasons behind one's own art, as in Dallapiccola's "Nascita di un libretto d'opera" ("Birth of an opera libretto"), an article that offers learned and subtle insights and lucid observations on the relationship between text and music and the perennial problem of bending literary language to the laws of a very different medium of expression.

> People often ask me why I write my own librettos. The answer is always the same: because collaboration with a poet would be a hindrance to my work as a composer. . . . By writing the libretto myself I can work it out with total freedom; I can organize the interplay of questions and answers along purely musical and constructive lines; I can decide, finally, where to exploit the power of "concentration" so characteristic of operatic music, . . . all of which means seeing where music permits the reduction of words to a minimum.[172]

There are not many other composers who have followed Dallapiccola's example. Among the few, though in a quite different cultural climate, are Nino Rota and Gian Carlo Menotti, the last but worthy survivors of an craftsman-like conception of operatic creation. More frequently composers have sought a literary collaborator who might, according to circumstances, be a poet, a journalist, or a stage director. These collaborations have included some prestigious names: thus Giorgio Federico Ghedini has worked with the poet and critic Salvatore Quasimodo (*Billy Budd*, 1949); Goffredo Petrassi with the poet and prose writer Eugenio Montale (*Il cordovano*, 1949) and with the painter Toti Scialoja (*La morte dell'aria*, 1950); Luigi Nono has worked with Angelo Maria Ripellino (*Intolleranza 1960*, 1960) and more recently with the philosopher Massimo Cacciari (*Prometeo*, 1984); Luciano Berio has collaborated with Edoardo Sanguineti (*Passaggio*, 1963) and with Italo Calvino (*La vera storia*, 1982). It is clear that these partnerships reflect

171. Ibid., 157.
172. Luigi Dallapiccola, "Nascita di un libretto d'opera," *Nuova rivista musicale italiana* 2 (1968): 605–24, also available in Dallapiccola, *Parole e musica,* ed. Fiamma Nicolodi (Milan: Il Saggiatore, 1980), 511–30, quotation 527–28.

an aspiration on the part of Italian composers (whose professional training is still conceived more in craftsman-like than in intellectual terms) to enter into the circuits of contemporary cultural debate. Other evidence of this trend can be seen in the proliferation of literary and philosophical references (relevant and irrelevant) in interviews, printed program notes, and essays.

Two other developments have been of genuine interest: some sectors of Italian culture have become attuned to the problems of contemporary music, and more recently there has been a rediscovery of the literary aspects of eighteenth- and nineteenth-century Italian opera. Now that such works can be viewed as a product from the distant past, they are open to an intellectual enjoyment detached from the polemics they once elicited. Finally, in even more recent years, an increasing number of scholars of theatrical communication and Italian, Latin, and Greek literature and culture have turned their attention to the opera libretto.

This promotion to the rank of an academic subject may mark the end of the adventure that began in 1600. Perhaps the renewed aspiration for a communicating art that seems manifest in the most recent generation of composers will bring on a rebirth of activity in operatic practice. Should that occur, and the professional relationship between librettist and composer be revived, we may be surprised by a reemergence of age-old occasions for dissent that for the moment seem to have no reason for being. It is unlikely that a remote possibility of this sort lead to a new phase of crisis for the man or woman of letters as such, given that the overall role of the intellectual today is so fraught with ideologies and new technologies.

BIBLIOGRAPHIC NOTE

There is no specific bibliography on the opera librettist; the only work entirely dedicated to the subject, Antonio Cassi Ramelli, *Libretti e librettisti* (Milan: Ceschina, 1973), is in reality little more than a collection of anecdotes. For information on individual librettists and bibliography on them, the reader is referred to the entries in *The New Grove Dictionary of Music and Musicians,* ed. Stanley Sadie, 20 vols. (London: Macmillan; Washington D.C.: Grove's Dictionaries of Music, 1980) and *New Grove Dictionary of Opera,* ed. Stanley Sadie, 4 vols. (London: Macmillan; New York: Grove's Dictionaries of Music, 1992), to be complemented, when necessary, by entries in the *Enciclopedia dello spettacolo,* ed. Sandro d'Amico, 9 vols. (Rome: Le Maschere, 1954–60), and the volumes published to date of the *Dizionario biografico degli italiani* (Rome: Istituto della Enciclopedia Italiana, 1960–). Little attention has been given to the figure of the librettist in the various histories and studies of the writing of librettos, with the exception (in part) of Patrick J. Smith, *The Tenth Muse: A Historical Study of the Opera Libretto* (New York: Alfred A. Knopf, 1970; London: Gollancz, 1971);

Kurt Honolka, *Kulturgeschichte des Librettos: Opern, Dichter, Operndichter* (Wilhelmshaven: Heinrichshofen, 1978); Daniela Goldin, *La vera fenice: Librettisti e libretti tra Sette e Ottocento* (Turin: Einaudi, 1985).

1. On the status and the work of the Italian man of letters, see the first two volumes of *Letteratura italiana,* ed. Alberto Asor Rosa, 8 vols. (Turin: Einaudi, 1982–91). A singular and penetrating analysis of the crisis of identity faced by the man of letters at a crucial moment in his history can be found in Gino Benzoni, *Gli affanni della cultura: Intellettuali e potere nell'Italia della Controriforma e barocca* (Milan: Feltrinelli, 1978); the condition of the early-nineteenth-century man of letters in Milan, the cultural capital of Italy, is examined in Marino Barengo, *Intellettuali e librai nella Milano della Restaurazione* (Turin: Einaudi, 1980).

2. The fundamental study on Giulio Rospigliosi's activities as a librettist and on court opera in Rome in the seventeenth century is Margaret Murata, *Operas for the Papal Court 1631–1668* (Ann Arbor, Mich.: UMI Research Press, 1981). On Venetian librettists see Simon Towneley Worsthorne, *Venetian Opera in the Seventeenth Century* (Oxford: Clarendon Press, 1954, 1968), especially chapter 8, "The Relations between Composer and Librettist." There is a collection of prefaces to librettos in Ellen Rosand, "In Defense of the Venetian Libretto," *Studi musicali* 9 (1980): 271–85. See also Rosand's more recent *Opera in Seventeenth-Century Venice: The Creation of a Genre* (Berkeley: University of California Press, 1991). Still an important text on Busenello is Arthur Livingston, *La vita veneziana nelle opere di Gian Francesco Busenello* (Venice: Callegari, 1913), to which I might add Francesco Degrada, "Gian Francesco Busenello e il libretto dell'*Incoronazione di Poppea,*" in *Il palazzo incantato: Studi sulla tradizione del melodramma dal Barocco al Romanticismo* (Fiesole: Discanto, 1979), 113–26, and Ellen Rosand, "Seneca and the Interpretation of *L'incoronazione di Poppea,*" *Journal of the American Musicological Society* 38 (1985): 34–71. On Minato's career see Nino Pirrotta, "Note su Minato," in *L'opera italiana a Vienna prima di Metastasio,* ed. Maria Teresa Muraro (Florence: Olschki, 1990), 127–63.

3. Little attention was paid to the figure of Apostolo Zeno before two studies by Elena Sala Di Felice: "Alla Vigilia del Metastasio: Zeno," in *Convegno indetto in occasione del II centenario della morte di Metastasio d'intesa con Arcadia, Accademia letteraria italiana, Istituto di studi romani, Società italiana di studi sul sec. XVIII: Roma, 25–27 maggio 1983,* Atti dei convegni lincei, 65 (Rome: Accademia Nazionale dei Lincei, 1985), 79–109, and "Dagli inganni felici allo specchio delle virtù: Diagramma di Apostolo Zeno," *Intersezioni* 6 (1986): 51–71. On Pariati see Giovanna Gronda et al., *La carriera di un librettista: Pietro Pariati da Reggio di Lombardia* (Bologna: Il Mulino, 1990). The Metastasio bicentenary in 1982 gave rise to a number of studies, for a critical review of which see Giovanna Gronda, "Metastasiana," *Rivista italiana di musicologia* 19 (1984): 314–32. The most important of these are by Elena Sala Di Felice, in particular her *Metastasio: Ideologia, drammaturgia, spettacolo* (Milan: Angeli, 1983) and a penetrating psychological portrait based on Metastasio's correspondence, "Metastasio sulla scena del mondo," *Italianistica* 13 (1984): 41–70. I might also mention three studies by Nino Pirrotta: "Metastasio and the Demands of

His Literary Environment," in *Crosscurrents and the Mainstream of Italian Serious Opera 1730–1790: A Symposium, February 11–13, 1982*, Studies in Music from the University of Western Ontario, vol. 7, no. 2 (1982): 10–27; "Metastasio e i teatri romani," in *Le muse galanti: La musica a Roma nel Settecento,* ed. Bruno Cagli (Rome: Istituto della Enciclopedia Italiana, 1985), 23–34; and "I musicisti nell'epistolario di Metastasio," in *Convegno indetto in occasione del II centenario della morte di Metastasio d'intesa con Arcadia, Accademia letteraria italiana, Istituto di studi romani, Società italiana di studi sul sec. XVIII: Roma, 25–27 maggio 1983,* Atti dei convegni lincei, 65 (Rome: Accademia Nazionale dei Lincei, 1985), 245–55. In the volume *Crosscurrents and the Mainstream,* there is an article on an important court librettist: Marita McClymonds, "Mattia Verazi and the Opera at Mannheim, Stuttgart and Ludwigsburg," 99–136. On Neapolitan librettists, Pietro Trinchera in particular, see Eugenio Battisti, "Per un'indagine sociologica sui librettisti napoletani buffi," *Letteratura* 8 (1960): 114–64, in which the sociological analysis concerns the librettos more than the librettists. There is an important summary of Goldoni's activities as librettist in Piero Weiss, "Goldoni poeta d'opere serie per musica," *Studi goldoniani* 3 (1973): 7–40. On opera-related caricatures see Daniela Goldin, "Un microgenere melodrammatico: L'opera nell'opera," in Goldin, *La vera fenice: Librettisti e libretti tra Sette e Ottocento* (Turin: Einaudi, 1985), 73–76.

4–5.   For material, often first-hand, on nineteenth-century librettists, see Francesco Regli, *Dizionario biografico dei più celebri poeti ed artisti melodrammatici . . . che fiorirono in Italia dal 1800 al 1860* (Turin, 1860; reprint, Bologna: Arnaldo Forni, 1990). Among the few monographs, one tendentious work that nonetheless presents a good deal of information is Emilia Branca, *Felice Romani ed i più riputati maestri di musica del suo tempo* (Turin, 1882). See also Alberto Cametti, *Un poeta melodrammatico romano: Appunti e notizie in gran parte inedite sopra Jacopo Ferretti e i musicisti del suo tempo* (Milan, [1898]); John Black, *The Italian Romantic Libretto: A Study of Salvatore Cammarano* (Edinburgh: The University Press, 1984); Alessandro Roccatagliati, *Felice Romani librettista* (Lucca: Libreria Italiana Musicale, 1996). Carlo Ritorni, *Ammaestramenti alla composizione d'ogni poema e d'ogni opera appartenente alla musica* (Milan, 1841) is an unusual "working manual" for librettists. There are useful observations on working methods in Rossini's times (Gaetano Rossi's in particular) in Sabine Henze-Döhring, "'Combinammo l'ossatura . . .': Voltaire und die Librettistik des frühen Ottocento," *Die Musikforschung* 36 (1983): 113–27, and in Maria Giovanna Miggiani, "Di alcuni termini e concetti prescrittivi in Gaetano Rossi," in *Le parole della musica, I: Studi sulla lingua della letteratura musicale in onore di Gianfranco Folena,* ed. Fiamma Nicolodi and Paolo Trovato (Florence: Olschki, 1994), 225–58. The genesis of Verdi's various operas is reconstructed in Julian Budden, *The Operas of Verdi,* 3 vols. (London: Cassell, 1973–81; rev. ed., Oxford: Clarendon Press, 1991). Among the various collections of Verdi's letters, the ones of particular importance for the argument here are *Re Lear e Ballo in maschera: Lettere di Giuseppe Verdi ad Antonio Somma,* ed. Alessandro Pascolato (Città di Castello: Lapi, 1902). Verdi's methods for working with his librettists are analyzed in exemplary fashion in Philip Gossett, "Verdi, Ghislanzoni, and *Aida:* The Uses of Convention," *Critical Inquiry* 1 (1974–75): 291–334.

Still fundamental for Boito is Piero Nardi, *Vita di Arrigo Boito* (Milan: Mondadori, 1942), to which we can now add Mario Lavagetto, introduction to Arrigo Boito, *Opere* (Milan: Garzanti, 1979). On the relations between D'Annunzio and composers, see the special issue, *A Gabriele D'Annunzio in memoriam,* of *Rivista musicale italiana* 43 (1939). For the reflections of a contemporary man of letters with experience in musical theater, see Edoardo Sanguineti, "Teatro con musica, senza musica," *Intersezioni* 4 (1984): 597–608.

— 5 —

The Opera Composer

ELVIDIO SURIAN

There are few Italian composers of some renown, from the early seventeenth century to our own, who were not involved in some manner and to some degree in the field of opera production. Some were in fact exclusively opera composers. Given the vast and broad diffusion of Italian opera, both in Italy and elsewhere, from around the mid-seventeenth century most of the Italian composers who had official and often prestigious positions in foreign capitals and foreign courts worked principally in the field of opera. Not surprisingly, even today outside Italy "Italian music" is often synonymous with bel canto and opera in the particularly Italian form of *melodramma*.[1] In Italy itself opera has for centuries been the predominant form of artistic musical expression; especially during the nineteenth century, all levels of Italian society shared a love of opera, and opera still has thriving historical and cultural roots in Italy today.

It is also just as true that for over a century music historians have been biased against Italian opera and opera composers. According to Richard Wagner's teleological vision of the history of opera (*Oper und Drama*, 1851), Italian *melodramma* was governed by "corrupt" cultural conventions that violated the laws of dramatic continuity; Italian opera composers were to blame for having accepted a role subordinate to singers and for having knuck-

---

1. During the eighteenth century Italian opera (Neapolitan opera in particular) even took on a mythical quality and became the symbol of an ideal category of sentiments. See, for example, the praise given it by Jean-Jacques Rousseau, *Dictionnaire de la musique* (Paris, 1768), s. v., "Génie."

led under to the theatrical conventions of the time. The founding fathers of German musicology followed Wagner's prejudiced, distorted view of Italian opera and its vicissitudes, and they laid the groundwork for the often dogmatic assumptions of later generations of historians of the opera.[2] One result was a tenacious historiographical prejudice in favor of the Wagnerian tradition that gave historians little incentive to investigate Italian opera. Italian music historians of the same period (the late nineteenth century and the early twentieth century) either embraced the Wagnerian ideas enthusiastically or were unable (or had little desire) to offer historiographical models of their own that were more relevant to the Italian opera tradition. We still suffer the consequences of this imbalance today: adequate critical studies and modern editions of the operas themselves are few in comparison with the enormous amount of documentation and musical source material available.

Many Italian opera composers still await the recognition of an appropriate musicological study of their careers and their development. In many cases what we do know about them is information published over a century ago (by François-Joseph Fétis, Francesco Florimo, and others) that is often inaccurate, incomplete, and not rarely scattered in locally published pieces that are hard to find, but that is nonetheless uncritically repeated in more recent dictionaries. There is very little documentation, for example, of the careers of a number of opera composers who were famous in their day, such as Leonardo Vinci, Geminiano Giacomelli, Nicola Logroscino, Pietro Auletta, and Sebastiano Nasolini. There is a romanticized biography of Alessandro Stradella, but despite the enormous amount of documentation available, we are still awaiting a definitive biography of Gioachino Rossini. What we do have is a large number of publications that are little more than glorified descriptions of the composers' works. Especially where Italian opera composers of the seventeenth and eighteenth centuries are concerned, there is not even a systematic, reliable catalog of their works. We are fortunate to have the information and the data collected by such scholarly organizations as the Répertoire international des sources musicales (RISM) and the Ufficio Ricerca Fondi Musicali (URFM) of Milan,[3] which can give a much more complete picture of the production of many opera composers than the entries in the

2. For an overview of the consequences of adopting Wagner's conception of *Musikdrama* in opera historiography, see Elvidio Surian, "Musical Historiography and Histories of Italian Opera," *Current Musicology* 36 (1983): 167–75.

3. An important result of the Milanese research center's activities has been the publication of Claudio Sartori's monumental *I libretti italiani a stampa dalle origini al 1800: Catalogo analitico con 16 indici*, 7 vols. (Cuneo: Bertola and Locatelli, 1990). This catalog, like many of those for individual collections, does not include mineteenth-century librettos. In addition to information on these librettos, the URFM is in the process of compiling a union catalog of music in Italian libraries and music of Italian composers preserved elsewhere. These files, as yet unpublished, provide an important starting point for research on the music of Italian opera.

standard musical dictionaries and encyclopedias. There is no complete, exhaustive catalog of the works of any Italian opera composer (with the single exception of Giovanni Paisiello) that equals the Mozart or Haydn catalogs, and there are even seventeenth-and eighteenth-century composers whose works have been completely lost (or nearly so), such as Benedetto Ferrari, Francesco Manelli, Giovanni Battista Lampugnani, Gaetano Latilla, Rinaldo da Capua, and others. The situation is totally different regarding composers after 1800, where there are endless masses of musical and documentary sources (letters, archival documents, journalistic pieces, librettos) on musical works, opera productions, and composers' biographies. Some of these documents have been published only in part or are scattered in books and a wide variety of journals. Biographers and critics of Rossini, Gaetano Donizetti, Giuseppe Verdi, Pietro Mascagni, and others have hardly touched the wealth of reviews and news published in periodicals during the nineteenth century.

The present attempt to trace a sociological portrait of the Italian opera composer is based on information regarding 133 composers (listed in the appendix to this chapter)—a sample that fairly accurately represents the socioprofessional characteristics of composers over the moderately long time span from the early seventeenth century to the twentieth century. The data sheet that was prepared for each of these composers includes information on

1. Social background
2. Schooling, professional training, technical apprenticeship
3. Place in the production system of opera, career, operas
4. Creative process, working methods, and schedules

Once collected, this information was organized, analyzed, and subdivided chronologically. The resulting analysis is not intended to furnish a complete, exhaustive survey of Italian opera composers (an impossible task, given the lacunae in current research) but rather to trace an overall, generic sketch of the figure of the composer and a picture of his social position over the long run.

Opera composers always tended to be clearly aware of their relations with the public and the importance of serving its needs.[4] The composer took care

4. Alessandro Scarlatti wrote that music "has as its end the enjoyment of the listener" (letter of 1 May 1706 to Ferdinando de' Medici, *granprincipe* of Tuscany; Mario Fabbri, *Alessandro Scarlatti e il principe Ferdinando de' Medici* (Florence: Olschki, 1961), 70–71. The listeners' satisfaction was also a prevailing concern for nineteenth-century opera composers. Bellini's continuing interest in the dramatic depiction of his characters, for example, is closely connected with his desire to please a broader theatrical public. Immediately after the performance in Genoa of *Bianca e Fernando,* Bellini wrote to Francesco Florimo (letter of 9 April 1828) that "the opera had the desired effect . . . to the point that the public was very content, especially with the second act"; Maria Rosaria Adamo and Friedrich Lippmann, *Vincenzo Bellini* (Turin: Edizioni RAI Radiotele-

not only to offer an artistic product that would meet with the approval of whoever had commissioned it (be it a ruler, an impresario, or a publisher) but also to seek favor with the paying public or the courtly audience. Throughout the centuries the composer had to take into account the particular organization for which he worked; that meant that he was never free from social and professional constraints of a number of types. His working methods, the rules that governed them, and his place in the production system changed (and changed greatly from the nineteenth century on), but the definitions of the sector in which he worked and of his specialized contributions remained almost unchanged. From the late seventeenth century on, when the laws of a market economy and of supply and demand began governing theatrical life and opera production (in Italy even more than elsewhere), the opera composer invested most of his professional energies in striving for success, financial success in particular. Since nearly everywhere in Italy opera productions were commercial ventures managed by an impresario (elsewhere they tended to be financed by courts, and even the Italian impresarial system always had to rely on government subsidies),[5] the opera composer could make substantial sums of money if he were willing to work under stress, at least for a certain period in his career.[6] Such earnings did not last long, however,

---

visione Italiana, 1981), 76. We can see Bellini's intent to conceive of musical drama in function of its "effect" (that is, its capacity to move the audience) in a phrase he used in a letter to his librettist, Carlo Pepoli, while preparing the production of *I puritani*: "Sculpt it in your head in adamantine letters: *Music drama must make people weep, must horrify, must die singing*"; Adamo and Lippmann, *Vincenzo Bellini*, 243. Amilcare Ponchielli also sought public acceptance: during the composition of *I Lituani*, he wrote to Giulio Ricordi (letter of 19 June 1874), "I am always afraid that my music will not satisfy myself or others!" In another letter (19 November 1874) he wrote, "I think that for the Italian public you should not caress the drama too much, or you will fall into rhythms that do not strike the ear"; Gaetano Cesari, *Amilcare Ponchielli nell'arte del suo tempo*, ed. Elia Santoro (Cremona: Cremona Produce, 1984), 46, 49.

    5. The fundamental study for an overview of the role of the impresario in the production system of Italian opera from the late eighteenth to the late nineteenth century is John Rosselli, *The Opera Industry in Italy from Cimarosa to Verdi: The Role of the Impresario* (Cambridge: Cambridge University Press, 1984), in Italian translation, in an amplified version, as *L'impresario d'opera: Arte e affari nel teatro musicale italiano dell'Ottocento* (Turin: Edizioni di Torino/Musica, 1985). See also chapter 2 of the present volume and Rosselli, "Agenti teatrali nel mondo dell'opera lirica italiana dell'Ottocento," *Rivista italiana di musicologia* 17 (1982): 134–54.

    6. John Mainwaring, an English clergyman, gave vivid testimony to the pace at which the opera composer in Italy had to work; see his *Memoirs of the Life of the Late George Frederic Handel* (London, 1760; reprint, with a forward by J. Merrill Knapp, New York: Da Capo Press, 1980). Mainwaring saw one of the causes for the "trifling and frothy" vocal music being composed in Italy as the "little time" that Italian composers had for composing, "For as soon as any rising genius has given some striking proof of his abilities, the Managers of almost every Opera in Italy, want to engage him to compose for them. The young fellow thinks his reputation is established, and endeavours to make the most of it, by undertaking to compose as much as it is possible to do in the time. This obliges him to write down any thing that first presents itself: and

given changing public tastes and fierce competition among composers (from the eighteenth century on). Because this was the case, the opera composer learned to safeguard his own interests by acquiring managerial skills and an impresarial savoir faire far beyond those of his colleagues in other branches of the musical profession. Verdi, for example, showed a good deal of enterprise in defending his financial interests in his dealings with his publisher, Ricordi, and with the firm's branches in Italy and abroad.

What nearly all the composers examined in this survey had in common was that they could not live by composing solely for the theater. Opera composition was precarious and exasperating work. The market demanded new operas for every season; moreover, the composer had to move constantly from one place to another because until well into the nineteenth century, the composer's contract usually stated that he must be present in the opera house at least for the first three performances of a new opera. For this reason composers aimed at obtaining a fixed post, either as a *maestro di cappella,* for the most part in an ecclesiastical institution, or a teaching position in one of the conservatories of Venice or Naples (in the eighteenth century) or in a state conservatory or a local music school (from the nineteenth century on). Such positions nearly always paid relatively less than what the composer could earn in the field of opera,[7] but they offered a better chance at long-term financial security, and they provided him certain benefits and supplementary payments after a number of years of satisfactory service. In view of their mod-

---

thus his Opera is chiefly made up of old worn-out passages hastily put together, without any new turn of expression, or harmony. Almost every Composer of genius in Italy is an instance of this" (170–71).

7. For example, Alessandro Scarlatti was paid a modest salary (120 ducats a year) in 1689 for teaching at the Conservatorio di Santa Maria di Loreto in Naples, whereas in 1685 he had earned more than twice that sum (300 ducats) for his operas. See Francesco Degrada, "L'opera napoletana," in *Storia dell'opera,* ed. Guglielmo Barblan and Alberto Basso, 3 vols. (Turin: Unione Tipografico-Editrice Torinese, 1977), vol. 1, pt. 1, 1:237–332, esp. 275. The financial situation of the *maestri di cappella* of Saint Mark's in Venice was not much better: during the entire eighteenth century their salary was still 400 ducats, just what Claudio Monteverdi and Francesco Cavalli had been paid nearly a century earlier. If, on the other hand, composers on fixed stipends failed to gain entry into the theatrical world to supplement their income, they risked indigence and even poverty. This seems to have been the case with Giuseppe Saratelli (ca. 1680–1762), *maestro di cappella* of Saint Mark's from 1747 to 1762, who did not write for the opera and who died "leaving two daughters in such squalid poverty that the procurators, by a decree dated 16 May 1762, took pity on them and granted them 100 ducats": Francesco Caffi, *Storia della musica sacra nella già cappella ducale di San Marco in Venezia dal 1318 al 1797,* 2 vols. (Venice, 1854; reprint, ed. Elvidio Surian, 2 vols. in 1, Florence: Olschki, 1987), 369 (page citation is to the original edition). On the low salaries of the maestros of Saint Mark's during the eighteenth century and on their attendant benefits (right to lodging and supplemental pay), see Giovanni Morelli and Elvidio Surian, "La musica strumentale e sacra e le sue istituzioni a Venezia," in *Storia della cultura veneta,* 6 vols. (Vicenza: Neri Pozza, 1976–86), 5:401–28, esp. 411–12.

est remuneration, composers frequently petitioned the school administrations or ecclesiastical institutions for which they worked for "artistic leaves of absence" during the opera seasons so that they could pursue their opera activities. A number of documents and minutes of decisions taken by the chapters of ecclesiastical institutions record requests and petitions from *maestri di cappella* for permission to travel. Posts whose contract terms included several months' absence per year—for instance, as court composer or as kapellmeister for the court opera of Vienna—were particularly desirable. Stefano Pavesi, for example, was able to retain his post in Vienna (1826–30) and at the same time hold the position of maestro of the cathedral of Crema (1818–30).[8] From Giuseppe Tricarico to Donizetti, the Italian opera composer could usually achieve greater financial security by going abroad, thanks to stipends and living allowances that were, on the average, much higher than in Italy. On occasion just a few years sojourn in a foreign court was enough to improve his financial situation and permit a return home to a life of ease.[9] When this happened the composer's opera production tended to fall drastically.[10]

Like their counterparts in the early twentieth century, Italian opera composers of the seventeenth century moved toward increasing professional specialization as they enjoyed greater social prestige.[11] While during the seventeenth century the composer wrote for the opera only sporadically during his

8. The position of "maestro di cappella di camera" or "compositore di corte" in Vienna was Donizetti's only institutional post from 1842 to 1845, a period during which he contemplated retiring from operatic life.

9. One case in point is that of Giuseppe Tricarico, who, after several years as *maestro di cappella* to the empress at the court in Vienna (1656?–1663), returned to his home town, Gallipoli, where he lived comfortably on the income from investments in lands, farms, olive orchards, and vineyards bought from his savings from his post in Vienna (see Giuseppe A. Pastore, "Giuseppe Tricarico da Gallipoli, musicista del secolo XVII," *Studi salentini* 5, no. 7 [1958–59]: 3–71). Similarly Antonio Lotti, after having spent two years at the court in Dresden (1717–19), returned to Venice with a carriage and horses, and from his will it appears he owned lands, a villa, and kept a large number of servants. Baldassare Galuppi, after three years of service in Russia (1765–68), had accumulated a sizable fortune, and at his death he was certainly one of the wealthiest composers in Italy.

10. This was true of Tricarico, Lotti, and Galuppi, but also of a number of other opera composers (Jommelli, Piccinni, and Spontini).

11. The social and cultural position of the Italian opera composer had begun to improve as early as the beginning of the eighteenth century. One indication of this was his growing influence within theatrical production systems, on which see Lorenzo Bianconi, "Condizione sociale e intellettuale del musicista di teatro ai tempi di Vivaldi," in *Antonio Vivaldi: Teatro musicale, cultura e società*, ed. Lorenzo Bianconi and Giovanni Morelli, 2 vols. Studi di musica veneta: Quaderni vivaldiani (Florence: Olschki, 1982), 2:371–88. According to Giovanni Morelli, "Morire di prestazioni: Sulla condizione intellettuale del musicista (teatrale, al tempo di Vivaldi)," in ibid., 389–414, when the opera composer took on the role of an intellectual, it was at the wish and on the order of the commissioning patron and as a reflection of the patron's will, therefore it was the patron who instigated an antischolarly, antischolastic, and anticounterpoint "modernity."

musical career (this was true, for example, not only of Giulio Caccini and Jacopo Peri, but also of Claudio Monteverdi, Stefano Landi, Marco Marazzoli, and Antonio Maria Abbatini), the situation was reversed during the nineteenth century, when the musical production of many Italian composers was largely confined to theatrical genres (as with Nasolini, Giuseppe Nicolini, Giuseppe Mosca, Vincenzo Bellini, Luigi and Federico Ricci, Verdi, Errico Petrella, Antonio Smareglia, Alfredo Catalani, Ruggero Leoncavallo, Giacomo Puccini, Mascagni, Francesco Cilea, Umberto Giordano, and still others who wrote almost exclusively for opera). It was for their operas that they achieved fame and success, then and now, in Italy and throughout the world, but with a difference: in the seventeenth century nearly all composers (for example, Francesco Cavalli, Antonio Cesti, Alessandro and Jacopo Melani, and Pietro Andrea Ziani) began their professional careers as *maestri di cappella* or organists in ecclesiastical institutions (for the most part in provincial towns) and only relatively late in life (at thirty years of age or later) began their theatrical careers; in later centuries composers began their opera careers at an extremely young age (at eighteen or twenty), and they usually focused their creative energies on opera immediately.

Increasingly favorable conditions for proprietary rights to the products of his own artistic labors provide one indication of the opera composer's improved social position and growing prestige. During the seventeenth century the opera composer's work was usually "expropriated": once the opera had been performed, the score was ceded to the theater (more precisely to the proprietor of the theater or to the impresario), who had the right to use the work again without making any further payment to the composer.[12] Printed opera librettos and even manuscript scores of this period often omit the composer's name. During the next century some progress was made in the composer's further rights to his own artistic creations, if only by possession of the score. It seems, for example, that when Antonio Vivaldi was involved in impresarial management of theatrical productions, he strove to retain exclusive rights to his scores and exercised (in advance of his times) a sort of copyright by which he profited financially from performances of his works.[13] Later

12. See Lorenzo Bianconi, *Il Seicento* (Turin: Edizioni di Torino/Musica, 1982), 83–91, in English translation as *Music in the Seventeenth Century*, trans. David Bryant (Cambridge: Cambridge University Press, 1987), 82–90. For example, the contract (Venice, 29 June 1667) between the composer Francesco Cavalli and the impresario Marco Faustini stipulated that "Sig.ʳ Franc.º Cavalli agrees to set to music . . . an opera . . . and, if need be, also to add, alter, and remove those things that may be necessary and proper to conform to the satisfaction of the said Sig.ʳ Faustini, who is to retain the originals"; quoted (in Italian) in Lorenzo Bianconi and Thomas Walker, "Production, Consumption, and Political Function of Seventeenth-Century Opera," *Early Music History* 4 (1984): 209–96, esp. 237.

13. See Reinhard Strohm, "Zu Vivaldis Opernschaffen," in *Venezia e il melodramma nel Settecento*, ed. Maria Teresa Muraro, 2 vols. (Florence: Olschki, 1978–81), 1:237–48; Strohm, "Vi-

in the same century a letter of Niccolò Jommelli to Duke Karl Eugen of Württemberg dated 24 February 1769 provides a detailed picture not only of Jommelli's conditions of employment but of those of other composers as well. After fifteen years of service (from 1754 to 1769) at the court at Ludwigsburg, Jommelli pressed his employer to grant him ownership of at least a copy of his own original scores. Here are the salient points in his long letter:

I have always left in the possession of V.A.S. [Your Highness] all my originals in my own hand of all the compositions that it has been my duty to do here during the past ten years. I have done so, not at all as a duty but only to show my sincere attachment to the adorable person of V.A.S. and to respond, with what has been a great sacrifice for me, to the many kindnesses and bounties that V.A.S. has deigned to continually heap upon me. Certainly no other composer or writer has allowed his autographs out of his hands or put them in the control of another. Neither Hasse and others at the court of Dresden, nor the many masters at the court in Vienna, nor the celebrated [Domenico] Scarlatti and others at the Spanish court. . . . In sum, none of the thousands and thousands of others who create music. And if, when I had the fortune to be accorded to the honorable service of V.A.S., such a request had been made of me, frankly I would have said no at any cost. On the contrary, since at the time I was promised upon entering this service the same prerogatives and distinctions that the most worthy Master Hasse had at the Dresden court, I would never have believed myself duty bound to something that was not expected of the aforementioned Hasse or of any other Master and composer of music.

If I forego the right to my own autographs, then why must I be prohibited from having copies of them? It is very just and necessary that an author have in his power and possession, under his own eyes, an example at least of his own production and work. . . . At least the copies of my works, even if I must give up my originals, are rightfully mine, but for the convenience, study, and benefit of myself, and not ever for the shameful commercial enterprise that has been done with them by so many others. I do not know who they are, but they must exist because not only outside, but even in Stuttgart itself, as everyone knows, my compositions are being circulated and sold, compositions that now I myself am being denied and that justly are my right to have.

V.A.S. as judge has given a clear example of this justice for which I ask. When you wanted to have the autographs of the compositions done here by Master [Giuseppe Antonio] Brescianello for the service of the Ducal Chapel, V.A.S., yourself, bought them from his widow, as can be seen from the decree issued after the death of the aforementioned master, my predecessor. And why was Brescianello permitted

---

valdi's Career as an Opera Producer," in Bianconi and Morelli, eds., *Antonio Vivaldi: Teatro musicale,* 1:11–63, now also available in Strohm, *Essays on Handel and Italian Opera* (Cambridge: Cambridge University Press, 1985), 122–63.

to have possession of his autographs, like so many others, and only I am not permitted mine, or at least copies?[14]

Rossini was perhaps the first to institute a new relationship among the composer, the commissioner, and the artistic product, probably thanks to the enormous success of his works over the years but also to his good relations with the impresario Domenico Barbaja (unfortunately their contracts have not come down to us). Barbaja's contracts with Donizetti for *Gianni di Calais* and *Il paria* (1828) explicitly state that "ownership of the music of the said two operas is to remain exclusively the management's, as is customary, and Sig. Donizetti cannot have copies of them made under any pretext, either in complete copies or in part."[15] A few years later, however, Rossini had this to say about his differences with Barbaja over the autograph manuscript of *Zelmira*.

> I own all my originals, being the custom and the law that after one year following the performance of an opera the author has the right to have back his autograph score. Have I perhaps robbed Barbaja's files of my originals? I have asked for them, and he has given them to me; why does he want them back now? . . . And if a contract can be found in which I have ceded the score of *Zelmira* I will pay any fine.[16]

Clearly, in the contracts he signed with the impresario, Rossini had taken pains to retain rights to his own scores. According to Nicola Vaccai,[17] by the 1830s it was customary in Italian opera houses to grant the composer not only the right to choose both the subject matter for the libretto and the poet who would write it but also to have proprietary rights to the score (all rights that had formerly been the impresario's). It was, however, from Verdi on that the composer definitively imposed his right to personal control of every aspect

14. Marita P. McClymonds, *Niccolò Jommelli: The Last Years, 1769–1774* (Ann Arbor: UMI Research Press, 1980), 694–98. When Jommelli left Stuttgart he left behind heavy debts that he had contracted during his service at court (see 70–71), and on another occasion before his return to Italy he attempted to obtain an advantageous life pension from the king of Portugal, with the obligation to send new works to Lisbon along with copies of all the operas he might write for other theaters. Jommelli's correspondence with the Portuguese court offers exceptional documentation, without equal among papers of other eighteenth-century Italian opera composers.

15. The contract is given in Alexander L. Ringer, "Aspetti socio-economici dell'opera italiana nel periodo donizettiano," in *Atti del primo convegno internazionale di studi donizettiani, 22–28 settembre 1975* (Bergamo: Azienda Autonoma di Turismo, 1983), 943–58, esp. 956–57.

16. Letter to his friend Carlo De Chiaro, 17 April 1823, in *Lettere di G. Rossini*, ed. Giuseppe Mazzatinti and F. and G. Manis (Florence: G. Barbera, 1902; reprint, Bologna: Arnaldo Forni, 1975), 27–28.

17. Giulio Vaccai, *Vita di Nicola Vaccaj* (Bologna, 1882), 181, 216.

of the production and that he held proprietary rights over an artistic product that was now considered capable of producing long-term income and was now the result of close collaboration between the composer and the music publisher. (This was a radical change from the previous custom: until well into the nineteenth century, one lump-sum payment was made to the composer for each opera that he composed, irrespective of its success.)

When an opera was widely performed, even in small provincial theaters, the composer's right to a share in the profits from the rental of orchestral parts and from printed piano-vocal scores might represent a good source of income.[18] In view of such future earnings, both the publisher and the composer (beginning with Verdi) acted with a common accord to protect the integrity of the work and prevent cuts, revisions, and the transfer of single pieces (of the composer's work or even from other composers' works) from one opera to another. Verdi was perhaps the first composer who insisted that his publisher see to it that contracts with the theaters contained a clause prohibiting any modification of the version of the score provided. Thus he wrote to Giovanni Ricordi (15 October 1847) regarding the Italian version of *Jérusalem*:

> It is still prohibited to make any intrusion into or mutilation of the score (with the exception of the ballet music, which can be removed) under pain of a fine of 1,000 francs, which I shall demand from you every time that score is played in major theaters. For second-rank theaters the same clause will likewise exist, and it will be up to you to study possible means for demanding the fine in case of infringement.[19]

Verdi and Ricordi strove together to safeguard and protect the composer's work, urging the Italian parliament to work out and pass the first law after the unification of Italy on literary and artistic copyright.[20]

From the time of Verdi on, the fortunes, prestige, and social position of the opera composer were in great part tied to music publishing. In the last

18. In 1850 Verdi demanded from Ricordi 30 percent of the income on the rental of instrumental parts and 40 percent on the sale of printed piano-vocal scores for a period of ten years; see Giuseppe Verdi, *I copialettere di Giuseppe Verdi,* ed. Gaetano Cesari and Alessandro Luzio (Milan: Stucchi Ceretti, 1913; reprint, Bologna: Arnaldo Forni, 1968), 93–94. This share in the profits must have been considerable for Verdi. Over a ten-year period the composer Filippo Marchetti earned for *Ruy Blas* (1869) alone more than 100,000 lire; see Francesco D'Arcais, "L'industria musicale in Italia," *Nuova antologia di scienze, lettere ed arti* 2d ser., 15 (15 May 1879): 133–48, esp. 145. On Verdi's earnings from his operas, see John Rosselli, "Verdi e la storia della retribuzione del compositore italiano," *Studi verdiani* 2 (1983): 11–28, esp. 21–25.

19. Verdi, *I copialettere,* 45.

20. The law was approved by the national parliament at Turin on 25 June 1865; see "Per la nuova legge sui diritti d'autore," in *Carteggi verdiani,* ed. Alessandro Luzio (Rome: Accademia Nazionale dei Lincei, 1947), 4:133–35; Nicola Tabanelli, "Verdi e la legge sul diritto d'autore," *Rivista musicale italiana* 46 (1942): 208–17.

analysis it was the publisher rather than the impresario who could most efficiently safeguard the composer's artistic interests, imposing conditions on the opera houses, determining the number of rehearsals, and freeing and protecting the composer from copyright infringements and plagiarism of his works. There was another side to the coin, however, and there are a number of cases in which the composer's image and his creative faculties were clearly hindered by music publishers.[21]

1. Social Background

We have little precise information on the social background of many composers, but as far as we know, seventeenth- and eighteenth-century opera composers came predominantly from families of professional musicians or were involved in music thanks to family tradition. There are many cases of entire generations of composers who wrote theatrical music and who were directly conditioned by a family environment that propelled them to early success. During the nineteenth and twentieth centuries, however, it is even clearer that the number of opera composers who came from musical families declined and that more of them came from a solid middle-class background. When the profession of opera composer was no longer considered to be a craft, the composer won a much more respectable position in society—a conquest due in large part, as we have seen, to the expanded opportunities offered by the music publishing houses. A number of opera composers were also of humble (even very humble) extraction. They tended to make every effort to become established in opera rather than in other sectors of musical production that offered less opportunity for social promotion. Composers from humble backgrounds, in fact, shared the characteristic of high productivity, continuing to compose without pause throughout their careers.

There have been few opera composers from aristocratic and upper-middle-class backgrounds who can be said to have had a genuine musical career in opera. It seems obvious that an aristocratic composer, who already enjoys an independent income, does not feel the same need for social advancement or professional success. At most he will take on composing for opera as a secondary activity carried on without excessive professional involvement. In spite of the advantages that family connections might offer (support for musical studies, contacts to aid entry into the production system, etc.), upper-class composers wrote very few operas, and those few fell within a brief span of

21. One composer typical in this regard was Antonio Smareglia, whose opera career met with a certain success in its initial stages but who was tenaciously opposed by Giulio Ricordi during the early 1900s, after which his fortunes declined precipitously (even though he had the support of Arturo Toscanini), and his operas were performed only in the province of Venezia Giulia.

time. One such case was the nobleman Alberto Franchetti; he studied in Germany at the best music schools, and later his father contributed generously to the exorbitant production costs of his first opera (*Asrael,* Reggio Emilia, 1888). An exception that proves the rule was Prince Michele Carafa di Colobrano. Intended for a military career and in fact a valorous officer in the army of Joachim Murat, he retired to private life at the return of the Bourbons to Naples, going back, as a professional, to the opera career that he had begun with considerable success as a dilettante in the 1820s.

Table 1 presents a classification of eighty-one Italian opera composers on whose family backgrounds we have reliable information. Composers are arranged by social extraction and chronology within each group.

2. *Schooling, Professional Training, Apprenticeship*

Before musical instruction in Italy became almost totally institutionalized—a movement that began in the post-Napoleonic era but was not completed until after national unification—the musician generally learned the fundamentals of his profession in the family, if someone in the family was already a musician, or from the *maestro di cappella* of the local cathedral. Thus a very young musician's early technical training was empirical; he learned his craft in a transfer of skills from teacher to pupil. Even after the institution of state-supported music schools (beginning around the mid-nineteenth century), a child still learned basic musical skills privately and locally. Amilcare Ponchielli, to pick one example, studied with his father and with local teachers before going to the conservatory in Milan (1843–54) for formal training. Catalani learned the rudiments of music from his father before he attended Lucca's Istituto di Musica; Mascagni studied with a baritone and an organist in his city of birth (Livorno); Giordano studied with a family friend; Riccardo Zandonai studied with the director of the local music school; and Gian Carlo Menotti and Nino Rota studied with their mothers. Budding composers who came from families of professional musicians presumably learned their musical ABCs within the family, along with further training as they became capable of it. A young musician must have been strongly motivated to learn the rudiments of his craft directly from his father and to set his sights on opera composition.[22]

Until the sixteenth century, musical instruction was humanistic and individual in nature: music was one of the many arts that the gentleman owed

---

22. After teaching his son his craft, the musician father often worked to help him gain entry into the profession. One good example of this is the apprehension that Alessandro Scarlatti expressed in a letter of 1705 to Ferdinando de' Medici concerning the professional future of the young Domenico Scarlatti; see Fabbri, *Alessandro Scarlatti,* 58–59.

TABLE 1. A Classification of Italian Operatic Composers

	Musical Families
Antonio Maria Abbatini	Uncle *maestro di cappella* in Città di Castello
Francesco Cavalli	Father *maestro di cappella* in Crema
Jacopo and Atto Melani	Father bell ringer; seven musician brothers
Giovanni Legrenzi	Father violinist
Alessandro Melani	Father bell ringer; seven musician brothers
Marc'Antonio Ziani	Uncle Pietro Andrea composer
Carlo Francesco Pollarolo	Father organist
Alessandro Scarlatti	Probably musicians in mother's family
Antonio Lotti	Father *maestro di cappella* in Hannover
Giovanni Bononcini	Father Giovanni Maria composer
Antonio Caldara	Father violinist
Antonio Maria Bononcini	Father Giovanni Maria composer
Antonio Vivaldi	Father violinist
Domenico Scarlatti	Father Alessandro composer
Riccardo Broschi	Father *maestro di cappella* at Andria and Barletta, brother Carlo the celebrated castrato Farinelli
Egidio Romualdo Duni	Father *maestro di cappella* at Matera
Gennaro Manna	Father musician, mother sister of Francesco Feo
Niccolò Piccinni	Father musician, mother sister of Gaetano Latilla
Pietro Alessandro Guglielmi	Father *maestro di cappella* at Massa
Gian Francesco de Majo	Father composer
Nicola Zingarelli	Father singing teacher
Luigi Caruso	Father *maestro di cappella* at Naples, brother a tenor
Gaetano Andreozzi	Nephew of Niccolò Jommelli
Luigi Cherubini	Father conductor-harpsichordist in Florentine theaters
Giuseppe Nicolini	Father *maestro di cappella* at Piacenza
Johann Simon Mayr	Father organist
Carlo Coccia	Father violinist
Gioachino Rossini	Father horn player (and *trombetta,* town trumpeter), mother a singer
Giovanni Pacini	Father a tenor
Giuseppe Persiani	Father violinist
Vincenzo Bellini	Father *maestro di cappella* at Catania
Luigi and Federico Ricci	Father pianist
Amilcare Ponchielli	Father organist
Alfredo Catalani	Grandfather and father musicians
Giacomo Puccini	Forbears and father musicians
Ildebrando Pizzetti	Father piano teacher
Gian Francesco Malipiero	Musicians in family
Nino Rota	Grandfather composer, mother pianist

	Middle-Class Origins
Jacopo Peri	Father public official
Claudio Monteverdi	Father physician-pharmacist
Alessandro Stradella	Father military governor
Tomaso Albinoni	Father paper wholesaler

TABLE 1. *Continued*

Middle-Class Origins

Nicola Logroscino	Father probably landowner
Giovanni Battista Pergolesi	Father agricultural expert
Niccolò Jommelli	Father wealthy wholesale merchant
Giacomo Tritto	Father shopkeeper
Antonio Salieri	Father shopkeeper
Gaspare Spontini	Father small farmer
Nicola Vaccai	Father physician
Giuseppe Verdi	Family of small landowners and shopkeepers
Errico Petrella	Father official in the Bourbon navy
Antonio Cagnoni	Father physician
Ruggero Leoncavallo	Father judge
Francesco Cilea	Father prominent lawyer
Umberto Giordano	Father pharmacist
Ermanno Wolf-Ferrari	Father painter
Luigi Dallapiccola	Father teacher
Gian Carlo Menotti	Father wealthy merchant
Luigi Nono	Father painter, uncle sculptor
Sylvano Bussotti	Uncle and brother painters

Lower-Class Background

Giulio Caccini	Father carpenter
Antonio Cesti	Ninth child of grocer-delicatessen owner
Francesco Feo	Father tailor
Baldassare Galuppi	Father barber
Tommaso Traetta	Father farmer
Antonio Sacchini	Father cook
Giovanni Paisiello	Father blacksmith
Domenico Cimarosa	Father mason; mother washerwoman
Francesco Bianchi	Proletarian background
Gaetano Donizetti	Father weaver
Pietro Mascagni	Father baker
Riccardo Zandonai	Father shoemaker

Aristocratic Background

Pirro Albergati Capacelli	Marquis
Emanuele d'Astorga	Baron
Giovanni Battista Cimador	Patrician family
Michele Carafa	Prince
Francesco Sampieri	Marquis
Arrigo Boito	Mother Polish noblewoman
Alberto Franchetti	Father baron, mother Rothschild

Note: Composers are arranged chronologically within each group.

it to himself to master, following the model of Baldassarre Castiglione's *Il cortegiano* (1528). From the seventeenth century on, however, musical training was increasingly aimed at forming a good craftsman who could furnish a service requiring specific skills, thus it became more standardized.[23] From roughly the mid-seventeenth century on, the four conservatories that were founded in Naples provided training for a labor force needed to supply music for the various functions (both religious and aristocratic) that took place in and around the city. After 1660 the Neapolitan conservatories put on productions of both sacred and comic dramatic works in an attempt to link musical instruction with the professional world and to provide their more advanced students with an opportunity to learn the latest techniques of theatrical production.[24] Thus when the young composer had completed his course of studies (at from eighteen to twenty years of age), he already had an entry into a theatrical career. This didactic method does not seem to have continued to be the rule in state-supported conservatories during the nineteenth century, although the little theater in the Milan Conservatory at times offered young composers a chance to perform their works at the end of the school year. Such productions included, for example, an operetta, *Rosalia di San Miniato* (1845), and the opera *I due Savoiardi* (1846) by Antonio Cagnoni, a lyric drama, *La Tirolese* (1855), by Ivan Zajc, and *La falce* (1875), Catalani's first opera. The same tradition seems to have been carried on at the Naples Conservatory, where Cilea's first opera, *Gina*, was put on in its little theater in 1889.

In the Naples conservatories and elsewhere, a young musician's instruction (students usually entered such schools at the age of twelve) was based principally on a rigorous training in formal techniques of traditional counterpoint. Throughout the seventeenth century the polyphonic madrigal continued to be indispensable for giving the student mastery of the language of polyphony.[25] In the eighteenth century the curriculum of the most famous Neapolitan schools was based on the study of *partimenti*—exercises on figured and nonfigured basses—and on counterpoint, singing, and solfège.[26] The professors in the Naples conservatories devoted much care and effort to their teaching, and it often took as much of their time as their professional opera activi-

23. Bianconi, *Music in the Seventeenth Century,* 65–66.

24. Michael F. Robinson, *Naples and Neapolitan Opera* (Oxford: Clarendon Press, 1972), 16–18.

25. See Elvidio Surian, "L'esordio teatrale del giovane Gasparini: Alcune considerazioni sull'apprendimento e tirocinio musicale nel Seicento," in *Francesco Gasparini (1661–1727),* ed. Fabrizio Della Seta and Franco Piperno (Florence: Olschki, 1981), 37–54, esp. 43–47.

26. On the curriculum and didactic methods of Neapolitan conservatories from the late seventeenth century on, see Salvatore di Giacomo, *Il Conservatorio di S. Onofrio a Capuana e quello di S. Maria della Pietà dei Turchini* (Palermo: Sandron, 1924), 87–90.

ties. This is clear from the solfège and counterpoint manuals that many of them—Nicola Porpora, Francesco Feo, Leonardo Leo, Giacomo Tritto, Fedele Fenaroli, Nicola Zingarelli, and others—compiled as aids to their teaching. Some of these works were printed, were circulated throughout much of Europe, and were still in use well into the nineteenth century. From what we know (and our knowledge is still fragmentary and full of gaps) the theoretical study of counterpoint was based on the treatises of Gioseffo Zarlino and Johann Joseph Fux. There is a portrait of Feo showing treatises by Domenico Scorpione, Fux, and Zarlino in the background.[27] In his prefatory letter to the first Italian translation (Carpi, 1761) of Fux's *Gradus ad Parnassum,* Niccolò Piccinni wrote, "I discovered its usefulness when the celebrated Professor Durante warmly recommended that I study it."[28]

Young musicians who trained privately or took lessons from established composers also followed programs of study based on the traditional forms of the past. Simon Mayr, Donizetti's teacher, stated that he gave theoretical lessons "without which practical exercises are always uncertain and overly mechanical,"[29] and he transcribed for his students' use a number of eighteenth-century works on musical theory. Vaccai first studied composition in Rome with the contrapuntalist Giuseppe Janacconi, *maestro di cappella* of Saint Peter's, and then took his diploma in 1811 at the Accademia di Santa Cecilia with an examination that included the improvisation of a fugue. Only then did Vaccai decide to go to Naples to study opera composition with Paisiello, a discipline "very different from the severe style taught by Janacconi."[30] Verdi tells us that his teacher, Vincenzo Lavigna, who had himself trained under Paisiello in Naples, spent three years having Verdi do nothing but "canons and fugues, fugues and canons in all kinds of sauces."[31] Verdi in turn attempted to transmit to his one pupil, Emanuele Muzio, the same course of

27. Bologna, Civico Museo Bibliografico Musicale. For a reproduction of this portrait, see *The New Grove Dictionary of Music and Musicians,* s. v. "Feo, Francesco," by Hanns-Bertold Dietz.

28. Piccinni studied at the Neapolitan Conservatorio di Sant'Onofrio in Capuana from 1742 to 1754, first with Leonardo Leo and then, after Leo's death in 1744, with Francesco Durante, a composer and teacher who never wrote for the opera stage.

29. John Allitt, "L'importanza di Simone Mayr nella formazione culturale e musicale di Gaetano Donizetti," in *Atti del primo convegno internazionale di studi donizettiani,* 333–49, esp. 337.

30. Vaccai, *Vita di Nicola Vaccaj,* 20–21.

31. Letter of 9 January 1871 to Francesco Florimo, in *Carteggi verdiani,* 4:126. For the competitive examination for the post of music teacher at Busseto (1836), Verdi spent an entire day (from eight o'clock in the morning to after six in the evening) composing a four-part fugue; see his letter of 29 February 1836 to Antonio Barezzi, in Gustavo Marchesi, *Verdi, merli e cucù: Cronache bussetane fra il 1819 e il 1839* (Busseto: Cassa di Risparmio di Parma e Monte di Credito su pegno di Busseto, 1979), 336.

studies that he himself had completed under the guidance of Lavigna, "improved, however, by himself": counterpoint, harmonizing a bass line, studying the treatises of Giuseppe Tartini and Francesco Antonio Vallotti and the music of "Beethoven, Mozart, Leinsdesdorf [Maximilian Joseph Leidesdorf], Schubert, Haydn, etc." [32]

During the seventeenth century a talented youngster who had already mastered the rudiments of musical composition and wanted to complete his technical training nearly always did a few years of practical apprenticeship, usually as a singer, in the chief ecclesiastical institution of his place of origin. [33] In the eighteenth century a number of composers attended one of the prestigious Neapolitan schools or were instructed by a famous master composer, while in the nineteenth century aspiring composers hoped to graduate from one of the best state schools, the Milan Conservatory in particular. From the late nineteenth century to our own day, a good many Italian composers have studied abroad. [34] Beginning in the early eighteenth century the Neapolitan conservatories trained a number of opera composers who later rose to fame in Italy and throughout Europe. [35] There were also a number of aspiring composers from outside Naples who went there to study with the famous masters in residence there, both in order to acquire a good musical training and in the hope that their teachers would facilitate their entry into the professional (and particularly into the opera) world. Non-Neapolitans studying in the Naples conservatories were admitted as paying boarders at an annual fee (25 ducats) that seems fairly high in comparison to the annual salaries that the leading

---

32. Luigi Agostino Garibaldi, *Giuseppe Verdi nelle lettere di Emanuele Muzio ad Antonio Barezzi* (Milan: Treves, 1931), 168 and 199; see also 161, 181.

33. In 1616 at the age of fourteen, Francesco Cavalli became a choirboy at Saint Mark's in Venice; later he became the organist there and finally, in his old age, *maestro di cappella*. At the age of eleven, Francesco Manelli was a choirboy in the cathedral of Tivoli, as were Giuseppe Tricarico in the cathedral of Gallipoli, Alessandro Melani (from the age of eleven to twenty-one) in the cathedral of Pistoia, Antonio Cesti (from age eight to fifteen) in the cathedral of Arezzo, Giovanni Domenico Freschi in the cathedral of Vicenza, and Alessandro Stradella in the Oratorio del Santo Crocifisso in Rome. We have no information on the early formal musical training of other composers of the age (Pietro Andrea Ziani, Giovanni Legrenzi, Antonio Sartorio, and Carlo Pallavicino).

34. Alberto Franchetti studied in the conservatories of Dresden and Munich, Alfredo Catalani at the Paris Conservatory; Ermanno Wolf-Ferrari at the Akademie der Tonkunst of Munich, Gian Francesco Malipiero at the conservatory in Vienna. Luigi Dallapiccola became familiar with German music during his years of internment at Graz (1917–18), Menotti studied at the Curtis Institute in Philadelphia, Luigi Nono studied in Darmstadt after 1950, and Sylvano Bussotti (who considers himself self-taught) made a number of trips abroad (to Paris, Darmstadt, Berlin, and the United States) during the period of his musical formation.

35. For an indicative (but incomplete) list, see Robinson, *Naples and Neapolitan Opera*, 16–18.

conservatories paid their most prominent teachers (around 100 ducats a year, and even less as the century progressed).[36] This may explain why young men from outside Naples felt they needed to find support from some nobleman or other influential person in order to pay for their studies in the conservatories: as the written regulations of these institutions stated,[37] they had to procure a "guarantor" who was a resident of the city.[38]

The leading center for the production of opera during the nineteenth century was Milan, which attracted young composers eager not so much to acquire adequate musical training as to have better access to professional opportunities in opera houses and music publishers than were available in provincial areas. Puccini, for example, went from Lucca to Milan (as his fellow Lucchese Catalani had done before him) not so much in search of a less provincial musical training—he had studied in Lucca with his father and his grandfather, both excellent musicians—as to seek new work opportunities to launch his career as an opera composer. Just as Verdi, at the beginning of the century, had needed financial support to study in Milan (which he received first from Antonio Barezzi, his future father-in-law, and then from the Monte di Pietà bank in his home town, Busseto), so Albina Puccini pressed the local nobility to help her son Giacomo obtain a scholarship offered to talented students by Queen Margherita. Albina Puccini also worked indefatigably to get Puccini's uncle, the physician Nicolao Cerù, to finance his studies in Mi-

---

36. Michael F. Robinson, "The Governors' Minutes of the Conservatory S. Maria di Loreto, Naples," *R.M.A. Research Chronicle* 10 (1972): 1–97, esp. 52–54, 94–97.

37. Ibid., 54.

38. Leonardo Leo, who came from Puglia, may have been admitted to the Conservatorio di Santa Maria della Pietà (1709) in Naples thanks to the recommendation of his uncle Teodomiro, a *doctor physicus;* Giovanni Battista Pergolesi, who came from the Marches, entered the Conservatorio dei Poveri di Gesù Cristo on the recommendation of Marquis Cardolo Maria Pianetti, who came from Iesi; a nobleman brought Pasquale Anfossi, a Ligurian, to Naples; an uncle who was a priest did the same for Giacomo Tritto, who was from Puglia; Duchess Ricciarda Cybo Gonzaga sponsored Pietro Alessandro Guglielmi, from Massa, at the Conservatorio di Santa Maria di Loreto; Nicola Porpora procured a free place in the Conservatorio di Sant'Onofrio for Giuseppe Gazzaniga, who was from Verona; a prelate from Cremona financed the Neapolitan studies of Francesco Bianchi; the duke of Castelnuovo maintained Giuseppe Nicolini, who was from Piacenza, at the Conservatorio di Sant'Onofrio; some wealthy gentlemen from Crema financed the Neapolitan studies of Stefano Pavesi; the professor Vincenzo Ciuffolotti (who had himself studied in Naples) recommended Gaspare Spontini, who came from the Marches, to the Conservatorio della Pietà dei Turchini. The tradition of having a local guarantor must have persisted in Naples even into the nineteenth century. For example, when Francesco Cilea came from Calabria to the conservatory of San Pietro a Majella at the age of thirteen, he was admitted thanks to a written guarantee signed by one Giacomo Correale, Francesco Florimo's personal physician and a friend of the young man's father: the document is published in Tomasino D'Amico, *Francesco Cilea* (Milan: Edizioni Curci, 1960), 27–28.

lan.[39] Mascagni, who was born in Livorno, received aid from Count Flo-restano de Larderel that enabled him to go to Milan to study at the Conservatory.

3. Entry into the Production System, Career, Opera Production

During the seventeenth century the composer's theatrical debut usually occurred when he was no longer in his youth.[40] For some opera composers of that period, of course, this relatively late beginning must be understood in historical terms: a genuine market for opera was created and expanded only after the midcentury, when theaters devoted exclusively to opera were inaugurated throughout Italy, both in the major cities and in outlying centers, and when these opera houses in turn created a growing demand for new operas and for recasting existent works. Another reason for a late start in opera composing was that the musical training of the composer of the early and mid-seventeenth century, as we have seen, took place within the context of church and chapel, where the talented youngster found ready possibilities for employment and was able to dedicate his energies to opera only when and if the opportunity arose. The situation changed completely after about 1680; the place of skilled singers—*virtuosi*—within the structure of opera changed as well.[41] If up to that point there had been some singers who, like certain composers, had earned their living as court *virtuosi* in the exclusive service of one prince or patron, the moment a "system" had been put into place—that is, a network of opera houses operating on the basis of a traveling repertory—performers took on more responsibility for the end result of an opera production. Artistic specialization increased, but so did professional specialization, with its attendant earnings differential. Just as the singers to a large extent determined the specific character of opera by the heightened stylization of arias, so the composers found that their talents necessarily had to

---

39. Mosco Carner, *Puccini: A Critical Biography,* 3d ed. (New York: Holmes and Meier, 1992), 21.

40. Some seventeenth-century composers and their ages when they first wrote an opera: Stefano Landi (33), Francesco Manelli (43), Marco Marazzoli (either about 35 or 29), Francesco Cavalli (37), Antonio Maria Abbatini (59?), Pietro Andrea Ziani (38), Giuseppe Tricarico (32), Jacopo Melani (34), Antonio Cesti (28), Antonio Sartorio (31), Bernardo Pasquini (35).

41. Reinhard Strohm, "Aspetti sociali dell'opera italiana del primo Settecento," *Musica/Realtà* 2, no. 5 (August 1981): 117–41, esp. 136–38. On the shifting relationships between aristocratic power and professional singers around 1700, see Sergio Durante, "Cantanti per Reggio (1696–1717): Note sul rapporto di dipendenza," in *Civiltà teatrale e Settecento emiliano,* ed. Susi Davoli (Bologna: Il Mulino, 1986), 301–7.

become more specialized.[42] Furthermore, specialization set in at the outset of
the composer's professional career.

Neapolitan schools in the early eighteenth century offered young composers a high level of technical training, but that preparation did not necessarily
mean that once they had completed their formal studies they were ready to
write operas, tragic or comic. Theatrical music had no "theory" behind it;
nor had it any didactic praxis. In fact there were hardly any theoretical, didactic, and critical texts on opera composition throughout the eighteenth century
and for part of the nineteenth century.

Until well into the 1800s there was no treatise specifically devoted to opera
composition written in Italy. As we have seen, Johann Joseph Fux's *Gradus
ad Parnassum* (Vienna, 1725), translated into Italian and published at Carpi
in 1761, was widely used by composition students at the conservatories of
Naples, but this treatise gave absolute precedence to training in the ecclesiastical style. At the end of the volume in its Italian translation (pp. 232–37), the
work treats the application of the recitative style to the field of secular music
(chamber music and theatrical music) by passing in review a certain number
of musical formulas corresponding to as many "affections" (scorn, compas-
sion, fear, violence, pleasure, love) and giving precepts on how to project the
various "parts of discourse" (the comma, the opening of a period, the full
stop, the question mark, the exclamation, the parenthesis, etc.).[43]

The first instructional manuals on composition that do more than treat
the study of counterpoint and church music came only after the institutional-
ization of musical training in the post-Napoleonic era. Bonifazio Asioli
(1769–1832) wrote a series of didactic works that had a notable influence on
several generations of composers; they were reprinted many times and long
remained in use in the music schools of Italy. By now harmony was included
among the topics studied by composition students (Asioli wrote no fewer
than three treatises on harmony). Counterpoint, which generally followed the
eighteenth-century tradition, had its own texts as well. Asioli's *Il maestro di
composizione, ossia Séguito del Trattato d'armonia* (Milan, 1832), his last
theoretical work, was the first Italian printed manual to devote notable space
to opera composition (all of book 3, while book 1 treated harmony and book
2 the fugue). In the "Vita di Bonifazio Asioli da Correggio" printed in a later

42. *Dizionario enciclopedico universale della musica e dei musicisti: Il lessico*, s.v. "Aria," by
Elvidio Surian.

43. Another work in the same theoretical tradition is a manuscript treatise of 396 pages (latter eighteenth century) by Giannantonio Banner of Padua entitled "Compendio musicale nel quale
con varij ragionamenti, regole, avvertimenti, ed esempij, si dimostra al Principiante . . . l'arte del
Contrapunto," Bologna, Civico Museo Bibliografico Musicale, EE 114. Chapter 12, on how to
compose recitatives and arias, reworks Fux's theories on the expression of the various affects and
on the musical realization of the "parts of discourse."

edition of that work (1834), Antonio Coli explains (xxviii) the didactic principles underlying the manual:

> Experience had already shown that the old methods of teaching music were bad. Ignorance of the integral numbers of the chords and the ridiculous plays on words to guide the student as he superimposes the parts onto a cantus firmus led to specific complaints from which the art drew absolutely no profit. These and other pernicious errors were manifest, but in spite of this, blind respect led many valiant men to hold their pens, to the point that I know of no one who has yet dared to give prejudice as mortal a blow as Asioli. He proposed a new method, and in the three volumes of the *Maestro di composizione* he develops it completely.

Anticipating by several years the first manuals on orchestration (Giuseppe Pilotti, 1836; Jean-Georges Kastner, 1837; and Hector Berlioz, 1843), Asioli gives, at the head of book 3, a general table of the human voices and the instruments used by the opera composer, noting the range, character, typical sounds, and properties of each. He then treats melodic composition (melodic rhythm, relationships between musical phrases, and the various poetic meters) and what he calls "imitation of sentiments"—expression of the various affects of the soul (poetic, amorous, choleric, etc.). He also treats the opera sinfonia, examining the periods, harmonic modulations, and principal divisions of the overture to Rossini's *La Cenerentola*, which he gives in complete orchestral score (90–137). He describes the requirements of writing for chorus and gives appropriate advice on the composition of concerted ensembles and arias, presenting as a model for the grand aria the scene "Qual densa notte! qual silenzio! quale" from *Gli Orazi e i Curiazi* of Domenico Cimarosa, which he analyses almost measure for measure, and prints the entire orchestral score (146–80). Asioli's many musical examples (most of which are printed in full score) concentrate on the leading composers of the immediate past: Paisiello, Cimarosa, Rossini, and Joseph Haydn.

It was in the best interests of the composer of the eighteenth and nineteenth centuries to start working in opera (which could represent a good source of income for him) at a young age, generally before he was twenty, and to learn the laws specific to opera composition as soon as possible. From the 1780s on, the usual way for a composer to get a start was by being commissioned (by an impresario or by his teacher) to rewrite a work composed by someone else and produced elsewhere, making additions to it and adapting it. This process enabled him to learn the techniques of his craft by direct practical experience and by imitation of the dominant models, and it remained standard practice throughout the eighteenth century.[44] In the nine-

---

44. Thus the first theatrical experience of the seventeen-year-old Alessandro Scarlatti was to collaborate in the *commedia in musica, La Rosmene* (Rome, 1677); that of Francesco Gasparini (at the age of twenty-five) was to add arias to *Il Roderico* (Livorno, 1687); at the age of twenty-

teenth century music publishers also offered the young composer training in opera writing by hiring him to make cuts and changes in operas in the repertory or to edit scores or make instrumental reductions for commercial purposes. According to Catalani, the Ricordi publishing firm hired Puccini "to make the necessary cuts in *Die Meistersinger* so as to adjust it, like clothes, to the shoulders of the good Milanese."[45] While Cilea was still a student in Naples, he did a transcription of Donizetti's *Lucia di Lammermoor*.[46] The young opera composer could also get good technical training (even in a place far from where he had studied) as a keyboard accompanist.[47]

Any young person who aspired to a career in opera found that the protection of a powerful or influential person and the support of a known composer were so necessary as to be indispensable. Especially from about 1650 to the early eighteenth century, the opera composer (like the singer, for that matter) had to have the support and the respect of some powerful person if he wanted to get anywhere in his profession. Nearly all of Cesti's opera career, for example, took place within the sphere of influence of the Medici family.[48] Composers linked to aristocratic circles in Rome in the late seventeenth and early

---

two, Giovanni Bononcini added new arias for a performance in Rome of Antonio Draghi's *L'Eraclea* in 1692; and at eighteen Domenico Scarlatti composed his own *L'Ottavia* and patched up Giovanni Legrenzi's *Il Giustino* (Naples, 1703). In the same period Giacomo Antonio Perti wrote the third act of *Atide* (Bologna, 1679); see Surian, "L'esordio teatrale del giovane Gasparini," 47–48. Often the young composer just out of a Naples conservatory began with a drama or sacred oratorio: Antonio Sacchini added some arias to the opera *Le donne dispettose* of Niccolò Piccinni (Naples, 1754) before he composed his own first short opera, *Fra Donato* (1756), performed in the little theater of the Conservatorio di Santa Maria di Loreto. The young Luigi Cherubini learned opera composition by following his teacher Giuseppe Sarti as he moved from Florence to Bologna and then to Milan (1779–82) and by composing all the arias for secondary characters for the operas that Sarti was writing; see Margery Stomne Selden, "Cherubini: The Italian 'Image,'" *Journal of the American Musicological Society* 17 (1964): 378–81.

45. Letter of 20 August 1889 to Giuseppe Depanis, in Carner, *Puccini: A Critical Biography*, 29.

46. D'Amico, *Francesco Cilea*, 29.

47. When he was twenty Baldassare Galuppi spent two years (1726–27) as a harpsichord accompanist at the Teatro della Pergola in Florence; Francesco Bianchi did the same (at the age of twenty-three) for three years (1775–78) at the Théâtre Italien in Paris; Luigi Mosca was for many years *maestro al cembalo* at the Teatro San Carlo in Naples (his entire opera career took place in that city); his brother Giuseppe Mosca was from 1803 to 1810 the keyboardist at the Théâtre Italien in Paris; at seventeen Sebastiano Nasolini was harpsichordist after 1787 at the Teatro San Pietro of Trieste (where his first opera, *La Nitteti* was produced in 1788); at twenty-six Vincenzo Lavigna (later Verdi's teacher) had the post of *maestro al cembalo* at La Scala in Milan (thanks to a recommendation from Giovanni Paisiello) from 1802 to 1832.

48. Cesti's debut in Venice with *Alessandro vincitor di se stesso* (1651) was probably due to the mediation of Mattias de' Medici with the Grimani family, as was his position (1652) at the court of Innsbruck (Ferdinando Carlo, archduke of the Tyrol, was a brother-in-law of the Medicis); see *Dizionario biografico degli italiani*, s. v. "Pietro Cesti," by Lorenzo Bianconi.

eighteenth centuries (the Ruspoli, Colonna, Borghese, and Ottoboni families) had an excellent entry into the opera field, since (except when the changing sociocultural policies of the popes interrupted theatrical life in Rome) these were families that kept up a dense network of relations and artistic exchanges in Italy and throughout Europe.[49] Nearly all of the fourteen theatrical works written by Bernardo Pasquini (who had connections with the Colonna, Pamphili, and Borghese families) were performed in noble palaces in Rome. It was by frequenting the Ottoboni, Ruspoli, and Colonna families that the Venetian Antonio Caldara landed the prestigious and well-paid post of maestro at the Viennese court (1716–36), and the brilliant opera careers in Italy and abroad of Giovanni and Antonio Maria Bononcini were certainly due to the familiar relations they established with Roman nobles during their early professional years. The Bononcinis, who enjoyed the protection of Francesco II d'Este, moved from Bologna to Rome (at a time when the papal legate in Bologna was Cardinal Benedetto Pamphili) and then to Vienna, where Giovanni became the favorite composer of the new emperor, Joseph I (1705), and where he helped his brother Antonio obtain a well-paid post at the imperial court. Less than two years after the death of Emperor Joseph in 1711, the Bononcini brothers had to return to Italy, because the emperor's successor, Charles VI, had fired them.[50] Francesco Gasparini wrote no more music dramas for production in Rome after 1721 (although he remained in that city), perhaps because his protector, Prince Marco Antonio Borghese, had moved to Naples as viceroy.

From the early 1700s and throughout the eighteenth century, Naples exported rather than imported music and musicians. The city had a plethora of young composers, and once they had completed their musical training in one or another of the city's conservatories, they found it difficult to find a perma-

---

49. On the support given by some aristocratic Roman families to musical activities (including varying degrees of involvement in opera) during the early eighteenth century, see especially Mercedes Viale Ferrero, "Antonio e Pietro Ottoboni e alcuni melodrammi da loro ideati o promossi a Roma," in *Venezia e il melodramma nel Settecento,* ed. Maria Teresa Muraro (Florence: Olschki, 1978–81), 1:271–94; Ursula Kirkendale, *Antonio Caldara: Sein Leben und seine venezianisch-römischen Oratorien* (Graz-Cologne: Böhlau, 1966); Ursula Kirkendale, "The Ruspoli Documents on Handel," *Journal of the American Musicological Society* 20 (1967): 222–73, 517–18; Franco Piperno, "Francesco Gasparini 'virtuoso dell'eccellentissimo sig. principe Ruspoli': Contributo alla biografia gaspariniana (1716–1718)," and Fabrizio Della Seta, "Francesco Gasparini, virtuoso del principe Borghese?" in *Francesco Gasparini (1661–1727),* ed. Fabrizio Della Seta and Franco Piperno (Florence: Olschki, 1981), 191–214 and 215–43, respectively; Fabrizio Della Seta, "I Borghese (1691–1731): La musica di una generazione," *Note d'archivio per la storia musicale* n. s. 1 (1983): 139–208.

50. See Lowell Lindgren, "Antonio Maria Bononcini e 'La conquista del vello d'oro' (Reggio Emilia, 1717)," in *Civiltà teatrale e Settecento emiliano,* ed. Susi Davoli (Bologna: Il Mulino, 1986), 309–33.

nent position in the public and private chapels of the capital.[51] One solution for a young opera composer was to procure the protection of a powerful noble, perhaps beginning his musical career in the noble's service as a harpsichord instructor or a singing teacher.[52] Even more often, however, the young composer who wanted to break into opera (and not only in Naples) had to attract the respect and the support of a composer who was already known and established, often the man from whom he had received his own training. It is not unlikely that master composers, like singing teachers with their pupils,[53] were repaid for their efforts with a percentage of their students' earnings in subsequent years. Josse de Villeneuve, an acute observer of the Italian musical scene of those years, noted, "In every town there are teachers who instruct without charge but who legally bind their pupils to pay them a share of whatever profits they may obtain from their art, once they have reached a

---

51. The *maestri di cappella* for the royal chapel in Naples were usually chosen from among composers who were already well known, in particular for their operatic works and for their reputation even outside the city. Alessandro Scarlatti, for example, was twice named *primo maestro della cappella reale*, in 1684 by a Spanish viceroy, and again in 1708 by an Austrian viceroy, both of whom admired his opera work, which they had encountered, the first as Spanish ambassador and the second as imperial ambassador in Rome.

52. In the year of Leonardo Vinci's opera debut (1719), the prince of Sansevero took him on for two years to give music lessons to his grandson; Niccolò Jommelli had the support of Marquis del Vasto for his first breakthrough in opera (1737); the young Niccolò Piccinni entered the opera scene in Naples in 1754 thanks to the protection of the duke of Ventimiglia; Nicola Zingarelli owed to the duchess of Castelpagano (whose singing teacher he was) the commission for a cantata put on at the Teatro San Carlo (1778) and was then recommended by her to the nobility in Milan (where at the age of barely thirty he had his first major successes). For even greater reason the foreigners who came to Italy to complete their musical training or promote their musical careers had to find support and protection. The success and the abundant musical production of the young Handel during his residence in Italy (1706–10) were undoubtedly facilitated by the aristocratic and diplomatic circles that he frequented, first in Florence (Ferdinando de' Medici), then in Rome (several German and English diplomats, Marquis Ruspoli), and in Naples and Venice (the cardinal and diplomat Vincenzo Grimani); see Reinhard Strohm, "Händel in Italia: Nuovi contributi," *Rivista italiana di musicologia* 9 (1974): 152–74. One extreme case was that of Johann Adolf Hasse, the most Italianized of the German composers, who established long-standing connections in Italy when he was a pupil of Nicola Porpora's (probably) and Alessandro Scarlatti's (certainly)—connections that he continued to cultivate after his marriage to the famous soprano Faustina Bordoni. After making his debut as a tenor in German opera houses, Hasse came to Italy, traveling (1722–24) from Venice to Florence, Rome, and Bologna, but producing no known operas. It was at Naples that he rapidly emerged as an opera composer under the protection of Marquis Vargas Maccina and Carlo Carmignano, an official in the court. From 1726 to 1730 Hasse wrote eight intermezzi and (the only such case for a foreigner in Italy) was even appointed *maestro sopranumerario* to the royal chapel of Naples (as stated in the libretto for his *Artaserse*, Venice, 1730); see, in *The New Grove Dictionary of Music and Musicians*, s.v. "Johann Adolf Hasse," by Sven Hansell..

53. See Strohm, "Aspetti sociali," 137, and the documentation cited in chapter 6, note 88.

certain age, and for a number of years following."[54] Later—after about the mid-nineteenth century—the beginning composer's entry into the field of opera was handled by his publisher, who set such contract terms as these:

1. The publisher gives no immediate remuneration;
2. The author will have 40 percent for ten years on the rental of his scores to the impresarios;
3. The publisher reserves a right of preemption for the second, and (on some occasions) the third, opera that will be written and produced by the young composer.[55]

There are many examples of young composers who gained entry to an opera company and were launched on an opera career thanks to an already established composer. The support of an illustrious colleague was necessary because after the mid-eighteenth century the supply of composers far exceeded demand in the opera field in Italy in general and in Naples in particular. The opposite was true of the market for virtuoso singers, who could command a high price for their voices and who, as a group, achieved economic independence early on.

It was Florian Leopold Gassmann who in 1766 brought the sixteen-year-old Antonio Salieri from Venice to Vienna, and at the age of twenty-four Salieri succeeded Gassmann in the post of composer to the imperial court. In 1769 Salieri met Christoph Willibald Gluck in Vienna; Gluck, a fellow Freemason, helped Salieri to get the commission for the inaugural opera for the Teatro alla Scala in Milan (*Europa riconosciuta,* 1778). Giacomo Tritto was protected by his fellow countryman Pasquale Cataro, whom he succeeded in 1787 as director of the Teatro San Carlo of Naples. Antonio Sacchini got Giuseppe Gazzaniga his first contract in Vienna (for *Il finto cieco,* 1786), an engagement that opened up a brilliant career for Gazzaniga, who received invitations to write for major theaters all over Europe. In 1803 Gazzaniga in turn introduced his pupil Pavesi in Venice, and in 1818 Pavesi succeeded Gazzaniga as *maestro di cappella* at the cathedral of Crema. Above all Paisiello seems to have had a circle of pupils whom he placed in the major centers of the opera market in Italy.[56] Paisiello protected Luigi Mosca at Naples; on his way to Paris in 1801, he accompanied Lavigna to Milan, arranged

---

54. Josse de Villeneuve, *Lettre sur le méchanisme de l'opéra italien,* in Robinson, *Naples and Neapolitan Opera,* 13.

55. D'Arcais, "L'industria musicale in Italia," 145–46.

56. It is noteworthy that an anonymous journalist writing for the *Allgemeine musikalische Zeitung* 10, no. 13 (23 December 1807): 205, pointed out Paisiello's tendency to make his pupils near copies of himself.

for his La Scala debut (with *La muta per amore,* 1802), and recommended him for the position of *maestro al cembalo* in that same theater (1802); he introduced Coccia to the Venetian theatrical scene by ceding a contract of his own to the younger man (1809). At the age of eighteen Rossini made his opera debut at Venice (1810) with *La cambiale di matrimonio,* thanks to the intervention of Giovanni Morandi, the composer-impresario-singing teacher from the Marches (whose wife was the singer Rosa Morandi, a family friend of the Rossinis).[57] Donizetti long enjoyed the aid of Mayr.[58] Luigi Ricci was recommended by Pietro Generali (with whom he had studied privately) for his public debut in Naples (1824). Antonio Bazzini presented to the publisher Giovannina Lucca his favorite pupil, Catalani (who dedicated his first opera, *La falce,* to his teacher). Pizzetti was protected by Giovanni Tebaldini, the director of the Parma Conservatory. Zandonai was introduced into the salons of Milan (where he met Giulio Ricordi) by Boito. After Zandonai we can say that the era of the Italian composer whose professional career typically began in opera had come to an end.

57. The full story of the circumstances that brought the young Rossini to his debut in Venice in 1810 is of more than anecdotal interest. The episode was related to Rossini's biographer Giuseppe Radiciotti by Arcangelo Boccoli, a music teacher at Senigallia and a pupil of Giovanni Morandi's: "For some years before the performance of *La cambiale di matrimonio,* the Rossinis and the Morandis, finding themselves in the same opera company, had become good friends, and among themselves they often talked about little Gioachino and about their hopes for his future. Later, in August 1810, when the Morandis were passing through Bologna on their way to Venice, Rossini's mother went to see them, and she spoke to the maestro of the great progress the young man was making and of his burning desire to write an opera and have it produced, and she recommended him warmly to [Morandi], someone who had ample opportunity to present [Rossini] to the public. Morandi promised [he would do so], and the occasion soon arose. Five new farces by five different composers were to be put on at the San Moisè. When [Pietro] Generali's *Adelina* was greeted with noisy disapproval, the composer of the fifth farce, a German (whose name Boccoli did not remember), backed out, leaving the management in a quandary. So Morandi thought of Rossini and wrote to him, asking him if he could come. Rossini's only response was to leave immediately, and after receiving the libretto from the theater's librettist, who at the time was Gaetano Rossi, he set it to music in only a few days. At the first rehearsal, however, the leading actors protested and refused to sing, demanding that the orchestral accompaniment, which they claimed was so loud that it covered their voices, be changed and toned down. Rossini went home (he was staying with the Morandis), locked himself in his room, and burst into tears. The maestro ran to console him, and he showed Rossini how to make the changes in the score required by opera conventions and demanded by the singers. The young man put his trust in Morandi's experience and his knowledge, so that the farce could be put on." See Giuseppe Radiciotti, *Lettere inedite di celebri musicisti* (Milan, 1892), 14–15.

58. It was probably Mayr who interceded with the impresario Paolo Zancla and the Bergamo librettist (and subsequently a major impresario) Bartolomeo Merelli to get Donizetti his first opera contract (for *Enrico di Borgogna,* Venice 1818); see Luigi Pilon, "Gli esordi operistici di Donizetti," in *Atti del primo convegno internazionale di studi donizettiani,* 1045–53.

Competition in the eighteenth century was keen, which meant that only rarely did a young composer make his name in the leading opera houses and in the major centers of the opera circuit. A number of composers who had been trained in Naples, for example, went to work first in Rome (at the time not a leading opera center), often beginning with an opera seria. (The connections and relations between Rome and Naples in the eighteenth century still await in-depth study.)[59] After launching their careers at Rome, the young opera composers might improve their fortunes by recycling their works at Naples or by going to Venice, the city that was at the time clearly the most important center of opera in Italy. Many other young composers must have found themselves in the same situation as the twenty-year-old Domenico Scarlatti when he sought a position outside Naples and Rome. His father, Alessandro, was clearly concerned when he wrote to Ferdinando de' Medici (30 May 1705) to ask him for letters of introduction for Domenico in Venice. [60]

> I have removed him by force from Naples, where his talent has plenty of scope, but it is not a talent for that place. I am also keeping him away from Rome, because Rome cannot put a roof over Music's head, and she lives there in beggary. This son, who is an eagle whose wings are grown, must not remain idle in his nest, and I must not keep him from flying. . . . My intention is that before he sets off to seek his fortune, he appear at the feet of Your Royal Highness.

Ferdinando gave Domenico (who stopped by Florence on his way to Venice) a letter of recommendation to present to the Venetian nobleman Alvise Morosini. Ferdinando wrote to Alessandro, "Your son Domenico truly has enough capital of talent and wit to make his fortune anywhere, but especially in *Venice, where worth finds all esteem and favor.*"[61]

59. Opera composers who trained at Naples and who successfully launched their careers (often with an opera seria) in Rome include Egidio Romualdo Duni (three serious operas produced in Rome, 1735–36); Niccolò Jommelli (*Ricimero re de' Goti*, 1740), Gennaro Manna (*Tito Manlio*, 1742), Gioacchino Cocchi (*Adelaide*, 1743), Niccolò Piccinni (between 1758 and 1773 he wrote new operas every year for Rome), Pietro Alessandro Guglielmi (*Tito Manlio*, 1763), Gaetano Andreozzi (his debut was in Rome with the oratorio *Giefte*, 1779), Giuseppe Mosca (*La vedova scaltra*, 1796), Gaspare Spontini (*Li puntigli delle donne*, 1796), and Carlo Coccia (*Il matrimonio per lettera*, 1807). It should also be noted that the first wave of opera buffa that swept over northern Italy and then all of Europe in the mid-eighteenth century was set off not by singers but by a number of composers from Naples who moved to Rome after about 1730, working in particular for the Teatro Valle; see Piero Weiss, "La diffusione del repertorio operistico nell'Italia del Settecento: Il caso dell'opera buffa," in *Civiltà teatrale e Settecento emiliano*, ed. Susi Davoli (Bologna: Il Mulino, 1986), 241–56, esp. 249–50.

60. See note 22.

61. Letter of 8 June 1705, quoted in Fabbri, *Alessandro Scarlatti*, 59 (emphasis added).

We know nothing of the years that Domenico Scarlatti spent in Venice (1705–9, but he probably did not remain in the city through that entire period), and it does not appear that any opera of his was produced on the stage. His "capital of talent and wit" and Ferdinando's support must not have been enough for him to make his mark and become established in the city's musical life. Venetian musical circles had been decidedly hostile to his father, Alessandro, whose only works produced in public in Venice during that period (*Il Mitridate Eupatore* and *Il trionfo della libertà*, performed in the Teatro San Giovanni Grisostomo during carnival 1707) were unfavorably received.[62] Admittedly competition was keen in Venice during those years. The major theaters under aristocratic management (San Giovanni Grisostomo, San Cassiano) were, to all intents and purposes, monopolized by Pollarolo, Gasparini, and Lotti (and later Albinoni), whose operas were also put on in many other Italian theaters, including those in Naples, after their Venetian debuts. Even Vivaldi found it difficult to launch his opera career in Venice in those years (1705–12), and his first opera was performed on the Venetian terraferma (in Vicenza, *Ottone in villa*, 1713).[63]

The musicians who wanted to break into opera at Naples had no other choice than to work for a while in comic opera, transferring to the tragic stage after a few years. Vinci, for example, wrote eight comedies before moving on to opera seria, a genre in which he soon won wide fame (thanks also in part to his collaboration with Pietro Metastasio). As is clear from petitions presented to the king and to the commission that administered the theater, a young opera composer at the start of his career could not possibly get an opera seria produced by the Teatro San Carlo in Naples.[64] In 1738 the minister charged with supervision of the Neapolitan royal theaters wrote to recommend the performance of a new opera by Logroscino at the San Carlo.

I do not hesitate to propose Logroscino, since he has set several comedies to music for the smaller theaters of this capital that have been applauded. The latest of them,

62. The long satire, "Contro il Scarlatti musico," by Bartolomeo Dotti gives eloquent proof of the Venetians' hostility toward Alessandro Scarlatti. The entire text of this satire is available in Lino Bianchi and Roberto Pagano, *Alessandro Scarlatti* (Turin: Edizione RAI Radiotelevisione, 1972), 185–89. See also *Colloquium Alessandro Scarlatti Würzburg,* ed. Wolfgang Osthoff and Jutta Ruile-Dronke (Tutzing: Schneider, 1979), 170 n. 278.

63. See Strohm, "Zu Vivaldis Opernschaffen," 240–43, and, more generally, Strohm "Vivaldi's Career."

64. The Teatro San Carlo was inaugurated 4 November 1737 with Domenico Sarro's *Achille in Sciro,* when Sarro, at fifty-eight, was far from a novice: *vice-maestro di cappella* at court from 1725 and maestro from 1735, his most important works had been staged regularly at the Teatro San Bartolomeo (the temple of opera seria in Naples before the opening of the San Carlo) from 1718 on.

which is now being performed at the Fiorentini, [was] well received by all the nobility, and, besides, last year he was invited to Rome, where he went and composed one of the comedies being performed there.[65]

In 1745 the administrative board that governed the theaters of Naples commissioned Gennaro Manna to compose an opera seria *(Lucio Vero)* for the San Carlo because, as they stated, he "composed with much grace and novelty and was among the best composer of this Capital."[66] However, Manna had launched his opera career in Rome and Venice. When Giuseppe Giordani petitioned that same committee in 1776, offering to write a work for the San Carlo, the petition was turned down because the composer, who was twenty-five at the time, had not yet written for the smaller Neapolitan theaters.[67] Giordani had to go north (to Modena and Florence, 1779–80), return to Naples and write comic operas (1781–82), and return to northern Italy (he was *maestro di cappella* at Fermo from 1789 to his death and also wrote for the local opera house). The situation at the San Carlo remained largely unchanged until well into the nineteenth century. Petrella wrote seven comic operas and opere semiserie (1829–52) for the lesser theaters of Naples. In 1835 a production of his opera seria *La Cimodocea* was turned down; only in 1854 did he receive a commission for *Marco Visconti*, a work that met with considerable success everywhere and even held its ground against Verdi's *Il trovatore*. Petrella later went to Milan with the support of the Lucca publishing firm, which prepared the way for a number of successful productions (all, however, had short runs).[68]

Especially from the mid-eighteenth century on, a number of composers trained in Naples moved as far north in Italy as they could to launch a full-fledged opera career: Sacchini went to Venice; Gian Francesco De Majo to Parma, Bologna, and Turin; Giovanni Battista Borghi to the Marches and Venice; Paisiello to Emilia and Venice; Cimarosa to Emilia; Luigi Caruso to Tuscany, Venice, and the Marches; Gaetano Andreozzi to Tuscany and Venice. During the nineteenth century composers young and old flooded into Milan from the outlying provinces to seek commissions and contacts with music publishers.

From the early 1700s until well into the 1800s, when the opera market in

---

65. *Enciclopedia dello spettacolo*, s. v. "Nicola Logroscino," by Ulisse Prota-Giurleo.

66. *Enciclopedia dello spettacolo*, s.v. "Gennaro Manna," by Ulisse Prota-Giurleo.

67. *Enciclopedia dello spettacolo*, s.v. "Giordano, Giuseppe [detto Giordaniello]," by Ulisse Prota-Giurleo.

68. Petrella's relations with the San Carlo and with Giovannina Lucca are documented in Franco Schlitzer, *Mondo teatrale dell'Ottocento* (Naples: Fiorentino, 1954), 183–212.

Italy was ruled by the iron law of profit, competition, and the vicissitudes of taste,[69] the opera composer, particularly when he was at the start of his career, had to advance rapidly from one success to another, carving out a place for himself thanks to a frantic workload made all the more difficult by having to travel up and down the Italian peninsula. From the earliest days of Italian opera it had been the composer's task to plan and coordinate the execution of his work (with the librettist and the set designer), which made his presence indispensable. Although opera composers of the early seventeenth century worked for the most part in one place, traveling only to fulfill a particularly important commission (as did Marazzoli and Cavalli, for instance), the development around 1680 of a genuine network for the circulation and exchange of operas among the various theaters of Italy changed the opera composer's professional life from a sedentary to an itinerant one. Theatrical contracts from the early 1700s to Donizetti's and Verdi's days continued to stipulate that the composer must be present in the theater for rehearsals and for at least the first three performances, which he was to conduct from the keyboard.[70] If

69. Until the last decades of the nineteenth century, when a stable repertory became the rule and opera taste became less of a factor, the often-repeated statement of Charles de Brosses ("Musical taste changes here at least every two years") remained true; see Charles de Brosses, *Lettres familières,* ed. Giuseppina Cafasso and Letizia Norci Cagiano de Azevedo, 3 vols. (Naples: Centre Jean Bérard, 1991; distributed by Boccard, Paris). Musical tastes in Italy continued to demand new works through the mid-nineteenth century. For an indication of the low esteem in which music of the past was held, see the review by C. Mellini in *L'Arpa: Giornale letterario, artistico, teatrale* (11 December 1854) of Francesco Caffi's *Storia della musica sacra . . . nella già cappella ducale di San Marco in Venezia dal 1318 al 1797* (Venice, 1854): "Music in Italy lives a rapid, agitated, febrile life: the genius of production multiplies novices and their accompanying pilgrims, and the cult of enthusiasm is totally directed toward them; for the past there is only forgetfulness. . . . It is true not only that Italians generally care little for the history of their own music; they are also much inclined to weary of any music that is not recent and to scorn that which they themselves had welcomed enthusiastically thirty years before." The negative opinion that a reviewer for *La gazzetta di Genova* (1 April 1839) expressed regarding a revival of Francesco Morlacchi's *Colombo* at the Teatro Carlo Felice (eleven years after its successful premiere at the same theater) requires no comment: "His music is no longer made for our ears"; see Edilio Frassoni, *Due secoli di lirica a Genova,* 2 vols. (Genoa: Cassa di Risparmio di Genova e Imperia, 1980), 1:151.

70. One of the very few pieces of visual evidence of how orchestras were directed in eighteenth-century Italian opera is a caricature by Pierleone Ghezzi showing Nicola Logroscino conducting the orchestra for a performance of his *Olimpiade* (Rome, 1753); see Pierluigi Petrobelli, "Il mondo del teatro in musica nelle caricature di Pierleone Ghezzi," in *Le muse galanti: La musica a Roma nel Settecento,* ed. Bruno Cagli (Rome: Istituto della Enciclopedia Italiana, 1985), 109–17, figure 2 (following page 112). The maestro's obligation to "sit at the keyboard" for the first performances of the opera is explicitly noted, for example, in the contract between Rossini and the owner-impresario of the Teatro Argentina of Rome for *Il barbiere di Siviglia* (1815) and in the contract between Donizetti and Alessandro Lanari for *Pia de' Tolomei* (1836); see Mario Rinaldi, *Due secoli di musica al Teatro Argentina,* 3 vols. (Florence: Olschki, 1978), 1: 494, and

the composer's presence was not required at the first performances and he simply delivered the score, his remuneration was lower.[71]

In order to maintain his prestige and his fame at the level he had acquired and to increase his earnings,[72] the opera composer needed to work at a fast pace. He would also be wise to concentrate on writing opere serie, as they paid better, in particular if the premiere of the work opened the opera season. From Alessandro Scarlatti's time to the early decades of the nineteenth century,[73] the most successful opera composers produced an average of from one to three operas per year, and in their periods of greatest activity they managed to write as many as four a year (see table 2). Exceptions to this rule were composers who were predominantly teachers (Feo, for example, wrote only sixteen operas in over a quarter century) and those who occupied permanent and well-paid positions in religious institutions (generally toward the end of their careers).[74] A sizable proportion of Piccinni's vast production (around

---

Jeremy Commons, "Una corrispondenza tra Alessandro Lanari e Donizetti," *Studi donizettiani* 3 (1978): 9–74, esp. 38–39.

71. On this question see the letter (1726) of the impresario of the Teatro della Pergola in Florence to Nicola Porpora quoted in Gino Conti, "Il Teatro La Pergola di Firenze e la stagione d'opera per il carnevale 1726–1727: Lettere di Luca Casimiro degli Albizzi a Vivaldi, Porpora ed altri," *Rivista italiana di musicologia* 15 (1980): 182–88, esp. 186.

72. Mayr, for example, declared that he was constrained by financial necessity alone to compose operas: see Giovanni Simone Mayr, *Zibaldone, preceduto dalle pagine autobiografiche,* ed. Arrigo Gazzaniga (Gorle-Bergamo: Gutenberg Editrice, 1977), 10.

73. Overall production figures for seventeenth-century composers are much lower than those for opera composers of the following century for another reason: as we have seen, the former began their operatic careers at a relatively mature age. Furthermore, except in late cases most of them were directly involved in the service of a court or worked for aristocratic patrons (who often commissioned celebratory works that were never repeated), and the opera market was not subject to inflation or governed by merciless laws of competition. A sampling of the total number of opera scores composed by some musicians of the period follows: Jacopo Peri, 7; Claudio Monteverdi, about 15; Stefano Landi, 2; Francesco Manelli, 11; Francesco Cavalli, 33; Marco Marazzoli, 8; Antonio Maria Abbatini, 3; Pietro Andrea Ziani, about 30; Giuseppe Tricarico, 6; Jacopo Melani, 9; Antonio Cesti, 14; Giovanni Legrenzi, 19; Francesco Provenzale, 8 or 9; Antonio Sartorio, 15; Carlo Pallavicino, 24; Pietro Simone Agostini, 7; Giovanni Maria Pagliardi, 7; Bernardo Pasquini, 14; Alessandro Melani, 8; Alessandro Stradella, 6. Cavalli wrote a relatively high number of operas (33), but he represents an exception rather than the rule as "the first in a long line of truly 'opera' composers," as Lorenzo Bianconi calls him (*Music in the Seventeenth Century,* 82). A difficult financial situation is probably the reason for the high number (about 30) of dramas composed by Pietro Andrea Ziani: after holding temporary positions as an organist in a number of Venetian churches, he was for two years (1657–59) *maestro di cappella* in the provincial city of Bergamo, then held secondary posts in Vienna, was refused (1676) the post of *maestro di cappella* of Saint Mark's in Venice, and only in the last four years of his life (after 1680) succeeded in being named maestro of the royal chapel in Naples.

74. Nearly all of the twenty-seven theatrical works of Giacomo Antonio Perti, for example, were composed in the decade between 1690 and 1700. From 1690 until his death in 1756, Perti was *maestro di cappella* at San Petronio in Bologna and wrote mostly sacred music.

TABLE 2. Total and Annual Production of Some Leading Italian Opera Composers from the Early 1700s to the 1800s

COMPOSER	NO. OF OPERAS	AVERAGE NO. PER YEAR
Alessandro Scarlatti (1660–1725)	114	2.7
Giovanni Bononcini (1670–1747)	about 56	1.2
Tomaso Albinoni (1671–1751)	about 80	1.7
Antonio Caldara (ca. 1670–1736)	90	1.9
Giuseppe Maria Orlandini (1675–1760)	49	1.3
Antonio Vivaldi (1678–1741)	94	3.6
Nicola Porpora (1686–1768)	50	1.4
Leonardo Leo (1694–1744)	50	1.6
Baldassare Galuppi (1706–85)	104	2.0
Niccolò Jommelli (1714–74)	85	2.5
Ferdinando Bertoni (1725–1813)	50	1.0
Tommaso Traetta (1727–79)	43	1.5
Pasquale Anfossi (1727–97)	about 76	2.2
Niccolò Piccinni (1728–1800)	about 120	3.0
Pietro Alessandro Guglielmi (1728–1804)	91	2.0
Giuseppe Sarti (1729–1802)	about 70	1.4
Giovanni Paisiello (1740–1816)	about 80	1.8
Giuseppe Gazzaniga (1743–1818)	about 50	1.2
Domenico Cimarosa (1749–1801)	65	2.2
Francesco Bianchi (1752–1810)	about 81	2.3
Ferdinando Paër (1771–1839)	55	1.2
Pietro Generali (1773–1832)	about 54	1.7
Stefano Pavesi (1779–1850)	about 70	2.5
Carlo Coccia (1782–1873)	about 40	1.1
Gioachino Rossini (1792–1868)	39	2.0
Saverio Mercadante (1795–1870)	about 60	1.5
Giovanni Pacini (1796–1867)	about 90	1.6
Gaetano Donizetti (1797–1848)	66	2.6

Note: The total number of operas is only indicative. Data for the eighteenth century is particularly problematic, and it is often difficult, at times impossible, and perhaps always arbitrary to distinguish among genuinely new scores and more or less extensive revisions of other composers' scores by the composer in question. The cases of Scarlatti, Albinoni, and Vivaldi are typical in this respect. On them see Reinhard Strohm, Italienische Opernarien des frühen Settecento (1720–1730), in Analecta musicologia, no. 16, 2 vols. (Cologne: Arno Volk, 1976), 2:258–59.

120 operas) was crowded into the fifteen years that he spent in Rome and Naples (1758–73), when he wrote twenty operas for Roman opera houses and thirty for theaters in Naples, or an average of more than three per year. Immediately after his debut in Venice with La cambiale di matrimonio (1810), Rossini had thirteen operas produced in just over three years, two of them at La Scala in Milan, one at La Fenice in Venice, and one at the Valle in Rome, all of which were among the major theaters of the age. Pacini's career also got off to an extremely rapid start: after his debut at the Teatro

Santa Radegonda of Milan (1813) with the farce *Annetta e Lucindo,* he had a dozen works produced in the following four years, nearly all of them one-act farces, for theaters in Florence, Pisa, Venice, and Milan before he had his first major success with *Adelaide e Comingio* (Milan, Teatro Re, 1817). Several years later (in 1822) Pacini built a villa at Viareggio; the impresario Barbaja then invited him to direct the San Carlo in Naples (1825), and by 1830, at the age of thirty-four and at the peak of his career, he had written forty theatrical works in sixteen years. He continued to compose successful operas: *Saffo,* his most famous, was written in 1840.[75] Verdi had a meteoric career as well: after his La Scala debut with *Oberto* (1839), he had three operas produced in the major theaters of Italy in as many years.

Beginning with Bellini Italian opera composers began to write fewer stage works and to demand compensation more in line with their talents.[76] During the course of the nineteenth century, they worked more and more closely with music publishers; with a degree of protection for their opera scores, they tended to produce fewer works than composers of the past (see table 3). During the last two or three decades of the nineteenth century, the opera composer began to have a greater personal responsibility for the success of his work: enormous sums of money were involved, the opinions of the newspaper critics bore a good deal of weight in many cases,[77] and one never knew how the public would receive an opera. That meant that the maturation period for a new opera was often long and fraught with problems in the choice of a subject, the composer's collaboration with the librettist, indecision regarding the length of the libretto or the score, and more.[78] Ponchielli was typical in this regard. After the disappointing experience of the failure of *I promessi sposi* in Cremona in 1856, Ponchielli went through a period of relative dissatisfaction and worked as a bandmaster in the provincial cities of Piacenza and Cremona (from 1861 to 1872); it took the respectable success (December 1872) of the same opera, revised for the Teatro Dal Verme in Milan, before Giulio Ricordi was willing to commission the composition of *I Lituani.* Ponchielli was assigned a top-notch librettist, Antonio Ghislanzoni, and the work

75. As far as we know Pacini was the first opera composer to write an extensive autobiography, which was published several years after his death; see Giovanni Pacini, *Le mie memorie artistiche* (Florence, 1875; reprint, Lucca: Maria Pacini Fazzi, 1981).

76. See Rosselli, "Verdi e la storia della retribuzione del compositore italiano."

77. For the case of one opera composer (Ponchielli) who was particularly sensitive to the reactions of the critics see Angelo Pompilio, "La carriera e le opere di Ponchielli nei giudizi della critica italiana (1856–1887)," in *Amilcare Ponchielli, 1834–1886: Saggi e ricerche nel 150° anniversario della nascita* (Casalmorano: Cassa Rurale ed Artigiana, 1984), 7–92.

78. On this question see Giovanni Morelli, "Suicidio e Pazza Gioia: Ponchielli e la poetica dell'Opera Italiana neo-nazional-popolare," in *Amilcare Ponchielli, 1834–1886,* 171–231, esp. 174–88.

TABLE 3. Overall Production and Length of Active Career of Some Leading Opera Composers from the 1800s to the 1900s

COMPOSER	NO. OF OPERAS	LENGTH OF ACTIVE CAREER
Vincenzo Bellini (1801–35)	10	9 years
Giuseppe Verdi(1813–1901)	32	54 years
Carlo Pedrotti (1817–93)	19	32 years
Antonio Cagnoni (1828–96)	20	33 years
Filippo Marchetti (1831–1902)	7	24 years
Amilcare Ponchielli (1834–86)	10	29 years
Arrigo Boito (1842–1918)	2	47 years
Antonio Smareglia (1854–1929)	9	35 years
Alfredo Catalani (1854–93)	5	17 years
Ruggero Leoncavallo (1857–1919)	10	27 years
Giacomo Puccini (1858–1924)	17	40 years*
Alberto Franchetti (1860–1942)	10	34 years
Pietro Mascagni (1863–1945)	17	45 years
Francesco Cilea (1866–1950)	6	18 years
Umberto Giordano (1867–1948)	13	37 years
Franco Alfano (1875–1954)	12	51 years
Italo Montemezzi (1875–1952)	7	38 years
Ermanno Wolf-Ferrari (1876–1948)	15	43 years
Ildebrando Pizzetti (1880–1968)	22	57 years
Gian Francesco Malipiero (1882–1973)	35	57 years
Riccardo Zandonai (1883–1944)	13	37 years
Luigi Dallapiccola (1904–75)	3	28 years
Gian Carlo Menotti (1911–)	17	36 years
Luigi Nono (1924–1990)	3	25 years
Sylvano Bussotti (1931–)	6	11 years

*Including revisions.

was scheduled for La Scala. This was an excellent opportunity for Ponchielli to get his opera career off to a new start, and he was well aware of his heavy responsibility, as confirmed by several passages in letters to Giulio Ricordi (June to December 1873), written while he was working on the opera: "I am always afraid that I will not satisfy myself and the others with my music. . . . If I do not succeed in this opera I will write no more—not even a polka— and go to some obscure village . . . as an organist!" (19 June). He feared not finishing in time for La Scala's scheduled production: "Even the orchestration is laborious. I am hard to satisfy; I cannot tell you how many times I have torn up a piece of music. . . . For me this is a horrifying responsibility: the public is waiting. It is true, they may be well-disposed, but they are still the public of La Scala" (28 June);[79] "But perhaps I think too much about what I am doing, and that is the reason for this snail's pace" (28 August); "I do not guarantee that anything will arrive there in time. . . . The passage that I am

79. Cesari, *Amilcare Ponchielli nell'arte del suo tempo*, 46.

about to do is too important, and I do not jot down a single note if I am not convinced that it is right" (November).[80]

In that era a single failure could threaten an opera composer's entire career. Right after the failure of *Regina Diaz* (Naples, 1894), Umberto Giordano was summarily fired by the Sonzogno publishing firm (which until that time had given him a monthly stipend of 200 lire). Giordano thought of directing a municipal band somewhere or perhaps opening a fencing school, and it was only thanks to heavy pressure on the part of Filippo Marchetti that Sonzogno was persuaded to give Giordano another chance. The result was the commission for *Andrea Chénier* (1896), a work that has played all the opera houses in the world. How profoundly the fiasco of the opening of *Madama Butterfly* (Milan, La Scala, 1904) affected Puccini is a familiar story: he waited six and a half years to complete his next opera, *La fanciulla del West* (New York, Metropolitan Opera House, 1910). Conversely there were a number of opera composers after the mid-nineteenth century who based a successful career in Italy and abroad on a single opera, whose royalties enabled them to live in prosperity.[81]

With the possible exception of Gian Carlo Menotti, we can say that the composer who concentrated all his professional activities on opera disappeared during the period between the two World Wars, and in particular after 1945. If by opera composer we understand a professional musician organically linked to the sphere of the opera house, we might go so far as to say that he does not exist in our own century. This is not the place for an analysis of the reasons for this decline, but we might note that the phenomenon (which has never been investigated seriously by historians of Italian music) has had an important effect on musical life in Italy. A number of contemporary composers have channeled a part of their creative energies into the new mass media of sound reproduction—film scores, radio, and television—rather than opera. It is those fields of musical production that seem to attract

---

80. Ibid., 47.

81. See the case of Marchetti's *Ruy Blas* (1869) mentioned in note 18. Opera composers who owed their fame uniquely or principally to a single work include Luigi and Federico Ricci (*Crispino e la comare,* a very successful opera from 1850 to the end of the century), Carlo Pedrotti (*Tutti in maschera,* 1856), Amilcare Ponchielli (*La Gioconda,* 1876), Pietro Mascagni (*Cavalleria rusticana,* 1890, a first work that immediately made the composer famous), Alfredo Catalani (*La Wally,* 1892, conducted by Arturo Toscanini in many European and American theaters and brought to the cinema in one of the earliest Italian sound films), Ruggero Leoncavallo (*I pagliacci,* 1892, a first opera, the winner of a contest sponsored by Sonzogno, the first complete opera to be recorded in Italy—by the G. & T. Company in 1907—and among the first to be televised in the United States, in 1951), Umberto Giordano (*Andrea Chénier,* 1896, and *Fedora,* 1898), Francesco Cilea (*Adriana Lecouvreur,* 1902), Italo Montemezzi (*L'amore dei tre re,* 1913, later a familiar part of the repertory in the United States), Riccardo Zandonai (*Francesca da Rimini,* 1914, produced almost yearly after that date, often in two or three theaters simultaneously).

the craftsman-musician today. Mascagni, Pizzetti, Dallapiccola, Menotti, Rota, and Bussotti have all written music for film, both before and after the advent of sound. The greater part of Rota's musical production has been for films (some eighty scores), which have brought him fame and fortune (the director Federico Fellini used Rota's music for all his films until 1979).[82]

Finally, the Italian opera composer has always (but in particular after the early eighteenth century) tied his fame and fortune to those of the virtuoso singer. It is no accident that so many composers combined their theatrical and private lives by marrying a *prima donna*.[83] A composer's operas were often directly launched, encouraged, and mantanied in the repertory by great singers. Moreover, the success or failure of a production was largely dependent on the performers—which was why, from Cavalli to Donizetti and after, singers were usually paid a good deal more than composers (though this was truer in Italy than abroad). The rapid rise of Hasse and Porpora after the 1720s was undeniably due in part to their collaboration with singers of the highest quality, chief among them Carlo Broschi, known as Farinelli. The brief career of Riccardo Broschi as an opera composer was concentrated in the years (1728–35) in which he followed his singer brother from one theater to another, writing highly virtuosic arias for him. When Riccardo Broschi returned to Naples alone (1737), he no longer got commissions for opera work; he became a wine merchant, and he later joined his brother in Madrid (around 1740). The great success (after 1758) of the Milanese singing teacher Lampugnani, both in Italy and throughout Europe, was due primarily to the companies of singers who had been his pupils and who sang his works wherever they went. The wide circulation given to the one surviving opera score of Giovanni Battista Cimador (the dramatic scene, *Pigmalione*, Venice, 1790) can be attributed to the tenor Matteo Babbini, who was typical of a new singer-actor acclaimed for his extraordinary dramatic gifts.[84] Rossini's career

82. For a profile of Rota as a film composer, see Sergio Miceli, *La musica nel film: Arte e artigianato* (Fiesole: Discanto, 1982), 249–59.

83. Opera composers who married singers include Claudio Monteverdi (who married Claudia Cattaneo), Francesco Manelli (Maddalena), Antonio Lotti (Santa Stella), Tomaso Albinoni (Margherita Rimondi), Antonio Caldara (Caterina Petrolli), Giuseppe Maria Orlandini (Maria Maddalena Bonavia), Johann Adolf Hasse (Faustina Bordoni), Niccolò Piccinni (Vincenza Sibilla), Pietro Alessandro Guglielmi (Maria Leli); Giuseppe Sarti (Camilla Pasi); Antonio Salieri (Teresa von Helferstorfer); Francesco Bianchi (Jane Jackson); Giuseppe Giordani (Emanuela Cosmi), Gaetano Andreozzi (Anna de Santi); Ferdinando Paër (Francesca Riccardi); Gioachino Rossini (Isabella Colbran); Giovanni Pacini (Marietta Albini); Giuseppe Persiani (Fanny Tacchinardi); Luigi Ricci (Ludmilla Stolz); Giuseppe Verdi (Giuseppina Strepponi); Amilcare Ponchielli (Teresina Brambilla); and Riccardo Zandonai (Tarquinia Tarquini).

84. On the circulation of Cimador's *Pigmalione*, see Giovanni Morelli and Elvidio Surian, "Pigmalione a Venezia," in *Venezia e il melodramma nel Settecento*, ed. Maria Teresa Muraro (Florence: Olschki, 1978–81), 147–68.

took a decided turn for the better during his Neapolitan period (1815–22), when he could call on the talents of the famous soprano Isabella Colbran (whom he married in 1822) and of one of the leading tenors of the age, Andrea Nozzari, who sang in all the Neapolitan premieres of Rossini's opere serie of those years. The opera *Tebaldo e Isolina* by Francesco Morlacchi (Venice, 1822) was revived many times in the next ten years, or until its two major male singers (Giovanni Battista Velluti and Gaetano Crivelli, both among the leading performers of the day) retired from the stage in 1831.[85] Later the world success of some of the operas of the verismo period (*I pagliacci, Cavalleria rusticana, Andrea Chénier, Adriana Lecouvreur,* and nearly all of Puccini's operas) was aided by the exceptional voices of leading singers. Such famous names as Enrico Caruso, Gilda dalla Rizza, Giuseppe De Luca, Tito Schipa, Beniamino Gigli, and a host of others gave the works an even wider distribution thanks to recordings of entire operas or selections.

4. The Creative Process: Work Methods and Schedules

Surprisingly few Italian musicologists (they can be counted on the fingers of one hand) have conducted systematic, well-organized investigations into the conception and material existence of opera by means of either direct documentation (letters, sketches, autograph scores, manuscript and printed librettos) or indirect documentation (notices, political and musical periodicals, diaries, and other reports).

From the outset the primary point of reference for *opera in musica* has been its poetic texts.[86] The term *dramma per musica* (the term that appears on the title pages of librettos and scores throughout the eighteenth century) refers, in fact, to the literary text that was to be "clothed in notes."[87]

85. On the contribution of these two singers to the success of *Tebaldo e Isolina,* see Elvidio Surian, "Morlacchi compositore operistico: Sua carriera e circolazione delle sue opere in Italia," in *Francesco Morlacchi e la musica del suo tempo (1784–1841),* ed. Biancamaria Brumana and Galliano Ciliberti (Florence: Olschki, 1986), 77–86.

86. In the dedication prefacing the libretto for *Euridice* (Florence, 1600), the poet Ottavio Rinuccini attributed to himself and to his patron Jacopo Corsi (rather than to the composer and singer Jacopo Peri) the concept of a new sort of theatrical spectacle. He stated that he had written the story of Daphne "solely to make a simple trial of what the music of our age could do"; Angelo Solerti, *Le origini del melodramma* (Turin: Bocca, 1903; reprint, Bologna: Arnaldo Forni, 1969), 40, Heinz Becker, ed., *Quellentexte zur Konzeption der europäischen Oper im 17. Jahrhundert* (Kassel and Basel: Bärenreiter, 1981), 16, and quoted here from Oliver Strunk, *Source Readings in Music History from Classical Antiquity through the Romantic Era* (New York: Norton, 1950), 368.

87. On the literary implications of the *dramma per musica* in the seventeenth and eighteenth centuries, see, respectively, Bianconi and Walker, "Production, consumption," 211–15, and Rein-

Throughout its history and even before it took on more concrete form in music, opera relied on a literary text that was consonant with music in the flow of its action and the disposition of its verse and that lent itself to music. This circumstance, along with reasons of a sociological nature, certainly helped to favor the librettist over the composer within the economic structure of opera from the seventeenth century until well into the nineteenth century. It was, for example, the librettist who followed through and coordinated the staging of the work. Whether the composer's subordinance to the librettist was real or presumed, it was only when figures like Bellini (and above all Verdi) came along that the situation was turned around and the composer dominated the poet. A clear indication of eighteenth-century attitudes is the peremptory set of instructions that Ferdinando de' Medici gave Alessandro Scarlatti when he sent him the first act of the libretto for *Lucio Manlio*. Ferdinando wrote, "Thus I desire that it be set to music by you, in the more fully developed form that you will learn about from Silvio Stampiglia, the author of the drama." The composer, who hastened to comply with the prince's request, replied, "In execution of what Your Royal Highness has deigned to impose upon me, I will be attentive to the ideas and inspirations that the poet may communicate to me for my greater comprehension and illumination [and will work] to assure all possible *agreement with the author's concept*."[88]

The task of the music was to respond to the fundamental unitary nature of the *dramma per musica* by appropriate alternation of the various types of solo pieces around which Italian opera continued to be constructed from the 1680s until just a few decades ago.[89] The music was also expected to provide variety within a set of paradigmatic emotional and psychological states and realistic situations and settings, and among differing but often deliberately stylized theatrical devices. The careful alternation among various sorts of arias was not governed by any well-defined written system or artistic code;[90] rather, the opera composer exercised his creative efforts within a set of conventions for composition and dramatic and dramaturgical structures that

---

hard Strohm, "Towards an Understanding of the *opera seria*," in *Essays on Handel and Italian Opera* (Cambridge: Cambridge University Press, 1985), 93–105, esp. 96–97.

88. Letters of 9 and 13 June 1705, in Fabbri, *Alessandro Scarlatti*, 61 (emphasis added).

89. See Reinhard Strohm, *Italienische Opernarien des frühen Settecento (1720–1730)*, in *Analecta musicologica*, no. 16, 2 vols. (Cologne: Arno Volk, 1976), 1:11–12. Not even in the age of so-called verismo did opera composers give up subdividing an opera into "numbers." The index to the score of *Andrea Chénier* (1896) lists the *appuntamenti* for every scene: "Introduzione," "Scena di Gérard," "Scena di Maddalena," and so forth. The index to the pocket version of the orchestral score of Leoncavallo's *I pagliacci* (1909) is similarly divided into *scene*.

90. This was the opinion of an attentive observer of Italian opera practice in the eighteenth century, John Brown, *Letters Upon the Poetry and Music of the Italian Opera* (ca. 1760) (Edinburgh, 1789), 41–42.

were tacitly understood but flexible and changed over time, and that, by the same token, the theatrical public had internalized as part of its "horizon of expectation."[91] In such a context the musical and poetic language of Italian opera could not avoid being founded on a repetitive rotation of highly stylized situations, schemes, and structures. Rinaldo da Capua gave Charles Burney an interesting report on repetition in musical language in eighteenth-century opera. Burney tells us,

> He thinks that [composers] have nothing left to do now, but to write themselves and others over again; and that the only chance which they have left for obtaining the reputation of novelty and invention, arises either from ignorance or want of memory in the public; as in everything, both in melody and modulation, that is worth doing, has already been often done. He . . . frankly confesses, that though he had written full as much as his neighbors, yet out of all his works, perhaps not above *one* new melody can be found. . . . And as to modulation, it must always be the same, to be natural and pleasing; what has not been given to the public being only the refuse of thousands, who have tried and rejected it, either as impracticable or displeasing. The only opportunity a composer has for introducing new modulation in songs, is in a short second part, in order to *fright* the hearer back to the first, to which it serves as a foil, by making it comparatively beautiful.[92]

It was probably the poetic design of the librettos themselves that urged the composer to stylize his own musical language as much as possible. We need only think, for example, of the long life that Metastasio's texts enjoyed. Jommelli may have expressed the thought of a number of other opera composers of his day (and of earlier and later times) when he openly declared his distaste for the poetic schemes then fashionable.

> I love, venerate, and kneel before the adored Metastasio and all of his works, but I wish that even he, adapting himself to the mode, would do something new, as everyone else wishes as well. Since I must draw out so many different ideas, not only different from my own, but also from those of so many other composers, always, always on the same words, it would make even a head of bronze spin.[93]

Many of the constraints on the composer derived from the rigid laws of the opera market and its strong consumer orientation. Until Verdi appeared on the scene, and aside from exceptional occasions when operas were put on

91. Lorenzo Bianconi, "Perché la storia dell'opera italiana?" *Musica/Realtà* 17, no. 17 (August 1985): 29–48, esp. 41–42.

92. Charles Burney, *An Eighteenth Century Musical Tour in France and Italy,* vol. 1. of *Dr. Burney's Musical Tours in Europe,* ed. Percy A. Scholes, 2 vols. (London: Oxford University Press, 1959), 235.

93. Letter to the librettist Gaetano Martinelli, Naples, 14 November 1769, in McClymonds, *Niccolò Jommelli: The Last Years,* 487–88.

with the direct participation of the composer, it was virtually unheard of for the score of a previous production to be used again without alteration; rather, it was taken for granted that the original composer or some other musician would insert new arias, cut recitatives, and switch around or compress entire scenes. There was no such concept as a "composer's work," and lifting a single piece from one dramatic context and transplanting it to a different one was a fairly frequent practice in Italian opera. Although in France, from the time of Lully on, scores were printed, either typographically or in elegant copperplate engravings, and enjoyed a royal "privilege" before the passing of the first copyright laws during the revolutionary and Napoleonic periods, in Italy the composer of the same period could claim no ownership rights whatsoever to his own work. When a score left his hands there were no rules governing its reproduction: copyists could make and distribute copies at will if the music had met with success and had created a demand. This situation also explains why the pasticcio became the normal fate of a theatrical work: it was not essential for all the various parts of a work to be written by one composer; instead, it became more important that those parts be disposed ingeniously so as to give the spectacle an organic dramatic quality and a musical unity at least from time to time.[94]

Verdi was the first composer to specify that his operas must be produced as he had written them, and from *Rigoletto* on he insisted firmly that this be done.[95] In this aim he was fortunate to have good relations with a publisher disposed (and able) to second his wishes, and in fact from 1859 on he did not deal directly with theatrical impresarios.[96] Before Verdi, when a work was revived its text was freely manipulated for the benefit of (when not by the hand of) virtuoso singers. Furthermore, if the impresario wished to make sure that the public would take an interest in the production, he had to maximize publicity regarding the musical gifts of his principal singers. Given their high degree of specialization and the demand for their services, famous singers dictated what was to be added, substituted, or written anew for their parts

---

94. *The New Grove Dictionary of Music and Musicians,* s.v. "Pasticcio," by Reinhard Strohm. See also *The New Grove Dictionary of Opera,* s. v. "Pasticcio," by Curtis Price.

95. To explain his refusal to write an aria for the singer Teresa De Giuli Borsi to be inserted into a revival of *Rigoletto,* Verdi noted, "If this *Rigoletto* can stand as it is, a new aria would be superfluous. And where would one put it? Verses and notes can be provided, but unless they are at the right time and in the right place, they will never make any effect. . . . I conceived *Rigoletto* without arias, without finales, as a long string of duets, because this was how I wanted it." This letter of 8 September 1852 to Carlo Antonio Borsi, the singer's husband, can be found in Giuseppe Verdi, *I copialettere,* 497, and is quoted here from *Letters of Giuseppe Verdi,* ed. and trans. Charles Osborne (New York: Holt, Rinehart and Winston, 1971), 87–88. See also *I copialettere,* 45.

96. Rosselli, "Verdi e la storia della retribuzione del compositore italiano," 20.

because they were aware that their personal success was, in the last analysis, what made the show as a whole a success.

The emphasis on singers could not help shaping the composer's creative processes and the way he produced a musical score. For that reason and others dictated by individual circumstances, the tasks of opera composers after the mid-seventeenth century necessarily went beyond producing a finished orchestral score. Modifications were made; entire sections or individual passages were replaced; revision, recasting, and elaboration of various sorts often took place before opening night, while the opera was still in rehearsal, or on the occasion of a revival. One might say that in general the autograph score of an opera represents only an initial stage of the composer's creative task—an important stage, but one that does not necessarily reflect his final conception of the opera. Indeed, it is probable that the opera composer did not even attempt to produce a "definitive" version of his opera scores. During the nineteenth century the printed editions of the piano-vocal scores of Italian operas were not always prepared with the active supervision or even the authorization of the composer, given that the publishers were intent on making the vocal score (and at times even the full orchestral score) available for sale as soon as possible after the opera's premiere. With the exception of *Rigoletto,* there is practically no theatrical work of Verdi's that remains intact in its original version. Until *Attila* (1846) Verdi subjected his own works to a number of modifications and revisions that were not an integral part of the "official" scores and that were written, for the most part, to satisfy the demands of individual singers and specific productions, often with the composer himself conducting.[97] Some modifications and changes in Verdi's later works (*Simon Boccanegra* and *Don Carlos,* for example) were dictated by practical concerns,[98] but still others were inspired by musical reasons and by an effort to

---

97. For a complete picture of the revisions never incorporated in the official printed versions of Verdi's scores, see David Rosen and David Lawton, "Verdi's Non-Definitive Revisions: The Early Operas," in *Atti del III congresso internazionale di studi verdiani, Milan, Piccola Scala, 12–17 giugno 1972* (Parma: Istituto di Studi Verdiani, 1974), 189–237.

98. For the revival of *Simon Boccanegra* in Reggio Emilia in 1857, Verdi changed, among other things, a difficult passage in the viola and cello parts because the players in that provincial city were unable to perform them; see Marcello Conati, *Il "Simon Boccanegra" di Verdi a Reggio Emilia (1857): Storia documentata: Alcune varianti alla prima edizione dell'opera* (Reggio Emilia: Teatro Municipale "Romolo Valli," 1984), 40–43. The original five-act version of *Don Carlos,* composed for Paris, was never performed. Because the work as written would have exceeded the time limit imposed by the management of the Paris Opéra (where operas had to be over by midnight), Verdi made several cuts in it during rehearsals (autumn 1867). On Verdi's many modifications in *Don Carlos* before 1884, see Andrew Porter's review of the edition of the score of the opera edited by Ursula Günther (Milan: Ricordi, 1980) in *Journal of the American Musicological Society* 35 (1982): 360–70.

try out better ways to adapt the musical and dramaturgical scheme to the dramatic action.[99] Puccini as well made radical changes in some of his works, on occasion long after the premiere.[100]

From the seventeenth century on the composer who wrote for the theater placed the vocal parts at the center of his compositional vision, privileging the voice as a structural element.[101] The poetic text represented the initial impetus for the musical idea, and the voice was the principal resource for enhancing the expressive charge of that idea. It was the composer's task not only to invent melodies but to create them in accordance with the vocal characteristics of predetermined performers. The principal referent for any specific opera production was thus not the score but the interpretation that a particular singer would give of the drama. Furthermore, because the com-

99. When Verdi revised *Simon Boccanegra* he made changes and accentuated the rhythms to support stage action and increase dramatic intensity; see Wolfgang Osthoff, "Die beiden *Boccanegra*-Fassungen und der Beginn von Verdis Spätwerk," *Analecta Musicologica* 1 (1963): 70–89, esp. 78–79. Even the changes Verdi made in the 1884 version of *Don Carlos* (on which he had been working since 1882) aimed primarily at greater fidelity to Schiller's drama and were made, for the most part, for artistic and musical reasons. Verdi wrote to Charles Nuitter on 28 September 1882, "On rereading Schiller I found some phrases that have a very powerful significance and [are] of immense scenic effect"; Ursula Günther and Gabriella Carrara Verdi, "Der Briefwechsel Verdi-Nuitter-Du Locle zur Revision des *Don Carlos*," *Analecta Musicologica* 15 (1975): 334–401, esp. 355. On Verdi's reasons for recasting a section of the duet between King Philip II and Posa, see Giorgio Pestelli, "Le riduzioni del tardo stile verdiano: Osservazioni su alcune varianti del *Don Carlos*," *Nuova rivista musicale italiana* 6 (1972): 372–90.

100. *Madama Butterfly* is a paradigmatic case. After the negative reception of the opera at its premiere at La Scala in Milan, 17 February 1904 (a reception in large part prepared in advance by a well-organized claque paid by rival composers), Puccini made cuts and changes in both the musical score and the poetic text, and the opera was presented with great success on 28 May of the same year at Brescia. The opera was then produced at Paris on 28 December of the same year with further cuts and changes made (during the long rehearsal period in the summer and autumn of 1906) at the request of the director of the Opéra Comique, Albert Carré, in the interest of adapting the opera to the tastes of the middle-class Parisian public. Concerning the complex events that persuaded the composer to revise his opera for the Paris production, see Julian Smith, "'Madame Butterfly': The Paris Première of 1906," in *Werk und Wiedergabe: Musiktheater exemplarisch interpretiert,* ed. Sigrid Wiesmann (Bayreuth: Mühl'scher Universitätsverlag Werner Fehr, 1980), 229–38, and Julian Smith, "A Metamorphic Tragedy," *Proceedings of the Royal Musical Association* 106 (1979/80): 105–14.

101. Even Richard Wagner, a composer whose works are usually contrasted to Italian opera traditions, first penciled in the vocal parts during a preliminary phase of the creative process. It was only after about 1850, with the writing of *Der Ring des Nibelungen,* that he changed his method of composition and sketched out the orchestral motifs in the first phases of creation. On Wagner's working methods see Robert Bailey, "The Evolution of Wagner's Compositional Procedure after *Lohengrin*," in International Musicological Society, *Report of the Eleventh Congress, Copenhagen 1972,* ed. Henrik Glahn, Søren Sørensen, and Peter Ryom (Copenhagen: Wilhelm Hansen, 1974), 1:240–44, esp. 241, and John Deathridge, "The Nomenclature of Wagner's Sketches," *Proceedings of the Royal Musical Association* 101 (1974/75): 75–83, esp. 77.

poser had little influence over the selection of the singers or their contracts, and because he had to create the score so that the vocal parts served their particular function, he had to know the vocal characteristics and acting talents of the singers hired for the premiere. To cite one example, when the Venetian impresario Marco Faustini invited Antonio Cesti to write an opera, his reaction was, "All that is left, as far as I am concerned, is to know who the singers are, and to see the poetry first." [102] Alessandro Scarlatti wrote from Rome to Ferdinando de' Medici, who had just sent him the first act of the libretto for *Il gran Tamerlano* to set to music,

> And, for my part, in order not to fail to grasp every [favorable] circumstance for fulfilling my duty, I will not withhold from asking reverently (when it will please Your Highness) for fuller information on the persons who are to perform it, not for any other reason than to adapt the music to the voices and the abilities of the same. . . . Adapting the music to the voice and the abilities of each singer is a method that must be followed for the greater security of the same [singers] and, in consequence, that will contribute to the happy outcome of the whole, which has as its aim the listener's enjoyment. [103]

From Monteverdi to Puccini there are innumerable direct statements from composers to the effect that an opera in the early stages of its creation was written not only with the various roles in mind but also for the specific singers who were to perform it. [104]

As regards the actual writing of the musical score, the composer most likely began with the creation of the vocal parts, composing first all the arias and later adding the recitatives. That procedure permitted him, should there be unforeseen changes in the cast, to switch the arias more easily from one point in the drama to another or to rewrite them in another key without having to lay out again the musical context of the recitatives. Historical documentation and specific studies of the question are lacking for seventeenth-

---

102. Letter of 16 May 1666 from Vienna, in Remo Giazotto, "Nel CCC anno della morte di Antonio Cesti: Ventidue [*recte:* 21] lettere ritrovate nell'Archivio di Stato di Venezia," *Nuova rivista musicale italiana* 3 (1969): 496–512, esp. 508. The reader will find pertinent commentary and an accurate reconstruction of the context of Cesti's letters (absent in Giazotto's essay) in Carl B. Schmidt, "An Episode in the History of Venetian Opera: The *Tito* Commission (1665–66)," *Journal of the American Musicological Society* 31 (1978): 442–66.

103. Letter of 1 May 1706, in Fabbri, *Alessandro Scarlatti*, 70–71.

104. Puccini may well have written *Turandot* with the singer Gilda dalla Rizza, his favorite interpreter, in mind, according to a letter he wrote (25 February 1924) to that singer: "I am not sure that Turandot can be for you, but certainly Liù (the slave), a principal part just like the other, would be a natural for la Gilda"; F. G. Rizzi, *Gilda Dalla Rizza: Verismo e Bel Canto* (Venice: Tipografia Commerciale, 1964), 65.

and eighteenth-century opera,[105] but there is some direct evidence for such methods in the nineteenth century.

As soon as Bellini received the contract for *La straniera* (June 1828), he began to sketch out preliminary ideas, as seen in a letter dated 21 June: "Every day I write melodies, but I have not yet been able to do cabalettas, and I hope they will come." A letter written a few days later (7 July) reveals that Bellini was sketching out the "melodies" two months before he began to write down the first pages of the score (September 1828): "I am attempting to accumulate a supply of melodies, and I am doing some that are not bad, which I hope, once I have the libretto, to put in place and develop effectively."[106] Before he actually wrote out the score proper, then, and without having the libretto at hand, Bellini was writing a series of sketches containing "melodies" that would later appear in the final autograph score. It is significant that no sketches of a complete opera of Bellini are known, only sketches of melodies he wrote *before* he had the poetic text of the opera in hand.[107]

---

105. We know some specifics concerning the compositional methods of George Frideric Handel, who might, in many ways and without stretching it too far, be considered an "Italian" opera composer. Different versions of a given aria are often patched into his autograph scores; presumably they were composed at various times to exploit the vocal resources of different singers. For *Tamerlano* (1724), see the description of the autograph score in J. Merrill Knapp, "Handel's *Tamerlano:* The Creation of an Opera," *Musical Quarterly* 56 (1970): 405–30, esp. 421–23. Handel composed his arias first, then went back and wrote the recitatives (but in the case of *Tamerlano,* he wrote the text of the recitatives first, adding the music after; see Knapp, 422). From the extant fragments of an unfinished opera (*Il Genserico,* begun in 1728), we can see that Handel had composed the arias for about half of the opera, but the recitatives had not yet been set to music. In the first phase of the composition of *Alcina* (1735), Handel omitted the recitatives completely, not even writing the text; see Reinhard Strohm, "Handel and his Italian Opera Texts," in *Essays on Handel and Italian Opera,* (Cambridge: Cambridge University Press, 1985), 34–79. Mozart's compositional method is known for at least for two of his opera scores (*Così fan tutte* and *La clemenza di Tito*): he wrote the ensemble numbers first, then the solo arias (probably after consulting with the leading singers), and the recitatives last. On Mozart's compositional methods and for further bibliographical information, see Alan Tyson, "Notes on the Composition of Mozart's *Così fan tutte," Journal of the American Musicological Society* 37 (1984): 356–401, esp. 362–63 and 366. That Italian opera composers continued to use similar compositional methods until the early decades of the nineteenth century is shown in Carlo Ritorni, *Ammaestramenti alla composizione d'ogni poema e d'ogni opera appartenente alla musica* (Milan, 1841), 53: "Thus the composer, when he sets out to do the score for a libretto, first looks at how many 'pieces' it contains that he must set, and he begins to work on them diligently, one by one, but without necessarily respecting their natural order. Sometimes the poet will hand them to him one at a time, also without following the dramatic order. When he has finished setting these to music and has joined them together to make up his dramatic display, he will recall the recitatives to mind; setting them to music is a material and uniform operation (even if they are wholly orchestrated) for which, if time and will are lacking, it would be sufficient to call upon a young pupil."

106. Quoted in Adamo and Lippmann, *Vincenzo Bellini,* 519.

107. For a discussion of Bellini's sketches, see ibid., 519–21. One anecdote relates that Bellini had composed the music for the aria "Or sei pago, o ciel tremendo" for *La straniera* even before

Verdi presumably operated in the same manner. From the two pages of *La traviata* published in facsimile from the original manuscript,[108] we can see that even before receiving Piave's libretto, the composer had sketched out some important melodies without vocal text, to which he added stage directions ("Margherita feels ill. Everyone disperses; only the Tenor remains" and so forth). The complete continuity draft of *Rigoletto* (the only major Verdian draft yet published in facsimile)[109] is preceded by eleven fragmentary sketches (of from two to twenty-five measures) probably noted down before the redaction of the continuity draft itself, most of which contain melodies without text. In the continuity draft the vocal parts clearly predominate over the other musical elements and are accompanied by a bass line, with cues for solo instruments indicated here and there.[110] It is well known that for Verdi the continuity draft represented the essential phase of composition that fixed the succession of musical ideas for the entire opera. Once that manuscript draft was finished, the subsequent task of orchestrating the score—the official and public text that later went to the copyists, the engravers, etc.—was a more mechanical operation that, at least until relatively late in his career, could be polished off in a few days. In fact when Verdi had finished the draft of *Rigo-*

---

he had the text: he played the aria on the piano for the librettist, Felice Romani, and persuaded Romani to write the verse on the spot (see ibid., 93–94). For more on the question of "prefabricated" melodies by Bellini that he later adapted to the poetic texts he received from the librettist, see the examination of melodic sketches later used in the score for *La sonnambula* in Friedrich Lippmann, "Belliniana," in *Il melodramma italiano dell'Ottocento: Studi e ricerche per Massimo Mila* (Turin: Einaudi, 1977), 281–317, esp. 299–303.

108. Carlo Gatti, *Verdi nelle immagini* (Milan: Garzanti, 1941), 64–65.

109. See Carlo Gatti, *L'abbozzo del "Rigoletto" di Giuseppe Verdi* (Milan: Ricordi, 1941). The document contains twenty-eight folios grouped in two fascicles. According to Gatti all of Verdi's drafts (from *Luisa Miller* on) are preserved at Sant'Agata by the composer's heirs. Verdi's sketches for *Stiffelio*, including a complete continuity draft, and the sketches for *La traviata* have recently been made available to the editors of *The Works of Giuseppe Verdi* (Chicago: University of Chicago Press; Milan: Ricordi). For a discussion of the *Stiffelio* sketches, see the essays by Philip Gossett and by Kathleen Kuzmick Hansell in *Verdi's Middle Period, 1849–1859: Source Studies, Analysis, and Performance Practice* (Chicago: University of Chicago Press, 1997). Gossett's essay has also appeared in *Cambridge Opera Journal* 5 (1993), 199–222. Regarding the newly released sketches for *La traviata*, see Fabrizio Della Seta's introduction to the critical edition of the opera, vol. 19 of *The Works of Giuseppe Verdi*. Della Seta is preparing a facsimile edition with transcription and commentary for publication by the Istituto Nazionale di Studi Verdiani, Parma.

110. The variants between the draft of the chorus "Urli, rapine" in the prologue to *Attila* and the definitive version in the autograph full score of the opera confirm the predominance of the melodic line in Verdi's creative process. The principal changes concern the refinement of the melodic movement in the vocal parts; see Michel Noiray and Roger Parker, "La composition d'*Attila*: Étude de quelques variantes," *Revue de musicologie* 62 (1976): 104–23. On the changes made by Verdi between the draft version and the final version of *I due Foscari* and *Rigoletto*, see Pierluigi Petrobelli, "Remarks on Verdi's Composing Process," in *Music in the Theater: Essays on Verdi and Other Composers*, trans. Roger Parker (Princeton: Princeton University Press, 1994), 48–74.

letto he wrote to Piave (letter of 5 February 1851): "Just today I have finished the opera. All I have left to do is the clean copy of the second act and the last piece."[111] A few days before (29 January 1851) Verdi had written to the director of La Fenice in Venice, "With the final duet done I have only to work five or six days on the orchestration."[112] Puccini too presumably worked to ready the musical texts of his operas in the same way as Verdi. First, in a preliminary phase, even before he had the versified text, he planned out the key musical ideas.[113] Second, he passed on to writing the "pianistic" drafts, at times written on systems of three, four, or more staves and even including details of orchestration.[114] Third, he completed the entire score, which was then sent off to the publisher.

Nearly all Italian opera composers from the early eighteenth century until late in the nineteenth century shared a characteristic ability to prepare an opera score in a very short time. Since there were usually only a few weeks between when a contract was signed for a work and when it went on the stage, and since the composer had to be present in the opera house several days before the premiere in order to make all the adaptations necessary, he had little time available to complete his work—three or four weeks or even less. Thus an opera had to be written in one creative impulse with no afterthoughts. George Frideric Handel, for example, completed *Tamerlano* in less than three weeks (3–23 July 1724). Piccinni wrote *La buona figliuola* (1760) in eighteen days. Pacini normally devoted three or four days to each of his one-act farces. Carlo Coccia composed *La donna selvaggia* (1813) in twelve days and *Donna Caritea* (1817) in a week. Rossini completed the six hundred pages of the score of *Il barbiere di Siviglia* in eighteen or nineteen days (Janu-

111. Franco Abbiati, *Giuseppe Verdi,* 4 vols. (Milan: Ricordi, 1959), 1: 105–6.

112. Marcello Conati, *La bottega della musica: Verdi e La Fenice* (Milan: Il Saggiatore, 1983), 250.

113. Puccini had conceived the waltz tune that Magda and Ruggero sing ("Dolcezza, ebrezza") in the second act of *La rondine* (a recurring theme denoting love that appears on several occasions in the course of the opera) even before he received Giuseppe Adami's words. Puccini wrote to his librettist from Torre del Lago on 11 November 1914: "So I am going ahead, and as I find that in the second act there is too little animation and none of the gaiety and cheerful noise that there should be, considering where the scene is laid, I have had the idea of lengthening the waltz by adding some music which will be livelier and have more *entrain* in it. This music I have, in fact, composed. It now only wants the *mise en scène*. This lively music must have its counterpart in some scene of unrestrained gaiety. And we need words. At a certain point the two lovers break into the love-song in waltz time, and this, I think, is going to fit in well. . . . In the meantime, I am forging ahead"; Giacomo Puccini, *Epistolario,* ed. Giuseppe Adami (Milan: Mondadori, 1928), 192, quoted here from *Letters of Giacomo Puccini,* ed. Giuseppe Adami, trans. Ena Makin, new rev. ed. by Mosco Carner (London: Harrap, 1974), 203.

114. At least this is what transpires from the inventory of Puccini drafts published in Alberto Cavalli, "I frammenti pucciniani di Celle," in *Critica pucciniana* (Lucca: Provincia di Lucca, 1976), 16–34.

ary–February 1816), and he received the libretto for *La Cenerentola* (which went on the stage 25 January 1817) barely a month earlier (26 December 1816). Donizetti composed *L'elisir d'amore* in two weeks (April 1832) and *Lucia di Lammermoor* in under six weeks (June and July 1832). Verdi wrote *La traviata* nonstop at Busseto from the end of January to 20 February 1853 (completing the orchestration in Venice in the first five or six days of March). Mascagni composed *Cavalleria rusticana* in two months.

Giuseppe Carpani put his finger on the right spot when, criticizing the lack of depth in opera in his day (the early nineteenth century), he stated that the basic cause was a "mania for novelty and . . . an aversion to studying the solid foundations of the art together with an eagerness for quick earnings and the haste with which musical works are written, at times in eight days."[115] Emilia Branca, the widow of the librettist Felice Romani, gave vivid testimony to Donizetti's facility and speed of composition.

> The Lombard maestro, all fire and energy, when he received from the poet the verses of *L'elisir*, set them mentally to music as he was reading them and then immediately transferred it to paper. He wrote as rapidly as he conceived, only rarely canceling out or correcting what he wrote.[116]

Once, when Donizetti arrived late for a dinner invitation at the Branca household, he excused himself by explaining,

> I started out for here a half hour ago, but passing by the Romani's house I entered to see if he had *something* to give me; in fact my worthy friend gave me an entire duet. As I was reading the beautiful poetry—as only he knows how to write—I was so inspired that without being aware of it I was reading it already with music. . . . I wanted to write it down immediately, as you can well understand. . . . This evening before I go to bed I will orchestrate it, tomorrow I will give it to the copyist to write out the parts, which he will deliver to the singers, etc., etc. Everything is going full steam ahead![117]

115. Giuseppe Carpani, *Le rossiane, ossia Lettere musico-teatrali* (Padua, 1824), 17. See also John Mainwaring, *Memoirs of the Life of the Late George Frederic Handel* on the pace of composition of Italian composers in Handel's time.

116. Emilia Branca, *Felice Romani ed i più riputati maestri di musica del suo tempo* (Turin, 1882), 218–19.

117. Ibid. The commonplace of melody that springs fully formed from the words has its roots in eighteenth-century Enlightenment theories on the evolution of spoken language. Many of the eighteenth-century figures who wrote on the relationship between music and declamation (Étienne Bonnot de Condillac, Jean-Jacques Rousseau, Francesco Algarotti, Ranieri de' Calzabigi, and others) are reviewed in Giorgio Pestelli, "Musica, linguaggio, declamazione: Il contributo di Condillac alla definizione del problema," in *Musica e spettacolo a Parma nel Settecento* (Parma: Università di Parma, 1984), 227–35. The idea of the composer who listens to a declamation of the poetic text and draws out its implicit melody is found in descriptions of Bellini's compositional methods (Adamo and Lippmann, *Vincenzo Bellini*, 133–34) and in Giuseppe Giacosa's account

The short time that opera composers in Italy had available for conceiving and writing down the musical text (normally the few weeks from the date of signing the contract and the delivery of the libretto to the date of the first performance) could not help having a direct influence on the compositional methods that the composer adopted as he wrote the score. The autograph full score of an opera was at once the first and final draft, ready to be used in the theater. Given the circumstances the composer simply did not have the leisure to devote himself as long as he might have wanted to all the preparatory tasks (sketches and drafts) that preceded the final redaction of the work. We know that Rossini (for whom we have only two known drafts, both dating from his Paris period) prepared the orchestral score by writing the part for the first violin (when it carried the melody) from beginning to end, together with the vocal parts and the bass of the harmony, after which he went on to complete the rest of the orchestral accompaniment.[118] Other opera composers, both before and after Rossini, used the same method of composition.[119] Verdi was the first Italian opera composer who was systematic (from at least 1850) about the preparatory tasks that preceded writing the definitive score (that is, the autograph score used for the premiere or as a copy text for publication). Verdi's method was one that Italian opera composers had followed only sporadically, and in and of itself it is an indication of Verdi's greater artistic and intellectual awareness as he realized his musical ideas. Yet dedicated as he was to building an image that would make him appear legendary in the eyes

---

of a visit to Sant'Agata in early autumn 1884, when Verdi was working on *Otello:* "Verdi would sometimes clutch the libretto and read several pieces aloud. . . . The voice, the accent, the cadences, the force, the anger expressed in that reading betrayed such an ardent kindling of the soul, magnified so immeasurably the sense of the words, that the source of the musical idea was clearly revealed to us. With our own eyes we saw, as it were, the flower of the melody blossom, and the words, given by his voice their utmost power, transmuted into waves of sound, sweeping away the endless anguish that sometimes assails the human soul"; Marcello Conati, *Interviste e incontri con Verdi* (Milan: Il Formichiere, 1980), 156, and quoted here from Conati, *Interviews and Encounters with Verdi,* trans. Richard Stokes (London: V. Gollancz, 1984), 161. In an essay entitled "Come scrive e come prova Giuseppe Verdi," which appeared in a special issue of *L'illustrazione italiana* (early February 1893, p. 24), published a few days before the premiere of *Falstaff,* Giulio Ricordi wrote that Verdi used to recite the verse lines of the libretto before he went on to tracing the musical outline of his operas.

118. See Philip Gossett, "Gioachino Rossini and the Conventions of Composition," *Acta Musicologica* 42 (1970): 48–59, esp. 51–52.

119. Mozart wrote his theatrical works in the same way as Rossini later did; see Alfred Einstein, *Mozart: His Character, His Work,* trans. Arthur Mendel and Nathan Broder (New York: Oxford University Press, 1962), 142. When Donizetti wrote out the score for *Anna Bolena,* he completed the orchestral parts after he had composed the vocal parts and even after having made changes (perhaps in collaboration with the singers) and variants in the melodic line; see Philip Gossett, *Anna Bolena and the Artistic Maturity of Gaetano Donizetti* (Oxford: Clarendon Press, 1985), 34–39.

of the public, Verdi took care, particularly in the years of his artistic maturity, to present an utterly romantic picture of himself as a composer of genius writing in one spontaneous burst of creative energy with no afterthoughts. This is clear in the advice that Verdi gave Umberto Giordano during a conversation. Giordano reports,

> I had the good fortune to visit him often. It would have been better if I had taken some notes of what the Maestro told me during the visits; but some things I can recall merely by exerting my memory. He once asked me, point-blank: "Giordano, what is your method of composition?" I replied: "Maestro, I cannot possibly speak to you of my method—but pray give me some advice." "Good," he replied, "I shall tell you immediately: never correct what you wrote on the previous day—you will not like it any more and you will mistakenly destroy all that you have done. Compose the first act, without pausing, without corrections; when you have done this, put the sheets of music to one side and start the second act. Proceed with the second act in exactly the same way, and then continue with the third and fourth acts. Then rest. When you have recovered your strength, revise and correct everything; you can be sure that this is the only way of avoiding error." Another time he recommended me to work every day, at any work to hand—[for] without such daily exercise the hand . . . grows stiff.[120]

Giulio Ricordi also encouraged the image of Verdi's legendary creative talents. During the rehearsals in Milan for *Falstaff,* the publisher reported,

> Giuseppe Verdi's autograph scores are admirable for their exactness. . . . The opera emerges spontaneously in one block. . . . Verdi writes very few sketches during the period of composition: [only] simple reminders, indications of musical impulses, and nothing more. . . . The facility with which Verdi conceives and writes an opera is absolutely phenomenal. . . . One should not believe that the celebrated maestro uses for his creation any haphazardly found musical reminders that he had sketched [earlier] on a page of music paper to use when needed. On the contrary, that [method of composing] is not admissible for one of the true and great composers of opera. It is the dramatic situation, the words, that excite and awaken the creative fantasy, and no successful operatic piece has been composed on a template of a little *motive* found here or there and hastily scratched onto paper for later use. Verdi, however, has never done this. . . . He does not even use very many sketches when he composes an opera. For his *Falstaff* he jotted down very few notes [*appunti*] that filled only two pages.[121]

120. Conati, *Interviste e incontri,* 363–64, and quoted here from Conati, *Interviews and Encounters with Verdi,* 384.

121. Giulio Ricordi, "Come scrive e come prova Giuseppe Verdi," quoted here from Ricordi, "How Giuseppe Verdi Writes and Rehearses," 150–51 in James A. Hepokoski, "Under the Eye of the Verdian Bear: Notes on the Rehearsals and Premiere of *Falstaff,*" *The Musical Quarterly* 71 (1985): 135–56; see esp. 141, which also discusses the reliability of Ricordi's testimony concerning Verdi's methods of composition.

Bellini's compositional methods, like Verdi's in his mature years, required more time than those of his contemporaries, thanks to his meticulous habits and his constant reflection on his musical ideas. As much is attested by a statement that Bellini made in 1832 to an admirer from Palermo, later published in letter form (surely not an authentic document but probably based on authentic statements).

> Since I propose to write few scores—not more than one per year—I use all the strength of my mind on them. Persuaded as I am that a great part of their success depends on the choice of an interesting subject, on clashing passions, on harmonious verse burning with expression, not to mention startling plot turns, I do my best, first of all, to have a perfect drama from a talented writer, which is why I have preferred Romani to all others—a most powerful mind, made for musical drama. When his work is finished I study attentively the personality of the characters, their ruling passions, and the sentiments that they express. Imbued by the emotions of each one of them, I imagine myself to be whichever one of them is speaking, and I make every effort to feel and to express myself efficaciously in their person. Knowing that music results from variety in the sounds and that the passions of men become evident when they speak in differently modulated tones, by an incessant observation of humankind I have drawn the spark of sentiment for my art. Then, closeted in my room, I begin to declaim the role of the character in the drama with all the warmth of passion, and at the same time I observe the inflections of my voice, the speeding up or the languor of the pronunciation in such a circumstance, in short, the accent and the tone of the expression that nature gives to man in prey to passion, and I find in them the musical motifs and the rhythms appropriate to display [emotions] and transmit them to others by means of harmony. I jot them down on paper right away, I try them out at the keyboard, and when I myself feel the corresponding emotion, I judge that I have been successful. If not I go back to seeking inspiration until I have reached my goal.[122]

Puccini's musical ideas, like Bellini's, needed time to ripen. (We should keep in mind, however, that the two composers worked in different eras and different historical contexts, in particular where relations with music publishing were concerned). There are still only very few published letters of Puccini that tell about his compositional methods, although many Puccini letters tell us about the various phases of the elaboration and redaction of the poetic texts for his operas (he always collaborated actively with his librettists) and about problems of staging. One letter written in November 1895 to Giulio Ricordi offers an interesting picture of Puccini's slow and meticulous compositional methods (he was working on the fourth scene of *La Bohème* at the time). Ricordi had urged Puccini to come to Milan to choose the singers for the first performances of the opera, which were imminent. Puccini answered,

---

122. Quoted in Adamo and Lippmann, *Vincenzo Bellini*, 133–34.

I agree with your letter entirely, but there is a difficulty.

Am I to finish this act or not? Am I to finish it in Milan? Is my presence so necessary? I can put in the metronome indications here. You have only to send me a metronome by parcel post and a copy of all that is printed, and I will do it at once. . . . I am orchestrating now, and in a day or two I shall send you some music. I am very well on with the composition and pleased with it. It has been rather troublesome, as I wanted it to be in some degree realistic and was anxious also to make all these little snatches slightly lyrical. And in this I have succeeded, for I wish there to be as much singing, as much *melody,* as possible.

The act is composed almost entirely of logical repetitions. The duet *Sono andati?* and Colline's *Vecchia zimarra* are almost the only exceptions. I think that I have found a good beginning for the duet and an effective climax, though it is nothing very new. But then, we don't have to split hairs, do we?

To conclude, therefore, leave me here in peace to drink in this splendid sunshine and enjoy this enchanting countryside. As soon as I write the word *Fine* I will fly to Milan, and I hope that will be around the *beginning of December.*[123]

If Puccini had lived in the mid-eighteenth century, he probably would not have had so many days to spend in the country writing one scene for an opera when the singers were already in rehearsal. He might even have suffered the fate of Leonardo Leo, who was put under house arrest (in Naples in 1738) at the request of the impresario so that he could complete the revision of his *Demetrio* on time.[124]

APPENDIX: ITALIAN OPERA COMPOSERS

List of the composers used in the statistical surveys and comprehensive analyses, organized in chronological order by year of birth.

Giulio Caccini (Rome or Tivoli, 1551–Florence, 1618)
Jacopo Peri (Rome, 1561–Florence, 1633)
Claudio Monteverdi (Cremona, 1567–Venice, 1643)
Stefano Landi (Rome, ca. 1586–1639)
Francesco Manelli (Tivoli, 1594–Parma, 1667)
Antonio Maria Abbatini (Città di Castello, 1595?–1679)

---

123. *Carteggi pucciniani,* ed. Eugenio Gara (Milan: Ricordi, 1958), 89, quoted from *Letters of Giacomo Puccini,* 133–34. See also the letters to Ricordi on *Madama Butterfly* of 3 May 1902 ("I am going slowly, as usual, but working carefully and with deliberation") and November 1902 ("If you only knew how I am racking my brains! The work to be done is not great, but it is essential to bind the whole story together with a closer logic than there is in Belasco's play"); Puccini, *Epistolario,* 146, 151, quoted from *Letters of Giacomo Puccini,* 153, 159.

124. This episode is documented in Giuseppe A. Pastore, *Leonardo Leo* (Galatina: Pajano, 1957), 54–56.

Francesco Cavalli (Crema, 1602–Venice, 1676)
Marco Marazzoli (Parma, ca. 1602 or 1608–Rome, 1662)
Pietro Andrea Ziani (Venice, 1616–Naples, 1684)
Giuseppe Tricarico (Gallipoli, 1623–1697)
Jacopo Melani (Pistoia, 1623–1676)
Antonio Cesti (Arezzo, 1623–Florence, 1669)
Atto Melani (Pistoia, 1626–Paris, 1714)
Giovanni Legrenzi (Clusone, 1626–Venice, 1690)
Francesco Provenzale (Naples, ca. 1626–1704)
Antonio Sartorio (Venice, 1630–1680)
Giovanni Domenico Freschi (Bassano, ca. 1630–Vicenza, 1710)
Carlo Pallavicino (Salò, ca. 1630?–Dresden, 1688)
Pietro Simone Agostini (Forlì, ca. 1635–Parma, 1680)
Giovanni Maria Pagliardi (Genoa, 1637–Florence, 1702)
Bernardo Pasquini (Massa e Cozzile, 1637–Rome, 1710)
Alessandro Melani (Pistoia, 1639–Rome, 1703)
Alessandro Stradella (Rome, 1639–Genoa, 1682)
Marc'Antonio Ziani (Venice, ca. 1653–Vienna, 1715)
Carlo Francesco Pollarolo (Brescia? ca. 1653–Venice, 1723)
Alessandro Scarlatti (Palermo, 1660–Naples, 1725)
Francesco Gasparini (Camaiore, 1661–Rome, 1727)
Giacomo Antonio Perti (Bologna, 1661–1756)
Pirro Albergati Capacelli (Bologna, 1663–1735)
Antonio Lotti (Venice or Hannover, ca. 1667–Venice, 1740)
Giovanni Bononcini (Modena, 1670–Vienna, 1747)
Tomaso Albinoni (Venice, 1671–1751)
Antonio Caldara (Venice, ca. 1671–Vienna, 1736)
Giuseppe Maria Orlandini (Florence, 1676–1760)
Antonio Maria Bononcini (Modena, 1677–1726)
Antonio Vivaldi (Venice, 1678–Vienna, 1741)
Domenico Sarro (Trani, 1679–Naples, 1744)
Emanuele d'Astorga (Augusta, 1680–Madrid? 1757?)
George Frideric Handel (Halle an der Saale, 1685–London, 1759)
Domenico Scarlatti (Naples, 1685–Madrid, 1757)
Nicola Porpora (Naples, 1686–1768)
Francesco Feo (Naples, 1691–1761)
Geminiano Giacomelli (Piacenza, ca. 1692–Loreto, 1740)
Leonardo Leo (S. Vito dei Normanni, 1694–Naples, 1744)
Leonardo Vinci (Strongoli, ca. 1696–Naples, 1730)
Nicola Logroscino (Bitonto, 1698–Palermo? 1765–67)
Riccardo Broschi (Naples, ca. 1698–Madrid, 1756)
Johann Adolf Hasse (Bergedorf, 1699–Venice, 1783)
Rinaldo da Capua (Capua or Naples, ca. 1705–Rome? ca. 1780)
Baldassare Galuppi (Burano, 1706–Venice, 1785)
Giovanni Battista Lampugnani (Milan, 1706–1788)

Pasquale Cafaro (Galatina, 1708–Naples, 1787)
Egidio Romualdo Duni (Matera, 1708–Paris, 1775)
Giovanni Battista Pergolesi (Iesi, 1710–Pozzuoli, 1736)
Gaetano Latilla (Bari, 1711–Naples, 1788)
Niccolò Jommelli (Aversa, 1714–Naples, 1774)
Gennaro Manna (Naples, 1715–1779)
Vincenzo Ciampi (Piacenza, 1719?–Venice, 1762)
Gioacchino Cocchi (Naples? ca. 1720–Venice? after 1788)
Ferdinando Bertoni (Salò, 1725–Desenzano, 1813)
Tommaso Traetta (Bitonto, 1727–Venice, 1779)
Pasquale Anfossi (Taggia, 1727–Rome, 1797)
Niccolò Piccinni (Bari, 1728–Passy, 1800)
Pietro Alessandro Guglielmi (Massa, 1728–Rome, 1804)
Giuseppe Sarti (Faenza, 1729–Berlin, 1802)
Antonio Sacchini (Florence, 1730–Paris, 1768)
Gian Francesco De Majo (Naples, 1732– 1770)
Giacomo Tritto (Altamura, 1733–Naples, 1824)
Giovanni Battista Borghi (Camerino, 1738–Loreto, 1796)
Giovanni Paisiello (Roccaforzata, 1740–Naples, 1816)
Giuseppe Gazzaniga (Verona, 1743–Crema, 1818)
Gennaro Astarita (Naples? ca. 1745–9–place unknown, after 1803)
Domenico Cimarosa (Aversa, 1749–Venice, 1801)
Antonio Salieri (Legnago, 1750–Vienna, 1825)
Giuseppe Giordani (Naples, 1751–Fermo, 1798)
Nicola Zingarelli (Naples, 1752–Torre del Greco, 1837)
Francesco Bianchi (Cremona, ca. 1752–Hammersmith, 1810)
Luigi Caruso (Naples, 1754–Perugia, 1823)
Gaetano Andreozzi (Aversa, 1755–Paris, 1826)
Wolfgang Amadeus Mozart (Salzburg, 1756–Vienna, 1791)
Luigi Cherubini (Florence, 1760–Paris, 1842)
Giovanni Battista Cimador (Venice, 1761–Bath, 1805)
Giuseppe Nicolini (Piacenza, 1762–1842)
Giovanni Simone Mayr (Mendorf, 1763–Bergamo, 1845)
Valentino Fioravanti (Rome, 1764–Capua, 1837)
Sabastiano Nasolini (Piacenza, ca. 1768–Naples? 1806? 1816?)
Ferdinando Paër (Parma, 1771–Paris, 1839)
Giuseppe Mosca (Naples, 1772–Messina, 1839)
Pietro Generali (Masserano, 1773–Novara, 1832)
Gaspare Spontini (Maiolati, 1774–1851)
Luigi Mosca (Naples, 1775–1824)
Vincenzo Lavigna (Altamura, 1776–Milan, 1836)
Stefano Pavesi (Casaletto Vaprio, 1779–Crema, 1850)
Carlo Coccia (Naples, 1782–Novara, 1873)
Francesco Morlacchi (Perugia, 1784–Innsbruck, 1841)
Pietro Raimondi (Rome, 1786–1853)

Michele Carafa (Naples, 1787–Paris, 1872)
Nicola Vaccai (Tolentino, 1790–Pesaro, 1848)
Francesco Sampieri (Bologna, 1790–Paris, 1863)
Gioachino Rossini (Pesaro, 1792–Passy, 1868)
Saverio Mercadante (Altamura, 1795–Naples, 1870)
Giovanni Pacini (Catania, 1796–Pescia, 1867)
Gaetano Donizetti (Bergamo, 1797–1848)
Giuseppe Persiani (Recanati, 1799–Paris, 1869)
Vincenzo Bellini (Catania, 1801–Puteaux, 1835)
Luigi Ricci (Naples? 1805–Prague, 1859)
Federico Ricci (Naples, 1809–Conegliano, 1877)
Giuseppe Verdi (Roncole, 1813–Milan, 1901)
Errico Petrella (Palermo, 1813–Genoa, 1877)
Carlo Pedrotti (Verona, 1817–1893)
Antonio Cagnoni (Godiasco, 1828–Bergamo, 1896)
Filippo Marchetti (Bolognola, 1831–Rome, 1902)
Amilcare Ponchielli (Paderno, 1834–Milan, 1886)
Arrigo Boito (Padua, 1842–Milan, 1918)
Antonio Smareglia (Pola, 1854–Grado, 1929)
Alfredo Catalani (Lucca, 1854–Milan, 1893)
Ruggero Leoncavallo (Naples, 1857–Montecatini, 1919)
Giacomo Puccini (Lucca, 1858–Brussels, 1924)
Alberto Franchetti (Turin, 1860–Viareggio, 1942)
Pietro Mascagni (Livorno, 1863–Rome, 1945)
Francesco Cilea (Palmi, 1866–Varazze, 1950)
Umberto Giordano (Foggia, 1867–Milan, 1948)
Franco Alfano (Posillipo, 1875–San Remo, 1954)
Italo Montemezzi (Vigasio, 1875–1952)
Ermanno Wolf-Ferrari (Venice, 1876–1948)
Ildebrando Pizzetti (Parma, 1880–Rome, 1968)
Gian Francesco Malipiero (Venice, 1882–Treviso, 1973)
Riccardo Zandonai (Sacco di Rovereto, 1883–Pesaro, 1944)
Luigi Dallapiccola (Pisino d'Istria, 1904–Florence, 1975)
Gian Carlo Menotti (Cadegliano, 1911–)
Nino Rota (Milan, 1911–Rome, 1979)
Luigi Nono (Venice, 1924–1990)
Sylvano Bussotti (Florence, 1931–)

—— 6 ——

The Opera Singer

SERGIO DURANTE

A chapter on singers is such a natural part of any history of Italian opera that it needs no justification. When it comes to defining what its content will be, however, we find we need to choose among several orientations, according to the different ways in which singers determined or influenced the shape of opera. For example, we might choose to concentrate on the sound that singers produced and offer the reader a history of vocalism, or we might simply give an orderly series of biographies of the "greats."[1] The first option would have the disadvantage of duplicating or replacing a discourse on style and would risk artificially separating singers from an analysis of opera's dramatic and musical elements. The biographical approach, on the other hand, inevitably becomes a list of information arbitrarily selected out of an endless literature. Neither choice would permit us to investigate further areas that, although not always directly connected with opera, are extremely important to the singer: the history of training methods and didactic literature, a study of the "labor market" (taking singers as a group rather than as individuals), or a consideration of the professional status of singers, long divided into those who worked in the theater and those whose duties were at a court or a church.

The moment we acknowledge that it would be useful to treat the subject of singers, however, we have to give up hope of doing a complete study, both

1. See, for example, Rodolfo Celletti, "La vocalità," and Gustavo Marchesi, "I cantanti," in *Storia dell'opera,* ed. Guglielmo Barblan and Alberto Basso, 3 vols. (Turin: Unione Tipografico-Editrice Torinese, 1977), 3:3–317 and 3:321–435, respectively.

because exhaustive studies of the related subtopics do not exist, and because the nuclei of basic problems for this type of study shift or change completely in the course of Italian opera's nearly four centuries of history. For example, the competition between church and theater to hire the best *virtuosi* was typical of the labor market between the late seventeenth and early eighteenth century, but it was nowhere to be seen a century later. For these reasons the present chapter will touch on a heterogeneous set of problems that affected singers, as individuals or as a group, and that for the most part concern their professional definition. In spite of a roughly chronological order, it will not be a complete history of singers running parallel to the history of opera. Within a deliberately elastic structure the biographies of individual artists and problems of vocalism will be evoked, but they will not dominate.

One of the most noticeable imbalances in this exposition will certainly be its emphasis on problems regarding singers of the eighteenth century. This focus depends in part on the recent proliferation of studies in this area reevaluating the singers' historical role; it also seems acceptable, however, to favor the century in which singers' performances became a central element in operatic spectacle.

1. *The Court Singer Mounts the Theatrical Machine*

To attempt to pick a date or a name as a point of departure for a discussion of opera singers would be taking for granted a professional role that really came into being only gradually. It is of course legitimate and practical to point to Jacopo Peri or Giulio Caccini as deans of the profession, but only in the sense that they were undeniably singers and certainly sang operas; considering them uniquely as opera singers, however, would mean isolating one particular segment out of a much broader range of activities. To do so would create the "opera singer," but it would not clarify how, where, and when the profession came to be defined. From the singers' point of view opera in its first decades was still a somewhat rare occurrence—a special event of unusual luster that was added to their more customary service in chambers or at table. Until operatic production became an ongoing activity, singers remained principally court musicians, a form of personal service that is reflected in printed descriptions of commemorative and celebratory spectacles, where singers' names appear—usually in a "high" style that borders on poetic eulogy—only inasmuch as they helped to magnify the lord or the court.[2] Minor performers'

2. It has been noted that the singers mentioned in these descriptions did not depend on the importance of their roles in the work to be performed but on their reputations or the political influence of their patrons: see Stuart Reiner, "La vag'Angioletta (and Others)," *Analecta Musicologica* 14 (1974): 26–88, esp. 48. It is symptomatic that both Jacopo Peri and Giulio Caccini, in

names were not mentioned at all. A simple listing of performers (the rule in eighteenth-century librettos) would have conferred an inappropriate importance to domestic servants and might even have proven unpleasantly destructive of the theatrical fiction.

Although descriptions and "librettos"[3] gave little information on the performers, contemporary letters show that they were recruited with great care. For the performance of Claudio Monteverdi's *Orfeo* in Mantua in 1607, the young Francesco Gonzaga went to great trouble to get the castrato Giovanni Gualberto Magli to come to Mantua from Florence, since he judged the sopranos available in Mantua inadequate to the task.[4] Magli was in fact asked to sing three parts: Music, Proserpina, and a third, unspecified role; the part of Euridice was also played by a castrato, Girolamo Bacchini (known as "Il Pretino," the little priest),[5] while the title role was performed by Francesco Rasi, a famous tenor who had already appeared in Peri's *Euridice* and in *Il rapimento di Cefalo* by Caccini, who was probably Rasi's teacher. Before Rasi began to sing operatic roles, he was already well known and highly esteemed as both a singer and a skilled performer on the chitarrone, and he was a poet and composer as well.

The combination of his vocal and instrumental talents—frequently the case with singers of this period—made Rasi perfect for the part of Orpheus, since he could accompany himself on the harp as he confronted the spirits of hell.[6] This must have been a favorite "number" of Rasi's, as he repeated it the following year in Turin, this time in the role of an aquatic Arion.

---

the prefaces to their two versions of *Euridice* (Florence, 1600), fail to mention the name of the singer who sang Euridice (a singer of the Caccini "clan" and in fact Giulio's sister-in-law) but do mention Vittoria Archilei, a performer much favored by the Medici family.

3. The text of the *Orfeo* performed in Mantua in 1607 was, in fact, printed in the form of a libretto: see Iain Fenlon, "Monteverdi's Mantuan *Orfeo*: Some New Documentation," *Early Music* 12 (1984): 163–72, for a reproduction of the title page.

4. Ibid., 166. Even beyond the singers' purely vocal capabilities, the *stile rappresentativo* made special demands. The following year Cherubino Ferrari wrote to the duke of Modena that "when Your Highness may have need of good singers to sing solos and to portray the emotions of the soul, as is sought in these works, I will find them, as I have also done for his Highness of Savoy"; Paolo Fabbri, "Inediti monteverdiani," *Rivista italiana di musicologia* 15 (1980): 71–85, 73.

5. Although Bacchini was at the time still a seminary student (see Reiner, "La vag'Angioletta," 58, n. 110), he anticipated a tradition (of limited scope) of opera singer-priests—a tradition that died out only toward the end of the century, when public theaters were judged an environment incompatible with holy orders. In Milan in 1697 performances of *L'Orosmonda* were shut down by the excommunication of a priest who was in the cast; see *L'epistolario di Ludovico Antonio Muratori,* ed. Matteo Campori, 13 vols. (Modena: Society Tipografica Modenese, 1901), letter of 2 January 1697 to Giovanni Jacopo Tori (no. 180).

6. On the instrument used in this performance (the *arpa doppia,* or double harp), see the exhaustive study of Elio Durante and Anna Martellotti, *L'arpa di Laura: Indagine organologica, artistica e archivistica sull'arpa estense* (Florence: Studio per Edizioni Scelti, 1982).

A majestic Arion emerged on the back of a dolphin from a break in the forest through which flows a river, and as he slithered through the water toward the spectators, the famous Rasis [Rasi] burst into song and, accompanying himself on the harp, made the glade ring with celestial harmony.[7]

The performance in question was not an opera but a festive occasion, but Rasi's presence helped establish a point of contact between it and the Mantuan *Orfeo*. Moreover, in Turin Rasi sang in the open air from the back of a "wriggling dolphin": a taste for the marvelous inspired an execution combining musical virtuosity with acrobatics, be they singing from a rocking boat or—as was more often the case—from a stage machine. This combination presented problems treated several years later by the anonymous author of *Il corago*, a treatise on stagecraft and performing techniques, who warned,

> When a singer has to sing from a machine, it must be stopped or else moving very slowly while the singer is performing so as not to disturb him, especially with some sudden movement that might on occasion be called for, because it is inappropriate, while he is being carried, that he have to worry about such things. Undeniably, however, at certain times and places—such as in fits of disdain, in sorrow, and other similar emotions—it is legitimate to use gestures to seek to express the inner passions of the soul more strongly.[8]

Just as the custom of singing from a stage machine was a professional requirement for singers of the early seventeenth century, so aspirations to become part of the court system, individually or as members of the staff, typified them from a social point of view. The Caccinis, who were firmly attached to the Medici court, gave Rasi an example to imitate when he attempted to gain an entry at the court of the duke of Mantua for his two sisters. Rasi wrote the duke,

> To my great satisfaction I have found my sisters excellently trained by Father Carlo Berti. . . . One of them is thirteen years of age, very beautiful, and of most noble fashioning, who sings and will sing divinely, and another is eleven years of age,

---

7. *Repertorio di feste alla corte dei Savoia (1346–1699)*, ed. Gualtiero Rizzi (Turin: Centro Studi Piemontesi, 1973), 8–9. Again in Casale Monferrato in 1611, "Neptune . . . playing a double harp and singing . . . was the marvelous Sig. Rasi"; *La drammaturgia musicale*, ed. Lorenzo Bianconi (Bologna: Il Mulino, 1986), 38 n. 42. One excellent study on Rasi is Warren Kirkendale, "Zur Biographie des ersten Orfeo, Francesco Rasi," in *Claudio Monteverdi: Festschrift Reinhold Hammerstein zum 70. Geburtstag*, ed. Ludwig Finscher (Laaber: Laaber-Verlag, 1986), 297–335, which, among other things, clarifies Rasi's honored position within the early opera casts. According to Emilio de' Cavalieri, he was not "a man to get along with the castratos" (Kirkendale, "Zur Biographie," 302).

8. *Il corago, o vero Alcune osservazioni per metter bene in scena le composizioni drammatiche*, ed. Paolo Fabbri and Angelo Pompilio (Florence: Olschki, 1983), 92.

who already sings and plays well. . . . I have thought it appropriate to tell you about them, hoping that they will please you—indeed, greatly if Your Highness will desire that they come to Mantua.[9]

The younger sister was sent to Mantua to study with Caccini, but after a few years neither sister had achieved the success Rasi had hoped for, and one went into a convent and the other was married.

A more successful example of integration into court circles comes from the family of Adriana Basile Baroni, "la bella Adriana." Singing in opera played only a minor role in her career: she may have taken part in a *Medoro* (perhaps *Lo sposalizio di Angelica e Medoro*) by Marco da Gagliano (Mantua, 1622?) and in other productions put on in Mantua.[10] That these performances were enough to make her an "opera singer" is dubious, to say the least, but it is useful nevertheless to mention some important events in her career.

Born around 1580 in Naples (perhaps in Posillipo)[11] and married to Muzio Baroni, Basile was first in the service of the prince of Stigliano, Don Luigi Carafa. Her virtues, musical and otherwise, were sung by poets great and small and abundantly documented in *Il teatro delle glorie della Signora Adriana Basile* (Venice, 1623). After winning widespread appreciation for singing performances "at Posillipo, at sea, in a *filluga* [a small boat] with her golden harp in hand,"[12] she attracted the eye of Vincenzo Gonzaga, who, after long and complicated negotiations, brought her to Mantua, where she arrived toward the end of June 1610. Adriana was by then one of the best-known singers of her time, and certainly the duke's own prestige had something to do with his eagerness to have her at his court. As she passed through Florence, Basile measured her talents against the best court musicians there.

> The singers were Signora Adriana, Signor Lelio Grilinzoni [Grillenzoni], Signor Zazzerino [Jacopo Peri], il Brandino [Antonio Brandi], and Gio. Gualberto [Magli], . . . and afterward everyone, with one voice, concluded that she was without peer. La Vittoria [Archilei] did not want to be heard when she learned that Signora Adriana was at the palace.[13]

This evaluation was biased, since it came from a Gonzaga agent, but Monteverdi thought Adriana superior to both Ippolita Recupito and Francesca Cac-

9. Letter of 28 August 1600 to the duke of Mantua, published in Alessandro Ademollo, *La bell'Adriana ed altre virtuose del suo tempo alla corte di Mantova* (Città di Castello, 1888), 32 n.

10. Ibid., 271.

11. This is Ademollo's conjecture, on the basis of writings of Adriana's brother, the poet Giovambattista Basile (ibid., 5).

12. So described by Pietro della Valle in a letter to Lelio Guidiccioni; ibid., 3.

13. Letter of Ottavio Gentile to Ferdinando Gonzaga of 16 June 1610; ibid., 136.

cini.[14] The question of who was best, however, was much more political than musical, and judgments given in correspondence reflect the writer's place in one circle or another and his desire to please his patrons. Thus Antimo Galli, in letters addressed to the Florentine secretary of state, Dimurgo Lambardi, gave first place to the Medici singer, bolstering his own opinion with the more authoritative one of Giambattista Marino.

> I do not want to forget to tell you that Cavalier Marini, one of the most famous poets today, being here for several months and I finding myself with him [and] hearing them praise La Adriana, I invited him to hear La Cecchina [Francesca Caccini] and then judge, but the man, being unable to believe that anyone else could compare, almost would not listen to me. Finally he allowed himself to be taken to listen [to La Cecchina] to settle the dispute . . . and he returned from [hearing] her yesterday evening singing her praises above all others in that profession.[15]

Others have quite sufficiently sung the praises of Adriana Basile and Francesca Caccini; what is more interesting for our purposes is that Basile reached the height of her fame without having theatrical activities play an important role in her career. Within a generation, however, talent on the stage was to become indispensable, even at court.[16]

Peri, Caccini and his family, Rasi, and the beautiful Adriana Basile are all examples of musicians who were fully integrated into the economic ambiance and the mentality of the late-Renaissance court. They moved in the highest artistic circles; they were people who were already musical aristocracy and who aspired to become social aristocracy as well. Adriana's singing earned her not only a notable amount of money but also the title of baroness of Piancerreto.

The second level of singers had considerable importance as well. The constant search for singers focused not only on the stars but also on promising youngsters, who were sought out and chosen with care.[17] A singer in the papal chapel, Paolo Facconi, acted as the duke of Mantua's agent in Rome, and in 1603 he sent north a promising thirteen-year-old, Caterina Martinelli, along

14. See the letter of 28 December 1610 in Claudio Monteverdi, *Lettere, dediche e prefazioni,* ed. Domenico De' Paoli (Rome: De Santis, 1973), 52.

15. Letter of 11 November 1623, in Anna Maria Crinò, "Virtuose di canto e poeti a Roma e a Firenze nella prima metà del Seicento," *Studi secenteschi* 1 (1960): 175–93, quote 180.

16. One of Adriana's sisters, Margherita Basile, was in fact appreciated for her dramatic talent: see the letter of Monteverdi of 7 May 1627 regarding the project for a production of *La finta pazza Licori* in which Margherita was to have the leading role; Ademollo, *La bell'Adriana,* 310 and 312; Monteverdi *Lettere,* 244.

17. On Guglielmo Gonzaga's policies regarding singers, see Pietro Canal, *Della musica in Mantova* (Venice, 1881; reprint ed., Bologna: Arnaldo Forni, 1977), 692–99, and passim. See also Richard Sherr, "Guglielmo Gonzaga and the Castrati," *Renaissance Quarterly* 33 (1980): 33–56.

with her teacher and her parents.[18] On another occasion Peri wrote to the duchess of Mantua.

> The most illustrious Signor D. Antonio Medici let me see and hear, on behalf of Your Most Serene Highness, some young girls in the hope of finding one who might be taught how to sing, and so I did: she has been attended to most solicitously, and I have not failed to provide her with a good teacher.[19]

No stone was left unturned in the search for young female singers: in 1607 Vincenzo Gonzaga asked the Marquis and Marchioness Bentivoglio of Ferrara to lend him a domestic servant of theirs whose musical training had just been started, and later Vincenzo attempted to get the young woman into his own service so that she could be sent for further study with Peri in Florence. A functionary in Mantua wrote to Bentivoglio about the negotiations.

> I have found such good will in Their Highnesses [the Gonzagas] toward the young woman about whom I have received word concerning a trial [engagement] that has given the good results hoped for in the play just sung, that not only are they willing to have Rasio [Rasi] or some other *virtuoso* give her lessons, but Her Most Serene Highness has thought . . . of sending her to Florence for at least a year in the house of La Zazarina [Peri's wife], . . . Her Highness having added to me that, if it may please your Most Illustrious Lordship, she much desires to keep [the girl] in her service.[20]

The maneuver came to naught, as Bentivoglio, who intended to take the singer to Rome with him, refused to give her up.

The histories of these musicians are so closely linked to those of their patrons that it would be a distortion to interpret their professional role in a modern sense. Even when they moved from one court to another, such moves were a reflection of political and diplomatic events and of the patron's need to show a prestigious image to the outside world. When in 1647 a company was being put together to send to Paris to perform Luigi Rossi's *Orfeo*, the trip stirred up competition among the singers of a number of Italian states. One of them wrote to the duke of Modena.

> Two other [singers] of Cardinal Antonio and Prince Mattias [de' Medici] sang, but Your Highness's two [singers] were again desired and ordered by the gentlemen, by

18. Caterina Martinelli died of small pox at the age of eighteen while she was preparing the title role in Monteverdi's *Arianna;* see Edmond Strainchamps, "The Life and Death of Caterina Martinelli: New Light on Monteverdi's *Arianna,*" *Early Music History* 5 (1985): 155–86.

19. Letter of 15 December 1608, in Ademollo, *La bell'Adriana,* 82.

20. Letter of Orazio Langosco to Enzo Bentivoglio of 18 February 1608; Reiner, "La vag'Angioletta," 41–42. The singer in question was Angiola Zanibelli.

the duke of Anguien [Enghien], and by the queen; and I, called in, approached and accompanied them in an aria that was again greeted with applause for all the high spirits of these youngsters, and truly I cannot omit to report to Your Highness (hearing Your Highness's name in the mouths of many gentlemen and on many occasions), that [the performance] was acclaimed and liked by all, and these honors that were brought to us were the effect of your grandeur.[21]

The singer's autonomy to move about depended above all on the good will of the prince. The less rosy side of the life of a minor courtier is documented in the career of Francesco Campagnolo, one of Monteverdi's singing students, who was obliged to leave Mantua to seek his fortune elsewhere in order to pay some debts he had incurred. The duke refused him both permission to leave and economic assistance (and since he was a native Mantuan, his stipend would have been extremely low). He finally did leave his homeland, but he was pursued to Salzburg by the duke, who attempted to have him imprisoned for lèse majesté.[22]

From the point of view of their professional training, the operatic performers considered thus far were singers who developed a particular competence in the stile rappresentativo, but from the very beginnings of Italian opera we can find cases of something like the opposite—that is, actors of the spoken theater who sang in opera. Singing had always been one of the actor's working tools; it was now becoming much more appreciated.

The use of an actress who was also a singer goes back as far as Monteverdi's *L'Arianna* (Mantua, 1608); when the sudden death of Caterina Martinelli, who was to sing the lead, made it necessary to find a last-minute replacement. La Florinda (Virginia Ramponi Andreini) stepped in for her, learned the part in six days, and performed the role with success. For the author of *Il corago*, actors were by no means a lesser choice but rather a way of following the taste of the greater part of the public.

> Above all, in order to be good at performing while singing, one must also be good at performing while speaking, from which we have seen that some who have had

21. Letter of 13 February 1674 of Venanzio Leopardi to the duke of Modena; Henry Prunières, *L'opéra italien en France avant Lulli* (Paris: Champion, 1913), 380–81. The duke was Louis II duc d'Enghien, prince de Condé; the queen was Marie-Thérèse of Spain, queen of France.

22. The entire episode is outlined in Campagnolo's letters, published in Herbert Seifert, "Beiträge zur Frühgeschichte der Monodie in Österreich," *Studien zur Musikwissenschaft* 31 (1980): 7–33. It is interesting to note that the singer made a heartfelt appeal to natural law: after declaring "because I was born and raised in that city they showed me much less esteem than they would have done for a foreigner," Campagnolo asked, "And what offense did I do to His Highness in defending myself from the necessities and miseries that afflicted me? Is it not perhaps a natural instinct, and one common to all animals, even those without reason, to defend themselves from whatever harms them?" (letter of 30 November 1617, 20–23).

particular grace in recitation have done marvels when they have also known how to sing. In this regard some wonder whether it is preferable to have a mediocre singer but a perfect actor or an excellent singer who has little or no talent for recitation. Experience has shown that although a few people who understand much about music prefer excellent singers whose recitation may be a bit cold, the common run of theatrical audiences takes greater satisfaction in perfect actors with mediocre voices and little musical skill.[23]

Even without the aesthetic and theatrical qualities implicit in the performance of an actor-singer, however, the economic and organizational structure of the companies of itinerant actors were soon to provide an important alternative model to court operatic productions.

2. Church, Theater, and School

Long before *opera in musica* was born and independent of its birth, Rome had one of the liveliest musical scenes on the Italian peninsula.[24] Rome offered work opportunities not only in the many permanent and semipermanent ecclesiastical chapels but also in the courts of cardinals and aristocrats, the various national colleges, the embassies, and the Oratorio of St. Philip Neri. Musicians and singers were in high demand, which meant that schools flourished. The satire *Contrasto musico* by Grazioso Uberti (Rome, 1630)[25] presents singing teachers and their flocks of warbling choirboys as contributing to the noise and confusion of city life. Aside from the young boys trained to sing in the churches, young girls were also schooled as singers, but they were prohibited from appearing on the public stage.[26]

The Barberini family's stage productions made use of a very large number of singers compared to the first Florentine and Mantuan operas, and two such productions—*San Bonifacio* (1638) and *La Genoinda* (1641)—were sung by

23. *Il corago*, 91.

24. Earlier than any other Italian city, Rome had a *vertuosa compagnia dei musici*—a corporation dedicated to the Virgin Mary, St. Gregory, and St. Cecilia that safeguarded the members' interests and guaranteed the prestige of the profession. It was officially recognized in 1585. On the history of that association, see Remo Giazotto, *Quattro secoli di storia dell'Accademia nazionale di Santa Cecilia*, 2 vols. (Rome: Accademia Nazionale di Santa Cecilia, 1970).

25. *Contrasto musico, opera dilettevole del signor Grazioso Uberti da Cesena* (Rome, 1630), available in part in Andrea della Corte, *Satire e grotteschi di musiche e di musicisti d'ogni tempo* (Turin: Unione Tipografico-Editrice Torinese, 1946), 113–35; for a recent edition see Grazioso Uberti, *Contrasto musico: Opera dilettevole*, ed. Giancarlo Rostirolla ([Lucca]: Libreria Musicale Italiana, 1991).

26. The exclusion of women from the public stage in Rome went back to 1588 and continued (with rare exceptions) until 1798. In this connection see Alessandro Ademollo, *I teatri di Roma nel secolo decimosettimo* (Rome, 1888), 136 and xxvii.

boys "under eleven or twelve years of age."[27] Although these are isolated cases, they demonstrate the enormous efficacy of the schools. In 1641 Marco Marazzoli observed that "all men in this world seek to send pupils to Rome to have them study because that is where the schooling is."[28]

Rome risked having its music schools proliferate beyond the city's capacities for absorption. As early as 1624 the Congregazione Romana dei Musici dedicated to St. Cecilia petitioned Pope Urban VIII and received a privilege over music schools, establishing that "in the future all individuals, clerical and lay, who wish to open a school of music in the said city and to teach music publicly in it can request and obtain permission . . . which must be given gratis, in writing, and furnished with the seal of that same confraternity."[29] The privilege was withdrawn after only two years on protest from the papal choristers, who held that they were unfairly threatened by an organization with a status lower than their own.[30] The original objective of the Congregation of St. Cecilia must have been more general, however, and analogous to the aims of the arts and crafts guilds—that is, to regulate access to employment and to control professional standards, "so that incompetents will absolutely not be permitted to open public schools of music in Rome."[31]

Around the 1640s Roman musical circles seemed saturated, as shown indirectly by the frequent appearance of Roman singers, male and female, touring other regions of Italy.[32] But the Romans who ended up, for example, on the Venetian stages belonged to a different professional sphere from that of the Barberinis' singers: the latter had little reason to move away from Rome, and if they did so (for instance, for festivities in Parma in 1617 and 1628) it was

27. See Margaret Murata, *Operas for the Papal Court 1631–1668* (Ann Arbor, Mich.: UMI Research Press, 1981), 290 (letter of 1 January 1638 from Giulio Rospigliosi to his brother Camillo) and 298 (letter of 2 February 1641 of Ottaviano Castelli to Giulio Mazzarino). The number of solo roles in the Barbarini operas from 1631 to 1643 ranged from eleven for *Il Sant'Alessio* to twenty-four for *Il palazzo incantato*, and from 1654 to 1668 from eight in *Dal male il bene* to sixteen in *La comica del cielo*. It was customary, however, for some singers to take two or more smaller roles.

28. From a letter published in part in Pier Maria Capponi, "L'educazione di una virtuosa nel secolo XVII," *Lo spettatore musicale* 3 (May 1968): 12–15, quote 15.

29. The papal brief is published in full in Giazotto, *Quattro secoli,* 1:93–96.

30. The papal choristers hastened to request the exemption of their own collegial group from the law rather than seeking its annulment—in other words, they had no objection to the Cecilians' control as long as it was limited to the lesser schools.

31. This was the reason given in the counter brief of 1626; see Giazotto, *Quattro secoli,* 1:105–8.

32. On this question see Nino Pirrotta, "Tre capitoli su Cesti," in *La scuola romana: G. Carissimi, A. Cesti, M. Marazzoli* (Siena: Ticci, 1953), 27–40; Pierluigi Petrobelli, "L'Ermiona di Pio Enea degli Obizzi ed i primi spettacoli d'opera veneziani," *Quaderni della Rassegna musicale* 3 (Turin: Einaudi, 1965): 125–41; and Lorenzo Bianconi and Thomas Walker, "Dalla *Finta pazza* alla *Veremonda:* Storie di Febiarmonici," *Rivista italiana di musicologia* 10 (1975): 379–454.

because their patrons wanted them to travel or had lent them to another court. The singers who made an independent decision to travel probably did so because Rome had become overcrowded, because the city prohibited females from singing in public, or simply because opera opportunities were opening up elsewhere. Thus we see in embryonic form two phenomena that were soon to become widespread: a higher degree of mobility for the singer than in the past, and the interaction of various places where operas were produced in a complex, market-driven system.

Roman singers also fed into the circuits of the so-called Febiarmonici—itinerant companies that traveled throughout Italy in the mid-seventeenth century offering opera productions at modest prices. These traveling companies included members from such a variety of places and backgrounds that it is of only secondary interest to quantify their geographic origins. It is more useful to understand singers' relations with various musical circles: the courts, the traveling companies, and the public theaters of Venice. We can suppose that there was a certain amount of osmosis between professional environments, different as they were. For example, Margherita Confalonieri, a Roman, sang with the Febiarmonici in Lucca in 1646 and in Genoa in 1647, but she also worked for the Venetian theaters.[33] When the theaters of the Serenissima were closed from 1645 to 1647, she must have returned to the traveling companies. We also find singers, such as Giovanni Paolo Bonelli, Francesco Pesarino, Antonio Agnadini, and Marco Antonio Brocchi, who moved from the itinerant companies to a court.[34] A position at a court must have been the most preferable situation, since no singers seemed to have moved from court to an itinerant existence.

The organizational modes of these companies and working conditions in them are eloquently described in the treatise *Della cristiana moderazione del teatro* (Florence, 1652), by the Jesuit Giovan Domenico Ottonelli. One passage in this work might even be read as "Statutes of the Febiarmonici":[35]

> These commercial actors and performing singers, according to what is common practice, have the following conditions.
>
> They are usually virtuosos either in singing, playing, dancing, designing new sets, building admirable stage machines, preparing and varying scenery with graceful facility, or in other things concerning musical production.
>
> They bring with them female performers—actresses, singers, or players—who are their wives or companions and who take leading parts in the musical dramas.

33. Bianconi and Walker, "Dalla *Finta pazza*," 399, 403.

34. Ibid., 403–4 and n. 115.

35. Ibid., 406. The passage is taken from book 4 of Ottonelli's *Ammonizioni a' recitanti*, reprinted in Fernando Taviani, *La commedia dell'arte e la società barocca: La fascinazione del teatro*, vol. 1 of *La commedia dell'arte: Storia Testi Documenti*, ed. Ferruccio Mariotti, 2 vols. (Rome: Bulzoni, 1969), 512.

They have in their repertory one, two, or more works composed by talented authors and diligently set to music from act to act, scene to scene, word for word, from the beginning to the end; and they have scores and separate parts to be sung by one or more voices, according to the number of performers needed for the musical drama.

They attempt to bring together enough *virtuosi* as members to enable the company, composed of paid performers, to mount productions by themselves with no need to call in other singers or musicians to help them; at times they succeed in this intent and at times not. When they do not achieve that end they do not give up, but rather, as soon as a company is partly formed, they go off to a principal city: they let it be known that they have come to present a new play set to music or a sung comedy most excellent for the beauty of its composition, for the artful harmony of the voices, and for the exquisite charm of its scenic effects.

One of their practices is to find out, if they do not already know, what singers or players, lay, ecclesiastical, or religious, might be in the city who could be invited—for payment, out of affection, or even, at times, almost forced through the intercession of important people—to accept taking on one or more tasks as an assisting musician in the public theater, thus making up the number sufficient to enable the drama or the musical play to be heard, seen, and enjoyed by the listeners and spectators.

It would be difficult and perhaps senseless to attempt an overall evaluation of the professional level of these singers (or, if you will, actors). To hear the derogatory tone of their rivals, they were second-class performers. Giulio Strozzi spoke of them in this vein when his *La finta pazza* was reprinted in 1644: "Some wandering musicians have variously had [the work] reprinted elsewhere and are going about performing it as something of their own . . . whereas in the mouth of Signora Anna Renzi . . . it stupefied Venice."[36] On the other side of the coin, the following year an otherwise anonymous "head of the academy of the Febiarmonici" promised that the same work would be

performed exceedingly well, there being, among other things, a bass whose equal cannot be heard on the stage, and also a woman who acts marvelously well, and all the other roles are extremely good, singers having been brought in from Rome. . . . Added to this are superb costumes, scene changes, aerial flights, dancing bears and monsters, and other novelties.[37]

We can perhaps read between the lines here that theatrical effects were more important than the singers' performances. This development might also

36. Claudio Sartori, "La prima diva della lirica italiana: Anna Renzi," *Nuova rivista musicale italiana* 2 (1968): 430–52, quotation 444.

37. Letter of 25 February 1645 to Francesco Barbolani; Bianconi and Walker, "Dalla *Finta pazza,*" 402 and n. 107. For another positive evaluation of the musicians, stage machines, and costumes, see 400, n. 98.

offer an interpretation of the growing importance of the comic roles in the versions of *La finta pazza* that were exported from Venice.[38] An emphasis on dramatic action does not necessarily jeopardize the vocal aspect of a performance, but undeniably, operational structures and methods of preparation can emphasize one or the other, and it is quite possible that because the Febiarmonici players kept a stable repertory limited to a few works, they were able to perfect (and modify) the characters they played from one season to another.

Even outside the itinerant companies, however, the leading singers of the time were remembered for their stage presence.[39] Two nearly contemporary descriptions of the singing of Loreto Vittori and Anna Renzi offer good examples:[40]

> [Loreto Vittori has a] graceful and splendid voice, able to execute any sort of variation and change, and such as to respond with agility to any stimulus, and it is in turn piercing, grave, flowing, slow, strong, light. . . . That true artist, when he has to portray the voice and the words of a man agitated by anger, makes use of a piercing, excited, often precipitous sort of voice; if he is to show compassion and sadness, a flexible, broken, weak sort of voice; if he is to express fear, a submissive, hesitating, humbled quality. . . . All of this is what the most authoritative voice teachers recommend, but he knows how to do it better than they. The ability not only to play the role but to make himself take on, as he sings, any shade of the soul's emotions is one of his natural talents. . . . And how admirable he is for the clarity of his voice and his limpid articulation of the words!

> [Anna Renzi] takes command of the stage, means what she says, and says it so clearly that ears could desire no more. She has a nimble tongue, a gentle, not affected or borrowed pronunciation, a full, sonorous voice, neither harsh nor raw, nor one that offends you by too much subtlety; [a voice] born of the humors of the chest and the throat, which, for such a good voice must be very warm in order to enlarge the passages, and humid enough to make them tender and soft. For this reason, she has excellent improvised ornaments and a robust and fast double trill. . . . She quietly observes the actions of others, and when later she must act them on stage, aided by her blood, which is copious in her, and by the bile that

38. Ibid., 423–24.

39. The best seventeenth-century singers differed in this respect from their counterparts of the following century, who at times based their success on their vocal endowments alone.

40. The description of Vittori comes from Janus Nicius Erythraeus (Gian Vittorio Rossi), *Pinacotheca altera* (Cologne [*recte* Amsterdam], 1645), 215–21, and it is taken here from the Italian version in Claudio Gallico, "La 'Querimonia' di Maddalena di Domenico Mazzocchi e l'interpretazione di Loreto Vittori," *Collectanea Historiae Musicae* 4 (1966): 133–47, quotation 145, a study that should be read along with the more recent one by Bianca Maria Antolini, "La carriera di cantante e compositore di Loreto Vittori," *Studi musicali* 7 (1978): 141–88. The passage on Renzi can be found in the compendium of testimonials, *Le glorie della signora Anna Renzi romana* (Venice, 1644); see Sartori, "La prima diva," 451–52.

puts a spark into her (and without which men cannot undertake great deeds), she shows the spirit and the excellence that she has learned through study and observation.

It might seem from reading these two descriptions that they show a common stylistic base in the predominance of the pathetic and the theatrical, but the two singers' theatricality is based on totally different premises. Vittori, with his ample palette of colors, was a good actor thanks to his innate gifts, and his technique (if one can use the term) consisted in identification with the character he was playing. Renzi, whose voice was perhaps less flexible, based her acting on attentive observation and study.[41]

Similarities, then, depend on how one reads the documents, and comparison is strongly conditioned by the subjective and inevitably generic nature of the sources: one can find nothing that cannot be applied, in the last analysis, to any qualified singer with a good stage presence. Descriptions of this sort can perhaps be better taken as documents regarding the sensibilities and the minds of the persons who wrote them than as objective descriptions of the singers themselves. In other words a written account is an extremely poor surrogate for a musical and theatrical event: it is a stimulus to the imagination more than probative testimony.

Above and beyond a vague stylistic similarity, the figures of Vittori and Renzi exemplify careers that were roughly contemporary but highly dissimilar from the professional, intellectual, and social points of view.

Loreto Vittori, born in Spoleto in 1600 in a family of modest social rank, was castrated and sent to study music in the singing school of the local cathedral. In 1617, when Maffeo Barberini, then bishop of Spoleto, left his diocese, he brought Vittori to Rome. In Rome Vittori may have studied singing with Francesco Soto and counterpoint with Giovanni Bernardino Nanino. He continued his studies in Florence, where he served Grand Duke Cosimo II and first demonstrated his talents as an opera singer. On his return to Rome at the insistent request of Cardinal Nephew Ludovico Ludovisi, Vittori was fairly well known. In January 1622 he was admitted to the papal chapel without having to go through the usual competitive examinations. Vittori seems to have laid the foundations for his wealth during this period, when Ludovisi had him sing for the high aristocracy and showered him with rich gifts. At

---

41. The distinction between the method of psychological identification and the method of imitation on the basis of a refined technical apparatus was defined particularly clearly in the following century by Francesco Riccoboni; see in particular Riccoboni, *L'arte del teatro* (Venice, 1762), a translation of the French original, *L'art du théâtre* (Paris, 1750). Although this treatise is devoted primarily to prose actors, Riccoboni also considered problems regarding opera, as can be seen from his frequent references to singers.

Florence in 1628, on the occasion of the wedding of Margaretta de' Medici and Edoardo Farnese, duke of Parma, Vittori sang the leading role in Gagliano's *Flora,* and he later spent a short time at Parma. Aside from his musical activities, Vittori had a keen interest in literature; he probably frequented the Accademia degli Umoristi, and he wrote (among other pieces) a comic-heroic poem, *La troia rapita,* published in 1662, in which one of the cantos was autobiographical. Vittori's rare appearances outside aristocratic circles probably took place at the Oratorio della Vallicella, where he sang (among other things) a lament of Mary Magdalene that became famous.

The only stain on Vittori's honor was the kidnapping of a young girl in 1637, an episode that he described as a "slight error of youthful desire" but that nonetheless forced him to spend two years in self-imposed exile from Rome. His dishonor seems to have been completely expunged only in 1640, when, taking the opportunity of presenting his Easter wishes to the pope, "the cavaliere Loreto threw himself at the holy feet to demand pardon for the public error committed two years before; Our Lord willingly listened to him, and then gave him absolution, which everyone heard."[42]

In 1639, during his exile from Rome, Vittori wrote and published *La Galatea,* a *dramma in musica* produced in Naples in 1644; in 1640 he set to music a *Sant'Ignazio* (now lost); and in 1642 he performed in Luigi Rossi's *Il palazzo d'Atlante.* During the following year he was ordained as a priest in a ceremony, recorded in the *Avvisi* of Rome, in which 150 singers divided into six choirs took part, thus providing a logical point of arrival in a process of assimilation into the society to which he belonged. There may be other details in the life of this notable personality that are worthy of note, but the ones of most interest for our purposes are those that help us to evaluate the significant differences between his career and a woman's career that was predominantly theatrical career.

Unlike Vittori, Anna Renzi's training took place wholly outside institutions. This is already an important difference between them: if a young boy with a beautiful voice had the possibility of being taken in as a choirboy in one of the many schools that existed in Italy, a woman had to turn to private teachers. In Renzi's case her teacher also became her mentor, her "agent," and a full partner in both her artistic and financial destiny. It is no surprise that the slim volume telling us most of what we know about her—*Le glorie della signora Anna Renzi romana*—is dedicated to her teacher, Filiberto Laurenzi, as the person who "has done much to lead this most promising young lady to so much excellence."[43] Indeed, it was thanks to Laurenzi that

---

42. See Antolini, "La carriera di cantante," 182, quoting the *Diario Sistino* for the year 1640.
43. Sartori, "La prima diva," 438.

his pupil, who was already well known in Roman circles, made the major move to the theaters of the Serenissima.[44] At Rome Renzi had sung Lucinda in *Il favorito del principe,* for which Laurenzi had written the music (1640), in a performance at the French embassy (where the prohibition of women singers on the stage did not pertain). The move to Venice was at the invitation of the composer Francesco Sacrati, who hired her to sing the lead in the highly acclaimed *La finta pazza,* but once she got to Venice she remained there for some time, appearing in *Il Bellerofonte* (1642), *La finta savia, L'incoronazione di Poppea* (1643), and other works, ending with *Le fortune di Rodope e Damira* in 1657.

Renzi's fame was closely connected with the theater, particularly with theaters managed by academies and commercial theaters. There was a significant difference in her financial status and that of Vittori. Vittori lived on his chapel appointment, and his wealth came in ways appropriate to his rank: according the *Nota de' musicisti di Roma che hanno a servire in Parma* (1628), as the principal singer he was "to be rewarded rather with a gift than with money."[45] Renzi was instead paid in cash. Given that direct contact with money was considered vulgar, we can understand her annoyance on reading what Giovan Francesco Loredano had to say about her in *Ragguaglio di Parnaso* (News of Parnassus) in a piece written for her entitled "Anna Rensi chiede luogo in Parnaso, e non vien ricevuta" (Anna Renzi requests a place in Parnassus and is not accepted). In Loredano's witty scenario the companions of the aspirant Muse who yearned in vain to be welcomed into Parnassus ask one another if her unexpected rejection was perhaps occasioned by Apollo's scorn at "seeing music . . . become the instrument of a little-honorable commerce, observing the greed of many who make use of a voice to enchant souls so that [people] would pay no attention to what they spend."[46] By the time Loredano makes it clear that Apollo rejects Renzi only because she would make the Muses jealous, the gaffe had already had its effect.

If Renzi had any literary interests, she left no trace of them, but she was judged to be "of great intellect, very imaginative, with a good memory."[47] Among her acknowledged qualities there was "honesty" of mores, a rare virtue among female singers. In fact an attempt to avoid the role of courtesan

---

44. Another Roman singer, Felicita Uga, had already been in Venice since 1634; see Elena Povoledo, "Una rappresentazione accademica a Venezia nel 1634," in *Studi sul teatro veneto fra rinascimento ed età barocca,* ed. Maria Teresa Muraro (Florence: Olschki, 1971), 119–69, esp. 136–37.

45. Emil Vogel, "Claudio Monteverdi," *Vierteljahrsschrift für Musikwissenschaft* 3 (1887): 315–450, quotation 437.

46. Bianconi and Walker, "Dalla *Finta Pazza,*" 418, from the 14th ed. of Loredano's *Bizzarrie academiche* (Bologna, 1676).

47. Sartori, "La prima diva," 452.

that was so often synonymous with the female singer's profession seems to have been behind her transfer to Venice. In this respect Renzi stood out as different from adventuresses such as Margherita Costa, Anna Maria Sardelli, or, later, the ill-famed "Giorgina,"[48] and she appears to have been an early but fairly well-defined example of female professionalism in opera. Thus she deserved her recognition as the "first diva of Italian opera."

Even though we might see Renzi as a forerunner of future developments in the profession, it would be a mistake to take her as a sign that a shift to an autonomous condition for the singer had already occurred. The courts and aristocratic circles continued to be the focus of the musical professions, both from the economic point of view and as a source of behavioral models. Power relationships did change—slowly and by no means in linear fashion—but there too it is easy to misinterpret certain outward signs of power. Such figures as Atto Melani or Francesco de Castris had important responsibilities within the Medici court, but the power they held was conceded to them and operated within the equilibrium of traditional hierarchies. The power to influence and guide taste did not yet exist in the autonomous or at least partially autonomous form that became typical a century later (and was hence considered deviant).

Precisely in Florence the policies of Prince Ferdinando carried over into the early eighteenth century the court's firm control over every aspect of musical life. As the *virtuosi* became the central element in operatic productions, it was increasingly urgent to be able to offer highly acclaimed singers, and Ferdinando pursued two parallel and complementary strategies to obtain them.[49] First he promoted and financed the studies of local singers and encouraged the formation of a "school," or more properly speaking he encouraged the formation of a nucleus of Tuscans who had been trained in the best schools throughout Italy. One Florentine singing teacher, Ippolito Fusai, was well known, and there are traces of another local musician, Antonio Rivani, who attracted pupils.[50] Raffaello Baldi was sent to Rome to study with Giuseppe Vecchi in 1692; Marina Orsati was sent to Ferrara to study with Giu-

48. On the colorful lives of these courtesans, see, respectively, the *Enciclopedia dello spettacolo,* s. v. "Margherita Costa," by Nino Pirrotta; Bianconi and Walker, "Dalla *Finta pazza,*" 440–44; and Giorgio Morelli, "Una celebre 'canterina' romana del Seicento, 'La Giorgina,'" *Studi secenteschi* 16 (1975): 157–80.

49. The question in treated in detail in Robert Lamar Weaver and Norma Wright Weaver, *A Chronology of Music in the Florentine Theater,* Detroit Studies in Musical Bibliography, nos. 30 and 70, 2 vols. (Detroit: Information Coordinators; Harmonie Park Press, 1978, 1993), 1:61–76.

50. There is reference to the teaching of Antonio Rivani, called Ciecolino, in Pierfrancesco Tosi, *Opinioni de' cantori antichi e moderni* (Bologna, 1723), 64–65, in English translation by John Ernest Galliard, *Observations on the Florid Song, or, Sentiments on the Ancient and Modern Singers* (London, 1742). On Rivani's theatrical activities, see Weaver and Weaver, *A Chronology of Music.*

seppe Antonio Aldrovandini in 1696; Andrea Guerri went to Bologna in 1704 to work with the most highly reputed teacher of the period, Francesco Antonio Pistocchi. Through his *virtuosi* Ferdinando also participated in the so-called ducal circuit, which consisted in regular exchanges of singers among the courts of north-central Italy. These included not only the principal centers—Mantua, Modena, and Florence—but also the Farnese family in Parma, the duchess of Zagarolo, Cardinal Benedetto Pamphili in Rome, and above all the Venetian theatrical aristocracy of the Grimani, Giustiniani, and Tron families.

There is no written document giving that circuit any official status, but its mechanisms seem clear: each prince maintained his own singers and might, on occasion, exchange them or borrow "adjuncts." The system seems to have been put into place toward the end of the 1680s, to judge from opera librettos that list not only the singers' names (and on occasion their places of origin) but also the names of their protectors. For example, performers were listed as follows for a production of *Oreste in Sparta* in Reggio Emilia in 1697.

MENELAO — Giovanni Battista Franceschini of His Most Serene Highness of
   Modena
ERMIONE — Margherita Salicola Suini of Saxony
PIRRO — Giovanni Battista Ruberti of His Most Serene Highness of Modena
PILADE — Antonio Ferrini of the *granprincipe* of Tuscany
ORESTE — Luigi Albarelli of His Most Serene Highness of Modena
ERSILLA — Anna Maria Lisi of the *granprincipessa* of Tuscany
NISO — Giovanni Battista Cattivelli of His Most Serene Highness of Mantua

In Florence the system operated efficiently thanks to *Granprincipe* Ferdinando de' Medici, who took a keen interest in theater, and who had something to say at all stages of the planning of productions and even about his singers' private lives. With Ferdinando's death in 1713, Medici promotion and guidance of singing schools came to an end, but the seed had been planted, and there were sufficient local singers to supply the growing demand for their services. During the first quarter of the eighteenth century, Florentine performers active in Venice were second only to the increasing numbers of Bolognese.[51]

As it had operated in Ferdinando's time, the system still relied upon the

---

51. For a statistical study of the singers active in Venice during the first quarter of the eighteenth century, see Sergio Durante, "Alcune considerazioni sui cantanti di teatro del primo Settecento e la loro formazione," in *Antonio Vivaldi: Teatro musicale, cultura e società*, ed. Lorenzo Bianconi and Giovanni Morelli, Studi di musica veneta: Quaderni vivaldiani (Florence: Olschki, 1982), 2:427–81, esp. 428–40.

"court" singer, but that term from an earlier age needs to be understood within a context that had changed profoundly since the early decades of the seventeenth century. The very existence of a "ducal circuit" is proof of the persistence of a dependent condition for singers, but it also indicates that the courts found it increasingly difficult to keep in their full-time service all the singers required for an opera season. When performers moved from one place to another, it was at bottom a way for their employers to share expenses. Moreover it was not enough to make sure that all roles would be covered, because the success of an opera was increasingly dependent on the presence of a star singer. The singers who were most in demand in the early eighteenth century—Margherita Salicola, Domenico Cecchi, Maria Maddalena Musi, Giovanni Francesco Grossi, Maria Domenica Pini, and Francesco Antonio Pistocchi (all castratos or women)—had their choice of offers from a number of potential protectors and could maintain relative freedom of movement. It is true that the princely employer had to grant leave to travel, but it is probable that such permission was guaranteed by contract. One such contract, offered by the duke of Mantua, Ferdinando Carlo Gonzaga, to the singer Clarice Gigli, included a clause stipulating that the singer had "liberty to assume obligations to perform with the absolute permission of His Highness, who will graciously assent." [52] There is no way of knowing whether this clause was an exception or the rule; it is true, however, that it would fit to perfection many singers who, while making much of their membership in the Mantua court, seem to have been more active elsewhere. This state of semidependence is probably best understood as the reflection of a policy of prestige that the last of the Gonzagas by then invested even in opera librettos. [53] Was the same thing true of other powerful persons in Italy? Clearly many questions remain unanswered, but it seems evident that the changing relations between patrons and their musical personnel were tending toward a greater liberty of movement for the latter. The singers' greater mobility contributed to the expansion and stabilization of the theatrical market, and at the same time it laid the foundations for the irresistible rise of the star singers in the eighteenth century.

---

52. This unusual document (in effect the draft of a very detailed contract) was published in Giovan Battista Cavalcaselle, *Tipi di scritture teatrali attraverso luoghi e tempi diversi: Contributo storico-giuridico* (Rome: Athenaeum, 1919), section 2, 12–13. It is discussed in Sergio Durante, "Cantanti per Reggio (1696–1717): Note sul rapporto di dipendenza," in *Civiltà teatrale e Settecento emiliano,* ed. Susi Davoli (Bologna: Il Mulino, 1986), 301–7.

53. On this problem, see Lorenzo Bianconi and Thomas Walker, "Production, Consumption, and Political Function of Seventeenth-Century Opera," *Early Music History* 4 (1984): 209–96, esp. 274–82.

The author of the first treatise on singing in the Italian language, Pierfrancesco Tosi, thought it strange that no one before him had attempted a project of the sort and that among so many professional singers "of the first Rank" no one had "undertaken to explain in the Art of Singing, any thing more than the first Elements, known to all, concealing the most necessary Rules for Singing well."[54] Before Tosi's book appeared in 1723, the secrets of the art of singing had been passed on orally. Although we can get some idea of singing styles from the detailed indications of performance practices included in many printed musical works, we know about the methods and materials of seventeenth-century teaching practices not from specific and exhaustive treatises but only indirectly through letters, memoirs, and reports. The very fact that sources are relatively scarce and occasional in nature is in itself indicative of a certain sort of learning process analogous to the transmission of a craft and, as with craftsmanship, of jealously guarded secrets. Furthermore the skills that the master passed on to the pupil are not necessarily to be understood as rationalized (or pseudorationalized) "techniques" in the modern sense. As late as 1677, for example, Bartolomeo Bismantova limited his "technical" advice to a brief description of how to work on trills; for all the rest he advised his pupils to listen to the leading singers of the day.[55] Singing methods could be apprehended much more easily through practice than in writing, and although Tosi agreed, fifty years later, that oral teaching was indispensable, the degree to which conceptualization was thought useful or possible had changed radically by then. Tosi, for instance, devoted an entire chapter to the trill.

This does not mean that a "pretechnical" phase reflected an inferior stage in the art of singing. The level of execution is not in question; it is the musician's attitude toward his or her own work that changed. The dedication with which musical excellence was pursued in certain Roman schools is astonishing to this day. A well-known passage in Giovanni Andrea Angelini Bontempi's *Historia musica* states,

> The schools of Rome obliged their pupils to devote a total of one hour per day to the singing of difficult, arduous things in order to gain experience. One hour practicing the trill, another on *passaggi,* a third on the study of letters, a fourth on training and other exercises—in the presence of the master and/or in front of the mirror—with the purpose of eliminating all unseemly movement of body, face,

54. Tosi, *Opinioni de' cantori,* 4, quoted from *Observations on the Florid Song,* 5–6.
55. Bartolomeo Bismantova, *Compendio musicale* (1677; facsimile reprint ed., Florence: Studio per Edizioni Scelti, 1979), 23.

brows, and mouth. All these were the morning activities. After noon, pupils underwent half an hour of theoretical training, half an hour of counterpoint on a cantus firmus, an hour of instruction and practice in counterpoint in open score, and a further hour in the study of letters; the remainder of the day was spent at the harpsichord or in the composition of some psalm, motet, canzonetta or other form of song, in accordance with individual flair and ability. These were the normal exercises for days on which pupils remained indoors. "Outdoor" exercises consisted of frequent trips to sing and listen to the echo outside Porta Angelica (toward Monte Mario), with the aim of increasing self-criticism of the scholar's tone of voice; participation in almost all the music of the various churches of Rome; observation of the performance styles of the many illustrious singers who flourished under Urban VIII; later, at home, practice in these manners of singing and description thereof to the maestro, who himself, in his efforts to impress them more firmly upon the minds of his pupils, added all necessary warnings and other remarks. These exercises and general training in the art of music are those given us in Rome by Virgilio Mazzocchi, illustrious professor and *maestro di cappella* of Saint Peter's.[56]

What we have here is a carefully organized, comprehensive didactic system that includes intelligently varied exercises appropriately placed through the day in order to obtain the maximum result with a minimum of tedium and fatigue. Singing practice was inextricably combined with the study of a keyboard instrument, theory, composition, and literary studies. The physical and intellectual demands made of students were impressive: they sang for four hours in the morning, and when the day ended they had completed more than eight hours of work. They had daily contact with their teacher, and what they learned was corroborated by expeditions outside the city and by discussions on what they had listened to.

It would also be useful to know the average length of a program of studies, the age of the students, and whether Mazzocchi accepted beginners or skimmed off the cream of the crop of young musicians in Rome. Finally we need to ask whether Mazzocchi's school can be considered representative of the general level of instruction during the seventeenth century or whether it was not perhaps an exception in which Bontempi could take rightful pride. To offer one possible comparison, toward the beginning of the century Marquis Enzo Bentivoglio had a boy soprano work for one hour every day on learning to "sing well and place his voice well" and another hour "having him attend to the study of counterpoint and composition." At the same time the young man took lessons from Cesare Marotta "three or four times a day"

56. Giovanni Andrea Angelini Bontempi, *Historia musica* (Perugia, 1695; reprint ed,. Bologna: Arnaldo Forni, 1979), 170, quoted (edited) from Lorenzo Bianconi, *Music in the Seventeenth Century,* trans. David Bryant (Cambridge: Cambridge University Press, 1987), 61.

to learn arias and *sonetti,* had harpsichord lessons from Girolamo Frescobaldi, and guitar lessons from the famous Ippolita Recupito (Marotta's
wife).[57] This young musician also studied full time on a daily basis, but his
studies were structured differently, were spread among a number of teachers,
and stressed instrumental music. There is no sign of literary studies, theory,
or composition. The young man was being trained to be a good "domestic"
singer, and his literary training was secondary. A young female singer also
connected with the Bentivoglio family, Angiola Zanibelli, was requested to
perform in an opera being put on in Mantua when she had been studying
music only for a few months. On her return from a successful debut she was
immediately offered a chance to teach another young female singer. She refused the invitation on the grounds that she lacked experience, thus showing
better sense than her patrons, but the episode nonetheless shows how widely
singers' levels of training might vary.[58]

Courses of study necessarily began with *bicinia,* two-part solfège exercises
that were written by a number of composers from Jhan Gero, Bernardino
Lupacchino dal Vasto, and Orlando di Lasso to Grammatico Metallo, Giovanni Matteo Asola, and Giuseppe Giamberti, and were reprinted several
times during the course of the century. These pieces were generally sung in
solmization, or, more precisely, sung by pronouncing the names of the notes,
with their appropriate mutations, in the six-note "Guidonian" system. The
student then went on to singing with words, probably using the simplest sacred and madrigal repertory. The teachers themselves may also have composed exercises for their own pupils (Bontempi's "difficult, arduous
things"?), but if such ad hoc practical exercises existed, they have left no
trace. Advanced students would have gone on to learn to sing in the recitative
style, the chamber style, and the aria style.[59]

57. See the letters of June and July 1615 quoted in Frederick Hammond, *Girolamo Frescobaldi* (Cambridge: Harvard University Press, 1983), 39 and n. 23. These documents are more
fully discussed in John Walter Hill, "Le 'Arie' di Frescobaldi e la cerchia musicale del cardinal
Montalto," in *Girolamo Frescobaldi nel VI centenario della nascita,* ed. Sergio Durante and
Dinko Fabris (Florence: Olschki, 1986), 215–32.

58. See Reiner, "La vag'Angioletta," 61–62. For other details relating to teaching and singing,
see Fenlon, "Monteverdi's Mantuan *Orfeo*," 167–68, which documents the custom of teaching
"parts" by memorizing the music first and the words only later. On the compositional talents of
the singers of the early seventeenth century, see Ademollo "La bell'Adriana," 234. Such talents
were not always and not necessarily accompanied by even a modest level of musical literacy, as
shown in Claudio Sartori, "Quindici lettere di Leonora Baroni, musicista analfabeta," *Studien zur
Musikwissenschaft* 25 (1962): 446–51, esp. 449.

59. See Capponi, "L'educazione d'una virtuosa." Italian teaching practices of the mid-
seventeenth century are documented indirectly in some parts of the treatise of Christoph Bernhard,
published in Joseph Müller-Blattau, *Die Kompositionslehre Heinrich Schützens in der Fassung
seines Schülers Christoph Bernhard,* 2d ed. (Kassel: Bärenreiter, 1963).

3. From Modena to Bologna: Criticism and Growth

Ludovico Antonio Muratori had understood that the fortunes of *opera in musica* would improve in the late seventeenth century, and his *Annali d'Italia* have particularly significant things to say about the phenomenon. Muratori considered the events he noted as relevant not only as they fitted in with the history of the theater or the history of literature but also in the broader sense, as part of a process of transformation of manners that reached its peak in the 1690s.

> Many years passed during which this province enjoyed peace and tranquillity; for that reason people thought of little else than entertainments and pleasures. Music, and particularly theater music, had risen to high esteem, and everywhere there appeared sumptuous operas, whose singers, male and female, were embellished with the adulterated titles of *virtuosi* and *virtuose*. . . . It became common practice at that time to pay two hundred, three hundred, and even more dobles apiece to the most melodious actors in the theaters, besides the large sums spent on the orchestra, the costumes, the scenery, and the lighting.[60]

Incomplete as they are, data on two representative centers of production, Venice and Florence, provide an idea of the quantitative growth of the theatrical market. From a total of forty-six productions in 1641 to 1650, opera in these two cities increased steadily (but with a noticeable surge from 1681 to 1690) to reach a total of 120 and more productions in 1691 to 1700. The information on these two major centers should be supplemented with data on the other cities, both in Italy and north of the Alps, that inaugurated more or less regular opera seasons toward the end of the century. That increased activity obviously had consequences for the performers: within only a few decades the demand for singers increased enormously (although not in the same proportion as the increase in productions).[61] At the same time the rise in costs to which Muratori refers seems to have continued uninterrupted until well into the eighteenth century, as Giovanni Carlo Bonlini (among others) attests.

> Once it was considered unusual if the expense for a beautiful voice exceeded 100 scudi; it was thought extraordinary, and anyone who was paid 120 for the first time

60. Ludovico Antonio Muratori, *Annali d'Italia dal principio dell'era volgare sino all'anno 1750 . . . e continuati sino all'anno 1827*, 40 vols. (Florence, 1827–28), 27: 270.

61. The demand for singers was affected by a decline in the average number of characters in the individual operas. Furthermore, an increase in the number of opera productions might lead to a more intensive use of the same cast of singers during any given season, but not necessarily to an increase in their absolute numbers, which depended on a larger number of productions and an increase in the number of cities with opera seasons.

became proverbial as the news passed from mouth to mouth. But if we compare
those bygone times with the present, [we see that] in our days it is becoming almost
common [to pay] the exorbitant price of more than 1,000 zecchini to anyone who
can boast of some special prerogative over the others in the profession. Example
has now given everyone immoderate demands.[62]

Although exhaustive financial and economic data on rising prices are lacking, circumstantial evidence shows a market situation in which the demand
for singers usually was greater than the supply. This meant that singers were
in a stronger contractual position than librettists, impresarios, and composers—a superiority expressed not only in high fees but in a dominant position
within the complex dynamics of forces competing to have their demands met.

At the beginning of the eighteenth century, Muratori, in his *Perfetta poesia
italiana,* had already described all the negative traits commonly associated
with singers. In his yearning for a type of music drama inspired by Arcadian
and classical ideals, Muratori argued that many if not all the defects of the
opera of his time came from disrespect for the traditional hierarchy of the
arts, where music was ancillary to poetry. It was perfectly clear to him, however, that "the taste of our times has constituted the entire essence of these
dramas in music, and their perfection [lies] in the choice of worthy singers."
But even as he was noting the chief source of the pleasure that these works
gave, he criticized them for "deformities" that made that same pleasure perni-
cious. His first accusation was moral.

> Everyone knows and feels the emotions that listening to fine singers in the theater
> arouse within us. Their singing always inspires a certain softness and sweetness
> that secretly serves to make the people ever more base and given to base loves as
> they drink in the affected languidness of the voices and enjoy the vilest emotions,
> embellished by unhealthy melody.

Among other things Muratori blamed opera for an "overwhelming use of
fast notes [eighth and sixteenth notes] and even notes of smaller value, by
which the gravity of the singing is broken up." He also criticized the fact that
"each actor takes it upon himself to command the poet and ask verses from
him according to his own imagination . . . so that poets are constrained to
weave and garb their dramas not as art and the argument require but as the

---

62. Giovanni Carlo Bonlini, *Le glorie della poesia e della musica* (Venice, 1730 [1731]), 183.
Bonlini was referring to *Paride,* given at the Teatro San Giovanni Grisostomo in 1720, and he was
alluding to Caterina Angiola Botteghi, called "La Centoventi," who was probably still remembered at the time; see Ademollo, *I teatri di Roma,* 139.

music desires." To end his list of complaints, Muratori criticized the poor quality of the acting, which he attributed to the performers' ignorance.[63]

Although hints of Muratori's assiduous frequentation of the opera houses and his lively passion for the opera pierce through his invective,[64] later critics noted and commented more on his negative remarks, thus perpetuating a substantially condemnatory historical evaluation of the "harmonic profession." Thus singers were made the scapegoat for presumed "imperfections" in opera by arguing from Muratori's theoretical literary premises and indiscriminately extending his criticism to cover an entire professional class. These generalizations, uncritically repeated, were persistent enough to have long-term, disconcerting results: even today, for example, some writers think it "philologically correct" in revivals of the eighteenth-century opera seria repertory to encourage singers to display an ineptitude on stage that in fact contemporaries found abhorrent. The acting abilities of the best *virtuosi* were appreciated just as much as their vocal capabilities and considered a rare virtue and a fundamental ingredient of a perfect performance. There is ample contemporary witness to this attitude, not only in treatises and correspondence but also in the vast production of sonnets in praise of singers printed on the occasion of individual productions. Such occasional pieces often commemorate not only the sweetness of the singer's voice but also his or her acting ability or the power of suggestion of a particular moment in the performance. The tone of such pieces is often justificatory, at times even hyperbolic, almost as if to compensate singers for the hostility shown them in more theoretical contexts.[65]

63. Ludovico Antonio Muratori, *Della perfetta poesia italiana* (Modena, 1706). This work had already been completed by 1702, as clarified by Ada Ruschioni, the editor of the modern edition, 2 vols. (Milan: Marzorati, 1971–72), from which the quotations have been taken (see 577, 573, 575, 576, and 577, respectively).

64. Muratori's passion for the theater is confirmed by a reading of his correspondence, in particular the letters to his friends Giovanni Jacopo Tori and Francesco Arisi; see *L'Epistolario di Ludovico Antonio Muratori*, esp. vol. 1.

65. Celebratory materials of this sort are scattered among the libraries and archives of Italy, where they still await a systematic survey. For examples, see the descriptions of some pieces in Zeno Davoli, *Stampe di autore e di interesse reggiano,* vol. 1 in *Le raccolte di stampe dei civici musei* (Reggio Emilia: Comune di Reggio Emilia, 1983), nos. 556ff. See also the collection described in Lowell E. Lindgren and Carl B. Schmidt, "A Collection of 137 Broadsides Concerning Theatre in Late Seventeenth-Century Italy: An Annotated Catalogue," *Harvard Library Bulletin* 28 (1980): 185–233. For an evaluation of the acting abilities and stage presence of some singers, see Giambattista Mancini, *Pensieri e riflessioni pratiche sopra il canto figurato* (Vienna, 1774), and the second edition, entitled *Riflessioni pratiche sul canto figurato* (Milan, 1777; reprint ed., Bologna: Arnaldo Forni, 1970), passim. Abundant documentation can be found in correspondence, in particular that of Metastasio, published in vols. 3 and 4 of Pietro Metastasio, *Tutte le opere,* ed. Bruno Brunelli, 5 vols. (Milan: Mondadori, 1947–54). The correspondence of Giovanni Battista Martini is also of prime importance; for a catalog, see Anne Schnoebelen, *Padre Martini's*

As the seventeenth century drew to a close, during the years when the ducal circuit prospered and operatic activities were rapidly expanding, Bologna became the principal center for Italian theatrical artists. Opera librettos, which in this period bear names and places of origin with a certain regularity, show an increasing proportion of Bolognese in opera houses all over the peninsula, among the singers in particular but also among the set designers and costumers.

This was in substance a new phenomenon (the Roman precedent had not been so clearly tied to opera) and one of notable importance in the professional history of the opera singer. This proliferation, rather than depending on the will of a prince, as had been the case in Florence, was a natural growth arising from a fortunate combination of socioeconomic circumstances beyond the control of any one person. An entire professional class came into being, concentrated within a particularly favorable urban context. It had its own hierarchy of rank, its own factions, even its own café and academy (the renowned Accademia Filarmonica), and it eventually became responsible— for good or ill—for the public image of the profession both in Italy and throughout Europe.[66]

A survey (undoubtedly incomplete) of the performers who gravitated toward Bologna between the late seventeenth and early eighteenth centuries has enabled scholars to identify 450 professional singers. Citizens of Bologna make up only a part of this group: students migrated to Bologna from elsewhere, and a good many singers also came from other places either to attend functions of the Accademia Filarmonica or to live permanently in the city. One libretto tells us that Anna Cosimi was a "*virtuosa* of the duke of Modena, a Roman living in Bologna"; another singer, Guglielmo Ettore, moved to Bologna from his native Sicily toward the middle of the century. It was not by chance, then, that after having traveled throughout Europe, Tosi came to Bologna to publish his treatise, or that Farinelli (Carlo Broschi), the most famous castrato of the century, chose Bologna as his permanent place of residence and became a Bolognese citizen. According to Charles de Brosses, Bo-

---

Collection of Letters in the Civico Museo Bibliografico Musicale in Bologna (New York: Pendragon Press, 1979). For opera circles in Handel's London, see *The Complete Letters of Lady Mary Wortley Montagu (1708–1751)*, ed. Robert Halsband, 3 vols. (Oxford: Clarendon Press, 1965).

66. There is ample testimony to these minor aspects of musical life in Bologna in Olivo Penna, *Cronologia, o sia Istoria generale di questa Accademia* [*Filarmonica*], MS, ca. 1736, in the archives of the academy. A partial copy of this fundamental source for Bolognese history has been published under the (erroneous) name of Giovanni Battista Martini as *Catalogo degli aggregati dell'Accademia Filarmonica di Bologna,* ed. Anne Schnoebelen (Bologna: Accademia Filarmonica, 1973), on which see Sergio Durante, "Note su un manoscritto 'martiniano'," in *Padre Martini: Musica e cultura nel Settecento europeo,* ed. Angelo Pompilio (Florence: Olschki, 1987), 123–33.

logna was the "great seminary of Italian music";[67] Johann Wilhelm von Archenholz called the city the "collection center for all the Italian composers,
castratos, and actors in search of an engagement." "They gather here," he
continued, "because from all lands people turn to this city to hire them. . . .
Hence the performances in Bologna must be numbered among the best in
Italy and are besides the least expensive in all of Europe."[68] Bologna's status
as a privileged market lasted at least until the early nineteenth century, when
the center for theatrical negotiations gradually shifted to Milan. As late as
1853 census figures show that there were ten theatrical agents in Bologna.[69]

If Bologna's decline can be explained by Milan's greater powers of attraction (it had become the capital of the Napoleonic Kingdom of Italy) and by
its prestigious theater,[70] the reasons for Bologna's ascendancy in the late seventeenth century are less clear. why Bologna and not Venice or Florence?
There is no simple answer to the question. One basic factor was certainly
Bologna's favorable geographic position at the center of an area of intense
operatic activity on all professional levels, extending from the most prestigious Venetian theater, the San Giovanni Grisostomo, to seasons in Modena,
Reggio, Ferrara, Cremona, Milan, Verona, Padua, and even to nearby provincial initiatives in towns like Cento, Budrio, Lugo, and Medicina. Another
important factor was Bologna's urban traditions, according to which "cul-

67. A study of Bolognese singers and the environment in which they operated, written by the
present author, is part of a research project on culture and civil life in eighteenth-century Emilia
Romagna under the auspices of the Region, the results of which should be published shortly. For
Cosimi see the libretto for the performance of the Metastasio-Hasse *Artaserse* in Bergamo, carnival 1738; for Ettore (a singer mentioned by Charles Burney, who heard him in 1770) see the
letter of Father Martini of 12 August 1761 to Andrea Bernasconi, Schnoebelen, *Padre Martini's
Collection*, no. 672. It should be noted in connection with Pierfrancesco Tosi that the current
interpretation that makes him something like a spokesman for a "Bolognese school" of reactionary tendencies is founded on erroneous and incomplete information. Although Tosi did come
from Cesena (but he was not the son of the Bolognese composer Giuseppe Felice), he had lived
for the most part in Genoa, and he became a "foreign" member of the Filarmonica in 1689.
His treatise brings together a cosmopolitan sort of experience that only a determinedly parochial
interpretation could limit to one locality. On Farinelli's residence in Bologna see Corrado Ricci,
Casanova e Farinelli a Bologna (Milan, 1890). To end the list see Charles de Brosses, *Lettres
familières écrites d'Italie*, available in a recent edition in French as *Lettres familières*, ed. Giuseppina Cafasso and Letizia Norchi Cagiano de Azevedo, 3 vols. (Naples: Centre Jean Bérard, 1991;
distribution by Boccard).

68. Johann Wilhelm von Archenholz, *England und Italien*, 2 vols. (Leipzig, 1785), 2:78.

69. Bologna, Archivio di Stato, Censimenti 1852–1859, file entitled "Statistica della Popolaz-
ione del Comune di Bologna riferibile al 1853," dated Rome, 15 March 1852, quadro VI.

70. On this problem, see John Rosselli, "Agenti teatrali nel mondo dell'opera lirica italiana
dell'Ottocento," *Rivista italiana di musicologia* 17 (1982): 134–54, esp. 138, and *The Opera
Industry in Italy from Cimarosa to Verdi: The Role of the Impresario* (Cambridge: Cambridge
University Press, 1984), 138–39 and 150.

ture, the arts, and the economy were . . . just as important as lineage and military valor."[71] Even the dynamics of the Bolognese nobility, which was relatively open to those with new fortunes, gave nonaristocratic classes a social mobility that they lacked elsewhere. We might also add that a large number of Bolognese intellectuals were at the various courts in Europe, where they were ready to support the engagement of their compatriots (the Garelli family in Vienna, Giovanni Ludovico Bianconi in Dresden). All these were pieces in a complex mosaic that also included a number of musical institutions: ecclesiastical chapels, conservatories,[72] and the Accademia Filarmonica. Finally, there were the various singing teachers into whose hands the prestige and the productivity of the local schools were entrusted. These included not only extremely famous names—Pistocchi, Antonio Maria Bernacchi, and Francesco Campeggi—but also prolific but lesser-known figures such as Agostino Filippucci and Giacomo Cesare Predieri, who between them could boast of having no fewer than thirty-six former pupils among the academicians of the Filarmonica, and others, such as Silvestro Costa and Antonio Desiderati, who were the first teachers, later forgotten, of singers who became famous.[73]

4. The Virtuosi: Background, Training, Itineraries, Specialties

The vast store of anecdotes about the uncouth attitudes and senseless obstinacy of eighteenth-century *virtuosi* provide constant amusement, but they also show that the singers' swift social promotion and the cultural imbalance that resulted from their sudden plunge into a different social sphere were part and parcel of a successful singing career. In their rapid rise to stardom the

71. Alfeo Giacomelli, "La dinamica della nobiltà bolognese nel XVIII secolo," in *Famiglie senatorie e istituzioni cittadine a Bologna nel Settecento*, Atti del primo colloquio, Bologna 2–3 February 1980 (Bologna: Istituto per la Storia di Bologna, 1980), 55–112, quotation 58.

72. There is some fragmentary information on conservatories in Durante, "Alcune considerazioni," 440–53.

73. There is abundant information on Bolognese singing teachers in Piero Mioli, "La scuola di canto bolognese nel Settecento," *Quadrivium* 22, no. 1 (1981): 5–59. Mioli unquestioningly accepts a notion of "school" that in reality is quite indefinite, and he takes from Rodolfo Celletti the dubious thesis that the history of singing can be interpreted as the evolution of the various vocal timbres. More solidly founded but more limited in its intentions is an old article by Lodovico Frati, "Antonio Bernacchi e la sua scuola di canto," *Rivista musicale italiana* 29 (1922): 473–91. Silvestro Costa, who became a member of the Accademia in 1700, was the teacher of Annibale Pio Fabbri, who subsequently studied with the more famous Francesco Antonio Pistocchi; Antonio Desiderati, who became an academician in 1684, was the teacher of Francesca Vanini and Antonio Bernacchi (as can be deduced from Olivo Penna's *Cronologia*, in the edition cited, fols. 36v and 58v).

virtuosi had little time to internalize the ways of the dominant class; in general they achieved little more than an imitation of outward forms.

Singers' family backgrounds can occasionally be guessed from their nicknames. The range was broad, but it probably excluded aristocratic origins. There were famous female singers nicknamed "La Coghetta" (little cook), "La Beccarina" (little butcher), "La Parrucchierina" (little wigmaker).[74] Often, however, music was a family tradition, as it was in the Belisani, Predieri, Laurenti, and Ristorini families. Vittoria Tesi was the daughter of a lackey of Francesco de Castris, a singer; Celeste Coltellini was the daughter of a librettist. Castratos were thought to have very low social origins, as Benedetto Marcello suggested in one of his satirical thrusts.

> If the singer were a contralto or a soprano, he would have some good friend to speak up for him in conversational gatherings and declare him (in the name of the truth) of civil and honorable family, adding that because of a most perilous infirmity he had agreed to undergo the incision; that besides he had a brother who was a professor of philosophy, another who was a physician, a sister who was a nun highly placed in her convent, another married to a citizen, etc., etc.[75]

When a family had a son castrated, it undeniably opened up concrete possibilities for economic advancement, but it was a move also chosen by some families who were not on the lowest rung of the social ladder. Pistocchi's father, for example, was a salaried employee of the chapel of San Petronio, Bologna's largest church, as was Giuseppe Segni's father; Gaetano Berenstadt's father was a drummer for the grand duke of Tuscany. One castrato who came closer to fitting Marcello's description was Matteo Sassano, the illegitimate son of a nineteen-year-old mother, raised by people outside the

---

74. These nicknames referred, respectively, to Caterina Gabrielli, Anna Maria Cecchi, and Anna Maria Peruzzi. Nicknames often derived from the singer's place of origin (there was more than one "Romanina" or "Senesino") or from a place name attached to the singer's teacher: thus "Il Cortoncino" (Antonio Archi) was from Florence, not Cortona, but he was the pupil of "Il Cortona," Domenico Cecchi, who was indeed born in that town; Francesco Segni was called "Il Finale," although he was from Bologna, because he taught school at Finale di Modena; his son, called "Il Finalino," was indeed born in Finale, though his fellow Filarmonici considered him Bolognese—see Penna, *Cronologia*, 43. Two singers each known as "La Polacca" (Silvia and Livia Nannini) were not Polish, any more than Margherita "di Sassonia" (Margherita Salicola Suini) was German, or Silvia Lodi, "La Spagnoletta," was Spanish. Other nicknames recalled some act that had brought the singer greater prestige, a famous dramatic role (Giovanni Francesco Grossi was called "Siface"), or a powerful protector (Giovanni Carestini was "Il Cusanino" because his patrons were the Cusani family).

75. Benedetto Marcello, *Il teatro alla moda* (Venice, 1720), modern edition, ed. A. Marianni (Milan: Rizzoli, 1959), 43.

family who had him castrated and later put him into the Conservatorio dei Poveri di Gesù Cristo in Naples.[76]

Admission to such charitable institutions had originally been limited to children who had lost at least one parent, but in Naples they were gradually transformed into hybrid institutions, partly musical orphan asylums and partly paid boarding schools. When a nonpaying pupil was admitted it was agreed that he would "serve" the conservatory for a determined number of years: in Sassano's case, ten years, but they could be only two, as for Angelo Caselli. This period of "service" did not refer to the length of the pupil's formal course of studies but to the amount of time during which his earnings (for the most part from processions, funerals, and other religious services) would be turned over to the school. These institutions admitted their first paying students in the late seventeenth century, but the practice became current only in the following century. Obviously a paying student was not obligated to long residence in the institution. The fees varied according to the individual's ability to pay and the school's interest in the pupil: in the Conservatory of Sant'Onofrio around 1760 to 1770, for example, castratos paid 10 ducats per year, as opposed to 24 to 30 ducats for other students.[77] In those days (just before Charles Burney's visits to Italy, which were to have an extraordinary importance for publicizing the Italian conservatories all over Europe), the Neapolitan schools had reached a notable level of renown, which meant that access to them had become proportionally more difficult.

Despite their undeniable prestige the role of those schools in the formation of opera singers has probably been exaggerated. Throughout the seventeenth century the normal career for the students trained in such schools was not on the stage but in the church, and in Naples even more forcefully than elsewhere, such authoritative persons as Geronimo della Marra, *cappellano maggiore* of the royal chapel, insisted that a clear division be made between sacred and secular music.[78] When Sassano, a singer of the royal chapel, made his operatic debut in 1697, it caused a scandal, and after that date, although prejudices against the theater reached feverish proportions, teachers found

76. On Berenstadt, a singular figure and both a singer and a man of letters, see the detailed study by Lowell E. Lindgren, "La carriera di Gaetano Berenstadt, contralto evirato (ca. 1690–1735)," *Rivista italiana di musicologia* 19 (1984): 36–112, and Carlo Vitali, "Gaetano Berenstadt tra Roma, Firenze e Napoli: Interessi culturali e frequentazioni erudite di un 'eunico letterato,'" in *Antonio Vivaldi: Teatro musicale, cultura e società,* ed. Lorenzo Bianconi and Giovanni Morelli, Studi di musica veneta: Quaderni vivaldiani (Florence: Olschki, 1982), 2:499–519. On Sassano, see Ulisse Prota-Giurleo, "Matteo Sassano detto 'Matteuccio,'" *Rivista italiana di musicologia* 1 (1966): 97–119.

77. See Salvatore di Giacomo, *Il Conservatorio di S. Onofrio a Capuana e quello di S. Maria della Pietà dei Turchini* (Palermo: Sandron, 1924), 107 and 114.

78. See Lino Bianchi and Roberto Pagano, *Alessandro Scarlatti* (Turin: Edizioni RAI Radiotelevisione Italiana, 1972), 72ff.

that it was increasingly to their economic advantage to give private instruction to the more promising students. In a well-known study on the Conservatory of Sant'Onofrio, Salvatore Di Giacomo observed that Carlo Broschi (Farinelli) and Gaetano Majorano (Caffarelli) had both been pupils of Nicola Porpora's, "but pupils to whom . . . he gave lessons at home, not in the Conservatory."[79] If admission to the conservatory was so sought after, it was not only in view of a theatrical career but also because there was the certitude of another career to fall back on. As Giambattista Mancini noted, if a student "did not have enough talent to succeed in secular life, he was redirected to an ecclesiastical career, and the directors of the conservatories made sure he would have an appropriate position and occupation among the various cathedrals."[80] On the whole the Neapolitan conservatories seem to have offered the opera houses of Italy highly qualified singers, but in limited numbers: of the thirty-one famous castratos surveyed by Angus Heriot, only three had attended a conservatory.

In Venice, a city famous for its four female conservatories, the life of the schools was completely separate from theatrical circles, and the girls educated in them were in fact discouraged from turning toward a theatrical profession, a choice that would mean ipso facto that the institution would lose the student's dowry. It is difficult to evaluate the impact of the less-well-known charitable institutions, perhaps because they were not as involved in public musical activities (or perhaps because Dr. Burney failed to mention them). There were conservatories nearly everywhere in Italy, from Bologna to Palermo and Gallipoli.[81] There were no fewer than three charity hospitals active in Bologna during the eighteenth century (Santi Pietro e Procolo, called "degli Esposti"; Santa Maria Maddalena or Sant'Onofrio; and the Ospedale dei Mendicanti, called "della Pietà"), and there were also the *scuole pie,* run by the civil authorities, which had well-attended classes in the singing of plainsong and polyphonic music. Since almost all the names of the students in these schools have been lost, it is impossible to evaluate the extent to which the schools contributed to the theater. We do know the names of a few teachers and that, unlike their Neapolitan counterparts, they taught plainchant and polyphony but not composition. One teacher, Pietro Antonio Fontana, was even an op-

79. See Di Giacomo, *Il Conservatorio di S. Onofrio,* 100.

80. Mancini, *Riflessioni pratiche,* 47.

81. On Palermo see Federico de Maria, *Il regio conservatorio di musica di Palermo* (Florence: Le Monnier, 1941), which gives documents from the seventeenth and eighteenth centuries that were lost during World War II; see also Roberto Pagano, "La Casa degli Spersi," in *Conservatorio di musica "Vincenzo Bellini": Annuario 1960–61* (Palermo: Conservatorio Vincenzo Bellini, 1962), 16–22. On the school in Gallipoli see Giuseppe A. Pastore, "Scuole musicali in Gallipoli," in *Informazioni archivistiche e bibliografiche sul Salento* (Galatone: Russo, 1957). For other references on conservatories, see n. 122.

era singer, which proves—if nothing else—that the Bolognese were less worried that secular music would contaminate sacred music. No Bolognese school took paying students, and although the schools did engage in public activities,[82] they never reached the levels of the school performances in Naples or Venice. As for the level of instruction in Bologna, an examination of the sight-reading exercises published for the use of the *scuole pie* suggests that they might have given students a solid base for further study, but they were certainly not adequate preparation for a professional career.[83] The city had an abundant supply of private teachers eager to take on that task.

According to the different urban contexts into which they fitted, the conservatories and other, similar institutions seem to have taken on differing organizational and didactic structures, and they proved capable of adapting to changing economic conditions. Still, the existence of such institutions should not be interpreted as a sign that musical training (even less, theatrical training) had become institutionalized; quite to the contrary, for the most part these remained the province of private instruction.

In his *Opinioni de' cantori antichi e moderni,* Tosi directed much of his advice to a hypothetical singing teacher, thus indirectly informing us of some of his own habits. For the first phase of his studies, a singing student normally turned to a "Master of a lower Rank,"[84] passing on to the top teachers only for advanced study, especially in how to sing arias, cadenzas, and *passi* (embellishments). A teacher as sought after as Pistocchi might have his students taught by a person he trusted, limiting his own efforts to hearing them from time to time to be sure they were mastering the style for which he was famous.[85]

Tosi's advice to a singer that he take the time to perfect his skills was observed by many of the most famous singers, but it is probable that most singers of average talent, prepared by "mercenary" and incompetent teachers, were launched in theatrical circuits as soon as they were capable of earning money. Giambattista Mancini speaks of the

> base interests that seem to govern the better part of the teachers, making no attempt to apply the good rules of the art and the precepts that were transmitted to them nor paying the necessary attention to the differing talent of their students, they

82. The Ospedale dei Mendicanti, for example, used its young students, dressed as angels, to accompany the dead to their tombs; see the documentation in the Archivio di Stato di Bologna, fondo "Mendicanti," *Libro giornale Y 1706–1711* (no. 336), passim.

83. For an example, see Angelo Michele Bertalotti, *Solfeggi a canto e alto dati alle stampe per comodo delli putti delle Scuole pie di Bologna* (Bologna, 1744).

84. Tosi, *Opinioni de' cantori,* 8, quoted from *Observations on the Florid Song,* 11.

85. See the documentation in Fabrizio Della Seta, "I Borghese (1691–1731): La musica di una generazione," *Note d'archivio per la storia musicale* n. s. 1 (1983): 139–208, esp. 164–67.

think only of starting them on their careers, with the objective of soon seeing them mount the stage and of realizing a profit, which they contract, on the earnings of their own students—who, appearing on the stage when they are still immature and often made proud by ephemeral applause, abandon their studies and advance no further in the secrets and the refinements of their art.[86]

Mancini himself had made his debut at the age of sixteen, but for him (and for many others) the beginning of public performance did not signal the end of his studies. One case in point is the houseful of students who lived with Francesco Gasparini, a well-known singing teacher and composer. Between 1717 and 1727 Gasparini lodged nine students in his house, most of whom later became quite successful professionals. The period of cohabitation ranged between one year and four years, and the students who remained the longest with him (Girolamo Bartoluzzi, Antonio Lottini, and Giacomo Raggi) were not the beginners but the more advanced students. It is clear that they were pursuing further studies with Gasparini after having trained with other teachers. An analogous case is that of Giacomo Calcina, who, after his first experiences on the stage, returned to Bologna to study with a new teacher. He was presented to the famous Padre Martini in these terms:[87]

> The bearer [of the present letter] is Sig. Giacomo Calcina. . . . The aforesaid comes to Bologna to gain a more solid foundation in music, wherefore I beg your fatherly grace to deign to recommend him to Sig. . . . Giovanardi so that he might assist him. Concerning the payment, if the young man turns out to need frequent lessons, payment will be arranged for; if not, he will content Sig. Giovanardi with gifts in kind. [I might] add that the young man has already been in Bologna and that Sig. Mazzoni taught him, but for good reasons he should no longer study with him. I am sorry I cannot send you someone who will do for an ecclesiastical career . . . but since [Calcina] has already sung on the stage in Turin and this carnival in Piacenza and done sufficiently well, his father thinks . . . it best to have him follow a theatrical curriculum.

In this case the student could permit himself the luxury of paying (or "gifting") the teacher, but often a student agreed to give his teacher a portion of his future earnings. A contract written in 1776 stipulated that two years of free lessons were to be given in exchange for a fourth of the student's earnings throughout his entire career. These were lessons from a very prominent

---

86. Mancini, *Riflessioni pratiche,* 43.

87. On Gasparini's students see Franco Piperno, "Francesco Gasparini, le sue abitazioni romane, i suoi allievi coabitanti (1717–1727)," *Esercizi: Arte, musica, spettacolo* 4 (1981): 104–15. The letter of recommendation was written by Teresa Bolognini Fontana (from Turin, 27 September 1752) and is no. 769 in the Schnoebelen catalog, *Padre Martini's Collection.*

teacher, however.[88] The teacher's claims might be less stringent and for a more limited time span; in any event they indicated a practical involvement in the student's professional career.

One eighteenth-century singing school that merits special mention is that of Antonio Maria Bernacchi, a Bolognese castrato and a good friend of Padre Martini's and Carlo Broschi's. Bernacchi, who was at the height of his fame when he decided to open a school, usually took singers who had already made their reputations: he gave lessons to Broschi (Farinelli) after the latter had studied with Porpora, to Giambattista Mancini after he had studied with Leonardo Leo, to Anton Raaff after his studies with Giovanni Ferrandini, to Vittoria Tesi after her period in Florence with Francesco Redi, and to Gioacchino Conti and Giuseppe Appiani when both men were well started in their careers. Some of these singers only took lessons for a few months, as in the case of the tenor Pietro Paolo Carnoli, or, like Farinelli, during one season when Bernacchi and he were working in the same theater. In other cases, however, students worked for years with Bernacchi, lived in his house, and had ongoing personal relations with their teacher. By 1739 Bernacchi was already surrounded by a "noble brigade" of students whose every activity he supervised: he wrote sight-reading exercises for them (as did most of the better teachers), and on occasion he helped them prepare music for performance. In September 1753 he asked his friend Martini for pieces for "Venturino" (Ventura Rocchetti) to sing in Alessandria not long after. This student must not have been among the most gifted, since the maestro commented that "you have to adapt to the wind that's blowing when you're dealing with boats with no oars." That may be why he asked the composer not to "oblige him to sustain above a delasolre [D above middle C in the solmization system], thus leaving [his voice] free and exposed; if you like you can incorporate a messa di voce on C solfaut [middle C]." Bernacchi then asked Martini "to have the parts copied out with the bass line [only], and send them along right away, because I am looking forward to rehearsing it with him myself." The maestro was fully aware of the resources of that particular voice, and he intended to bring out the best in it with the proper instrumentation. On another occasion he asked to have the solo portions of a motet extended so as to show off the

---

88. This contract, drawn up between the teacher, Giuseppe Santarelli (who had been an opera singer and, after 1749, a papal chorister), and Clementina Closè, is in the Masseangeli manuscript collection at the Accademia Filarmonica of Bologna; it is described in the *Catalogo della collezione d'autografi lasciata alla R. Accademia Filarmonica di Bologna* (Bologna, 1881), 362. Another document from a few years earlier, regarding a less famous teacher, stipulates that he was to receive one-fifth of the student's earnings for only three years: see *Parma, Conservatorio di musica: Studi e ricerche*, ed. Guido Piamonte and Gaspare Nello Vetro (Parma: Battei, n.d.), 39, which also includes the *Sistema da osservarsi dalla scuola de' cantanti stabilita dalla Reale Direzione Generale de' spettacoli, e diretta dal sig.r maestro Francesco Poncini*.

abilities of some other students.[89] That particular exchange concerned sacred music, to be supplied by a friend who was happy to comply, but singers' requests to composers for music for the theater were not much different. Singers' requests, then, were not necessarily capricious, pretentious, or unreasonable; they were part of the painstaking preparation on which the success of a performance depended.

Bernacchi's school provides a paradigm of a small but compact community tied together by personal as well as artistic relations, but it would be mistaken to think that the singers associated in this way were all marked by one style rigidly imposed by their teacher. To the contrary each student was encouraged to follow his own inclinations and vocal capabilities. The teacher did not produce copies of himself but rather gave his students the techniques they needed in order to extend their own capabilities in all possible directions.[90] Developing vocal agility did not ipso facto exclude practice of the "pathetic" style, and working for a pure, sweet tone did not exclude the study of recitation. It is difficult to define Bernacchi's own singing style: Francesco Algarotti called him the "Marino of modern license,"[91] but Metastasio called him a "great teacher of how to place, expand, and sustain the voice; of how to finish with clarity whatever one takes on, and of how always to subject ability to reason."[92] They were probably both right, each on his own terms. Our task is to note their judgments without making facile and definitive stylistic classifications of our own. Flexibility and a facility in passing from one style to another increased a singer's chances of success, and not coincidentally the two leading Italian theorists of the century (Tosi and Mancini) agreed that the "universal singer"—that is, the singer who could shine in all styles—was the supreme goal. Bernacchi himself was such a singer: in London in 1729 "he did not please the first evening, but on the second, he changed method

89. On Bernacchi and his school see the letter of Giambattista Mancini to Padre Martini of 4 January 1769, in Schnoebelen, *Padre Martini's Collection*, no. 2876. On lessons to Farinelli see Giovenale Sacchi, *Vita del cavaliere don Carlo Broschi* (Venice, 1784), 13; letter of Francesco Benzoni to Martini of 21 July 1739; letter of Bernacchi to Martini of 7 September 1753; letter of Bernacchi to Martini, n.d. (published in part in Frati, "Antonio Bernacchi," 483), all in Schnoebelen, *Padre Martini's Collection*, nos. 628, 660, and 666, respectively.

90. Mancini (who had studied with Bernacchi) stated, "A worthy and competent teacher cannot simply keep to one manner of instructing his students; but . . . in order to form perfect singers, he must have a thorough grasp of various manners of handling them, and then apply these judiciously in each practical case as need dictates"; Mancini, *Riflessioni pratiche*, 24.

91. Francesco Algarotti, *Saggio sopra l'opera in musica*, 2d ed. (Livorno, 1763; reprint ed., Bologna: FARAP, 1975). The first edition of this work, published in 1755 when the singer was still alive, does not mention Bernacchi; a modern edition is of the first edition is available, ed. Giovanni da Pozzo (Bari: Laterza: 1963). The poet Giambattista Marino (1569–1625) was known for his florid, highly elaborated style.

92. Letter of 21 January 1753 from Vienna, in Metastasio, *Tutte le opere*, 3:784–85.

and pleased."[93] The "graduates" of his school met with varying success. On the one hand there was Ventura Rocchetti, whom a fellow performer (in 1753) judged to be "an old-fashioned singer, full of trills, mordents, acciaccaturas, and appoggiaturas a half-measure long."[94] On the other hand there were students like Tommaso Guarducci, Giovanni Tedeschi, and the tenors Anton Raaff and Carlo Carlani, who became famous and "with universal approval, distinguished themselves, each in his varied, refined, and appropriate style."[95]

In short a school might give a singer a useful general framework, but schools should not be seen automatically as a determining factor from a stylistic point of view. The relationship between the teacher and the student was not a linear, evolutionary process involving the preservation of a specific style. Furthermore, during the course of a career in opera, every singer went through a number of phases. After listening to the authoritative advice of Emperor Charles VI, Farinelli turned to a more moderated style than in his younger years. Farinelli was then famous, and he could permit himself the luxury of developing aristocratic tastes, but his universal fame had been won by dazzling a less sophisticated public with his virtuosity and stunning his hearers with his "superhuman" vocal gifts.[96]

It is not realistic to associate either schools or individual singers with inflexible stylistic ideals; both teachers and their pupils were in touch with a living theatrical tradition and with the dynamic evolution of taste. An aria that was a great success in Vienna might bore the Bolognese; a cadenza that sent the Venetian audience in the Teatro Sant'Angelo into a frenzy of enthusiasm might be thought tiresome by the public of the Teatro San Giovanni Grisostomo in that same city. Style changed to follow the elusive ups and downs of personal and local taste.

---

93. Letter of Paolo Rolli to Giuseppe Riva, December 1729, in Sesto Fassini, *Il melodramma italiano a Londra nella prima metà del Settecento* (Turin, 1914; reprint ed., Bologna: Arnaldo Forni, 1979), 86–87.

94. Such was the opinion of the singer Giuseppe Tibaldi, expressed in a letter of 10 January 1753 to Martini, published and discussed in Pierluigi Petrobelli, "Un cantante fischiato e le appoggiature di mezza battuta: Cronaca teatrale e prassi esecutive alla metà del '700," in *Studies in Renaissance and Baroque Music in Honor of Arthur Mendel*, ed. Robert L. Marshall (Kassel: Bärenreiter; Hackensack, N.J.: Boonin, 1974), 363–76, quotation 365–66.

95. Mancini, *Riflessioni pratiche*, 22.

96. The episode is referred to in Charles Burney, *The Present State of Music in France and Italy* (London,1771), 207–8, and in a slightly different version in Sacchi, *Vita del cavaliere don Carlo Broschi*, 15, where it is dated as occurring in 1732. On Broschi/Farinelli's career see also Robert Freeman, "Farinello and His Repertory," in *Studies in Renaissance and Baroque Music in Honor of Arthur Mendel*, ed. Robert L. Marshall (Kassel: Bärenreiter; Hackensack, N.J.: Boonin, 1974), 301–30.

A discussion of private schools requires a comment on the situation of female singers, which was notably different from that of their male counterparts. Mental attitudes as well as social structures excluded women from the organized musical associations, which offered their members not only the immaterial benefits of honor and status but medical and financial assistance in case of need. Female teachers continued to be a rarity, and it would simply have been unthinkable for a female student to lodge in the house of a male teacher. Furthermore, a *virtuosa* was not expected to have the same level of preparation as her male counterpart, and it is not coincidental that the term *canterina,* with its light but affectionately disparaging tone, existed only in the feminine. Marcello mocked the *canterina* for using a professional accessory typical of the "weaker sex," the *libro dei passi* (book of ornamentations): "She will have the embellishments, the variations, the fine ornaments, etc., written for her by Maestro Crica [crack-voice] in the usual book written for that purpose, which she will carry with her through all lands."[97] Tosi agreed that it was characteristic of female singers to have ornaments written down rather than to be able to improvise them, and he exhorted all who aspired to becoming good singers not to imitate them. Female singers were often accompanied on their travels or assisted locally by a teacher who would act as a vocal coach, teaching them their roles and the indispensable embellishments. One contract written in Turin in 1765 explicitly stated the theater's obligation to procure "for Signora Suardi a coach for the music . . . whenever she shall have need of one."[98]

Obviously there were exceptions to the rule. One was the famous Francesca Vanini Boschi, who "for the glory of her sex, has shown that the women who study can teach even good men the rarest artifice with the same rules." Moreover, in light of later developments in the profession, it seems prophetic that as early as 1723, Tosi praised two women, Francesca Cuzzoni and Faustina Bordoni, as supreme in their profession.[99] Several decades had to pass, however, before a *prima donna,* Anna Maria Pellegrini Celoni, published a

---

97. Marcello, *Il teatro alla moda,* 46.

98. On the interesting figure of the teacher of female singers, Gaetano Benati, see Durante, "Alcune considerazioni," 450, 465–69; Eleanor Selfridge-Field, "Marcello, Sant'Angelo, and *Il teatro alla moda,*" in *Antonio Vivaldi: Teatro musicale, cultura e società,* ed. Lorenzo Bianconi and Giovanni Morelli, Studi di musica veneta: Quaderni vivaldiani (Florence: Olschki, 1982), 2:533–46, esp. 539–40. The Turin contract is published in Marie-Thérèse Bouquet, *Il teatro di corte: Dalle origini al 1788,* vol. 1 of *La Storia del Teatro Regio di Torino,* ed. Alberto Basso, 5 vols. (Turin: Cassa di Risparmio di Torino, 1976–83), 229; the chapter on singers in that same volume (pages 224–37) presents a wealth of information on contract terms and theatrical practices.

99. Tosi, *Opinioni de' cantori,* 65, 98.

treatise on singing or before the Accademia Filarmonica of Bologna sponsored funeral ceremonies for a female member.[100]

— ‒

During the course of the first century of the history of opera, relations between the church and the theater concerning singers underwent a radical
change: while initially the theater had made extensive use of ecclesiastical
singers, by the beginning of the eighteenth century it was the churches that
were borrowing famous voices from the theater. On the stage a singer could
achieve fame and wealth; the chapel offered advantages of a different sort—
stability, a secure position, and (almost always) a guarantee of a pension on
retirement. In Loreto, the seat of a famous chapel, admission to the choir and
to its benefits was granted by an open competition in three stages:

> Singing in public in church, before a full gathering of the people, singers, *maestro
> di cappella,* the organist, and the governor, first a plainchant antiphon sung alone;
> second, a three-voiced or four-voiced piece by Palestina [Palestrina]; third, a new
> solo composition with organ accompaniment. After which the candidate passes on
> to election by vote, which is done here by ballot. The competitors must present
> themselves before the jury with their baptismal certificates, because if someone is
> of advanced age he will not be admitted to the competition; that is, after reaching
> forty years of age or thereabouts it is unlikely [for anyone] to be admitted.[101]

A post as an ecclesiastical singer did not necessarily exclude theatrical activities, particularly since the chapels did not require their singers all the time.
There is ample documentation of forms of dual employment, for example, in
Venice among the singers at Saint Mark's basilica in the late seventeenth to
the early eighteenth centuries. When it proved impossible to reconcile the two
sorts of service, it was the theater that won out: Saint Mark's fired many of
its choristers who were also opera singers precisely for having deserted the
chapel for theatrical engagements.[102] Behind its severe facade, however, the

---

100. The treatise was Anna Maria Pellegrini Celoni's, *Grammatica o siano regole di ben cantare* (Rome, 1810), a highly esteemed method that was also published in German translation. The
solemn funeral mass is mentioned in Pietro Giordani, *Elogio a Maria Brizzi Giorgi* (Bologna,
1813).

101. Letter of Andrea Basili to Padre Martini of 17 November 1767, Schnoebelen, *Padre
Martini's Collection,* no. 502.

102. See Olga Termini, "Singers at San Marco in Venice: The Competition between Church
and Theatre (c 1675–c 1725)," *Royal Musical Association Research Chronicle* 17 (1981): 65–96.
For exchanges between theatrical and ecclesiastical circles in Rome, see Giancarlo Rostirolla,
"Maestri di cappella, organisti, cantanti e strumentisti attivi in Roma nella metà Settecento," *Note
d'archivio* n.s. 2 (1984): 195–269.

church really had little choice in the matter, since it found it impossible to keep increasingly costly professional singers on a full-time basis. The highest salary paid to a chorister in Saint Mark's in the early 1700s, 960 Venetian lire per year, was a good deal lower than a similar singer's earnings for a theatrical season (which in 1720 might reach something like 17,000 Venetian lire).[103] Consequently it became increasingly customary for singers to accept church engagements only for the few main holidays—Christmas, Holy Week, and Ascension Day.

Even outside Venice ecclesiastical institutions called more and more often on the "good heart" of the latest fashionable opera singers to bolster a reputation that their increasingly mediocre choirs no longer could guarantee. In Bologna, a city that never lacked singers, Senator Francesco Albergati had to turn to the influential Padre Martini to obtain opera singers at a reasonable price.[104]

> I beg of you to . . . persuade Signor Giuseppe Tibaldi and Signor Aprili [Giuseppe Aprile] to sing in San Petronio on the occasion of the music of our Signor Zanotti. They will certainly do for you what they would not do for me, and they are right. Please urge them to do this, as it were, out of devotion, because the church can offer them very little.

Things were not much different in Rome, where the *maestro di cappella* of the basilica of Saint John Lateran, Girolamo Chiti, complained, "We are in a famine of sopranos, and here in San Giovanni if those castratos [the opera singers who happened to be in Rome at the time] do not offer themselves, I don't know what we will do." Since these were among the greatest churches of Italy, we can well imagine the situation in lesser churches. In Forlì, for example, singers "not presently employed in the theater" were sought for two church services and an oratorio. This risky enterprise was to be prepared, with perhaps a rehearsal or two, in the following manner.[105]

> It is the custom for [the singers] to bring with them whatever arias they prefer, with the violin and bass parts, which [arias] will be adapted here to the appropriate

103. The comparison is based on the earnings of Antonio Formenti until 1714; see Termini, "Singers at San Marco," 83, and on the 1,000 zecchini paid to Faustina Bordoni in 1724, see the letter of Francesco Bettoni to Pierfrancesco Tosi of 24 February 1724, Bologna, Civico Museo Bibliografico musicale, Ep. Cod. 63, P. 141, 20, 1, computed in Venetian lire on the basis of the rates given in Bianconi and Walker, "Production, Consumption," 282–83.

104. Letter of Francesco Albergati to Padre Martini of 9 September 1761, in Schnoebelen, *Padre Martini's Collection,* no. 164.

105. The quotations that follow are from a letter of Girolamo Chiti to Padre Martini of 20 February 1748 and a letter of Ignazio Cirri to the same of 5 March 1788, respectively nos. 1383 and 1688 in Schnoebelen, *Padre Martini's Collection.*

meaning [by changing the text] and fitted into the recitatives that we have. We need two arias for the soprano and two others for the contralto, and also a duet for the same with its instrumental parts.

In this way the singers brought theatrical music and the practices of the opera house into the churches.

— ‑—

Among the many theater singers the so-called buffi formed a distinct sub-group. The term was at first used for performers in intermezzi; later, for those who specialized in comic works. This entire category of singers has long suffered from a summary and negative judgment that took them to task for vocal insufficiencies and exaggerated histrionics but was for the most part based on generalizations and on a hasty interpretation of contemporaneous sources. Critics set a higher standard for the buffo singers, taking as defects what would have been praised in singers of opera seria. The paradox that they were reproached for being too much actors and too little singers emphasizes the contradictions in a critical stance that as a matter of principle refused to recognize the importance of execution.[106]

More thoughtful evaluations have stressed the positive aspects of a happy combination of vocal qualities and stagecraft in the leading buffi, pointing out that theirs was a type of acting and a vocal style that was different from but not inferior to that of opera seria. The very famous duo of Antonio Ristorini and Rosa Ungarelli was called "a marvel of nature"; Ungarelli's acting in particular "would have moved a stone . . . with words that would have liquified bronze."[107] These singers may have stressed acting, but the scores show that their musical training could not have been substandard. The notion that the buffi were singers trained in the lesser schools is just as unfounded: their numbers included former students of Gasparini and Pistocchi and many members of the Accademia Filarmonica of Bologna.

Beyond such value judgments of the buffi, studies of their activities and travels have made important contributions to our knowledge of how the repertory circulated. At least three distinct phases in the organization of their

106. On problems regarding the singers of buffo roles in the first half of the eighteenth century, see Charles E. Troy, *The Comic Intermezzo: A Study in the History of Eighteenth-Century Italian Opera* (Ann Arbor, Mich.: UMI Research Press, 1979). See also (and especially) Franco Piperno, "Appunti sulla configurazione sociale e professionale delle 'parte buffe' al tempo di Vivaldi," in *Antonio Vivaldi: Teatro musicale, cultura e società*, ed. Lorenzo Bianconi and Giovanni Morelli, Studi di musica veneta: Quaderni vivaldiani (Florence: Olschki, 1982), 483–97; Franco Piperno, "Buffe e buffi (considerazioni sulla professionalità degli interpreti di scene buffe ed intermezzi)," *Rivista italiana di musicologia* 17 (1982): 240–84.

107. Piperno, "Appunti sulla configurazione sociale," 485.

operations have been identified for the first half of the eighteenth century. In the first of these the buffo singers were associated with "serious" singers on a equal footing in productions that included comic scenes; in a second phase fixed pairs of buffi traveled from one theater to another, ready to offer a vast repertory of two-character intermezzi that could be put on between the acts of any opera; in the third phase (after 1730) the fixed duos tended to disappear as individual buffo singers traveled, performing on each occasion with a partner who specialized in the complementary roles of the same repertory. The long-lasting success of Pergolesi's *La serva padrona* can be explained not only by the excellence of its music but by its exceptionally broad diffusion, given that the score came onto the opera circuit at a time when the sort of singers best capable of performing it reached a high point in their mobility.[108]

Many questions remain unanswered regarding the connections between the singers of intermezzi and the protagonists of the full-scale comic operas that became increasingly popular during the first half of the eighteenth century. When demand increased, where did the increased numbers of singers come from? What were the consequences of this change within the professional sphere of opera seria? From 1720 to 1770 in Venice the proportions of productions of opera seria and opera buffa were inverted in favor of the latter, bringing a parallel change in personnel requirements. For the first time there was less call for the older style of *virtuoso*, hence for castratos. One might be tempted to draw a connection between this decline in demand and Mancini's heartfelt declaration of a "crisis" among the singing schools in Italy. One might also entertain the notion that the reasons Mancini gave for that crisis (a lack of excellent church singers, the greed of teachers who pushed their students into a premature debut) were perhaps the early effects of new market conditions. Finally the question is inevitably connected with the definitive disappearance of the castratos in the early nineteenth century, a phenomenon that remains enigmatic only if it is considered to be sudden[109] rather than being recognized as the end result of a gradual decline in demand over the long run.

In opera seria, which was long considered the more prestigious genre for

108. See Franco Piperno, "Gli interpreti buffi di Pergolesi: Note sulla diffusione della *Serva Padrona*," in *Studi pergolesiani/Pergolesi Studies*, ed. Francesco Degrada, 2 vols. (Florence: La Nuova Italia, 1986), 1:166–77, and "Note sulla diffusione degli intermezzi di J. A. Hasse (1726–1741)," *Analecta Musicologica* 25 (1987): 267–86. On opera buffa itself see Piero Weiss, "La diffusione del repertorio operistico nell'Italia del Settecento: Il caso dell'opera buffa," in *Civiltà teatrale e Settecento emiliano*, ed. Susi Davoli (Bologna: Il Mulino, 1986), 241–56. On the consequences of the buffo singer Celeste Resse Gismondi's move to London, see Reinhard Strohm, "Comic Traditions in Handel's *Orlando*," in *Essays on Handel and Italian Opera* (Cambridge: Cambridge University Press, 1985), 249–69, 287–88.

109. As, for example, in Angus Heriot, *The Castrati in Opera* (London: Secker and Warburg, 1956), 9–22.

a singer in spite of its declining popularity, various combinations of gender and vocal register were possible when putting together a singer and a role. Women's roles could be taken by "natural" female voices or by castratos; the latter were in fact obligatory in states or cities that did not permit public performances by female singers (the Papal States, with the exception of Bologna and the other provinces governed by a legate, Vienna, and the Palatinate). Male roles could be assigned to a man (castrato or not) or to a woman, vocal tessitura could be high or low, and there was no established, necessary relationship between males roles and an actual male vocal range.[110] One emblematic case was the serenata by Johann Adolphe Hasse in *Antonio e Cleopatra,* which was performed in Naples in 1725 with Farinelli in the leading female role and Vittoria Tesi as the male lead.

Statistically it was the age of the character rather than his or her gender that quite observably determined the choice of tessitura. The rule was, the younger the character, the higher the voice. The fact that male voices become lower with puberty may have created some semblance of justification for this rule, even when the characters were not in fact adolescents. For the most part the castratos monopolized the young lovers' and heroes' parts, while female singers, who in many cases specialized in roles *en travesti,* sang the role of the *secondo uomo* and often the male lead. The most famous among these— Lucia Lancetti, Anna Maria Laurenti, Antonia Margherita Merighi, and Vittoria Tesi—were mezzo-sopranos or contraltos. Obviously if the character was involved in a transsexual disguise, the use of a woman or a castrato added to the efficacy of the portrayal. A lower voice, on the other hand, denoted age or wisdom. Tenors played fathers, advisors, or traitors, all parts important for moving the plot along or winding it up,[111] while basses played older men or persons endowed with magical or supernatural powers.

Within this general picture there were conspicuous exceptions, in particular as regards the careers of some tenors who worked their way up from secondary parts to play male leads. Annibale Pio Fabbri was already a *primo uomo* in *L'incoronazione di Dario* (Venice, 1717) and sang the title role in an *Artaserse* in a company that included several castratos (Rome, 1721). The same was true of many others among the leading tenors of the century: Carlo

110. On this problem see Roger Covell, "Voice Registers as an Index of Age and Status in Opera Seria," in *Opera and Vivaldi,* ed. Michael Collins and Elise K. Kirk (Austin: University of Texas Press, 1984), 193–210, even though this study takes for granted the idea that the relationship between the character and the vocal register was regulated a priori by a convention of an essentially aesthetic and symbolic nature. Such a convention was in fact subject to other conditions; it was the status of the singer and not the importance of the character that played the greater role in determining the choice of vocal register (making the latter not so much a choice as a consequence).

111. A second-string castrato, especially if he were no longer in his first youth, could also take such roles; see Lindgren, "La carriera di Gaetano Berenstadt," 39, 42, and passim.

Carlani, Gregorio Babbi, Giovanni Paita, Giovanni Battista Pinacci, Francesco Borosini, Giuseppe Tibaldi, Anton Raaff, and Angelo Amorevoli. Another factor that might be just as decisive as the relationship between age and register was the status of the performer, who might have the lead role in an opera even though he was not a soprano or a contralto. Moreover, the vocal art of the tenors and basses, understood as a complex of figurations and stylistic elements in performance practice, was no different from that of the higher voices; indeed, the lower voices stood out to the extent that they could imitate the soprano.[112]

In any case the relationship between the role and the vocal register should not be understood as rigid; opera was still made up of a series of discrete and adaptable, if not actually interchangeable, units. Just as it was acceptable to alter the dramatic text and desirable to update the musical score, it was also perfectly legitimate to have Alexander the Great be a tenor rather than a soprano or, paradoxically and at the other extreme, to have a castrato play a father. This characteristic elasticity of vocal register thus took on a dramatic function very different from the one it would have in the age of romanticism, for example, when the role (and hence the singer's contribution to a role) was conceived of and fixed musically within well-defined limits. In eighteenth-century opera seria, singers who performed the lead established an ongoing relationship with their own previous roles.[113] A *primo uomo* or a *prima donna* usually sang the same role in successive productions of a given dramatic text, whether the music changed or not. This detail reveals both the accessory nature of the musical score and the central importance of the relationship between voice and the character being played—taking "voice" to mean not a type or a register but the specific voice of one singer or another and "character" to indicate the result of a protracted relationship between an actor and a text (through a variety of musical scores). This relationship

112. Even a bass might appear in a title role if he was an exceptionally fine singer, as was the case with the very famous Antonfrancesco Carli, who sang leads (*Rodomonte sdegnato* and *Lucio Papirio* [Venice, Teatro Sant'Angelo, 1714 and 1715, respectively] and other operas). Still, the *stile di basso* (bass style) was a precise notion for the operatic composer of the early eighteenth century. Benedetto Marcello used the term in his *Teatro alla moda* (23): "Some arias will be composed in *stile di basso* even though they are meant for contraltos and sopranos." He was most probably referring to a systematic use of large intervals, at times of more than an octave. Even the bass parts that were "soprano-like" in their figuration, however, were not soprano parts simply "transposed" to a bass register. Rather, they used the voice in a relatively lower register than the one best suited to high voices.

113. See Reinhard Strohm, "Metastasios *Alessandro nell'Indie* und seine frühesten Vertonungen," in *Probleme der Händelschen Oper (inbesondere am Beispiel "Poro")*, ed. Walther Siegmund-Schultze (Halle: Martin-Luther-Universität, 1982), 40–61, esp. 50 and 55–59, in English translation as "Metastasio's *Alessandro nell'Indie* and its Earliest Settings," in *Essays on Handel and Italian Opera*, 232–48.

generated a quite particular sort of identity between the interpreter and the role.

Eighteenth-century librettos very seldom use the terms "soprano," "contralto," "tenor," and "bass," and when the terms do appear they refer to the singer, never to the character in the drama. They are thus indications that require interpretation: for instance, it was an affectation typical of castratos to consider themselves sopranos rather than contraltos. Moreover, the musical definition of those terms did not correspond to the modern one, not only (and not so much) because vocal tessitura has shifted higher or lower but rather because there was no fixed definition of vocal ranges comparable to the one that arose during the course of the nineteenth century in connection with a relatively stable repertory. Leaving terms aside, then, the surest way to ascertain the range of an eighteenth-century singer is the obvious one of direct examination of the scores written for him or her, keeping in mind, however, that pitch varied from one part of Italy to another.[114]

5. An Italian "School": Images and Economic Conditions

At the beginning of the twentieth century, Luigi Leonesi, himself a teacher, defined the eighteenth century as the golden age of the singing schools. Although this explicit mythmaking was part of an ongoing quarrel with the view of the vocal art proposed by the verismo school and the Wagnerian school, it was not completely unfounded. The two major theorists of the eighteenth century, Tosi and Mancini, handed down through their treatises the record of a didactic system that (within the horizon of expectations of its age) had reached a high point in maturity and efficacy. Tosi's *Opinioni de' cantori antichi e moderni* and Mancini's *Riflessioni pratiche sopra il canto figurato* contain clear and, insofar as possible, exhaustive precepts; even today they are required reading for anyone interested in the vocal art of the eighteenth century. Scholars have concentrated on the similarities between the two works

---

114. In this connection Tosi remarked, "Let him [the Master] always use the Scholar to the Pitch of Lombardy [that is, northern Italy in general] and not that of Rome" (*Opinioni de' cantori*, 16; *Observations on the Florid Song*, 26). Tosi's English translator, John Ernest Galliard, adds that "the pitch of Lombardy, or Venice, is something more than half a tone higher than in Rome" (*Observations on the Florid Song*, 27). This testimony is contradicted by the more trustworthy evidence of Marquis Gian Giuseppe Orsi, who states in his "Annotazioni" to Muratori's *La perfetta poesia italiana*, "The choir singer of Rome [sings] higher than the Bologna chorister by a tone; and thus all our organs, harpsichords, or other instruments are regularly tuned one tone lower than the Roman ones." Orsi's manuscript, preserved in Modena at the Biblioteca Estense, Archivio muratoriano, filza VI, fasc. 4, has been published in part in Marta Lucchi, "Problemi di estetica musicale negli scritti di L. A. Muratori," in *Aspetti e problemi del Settecento modenese* (Modena: Aedes Muratoriana, 1982), 219–40, esp. 232.

(almost as if they could provide a homogeneous base for Italian "bel canto") and have ignored their differences, which are obvious and significant. In fact by examining where these two works disagree, we can discern how teaching changed over time. We can note in Mancini, for example, the definitive abandonment of the Guidonian sight-reading system and its mutations. Moreover, Mancini includes two chapters that clearly contain new materials. Chapter 2 gives a historical treatment of singing schools from the late seventeenth century; Chapter 3 contains admonitions to parents who might be thinking of having their son castrated. Such materials were the result of a changing context, but many aspects of teaching also changed from one work to the other. For example, Tosi stresses the importance of making a clear distinction between three types of recitative (*da chiesa* for a religious setting; *da camera* for chamber performance; *da teatro* for the opera stage). Mancini considers the distinction incomprehensible and abandons it. All of Tosi's quarrels with virtuosity are forgotten in Mancini, who, on the other hand, shows a particular interest in vocal agility and theorizes about the many techniques of florid singing—"natural" agility, the *martellato* ("hammered" repetition of one note), the *arpeggiato*, the *canto di sbalzo* (leaping), etc. Tosi devotes an entire chapter of his treatise to *passi* (which Galliard translates as "graces"), not to be confused with *passaggi* (improvised, ornamented passages in general); Mancini refers to them only incidentally. It is worth noting in passing that by the midcentury, the German translator of Tosi's *Opinioni*, Johann Friedrich Agricola, was unfamiliar with the *strascino*, a form of ornamentation that Tosi considered of capital importance.

Priorities and interests changed, then: embellishments of an "emotional" *(affettuoso)* sort, particularly as used in slow and moderately slow arias, were replaced in Mancini's treatise by an interest in vocal agility and the bravura style, elements that were increasingly practiced, investigated, and cataloged. Mancini's treatise also shows, both in its general outline and its language, more and more exclusive emphasis on the *virtuoso* as a singer of opera: while Tosi's lessons were addressed to a singer who could perform with equal ease in the three styles of church, chamber, and theater, Mancini's ideal reader was a theatrical singer who, if he should chance to sing elsewhere, transferred operatic style to the new venue. What remained unchanged from one treatise to the other was the theory of a fusion in timbre to give a smooth transition between chest tones and head tones, and a preference for a pure, "sweet" timbre and a light voice production that facilitated rapid vocalization with an unforced but carrying sonority.

As for their literary qualities, Mancini's treatise lacked the rhetorical color and the polemical thrust that made Tosi's *Opinioni* (an extremely hybrid work halfway between a pamphlet and a genuine treatise) so successful. Later theorists, who showed an increasing interest in giving their own treatises a (genuine or presumed) scientific cast, took Mancini's *Riflessioni* as their model, at least for its focus on specifics and its methodical cast. Obviously it would be unjust to interpret all the differences between Tosi's and Mancini's works as demonstrating an evolution; they were often simple differences in method (even of apparently unimportant detail) of the sort that always sets one school and one teacher apart from another.

A new sort of didactic materials began to be popular early in the eighteenth century, when sight-reading exercises for voice with basso continuo were added to the ample and continuing production of unaccompanied *bicinia*. Such solmization exercises (*solfeggi*) with bass were composed by all the best singing teachers, who tailored them to the measure of their own students. Rarely published, they have survived, for the most part, in manuscript form. As works of a purely functional nature, not intended for concert performance, they have been ignored by musicologists and—more surprisingly— by vocal teachers, even though they are potentially one of the most efficacious means for reconstructing eighteenth-century vocal styles. They include actual solmization exercises of medium difficulty and vocalization exercises of an extremely high level of difficulty. Such more properly technical exercises were used in combination with the study of the madrigal repertory and, in particular, the cantatas of Alessandro Scarlatti, Emanuele d'Astorga, Gasparini, Marcello, and Porpora, all masters of the first half of the century but already considered canonical by Mancini's time. Duets with bass accompaniment (not to be confused with the beginners' *bicinia*) were used to perfect intonation and to work on homogeneous voice production in all registers.

Although such theoretical documents are clear and give explicit advice regarding a course of study and systems for learning, they are ambiguous on the level of aesthetics. Some of Tosi's statements are even contradictory: for example, he warmly defends the "pathetic" style, but he also recommends that the student work on *passaggi,* and he even praises the greatest exponent of vocal agility, Faustina Bordoni. Here he is guilty of the same inconsistency that he reproaches in singers who, according to him, "praise the Pathetick, yet sing the *Allegro*." Tosi declares himself incapable of understanding why the pathetic style should be in decline: "Ask all the Musicians in general, what their thoughts are of the Pathetick, they all agree in the same Opinion (a thing that seldom happens) and answer, that the *Pathetick* is what most sweetly affects the Soul, and is the strongest Basis of Harmony." [115] It is clear that the theorists were unable to produce a justification for the fast spreading "allegro" style and limited their efforts to reiterating the dominant literary ideol-

---

115. Tosi, *Opinioni de' cantori,* 68–69; quoted from *Observations on the Florid Song,* 108, 107.

ogy. This made a dual morality ("praising the pathetic and singing the allegro") imperative. The only alternative was to find a scapegoat: the singer attributed ultimate responsibility for bad taste to the public. Vincenzio Martinelli used that argument to defend Porpora's pupils.

> If at times these [students] have let themselves be carried away, floating through the clouds, as one might say, with their warblings and their cadenzas, this must be imputed to the extremely bad taste that has sprung up everywhere, which has made them fear not being held accomplished and expert as much as the others if from time to time they too do not do such demonstrations, rather than [being imputed] to their own lack of standards, since they are, as I have many times been told, the first to give similar extravagances their due blame.[116]

Twenty-five years later (a quarter century that had seen, among other things, the appearance of Gluck's "reformed" operas), the composer and singer Giuseppe Millico dusted off roughly the same arguments in his preface to his score for *La pietà d'amore*.

> Observant critics will find my music not totally purified of certain errors that are condemned by true good taste, and they will observe one or two brief warblings and some repetitions of words. . . . I myself recognize this defect, and I have overlooked it, but not without a reason: I have not thought it proper suddenly to go against the genius of a nation already seduced by the vivacity of some singers who work at resembling the gracious warblings of the nightingales more than [at producing] solid melody that penetrates the heart.[117]

Arguments that had been formulated at the beginning of the century thus reemerged periodically, and, in the absence of more telling comparisons from the musical sources themselves, their musical referent is too generic to be interpreted as indications of genuine changes in style. In reality the dispute between the pathetic style and the *stile d'agilità* cropped up with every reappearance of the notion that opera should be "tragedy in music." Furthermore, anyone interested in stylistic analysis needs to keep in mind that the musical referent of terms such as "allegro" and "pathetic" changed through time. For example, the famous "pathetic aria" that Ventura Rocchetti sang in the third

---

116. Vincenzio Martinelli, *Lettere familiari e critiche* (London, 1758), 362–63, quoted in Durante, "Alcune considerazioni," 464–65.

117. Ludwig Finscher, "Der Opernsänger als Komponist: Giuseppe Millico und seine Oper *La pietà d'amore*," in *Opernstudien: Anna Amalie Abert zum 65. Geburtstag*, ed. Klaus Hortschansky (Tutzing: Schneider, 1975), 57–90, quotation 69.

act of Niccolò Jommelli's *Attilio Regolo* (Rome, 1753),[118] with its long vocalizations (up to sixty-eight consecutive notes) and its melodic line broken by jumps of as much as an octave and a fifth, represented a type of the "pathetic" that was in reality a far cry from the "pathetic" that Tosi loved, which was a more legato, for the most part syllabic style of singing that gave the singer a chance to shine in the improvisation of tasteful *passi* and skillful rhythmic variations. Tracing a change in style thus cannot be limited to defining when the "pathetic" predominated over the "allegro" or vice versa but must discern what distinguished the "pathetic" in the 1720s from the "pathetic" of the 1750s or the 1790s. Only then can we understand how the singing schools responded to changing needs.

Millico had something to say on the subject (in which Gluck's influence is clear). Millico exhorted singers "to exercise their natural voice . . . so as to make it as obedient and flexible as dough, so that it can change and take all colors, even at times to the point of becoming harsh and strident if the violence of a passion should require it."[119] What Millico had in mind here was an original use of the voice to respond to the ideals of the Gluckian reform. It is clear that his vision differs from the earlier ideal of pure *soavità,* but it would be hazardous to speak of a "new school." These were perhaps the first signs of a tendency that would develop during the first half of the nineteenth century. We can see reflections of the same tendency in treatises on vocal music, not so much in positive terms in the more advanced works as indirectly in the more reactionary works, where such novelties are pilloried in the name of eighteenth-century ideals that were on the decline. We learn, for instance, from a passage in a treatise by Heinrich Ferdinand Mannstein (1835) complaining about Bernacchi's method that basses no longer worked on the transition from one register to another and that the basic exercise of holding a note, varying its intensity *(filare i suoni)* was practiced less and less. Mannstein stated that he was scandalized that the "false opinion" was gaining ground that "true talent has no need of cultivation or study; there are some who even claim that studies are harmful and that [a singer] shines more

118. See Petrobelli, "Un cantante fischiato," 372–73.

119. Quoted in Finscher, "Der Opernsänger," 70. A yearning for a new vocal style appears as well in a letter from Metastasio to Saverio Mattei (5 April 1770); see Metastasio, *Tutte le opere,* 4:813–19. He deplores the voice of the "modern" singers of his day, "weakened in the arpeggios, the trills, and the runs," where he would prefer them "firm and robust . . . that shake the organs of our hearing with a force equal to [our] delight and that thrust forward their effects to penetrate the very depths of our souls." The French vocal tradition may have had an influence on Italian styles: Pierre-Louis Ginguené passed on the anecdote that Tommaso Traetta noted on the score of *Sofonisba* (Vienna, 1762) that he wanted the singer to produce an *urlo alla francese* (a French-style bellow)—see Amintore Galli, *Estetica della musica: ossia, Del bello nella musica sacra, teatrale e da concerto in ordine alla sua storia* (Turin: Bocca, 1900; reprint ed., Bologna: Arnaldo Forni, 1979), 573 n.2.

brilliantly when everything is permitted to come directly from the hands of nature." [120]

The very foundations of the old didactic system seem to be under attack here in the name of a conception—typical of a transitional phase—of dramatic singing that was markedly original, though confused and undisciplined.

Toward the end of the eighteenth century, the art of singing, as practiced in Italy, enjoyed singular prestige throughout Europe, thanks to the growing circulation of Italian opera and Italian singers, but also thanks to the emigration of singing teachers and the diffusion of their teaching methods.

John Galliard's translation of Tosi's *Opinioni*, which bristled with explanatory notes, had already been published in 1742 in London, and at the end of the century the uninterrupted success of Italian methods was rekindled by the *Instruction of Mr. Tenducci to His Students* (London, ca. 1785) and Giuseppe Aprile's *The Modern Italian Method of Singing* (London, 1791). In German lands the presence of Italian singers and composers in the courts often went along with the establishment of a singing school, as with Ferrandini's school in Munich, Porpora's in Dresden, Mancini's in Vienna, and many others. In 1757 Johann Friedrich Agricola published a heavily annotated edition of Tosi's treatise. The success of Italian teaching methods was even more noteworthy in France, a nation by tradition less favorable to Italian tastes and one that had long remained self-sufficient and cultivated a solid local tradition. In 1776 the French translation of Mancini's *Pensieri e riflessioni pratiche* was published in Paris (as *L'art du chant figuré*), and several collections of Italian *solfeggi* that had circulated in manuscript in their homeland were printed in France. The preface of the *Solfèges d'Italie*, signed by Lévesque and Bêche, explained,

> The editors of this work, seeking to make available the solfèges of the great masters of Italy, at first had no other intention than the training of the young persons of the royal chapel whose education has been entrusted to them. The rapid progress in music of these young persons, thanks to these learned precepts, has given rise to the idea of bringing together a large number of [such exercises], from which we have chosen the ones that make up this method. [121]

Even after the French Revolution Italian teaching methods dominated the field: one of the authors of the *Méthode de chant du Conservatoire* (Paris,

---

120. Heinrich Ferdinand Mannstein, *Das System der grossen Gesangschule des Bernacchi von Bologna . . . nebst klassischen, bisher ungedruckten Singübungen von Meistern aus derselben Schule* (Dresden, [ca. 1835]), 68.

121. Lévesque and Bêche, *Solfèges d'Italie avec la basse chiffrée, composés par Leo, Durante, Scarlatti, Hasse, Porpora, Mazzoni, Bernacchi, David, Perez etc.*, 2d ed. (Paris, 1772), [3]. On the French vocal school of the seventeenth and eighteenth centuries, see the works listed in the anno-

1804) was an Italian, Bernardo Mengozzi; in 1811 Girolamo Crescentini published a widely used collection of vocalization exercises. The diffusion of Italian teaching techniques paralleled a growth in the number of local singing schools in France and elsewhere that brought the original quasi monopoly of Italian singers to an end. Schools existed all over the European continent, which makes it more problematic to see vocal styles and didactic methods as exclusively Italian.

From the institutional point of view, the political turmoil that followed the French Revolution and then the Italian Risorgimento was of particular importance in that public music schools were established in which the teaching of singing was always a prime objective. During the first half of the nineteenth century, the old conservatories (at least the ones that had survived) passed from ecclesiastical or mixed administration to the exclusive control of the civil authorities in a gradual process that varied from one local situation to another. Slowly but inexorably the charitable function of the music schools diminished and boarders disappeared. A number of new schools sprang up under the greatest variety of forms: in Piacenza an academy was transformed into a music school; in Florence a music school and an art school were combined into one; in Lucca the music school was an emanation of the local church; in Viareggio it was a private initiative, and so forth. Whatever their origin, however, the schools came to be structured almost exclusively as a function of the opera house, for which they were to furnish instrumental musicians, chorus, and solo singers. Singing schools often aimed exclusively at furnishing singers for the chorus—even just semiprofessionals to be employed during the local opera season—rather than soloists. Indeed, it was not in the interests of provincial cities to invest too much in the preparation of artists who would leave as soon as possible to seek their fortunes in the major centers. Obviously singers in the choral schools provided the pool from which talented youngsters were selected, but their further training necessarily continued in the major centers: singers did not normally move on from the school to the opera house but rather from peripheral areas to the principal cities, Milan in particular, where they could seek advanced training from one of the leading teachers and could make contact with an agent. It was from Milan that nineteenth-century singers launched their careers, perhaps even with a debut back in a provincial opera house. Without adequate historical studies, both general and comparative, it is difficult to evaluate the relative weight or function of the public schools as compared with private teaching with respect to opera, aside from noting the obvious differences between the most presti-

---

tated bibliography in Jane Arger, *Les agréments et le rythme: Leur représentation graphique dans la musique vocale française du XVIIIe siècle . . .* (Paris: Rouart Lerolle, [1921]).

gious institutions and those in the hinterland in terms of their students' scholastic and professional success.[122]

6. Bel Canto: The Market and the Myth

In the context of nineteenth-century Italian music, some scholars—with good reason—have spoken of a genuine opera "industry," and the expression is just as valid when applied to singers. The increasing concentration of musical personnel in the principal cities brought a need to structure recruitment: artisanal forms of mediation disappeared and the agent became an important figure. New sorts of contracts became common: for example, long-term arrangements in which the artist became an employee of the agent, from whom he received a fixed salary, in exchange for which the agent had the right (and assumed the risk) to have the singer perform where and when he, the agent, thought most appropriate and even to cede the singer to another agent or an impresario who would pay the current market price for the singer's services. An agent whose singers were readily (almost constantly) available was in a position to use their productive capabilities to the maximum, moving them from season to season like pawns in a chess game. This system produced a new pace of employment; it was a genuine exploitation, but one that was welcomed by the singers themselves, especially if they were at the start of their careers. Artists also drove themselves hard, agreeing to take on as many as five or six performances a week, and they were pressured to do so by the opera houses, which only rarely could afford double casts. The other side of this intensive exploitation was an underemployment of minor singers, which meant that many opera houses in provincial towns could hire them at extremely low fees. There was an even greater salary gap than in the past be-

---

122. During the Fascist period the Ministry of National Education commissioned a series of studies on public music schools, published in Florence by Le Monnier. Noteworthy among them are Adelmo Damerini, *Il regio conservatorio "Luigi Cherubini" di Firenze* (1941) and *L'istituto musicale "Giovanni Pacini" di Lucca* (1942); Arnaldo Furlotti, *Il regio conservatorio di musica "Arrigo Boito" di Parma* (1942); Carlo Censi, *Il liceo musicale "Giuseppe Nicolini" di Piacenza* (n.d.); Carlo Righini, *Il liceo musicale "Gerolamo Frescobaldi" di Ferrara* (1941); Federico De Maria, *Il regio conservatorio di musica di Palermo* (1941); Federico Mompellio, *Il regio conservatorio di musica "Giuseppe Verdi" di Milano* (1941); and Sergio Leoni, *L'istituto musicale "Cesare Pollini" di Padova* (1941). Although these works, almost without exception, are blatant apologias for the commissioning institution, they are nonetheless extremely useful for documenting the overall picture of school instruction in the nineteenth century, and in some cases they transmit documents destroyed during World War II that are irretrievably lost. Among more recent works one might note Alberto Basso, *Il conservatorio di musica "Giuseppe Verdi" di Torino* (Turin: Unione Tipografico-EditriceTorinese, 1971).

tween the major circuits on the one hand and the minor circuits that acted both as a pool for new talent and a limbo for second-rate artists on the other. All in all it was a system that fitted in well with the criteria of a liberal, free-market economy and that could count on an ample and perennial supply of professional singers in search of work.[123] Artists no longer could find the same possibilities for employment as they had under the old regime with noble families and ecclesiastical institutions.

Within a system that was growing both in size and complexity, new channels of information were needed on the capabilities, the success, and the availability of singers—one review in 1861 noted that in Milan alone there were 427 vocal soloists. A number of periodicals sprang up to provide theatrical information, some aimed at the "fans" and the general public but others aimed at impresaros and the artists themselves. In Naples *Il palcoscenico,* a daily, promised in its inaugural issue that it would reveal "the lives of all the artists of both sexes, under contract and awaiting contracts, and all the operations of the impresaros."[124] Such publications were connected (some more directly, some less) with agencies and interest groups whose official voice they were. Hence the news they reported should be subjected to scrutiny to discern their editors' and owners' agendas, both hidden and open. Some periodicals, for example, were owned by music publishing houses: Ricordi *(La gazzetta musicale di Milano),* Lucca *(L'Italia musicale)* and, later, Sonzogno *(Il teatro illustrato).* The most openly factious reviews were usually the ones produced informally by the various agencies, who used them both as a publicity medium for their stables of artists and as a source of supplementary earnings, since it was the singers themselves who bought subscriptions under the tacit agreement that by doing so they would receive publicity. This was a game everyone knew about. *L'Italia musicale* published a satirical piece in 1847 that explained how a singer should launch his or her career. The young singer, "once he has finished his studies (or, to put it better, has learned a couple of operas) will find, thanks to contacts and without disbursing a penny, a contract for some provincial opera house. Immediately he will subscribe to a number of journals and will be announced as a 'new artist' of great promise."[125] In other words, this was a more or less open form of paid publicity that had little to do with journalism in the modern sense. Still,

---

123. On the relationship between singers and agents between the late eighteenth century and the end of the nineteenth century and on the working of the labor market in general, see the studies of John Rosselli cited in note 70 and in chapter 2, in particular section 5.

124. *Il palcoscenico,* Naples, no. 1, 25 September 1849. On the crowding of the Milan market, see Rosselli, *The Opera Industry,* 150. For a rare memoir documenting the opera scene in Milan, see Lucius [pseudonym of an unknown author], *American and Italian Cantatrici, or, A Year at the Singing Schools of Milan* (London, 1867).

125. *L'Italia musicale,* 1, no. 7, August 1847.

34. Anton Maria Zanetti, caricature of Farinelli (Carlo Broschi), "In *Catone in Utica* in 1729" (Venice, Fondazione Cini). The singer, who was already famous (he was twenty-four at the time), is shown in his role of *Arbace* in the production of Metastasio's opera with music by Leonardo Leo given at the Teatro San Giovanni Grisostomo in Venice. Other Zanetti caricatures of a lanky Farinelli show him "in abito da galla" and "in abito da viaggio" (in formal attire; dressed for travel).

35. Pierleone Ghezzi, caricature of Farinelli (Rome, Biblioteca Apostolica Vaticana). Significantly, the picture has none of the usual attributes with which Ghezzi used to decorate his drawings: the singer was so famous that the artist did not need to add his name or allude to his reputation with descriptive remarks.

36. This engraving, which shows an unusually merry Farinelli, appeared facing the title page of the ode *In lode del signor Carlo Broschi detto Farinello, musico celebre,* by Tommaso Crudeli (Florence: Albizzini, 1734). The inscription emphasizes the original and daring nature of Farinelli's vocal style, hailed in the ode as a new Jason. Like the singer, the poet Crudeli opened new paths: he was one of the first Freemasons in Florence and a declared atheist; in 1739 he fell victim to one of the last throes of the Inquisition. These circumstances give Crudeli's appreciation of the iconoclastic elements in Farinelli's art a particular savor: "Now he sings; the agile winged voice / on voluble wheels / in a thousand turns floats / along the airy paths; / now sweet and freed / on tremulous notes / it distills new pleasures in our hearts; / now holding close to its sides / its sweeping wings, / with daring and free flight / it grows golden in the rays of the eternal light; / now with wearied course / with happy disorder it begins [again], / and ravishes [with] a grace, a beauty / that lurked, hidden, beyond art." (Milan, Raccolta delle Stampe "Achille Bertarelli")

37. Bartolomeo Nazari, portrait of Carlo Broschi, oil on canvas, 1734 (London, Royal College of Music). If the caricature in plate 35 shows the viewpoint of an artist-observer and the engraving in plate 36 a prestigious and attractive image, this oil shows a more intimate view: Farinelli is at ease in ordinary clothes and in his own domestic space. The engraving (plate 36) praised him as a servant of the emperor; here the presence of the dog in the lower-right corner shows him as master, while the keyboard instrument insists on his status as a *musicus* (leading castrato singer) rather than a simple *phonascus* (singer).

38. Jacopo Amigoni, group portrait commissioned by Farinelli, ca. 1750, oil on canvas (Melbourne, National Gallery of Victoria, Felton Bequest, 1949–50). From left to right: Metastasio, the Milanese soprano Teresa Castellini, Farinelli, the painter, an unidentified boy with a dog whose collar, on closer inspection, shows that he belongs to Farinelli. The commission of the painting is related to Metastasio's infatuation with the beautiful Castellini, documented in letters he sent to Farinelli (whom he always addressed as "my dear twin") from Vienna; the picture shows a desired but impossible meeting. The sheet of music Farinelli and Castellini are holding contains Metastasio's famous canzonetta "La partenza," for which Farinelli himself composed the music. This picture, crowded with personal references and allusions, is of obvious interest as a reflection of the commissioner's life.

39. Jacopo Amigoni, portrait of Farinelli, ca. 1750–52, oil on canvas (Stuttgart, Staatsgalerie). The singer, who wears the insignia of the order of Calatrava (as he does in the group portrait in plate 38), is depicted near the royal villa of the King of Spain at Aranjuez. Here Farinelli poses in the guise of an enlightened superintendent of court entertainments. In his left hand he holds a sheet containing the aria "Vi conosco, amate stelle" from Metastasio's *Zenobia,* set to music by Gaetano Latilla (Turin, 1742). The aria, which was not composed for Broschi but for another pupil of Porpora, Felice Salimbeni, seems to act as a musical emblem of the melancholy and affectionate character of the singer.

40. Corrado Giaquinto, portrait of Farinelli, oil on canvas (Bologna, Civico Museo Bibliografico Musicale). In the background there is a dual portrait of the king and queen of Spain, Ferdinando VI and Maria Barbara, and, behind the singer, the portrait of the artist. This triumphal picture summarizes and clearly portrays Farinelli's extraordinary social ascent as well as his prominence in eighteenth-century opera. The presence of his noble protectors recalls, however, that the highest honors (here again Farinelli is wearing the insignia of the order of Calatrava) are a reflection of the glory of his patrons.

41. *Il Parnaso canoro* ("The Parnassus of Song") in an engraving by Antonio Fedi. The preceding illustrations have shown images obviously commissioned by Farinelli himself; this one, which dates from between 1801 and 1807, shows his place in his profession. He is, predictably, at the highest level, along with equally legendary singers. The portraits in this series of idealized "medallions" celebrating the "great" singers of the past are for the most part imaginary: Farinelli died in 1782, and he and the others were remembered by their name and their fame.

42. The first stage photograph of Enrico Caruso, who made his debut at the age of twenty-two in the part of Turiddu in Mascagni's *Cavalleria rusticana* in Caserta (1895). The pose obviously invokes the famous toast *(brindisi)* in that opera.

43. Caruso published hundreds of caricatures in the newspaper of the Italian colony in New York, *La follia*. This one is a humorous self-portrait of Caruso as Dick Johnson in Puccini's *La fanciulla del West*.

44. Once again, Caruso as Dick Johnson in Puccini's *La fanciulla del West*. The photograph seems to have been taken in the thick of the action during a performance, but it is in reality a carefully posed studio shot documenting a key scene. It is still highly valuable as testimony to the actual staging, which was much appreciated by Puccini.

45. An advertisement from *Theater Magazine*, December 1919. Caruso leads the procession of "great artists" who will "sing in your home on Christmas morning." Listening to recorded music was still an exceptional event that lent solemnity to family gatherings. The spread of sound recordings was bolstered in some measure by the star system in opera.

46. Caruso as a cinema actor: this still from the film *My Cousin* (1918) shows Caruso in the dual role of a tenor and his cousin. The character was Italian, and in fact Caruso's great success in the United States was connected, ideologically, with the great waves of Italian immigration.

47. At the outbreak of World War I, the stars of New York's Metropolitan Opera were scattered throughout Europe. Called in haste to Naples, they then embarked on the "Canopic" for New York on 20 October 1914. This group photograph presents a picture of this "Musical Parnassus" on its way to the New World: Caruso (in a black beret) stands among his fellow singers, but perhaps the stars of the group are Arturo Toscanini (second row, center, with a bow tie and a moustache) and the director of the Metropolitan Opera, Giulio Gatti-Casazza (center, with beard and moustache).

48. Caruso in a prophetic photograph: air transport was to have profound effects on the movements of the major singers. Especially after World War II, air travel created an operatic market on
a worldwide scale.

Enrico Caruso (1873–1921)

As Radames in *Aïda*

As Dick Johnson in *La Fanciulla del West*

As Canio in *I Pagliacci*

PLATE 5

49. A late version of the myth of Caruso, between fetishism and popularization, appears in this set of paper dolls representing him in his most famous roles, printed in the United States in 1984, sixty-three years after his death. Once again, among his other famous roles, Caruso is featured in "western" clothes (which did not particularly favor his portly figure) in the role of Dick Johnson in Puccini's *La fanciulla del West*.

thanks to the enormous quantity of news that such journals reported, they are a priceless source of information on singers' careers, on critical and aesthetic debate on singing, and on the music schools. The sections that were presumably of greatest interest to insiders regarded contracts, which were announced far ahead of time and in telegraphic form. For example, *La rivista teatrale* of Rome (5 October 1837) announced for the following carnival season

Trieste — Rita Gabussi and Giuseppina Lozzano *prime donne*
Milano—Teatro Re — Santina Ferlotti *prima donna*
Vicenza — Fanny Maray *prima donna*
Pisa — Antonio Rivarola *basso comico*
. . .

Twenty-four artists under contract for the new theater of Algiers left Bologna for Corfù last August, among them singers, orchestral musicians, [scene] painters, male and female chorus singers, prompters, music copyists, and others.

There are also a large number of highly laudatory biographies of individual artists that nonetheless give a rich store of information on the singers' relations with composers and impresarios. Such biographies were written to enhance the artists' reputations and (at times) defend them, professionally and in their private lives, especially if there were any hint that the values of bourgeois respectability characteristic of all professional people in the nineteenth century seemed threatened. When this occurred, sharp and emotional denials were sent out.

Base envy and professional jealousy induced a female singer whose name will not be mentioned here to spread about in Milan and elsewhere the false rumor that the Salvi-Speck [Spech] couple had separated. To honor truth we are authorized to deny this calumny, and we can assure [our readers] that both Signora Adelina Speck [Spech] and Lorenzo Salvi, her husband, live together in the greatest harmony and that they both are singing in the royal theaters of Naples (for a sizable fee) and, more important, inspiring in that audience a lively desire to hear them and sing their praises again and again.

Details of these singers' private lives are given here, significantly, in close connection with information on their professional success, almost as if to declare that an artist's overall public image determined his or her worth.[126]

126. This denial appeared in *La rivista teatrale*, 4, no. 22, October 1837. Critics of the most reactionary, diehard sort tenaciously fixed on the less edifying aspects of the behavior of theatrical artists. Leonardo Perosa, after exhausting the ritual complaints about the lack "of expression, agility, [and] grace" in a performance, thundered, "Other and more serious reproaches must be made both against the *cantatrici* for the provocative license of their mode of dress and the comic male singers for that stage business [*lazzi*] and those licentious asides that they add, on their own, against the buffoonery of the music and the words, and against many of both the former and the

Periodicals were also the most appropriate place for aesthetic or critical comments (which followed a nearly obligatory scheme) on the singing schools, the advances they had made, and their decadence. One headline echoed another, reiterating recriminations, discussions, and polemics (often quite vaguely defined) in which happenings in the theatrical world were adjusted to support the arguments of one side or another. In one typical instance some attributed the fashion for *canto di forza* (a dramatic delivery forcing the voice) to one or more individual composers, while others claimed that it was a vice in particular singers, and that it would reappear periodically.[127] Since we have no thorough studies of this sort of literature, wisdom dictates avoiding making judgments of dubious value based on only a few selected documents. I might note, finally, that such periodicals also published historical articles, in particular on eighteenth-century singers. For the most part, however, such articles lacked focus, were inaccurate, borrowed heavily from Mancini's *Riflessioni,* and were full of hearsay and legend.[128]

---

latter for a life so intemperate that they bring dishonor to themselves and to their art. All of these are disorders that, added to the frequent immorality of the plays and to the undisciplined conduct of many of the spectators, serve to impinge on the virtue of many innocent souls, and against them the severe voice of teachers of healthy morals will always be raised"; Leonardo Perosa, *Della origine, dei progressi e degli effetti del melodramma in Italia* (Venice, 1864), 53.

127. For contrasting opinions on this matter, see Alberto Mazzucato in *La gazzetta musicale di Milano,* 3, 25 October 1844, 141–42, and a series of anonymous articles entitled "Degli odierni studi del canto," *La gazzetta musicale di Milano,* 18, 3 and 17 June 1860, 177–79 and 195–97, respectively, for one side, and "Cantanti e maestri di canto," *L'Italia musicale* 6, nos. 9ff., 1854, for the other side.

128. The eighteenth-century singer was already a mythic figure that kindled the imagination of novelists. Balzac used the elusive psychological and sexual status of a transvestite castrato, Zerbinella, as the turning point of the plot of his *Sarrasine* (1830), even though the character's profession is close to irrelevant. Giuseppe Rovani chose as the protagonist of his "cyclical" novel *Cento anni* (1856–64) the tenor Angelo Amorevoli, one of the most famous singers of the mid-eighteenth century. Rovani makes Amorevoli into a nineteenth-century tenor, even endowed with the fateful high C: "Frenetic applause followed that privileged C, which had the attribute of both force and sweetness. . . . There is nothing in the world that better penetrates the human breast than a voice on that note [*di quella chiave*]"; Giuseppe Rovani, *Cento anni,* ed. Piero Nardi (Florence: Vallecchi, 1972), 270. Rovani further fictionalized his character by changing Amorevoli's first name from Angelo to the sharper "Curzio." Other novelists invented their singers out of whole cloth. In "The Wicked Voice," a short story by Vernon Lee (Violet Paget) published in 1892 in her *Hauntings: Fantastic Stories* (London: William Heinemann; New York: F. F. Lovell, 1890), 195–237, the narrator, a young opera composer who "has despised the new-fangled nonsense of Wagner and returned boldly to the traditions of Handel and Gluck and the divine Mozart," is haunted by the singing ghost of a castrato, Balthasar Cesari, nicknamed Zaffirino ("O cursed human voice, violin of flesh and blood! . . . O execrable art of singing"), who reduces the unfortunate composer to consumption, then to creative impotence. It would make no sense to accuse such works of being historically inaccurate; they engage us (when they do) because they show that fiction showed an interest in the eighteenth-century singer long before music historiography did. Vernon Lee—that is, Violet Paget—even wrote a *Studies of the Eighteenth Century in Italy,* pub-

The change in the old theatrical hierarchies showed in the decline in singers' earnings as against those of composers even more than it did in the growing role of agents. In the seventeenth and eighteenth centuries an opera score cost less than the services of a *primo uomo* or a *prima donna;* beginning with Gioachino Rossini and Vincenzo Bellini, the situation was reversed. This change was an economic reflection of a profound change in the values assigned to composition and execution.

The Rossinian repertory can be seen as a threshold between past and future in other ways as well: although a taste for vocal agility and ornamentation survived in Rossini's operas, it was now the composer who took stylistic responsibility for them by writing out the flourishes and cadenzas that earlier tradition had left to the singer's improvisation. Furthermore, a more stable repertory than in the past brought a radical shift of perspective for the performer: sooner or later a singer would have to take on a role not written to measure and thus would have to adapt his or her vocal and dramatic talents to that role. The interpreter became secondary to the score, reversing the custom of the previous century. Modifications, adjustments, and variants in the musical text continued to be part of normal practice, but compromises were made more and more in the composer's favor, and changes were ever more respectful of the musical score.

The *stile d'agilità* that had been ushered out the door in serious opera returned through the window of opera buffa, almost as if it were an ineradicable part of the singer's profession. The sharp division between the professional skills required of "serious" and of "comic" singers disappeared, however: interpreters of Rossini's operas — Maria Teresa Belloc Giorgi, Rosa Morandi, Geltrude Righetti Giorgi, Francesca Festa, and Isabella Colbran — were all complete artists who excelled in all genres: the serious, the semiserious, and the buffo. The bass Luigi Lablache was the model for male singers. His voice had both agility and volume, and he could "take on almost any physiognomy, express all personalities, buffo or serious, tragic or sentimental . . . a true Proteus." The new roles demanded stamina as well: Carlo Blasis

---

lished in Italian as *Il Settecento in Italia: Letteratura, teatro, musica,* in 1880. In a more recent novel, Dominique Fernandez's *Porporino,* the novelist imagines the discovery of the memoirs of a singer (Antonio Del Prato, a fictional character, although the nickname "Porporino" was actually used for Antonio Hubert). The gripping plot is in reality based, as the preface declares, on the concerns of the generation of 1968: "Admittedly, it is very tempting to establish a relationship between the hippie protest of our century and the fashion for castratos of another [century]," and "They had more than just the complex; they had real castration"; Dominique Fernandez, *Porporino, ou, Les mystères de Naples* (Paris: Grasset, 1974), 13. Obviously historical accuracy does not affect the success of such works of fiction. They can be compared with a truly autobiographical work, the *Memorie dell'abate D. Bonifacio Pecorone . . . musico della real cappella di Napoli* (Naples, 1729), which clearly shows how remote the sophisticated, twentieth-century imagination is from the late feudal mentality of the genuine article.

observed about the title role in Rossini's *Otello* that "from his first appearance to his final exit . . . he is singing and continually in action; it [is] a gigantic effort, totally unknown to the singers of the last century."[129] Even the characters in the operas had acquired a precise musical identity: while Alexander the Great in an opera based on Metastasio's text was a role defined (if at all) by the text of the libretto, a Tancred or a Norma came to be defined, once and for all, by the musical score.

From the more strictly technical, vocal point of view, Rossini's era has been spoken of as a "restoration," almost as if the political restoration required a musical counterpart (or perhaps the term simply stresses continuity with the past). Contemporary descriptions of the tenor Giovanni Battista Rubini, for example, seem to reflect fundamental aspects of "classical" technique.

> Rubini's voice is a tenor in the fullest sense of the word. It begins at Mi [E] and rises in chest tones to high Si [B]; it continues in head tones up to Fa [F], always with perfect voice production as regards intonation and homogeneity. . . . As for its strength, it is never inferior to what is demanded of it by the most intense dramatic expression, but that strength never offends the ear with overly rough bursts. . . . One of the wonders of the art is revealed, above all, in the transition from his chest voice to his head tones and vice versa. When he has reached the limits of the chest register . . . the shift to enter into the head voice happens in such a marvelous manner that it is impossible to tell at what moment it occurs. . . . There is no singer with a more agile, lighter, more flexible throat than Rubini.[130]

The French tenor Gilbert Duprez, whose career immediately followed Rubini's, was given credit (or held responsible) for having popularized an original style much appreciated by his contemporaries. In particular Duprez was famous for the "invention" of the "chest high C," which he first introduced in the stretta of the aria in the fourth act of *Guillaume Tell,* a passage that Rossini had written for the tenor Adolphe Nourrit, who executed it in falsetto, as tradition dictated. Duprez's chest high C was only the most obvious exploit in a use of vocal means that was original in other ways as well. Duprez injected life into the recitative, which he claimed to "sing" rather than "recite," like many of his colleagues, and in general he gave his performances a particularly dramatic impetus, supported by a more energetic voice production that altered the traditional use of vocal registers. He did not abandon

---

129. See the studies of John Rosselli cited in n. 70. On vocal agility see Nicola Tacchinardi, *Dell'opera in musica sul teatro italiano e de' suoi difetti,* 2d ed. (Florence, 1833), 24ff. On the singers mentioned see Vittorio Della Croce, *Una giacobina piemontese alla Scala: La primadonna Teresa Belloc* (Turin: EDA, 1978); Léon and Marie-Pierre Yves Escudier, *Études biographiques sur les chanteurs contemporains, précédées d'une esquisse sur l'art du chant* (Paris, 1840), 68; Carlo Blasis, *The Code of Terpsichore* (London, 1828), 245.

130. Escudier and Escudier, *Études biographiques sur les chanteurs,* 64.

head tones, but the very fact of privileging chest voice production for high notes changed their function. That is, there was less emphasis on the problem of a smooth transition from chest production to head tones and on trying to make the tones as identical and homogeneous as possible. Forcing the voice inevitably had other, physical results: agility was diminished and the singer's vocal resources deteriorated more rapidly. Whereas Anton Raaff, Mozart's Idomeneo, still cut a fine figure on the opera stage at the age of sixty-six, Duprez's voice was already showing signs of deterioration when he was thirty-nine. But it was his abundant gifts as an actor rather than his voice that galvanized the auditorium. Gustave-Hippolyte Roger tells us, with regard to an *Otello* in 1849 (when Duprez was forty-three),

> Duprez, today, electrified us all. What daring! A terrifying old lion! How he hurled his guts in the audience's face! For those are no longer notes that one hears. They are the explosion of a breast crushed by an elephant's foot! That's his own blood, his own life, that he is squandering to entice from the public those cries of "Bravo!" with which the Romans honored the dying gladiator. There is a certain nobility about it. For despite the inequalities of a voice more blemished by passion than time, his good schooling prevails, and he finds even in his deficiencies the means of sustaining style. When this man is gone the world will not hear his like again.[131]

But if Duprez had no equal, he had plenty of imitators. The chest high C became "a new golden fleece, in search of which some of the new Argonauts have lost the feeble means they might have had [and] others their best natural gifts." Duprez, in a very different way from Faustina Bordoni a hundred years earlier, was the brand new muse who embodied all the features of a developing trend. Indeed, in 1829, two years before the famous chest high C made its appearance, the director of the Théâtre Italien of Paris wrote to a friend that Italian audiences applauded singers and demanded curtain calls only when they heard "the howling of furies." In that same period Nicola Tacchinardi defined the vocal characteristics of the *tenore di forza,* and *di forza* roles had been mentioned as early as the late eighteenth century. Thus it is highly likely that the importance of Duprez and his famous high C was exaggerated by a typically nineteenth-century taste for personages of heroic stature and actions of a definitive and historic scope—in short by a strictly *événimentiel* approach to the history of music focused on personages and events.

---

131. Gustave-Hippolyte Roger, *Le Carnet d'un ténor* (Paris, 1880), quoted from Henry Pleasants, *The Great Singers, from the Dawn of Opera to Our Own Times* (New York: Simon and Schuster, 1966), 165–70, quotation 169. On the *canto di forza* see Tacchinardi, *Dell'opera in musica,* 15ff.; for testimony from forty years earlier, see Marcello Conati, "Un 'Sackspear' per 'Jommellino,'" introductory essay to Giuseppe Foppa and Gaetano Andreozzi, *Amleto,* Drammaturgia musicale veneta, no. 26 (Milan: Ricordi, 1984), xiii.

Basically the same attitude gave rise to criticism of the leading composers, who were accused of being behind excessive use of the "forced" style of singing by using a syllabic (rather than an ornamented) melodic line, making the vocal tessitura higher, and introducing unison duets, which invited singers to compete with one another in volume.

Beyond such obviously sterile polemics and accusations lay the hard fact of the renovation of the entire vocabulary of opera and of the singing style. In Verdi's operas, for example, a progressive lessening in the use of ornamentation, the use of relatively high tessitura in declamation, and the density of some of his orchestral accompaniments contributed to a more dynamic delivery and less concentration on vocal agility. The critic Paul Scudo stated polemically that "you do not need to know how to sing in order to produce dramatic musical effects."[132] But it was one thing to blame some singers for an overuse of *canto di forza* and quite another thing to see composers as its cause. Verdi's vocal writing (and not only Verdi's) varies widely according to an extremely subtle definition of character and shifting psychological state. The choice of an interpretation based *only* on the effects of dramatic vocal production is obviously too narrow, and Verdi would have been the first to call it entirely improper. Indeed, Verdi's singers ran the gamut of preromantic vocal styles: Leone Giraldoni, one of the most highly esteemed interpreters of Verdi operas, went as far as to theorize on "dramatic effects and accents," which he reduced to schematic form for the use of his students.[133] Enrico delle

---

132. Paul Scudo, *Critique et littérature musicales* (Paris, 1859), quoted in Rodolfo Celletti, "La vocalità," in *Storia dell'opera,* ed. Guglielmo Barblan and Alberto Basso, 3 vols. (Turin: Unione Tipografico-Editrice Torinese, 1977),vol. 3, pt. 1, 3–317, quotation 209, and, in general, chapter 3, "La vocalità romantica," 105–262.

133. Leone Giraldoni, *Guida teorico-pratica ad uso dell'artista cantante* (Bologna, 1864), 48. How Giraldoni presented *slancio* (dynamic delivery) is a characteristic example of his attention to the details of execution, but it also demonstrates the terminological problems inherent in his material. For instance, while the term *accento* (emphasis) often appears in the literature on Verdi with a specific meaning, for Giraldoni it had a more general sense (in itself not without ambiguity), covering a number of stylistic devices, among them, precisely, *slancio:* "There are . . . sentiments that the timbres ["mixed," "closed," and "open"] are insufficient to make clear, hence the voice must have recourse to other means or emphases [*accenti*]; as, for example, the *strascinamento* [downward glide] of the voice, the *staccato,* the *slancio,* etc." While the first two of these could be used to express, respectively, "emotional stress" *(strazio)* and "sobbing" *(singhiozzo), lo slancio* "will characterize, in particular, any energetic and dramatic sentiment, a distinctive characteristic of modern music, which the famous maestro Verdi has garbed in new forms. . . . I recommend not rendering this *accento* by means of short chest tones [*colpi di petto*] . . . What is needed instead is [to have] the sound abandon the throat as soon as it is attacked with force; and when I say abandon the throat, I do not mean that one must abandon the sound; and here I beg the reader please to refer to the article that treats the *messa di voce* [crescendo-decrescendo]; the *slancio,* properly speaking, is no other than a successive passage of the voice from forte to piano on the same note, and nearly instantly" (47–48).

Sedie, in his *Riflessioni sulle cause della decadenza della scuola di canto in Italia* (Paris, 1881), explicitly rejected a return to the older tradition that some critics had proposed, exhorting schools to work instead to raise the level of singing instruction to match the ideal level of composition. In particular he suggested that schools teach control of "that infinity of timbres by means of which the various emotions of the soul are truthfully expressed." Volume and even intonation came after flexibility of timbre and dramatic accents: "Landi possessed a small and uncertain voice, but what a moving actor! Giorgio Ronconi's pitch was often dubious, but his power of expression, his moving accents, and his telling gestures made him famous."[134]

If Verdi cannot be explained by the easy choice of athletic vocal delivery, it is just as simplistic to approach the problem of the interpretation of Verdi's operas solely from the vocal point of view, especially when we are aware of the care that the composer took over the staging of his works and his interest in their overall dramatic impact—that is, in words, gestures, individual actors' moves, and the blocking of chorus and crowd movements.[135]

Even when the composer did not insist on dramatic efficacy and a strict respect of the spirit of the musical score, those same demands were made in much of nineteenth-century didactic literature. If such works agreed with composers on general principles, however, they offered a broad variety of practical solutions. On a strictly technical level, for example, the manuals proposed fundamentally different methods of breathing: Leone Giraldoni, who advocated diaphragmatic breathing, criticized the rib-cage breathing that was the official method taught at the Paris Conservatory. It would be tempting to attribute contradictions to differences between a French school and an Italian school if these terms were not in themselves too schematic: authors who might be grouped under the "Italian" archetype did not necessarily achieve the same results. Two nearly contemporary teachers, Heinrich Panofka and Giraldoni, held diametrically opposed methodological positions on such basic questions as sound production. If we move from general principles to an analysis of specific didactic materials, the "school" shatters into a number of "schools," perhaps as many as there were teachers. Obviously

---

134. Quoted from an anonymous review of Delle Sedie, *Riflessioni*, in *Il teatro illustrato*, 1, no. 2, February 1881.

135. On this question see Elvidio Surian, "Aspetti espliciti ed impliciti di regia teatrale (didascalie musicali) presenti nella partitura di un'opera verdiana dell'età di mezzo," in *Tornando a "Stiffelio,"* ed. Giovanni Morelli (Florence: Olschki, 1987), 189–201. That Giraldoni was interested in all aspects of stage performance is evident from his advice on the choice of the singer's costumes and props: "There is nothing easier for a conscientious artist than to protect himself against mistakes in costuming. If some doubt comes into his mind, he should go consult the libraries or the art museums, which exist in all civilized cities, and he will find there all the information and documentation he needs to assure himself that he will not fall into error"; Giraldoni, *Guida teorico-pratica*, 68.

there were similarities among methods; at times they even throw light on persisting notions connecting works of different times and places. The call for a
"scientific" approach to the art of singing, one expressed in its mature form
in the physiological and didactic studies of Manuel García, can be seen in the
same years in the lesser-known Luca Cagnazzi and was clearly expressed at
the beginning of the century in a treatise by Marcello Perrino (Naples, 1810)
as a hope (or at least a passing wish) for a more philosophical approach to vocalism.

> Few, in fact very few, . . . have been those who, with no other ambition than to
> assign some practical rules to that science, leaving aside the studies that are proper
> to philosophy (that is, by turning principally to investigate all that by nature has
> been disposed and ordained to that purpose), have limited themselves to pure mech-
> anism of the art and not strayed from it. Having thus concentrated their studies
> ever more on the effects without ever searching for the causes from which the per-
> fection of singing derives, they have floundered in doubt and ignorance of the true
> principles of art, which, instead of developing and improving, have remained, to
> the contrary, ever more enveloped in obscurity and error.[136]

Despite impassioned efforts on the part of teachers and physiologists,
however, a description of vocal phenomena did little to resolve the highly
empirical problem of singing well, and some years later Panofka could smile
at a half century of positivistic faith and declare it useless to

> fatigue the brain of a poor student by telling him that to produce this or that sound
> in this or that register he has to set into motion the cricoid cartilage or the thyroid
> cartilage or whatever other bone might be called for. It would be the same as if a
> ballet master explained to a student the movements that the various muscles must
> make in order to execute some step or other. And furthermore, what are all these
> theories that are based on physiology? Hypotheses! Nothing but hypotheses sus-
> tained by famous physiologists and combatted by other equally famous physiolo-
> gists.[137]

In this case, Panofka and Giraldoni seem to agree.
    A history of vocal teaching in the nineteenth century would presuppose
careful analysis of the similarities and differences in every single technical
problem treated by every method along with a systematic study of terminology—enormous tasks that have up to now discouraged scholars. Terms grew
in number and increased in specificity, and anyone who searches the diction-

---

136. Marcello Perrino, *Osservazioni sul canto* (Naples, 1810), 5.
137. Heinrich Panofka, *Voci e cantanti: Ventotto capitoli di considerazioni generali sulla voce
e sull'arte del canto,* trans. Vincenzo Meini (Florence, 1871; reprint ed., Bologna: Arnaldo Forni,
1984), 26.

aries to clarify the meanings of the ones used—to pick one example—to classify voices from the nineteenth to the twentieth centuries (a task that may prove easy for the *tenore di forza,* but a little less so for *mezzo contralto* or *soprano sfogato*) will find, with luck, the current meaning of the term. But it would be equally important to know when, where, and in what circumstance the "crystallization" of each term took place.

It has been absolutely imperative to ask that sort of question regarding one overused expression—*bel canto*—which both says it all and says nothing. Results have not been totally satisfactory: according to Henry Pleasants, one of the most reliable scholars of the "great singers," "it is probably a reasonable supposition . . . that the term *bel canto* evolved from the sulphur of pro- and anti-Wagnerian invective, employed by the Wagnerians pejoratively, by others as a symbol of the assumed virtues of the older Italian vocal tradition." More recently Owen Jander has connected the use of the term to an earlier date and a different context, claiming that Rossini employed it in 1858 (in a conversation that actually had nothing to do with Wagner). In point of fact Giovanni Pacini used the term twenty years or so before then in an official document, the program of studies of the school that he directed in Lucca, where he spoke of *bel canto* in connection with an advanced training class in vocalization, voice modulation, syllabification of texts, breathing, and ornamentation. The study of bel canto followed two years of solmization and *meloplasto,* a method of voice placement that Pacini himself had invented. It is impossible to tell whether the term *bel canto* was then a neologism, but the fact remains that its meaning was much less generic than scholars generally hold it to have been.[138]

It is true that didactic materials have been perused, frequently and assiduously, but with critical interests in mind rather than from a historical point of view. That is, treatises and memoirs have been (and are still being) scrutinized in search of models for critical categories to be applied to present-day interpreters of the operatic repertory. When, as is often the case, this operation is conducted with extreme nonchalance in the interpretation of sources and with an intent to seek authoritative norms, it can lead to pure mystification. It seems difficult to be detached or disinterested in treating a subject that is a living part of opera today: the repertory of our opera houses is still in large measure from the nineteenth century, as are the teaching methods of our conservatories. From the point of view of the culture of singing, the nineteenth century seems to have lasted well beyond its chronological limits. Or so it appears when we hear opera aficionados speaking (more or less perti-

---

138. On the use of the term *bel canto,* see Pleasants, *The Great Singers,* 19–20; *The New Grove Dictionary of Music and Musicians,* s.v. "Bel canto," by Owen Jander; Damerini, *L'istituto musicale "Giovanni Pacini,"* 74–81.

nently) about artists who have been dead for a century and a half with the authority of someone who had heard them in the opera house the night before.

6. The Voice Mirrored

One of the changes of greatest consequence for the professional status of the singer, whether in the Italian tradition or not, was the invention of mechanical systems of reproduction—first sound recordings and then, more recently, audiovisual techniques. Recordings of the "great voices" have introduced a totally new form of listening, one that fixes a singer's execution in memory to a very different degree from the frivolous occasional verse or the impressionistic descriptions of nineteenth-century opera critics. The listener has moved from the memory of an event to possession of a concrete semblance of that event. The particular nature of the sound document has permitted a study of performance practices of the late nineteenth century that contributes to a better understanding of the relationship between the text and the executor; still, recordings are incapable of satisfying our curiosity completely.[139] In some cases recordings even raise new problems. Beginning roughly with the first artists of the so-called verismo school, we have available sound documentation that, although incomplete, attests to a mannered, legato style still inclined to introduce ornamentation and trills. Vocal volume, on the other hand, does not seem to have been essential, to judge from the recordings of Gemma Bellincioni, Emma Calvé, Fernando de Lucia, or Alfonso Garulli. Still, Rodolfo Celletti has observed that the sound recordings contrast with the descriptions of music critics of the time who, "with superabundant astonishment speak of uncontrollable emotions, savage outbursts, terrifying anger, anguished cries, desperate passions."[140] The contradiction raises a historiographical problem that some have attempted to resolve by hypothesizing that the spectator in the opera house was struck more by the crudeness of the subject matter treated than by an execution pushed to emotional limits. This hypothesis presumes, perhaps too optimistically, that the performance recorded on disks and the live performance were identical, whereas they may be subtly but substantially different. And although the gap between live and recorded performance is less noticeable in recordings of more recent years, we must admit that for the older recordings the very rudimentary nature of the technical means that were used could impose constraints and limitations on the artist's interpretation. In short we cannot use sound recordings as his-

---

139. See Will Crutchfield, "Vocal Ornamentation in Verdi: The Phonographic Evidence," *19th-Century Music* 7 (1983–84): 3–54.
140. Celletti, "La vocalità," 293.

torical sources without applying critical judgment to them or without considering the physical conditions under which they were made.

Thanks to sound recordings the opera singer of the twentieth century has come to be known and heard in a new manner: the two spheres of operation (live performance and recording) quite obviously interact, but they are nonetheless distinct, and the listeners for the two genres coincide only in part. The singer's task (that of the singers who record, at least) is made easier in some ways by the opportunity to repeat an unsatisfactory passage in the studio (or to manipulate it technologically). On the other hand recordings create very high and quite specific expectations in the listener that in turn make performance in the opera house a more arduous enterprise and that severely limit the listener's horizon of expectations. Interpretations differ less and less, which works all to the advantage of rapid delivery of the product: the singers most in demand can produce the standard repertory, without rehearsal, in Milan today and the day after tomorrow in New York.

It sometimes happens that an opera will be recorded when it has never been produced on stage with that cast, almost as if to prepare the singers and future spectators in a public rehearsal. When this happens the recording is both an attractive publicity device and a symbol of success: the singer *di cartello* (of high repute) has been replaced by the singer who can boast a hefty discography, and access to the recording market, among other things, opens the doors to the specialized critical periodicals. Even the most important music dictionaries limit their entries to artists with a discography to their credit, and the mediation of the sound-recording critic—a new figure who has inherited, for good and bad, the journalistic tradition of the nineteenth century but who wields a much greater influence on public opinion—becomes enormously important to an artist's success.

The sort of recording most clearly conceived to show off the singer comprises selections from different operas, but the interpreter, indeed the entire cast, is no less fundamental to the success of a recording of a complete work. The complete work in fact becomes multiple: there is not just one *Traviata* but one for each cast that has recorded it—if not more, given that a work can be recorded anew after a reasonable lapse of time. It is, however, especially the periodic introduction of new systems of reproduction that has assured the renewal of the market: new recordings are justified primarily by ongoing improvements in the *sound*—a new notion born with the recording media and with the separation of the recording process from vocal or instrumental phonic values. Hence a new hedonism has appeared that is largely indifferent to traditional dramatic and interpretive values and that is capable of judging a "live" performance disagreeable because the listener must renounce total immersion and the comfort of floating in the "sound of the compact disk."

In short anyone who might wish to write a history of singing in the twentieth century cannot ignore the market for recordings. This is just as true in Italy as it is in other countries, both on the level of the production of recordings (where Italy at first played a leading role, then for many decades that of a bit player, and now today a secondary lead) and on the level of operatic repertory and artistic personnel. The continuing fortunes of the nineteenth-century repertory certainly cannot be said to lead to stagnation because the singers (with the blessings of the recording industry) have continued to innovate. Suffice it to recall the extraordinary importance of one artist, Maria Callas, who is considered responsible for the technical and stylistic recovery of a vocalism belonging to the repertory of the early nineteenth century (from Luigi Cherubini's *Medea* to Gaspare Spontini's *La vestale*) and even further back, as far back as Gluck's *Alceste*.[141] Whatever the judgment of future historians may be, starting with Callas and continuing with such singers as Joan Sutherland, Montserrat Caballé, and Marilyn Horne, the repertory has undeniably been enlarged, both in recordings and on stage. The renewed interest in repertory today continues to extend back from romantic and preromantic opera to "forgotten" nineteenth-century works and back to the operas of the seventeenth and eighteenth centuries. Concerning the latter, however, historical prejudices present an obstacle just as serious as the scarcity of singers truly adequate to the roles. This enlargement of possible choices has certainly interested opera singers more than the contemporary repertory, which presents difficulties of execution not sufficiently compensated by an enthusiastic but numerically very limited audience.

In spite of Cathy Berberian's invitation to singers thirty years ago to make their own "an infinite range of vocal styles embracing all of musical history,"[142] singers have rarely accepted the challenge. What we see instead are singers who specialize in specific "areas" of the repertory—the seventeenth and eighteenth centuries (as if they were a homogeneous period!), the nineteenth century, the "contemporary," or Wagner. Other singers, more daring ones perhaps, range over two or three centuries: Marilyn Horne has gone backwards in time from Rossini to Vivaldi; René Jacobs, a countertenor trained in the repertory of the sixteenth and seventeenth centuries, has moved in the opposite direction, to the point that he did a concert performance of the famous cavatina from Rossini's *Tancredi,* a *primo uomo* role written, in the absence of a castrato, for Adelaide Malanotte. This seems almost a joke,

---

141. Among the many things that have been written on Maria Callas, see in particular the "Processo alla Callas," a "trial" and roundtable debate involving Rodolfo Celletti, Fedele D'Amico, Eugenio Gara, Gianandrea Gavazzeni, Giorgio Gualerzi, and Luchino Visconti, published in *Nuova rivista musicale italiana* 12 (1978): 7–28.

142. Cathy Berberian, "La nuova vocalità nell'opera contemporanea," *Discoteca* 42 (1966): 34–35.

playing on the uncertain borderline between scholarly execution and histori-cal falsity.

If on the one hand the recording industry and its attendant market have to some degree leveled interpretive expectations, on the other hand taste has been expanded to include the entire history of opera. The résumé of a singer embraces operas far apart in time and style; conversely, the number of operas in which a singer performs during the course of his or her career is relatively smaller than was true of professional singers in the nineteenth century.[143]

The profound changes that have taken place during the last decades have gone beyond national boundaries. Given the internationalization of taste that the market for recordings has produced and the success of excellent non-Italian artists, it is legitimate to repeat a question that already came up, although with less urgency, in the nineteenth century: is there still a specifically Italian school of singing? and if so, within what limits and in what sense?[144] One factor contributing to an Italian "identity" may lie in the programs of study in Italian conservatories, which, although they labor under the weight of the half century that has passed since their founding, have certain positive as-pects. Such programs foster not only in-depth study of vocal techniques but study of the scenic arts, the history of costume and stage sets, makeup, an investigation of the historical and psychological aspects of opera characters, dramatic analysis of the libretto, and a knowledge of literature. One could not ask for more for a harmonious preparation for well-trained, fully aware students. What remains to be seen, however, is whether these programs still produce adequate results. Behind the uniformity required by current legisla-tion throughout Italy, there lies a reality that ranges from the very highest level of preparation in some places to the most fraudulent sort of commerce in diplomas in others. Efforts toward a critical investigation and knowledge of a precious didactic heritage are struggling against the inertia of a pedagogi-cal provincialism determined to perpetuate the myths of bel canto.

Obviously this problem is not Italy's alone. But perhaps it is in Italy more

143. See, for example, the chronology of Giovanni Battista Rubini's appearances documented in Bruce Brewer, "Giovan Battista Rubini: A Performance Study," *The Donizetti Society Journal* 4 (1980): 117–65, esp. 160ff.

144. A parallel and perhaps less ephemeral question regards the differing working conditions of the singer in various countries and the relative consequences for the ultimate musical result. One of the most notable variants involved in this question is the difference between a recruitment system based on the "season" or the individual production (the rule in Italy) as opposed to the system in which an opera house takes on a number of artists and employs them on a permanent basis (the system in Germany, among other places).

than elsewhere that we see the best and the worst of this profession, perennially hovering between the call of the intellect and the demands of the audience.

— —

Although more than ten years have elapsed between the first appearance of this chapter in Italian and the revisions for the English translation, the literature on singers has not changed substantially. On the whole it is still divided between the "mythographical" and the "historiographical" genres. Both have a right to exist, but it should be clear that they are directed to distinct goals. In recent years the mythification of opera stars has become increasingly a visual phenomenon, and only to a comparatively lesser degree does the process still rely on advertising tools of a literary nature, such as the memoirs, broadsides, or periodicals of earlier days. Where this phenomenon appears most clearly is in the worldwide fetish for a few exceptional singers (e.g., Luciano Pavarotti or the "three tenors"). Female singers have not been involved to the same extent, though many *prime donne* are (at least) as "great" as their male counterparts. In order to clarify these processes, future historians will do well to study the marketing policies of the leading recording companies. It seems clear in any case that by far the greatest number of people of the present generation will experience only bits and pieces of opera through compilations mixing popular songs and opera excerpts. It remains to be seen whether or not this limited kind of exposure will be sufficient to sustain the vitality of opera as a distinct theatrical genre.

BIBLIOGRAPHIC NOTE

This note does not claim to furnish more than a overall guide to the types of documents and studies useful for a deeper understanding of problems regarding singers. The material is vast and heterogenous in its bibliographic forms, its target audience, its ends, and its language.

Information on the lives and the careers of singers is scattered in general works on opera, chronologies, or anecdotal histories, where it often functions to lend a touch of erudite color to the narrative. Among such works are Taddeo Wiel, *I teatri musicali veneziani del Settecento* (Venice, 1897; reprint ed., Bologna: Arnaldo Forni, 1978), and Antonio Paglicci Brozzi, *Contributo alla storia del teatro: Il teatro a Milano nel secolo XVII* (Milan, 1892). Recently scholars have been aware of the need for closer study of theatrical customs and contractual procedures: see, for instance, the works of Marie-Thérèse Bouquet and of Robert Lamar Weaver and Norma Wright Weaver cited in notes 98 and 49. Biancamaria Brumana and Michelangelo Pascale, "Il teatro musicale a Perugia nel Settecento: Una cronologia dai libretti," *Esercizi: Arte, musica, spettacolo* 6 (1983): 71–134, attempts to discern the level of a theater's prestige through a systematic examination of its singing companies. Chronologies can also provide a base for reconstructing the careers of artists for whom no biography exists. One useful example is Claudio Sartori, *I libretti italiani a stampa dalle origini al 1800: Catalogo analitico con 16 indici,* 7 vols. (Cuneo: Bertola and Locatelli, 1990), which gives information regarding the singers mentioned in librettos. Obviously there are entries on the various singers' biographies in dictionaries and encyclopedias. Among the more useful are *Enciclopedia dello spettacolo,* ed. Sandro d'Amico, 9 vols. (Rome: Le Maschere, 1954–62), and the more recent *Dizionario enciclopedico universale della musica e dei musicisti: Le biografie,* ed. Alberto Basso, 8 vols. and an appendix (Turin: Unione Tipografico-Editrice Torinese, 1986–90). One can usually depend on the entries in the *New Grove Dictionary of Music and Musicians,* ed. Stanley Sadie, 20 vols. (London: Macmillan; Washington, D.C.: Grove's Dictionaries of Music, 1980), and in the recent *The New Grove Dictionary of Opera,* ed. Stanley Sadie, 4 vols. (London: Macmillan; New York: Grove's Dictionaries of Music, 1992). Grove has announced the publication of a dictionary dedicated exclusively to singers.

There are some works that are dated but have not been replaced, such as Ernst Ludwig Gerber, *Historisch-biographisches Lexicon der Tonkünstler,* 2d ed., 4 vols. (Leipzig, 1810–14; reprint ed., Graz: Akademische Druck- und Verlagsanstalt, 1966–77); Carlo Gervasoni, *Nuova teoria di musica, ricavata dalla odierna pratica* (Parma, 1812) (with biographical sketches of singers); Pietro Lichtenthal, *Dizionario e bibliografia della musica* (Milan, 1826; reprint of the Milan, 1836 edition, 4 vols., Bologna: Arnaldo Forni, 1970). For a work limited to singers who have made recordings, see *Le grandi voci: Dizionario critico-biografico dei cantanti,* ed. Rodolfo Celletti (Rome: Istituto per la Collaborazione Culturale, 1964), and Karl Josef Kutsch, *Unvergängliche Stimmen: Sängerlexikon* (Bern: Francke, 1982). Though limited to one center for the production of operas or to one opera house (for the most part outside of Italy), nonetheless useful are Philip H. Highfill, Jr., Kalman A. Burnim, and Edward A. Langhans, *A Biographical Dictionary of Actors, Actresses, Musicians, Dancers, Managers, and Other Stage Personnel in London, 1660–1800,* 16 vols. (Carbondale, Ill.: Southern Illinois University Press, 1973–93), and Jean Gourret, *Dictionnaire des chanteurs de l'Opéra de Paris* (Paris: Albatros, 1982).

At times the biographical entries in dictionaries omit bibliographies (this is true, for example, of the singers of Handel's operas whose biographies appear in the *New Grove*), which means that a bibliography has to be reconstructed by guesswork or by cross reference to other reference works. Individual biographies, however, generally provide a mass of bibliographic material that is interesting not only for the artist in question but more generally for a study of singers as a professional class. A useful orientation can be found in the bibliographies in Andrew Farkas, *Opera and Concert Singers: An Annotated International Bibliography of Books and Pamphlets* (New York: Garland, 1985), and Robert H. Cowden, *Concert and Opera Singers: A Bibliography of Biographical Materials* (Westport, Conn.: Greenwood, 1985). Within bibliography as a whole we can distinguish various "genres," beginning with laudatory and commemorative lives, such as Giovenale Sacchi, *Vita del cavaliere don Carlo Broschi*

(Venice, 1784), and Carlo Pancaldi, *Vita di Lorenzo Gibelli, celebre contrappuntista e cantore* (Bologna, 1830), and similar works on Gasparo Pacchierotti, Brigida Banti, and many other singers. Scholarly studies dedicated to individual artists include Alessandro Ademollo, "Le cantanti italiane celebri del secolo decimottavo: Vittoria Tesi," *Nuova antologia di scienze, lettere ed arti* 106 (1889): 308–27, "Margherita Salicola," *Nuova antologia di lettere, scienze ed arti* 107 (1890): 524–53, "La più famosa delle cantanti italiane nella seconda metà del Settecento: Caterina Gabrielli," *La gazzetta musicale di Milano* 45, no. 28 (1890): 446–47, no. 29 (1890): 461–62, no. 30 (1890): 478–80, no. 31 (1890):490–91, no. 32 (1890):510, no. 33 (1890): 520–21, no. 34 (1890): 543–45, no. 35 (1890):558–59. By the same author, but with more accurate references to sources, see *La bell'Adriana ed altre virtuose del suo tempo alla corte di Mantova* (Città di Castello, 1888). Reliable studies for the biography of the major stars of Neapolitan bel canto are Eugenio Faustini-Fasini, "Il Cav. Nicola Grimaldi detto 'Nicolino,' " *Note d'archivio* 12 (1935): 297–316, and "Gaetano Majorano detto 'Caffarelli'," *Note d'archivio* 15 (1938): 121–28, 157–70, 258–70. Good documentation on the economic and social status of a successful female singer between the seventeenth and eighteenth centuries can be found in Giuseppe Cosentino, *La Mignatta: Maria Maddalena Musi, cantatrice bolognese famosa 1669–1751* (Bologna: Zanichelli, 1930). More recent studies (aside from those of Ulisse Prota-Giurleo, Carlo Sartori, Bianca Maria Antolini, and Lowell E. Lindgren cited in notes 76, 36, and 40) include Claudio Sartori, "Profilo di una cantante della fine del secolo XVII: Barbara Riccioni," in *Festschrift Karl Gustav Fellerer zum sechzigsten Geburtstag*, ed. Heinrich Hüschen (Regensburg: Bosse, 1962), 454–60.

The first (and among the most interesting) singers' autobiographies include, in chronological order, the verse autobiography of Filippo Balatri, *Frutti del mondo*, ed. Karl Vossler (Palermo: Sandron, 1924), partially reprinted in Angus Heriot, *The Castrati in Opera* (London: Secker and Warburg, 1956), 231–52, and the *Memorie dell'abate D. Bonifacio Pecorone* (Venice, 1729), a work that is significant for the documentation of a way of thinking but is not specifically of interest for the history of opera. For opera singers' memoirs see Michael Kelly, *Reminiscences* (London, 1826), a work available in two modern editions, one edited by Alec Hyatt King (New York: Da Capo Press, 1968) and the other edited by Roger Fiske (London: Oxford University Press, 1975). See also Gilbert-Louis Duprez, *Souvenirs d'un chanteur* (Paris, 1880); Victor Maurel, *Dix ans de carrière 1887–1897* (Paris, 1897). For the opera scene in America and England, see Clara Louise Kellogg, *Memoirs of an American Prima Donna* (New York: Putnam, 1913). Among more recent publications by singers and aimed particularly at fans, see Titta Ruffo, *La mia parabola: Memorie*, ed. Titta Ruffo, Jr. (Rome: Staderini, 1977); Beverly Sills, *Bubbles: A Self-Portrait* (Indianapolis: Bobbs-Merril, 1976); Luciano Pavarotti, with William Wright, *Pavarotti: My Own Story* (Garden City, N.Y.: Doubleday, 1981); Marilyn Horne and Jane Scovell, *Marilyn Horne: My Life* (New York: Athenaeum, 1983).

At times a variously defined group of singers can be the object of a study: singers of one city in Daniele Rubboli, *Cronache di voci modenesi* (Milan: Nuove Edizioni, 1981); singers in one theater in Eugenio Gara, *Cantarono alla Scala* (Milan: Electa, 1975); singers connected with the works of one composer in Leonardo Bragaglia,

Verdi e i suoi interpreti, 1839–1978 (Rome: Bulzoni, 1979), and Denis Arnold, "Monteverdi's Singers," *Musical Times* 111 (1970): 982–85. There are many examples of works on singers grouped by status in the theater, the *prima donna* in particular, among them Henry Sutherland Edwards, *The Prima Donna: Her History and Surroundings from the Seventeenth to the Nineteenth Century* (London, 1888); Hermann Klein, *Great Women Singers of My Time* (London, 1931; reprint, Freeport, N.Y.: Books for Libraries Press, 1968); Charles Dupêchez, *Les Divas* (Paris: Ramsay, 1980); Kurt Honolka, *Die grossen Primadonnen: Vom Barock bis zur Gegenwart* (Wilhelmshaven: Heinrichshofen, 1982). For a Lacanian analysis from a feminist viewpoint, see Catherine Clément, *L'Opéra; ou, La défaite des femmes* (Paris: Grasset, 1979), in English translation as *Opera; or, The Undoing of Women*, trans. Betsy Wing (Minneapolis: University of Minnesota Press, 1985). Documents of operatic fetishism include Gustav Kobbé, *Opera Singers: A Pictorial Souvenir* (Boston: Ditson, 1906), and Frederick C. Schang, *Visiting Cards of Prima Donnas* (New York: Vantage, 1977). One work that is interesting for its abundant pictorial material is *The Great Opera Stars in Historic Photographs: 343 Portraits from the 1850s to the 1940s*, ed. James Camner (New York: Dover, 1978). Unlike many slipshod biographies of "great" singers, some recent publications show careful documentation: *Titta Ruffo: An Anthology*, ed. Andrew Farkas (Westport, Conn.: Greenwood, 1984); Howard Bushnell, *Maria Malibran: A Biography of the Singer* (University Park, Penn.: Pennsylvania State University Press, 1979).

There are many works on individual aspects of opera singing or historiographic problems more or less directly connected with operatic singers. Works with a newer point of view include the studies of Robert Freeman and Pierluigi Petrobelli cited in notes 96 and 94, and Elvidio Surian, "Metastasio, i nuovi cantanti, il nuovo stile: Verso il classicismo," in *Venezia e il melodramma nel Settecento*, ed. Maria Teresa Muraro, 2 vols. (Florence: Olschki, 1978–81), 1:341–62, which attempts to analyze the influence of singers on public taste and on composers. On antivirtuoso polemics around 1727, see Francesco Degrada, "Giuseppe Riva e il suo 'Avviso ai compositori ed ai cantanti,'" *Analecta musicologica* 4 (1967): 112–23, also available in Degrada, *Il palazzo incantato: Studi sulla tradizione del melodramma dal Barocco al Romanticismo* (Fiesole: Discanto, 1979), 27–39. On the problem of the relationship between church activities and theatrical activities, see the studies of Olga Termini and Giancarlo Rostirolla cited in note 102. On the social and professional status of the buffo singers during the first half of the eighteenth century, see the studies of Franco Piperno, Piero Weiss, and Reinhard Strohm cited in notes 106 and 108. In addition to the studies of Sergio Durante (cited in notes 51 and 52) on singers in Venice in the early eighteenth century and on their reliance on aristocratic patrons, there is information on the influence of Neapolitan singers on Venice as an operatic center in the 1730s in Sylvie Mamy, "Il teatro alla moda dei rosignoli: I cantanti napoletani al San Giovanni Grisostomo (*Merope*, 1734)," introductory essay to Apostolo Zeno, Domenico Lalli, and Geminiano Giacomelli, *La Merope*, Drammaturgia musicale veneta, no. 18 (Milan: Ricordi, 1984). On the relationship between the singer and the role see (aside from Reinhard Strohm's study cited in note 113) Joseph R. Roach, "Cavaliere Nicolini: London's First Opera Star," *Educational Theatre Journal* 28 (1976): 189–205, a work to be approached with some caution for its uninformed references to Neapolitan conservatories. On the relationship of voice to role in opera seria during the early eighteenth century, see the study by Roger Covell cited in note 110.

A wave of recent publications confirms the current popularity of the eighteenth century as a field for historical and stylistic studies on the role of singers: Klaus Hortschansky, "Die Rolle des Sängers im Drama Metastasios: Giovanni Carestini als Timante in *Demofoonte*," and Sylvie Mamy, "Les Révisions pour Giovanni Carestini du rôle de Timante dans le *Demofoonte* de J. A. Hasse (Venise, 1749)," in *Metastasio e il mondo musicale,* ed. Maria Teresa Muraro (Florence: Olschki, 1986), 207–34 and 235–73, respectively; Dale E. Monson, "Galuppi, Tenducci, and *Motezuma*: A Commentary on the History and Musical Style of Opera Seria after 1750," in *Galuppiana 1985: Studi e richerche,* ed. Maria Teresa Muraro and Franco Rossi (Florence: Olschki, 1986), 279–300; John A. Rice, "Sense, Sensibility, and Opera Seria: An Epistolary Debate," *Studi musicali* 15 (1986): 101–38, on Luigi Marchesi.

Primary sources for the nineteenth century include the works of Nicola Tacchinardi and Heinrich Panofka cited in notes 129 and 137. For a more focused technical study, see Austin Caswell, "Mme Cinti-Damoreau and the Embellishment of Italian Opera in Paris: 1820–1845," *Journal of the American Musicological Society* 28 (1975): 459–92. Among the many writings of Rodolfo Celletti on this topic, see his entry on "La vocalità" in *Storia dell'opera,* cited in note 1, especially the chapter on the nineteenth century. For a useful introduction to problems of vocalism (but one which contains some inaccuracies), see Celletti, *Storia del belcanto* (Fiesole: Discanto, 1983), in English translation as *A History of Bel Canto,* trans. Frederick Fuller (Oxford: Clarendon Press; New York: Oxford University Press, 1991). For a teacher's view of Celletti's criteria and critical categories, see Elio Battaglia, "L'esperto della vocalità," *Nuova rivista musicale italiana* 12 (1978): 67–82. On the categorization of vocal types, see Philippe-Joseph Salazar, *Idéologies de l'opéra* (Paris: Presses Universitaires de France, 1980), chapter 3.

Regarding the castratos see Anton Giulio Bragaglia, *Degli "evirati cantori": Contributo alla storia del teatro* (Florence: Sansoni, 1954), and the work of Angus Heriot cited above. Both works are anecdotal but give useful bibliographic information. On iconography, caricature in particular, see Pierluigi Petrobelli, "Il musicista di teatro settecentesco nelle caricature di Pierleone Ghezzi," in *Antonio Vivaldi: Teatro musicale, cultura e società,* ed. Lorenzo Bianconi and Giovanni Morelli, Studi di musica veneta: Quaderni vivaldiani, 2 vols. (Florence: Olschki, 1982), 2:415–26, "Il mondo del teatro in musica nelle caricature di Pierleone Ghezzi," in *Le muse galanti: La musica a Roma nel Settecento,* ed. Bruno Cagli (Rome: Istituto della Enciclopedia Italiana, 1985), 109–17. The same volume contains a (rather generic) study by Celletti on singers in Rome during the eighteenth century, pages 101–7. On the circulation of caricatures see Edward Croft-Murray, *An Album of Eighteenth-Century Venetian Caricatures, Formerly in the Collection of Count Algarotti* (Toronto: Art Gallery of Ontario, 1980), "Venetian Caricatures," in *Venetian Drawings of the XVII and XVIII Centuries in the Collection of Her Majesty the Queen at Windsor Castle,* ed. Anthony Blunt and Edward Croft-Murray (London: Phaedon Press, 1957), 137–210. One important work is the catalog, *Le caricature di Anton Maria Zanetti,* ed. Alessandro

Bettagno (Vicenza: Neri Pozza, 1969). For photographic documentation see *The Great Opera Stars in Historic Photographs,* cited above.

Extremely interesting as sources, both from the biographical viewpoint and as an indication of taste, are the verse compositions in praise of individual singers or entire companies, which were usually published in the form of broadsides. There is no complete listing of these materials, but one collection, preserved in the Houghton Library at Harvard University, is described in the article by Lowell E. Lindgren and Carl B. Schmidt cited in note 65. Similar materials are scattered in Italian libraries and archives and are occasionally described in special catalogs such as the one by Zeno Davoli cited in note 65, 22ff. A sheet of the sort in praise of Violante Vestri is reproduced in *The New Grove Dictionary of Music and Musicians,* s.v. "Milan." Less frequently there were collections of pieces in praise of one exceptionally fine singer, such as *Le glorie della Signora Anna Renzi romana* (Venice, 1644), mentioned in note 40, or later the *Rime di vari autori in lode della celeberrima signora Faustina Bordoni Hasse* ([Venice], 1739). Such works usually contain poetry of little worth, but there were exceptions: Muratori thought well enough of a few sonnets of the sort to include them in his edition of the *Rime varie* of Carlo Maria Maggi, 4 vols. (Milan, 1700), vol. 3; an ode of Tommaso Crudeli, *In lode del signor Carlo Broschi detto Farinello, musico celebre* (Florence, 1734), is recognized as one of the most representative examples of eighteenth-century lyric poetry. The genre continued to be cultivated into the following century, but it tended to be dedicated to female singers exclusively.

For information on teaching in the conservatories, the classic work on the Neapolitan school is Salvatore di Giacomo, *I quattro antichi conservatorii di musica a Napoli,* 2 vols. (Palermo: Sandron, 1924–28); for more recent studies see Helmut Hucke, "Verfassung und Entwicklung der alten neapolitanischen Konservatorien," in *Festschrift Helmuth Osthoff zum 65. Geburtstage,* ed. Lothar Hoffmann-Erbrecht and Helmut Hucke (Tutzing: Schneider, 1961), 139–54; Michael F. Robinson, "The Governors' Minutes of the Conservatory S. Maria di Loreto, Naples," *R. M. A. Research Chronicle* 10 (1972): 1–97. For Venice see Giancarlo Rostirolla, "L'organizzazione musicale nell'Ospedale veneziano della Pietà al tempo di Vivaldi," *Nuova rivista musicale italiana* 13 (1979): 168–95, and a useful exhibition catalog, *Arte e musica all'Ospedaletto: Schede d'archivio sull'attività musicale degli ospedali dei Derelitti e dei Mendicanti di Venezia (sec. XVI–XVII)* (Venice: Stamperia di Venezia, 1978). For information on the many singers who trained in Rome during the seventeenth century, see Thomas D. Culley, *Jesuits and Music: A Study of the Musicians Connected with the German College in Rome During the Seventeenth Century and of their Activities in Northern Europe* (Rome: Jesuit Historical Institute; St. Louis, Mo.: St. Louis University Press, 1970). A number of studies sponsored during the Fascist era by the Ministry of National Education refer principally to nineteenth-century conservatories, at times providing information on early years (see note 122). Among more recent studies, in addition to the one by Alberto Basso and the one on the Conservatorio di Parma cited in note 122, see *Il Conservatorio di musica "Benedetto Marcello" di Venezia,* ed. Pietro Verardo (Venice: Stamperia di Venezia, 1977).

On didactic sources, see *Die Musik in Geschichte und Gegenwart,* s.v. "Gesangspädagogik," by Arnold Geering. On the *bicinia,* see Jean Van Altena, "The Textless

Duo in Italian Printed Sources of the Sixteenth and First Half of the Seventeenth Centuries" (Ph.D. diss., Northwestern University, 1979).

On problems regarding discography see Michael Scott, *The Record of Singing to 1914*, 3 vols., records (London: Duckworth; New York: Scribner, 1977); Carlo Marinelli, *Opere in disco da Monteverdi a Berg* (Fiesole: Discanto, 1982); Lorenzo Bianconi, preface to vol. 1 of Susanna Gozzi and Alessandro Roccatagliati, *Catalogo della discoteca storica "Arrigo ed Egle Agosti" di Reggio Emilia* (Florence: Olschki, 1985–). Although it lacks rigor, Cornelius L. Reid, *A Dictionary of Vocal Terminology: An Analysis* (New York: Patelson, 1983) is useful on terminology

———

Since this chapter was first published, many studies related to the subject have appeared. The most important of these is John Rosselli, *Singers of Italian Opera: The History of a Profession* (Cambridge: Cambridge University Press, 1992), reviewed by Sergio Durante in *Notes* ser. 2, vol. 52, no. 1 (1995): 75–77. This book was preceded by a notable series of essays by Rosselli, including "L'apprendistato del cantante italiano: Rapporti contrattuali fra allievi e insegnanti dal Cinquecento al Novecento," *Rivista Italiana di Musicologia* 23 (1988) 157–81; "The Castrati as a Professional Group and a Social Phenomenon, 1550–1850," *Acta musicologica* 60 (1988): 143–79; and "From Princely Service to the Open Market: Singers of Italian Opera and their Patrons 1600–1850," *Cambridge Opera Journal* 1, no. 1 (1989): 1–32.

Relevant problems of the schooling systems in different periods and places were discussed at the study session of the fourteenth congress of the International Musicological Society in Bologna, "Condizioni materiali e forme di trasmissione del sapere musicale: Il caso delle scuole di canto." The papers given there by John Rosselli, Philippe Lescat, Sylvie Mamy, and Ellen Rosand are now published in *Atti del XIV Congresso della Società Internazionale di Musicologia: Trasmissione e recezione delle forme di cultura musicale*, vol. 2, *Study Sessions*, ed. Angelo Pompilio, Donatella Restani, Lorenzo Bianconi, and F. Alberto Gallo (Turin: Edizioni di Torino, 1990), 171–225.

On the question of the different Italian pitch standards (mentioned in note 114), see Partrizio Barbieri, "Il corista bolognese, secondo il rilevamento di V. F. Stancari," *L'organo* 18 (1980; published in 1983): 15–29.

On individual singers of historical importance, see N. Lucarelli, *Domenico Bruni (1758–1821): Biografia di un cantante evirato* (Città di Castello: Comune di Umbertide, [1987]); Carlo Vitali, "Ein 'Star' barocken Kirchengesangs: Lorenzo Gaggiotti," *Kirchenmusikalisches Jahrbuch* 76 (1992): 59–71.

Important letters of one of the greatest singing stars of all time, Farinelli, are available in Carlo Vitali, "Da 'schiavottiello' a 'fedele amico': Lettere (1731–1749) di Carlo Broschi Farinelli al conte Sicinio Pepoli," *Nuova rivista musicale italiana* (1992): 1–36. Also on Farinelli see the nonscholarly Sandro Cappelletto, *La voce perduta: Vita di Farinelli evirato cantore* (Turin: Edizioni di Torino, 1995).

Archival items are published in Paola Besutti, *La corte musicale di Fernando Carlo Gonzaga ultimo duca di Mantova: Musici, cantanti e teatro d'opera tra il 1665 e il 1707* (Mantua: Arcari, 1989).

For an important but little-known discussion of aesthetics and singers, see John A. Rice, "Benedetto Frizzi on Singers, Composers, and Opera in Late Eighteenth-Century Italy," *Studi musicali* 23 (1994): 367–93.

For an analysis of registers with potentially broad consequences, see Harold S. Powers, "Il 'do del baritono' nel 'gioco delle parti' verdiano," in *Opera e libretto II,* ed. Giovanni Morelli (Florence: Olschki, 1993), 267–81.

For an example of the problems involved in the interpretation of singers' technical vocabulary, see Sergio Durante, "Strutture mentali e vocabolario di un cantore antico/ moderno: Preliminari per una lettura delle fonti didattische settecentesche," in *Alessandro Scarlatti und seine Zeit,* ed. Max Lütolf (Bern: Paul Haupt, 1995), 38–54. For a comprehensive study of nineteenth-century Italian treatises on singing, see Marco Beghelli, "I trattati di canto italiani dell'Ottocento: Bibliografia, caratteri generali, prassi esecutiva, lessico," unpublished doctoral dissertation, University of Bologna, 1995. Also useful is the entry in *The New Grove Dictionary of Opera,* s.v. "Singing. A Bibliography."

Index of Names

Abbado, Claudio, 217
Abbatini, Antonio Maria, 297, 309n, 321n
Abert, Hermann, xii
Acciaiuoli, Filippo, 23, 238
Adamberger, Valentino, 45n
Adami, Giuseppe, 278, 336n
Ademollo, Alessandro, 349n
Adorno, Giacinto, 18
Adorno, Theodor Wiesengrund, 215
Adorno family, 18–19, 29, 34
Affligio, Giuseppe, 117
Agnadini, Antonio, 355
Agostini, Pietro Simone, 321n
Agricola, Johann Friedrich, 389, 393
Albarelli, Luigi, 362
Albergati, Francesco, 383
Albertini, Luigi, 191
Albini, Marietta, 326n
Albinoni, Tomaso, 53, 61–62, 243n, 318, 326n
Albizzi, Luca Casimiro degli, 56
Aldrovandini, Giuseppe Antonio Vincenzo, 361–62
Alessandri, Antonio degli, 61n
Alfano, Franco, 213
Alfieri, Vittorio, 266
Algarotti, Francesco, 337n, 379
Alibert, Count Giacomo d', 12, 20, 23
Alovar, Pietro (Pierre Alouard), 48
Amorevoli, Angelo, 387, 398n

Andreozzi, Gaetano, 317n, 319, 326n
Anfossi, Pasquale, 57, 68, 308n
Angelini (singer), 173
Angiolini, Gasparo (Domenico Maria Angiolo Gasparini), 46–47
Anichini, Caterina, 48
Apolloni, Giovanni Filippo, 238
Appiani, Giuseppe, 378
Aprile, Giuseppe, 251, 383, 393
Aquilanti, Francesco, 46
Archenholz, Johann Wilhelm von, 371
Archi, Antonio (Il Cortoncino), 373n
Archilei, Vittoria, 347n, 349
Arena, Giuseppe, 52
Aristotle, 254
Armano, Baldassare, 41n
Arner, Carlo, 190
Artaria (publishing firm), 158
Arteaga, Stefano (Esteban), 46
Aschieri, Caterina, 48
Asioli, Bonifazio, 310–11
Asola, Giovanni Matteo, 366
Asor Rosa, Alberto, 240
Astorga, Emanuele d', 352, 390
Auletta, Pietro, 64, 292
Aureli, Aurelio, 3, 235, 236, 239
Azeglio, Massimo Taparelli d', 260

Babbi, Gregorio, 387
Babbini, Matteo, 326

Baccelli, Guido, 167, 171
Bacchini, Girolamo (Il pretino), 347
Badoaro, Giacomo, 16, 235
Baglioni, Francesco, 65–66
Baillou, Luigi de, 49
Baldi, Raffaello, 361
Balochino, Carlo, 106, 113, 117–18, 138, 155
Balzac, Honoré de, 398n
Banner, Giannantonio, 310n
Barbaja, Domenico, 85, 102, 105–6, 113, 117–18, 123, 126n, 127–28, 141, 143, 145, 158, 174, 299, 323
Barberini, Cardinal Antonio, 7, 238
Barberini, Cardinal Francesco, 7
Barberini, Maffeo Vincenzo, bishop of Spoleto, 358. *See also* Urban VIII (Maffeo Vincenzo Barberini)
Barberini family, 5, 20, 109, 353, 354
Barbieri, Fedora, 212
Barbieri-Nini, Marianna, 94, 105, 137
Bardella, Francesco, 19
Barezzi, Antonio, 308
Barlocci, Giovanni Gualberto, 65n
Baroni, Muzio, 349
Bartók, Béla, 197, 204, 209
Bartoluzzi, Girolamo, 377
Basile Baroni, Adriana, 349–50
Basile, Giovambattista, 349n
Basile, Margherita, 350n
Bassi, Carolina, 263
Bastianini, Ettore, 212
Battistini, Vincenzo, 135
Baumol, William J., 223
Bava Beccaris, Fiorenzo, 179
Bazzini, Antonio, 316
Bêche, Jean-Louis, 393
Beethoven, Ludwig van, 307
Belasco, David, 341
Belisani family, 373
Belli, Giuseppe Gioachino, 148
Bellincioni, Gemma, 406
Bellini, Vincenzo, 119, 136, 142–43, 147, 151–52, 183, 187, 196, 199, 258, 265–66, 272–75, 293n, 297, 323, 328, 334, 337n, 340, 399
Belloc-Giorgi, Maria Teresa, 399
Benati, Gaetano, 381n
Benelli, Giovanni Battista, 154
Benti-Bulgarelli, Marianna, 53
Bentivoglio, Enzo, 351, 365–66

Bentivoglio family, 366
Benvenuto, Matteo, 66n
Berberian, Cathy, 408
Beregan, Nicolò, 16
Berenstadt, Gaetano, 373, 374n
Berg, Alban, 197, 204, 209
Berio, Luciano, 215, 285
Berio di Salsa, Francesco, 271
Berlioz, Hector, 146, 311
Bernacchi, Antonio Maria, 44, 372, 378–80, 392
Bertati, Giovanni, 68, 271
Berti, Carlo, 348
Bertoni, Ferdinando, 51n, 251, 269
Berzezio, Vittorio, 272
Besci, Paolo Pompeo, 26n
Bezzi, Tomaso, 13
Biaggi, Girolamo Alessandro, 169
Biancardi, Sebastiano (Domenico Lalli), 251n, 252
Bianchi, Bernardino, 12, 24
Bianchi, Francesco, 308n, 312n, 326n
Bianchi, Giovanni, 42n
Bianconi, Giovanni Ludovico, 372
Bibiena Galli family, 55
Bisaccioni, Maiolino, 16, 235
Bismantova, Bartolomeo, 364
Bizet, Georges, xii, 175, 188
Blasis, Carlo, 399–400
Blume, Bianca, 176
Boccabadati, Luigia, 113
Boccacci, Costantino, 129, 172
Bocchini, Arturo, 205
Boccoli, Arcangelo, 316n
Boito, Arrigo, 169, 179, 183, 189, 194, 274–78, 316
Bogianckino, Massimo, 218n
Bolognini Fontana, Teresa, 377n
Bonavia, Maria Maddalena, 326n
Bonelli, Giovanni Paolo, 355
Bonlini, Giovanni Carlo, 367–68
Bonola, Giovanni Battista, 144
Bononcini, Antonio Maria, 313
Bononcini, Giovanni, 312n, 313
Bontempi, Giovanni Andrea Angelini, 364–66
Bordoni, Faustina, 23–24, 44n, 314n, 326n, 381, 383n, 390, 401
Boretti, Giovanni Antonio, 3
Borghese, Prince Marco Antonio, 313
Borghese family, 313

Borghi, Giovanni Battista, 319
Borosini, Francesco, 387
Borrelli, Enzo, 214
Borromeo, Count Vitaliano, 14n
Borsa, Matteo, 47
Borsi, Carlo Antonio, 330n
Boselli, Paolo, 167
Bossi, Marco Enrico, 192
Bottai, Giuseppe, 193
Botteghi, Caterina Angiola (La Centoventi), 368n
Bragaglia, Anton Giulio, 196
Brambilla, Teresa (Teresina), 140, 326n
Branca, Emilia, 271–72, 337
Branca family, 337
Brandi, Antonio (Il Brandino), 349
Brenna, Guglielmo, 106, 258–59
Brescianello, Giuseppe Antonio, 298–99
Britten, Benjamin, 210, 213
Brivio, Giuseppe Ferdinando, 52
Brocchi, Marco Antonio, 355
Brogi, Caterina, 63–65
Broglio, Emilio, 169
Broschi, Carlo (Farinelli), 24, 44, 229, 246, 248, 326, 370, 371n, 375, 378, 380, 386
Broschi, Riccardo, 326
Brosses, Charles de, 31–32, 43n, 51, 61, 70n, 320n, 370–71
Brugnoli, Amalia, 112n
Bucchi, Valentino, 213
Buffa and Company (publishing firm), 184
Buratti, Pietro, 42n
Burcardi, Filippo, 145
Burney, Charles, 43n, 58n, 66n, 67n, 329, 371n, 374–75, 380n
Busenello, Giovanni Francesco, 11, 16, 235–36
Busoni, Ferruccio Benvenuto, 197, 209
Bussotti, Sylvano, 215, 307n, 326
Buti, Francesco, 238

Caballé, Montserrat, 408
Cacciari, Massimo, 285
Caccini, Francesca (La Cecchina), 348–50
Caccini, Giulio, 232–33, 297, 346–50
Cafaro, Pasquale (Caffariello), 23, 44, 315
Cagnazzi, Luca, 404
Cagnoni, Antonio, 187, 305
Calcina, Giacomo, 377
Caldara, Antonio, 313, 326n

Caldara, Emilio, 191
Caldesi, Vincenzo, 121n
Callas, Maria (Maria Anna Kalogeropoulos), 212, 408
Calvé, Emma, 406
Calvino, Italo, 285
Calzabigi, Ranieri de', 252–53, 271, 337n
Cammarano, Salvadore, 268, 274
Campagnolo, Francesco, 352
Campanini, Barbara, 48
Campanini, Domitilla, 48
Campeggi, Francesco, 372
Campigli, Andrea, 115
Campioni, Giustina, 48
Camuri, Pietro, 124
Canavasso, Vittorio Amedeo, 49
Canedi, Ippolito, 99n
Canori, Guglielmo, 172
Canovetti, Cesare, 131–32
Canovetti, Cosimo, 131–32
Cantù, Cesare, 183
Canziani, Giovanni, 32, 47n, 48
Capranica, Bartolomeo, 102
Capranica family, 116
Capua, Rinaldo da, 63, 65, 293, 329
Carafa, Cardinal Gian Pietro, 240
Carafa, Luigi, prince of Stigliano, 349
Carafa, Prince Michele, di Colobrano, 302
Carasale, Antonio, 37
Carducci, Giosue, 183
Carelli, Emma, 182, 193–94
Carestini, Giovanni (Il Cusanino), 373n
Carlani, Carlo, 380, 386–87
Carli, Antonfrancesco, 387n
Carlo Alberto of Savoy-Carignano, king of Sardinia, 257
Carlo Emanuele III, duke of Savoy, 5n, 38
Carlo Felice, king of Sardinia, 100
Carmignano, Carlo, 314n
Carminati, Giovanni Battista, 271
Carnoli, Pietro Paolo, 378
Carpani, Giuseppe, 337
Carré, Albert, 332n
Carteri, Rosanna, 212
Cartoni, Pietro, 115–16
Cartoni family, 157
Caruso, Enrico, 178, 327
Caruso, Luigi, 319
Casanova, Giovanni Giacomo, 253
Casella, Alfredo, 196, 197

Caselli, Angelo, 374
Casini, Cesare Augusto, 271
Casorati, Felice, 196
Castelli, Anna, 61
Castelpagano, duchess of, 314n
Castelnuovo, duke of, 308n
Casti, Giovanni Battista, da Montefiascone, 253–54, 271, 278
Castiglione, Baldassarre, 305
Castris, Francesco de, 361, 373
Catalani, Alfredo, 158, 160, 187, 189, 297, 302, 305, 307n, 308, 312, 316, 325n
Cattaneo, Claudia, 326n
Cattivelli, Giovanni Battista, 362
Cavalieri, Emilio de', 232, 348n
Cavalli, Francesco, 11, 15, 22–23, 26n, 229, 235–36, 295n, 297, 307n, 309n, 320, 321n, 326
Cavallotti, Felice, 183
Cavana, Giovanni Battista, 62
Cavour, Camillo Benso, conte di, 81, 167
Cecchi, Anna Maria (La Beccarina), 373
Cecchi, Domenico (Il Cortona), 363, 373n
Celletti, Rodolfo, 372n, 406, 408n
Cencelli (librettist), 271
Cencetti, Giovanni Battista, 187
Cerquetti, Anita, 212
Cerù, Nicolao, 308
Cesti, Antonio, 12, 239, 297, 307n, 309n, 312, 321n, 333
Charles, Bourbon king of Naples and Sicily (later Charles III, king of Spain), 37, 42, 46, 100
Charles VI, Holy Roman Emperor, 243, 247, 313, 380
Cherubini, Luigi, 196, 312n, 408
Chiari, Pietro, 68, 71
Chigi, Cardinal Flavio, 238
Chigi family, 14n, 238
Chinzer, Giovanni, 23
Chiti, Girolamo, 383
Christina, queen of Sweden, 20, 238
Ciacchi, Cesare, 171
Ciampi, Vincenzo, 64
Cicognini, Giacinto Andrea, 12, 15, 235, 238
Cigna-Santi, Vittorio Amedeo, 45n, 51n, 251
Cilea, Francesco, 192, 199, 297, 305, 308n, 312, 325n
Cimador, Giovanni Battista, 326
Cimarosa, Domenico, 57, 68, 101, 311, 319

Cirillo, Francesco, 12
Ciuffolotti, Vincenzo, 308n
Civinini, Guelfo, 278
Clement IX, pope (Giulio Rospigliosi), 16, 20
Clement X, pope (Emilio Altieri), 20
Clement XI, pope (Giovanni Francesco Albani), 39
Clement XII, pope (Lorenzo Corsini), 39
Clerico, Francesco, 47, 48
Closè, Clementina, 378n
Cocchi, Gioacchino, 65, 317n
Coccia, Carlo, 102, 135, 316, 317n, 336
Colbran, Isabella Angela, 117, 326n, 327, 399
Coli, Antonio, 311
Colombina, Giacomo, 42n
Colonna, Cardinal Carlo, 55
Colonna family, 238, 313
Coltellini, Celeste, 373
Comarolo, Giovanni, 42n
Comarolo, Pietro, 42n
Conati, Marcello, 156
Condillac, Étienne Bonnot de, 337n
Confalonieri, Margherita, 355
Consalvi, Cardinal Ercole, 101
Contarini family, 14n
Conti, Gioacchino (Gizziello), 54, 378
Copeau, Jacques, 106
Coppino, Michele, 167
Corazza, Carlotta, 120
Corneille, Pierre, xii
Corona, Achille, 218
Corradi, Giulio Cesare, 11
Corrado, Gioacchino, 63–64
Correale, Giacomo, 308n
Correr, Count Giacomo, 102
Correr, Marc'Antonio, 22
Corsi, Jacopo, 232, 327n
Corticelli, Mauro, 130, 132
Cosimi, Anna, 370, 371n
Cosimo II de' Medici, grand duke of Tuscany, 358
Cosmi, Emanuela, 326n
Costa, Margherita, 361
Costa, Silvestro, 372
Costanzi, Domenico, 181
Cotogni, Antonio, 173
Cottrau, Teodoro, 184, 187
Coyer, Gabriel-François, 43n, 70n
Cremonini, Cesare, 245

Crescentini, Girolamo, 44, 73, 394
Crescimbeni, Giovanni Mario, 241
Crespi, Teresa, 72
Cricchi, Domenico, 61, 63
Crivelli, Gaetano, 327
Crivelli, Giuseppe, 106, 117, 122
Curioni, Alberico, 112
Cusani family, 373n
Cuzzoni, Francesca, 381
Cybo Gonzaga, Ricciarda, duchess of, 308n

Dallapiccola, Luigi, 196–97, 199, 209, 213–14, 285, 307n, 326
Dalla Rizza, Gilda, 327, 333n
D'Amico, Fedele, 214, 408n
D'Annunzio, Gabriele, 275, 281–82, 283
Da Ponte, Lorenzo, 68, 253–55, 271
D'Arcais, Francesco, 176–77
D'Atri, Nicola, 192
David, Domenico, 50
David, Giacomo, 44
De Amicis, Anna Lucia, 73
De Bassini, Achille, 146
Debussy, Claude, 181
De Chiaro, Carlo, 299n
De Chirico, Giorgio, 196
De Gamerra, Giovanni, 253
De Giuli Borsi, Teresa, 330n
Delibes, Clément-Philibert-Léo, 188
Delisle, Jean-Philippe, 42n
Delle Sedie, Enrico, 402–3
Del Monaco, Mario, 212
De Luca, Giuseppe, 327
De Lucia, Fernando, 406
De Majo, Gian Francesco, 319
Dent, Edward J., 203
De Pirro, Nicola, 195, 197, 209
De Pisis, Filippo (Filippo Tibertelli), 196
De Sanctis, Francesco, 183, 240, 246, 248
De Santi, Anna, 326n
Desiderati, Antonio, 372
Di Giacomo, Salvatore, 375
Dionisotti, Carlo, xiii
Di Stefano, Giuseppe, 212
Donizetti, Gaetano, 118–19, 136, 142–43, 145, 149, 152n, 187, 199, 229, 258, 266–67, 272, 275, 293, 296, 298, 306, 312, 316, 320, 326, 337, 338n
Donzelli, Domenico, 94, 263
Dotti, Angiola, 6n

Dotti, Bartolomeo, 318n
Dotti, Geltrude, 66n
Dottori, Carlo de', 239–40, 250
Draghi, Antonio, 240, 312n
Duni, Egidio Romualdo, 317n
Duodo, Alvise, 22
Duprez, Gilbert-Louis, 119–20, 123, 139, 140, 400–401
Durante, Francesco, 306
Durazzo, Eugenio, 19
Duse troupe, 83
Dutillieu, Pierre, 49

Egk, Werner, 203
Enghien, duke of (Louis II, duc d'Enghien, prince de Condé), 352
Erba, Luigi, 180
Este. *See under individual names* Ettore, Guglielmo, 370, 371n
Eugenio of Savoy, 36
Eximeno, Antonio, 249

Fabbri, Annibale Pio, 372n, 386
Fabrici, Natale, 106
Fabrizi, Vincenzo, 68
Facconi, Paolo, 350
Faini, Anna, 44n, 64
Fancelli, Giuseppe, 173, 178
Farinacci, Roberto, 193, 202
Farinelli. *See* Broschi, Carlo (Farinelli)
Farnese, Edoardo, duke of Parma, 359
Farnese family, 362
Faustini, Giovanni, 15–16, 235
Faustini, Marco, 17–18, 22, 25n, 297n, 333
Favier, Jean, 48
Federici, Domenico, 239
Federico, Gennaro Antonio, 60–61, 63, 65
Felice, Giuseppe, 371n
Fellini, Federico, 326
Fenaroli, Fedele, 306
Feo, Francesco, 306, 321
Ferdinand IV (Ferdinando di Borbone), king of Naples, 71n
Ferdinando II, king of Naples, 124
Ferdinando I de' Medici, grand duke of Tuscany, 3, 14n, 19, 23
Ferdinando Carlo, archduke of the Tyrol, 312n
Ferlotti, Santina, 397
Fernandez, Dominique, 399n

Ferrandini, Giovanni, 378, 393
Ferrari, Angelo, 171
Ferrari, Benedetto, 8, 9, 14, 16, 22, 235, 293
Ferrari, Cherubino, 347n
Ferrero, Giovanni, 186, 189
Ferretti, Jacopo, 256, 267–68, 270–71
Ferrini, Antonio Romolo, 362
Festa, Francesca, 399
Fétis, François-Joseph, 292
Filippo di Borbone, duke of Parma, 37
Filippucci, Agostino, 372
Fink, Gottfried Wilhelm, xii
Fischietti, Domenico, 68
Flauto, Vincenzio, 115, 123
Floridia, Pietro, 274
Florimo, Francesco, 266, 292, 308n
Flotow, Friedrich von, 187
Fontana, Carlo, 218n
Fontana, Pietro Antonio, 375–76
Foppa, Giuseppe Maria, 257, 269–70, 282
Formenti, Antonio, 383n
Forti (singer), 263
Fortis, Leone, 276–77
Forzano, Giovacchino, 278
Foscolo, Ugo, 42n
Fragonard, Jean-Honoré, 43n
Franceschini, Giovanni Battista, 362
Franceschini, Giuseppe, 66n
Francesco II d'Este, duke of Modena and
    Reggio Emilia, 13, 313
Francesco III d'Este, duke of Modena, 37
Francesco IV of Austro-Este, duke of
    Modena, 153
Franchetti, Alberto, 302, 307n
Francia, Osea, 121n
Frazzi, Vito, 199
Freschi, Giovanni Domenico, 307n
Frescobaldi, Girolamo, 366
Frezzolini, Erminia, 140, 149
Fricci, Antonietta 2, 3
Frigemelica, Girolamo (nephew), 240
Frigimelica, Girolamo (uncle), 240
Frigimelica Roberti, Girolamo, 17
Frugoni, Carlo Innocenzo, 250
Fusai, Ippolito, 361
Fux, Johann Joseph, 306, 310

Gabrielli, Caterina (La Coghetta), 251, 373
Gabussi, Rita, 397
Gaggiotti, Pellegrino, 63, 64

Gagliano, Marco da, 232–33, 349, 359
Galiani, Ferdinando, 250n
Galilei, Galileo, 238
Galli, Antimo, 350
Galli, Filippo, 263
Galliard, John Ernest, 388n, 389, 393
Galliari family, 55
Gallignani, Giuseppe, 179
Galuppi, Baldassare, 52, 54–55, 57, 65–66,
    68, 269, 296n, 312n
Gara, Eugenio, 408n
García, Manuel Patricio Rodriguez, 404
Garelli family, 372
Garulli, Alfonso, 406
Gasparini, Francesco, 62, 311n, 313, 318,
    377, 384, 390
Gasparini, Michelangelo, 23, 54n
Gassmann, Florian Leopold, 59n, 68, 315
Gatti, Carlo, 197, 335n
Gatti, Guido M., 196
Gatti-Casazza, Giulio, 179–80
Gavazzeni, Gianandrea, 408n
Gazzaniga, Giuseppe, 45n, 68, 308n, 315
Generali, Pietro, 316
Gentile, Giovanni, 167
Gero, Jhan, 366
Gérod (dancer), 173
Ghedini, Giorgio Federico, 196–97, 285
Ghelli, Antonio, 124
Ghezzi, Ambrogio, 72
Ghezzi, Pierleone, pl. 35; 24n, 320n
Ghislanzoni, Alberto, 202n
Ghislanzoni, Antonio, 154, 267, 273–74,
    278, 323
Giacomelli, Geminiano, 292
Giacosa, Giuseppe, 190, 278–80, 337n
Giamberti, Giuseppe, 366
Gigli, Beniamino, 327
Gigli, Clarice, 363
Gigli, Girolamo, 16, 243n, 252
Ginguené, Pierre-Louis, 392n
Giolitti, Giovanni, 188, 205
Giordani, Giuseppe, 319, 326n
Giordano, Umberto, 199, 275, 297, 302, 325,
    339
Giorgina (singer), 361
Giovanardi (Zanardi), Nicolò, 377
Giovanetti, Italo, 99n
Giraldoni, Leone, 402–4
Girard, Bernardo, 187

Giudici e Strada (publishing firm), 184
Giustiniani family, 18, 362
Glossop, Joseph, 115
Gluck, Christoph Willibald, xii, 50, 52, 55–56, 58, 315, 391–92, 398n, 408
Gobatti, Stefano, 151
Gobbi, Tito, 212
Goethe, Johann Wolfgang, 276
Goldmark, Karl, 187
Goldoni, Carlo, 19, 63, 65–66, 68, 137, 251n, 252–53
Gomes, Antônio Carlos, 185
Gomez, Italo, 218n
Gonzaga, Cardinal Ferdinando, 233
Gonzaga, Ferdinando Carlo, duke of Mantua, 363
Gonzaga, Francesco, 5n, 347
Gonzaga, Guglielmo, duke of Mantua, 350
Gonzaga, Vincenzo I, duke of Mantua, 349, 351
Gonzaga family, 233
Gorrio, Tobia. *See* Arrigo Boito
Gounod, Charles, xiii, 187
Gozzi, Gasparo, 48n, 58n
Grandi, Tommaso, 68
Grassi, Paolo, 218
Gravina, Gian Vincenzo, 241, 245–46
Graziosi, Giorgio, 212
Grazzini, Antonfrancesco, 47
Gregory XVI, pope (Bartolomeo Albert Cappellari), 257
Grillenzoni, Lelio, 349
Grimaldi, Nicola, 44n, 53
Grimani, Cardinal Vincenzo, 13, 55, 314n
Grimani family, 11, 17–18, 23–24, 34, 252, 312, 362
Grisi, Giulia, 146
Grossatesta, Gaetano, 46
Grossi, Giovanni Francesco (Siface), 363, 373n
Guagni, Domenico, 23
Gualerzi, Giorgio, 408n
Guarducci, Tommaso, 380
Guarini, Battista, 246
Guastalla, Claudio, 203
Guerri, Andrea, 362
Gugliantini, Pietro, 46
Guglielmi, Pietro Alessandro, 57n, 68, 308n, 317n, 326n
Gui, Vittorio, 196, 208

Guicciardini family, 105
Guidi, Giovanni Gualberto, 187–88
Guillion, Alberto, 262n

Halévy, Fromental, 185
Handel, George Frideric, xii, 35, 55, 314n, 334n, 336, 370n, 398n
Hasse, Johann Adolf, 51n, 52, 55, 60–61, 63, 64, 229, 246, 262, 298, 314n, 326, 371n, 386
Haydn, Franz Josef, 293, 307, 311
Heiberger, Giuseppe, 67
Heidegger, John Jacop, 35, 55n
Helferstorfer, Teresa von, 326n
Henry, Louis, 112n
Heriot, Angus, 375
Hervé (Florimond Ronger), 188
Hindemith, Paul, 196, 204, 209, 210
Hitler, Adolph, 202, 204
Horne, Marilyn, 408
Hubert, Antonio (Porporino), 399n
Hugo, Victor, 259, 284

Illica, Luigi, 278–82
Imer, Giuseppe, 60n
Innocent XI, pope (Benedetto Odescalchi), 39
Innocent XII, pope (Antonio Pignatelli), 20, 39
Isola, Anna, 63
Ivanovich, Cristoforo, 10n, 18, 236–38, 239, 251

Jackson, Jane, 326n
Jacobs, René, 408
Jacovacci, Vincenzo, 95n, 116, 121, 125, 149, 158, 186
Janacconi, Giuseppe, 306
Jander, Owen, 405
Jommelli, Niccolò, 44n, 52, 54, 57, 60n, 296n, 298–99, 314n, 317n, 329, 392
Joseph I, Holy Roman emperor, 313
Joseph II, Holy Roman emperor, 97, 254
Juvarra, Filippo, 55

Karl Eugen, duke of Württemberg, 298
Kastner, Jean-Georges, 311
Krauss, Gabrielle, 174

Lablache, Luigi, 147, 399
Labroca, Mario, 196–98, 284

Lalande, Joseph-Jérôme Le Français de, 43n, 61
Lambardi, Dimurgo, 350
Lambertini, Domenica, 72
Lapugnani, Giovanni Battista, 66n, 293, 326
Lanari, Alessandro, 94, 103, 105–6, 113, 119–20, 122–25, 128, 131–35, 143–46, 154, 158, 169, 171n
Lanari, Antonio, 105, 120, 129–31, 320n
Lancetti, Lucia, 386
Lancetti, Vincenzo, 262
Landi, Stefano, 297, 309n, 321n, 403
La Pira, Giorgio, 214
Larderel, Florestano de, 309
Laschi, Filippo, 64, 72
Lasso, Orlando di, 366
Latilla, Gaetano, 64–65, 293
Laurenti, Anna Maria, 386
Laurenti family, 373
Laurenzi, Filiberto, 359–60
Lavagetto, Mario, 109
Lavaggi, Alessandro, 173
Lavigna, Vincenzo, 306–7, 312n, 315–16
Lecocq, Alexandre-Charles, 188
Le Compte, Claude, 188
Lee, Vernon (Violet Paget), 398n
Lefèvre, Domenico, 46
Legrenzi, Giovanni, 307n, 312n, 321n
Lehár, Franz, 206
Leidesdorf, Maximilian Josef, 307
Leli, Maria, 326n
Le Messier, Giuseppe Antonio, 49
Leo, Leonardo, 63, 246, 306, 308n, 341, 378
Leo, Teodomiro, 308n
Leonardi, Giovanni, 72
Leoncavallo, Ruggero, 171, 297, 325n, 328n
Leonesi, Luigi, 388
Leopardi, Giacomo, 265
Leopold I, Holy Roman emperor, 239–40
Le Picq, Charles, 32, 48
Levesque, Nicolò, 46
Lévesque (author), 393
Lisi, Anna Maria, 362
Livigni, Filippo, 68
Lodi, Silvia (La Spagnoletta), 373n
Logroscino, Nicola, 1, 292, 318–19, 320n
Lombardo, Carlo, 207
Lombardo Radice, Giuseppe, 167
Loredan family, 109

Loredano, Giovan Francesco, 360
Lorenzi, Giambattista, 251
Lorini, Achille, 120
Lotti, Antonio, 296n, 318, 326n
Lottini, Antonio, 23, 44n, 377
Lozzano, Giuseppina, 397
Lucca, Francesco, 159–60, 187
Lucca, Giovanna Strazza, 159, 187, 316
Lucca (publishing firm), 158–59, 176, 184–85, 188, 319, 396
Luchesi, Pompeo, 251
Ludovisi, Cardinal Ludovico, 358
Lully, Jean-Baptiste, 330
Lupacchino dal Vasto, Bernardino, 366

Maccari, Mino, 196
Maderna, Bruno, 215
Maffei, Andrea, 268, 273n
Maffei, Scipione, xiv, 242
Magagnoli, Ginevra, 63, 64
Maggi, Carlo Maria, 241
Magli, Giovanni Gualberto, 347, 349
Magliabechi, Antonio, 243
Magotti, Alessandro, 144
Magotti, Antonio, 144
Mainwaring, John, 294n
Majorano, Gaetano (Caffarelli), 375
Malanotte, Adelaide, 408
Malibran, Maria Felicita, 94, 154
Malipiero, Gian Francesco, 196–97, 207, 213, 283–84, 307n
Mallio (librettist), 271
Mamiani della Rovere, Terenzio, 266
Mancini, Giambattista, 375–79, 385, 388–90, 393, 398
Manelli, Francesco, 8–9, 10n, 14, 16, 293, 307n, 309n, 321n, 326n
Manelli, Maddalena, 326n
Mann, Thomas, 278
Manna, Gennaro, 317n, 319
Mannstein, Heinrich Ferdinand, 392–93
Mantelli, Alberto, 215
Mantua, duke of, 23, 239, 348, 350, 352. *See also under* Gonzaga
Mantua, duchess of, 233–34, 351
Manzoni, Alessandro, 275
Manzotti, Luigi, 184
Manzuoli, Giovanni, 73
Maray, Fanny, 397

Marazzoli, Marco, 297, 309n, 320, 321n, 354

Marcello, Benedetto, 252–53, 373, 381, 387n, 390

Marcello family, 18

Marchesini, Santa, 62

Marchetti, Filippo, 185, 187, 300n, 325

Marchetti, Giovanni, 122n

Marenco, Romualdo, 184

Marescalchi, Luigi, 49

Margaret Theresa of Spain, 239

Margherita di Savoia, queen of Italy, 308

Mari, Luigi, 139

Maria Teresa, empress of Austria, 38

Mariani, Angelo, 166

Marie-Thérèse of Spain, queen of France, 352

Marin, Carlo Antonio, 19n

Marino, Giambattista, 246, 350, 379

Marmi, Antonfrancesco, 243

Marotta, Cesare, 365, 366

Marra, Geronimo della, 374

Martello, Pier Jacopo, 252

Martín y Soler, Vicente, 68

Martinelli, Caterina, 350–52

Martinelli, Gaetano, 329n

Martinelli, Vincenzio, 391

Martini, Giovanni Battista, 369n, 371n, 377–78, 383

Marx brothers, 112

Marzi brothers, 129, 157

Masaniello (Tommaso Aniello), 3

Mascagni, Pietro, 171, 182, 185, 188, 192, 199, 229, 275, 293, 297, 302, 309, 325n, 326

Masini, Angelo, 178

Massenet, Jules, 160, 178, 188

Mattei, Saverio, 60n, 250n

Mauro family, 23, 55

Mayr, Simon, 96, 142, 269, 306, 316, 321n

Mazzanti, Ferdinando, 72

Mazzocchi, Virgilio, 365

Mazzoni, Antonio Maria, 372

Mazzucato, Alberto, 398n

Mazzuchelli, Giammaria, xiv

Medebac, Girolamo, 60n

Medici, Cardinal Antonio de', 351

Medici, Granprincipe Ferdinando de', 14n, 19, 23, 238, 302n, 314n, 317–18, 328, 333, 361–62

Medici, Cardinal Giancarlo de', 238

Medici, Margaretta de', 359

Medici, Mattias de', 238, 312n, 351

Medici family, 3, 20, 23, 312, 347n, 348, 350, 361, 362. *For grand dukes, see under name*

Medinaceli (Spanish viceroy), 12

Melani, Alessandro, 297, 307n, 320n

Melani, Atto, 361

Melani, Jacopo, 297, 309n, 320n

Mellini, Eugenia, 65

Melosio, Francesco, 236

Mengozzi, Bernardo, 394

Menichelli, Niccola, 66n

Menichelli, Teresa, 66n

Menotti, Gian Carlo, 213–14, 285, 302, 307n, 325–26

Mercadante, Giuseppe Saverio Raffaele, 135, 143, 159, 272

Merelli, Bartolomeo, 106, 118–19, 122, 136, 144–46, 154, 158, 187, 316n

Méric-Lalande, Henriette, 94

Merighi, Antonia Margherita, 386

Metallo, Grammatico, 366

Metastasio, Pietro, xii, 32, 49–55, 57–59, 230, 242, 244, 245–51, 254–56, 262, 269, 270–72, 280, 318, 329, 369n, 371n, 379, 392, 400

Meyerbeer, Giacomo, xii, xiii, 94, 142, 155, 159, 160, 175, 187, 257, 264, 272, 274

Michelangelo Buonaroti, 231n

Mila, Massimo, 215

Milhaud, Darius, 209, 213

Millico, Vito Giuseppe, 45n, 391–92

Milloss, Aurel M., 197

Minato, Nicolò, 15, 235, 239

Mioli, Piero, 372n

Mitropoulos, Dimitri, 217

Mocchi, Walter, 171, 181–82, 193

Modena, duke of, 9n, 23, 70, 92, 347n, 351, 370. *See also under given names*

Molière, 63

Molinari, Bernardino, 192

Molza, Nicolò, 43

Monaldi, Gino, 171–72, 178

Moniglia, Giovanni Andrea, 16–17, 64, 238

Montale, Eugenio, 285

Montefiascone, Giambattista da. *See* Casti, Giovanni Battista, da Montefiascone

Montefiore, Tommaso, 186
Montemezzi, Italo, 325n
Montesquieu, Charles de Secondat, baron de
    La Brède et de, 43n
Monteverdi, Claudio, 3, 4, 6, 196, 199, 202,
    295n, 297, 321n, 326n, 333, 347, 349,
    350n, 351n, 352
Monti, Teresa, 66n
Monti, Vincenzo, 109
Monticelli, Angelo Maria, 48
Monza, Carlo (Monzino), 32, 57
Morandi, Giovanni, 316
Morandi, Rosa, 316, 399
Moreno, Filippo, 122n
Morlacchi, Francesco, 257, 320n, 327
Morosini, Alvise, 317
Morosini, Livio, 155
Mosca, Giuseppe, 297, 312n, 317n
Mosca, Luigi, 312n, 315
Mozart, Wolfgang Amadeus, xii–xiii, 118,
    203, 255, 293, 307, 334n, 338n, 398n, 401
Mulè, Giuseppe, 192, 199, 202n
Murat, Joachim, 302
Muratori, Ludovico Antonio, xiv, 241–43,
    245, 367, 368–69
Musella, Antonio, 174–75
Musi, Maria Maddalena, 363
Musich, Eugenio, 143–44
Mussolini, Benito, 192–93, 202, 206–7
Mussorgsky, Modest Petrovich, 196
Muzio, Emanuele, 152, 306

Nanino, Giovanni Bernardino, 358
Nannini, Livia (La Polacca), 373n
Nannini, Silvia (La Polacca), 373n
Napoli-Signorelli, Pietro, 251n
Nasolini, Sebastiano, 292, 297, 312n
Nicolai, Carl Otto Ehrenfried, 142
Nicolini, Giuseppe, 297, 308n
Nicolini, Mariano, 46n
Nini, Alessandro, 258
Nono, Luigi, 215, 285, 307n
Noris, Matteo, 235
Nourrit, Adolphe, 150, 400
Novello, Clara Anastasia, 112
Noverre, Jean-Georges, 46–47, 49
Nozzari, Andrea, 139, 327

Obizzi, Pio Enea degli, 7, 9, 34, 238
Offenbach, Jacques, 188

Oñate, Inigo Vélez de Guevara y Taxis, count
    of, 3, 11
Orefice, Giacomo, 181
Orff, Carl, 203
Orlandini, Giuseppe Maria, 60–64, 326n
Orsati, Marina, 361
Orsatto, Giovanni, 27
Orsi, Gian Giuseppe, 388n
Ottajano de' Medici, Prince Giuseppe, 123
Ottani, Martino, 57
Ottoboni family, 313
Ottonelli, Giovan Domenico, 355–56

Pacchiarotti (Pacchierotti), Gasparo, 44
Pacini, Giovanni, 109, 145, 151, 256, 258,
    272, 322–23, 326n, 336, 405
Pacini, Pietro, 152n
Padovani, Antonio, 99n
Paër, Ferdinando, 326n
Pagliardi, Giovanni Maria, 321n
Paisiello, Giovanni, 44n, 57, 59nn, 67n, 68,
    69n, 71n, 251, 293, 306, 311, 312n, 315–
    16, 319
Paita, Giovanni, 387
Palestrina, Giovanni Pierluigi da, 382
Pallavicino, Carlo, 11, 307n, 321n
Pallavicino, Nicolò Maria, 19
Palomba, Antonio, 63–65
Pampani, Antonio Gaetano, 53
Pamphili, Cardinal Benedetto, 313, 362
Pamphili family, 313
Pannocchieschi, Francesco de', 29n
Panofka, Heinrich, 403, 404
Panzieri, Lorenzo, 113n, 122, 135n
Paradisi, Agostino, 45n
Pariati, Pietro, 61, 242n, 243–44, 247, 279
Pasi, Camilla, 326n
Pasquini, Bernardo, 309n, 313, 321n
Pasta, Giuditta Maria Costanza, 94–96, 99,
    102, 137, 154, 230
Paterni, Giovanni, 116
Paterni family, 157
Patti, Adelina, 98–99, 178
Pavarotti, Luciano, 410
Pavesi, Stefano, 135–36, 296, 308n, 315
Pazzi family, 105
Pedrotti, Carlo, 325n
Pekáry, István, 197
Pellegrini Celoni, Anna Maria, 381–82
Penni, Serafina, 72

Peñaranda (Spanish viceroy), 12
Pepoli, Carlo, 265–66, 294n
Peregallo, Mario, 214, 217
Perez, Davide, 54, 64
Pergolesi, Giovanni Battista, 60–61, 63–64,
    197, 308n, 385
Peri, Jacopo (Zazzerino), 232–33, 321n,
    327n, 346–47, 349–51
Perosa, Leonardo, 397n
Perrino, Marcello, 404
Persiani, Giuseppe, 326n
Perti, Giacomo Antonio, 312n, 321n
Pertici, Pietro, 63–66
Peruzzi, Anna Maria (La Parrucchierina), 373
Pesarino, Francesco, 355
Pescetti, Giovanni Battista, 54
Pestalozza, Luigi, 218n
Petrassi, Goffredo, 197, 213, 285
Petrella, Errico, 159n, 297, 319
Petri, Mario, 212
Petrolli, Caterina, 326n
Peverelli, Antonio, 36
Piacentini, Marcello, 194
Pianetti, Cardolo Maria, 308n
Piave, Francesco Maria, 230, 255–61, 267–
    68, 273–74, 277–78, 284, 335–36
Piccinni, Niccolò, 56–57, 58n, 67n, 68, 199,
    296n, 306, 312n, 314n, 317n, 321–22,
    326n, 336
Picena (impresario), 123
Pietro Leopoldo I, grand duke of Tuscany, 38,
    71n, 132
Pigna e Rovida (publishing firm), 184
Pignatelli, Antonio. *See* Pope Innocent XII
Pilo, Rosolino, 153
Pilotti, Giuseppe, 311
Pinacci, Giovanni Battista, 23, 387
Pini, Maria Domenica, 363
Piontelli, Luigi, 134, 189
Pirandello, Luigi, 207, 284–85
Pisaroni, Rosmunda, 105
Pistocchi, Francesco Antonio, 229, 362–63,
    372, 373, 376, 384
Pitrot, Antoine, 48
Pius IX, pope (Giovanni Maria Mastai-
    Ferretti), 102
Pizzetti, Ildebrando, 196, 199, 203, 207, 213,
    283, 316, 326
Pizzi, Gioacchino, 271
Platania, Pietro, 185

Pleasants, Henry, 405
Podrecca, Guido, 186, 191
Poggi, Antonio, 149
Poli, Giovanna, 64
Pollarolo, Carlo Francesco, 251, 318
Polvini, Giuseppe, 24
Pompadour, Madame de (Jeanne-Antoinette
    Poisson, marquise de), 253
Pompeati, Teresa, 72
Ponchielli, Amilcare, 158, 294n, 302, 323–25
Poncini Zilioli, Francesco, 42n
Poniatowski family, 152
Ponzo, Giuseppe, 251
Porpora, Nicola, 56, 246, 306, 308n, 314n,
    321n, 326, 375, 378, 390–91, 393
Porrino, Ennio, 203
Porro, Carlo, 180
Porta, Carlo, 90, 262–63
Poulenc, Francis, 213
Praga, Marco, 281
Prampolini, Enrico, 196–97
Prandelli, Giacinto, 212
Predieri, Giacomo Cesare, 372
Predieri family, 373
Prokofiev, Sergei, 213
Provenzale, Francesco, 321n
Prunati, Sante, 23
Psalidi, Antonio, 42n
Psalidi, Francesco, 42n
Puccini, Albina, 308
Puccini, Giacomo, xii, 158, 171, 192, 213,
    275, 278–82, 283, 297, 308–9, 312, 325,
    327, 332–33, 336, 340–41

Quadrio, Francesco Saverio, xiv, 241
Quasimodo, Salvatore, 285
Querzoli, Anna, 64
Querzoli, Vittoria, 64, 72

Raaff, Anton, 378, 380, 387, 401
Radiciotti, Giuseppe, 316n
Raggi, Giacomo, 377
Ramponi Andreini, Virginia (La Florinda),
    352
Ranzato, Virgilio, 207
Rasi, Francesco, 347–51
Rasori, Giovanni, 47
Ratti, Leopoldo, 187
Rauzzini, Venanzio, 73
Razetti, Alessio, 49

Recupito Marotta, Ippolita, 349, 366
Redi, Francesco, 378
Regli, Francesco, 273n
Reinhardt, Max, 196
Remorini, Ranieri, 263
Renzi, Anna, 21, 356–61
Respighi, Ottorino, 196–97, 199, 203
Resse Gismondi, Celeste, 64, 385n
Riccardi, Francesca, 326n
Ricci, Agata, 72
Ricci, Federico, 297, 325n
Ricci, Francesco Benedetto, 117
Ricci, Luigi, 297, 316, 325n, 326n
Ricci, Sebastiano, 23
Riccitelli, Primo, 192
Riccoboni, Francesco, 358n
Ricordi, Giovanni, 136, 300
Ricordi, Giulio, 180, 186, 190, 278, 179,
    280, 301n, 316, 323–24, 339–40
Ricordi, Tito, 186–87, 281
Ricordi (publishing firm), 158–60, 167, 184,
    187–88, 281, 295, 312, 396
Righenzi, Carlo, 15
Righetti Giorgi, Geltrude, 399
Rimondi, Margherita, 326n
Rinaldo d'Este, duke of Modena, 13, 37
Rinuccini, Ottavio, 3, 232–34, 327n
Rinuccini, Pierfrancesco, 234
Ripellino, Angelo Maria, 285
Ristorini, Antonio, 44n, 61–62, 384
Ristorini, Giuseppe, 65
Ristorini family, 373
Ritorni, Carlo, 97, 104
Rivani, Antonio (Ciecolino), 361
Rivarola, Antonio, 397
Rocca, Lodovico, 203, 213
Roccaforte, Gaetano, 271
Rocchetti, Ventura, 378, 380, 391–92
Roger, Gustave-Hippolyte, 401
Rognoni, Luigi, 215
Rolli, Paolo, 51, 251n, 380n
Romandiolo (impresario), 124
Romanelli, Luigi, 256n
Romani, Felice, 255, 257–58, 263, 265–67,
    271–73, 282, 335n, 337
Romani, Pietro, 119
Ronconi, Giorgio, 112n, 403
Ronzani, Domenico, 115
Ronzi de Begnis, Giuseppina, 94
Rosmini, Enrico, 183

Rospigliosi, Giulio, 16, 234. *See also* Clement
    IX, pope (Giulio Rospigliosi)
Rosselli, Carlo, 207
Rosselli, Sabatino, 207
Rossellini, Renzo, 213
Rossi, Gaetano, 257, 262n, 264, 270n, 316n
Rossi, Lauro, 159, 168–69, 187
Rossi, Luigi, 351, 359
Rossi-Brighenti (dancer), 173
Rossi Melocchi, Cosimo, 61
Rossini, Gioachino Antonio, xii, 89, 95–97,
    102, 116–18, 141, 152, 158, 181, 187, 196,
    199, 202, 211, 214, 262, 269–70, 274–75,
    292–93, 299, 311, 316, 320n, 322, 326–27,
    336–38, 399, 400, 405, 408
Rota, Nino, 213, 285, 302, 326
Rousseau, Jean-Jacques, 291n, 337n
Rovaglia, Pietro, 153
Rovani, Giuseppe, 274, 275, 398n
Ruberti (Roberti), Giovanni Battista, 362
Rubini, Giovanni Battista, 146, 400, 409n
Ruspoli, Marquis, 314n
Ruspoli family, 313
Ruvinetti, Rosa, 63

Sacchini, Antonio, 60n, 68, 312n, 315, 319
Sacrati, Francesco, 15, 360
Saddumene, Bernardo, 60–61, 63, 66n
Saint-Saëns, Camille, 188
Salani, G. (impresario), 122n
Salicola Suini, Margherita, 251, 362–63,
    373n
Salieri, Antonio, 68, 254–55, 315, 326n
Salvi, Antonio, 17, 54n, 60–61, 238
Salvi, Lorenzo, 397
Salviucci, Paolo, 211
Salvoni, Luigi Bernardo, 34n
Samengo, Paolo, 112n
Sances, Giovanni Felice, 7
Sanguineti, Edoardo, 285
Sanguineti, Francesco, 137, 143–44
San Martino Valperga, Enrico di, 197, 202
Sansevero, Paolo di Sangro, prince of, 314n
Santarelli, Giuseppe, 378n
Santley, Charles, 137
Santurini, Francesco, 18, 24, 27, 30
Saratelli, Giuseppe, 295n
Sardelli, Anna Maria, 361
Sarro, Domenico, 53, 54n, 57, 318n
Sarti, Giuseppe, 44n, 68, 312n, 326n

Sartorio, Antonio, 307n, 309n, 321n

Sassano, Matteo, 373–74

Saunier, Vincent, 48

Sauveterre, François, 46

Savoia-Nemours, Maria Giovanna Battista di, duchess of Savoy (Madama Reale), 5

Savoy, house of, 347. *See also under individual given names* Sbarra, Francesco, 12, 239, 240

Scalaberni, Luigi, 176, 178

Scappi, Antonio, 27

Scarlatti, Alessandro, xii, 26n, 34, 197, 199, 242n, 293n, 295n, 302n, 311n, 314n, 317–18, 321, 328, 333, 390

Scarlatti, Domenico, 298, 302n, 312n, 317–18

Scelba, Mario, 214

Scherli, Leopoldo Maria, 66n

Schiassi, Gaetano Maria, 52

Schiller, Friedrich, 284, 332n

Schipa, Tito, 327

Schubert, Franz, 307

Schultze, Norbert, 203

Schürmann, Joseph Johan, 171

Schütz, Amalia, 94

Scialoja, Toti, 285

Scoccimarro, Mauro, 210

Scorpione, Domenico, 306

Scotto, Ottavio, 171

Scudo, Paul, 402

Segni, Francesco (Il Finale), 373n

Segni, Giuseppe Maria (Il Finalino), 373

Sellitto, Giuseppe, 60, 63, 64

Senesino, Il (Francesco Bernardi), 44n, 48

Serafin, Tullio, 197

Sforza-Cesarini family, 116

Shakespeare, William, 277

Sharp, Samuel, 43n

Shostakovich, Dmitry, 204

Sibilla, Vincenza, 326n

Siepi, Cesare, 212

Simionato, Giulietta, 212

Simoni, Giovanni, 66n

Simoni, Renato, 278

Sironi, Mario, 196

Smareglia, Antonio, 186, 297, 301n

Solera, Temistocle, 261–62

Soliva, Carlo Evasio, 263

Somma, Antonio, 206, 268

Sonzogno, Edoardo, 183, 188

Sonzogno (publishing firm), 159–60, 175, 184, 187–88, 325, 396

Soto, Francesco, 358

Spech, Adelina, 397

Spontini, Gaspare, 196, 296n, 308n, 317n

Stagno, Roberto, 99

Stampiglia, Silvio, 34, 242, 328

Steffani, Agostino, xii

Stella, Antonietta, 212

Stella, Santa, 326n

Stendhal (Henri Beyle), 147

Sterbini, Cesare, 271

Stolz, Ludmilla, 326n

Stolz, Teresa, 173, 174, 176

Stolzmann, Anna, 172

Stradella, Alessandro, 292, 307n, 321n

Strakosch, Maurice, 171

Strakosch, Roberto, 171, 178

Strauss, Richard, 203

Stravinsky, Igor, 196, 209

Strazza, Giovannina. *See* Lucca, Giovanna Strazza

Strepponi, Giuseppina, 139, 326n

Striggio, Alessandro, 4

Strozzi, Giulio, 10–11, 15–16, 235, 356

Suardi, Teresa, 381

Suares Carducci, Vittoria, 61n

Sutherland, Joan, 408

Tacchinardi, Nicola, 122, 401

Tacchinardi-Persiani, Fanny, 138, 155, 326n

Taddei, Giuseppe, 212

Tadolini Savonari, Eugenia, 140

Tagliabue, Carlo, 212

Tagliavini, Ferruccio, 212

Tamagno, Francesco, 178

Tamburi, Orfeo, 196

Tamburini, Antonio, 146

Tamburini, Zaira, 122n

Tarquini, Tarquinia, 326n

Tartini, Giuseppe, 307

Tasso, Torquato, 240, 246

Tebaldi, Renata, 212, 230

Tebaldini, Giovanni, 316

Tedeschi, Giovanni, 380

Tesi, Vittoria, 373, 378, 386

Thomas, Ambroise, 188

Tibaldi, Giuseppe Luigi, 380n, 383, 387

Tiby, Ottavio, 198

Tillot, Guillaume du, 37

Tinti, Ercole, 134
Tiraboschi, Girolamo, xiv, 241
Tommasini, Vincenzo, 197
Tonelli, Anna, 61–62, 64
Toni, Alceo, 199
Torelli, Gasparo, 18
Torelli, Giacomo, 21
Torlonia family, 116
Toscanini, Arturo, 131, 179–80, 181, 191–92, 209, 301n, 325n
Tosi, Adelaide, 265
Tosi, Pierfrancesco, 364, 370, 371n, 376, 379, 381, 388–90, 392–93
Traetta, Tommaso, 57, 71, 392n
Trento, Vittorio, 49
Tricarico, Giuseppe, 296, 307n, 309n, 321n
Trinchera, Pietro, 252
Tritto, Giacomo, 306, 308n, 315
Tron family, 8, 18, 362

Uberti, Grazioso, 353
Uffenbach, Johann Friedrich Armand von, 43n
Uga, Felicita, 360n
Ughi, Nicolò degli, 20
Ungarelli, Rosa, 44n, 61–62, 384
Ungher, Carolina, 94, 146
Urban VIII, pope (Maffeo Vincenzo Barberini), 7, 20, 354, 359, 365
Uzeda, Juan Francisco Pacheco Tellez Girón, duke of, 22, 36

Vaccai, Nicola, 135, 136, 299, 306
Valle, Giovanni, 126
Vallisnieri, Antonio, 243
Vallotti, Francesco Antonio, 307
Vanini Boschi, Francesca, 372n, 381
Vargas Maccina, Marquis, 314n
Vasto, Marquis del, 314n
Vecchi, Giuseppe, 361
Velluti, Giovanni Battista, 327
Vendramin, Paolo, 235
Vendramin family, 18, 91n
Ventimiglia, duke of, 314n
Venturini, Genesio, 184
Verdi, Giuseppe, xii, 82, 99, 109–10, 116, 118–19, 136, 139, 141–42, 146, 150, 152, 158–59, 167, 171, 174–75, 178, 182–87, 202, 206, 256, 257–60, 261, 267–68, 273–

77, 281, 284, 293, 295, 297–99, 306–8, 312n, 319–20, 323, 326n, 328, 329, 330–31, 332n, 335–36, 338–40, 402–3
Verga, Giovanni, 183, 275n
Véron, Louis, 115
Viganò, Onorato, 48, 115
Viganò, Salvatore, 96
Villeneuve, Josse de (Jost de Villeneuve), 314
Villifranchi, Giovanni Cosimo, 17, 64, 238
Vinci, Leonardo, 32, 52, 55, 64, 246, 292, 314n, 318
Visconti, Luchino, 214, 408n
Visconti di Modrone, Carlo, 115, 179
Visconti di Modrone, Guido, 179–80
Vitali, Buonafede, 60n
Vittori, Loreto, 357–60
Vittorio Amedeo II of Savoy, king of Sardinia-Piedmont, 23, '36
Vittorio Emanuele I of Savoy, king of Sardinia, 84, 128
Vivaldi, Antonio, 23, 56, 197, 199, 253, 297, 318, 408
Vlad, Roman, 215

Wagner, Richard, xi–xiii, 179, 187–88, 274–76, 291–92, 332n, 388, 398n, 405, 408
Webern, Anton, 215
Weill, Kurt, 210
Wolf-Ferrari, Ermanno, 199, 307n

Zacj, Ivan, 305
Zafred, Mario, 214–15
Zagarolo, duchess of (Maria Pallavicini Rospigliosi), 362
Zanardini, Angelo, 274
Zancla, Paolo, 316n
Zandonai, Riccardo, 199, 302, 316, 325n, 326n
Zangarini, Carlo, 278
Zanibelli, Angiola, 351n, 366
Zanotti, Giovan Calisto Andrea, 383
Zarlino, Gioseffo, 306
Zeno, Apostolo, 49, 51, 242–49, 251–53, 270–72, 279
Ziani, Pietro Andrea, 297, 307n, 309n, 321n
Zingarelli, Nicola, 306, 314n
Zini (librettist), 71n
Zuancarli, Polifilo, 22
Zurlo, Leopoldo, 205–7

Index of Operas and Ballets

Achille in Sciro, Sarro, 318n

Adelaide, Cocchi, 317n

Adelaide e Comingio, Pacini, 323

Adelasia e Aleramo, Mayr, 142n

Adelia, Donizetti, 149

Adelina, Generali, 316n

Adriana Lecouvreur, Cilea, 325n, 327

Africaine (L'), Meyerbeer, 160

Agrippina, Grimani/Handel, 55

Aida, Ghislanzoni/Verdi, 127, 175–76, 186, 273

Alceste, Gluck, 58n, 408

Alcina, Handel, 334n

Alessandro nell'Indie, Metastasio, 50, 111n

Alessandro vincitor di se stesso, Sbarra/Cesti, 12, 312n

Allan Cameron, Piave/Verdi, 258–59

Amahl and the Night Visitors, Menotti, 214

Amore artigiano (L'), Gassmann, 59n

Amore contadino (L'), Goldoni/Lampugnani, 66n–67n

Amore dei tre re (L'), Montemezzi, 325n

Andrea Chénier, U. Giordano, 325, 327, 328n

Andromeda, Ferrari/Manelli, 8–9, 22

Andromeda (L'), Ascanio Pio di Savoia, 7n

Anna Bolena, Donizetti, 338n

Annetta e Lucindo, Pacini, 323

Antigona, Galuppi, 57

Antigono, Metastasio, 50

Antonio e Cleopatra, Hasse, 386

Apollon Musagète, Stravinsky, 196

Arcifanfano re dei matti, Goldoni/Galuppi, 66

Arianna (L'), Rinuccini/Monteverdi, 3, 6, 233–34, 351–52

Aristodemo, Dottori, 240

Arsace (Salvi): Gasparini, 54n; Sarro, 54n

Artaserse (Metastasio), 50, 51, 54, 57, 371, 386; Arena, 52; Brivio, 52; Galuppi, 52, 54; Gluck, 52; Hasse, 51–52, 55, 314n, 371; Jommelli, 52, 54; Pampani, 54; Perez, 54; Pescetti, 54; Schiassi, 52; Vinci, 51, 52, 55

Arte di far libretti (L'), Ghislanzoni, 273

Asrael, Franchetti, 302

Assassinio nella catterale, Pizzetti, 213

Assedio di Calais (L'), 117

Atide, Perti, 312n

Attila, Verdi, 119n, 331, 335n

Attilio Regolo, Metastasio/Jommelli, 392

Ballo delle ingrate (Il), Rinuccini/Monteverdi, 233

Ballo in maschera (Un), Somma/Verdi, 109, 116, 142, 206

Barbiere di Siviglia (Il), Rossini, 152, 320n, 336

Beatrice di Tenda, Bellini, 119n, 152

Bellerofonte (Il), 360

Bianca e Fernando, Bellini, 111n, 293n

Billy Budd, Quasimodo/Ghedini, 285

Bohème (La), Puccini, 340–41

Buona figliuola (La), Goldoni/Piccinni, 68, 336

Calipso, Ottani, 57
Cambiale di matrimonio (La), Rossini, 270,
  316, 322
Cappello di paglia di Firenze (Il), Rota, 213
Capuleti e i Montecchi (I), Bellini, 119n
Cardillac, Hindemith, 210
Carmen, Bizet, 175
Caterina di Guisa, Romani/Coccia, 271
Catone in Utica, Metastasio/Leo, 50
Cavalleria rusticana, Mascagni, 185, 188,
  325n, 327, 337
Cenerentola (La), ossia La bontà in trionfo,
  Ferretti/Rossini, 116, 270, 311, 337
Chi soffre speri, 5n
Cimodocea (La), Petrella, 319
Cin-ci-là, Lombardo/Ranzato, 207
Claudio Cesare, Aureli, 236
Clemenza di Tito (La), Mozart, 334n
Colombo, Morlacchi, 320n
Colonello (Il), Heiberger, 67
Comica del cielo (La), 354n
Commedia in commedia (La), Rinaldo da
  Capua, 65
Compagnacci (I), Riccitelli, 192
Contadina (La), Saddumene/Hasse, 61
Contrabasso (Il), Bucchi, 213
Cordovano (Il), Montale/Petrassi, 213, 285
Coriolano (Il) [ballet], 32
Corsaro (Il), Verdi, 141, 159
Cosa rara (Una), ossia Bellezza ed onestà, Da
  Ponte/Martín y Soler, 68
Così fan tutte, Mozart, 334n
Costanza (La), Saddumene, 65n–66n
Crispino e la comare, Ricci and Ricci, 325n
Cromvello, Piave/Verdi, 258–59, 268. See also
  Allan Cameron

Dafne (La) (Rinuccini): Gagliano, 6, 232;
  Peri, 232–33
Dal finto il vero, Zini/Paisiello, 71n
Dal male il bene, 354n
David, Milhaud, 213
Dèbora e Jaéle, Pizzetti, 203
Delia (La), Strozzi/Manelli, 10n
Demetrio (Metastasio), 50; Leo, 341; Ponzo,
  251
Demofoonte, Metastasio, 50
Dialogues des carmélites (Les), Poulenc, 213
Dibuk (Il), Rocca, 203
Didone (La), Busenello/Cavalli, 11

Didone abbandonata (Metastasio): Albinoni,
  53; Porpora, 54; Sarro, 53
Don Carlos (Don Carlo), Méry and du Locle/
  Verdi, 127, 176, 184, 217, 331, 332n
Donna bianca d'Avenello (La), Pavesi, 136n
Donna Caritea, regina di Spagna, Coccia, 336
Donna del lago (La), Rossini, 96
Donna selvaggia (La), Coccia, 336
Donne dispettose (Le), Piccinni, 312n
Don Pasquale, Donizetti, 175
Dottor Antonio (Il), Alfano, 213
Duca di Scilla (Il), Petrella, 159n
Due contesse (Le), Paisiello, 69n
Due Foscari (I), Verdi, 109, 335n
Due Savoiardi (I), Cagnoni, 305

Ebrea (L'). See *La Juive Egisto*, Faustini/
  Cavalli, 15
Eleonora di Toledo, Pacini, 152n
Eliogabalo, Aureli/Boretti, 3
Elisabetta regina d'Inghilterra, Rossini, 118
Elisir d'amore (L'), Donizetti, 337
Enrico di Borgogna, Donizetti, 316n
Eraclea (L'), o vero Il ratto delle Sabine,
  Draghi, 312n
Ermiona, Obizzi/Sances, 7–9
Ernani, Piave/Verdi, 110, 259, 268, 273
Eroe cinese (L'), Metastasio, 50
Étoile du nord (L') (La stella del nord),
  Meyerbeer, 175
Euridice (L') (Rinuccini): Caccini, 232–33;
  Peri, 327n, 347
Europa riconosciuta, Verazi/Salieri, 315
Excelsior [ballet], Manzotti/Marenco, 184
Ezio, Metastasio, 50

Falce (La), Catalani, 315–16
Falstaff, Boito/Verdi, 339
Fanciulla del West (La), Puccini, 99, 325
Favola del figlio cambiato (La), Pirandello/
  Malipiero, 207, 284–85
Favorito del principe (Il), Lorenzi, 360
Fedora, U. Giordano, 325n
Fedra, D'Annunzio/Pizzeti, 283
Filosofo di campagna (Il), Goldoni/
  Galuppi, 68
Finta cameriera (La), Latilla, 65, 66
Finta pazza (La), Strozzi/Sacrati, 15, 356–57,
  360
Finta pazza Licori (La), Monteverdi, 350n

Finta savia (La), 360
Finto cieco (Il), Gazzaniga, 315
Flora (La), Gagliano, 359
Fortune di Rodope e Damira (Le), 360
Forza del destino (La) (Don Alvaro), Maffei/
  Verdi, 268
Forza della virtù (La), Metastasio/David, 50
Fra Donato, Sacchini, 312n
Francesca da Rimini, Zandonai, 325n
Frascatana (La), Livigni/Paisiello, 68

Galatea (La), Vittori, 359
Gelosia per gelosia, Piccinni, 67n
Gelosie villane (Le), Grandi/Sarti, 68
Geloso in cimento (Il), Bertati/Anfossi, 68
Gengis-Kan, Anfossi, 57
Genoinda (La), o vero L'innocenza difesa,
  353
Genserico (Il), Handel, 334n
Gianni di Calais, Donizetti, 299
Giannina e Bernardone, Livigny/Cimarosa, 68
Giasone (Il), Cicognini/Cavalli, 15
Giefte [oratorio], Andreozzi, 317n
Gina, Cilea, 305
Ginevra di Scozia, Mayr, 96
Gioconda (La), Boito/Ponchielli, 276, 325n
Gismondo (Il), Federico/Latilla, 65
Gita in campagna (La), Peregallo, 213, 217
Giuditta, Lehár, 206
Giulio Sabino, Sarti, 57
Giustino (Il), Legrenzi, 312n
Goti (I), Gobatti, 151
Gran Tamerlano (Il), A. Scarlatti, 333
Griselda, Zeno/Albinoni, 243n
Griselda (La), Zeno-Goldoni/Vivaldi, 253
Guarany (Il), Gomes, 184–85
Guerra (La), Rossellini, 213
Guillaume Tell, Rossini, 400

Hérodiade, Massenet, 160
Hin und Zurück, Hindemith, 196
*Hôtellerie portugaise (L') (La locanda portogh-
  ese)*, Cherubini, 196
Huguenots (Les) (Gli Ugonotti), Scribe/
  Meyerbeer, 184

Ifigenia in Aulide, Cigna-Santi/Bertoni, 51n,
  129, 251
Ifigenia in Tauride, Traetta, 57
Incoronazione di Dario (L'), 386

Incoronazione di Poppea (L'), 360
Inganno felice (L'), Foppa/Rossini, 270
Intolleranza 1960, Ripellino/Nono, 285
Ipermestra, Metastasio, 50; Vivaldi, 56
Ismalia, ossia Morte ed amore, Romani/
  Mercadante, 271
Issipile, Metastasio, 50

Jérusalem, Verdi, 300
Job, Dallapiccola, 213
Juive (La) (L'Ebrea), 139

Lisetta e Astrobolo, Gasparini, 62
Lituani (I), Ghislanzoni/Ponchielli, 294n,
  323–24
*Locanda portoghese (La) (L'hôtellerie portu-
  gaise)*, Cherubini, 196
Lohengrin, Wagner, 175–76, 188
Lombardi alla prima crociata (I), Solera/
  Verdi, 258, 268
Lucia di Lammermoor, Donizetti, 110, 119n,
  123, 139, 140, 312, 337
Lucio Manlio, l'imperioso, Stampiglia/A. Scar-
  latti, 328
Lucio Papirio, Predieri, 387n
Lucio Vero, Manna, 319
Lucrezia Borgia, Donizetti, 152n
Luisa Miller, Verdi, 335n
Lulu, Berg, 209

Macbeth, Verdi, 119, 184
Madama Butterfly, Puccini, 152, 206, 325,
  332n, 341n
*Madama Dulcinea e il cuoco del marchese del
  Bosco*, Orlandini, 62
Maestra (La), Polomba/Cocchi, 65
Maga fulminata (La), Ferrari/Manelli, 9n
Mahagonny, Weill, 210
Malek Adel, Rossi/Meyerbeer, 264
Manon Lescaut, Puccini, 278
Marco Visconti, Petrella, 319
Maria d'Alessandria, Ghedini, 197
Maria di Rudenz, Donizetti, 119n
Marriage (The), Mussorgsky, 196
Masnadieri (I), Maffei/Verdi, 159, 268
Matrimonio per lettera (Il), Coccia, 317n
Medea, Cherubini, 408
Medonte re d'Epiro, Sarti, 57, 68
Mefistofele, Boito, 276

Meistersinger von Nürnberg (Die), Wagner, 312

Mercato di Malmantile (Il), Goldoni/ Fischietti, 68

Miraculous Mandarin (The), Bartók, 197

Mitridate Eupatore (Il), A. Scarlatti, 318

Monacella della fontana (La), Mulè, 192

Monsieur de Porsugnacco, Orlandini, 62–63

Morte dell'aria (La), Scialoja/Petrassi, 213, 285

Mosè in Egitto, Rossini, 96, 118, 196

Muta per amore (La), ossia Il medico per forza, Lavigna, 316

Nabucco (Nabucodonosor), Solera/Verdi, 118, 209, 258, 268

Nerone, Boito, 194, 277

Nitteti (La) (Metastasio), 32, 50; Monza, 32; Nasolini, 312n

Norma, Romani/Bellini, 104, 137, 139, 157, 175, 258, 265, 271

Oberto conte di S. Bonifacio, Verdi, 323

Olimpiade (L') (Metastasio), 50, 256; Cimarosa, 57; Hasse, 51n–52n, 131; Logroscino, 320n

Orazi (Gli), Guastalla/Porrino, 213

Orazi e i Curiazi (Gli), Cimarosa, 57, 311

Orazio, Palomba/Auletta, 64

Oreste in Sparta (L'), Luchesi/Pollarolo, 251, 362

Orfeide (L'), Malipiero, 283

Orfeo (L') (Striggio): Monteverdi, 4, 5, 6, 347, 348; Rossi, 351

Orontea regina d'Egitto, Cicognini/Cirillo, 12

Orosmonda (L'), 347n

Orsèolo, Pizzetti, 207

Otello, Boito/Verdi, 172, 178, 274, 277, 338n

Otello, ossia Il moro di Venezia, Rossini, 400–401

Ottavia restituita al trono (L'), D. Scarlatti, 312n

Ottone in villa, Vivaldi, 318

Palazzo d'Atlante (Il), Luigi Rossi, 359

Pagliacci (I), Leoncavallo, 325n, 327, 328n

Palazzo incantato (Il), 354n

Paria (Il), Donizetti, 299

Paride, 368n

Parisina (La), Romani/Donizetti, 119n, 271

Passaggio, Sanguineti/Berio, 285

Pastor regio (Il), Ferrari, 235n

Pelléas et Mélisande, Debussy, 181

Perseo e Andromeda, Cigna-Santi/Gazzaniga, 45n

Pia de' Tolomei, Donizetti, 119n, 320n

Piccolo Marat (Il), 198

Pietà d'amore (La), Millico, 391

Pigmalione, Cimador, 326

Pimpinone, Pariati/Albinoni, 61–62

Pirata (Il), Romani/Bellini, 272

Pirro, Paisiello, 57

Poliuto, Donizetti, 143

Prigioniero (Il), Dallapiccola, 213–14

Profeta (Il) (Le Prophète), 184

Promessi sposi (I), Ponchielli, 323

Prometeo, Cacciari/Nono, 285

Puntigli delle donne (Li), Spontini, 317n

Puritani (I), Pepoli/Bellini, 143, 183, 196, 265, 274, 294n

Rake's Progress (The), Stravinsky, 210

Rape of Lucretia (The), Britten, 213

Rapimento di Cefalo (Il), Caccini, 347

Re pastore (Il), Metastasio, 50

Regina Diaz, U. Giordano, 325

Reine de Chypre (La) (La regina di Cipro), Halévy, 185

Ricimero re de' Goti, Jommelli, 317n

Rigoletto, Piave/Verdi, 109, 267, 274, 330, 331, 335–36

Ring des Nibelungen (Der), Wagner, 332n

Ritorno di Ulisse in patria (Il), Monteverdi, 196

Roderico (Il), Gasparini, 311n

Rodomonte sdegnato, 387n

Roi de Lahore (Le), Massenet, 160

Romolo ed Ersilia, Metastasio, 50

Rondine (La), Adami/Puccini, 336

Rosalia di San Miniato, 305

Rosmene (La), A. Scarlatti, 311n

Rosmonda d'Inghilterra, Donizetti, 119n

Ruggiero (Il), ovvero L'eroica gratitudine, Metastasio, 50

Ruy Blas, Marchetti, 185, 300n, 325n

Saffo, Pacini, 323

San Bonifacio, 353

Sant'Alessio (Il), 354n

Sant'Ignazio di Loyola, Vittori, 359

Schwarzer Peter, Schultze, 203
Semiramide, Metastasio, 50; Rossi/Rossini, 89, 257, 270n
Serpilla e Bacocco, Salvi/Orlandini, 61–62
Serva nobile (La), Moniglia, 64
Serva padrona (La), Federico/Pergolesi, 61, 63, 385
Serve rivali (Le), Chiari/Traetta, 71n
Siface, Metastasio, 50
Simon Boccanegra, Verdi, 159n, 331, 332n
Socrate immaginario (Il), Lorenzi/Paisiello, 59, 251
Sofonisba, Traetta, 392n
Sonnambula (La), Bellini, 151, 335n
Speziale in villa (Lo), Villifranchi/ Orlandini, 64
Sposa fedele (La), Chiari/Guglielmi, 68
Sposalizio di Angelica e Medoro (Lo), Gagliano, 349
Stella del nord (La). See L'Étoile du nord Stiffelio, Verdi, 335n
Straniera (La), Romani/Bellini, 334

Tamerlano, Handel, 334n, 336
Tancredi, Rossi/Rossini, 257, 408
Tebaldo e Isolina, Morlacchi, 327
Telemaco (Il) [ballet], 32
Testa di bronzo (La), o sia La capanna solitaria, Romani/Soliva, 263
Tirolese (La), Zaje, 303
Tito Manlio, Guglielmi, 317n; Manna, 317n
Tito Sempronio Gracco, Stampiglia/A. Scarlatti, 34–35
Torneo notturno, Malipiero, 196, 284
Tosca, Sardou-Illica-Giacosa/Puccini, 211, 279, 280

Traviata (La), Piave/Verdi, 133, 260, 262, 335, 337, 407
Trionfo della libertà (Il), A. Scarlatti, 318
Trionfo di Clelia (Il), Metastasio, 50; Gluck, 50
Trionfo di Partenope liberata (Il), 3
Trovatore (Il), Verdi, 175–76, 179–80, 256, 262, 319
Turandot, Adami-Simoni/Puccini, 198, 273, 333n
Turn of the Screw (The), Britten, 210
Tutti in maschera, Pedrotti, 325n

Ugonotti (Gli). See Les Huguenots Uragano (L'), Rocca, 213

Vanna Lupa, Pizzetti, 213
Vedova scaltra (La), Mosca, 317n
Venere prigioniera, Malipiero, 213
Vera storia (La), Calvino/Berio, 285
Veremonda, l'amazzone d'Aragona, Strozzi/ Cavalli, 11
Vespasiano (Il), Corradi/Pallavicino, 11
Vestale (La), Spontini, 196, 408
Virginia, Vaccai, 136

Wally (La), Catalani, 189–90, 325n
War and Peace, Prokofiev, 213
Wozzeck, Berg, 197, 217

Xerse (Il), Minato/Cavalli, 15

Zelmira, Rossini, 118, 299
Zenobia, Metastasio, 50
Zite 'ngalera (Li), Saddumene, 66n

Index of Theatrical Venues

Alessandria, 33
Algiers, 397
Ancona, 28
Anghiari, 176
Arezzo, 33
Assisi, 99
Athens, 98, 131

Barbara, 176
Bari, 141, 157, 219; Petruzelli, 181
Bergamo, 27, 83, 219, 371n; Cerri (later Sociale), 156; delle Novità, 196–97
Bologna, xiii, 7, 15, 31, 55, 83, 86–88, 102, 104, 107–8, 111, 114–15, 120, 122, 126–27, 144, 147, 198, 312n, 370–71, 383, 386; Brunetti, 125; Comunale, 38, 40–41, 42, 45, 50, 58n, 83, 90, 123, 125–26, 130, 134, 166, 168, 176, 219, 222; Contavalli, 122n; del Corso, 121, 125, 132; Formagliari, 20, 38, 42n, 105; Malvezzi, 20, 38, 40, 42, 65; della Sala, 20
Brescia, 27, 66n, 219, 332n
Budrio, 371
Buenos Aires, 170, 181, 185; Coliseo, 182

Cadiz, 131
Cagliari, G. P. da Palestrina, 210, 219
Cairo, 98, 178
Camerino, 33
Caracas, 95, 170

Catania, 219; Bellini, 168
Cento, 371
Cesena, 87n, 105, 114, 152–53
Chicago, 170
Como, 219
Cosenza, 219
Constantinople, 95, 131, 156
Cremona, 88, 219, 323, 371; Nazari, 38, 40n, 70n

Dresden, 52

Faenza, 33, 107, 112, 121n, 156; Comunale, 169
Fano, Fortuna, 69
Fermo, 319
Ferrara, 7, 15, 52, 219, 371
Florence, xii–xiv, 3, 4, 7, 15, 20–21, 23, 36n, 61n, 66n, 88, 98, 105, 119, 122, 202, 213, 232, 238, 323, 327n, 347n, 353, 362, 367, 394; Alfieri, 87; Cocomero, 20, 43, 64–65, 67n, 68–69, 71n, 92n; Coletti, 69; Comunale, 189, 198, 208, 209, 214, 219; Immobili (see La Pergola); Pagliano, 147, 157–58, 176, 178; La Pergola, 20, 21n, 38, 42, 45n, 47n, 56, 59n, 69, 88, 98, 106, 108, 115, 119, 122, 131–32, 134, 147, 156, 166, 168–69, 176–77, 312n, 321n; Politeama Vittorio Emanuele II, 189, 196; Tintori, 69
Foggia, 157

Foligno, 119
Forlì, 169, 383–84; della Comune, 169
Forlimpopoli, 156

Genoa, xiii, 15, 17, 18–19, 38, 119, 128, 131,
143, 198, 208, 293, 355; Carlo Felice,
111n, 134, 137, 148, 156, 166, 168, 173–
74, 181, 320n; Comunale, 219; Falcone, 15,
18–19, 29; Sant'Agostino, 19

Havana, 95, 120, 135, 168, 170

Innsbruck, 50

Jesi, 219

Lecce, 157–58, 219; Politeama Principe, 158
Lima, 170
Lisbon, 54, 170, 178
Livorno, 19, 82, 85, 101, 105, 119, 125, 150,
219
London, 24, 35, 95, 135, 141, 178, 370n;
Haymarket, 55n; Royal Academy of Music,
22n, 55n
Lucca, xiii, 15, 113, 116–17, 119, 133–34,
152, 219, 355, 394; Castiglioncelli, 86; Gi-
glio, 152n; Pantera, 152n; Pubblico, 71
Lugo, 25n, 28, 33, 371

Macerata, 219
Madrid, 50, 95, 135, 159
Malta, 98, 141
Manchester, 95
Mantua, xiii, 3–7, 27, 219, 233, 347–49, 352,
353, 362, 366
Medicina, 371
Milan, xiii, 15, 36n, 50, 57, 81, 87, 96, 98,
111–15, 117, 127, 141, 144, 213, 251, 305,
323, 339, 340, 347, 371, 394, 396–97; Canobbiana, 118, 136, 188; Carcano, 151;
Conservatorio, 305; Dal Verme, 157, 323;
Interinale, 71; Lirico Internazionale, 188;
Re, 323, 397; Regio Ducale, 36, 38, 42, 54,
69; La Scala, 38, 42, 71, 82–83, 86–91, 95–
97, 100–4, 107, 115, 117–18, 122, 126,
139, 151, 155–57, 160, 166, 168, 172,
176–81, 188–92, 195–98, 202, 208–9, 217–
19, 223, 260, 262–63, 276, 312n, 315–16,
322–25, 332n; Santa Radegonda, 188,
322–23

Modena, 16, 87n, 95, 98, 112, 114, 139,
147, 149, 153, 219, 362, 371; Ducale, 43;
Rangone, 72
Montevideo, 170; Solis, 182

Naples, xiii–xiv, 3, 5, 11–12, 15, 31, 36n, 38,
52, 54n, 62–63, 65, 67n, 84–85, 87–88, 91–
92, 96–98, 102–3, 111, 113, 117–18, 123,
127, 132, 143, 146, 155, 159, 198, 213,
251, 305, 312n, 316–17, 319, 322, 325,
327, 386, 397; Bellini, 175; Concervatorio
di Santa Maria di Loreto, 312n; La Fenice,
157; Fiorentini, 69, 71n, 319; del Fondo,
69; Nuovo, 43, 64–65, 69, 71n, 72; di Palazzo reale, 11–12; San Bartolomeo, 11–12,
15, 34, 37, 42, 64, 72, 318n; San Carlino,
88; San Carlo, 37, 42–43, 45–46, 69, 72–
73, 84–85, 90, 95, 97–98, 100, 108, 111n,
115, 117, 127, 139, 150, 155–56, 168, 172,
174–75, 181, 219, 265n, 312n, 314n, 315,
318–19, 323
New Orleans, 168
New York, 95, 120, 135, 170; Metropolitan
Opera House, 180, 325
Novara, 33, 219; Nuovo, 38

Odessa, 95

Padua, 7–9, 46n, 55, 61, 83, 88, 109, 111,
125, 131, 152, 371; Nuovo, 38, 42, 54,
70n, 86
Palermo, xiii, 22, 96, 152, 198, 213; Bellini,
168; Carolino, 86, 153, 156; Massimo, 219;
Santa Cecilia, 22, 36, 42, 69; Santa Lucia,
69
Paris, 62, 97, 115, 135, 141, 143, 351; Thé-
âtre Italien, 312n, 401; Opéra, 95, 115,
150, 159, 167, 331n; Opéra Comique, 332n
Parma, xiii, 7, 16, 36n, 37, 38, 41, 87, 98,
104, 111–12, 114, 122, 133–34, 147, 152–
53, 219, 250, 362; Regio Ducale, 42n, 101,
108, 110
Patras, 95
Pavia, 41; Nuovo, 41
Perugia, 28, 119
Pesaro, 27, 28, 55, 156, 169
Philadelphia, 170
Piacenza, 7, 15–16, 133, 149, 219, 377, 394;
Municipale, 86

Pisa, 119, 131, 134, 219, 323, 397
Pistoia, 28, 41; dei Risvegliati, 22, 41n, 61
Prato, 33

Ravenna, 219
Recanati, 33, 86
Reggio Emilia, 13, 15, 22–23, 25n, 27–28,
    37–38, 53–54, 83, 147, 148–49, 152, 184,
    219, 251, 302, 362, 371; della Comunità,
    13; Municipale, 84, 191; Pubblico, 69–70
Rimini, 15, 108, 169
Rio de Janeiro, 98, 170; Municipal, 182
Rome, xiii–xiv, 5, 7, 20, 23, 31, 39, 49–50,
    52, 61n, 67, 88, 90, 94, 101, 107, 109, 113,
    115–16, 148, 160, 172, 213, 238, 312–13,
    317, 319, 322, 360, 362, 383, 386, 392; Ac-
    cademia di Santa Cecilia, 208, 210, 219;
    Adriano, 208; Alibert, 35, 39, 57, 67 (*see
    also* delle Dame); Anfiteatro Corea, 156–57;
    Apollo, 86, 88, 149, 166, 169, 176–77,
    184, 186; Argentina, 34n, 35, 39, 40, 42,
    43n, 54, 57, 69, 70n, 88, 156, 168, 171,
    185, 320n; delle Arti, 196; Capranica, 39,
    43n, 69; Costanzi, 158, 168, 171, 181–82,
    188–89, 191, 193, 211; delle Dame, 50, 67,
    69; Granari, 69; Opera, 202, 211–12, 219;
    Pace, 43n, 69; Pallacorda, 43n, 69; Po-
    liteama, 157; Reale; Reale dell' Opera, 194,
    197–98, 207; Rucellai, 69; Tordinona (later
    Apollo), 20, 34, 39, 43n, 156, 238; Valle,
    43, 64–65, 66n, 69, 85, 86n, 95, 102, 111,
    116, 317n, 322
Rosario, Opera, 182
Rovigo, 219

Salerno, 157
San Francisco, 98, 170
San Giovanni in Persiceto, 61
Santiago (Chile), 170
São Paulo, Municipal, 182
Sassari, 219
Senigallia, 25n, 28, 33, 92, 103, 107, 113,
    119, 130–31, 169; Condominiale (Pub-
    blico), 38; La Fenice, 169; Pubblico, 70

Siena, 33, 61n, 119, 196
Spoleto, 28; Nobile, 29

Taranto, 157
Treviso, 27, 219
Trieste, 82, 96, 101, 119, 198, 397; Comu-
    nale, 85, 177; San Pietro, 312n; Verdi, 219
Turin, 3, 5, 7, 12, 15, 23, 36, 38, 51n, 57, 73,
    84–85, 92, 97–99, 115, 119, 152, 198, 251,
    348, 377, 381; Auditorium of the Rai, 209;
    Carignano, 43, 69, 71n, 72; Grondana, 72;
    Lirico, 208; Regio, 36, 41n, 42–48, 51n,
    52n, 56, 69n, 71n, 72, 84, 94, 127, 155,
    168, 177–79, 181, 189, 208, 219; di Torino,
    196; Vittorio Emanuele, 157, 208

Udine, 27

Varese, 33
Venice, xiii–xiv, 3n, 8–12, 14–19, 27, 29–30,
    32, 40, 52–53, 54n, 65, 72, 82, 88, 98, 115,
    122, 125, 160, 198, 209, 235–38, 251–52,
    312n, 314n, 316, 317, 319, 323, 327, 333,
    354–56, 360, 362, 367, 382–83, 385–86;
    La Fenice, 86, 89, 91n, 95–98, 102, 105–6,
    108–9, 115, 119, 122, 133–34, 136, 140,
    156, 166, 168, 173, 208, 219, 258, 260–61,
    322, 336; Novissimo, 21, 26, 30, 34; San
    Benedetto, 32n, 34n, 69; San Cassiano, 8,
    9n, 18, 22, 24, 62; San Giovanni Grisos-
    tomo, 11–13, 18, 24, 54–55, 69, 83, 318,
    368n, 371, 380; San Luca, 18, 91n, 148;
    San Moisè, 18, 30, 66, 270, 316n; San Sa-
    muele, 18; Sant'Angelo, 18, 27, 66n, 380,
    387n; Sant'Apollinare, 22; Santi Giovanni e
    Paolo, 10n, 12, 17–18, 22
Verona, 15, 371; Amphitheater, 198,
    219; dell'Accademia Filarmonica, 38; de'
    Temperati, 23
Viareggio, 394
Vicenza, 27–28, 125, 318, 397
Vienna, 49–50, 52, 117, 138, 239–40, 242–
    47, 296, 386, 392n; Kärntnertortheater, 118
Viterbo, 131
Voghera, 152